SINGLE SUBJECT
RESEARCH IN
SPECIAL EDUCATION

James W. Tawney
The Pennsylvania State University

David L. Gast
University of Kentucky

SINGLE SUBJECT RESEARCH IN SPECIAL EDUCATION

Charles E. Merrill Publishing Company
A Bell & Howell Company
Columbus Toronto London Sydney

Published by
Charles E. Merrill Publishing Company
A Bell & Howell Company
Columbus, Ohio 43216

This book was set in Garamond.
Production Coordination: Martha Morss

Library of Congress Catalog Card Number: 83-062581
International Standard Book Number: 0-675-20135-7
Printed in the United States of America

1 2 3 4 5 6 7 8—88 87 86 85 84

To our parents

CONTENTS

9
Withdrawal and Reversal Designs

10
Multiple Baseline Designs

11
Variations of the Multiple Baseline Design:
Multiple Probe and Changing Criterion Designs

12
Comparative Intervention Designs

SECTION FOUR
WRITING TASKS AND ETHICAL BEHAVIOR

13
Writing Tasks for Single Subject Research

14

Ethical Principles and Practices

PREFACE

Typically, the preface to a text offers a general description of the intended audience, a statement of purpose, and a listing of the unique properties that distinguish the book from others. The nature of our subject, however, dictates that we do something more. This text is about how to conduct single subject research in classroom settings with students who show learning or behavior disorders. The activities we propose are based on the emergence of an instructional technology that emphasizes precise specification of observable behavior. Thus we will be precise about *who* might use this book, *how* it might best be used, and to *what* end.

The Audience

This text is suited to graduate students enrolled in programs in special education or applied behavior analysis. Predominately these will be master's degree students, many of whom have teaching experience. We assume that this experience has led students to raise many questions about student behavior, about the effectiveness of instructional materials, or about the effectiveness of instructional procedures they have used. Thus, their teaching experience has lead to the formulation of research questions. We assume, further, that once through the graduate program, many students will return to the classroom and assume the role of a teacher-researcher.

This text should prove useful to doctoral students who are introduced to single subject methodology as part of their research requirements and to students who enter graduate programs without a list of research questions derived from teaching experience. We suggest, however, that those who lack classroom experience should gain some, as soon as possible, by seeking out faculty engaged in classroom-based research and volunteering to work in classrooms. Only in the classroom can they see what happens when certain instructional procedures are applied to educational problems.

The Plan

This book begins with the premise that applied behavior analysis is an integral part of contemporary special education. The field of contemporary special education has experienced great difficulties in its short history. On one hand, it has shown rapid growth. On the other, the effectiveness of its practices have been called into question. We have outlined a brief history of special education, focusing on the problems that have confronted the field.

The history of applied behavior analysis is traced, beginning with Skinner's laboratory. The experimental analysis of behavior moved from the laboratory to the natural environment, from rat and pigeon subjects to humans, and the principles of operant conditioning became employed in special education. Key studies of historical value are identified and some of them are described in detail. Several key individuals at a few institutions were responsible for the behavioral influence in special education. Our discussion assumes that students have a basic knowledge of terminology and further that they will go to the original studies to gain a full understanding of them. In some cases the key elements of these studies have been identified, but since contemporary history is largely in the eye of the beholder, we acknowledge, and encourage, other interpretations.

The underlying recommendation of this text is that teaching should become more scientific. A look at the critical similarities and differences between technology and research reveals that they are really not so different. Another theme is that single subject research methodology is uniquely suited to classroom-based research with handicapped students. Though we have identified some of the problems with early experimental-control studies in special education, we have chosen not to describe group methodology or to develop a strong rationale to show why the approach we have emphasized is better than the other. The reasons are simple: both are appropriate for the purposes they serve, and graduate students are generally exposed to both methodologies. We briefly discuss general measurement problems in the classroom.

This text is primarily a "how to" book; it shows the student how to conduct single subject research. Design options are presented, selected studies are analyzed, and specific cautions or conditions are presented. These studies are intended to assist the student in conducting research that is replicable and publishable. To that end, we have included chapters on how to write theses, articles, and grants. Finally, we discuss ethical procedures, with the aim of guiding the professional behavior of the student.

The Outcome

Our goal, at the least, is to provide teachers with the skills required to conduct classroom-based research, but we have some other goals too. The teacher-researcher is a new type of professional. A data base in special education is lacking, but single subject research can provide that data base. Data collection practices are changing slowly. Where once there was no data collection tradition, now, to the extent that teachers employ systematic instruction procedures, the trend toward documenting learning is growing. We believe that educational practice should move a step further. Not only should teachers take data, they should teach within the structure of research designs that will enable them to demonstrate a functional relationship between their teaching and changes in a child's behavior. The result will be empirical verification of instruction. Simply put, we wish to enable teachers and other interventionists to say and to document that "my kids have changed" (for the better, of course) "and I can show, with confidence, that I was responsible for the change."

Acknowledgments

Many people assisted us in preparing this text, and we are grateful to each of them. A major part of the historical research (Chapters 1 and 2) was completed while Jim Tawney was a postdoctoral fellow at the University of California–Santa Barbara. Mel Semmel kindly placed many excellent resources at his disposal there. James R. Skouge coauthored Chapters 10 and 11 and Carol Chase Thomas (University of North Carolina, Wilmington) Chapter 12. Both worked closely with David Gast as doctoral students at the University of Kentucky. Mark Woolery provided constructive feedback on the manuscript. Norris Haring made especially helpful comments on the historical chapter. A special acknowledgement is due to Sidney Bijou and Samuel Kirk for enduring yet another interview on early developments in behavior analysis and in special education. Ms. Connie Fugate (University of Kentucky) and Glenda Carelas and Janis Leitzell (The Pennsylvania State University) typed the manuscript competently. The project was initiated with the enthusiastic support of Marianne Taflinger, and Vicki Knight ensured its smooth progress toward a completed manuscript. Finally, a special note of appreciation is extended to Bill Heward (Ohio State University), who read the prospectus and pointed out the need for a *readable* text on single subject design, and to Tom Lovitt (University of Washington) and Phil Strain (Western Psychiatric Institute and Clinic, University of Pittsburgh) for their valuable recommendations.

SECTION ONE

BEHAVIORAL RESEARCH IN EDUCATIONAL SETTINGS

1

INTRODUCTION

The year 1960 marks the beginning of contemporary special education. While the selection of that date is clearly arbitrary, there is a rationale for it. Prior to that time, introductory texts in special education typically described the European influence on the development of educational programs for the deaf, blind, and retarded in the United States. These programs grew slowly, but steadily, until they were interrupted by global conflict. A few books were published that attempted to define special education and suggest educational practices—though in a general and tentative manner.

The growth of special education programs resumed after World War II. During the 1950s, the country attempted to heal the wounds of war, shift to a peacetime economy, and reorder its social priorities, resulting in a reorganization of special education programs and practices.

Efforts of parents and educators during the period of reorganization resulted in the expansion of programs for the handicapped in the sixties and set the stage for a period of civil rights activism in the seventies. Parents of the handicapped organized the National Association for Retarded Children (Lippman & Goldberg, 1973), which is now the Association for Retarded Citizens (ARC). Thus began the efforts of parents to advocate as they lobbied for programs for lower functioning retarded students. The year 1958 marked the enactment of P.L. 85-926. This law provided funds to establish university training programs for classroom teachers and doctoral level teacher trainers in the area of mental retardation. The first trainees entered a limited number of established programs in 1959. In turn, the first generation of teachers and teacher trainers staffed the public school programs and the teacher training programs that marked the beginning of contemporary special education.

This chapter was written by **James W. Tawney** and **David L. Gast**.

Stages in Contemporary Special Education

Contemporary special education has evolved through three roughly delineated periods.

1960s	A period of *rapid expansion* of programs for the handicapped
1970s	A period of *activism* for handicapped students who were viewed as a disenfranchised minority
1980s	A period of *uncertainty* (and potential retrenchment)

The Sixties

During the 1960s, the number of programs for the handicapped increased
rapidly. Teachers filled newly funded classroom programs. As training programs were established at the university level, there then began a search for a
content of instruction for children and, in turn, for the university curriculum.
The first strategies were simple: slow down, or water down, the traditional
school curriculum; create experiential and vocationally oriented curricula; or
shift to a focus on social development as a primary educational goal.

The first step in the intervention process was to identify the difficult-to-
learn or difficult-to-control child and place him or her in a self-contained
special classroom. There, away from competition with normal students, content modification strategies were employed with smaller and presumably
homogeneous groups of students. Social behavior problems were expected
to disappear in this supportive environment. If they did not, traditional
disciplinary practices were employed to maintain classroom control.

Programs for the moderately retarded began their slow growth during the
mid sixties. A second piece of landmark legislation, P.L. 88-164, was enacted
in 1963. This law provided funding for centers for programmatic research in
mental retardation and broadened the scope of training teacher support to
other areas of exceptionality. This law and P.L. 85-926 set the stage for
continuing amendments and new legislation that expanded and wrought
major changes in special education practices in the 1970s. President Johnson's
Great Society programs, particularly Head Start and Follow-Through, focused
national attention on the deleterious effects of poverty, poor living environments,
and the cross-generational effects of cultural deprivation. The relationship
between poverty and retarded development created additional interest in
special education practices for the mildly retarded, particularly the cultural-
familial type of mental retardation (Robinson & Robinson, 1965).

The Seventies

The 1970s can best be described as a period of activism—activism which
occurred on several fronts and created multiple meanings of the word.

The civil rights activism of the previous decade emerged full blown when
the rights of handicapped individuals were closely examined in the seventies.
In California, two suits, *Diana* in 1970 and *Larry P* in 1973, charged that then
current testing and placement practices resulted in de facto segregation for
Hispanic and other nonwhite students. The claim was based on the
overrepresentation of nonwhite students in special education classes. In 1971,
parents in Pennsylvania charged the state with failure to provide equal access
to educational opportunity to severely mentally retarded students. This suit,
settled by consent decree, established that the state's department of education
was responsible for mentally retarded students. A similar suit, filed in the
District of Columbia, extended that basic right to all handicapped students.

These suits, and the hundred or more that followed, resulted in changes in state laws and regulations. In 1975, P.L. 94-142 was enacted. This new federal law, The Education for All Handicapped Act, promised many benefits:

A free appropriate public education for handicapped individuals from birth to adulthood,

Education in the least restrictive environment for all handicapped students (a provision designed, for the most part, to end the practice of educating mildly handicapped students in self-contained classrooms),

An end to discriminatory testing practices,

An individualized educational plan and program for all handicapped students,

Parent involvement in all phases of the educational assessment and instructional process,

A requirement stopping just short of teacher accountability for student achievement of written educational goals,

A procedure (due process) to guarantee parents' access to the civil courts to challenge educational decisions,

State level responsibility to insure that all provisions of the law were met,

A system of monitoring to insure state and local compliance with the provisions of the law, and

Massive federal support for these educational changes.

Federal regulations, published in 1977, set out the requirements of the law in explicit detail—or so it seemed at the onset.

The litigation and legislation focused national attention on special education practices and created new forms of activism. The law provided a forum for parents to advocate for their own children. Special educators at the university level actively promoted the return of mildly handicapped students to the regular classroom (Cartwright & Cartwright, 1972; Lilly, 1970). Others saw the courts and due process hearings as an opportunity to advocate for changes in educational practice. In a very real sense, the emerging discipline of contemporary special education was caught short at the onset by social events set in motion in the 1954 *Brown* v. *Board of Education* decision. Forced to examine its practices, special education experienced a renewed sense of commitment to quality programming for handicapped students.

Educational practices in the seventies were typified by a focus on the individual. The general curriculum strategies of the sixties were replaced by individualized instructional strategies: student-specific diagnostic-prescriptive models and curricula designed to match the learning style or learning modality strengths of the student. Social behavior change (behavior modification) strategies were incorporated in special education, focusing on problem behaviors of individual students as well as group control (token economy systems). Contingency contracting, or performance contracting, introduced learning systems to special education that provided academic programming as well as social behavior change. Highly precise instructional models, initially developed in the sixties (Haring & Schiefelbusch, 1967), came into widespread usage in the seventies—particularly with moderately and severely developmentally retarded students.

Process-oriented procedures were applied to the academic problems of learning disabled students. Severely and profoundly retarded, multihandicapped students were brought into the public education system through the external forces described earlier; these educational programs were structured for highly individualized programming. Low student to teacher/aide ratios were then and are still common.

Specific curriculum development expanded during this era into such areas as leisure time and physical education/recreation, career planning, science education, novel approaches to reading, specific language training, self-help skill development for moderately retarded students, and basic response shaping (repertoire building) for lower functioning students. And, with the most handicapped students, school systems were made responsible through the individualized educational plan (IEP) for coordinating the delivery of support services: physical therapy, specific nursing or health maintenance activities, speech therapy, and other related services. Toward the end of this period, some special educators understood and articulated the need to progress from systems of data-based instruction to systems that would allow empirical verification of the effects of intervention in the classroom—one of the basic goals of this text.

The cumulative effect of the developmental efforts of the seventies, then, was to set the stage for a new era of intensive programming for handicapped students in the 1980s. Having moved from global to highly specific curricula, instructional procedures, and behavioral control strategies, it appeared that the goal of demonstrably effective, individualized instruction for each handicapped child—from birth, if necessary, and continuing as long as necessary— might be met.

The decade ended on a less than optimistic note, however. The promise for handicapped students was dimmed by many pragmatic considerations: partial funding of legislation, logistical difficulties in developing plans and programs for *all* handicapped students, active resistance to federal intervention at the state and local levels, realization that parent advocates were really few in number and that many parents cared little about providing input into the educational process, the high cost of educating the most severely handicapped students, and teachers' inability to document students' progress. A steadily worsening economy, in turn, shifted attention from the problems of the handicapped to more personal concerns—the family budget.

The Eighties

The 1980s are unfolding in front of us. The future of programs for the handicapped is uncertain to say the least. The administration of the early eighties has been urging that current federal programs be returned to the states, shorn of the constraints that earmarked funds for the handicapped. There is as yet no public or professional acknowledgment of the civil rights issues that brought education for the handicapped to the attention of the courts and Congress in the first place. And, unfortunately, the effects of a change in direction in federal policies and federal budget management may not be apparent until four or five years have passed. Thus, programs for the handicapped exist in a state of uncertainty. Some (Tawney, 1982) have suggested that the future of public education as a whole is uncertain and that new forms of education may emerge to take its place. But that possibility exists somewhere in the distant future.

The Missing Era of Empiricism

Nowhere in this discussion has there been mention of an *era of empiricism* in special education—though perhaps the groundwork for such an era is being developed at the present time.

There have been periodic attempts, on a small scale, to evaluate the effectiveness of special education programs in the United States. These evaluative efforts, when analyzed together (Guskin & Spicker, 1968; Kirk, 1964), have failed to demonstrate significant benefits to the students enrolled in special education programs. Many reasons have been proposed to explain these findings, and some are elaborated in later chapters.

There are, too, many reasons why there has been no tradition of empiricism in contemporary special education. First, the field is new, as it is viewed here, and many of the initial efforts were of a developmental nature. The initial tasks of the field were to develop a content of instruction for teachers-in-training and for handicapped students.

Next, the first generation of doctoral level special educators, in many programs, were not trained as researchers. Rather, they were trained to teach teachers, to develop and administer teacher training programs, and to administer programs in state departments of education or local school systems. In only a few places (University of Illinois, Syracuse University, George Peabody College for Teachers) was there an early emphasis on training researchers. Only recently have doctoral level programs in special education assumed a research orientation. Prehm (1980) notes that scholarship is not highly developed in special education and that according to Arlin (1977), the majority of educational researchers rarely publish more than one study once they have completed the doctorate.

A third and major reason for a lack of empiricism is that special education did not emerge from the regular public education system in a logical, evolutionary manner. Instead the field was established from the outset by external forces. Schooling, it should be remembered, was once considered an endeavor for a white, middle-class, average or above population—a pervasive belief on the part of regular educators that was in large part responsible for the civil rights activism of the sixties. This belief remains with some individuals today and in large part is responsible for the resistance to mainstreaming of special education students.

Because special education evolved as a result of external forces, events moved faster than the field's ability to respond. Opportunities for systematic program development and evaluation were lost in the political climate of the times. In the early sixties, after the impact of P.L. 85-926, the major concern was to find and certify teachers to staff the classrooms for handicapped students. There was little knowledge of what to teach and how to teach it, let alone how to measure it. Although there were some attempts to develop curricula, or academic programs based on the unique characteristics of handicapped learners (as they were drawn from the literature of experimental or clinical psychology), these developed slowly. And they were abandoned, or deemphasized, during the seventies when political movements to mainstream the mildly handicapped and bring the severely handicapped into the public education system were initiated. Under court-ordered guidelines, major changes in educational practices were initiated. The eventual direction of change was not fully conceptualized at the outset: performance evaluation systems were in short supply, and the time to plan and the funds for systematic evaluation were absent. Consequently, particularly with the mainstreaming movement, the opportunity to document that it was more effective than traditional practice was lost. Though numerous small-scale studies of mainstreaming were conducted, an analysis made by Semmel, Gottlieb, and Robinson (1979) showed no evidence—that is, no empirically sound data—that educating mildly handicapped students in regular education with support services is an effective practice.

Another reason for failure to develop an empirical tradition in special education may be in the lack of fit between traditional statistical analysis and the characteristics of handicapped populations. From the thirties to the present, investigators have attempted to apply the laboratory study group comparison technique to the educational environment and to groups of handicapped students presumed to be homogeneous in composition by virtue of their common categorical label. As noted, these efforts have been singularly unspectacular. Even though, early on, Kirk (1964), a pioneer in special education, argued for a better way to assess the effects of intervention, it is only recently that an alternative strategy, single subject research design, has been employed.

Finally, there was little demand for teachers to collect data on student performance in the first contemporary programs for mildly handicapped students. In programs that focused on social or vocational skill development, the departure from the traditional curriculum rendered group achievement tests invalid for the "new" curriculum. Where the pace of the regular curriculum was slowed, there was no expectation that students would continue to perform at grade level. Little attention was given to the development of alternative evaluation systems (trial-by-trial data collection, etc.) Instead, concerns focused on more general ways to report progress to parents than the A-B-C grading system for, respectively, 90-80-70 percent correct responding on the traditional curriculum. This situation, in turn, led to a search for an alternative way to describe passage through the school years—certificates of attendance rather than certificates of achievement. One consequence of this shift to a "nongraded" curriculum was that specific performance criteria (individual student skill/content acquisition data) were abandoned early on.

This tradition began to change, however, in the late sixties and early seventies. Several factors accounted for the change: the development of systematic instructional models, such as the precision teaching model; the emerging impact of applied behavior analysis, which was present at the outset of the development of contemporary special education; a technological shift in society, eventually reflected in public education; public pressure for accountability in education; and, finally, the requirements for objective evaluation criteria incorporated in P.L. 94-142. Though this law specifically indicated that teachers were not held accountable for student's failure to achieve short-term objectives, an equally potent "accountability" provision was incorporated. The law requires that parents give their approval of the child's placement, plan, and educational program. Further, parent consent is voluntary and can be revoked at any time when, for example, parents are dissatisfied with their child's progress. Due process procedures allow parents and the schools to pursue their disagreements from the classroom to hearings at the local and state levels and then into the civil courts system. This has provided a powerful impetus for a shift to data-based *and* empirically verified instructional systems.

The Behavior-Analytic Tradition in Contemporary Special Education

What has been the influence of behavior(ism) *on* the field of special education? There is an implicit assumption when asking this question that a recent approach, behavioral intervention, has impacted on an existing field—special education. Typically, this is how the relationship between special education and behaviorism has been viewed—if considered at all.

The relationship between the fields is really quite different. In fact, behavioral influences have been present from the beginning of contemporary special education. And a case can be made that the behavioral influence has been the strongest and most productive of the intervention strategies that have become part of special education practice, a belief expressed by MacMillan and Morrison (1980, pp. 22–23). Whether that argument is accepted is, of course, a matter of personal interpretation.

What is the justification for this point of view? Part of the answer is found in the relationships between special education and psychology training programs as they have existed at key universities. Typically, doctoral students in special education take an emphasis, or minor, in related fields—often psychology. The behavioral influence has been reflected in subsequent research of special educators trained at universities with strong behavioral programs (e.g., the University of Kansas and the University of Illinois). Key writings of the major behaviorists found a receptive audience among the first generation of special educators—those who were searching for a content of instruction and a teaching methodology for a rapidly expanding field.

Part of the answer is found in a transformation that occurred in the treatment of mentally disturbed individuals in the 1960s. While programs for the handicapped were developing in the schools, the community mental health movement was growing. These movements were stimulated, in large part, by the same factors: postwar awareness of the presence and magnitude of handicapping conditions and the personal interest of the Kennedy administration in these areas. Thus, as public school classes grew, a new generation of psychologists, among them applied behavior analysts, moved from institutional settings into the community where they began working with the school-centered problems of conduct-disordered and other troubled students.

Part of the answer is that key behaviorists experimented with mentally retarded and disturbed populations as they developed their nontraditional procedures; the results of their research were then employed in special education.

Still another answer is that the first generation of special educators included behavioral psychologists who incorporated the principles of behaviorism into their teacher training programs. Reinforcement strategies were incorporated into curriculum materials for handicapped students; for example, the Peabody Language Development Kits (PLDK) contained plastic chips that could be used for reinforcers. Reinforcement and intensive response shaping strategies were incorporated into the Direct Instruction System for Teaching Arithmetic and Reading (DISTAR) materials. Developed by Bereiter, Englemann, and others at the University of Illinois in the mid sixties for culturally disadvantaged students in preschool programs, those materials strongly influenced early education programs and programs for the mildly and moderately retarded. At the same time, highly specific instructional procedures, generally referred to as systematic instruction, were developed by behaviorally trained special educators. Thus, incorporation and use of reinforcement procedures contributed to the growth of behavioral technology in special education.

The key to understanding the relationship between the two fields is in the temporal contiguity in developments in each area. Work in progress in the fifties and reported in the sixties shows the early extension of behavioral principles and intervention strategies with handicapped populations (Barrett & Lindsley, 1962; Bijou, 1963; Bijou & Orlando, 1961; Birnbrauer & Lawler, 1964; Ferster & DeMyer, 1961; Lindsley, 1965; Orlando & Bijou, 1960; Zimmerman & Zimmerman, 1962). These early studies greatly influenced special education practice and contributed to its behavior-analytic tradition. *Educating Emotionally Disturbed Children* (Haring & Phillips, 1962) also had a major effect.

A Note on Terminology

To this point, the rich diversity of behavioral terminology has, by design, remained untapped. The terms *behavior-analytic tradition, behavioral intervention, behavior(ism), behavioral influence,* and *behavioral psychology* have been used in the most general sense—to denote a focus on the behavior of an organism.

Behavioral psychology may be considered a broad discipline within psychology that focuses attention on the study and manipulation of organism-environment interactions. The field encompasses a multitude of behavioral intervention techniques. Kazdin (1978) has described the range of practices in an exhaustive history of behavior modification.

Operant conditioning is a procedure that modifies behavior by the manipulation of consequent events. The term is attributed to Skinner (1935) who posed a new type of learning paradigm. In contrast to traditional classical conditioning studies where behavioral change was effected by the arrangement of antecedents, operant learning was shown to be shaped by the arrangement of consequent events.

The term *experimental analysis of behavior* (EAB) also has been attributed to Skinner (1953). EAB refers to the experimental analysis of observable interactions between the organism and the environment. More specifically, it refers primarily to the study of operant conditioning in the laboratory, primarily with infrahuman subjects.

Applied behavior analysis refers to the study of observable organism-environment interaction, primarily with human subjects in the natural environment. The term *applied* reflects a focus on practical learning problems: the acceleration of academic targets (speech or sound production, computation of arithmetic problems), the acceleration of positive social behaviors (cooperative play, appropriate toy play), or the deceleration of disturbing or destructive social behaviors (uncontrolled screaming, head banging, verbal abusive statements).

The term *behavior modification* has acquired many technical and nontechnical meanings. In its broadest sense, it refers to any strategy to change behavior. Within psychology, the term is restricted to practices that manipulate observable behavior to demonstrate a functional relationship between intervention and behavior change. Within special education, the term is generally associated with intervention programs designed to change the observable behavior of students by careful arrangement of consequent events. Or, it may refer to group social control projects, e.g., token economies.

Behavior therapy, a term little used in special education, refers primarily to clinical treatment of so-called behavior disorders.

Behavioral principles refer to those empirically verifiable events or arranged contingencies that are known to change the rate, magnitude, or intensity of responses. These principles have been elaborated in numerous texts on behaviorism such as those by Bijou and Baer (1961), Ferster, Culbertson, and Boren (1975), and Holland and Skinner (1961), to name only a few.

In the present context, *behavioral intervention* refers to any educational intervention designed to accelerate academic (instructional) behavior or to accelerate or decelerate social behavior that utilizes the principles of operant conditioning to accomplish the desired behavior change.

In special education, the term *behavior-analytic tradition* refers to a philosophy of education—a philosophy that is grounded in the analysis of observable interactions between the organism (student) and the environment (schooling: the physical environment, the teacher, and other interventionists). From this perspective, student behavior change is accomplished by careful arrangement of consequent events (contingencies of reinforcement), following established principles of operant conditioning. In the instructional setting, careful attention also is paid to the arrangement of antecedents (instructional materials). Thus, when a student demonstrates high rates of correct responses to such stimuli and is then reinforced, that student is said to be *under instructional control.*

Single subject research design is an integral part of the behavior-analytic tradition. The term refers to a research strategy developed to document changes in the behavior of the individual subject. Through the accurate selection and utilization of the family of designs described in this text, it is possible to demonstrate a functional relationship between intervention and a change in behavior. *To demonstrate a functional relationship* means simply that the experimenter, teacher, and interventionist have confidence, through empirical verification, that behavior change occurred because the intervention occurred, and for no other likely reason.

SUMMARY

This introduction has presented a brief sketch of contemporary special education. We have described how contemporary special education and contemporary applied behavior analysis have developed as parallel disciplines and have documented presence of a behavior-analytic tradition in contemporary special education. In the next chapter, the extensive history of applied behavior analysis and its influence within special education is traced. The remainder of the book presents single subject research methodology and shows the student-researcher how to conduct studies in applied settings.

2

THE BEHAVIORAL REVOLUTION

The behavior-analytic tradition in special education can be traced directly to Skinner's early experiments in the 1930s. From the Skinner box and the pigeon, the principles of operant conditioning were identified as a type of learning distinct from classical conditioning. Skinner's work received careful attention among psychologists. When he presented these basic principles in fictionalized form in *Walden Two* (Skinner, 1948), he introduced operant conditioning to the general public, who reacted with a mixture of enthusiasm and condemnation. Through the 1950s, the parameters of the operant paradigm were explored in the laboratory. Tentatively at first, they were employed in clinical settings with disturbed clients. Spurred by critical evaluations (Eysenck, 1952) of traditional psychotherapy techniques, clinical psychologists sought other intervention models, among them operant conditioning. Later they extended their interests to the handicapped and to the natural environment. In those areas where the interests of special educators and psychologists meshed, there was a rapid acceleration of the use of operant conditioning in programs for the handicapped student, the development of token economies, individual behavior modification projects conducted by teacher consultants, and integration of reinforcement techniques in systematic instruction systems.

This chapter traces the growth of applied behavior analysis and single subject research design in special education. The careers of major behaviorists and their contributions are described. Links, diffusion points, or conjunctions between psychology and special education are identified, as are those special educators who received training from the pioneers in behavioral psychology or who were trained in the first behaviorally oriented special

This chapter was written by **James W. Tawney** and **David L. Gast**.

education programs. The students of the first generation of behavioral special educators are identified also, though the diffusion has become so widespread that many surely have been missed. To them, we apologize in advance.

B.F. Skinner

Overview: Skinner's Contributions in Perspective

Educated in the liberal arts tradition, frustrated as a budding novelist, B.F. Skinner entered Harvard to study psychology. His doctoral thesis was completed in 1931. From then until 1957, journal publication of studies of the rat and pigeon were quickly followed by nontechnical or fictional descriptions of operant behavior and its social applications. The cumulative knowledge derived from studies conducted from 1930 to 1937 was published in 1938 in *The Behavior of Organisms*. The principles of operant behavior were incorporated into his Utopia, *Walden Two*, published in 1948. *Science and Human Behavior*, published in 1953, raised the possibility of a scientific analysis of human behavior, described the principles of operant conditioning, and suggested how these might be applied to the design of a culture. In 1957, Skinner and Charles Ferster published *Schedules of Reinforcement*, a compendium of laboratory studies. Skinner (1957) also published *Verbal Behavior*, a book he later (Skinner, 1973, p. 261) described as an interpretation of the way that contingencies of reinforcement might account for the development of language (verbal behavior). Since 1957, Skinner has lectured extensively on operant conditioning and the experimental analysis of behavior. These lectures, in turn, have been widely published in psychology journals.

Eventually Skinner extended his experimental analysis to education and the instructional process. His papers in this area were published in 1968 as *The Technology of Teaching*. This collection of seven reprinted and four original chapters, influential in the conceptualization of teaching as a scientific process, contributed significantly to the development of instructional technology (systematic instructional procedures).

In 1971, *Beyond Freedom and Dignity* was published. This book suggested that a technology of behavior might solve major world problems, but in the process prized values of the autonomous human being (freedom and dignity) would have to be set aside. Skinner's suggestions were attacked immediately by scientists, philosophers, and theologians. Subsequently, Skinner's attention turned to defending his position. Harvey Wheeler (1973), at a symposium organized by the Center for the Study of Democratic Institutions to analyze *Beyond Freedom and Dignity*, put it this way: "Chafing under the attacks on *Beyond Freedom and Dignity*, Skinner now plans a new book, not on operant conditioning, but on the philosophy of behaviorism" (p. 13). That book, *About Behaviorism*, was published in 1974. Most recently Skinner has been working on his autobiography (Skinner, 1976, 1979) and publication of the notes and observations generated daily over the span of his career.

Skinner's influence on psychology has been pervasive. Through his practical applications (a pigeon-controlled missile guidance system during World War II and an air crib—a controlled infant environment) and his nontechnical writing, he has kept the science of behavior in the public eye. In the design of a culture, he naturally addressed the problems confronting public education: the punitive nature of the classroom, inefficient instruction, unsystematic feedback, nonscientific (non-data-based) analysis of pupil error, and failure to develop thinking and creative behavior. He has influenced other psychologists and educators whose subsequent efforts have contributed to effective programs for handicapped students. Skinner has frequently been misunderstood, or so he believes (Skinner, 1973, p. 256). His contributions transcend the development of a methodology for the single subject useful in classroom settings or a system of behavior analysis or suggestions for a technology of instruction. For these reasons, and because the contributions of pioneers are often paraphrased or abstracted when described by others, this history begins with the early Skinner and his original contributions.

**Scientist,
Philosopher,
Social Engineer**

It is one thing to be a teacher, a psychologist, or a school administrator. It is yet another to be a visionary scientist and philosopher. Skinner's critics have asked, *What, or who, is Skinner?* The public and the professionals (nonscientists) who have attacked him are generally unaware that the principles of operant conditioning were derived from the experimental laboratory. Some critics have been reluctant to accept Skinner's premise that laboratory findings obtained on infrahuman species may be helpful in solving the problems of human beings in the natural environment. And some acknowledge Skinner's expertise in psychology but feel that his social applications wander far afield. Wheeler (1973) has suggested that Skinner tends to intermix a philosophy of behaviorism, a science of the contingencies of reinforcement, and a technology of operant conditioning. These three areas, and the distinctions among them, are critical to understanding Skinner and the impact of the behavior-analytic tradition in special education.

Scientist

For nearly 30 years, Skinner published findings from the experimental laboratory. He and his associates studied the behavior of individual rat or pigeon subjects. From this body of work came these contributions: discovery of operant conditioning as a type distinct from classical (Pavlovian) conditioning, a set of principles of operant conditioning, data showing the effects of the manipulation of reinforcement contingencies on the rate of the behavior of the organism under study, a methodology for the study of the single organism, a strategy for the experimental analysis of behavior, and a commitment to the study of behavior, i.e., the observable behavior of the organism.

Later he would refer, in general terms, to the experimental and applied behavioral research of others in defense of his position as a behaviorist.

Philosopher

For our purposes, a philosopher can be defined as one who holds and expounds on an organized set of beliefs. Skinner, as a philosopher, may be viewed as one who has promoted a belief that a science of behavior has the potential to solve world (social) problems and, in so doing, to create a new and radically different culture. He developed a blueprint for that society in *Walden Two*. There, and in *Beyond Freedom and Dignity,* he describes the value systems that form the basis of this society. His belief, or philosophy, that the locus of control rests within the culture (environment) and not in the internalized and self-selected value system of the autonomous human being puts him at odds with other philosophers and theologians.

Some consider Skinner to be more philosopher than scientist. Wheeler (1973), summarizing the early influences of Skinner, notes that Skinner did not begin as an undergraduate major in psychology. Rather, he entered Harvard as an admirer of the philosopher Bertrand Russell, who introduced him to Watsonian behaviorism. "Empiricism, positivism, behaviorism—these were Skinner's philosophic antecedents, and the precedence of philosophy over science is important. The precedence has persisted" (Wheeler, 1973, p. 13).

Social Engineer

Walden Two described every aspect of life in a Utopian society. Efficient environmental design, work for credit for a communal existence, novel approaches to mating, child rearing, and education, extinction of destructive negative emotions and careful shaping of positive forms of behavior, loose organizational/governmental control, the absence of coercive control, and a reinterpretation of "freedom"—all are present in *Walden Two*. The concepts and principles originated in the laboratory and were applied directly to the design of a culture—even Skinner's work on schedule control. Frazier, the protagonist in *Walden Two,* describes how the community confronted the problem of reinforcing infants' exploratory behavior.

> We made a survey of the motives of the unhampered child and found more than we could use. Our engineering job was to preserve them by fortifying the child against discouragement. We introduce discouragement as carefully as we introduce any other emotional situation, beginning at about six months. Some of the toys in our air-conditioned cubicles are designed to build perseverance. A bit of a tune from a music box, or a pattern of flashing lights, is arranged to follow an appropriate response—say, pulling on a string. Later the string must be pulled twice, later still three or five or ten times. It's possible to build up fantastically perseverative behavior without encountering frustration or rage. (Skinner, 1948, p. 101)

The reader who has completed a basic course in psychology will immediately recognize that Skinner is describing the shaping of a durable response by thinning or "leaning" a fixed ratio schedule, respectively FR1, FR2, FR3, FR5, FR10.

Walden Two documents Skinner's credentials as a social engineer. Social applications of operant behavior are present in *Science and Human Behavior:* the design of a culture, issues of control (and counter-control) of behavior, and the use of operant technology by controlling agencies. In both books, Skinner suggests that traditional values and principles may be abandoned in the design of an Utopian society. Thus it comes as no surprise when Skinner states in *Beyond Freedom and Dignity* that the world needs a technology of behavior, but the development of such a technology is hampered by prescientific thinking.

> As the interaction between organism and environment has come to be understood, however, effects once assigned to states of mind, feelings and traits are beginning to be traced to accessible conditions, and a technology of behavior may therefore become available. It will not solve our problems, however, until it replaces traditional prescientific views, and these are strongly entrenched. Freedom and dignity illustrate the difficulty. They are the possessions of the autonomous man of traditional theory, and they are essential to practices in which a person is held responsible for his conduct and given credit for his achievements. A scientific

analysis shifts both the responsibility and the achievement to the environment. It also raises questions concerning "values." Who will use a technology and to what ends? (Skinner, 1971, pp. 22–23)

Thus we see three facets of Skinner—scientist, philosopher, social engineer. The quotations show how a scientific procedure, developed in the laboratory, is translated into a component of a culture. The problem of values is of pervasive concern and, in typical fashion, confronted directly.

The Reflex and Discovery of Operant Conditioning

In contemporary society, when a term acquires multiple referents, which overlap and extend beyond the original definition, it is said to have acquired surplus meaning. One who uses the term then may have said too much, i.e., the statement carries too much meaning. It goes beyond the data, so to speak. In a sense, Skinner's first and enduring interest has been to develop a description of behavior that has no surplus meaning. To this end he restricted his observations to only the data he could see—the observable interaction of the organism and the environment.

Skinner (1931) proposed that the study of behavior should focus on two areas, the characteristics of the correlation between stimulus and response (as these were varied systematically) and the effect of these variations on a third set of variables—reflex strength. He summarized his position: "From the point of view of scientific method, any law describing the behavior of organisms must be reducible to one of the forms herein discussed. The description of behavior, that is to say, is adequately embraced by the principles of the reflex" (p. 455). The concept of the reflex was modified, however, as Skinner discovered the operant.

In 1935, Skinner published a paper describing two types of conditioning. He described six differences between his Type I and Type II, the classical conditioning paradigm. In response to a criticism of this paper, Skinner (1937) elaborated on this distinction, using the now familiar operant-respondent terminology for the first time (Skinner, 1961, p. 376). The term *correlated with* was, in a sense, replaced by the more familiar *contingent upon,* i.e., the strength (frequency of occurrence of) an operant is contingent upon subsequent reinforcement. In this paper, Skinner clarifies the status of antecedent stimuli in the operant paradigm through the use of the term *discriminative stimulus.* Remember that the presence of a controlling, antecedent (eliciting) stimulus is a key feature of classical conditioning. A key distinction between operant and respondent conditioning is the absence of a controlling antecedent. However, antecedent stimuli, present when an operant is reinforced, may acquire discriminative properties, i.e., having been reinforced for responding when these stimuli are present; S may then respond in their presence (and continue to do so if the response is increased or maintained by the reinforcer which follows the response).

Implications for the Teacher-Researcher
Skinner's early contributions created a new behavioral psychology and have had a pervasive influence in contemporary behavior analysis. His work resulted in a focus on organism-environment interaction, an adherence to a precise language system (one devoid of surplus meaning), discovery of the operant conditioning paradigm, and elaboration of the paradigm.

The implications for the teacher-researcher are clear. Skinner's contributions can be translated into principles for working in the classroom environment.

1. Focus on the interaction of the student within his environment and avoid hypothesizing causes for behaviors that are removed from the interaction.

2. Be precise in describing the nature of academic or social behavior problems. Confine the description to observable events and their temporal relationships.

3. Child behavior is shaped by well-established principles that, when appropriately applied, will expand the child's repertoire of appropriate (adaptive, creative) responses.

4. It is possible to set the stage for responding by arranging discriminative stimuli. Careful sequencing of antecedents and arrangement of contingencies of reinforcement are critical to the establishment of systematic instruction, or data-based integrated learning systems.

The Experimental Analysis of Behavior

In *The Behavior of Organisms,* Skinner (1938) described a system of behavior, defined a research methodology, and presented data on various stimulus and response manipulations. This book set the stage for the study of operant behavior.

Later, Skinner and an associate (Ferster & Skinner, 1957) presented data on an extensive number of experiments, showing the effects of different schedules of reinforcement on the probability of occurrence of a behavior. These studies in schedule control form the basis for most of what is known about shaping specific patterns of behavior across species, the rat or pigeon in the laboratory as well as the student in the public school classroom.

Skinner's contributions to a methodology for the experimental analysis of behavior will become apparent to the reader as a methodology for data collection on applied problems in the natural setting (to the extent that a public school can be called a natural environment) is developed in subsequent chapters.

Educational Problems and the Technology of Teaching

The design of an educational system is an integral part of Skinner's preoccupation with the design of a culture: a design based on a technology of behavior. *The Technology of Teaching* (Skinner, 1968) contains papers written primarily between 1954 and 1968. During this period, key events were unfolding in public education:

1. Rapid expansion of schools to accommmodate the post World War II baby boom,

2. Major reorganization of math and science curricula as a result of the Sputnik era thrust to gain world superiority in science, technology, and space exploration,

3. Development of computer hardware leading to the first systems of *computer-assisted instruction* (CAI),

4. The growth of programs for handicapped students,

5. Dissatisfaction with public education, later in this period, as a result of the civil rights movement,

6. Growth of the Great Society programs, Head Start and Follow-Through for the culturally disadvantaged.

This period can be typified as a period of growth in some areas, as a time when public education was subjected to intense critical analysis and when there was great interest in improving education through the use of technology, through behavioral engineering and through systems for individualizing instruction. The titles of Skinner's works on teaching reflect the tenor of the times, e.g., "Why Teachers Fail," "The Science of Learning and the Art of Teaching," "Why We Need Teaching Machines," "The Technology of Teaching."

Skinner's interest in teaching and the instructional process moved in three directions: application of a technology of behavior to the classroom (the technology of teaching), development of teaching machines, and design of programmed instruction.

The Technology of Teaching

Skinner's papers on education reflect two major themes, the defective nature of the educational system, as he viewed it, and great enthusiasm for the potential benefits of major educational change based on a technology of behavior, teaching machines, and programmed instruction. His first paper, "The Science of Learning and the Art of Teaching," originally presented and published in 1954, illustrates Skinner's perspective. Again, his criticisms of the status of education of the time were externally validated, in a broad sense, by then present general dissatisfaction with public education.

Skinner felt that the major problem with the educational system was the widespread use of aversive control, i.e., children study to avoid punishment. His specific criticisms were that schools control behavior through aversive consequences, contingencies of reinforcement are loosely arranged, and reinforcement of correct responses occurs infrequently and thus exerts weak control over students' study behavior.

In "The Science of Learning and the Art of Teaching," Skinner discusses contingencies of reinforcement, the distinction between acquisition and maintenance of a behavior, and the effect of schedule control. He presents behavioral analogs to nonbehavioral terms (motivation). He talks about schedule control, stimulus control, discriminative stimuli, complex behaviors shaped by complex contingencies, shaping complex behavior by successive approximations, and rate as the datum of behavioral change. In essence, his brief paper contains a short course in operant conditioning.

Turning to the educational environment, Skinner suggests that teaching may be improved by identifying positive reinforcers, including artificial ones, and dispensing them contingently (best done by a teaching machine) to shape complex patterns of behavior. He concludes:

> There is a simple job to be done. The task can be stated in concrete terms. The necessary techniques are known. The equipment needed can easily be provided. Nothing stands in the way but cultural inertia ... we are on the threshold of an exciting and revolutionary period, in which the scientific study of man will be put to work in man's best interests. Education must play its part. It must accept the fact that a sweeping revision of educational practices is possible and inevitable. When it has done this, we may look forward with confidence to a school system which is aware of the nature of its tasks, secure in its methods, and generously supported by the informed and effective citizens whom education itself will create. (Skinner, 1968, p. 28)

Time has shown that Skinner's enthusiasm was warranted in some instances and not others. The application of a technology of behavior has occurred in special education but had little impact on regular education. The interest in instructional technology failed to reach fruition. Only now, several years after the publication of this paper, has there been renewed interest and forward movement in this area.

Skinner may have said too much, for once, in his enthusiasm for transforming education. For example Skinner (1968) also said, in developing a rationale for the teaching machine, "The simple fact is that, as a mere reinforcing mechanism, the teacher is out of date" (p. 22). Though there is a basis for that belief, the statement was hardly politic, given that teachers' first reactions to "automation" in the classroom were that they would lose their jobs.

However, in other areas, Skinner's arguments were well founded, as current problems in education bear out. In "Why Teachers Fail," he elaborated on the effects of aversive control. Arguing that aversive control is weak, he suggested that students may escape, in subtle ways, or counterattack. He said:

> Vandalism is another form of counterattack which is growing steadily more serious. Many cities maintain special police forces to guard school buildings on weekends. Schools are now designed so that windows cannot be easily broken from the street. *A more sweeping counterattack comes later when, as taxpayers or alumni, former students refuse to support educational institutions. Anti-intellectualism is often a general attack on all that education represents.* [italics added] (Skinner, 1968, p. 98)

While there are many factors which contribute to the current malaise in public education, perhaps Skinner identified a major source of dissatisfaction.

To what extent has Skinner contributed to the development of a technology of behavior in educational settings? His papers had little direct impact on educational practice at the time. They did, however, show that laboratory techniques and behavior analysis could be applied to educational problems. Typically, the principles of operant behavior were illustrated by describing how the behavior of a pigeon was shaped; then the principles were applied to a specific educational problem. It remained for Skinner's associates and a new generation of psychologists and special educators to translate these principles into widespread practice. These practices, as shown in subsequent chapters, came in the form of token economies, the development of artificial or prosthetic educational environments, a shift to positive forms of behavior control, and the development of sophisticated instructional procedures.

In summary, Skinner's contributions to education were the development of an experimental analysis of behavior, the application of an experimental analysis to the classroom environment, and exposure of the aversive nature of education practices. He introduced the notion that while education may not be a science, it is amenable to a technological/scientific analysis. Finally, he proposed that the experimental analysis of behavior had a critical role in the design of a future culture. These principles, translated into a technology of teaching, gave education a central role in cultural reform. But it cannot be said that, in general education, the promise of educational and cultural reform has been fulfilled.

Teaching Machines and Programmed Instruction

Skinner's interest in teaching machines and programmed instruction evolved naturally from the laboratory setting. In the Skinner box, stimuli were carefully controlled and precisely changed. Subjects' responses were reinforced immediately according to a defined schedule of reinforcement. Thus, with precise environmental control, complex and elaborate behaviors were shaped. Teaching machines and programmed instruction, according to Skinner, held promise to achieve instructional control in the educational setting. The problem was the same for both environments and for human and infrahuman subjects: to arrange the contingencies of reinforcement in the presence of carefully constructed stimuli to produce a change in behavior, in the desired direction, and in an efficient and effective manner.

Teaching machines could do what teachers could not do, Skinner proposed. Carefully constructed stimuli (programmed instruction) could lead the student, in small steps, through complex content. Careful content analysis and content programming could increase the probability of students' correct responding. Text materials and teaching machines could be designed to provide immediate feedback to the student. Teaching machines could be programmed to provide an array of reinforcers for a correct response. In addition to efficiency and effectiveness, they could provide individualized instruction, learner-paced instruction, infinite patience, error free operation (once fully programmed), and immediate reinforcement of correct responses or correction of errors.

Skinner's contributions to advances in teaching machines and programmed instruction were limited in the context of the total scope of development in the 1960s. His efforts were important because they illustrated how laboratory procedures and instrumentation could be used in the classroom. His major contributions to education from this body of work can be summarized. Educators should focus on positive control of behavior, encourage correct responding by fine grain sequencing of instructional stimuli, and encourage immediate feedback as a component of individualized instruction.

Skinner's Students and Associates

The growth of applied behavior analysis in special education settings can be traced directly to Skinner's work and to the work of his students and associates. This section identifies those individuals and briefly describes the nature of their work. Later sections describe the contributions of these individuals in detail and identify others they trained or with whom they collaborated.

Skinner's professional career was spent at the University of Minnesota, the University of Indiana, and at Harvard. While a department chairman at Indiana, he appointed Sidney Bijou as an assistant professor (Etzel, LeBlanc, & Baer, 1977). Bijou later studied with Skinner at Harvard on a postdoctoral fellowship. Bijou was influential in the area of mental (developmental) retardation. At Harvard, Ogden Lindsley and Nathan Azrin studied under Skinner. Lindsley and Skinner extended the principles of operant conditioning from animals to the behavior of psychotics, Lindsley and Azrin to the cooperative behavior of young children, and Azrin, later, to the design of a token economy in a mental institution.

Charles Ferster, who worked with Skinner in the Harvard laboratory (Ferster & Skinner, 1957), later (at Indiana University) began a study of the behavior of autistic children. Lindsley, Azrin, and Ferster, each in a different way, encouraged the development of prosthetic or artificial environments where the contingencies of reinforcement could be carefully controlled. Critical elements of these environments were translated into more natural environments (the classroom setting), e.g., the token economy developed by O'Leary and Becker (1967).

Sidney W. Bijou

For nearly 50 years, Sidney Bijou has studied and written about the behavior of retarded persons. When the 20th century ends, there is every likelihood that his contributions will stand as the most pervasive influence on the field of "retardation." The scope of Bijou's influence is broad. He has demonstrated the principles of operant conditioning with children, developed, with Donald Baer, a functional analysis of child development, extended this functional analysis to retarded development, organized early efforts to develop token economy systems with retarded students, contributed to the development of technology of instruction, promoted the development of applied behavior analysis with retarded students, developed a methodology for studying child behavior in natural settings, and trained and/or collaborated with behavioral psychologists who are now making contributions to the study of retarded behavior in applied settings.

The nature of these contributions is described here. His early professional activities are listed as are his contributions to theory and research methodology.

Historical Background

Bijou obtained his master's degree at Columbia and his doctorate at the University of Iowa. His master's thesis contributed to the standardization of an individual performance test for retarded children (Etzel, LeBlanc, & Baer, 1977). While at Iowa, he studied with Lewin, a Gestalt psychologist, and with Spence who, at the time, was collaborating in the formulation of the Hull-Spence learning theory. Bijou's first position after receiving his PhD was at the Wayne County Training School in Michigan, a residential institution for the mildly retarded. This facility was a training ground for researchers who later made contributions in special education. For example, Samuel Kirk, a pioneer in special education, preceded Bijou at the center. Alfred Strauss, who developed the Strauss-Lehntinen method for educating brain-injured children, worked there as did Heinz Werner, who also wrote in the area of brain injury. For example, Bijou and Werner (1945) collaborated on a study of language problems in brain-injured and non-brain-injured mentally deficient individuals.

From 1938 through the mid forties, Bijou's writing represented the interests of a clinical psychologist: the development of the Wide Range Achievement Test (Bijou & Jastak, 1941), studying experimental neuroses in the rat (Bijou, 1942), vocabulary analysis in mentally deficient children (Bijou & Werner, 1944), and the problem of pseudofeeblemindedness (Bijou, 1939).

Bijou's career was interrupted by World War II. Subsequent to the war, he joined the faculty at the University of Indiana. After two years, he went to the University of Washington where he set up laboratories to study child behavior. During this period, 1948 to 1965, his interest shifted to experimental analysis of behavior. This shift was accelerated after his postdoctoral year at Harvard, spent studying complex concept acquisition in normal and retarded students (Bijou, 1968). After his return to Washington, he established an experimental classroom based on operant principles. One outcome of this, the Rainier project, was a series of reports on the development of a token economy.

From 1965 to 1975, Bijou worked at the University of Illinois where his research with children continued in the Child Behavior Laboratory at the Colonel Wolfe School. (At various times during this period, this building also housed Karnes' projects on teaching culturally disadvantaged preschoolers and some of the Bereiter-Englemann staff who were working on early versions of the DISTAR materials.) Bijou's experimental laboratory was also housed in the school. His courses at Illinois were attended by graduate students in psychology and special education.

In 1975, Bijou moved to the University of Arizona in the Department of Special Education. It is interesting to note, looking at his influence on special education, that he and Samuel Kirk held positions at the Wayne County Training School, then Illinois, and now Arizona. At Illinois, through Kirk's influence, graduate students were encouraged to enroll in Bijou's courses. The number of students was not large, however, and it was through Baer and others in the original Washington group that many behaviorally oriented special educators were subsequently trained at the University of Kansas.

Theory of Child Development

As Bijou describes it (Etzel, LeBlanc, & Baer, 1977, pp. 587–589), he was trained in the Hullian tradition. Although Skinner recruited Bijou at Indiana, he had little immediate influence on him at the time. Skinner had started work on *Science and Human Behavior* at Indiana, and Bijou was aware that the book was in progress. When Bijou moved to Washington, he first experimented with doll play techniques with children. When this line of research produced less than he hoped for, Bijou began to examine other approaches. During this period, *Science and Human Behavior* was published (Skinner, 1953). It had a major impact on Bijou and was influential in his formulation of a theory of child development and methodology. Bijou's philosophy of science was influenced by Jacob Kantor, a faculty member at Indiana and a proponent of interbehavioral psychology (Kantor, 1958).

Bijou and Baer (1961) published a theory of child development that differed markedly from then current developmental (maturational) theories. The difference, of course, was the focus on child behavior and the interaction of the organism (child) and his environment. It is important to examine critical features of this theory because it forms the basis for Bijou's functional analysis of retarded behavior; it, too, is a radical departure from traditional conceptualizations of "mental" retardation.

Three terms are critical to a full understanding of a behavior analysis of child development: *psychological development, natural science,* and *theory.*

Psychological development refers to progressive changes in child-environment interactions. Analyzing the changes in interactions is the focus of this approach. Bijou and Baer (1961) restrict the use of the term *theory* to general statements of principle drawn from observations of interactions.

A *natural science* approach is one that applies a particular method to the analysis of observable events. Here the scientific domain is child behavior and the method is systematic behavior analysis. The organism (child) is viewed as an interrelated cluster of responses and stimuli in continuous interaction with the environment from birth to death (Bijou & Baer, 1961, p. 25). The formulation B = (f)S—behavior is a function of stimuli (stimulus events)—served, in 1961, to represent the behavior-analysis model for describing changes in behavior.

The relationship of this behavior analysis to Skinner's experimental analysis of behavior is clear. Bijou's experiments with children, from this systematic or functional approach, were among the first extensions of operant conditioning from rats to humans and from the experimental laboratory to a larger environmental domain.

Functional Analysis of Retarded Development

In a series of papers (Bijou, 1963, 1966; Bijou & Dunitz-Johnson, 1981), Bijou has extended a theory of child development to retarded development. In the same way that a functional analysis of child development eschews hypothetical constructs such as maturation, ego development, and so on, the extension to retarded development eschews hypothetical constructs typically invoked to describe "mental" retardation, e.g., lowered intelligence, brain damage (inferred from test performance), or deficits in mental processes such as memory or central organizational rehearsal strategies. Instead, from a natural science approach, retarded development is accounted for by the nature of child-environment interactions.

> It is suggested that developmental retardation be treated as observable, objectively defined stimulus-response relationships without recourse to hypothetical mental constructs such as "defective intelligence" and hypothetical biological abnormalities such as "clinically inferred brain injury." *From this point of view, a retarded individual is one who has a limited repertoire of behavior shaped by events that constitute his history.* Retardation is not conceived of as a symptom. A promising objective for behavioral research on retardation is an analysis of the observable conditions which produce *retarded behavior,* not *retarded mentality.* (Bijou, 1966, p. 2)

Bijou introduced the term *developmental* retardation to replace the term *mental* retardation. Special educators typically have not attended to the major conceptual difference between these terms which, semantically, appear nearly identical. The critical difference is that developmental retardation is a function of observable social, physical, and biological conditions rather than a manifestation of a hypothetical construct (Bijou, 1966, p. 3). Four conditions contribute to retarded development: abnormal anatomical structure and physiological functioning, inadequate discrimination, consequences of contingent aversive stimulation, and reinforcement of aversive behaviors (Bijou, 1966, p. 6). In the 1966 version of this article, Bijou described how each of these conditions contributed to retarded behavior. In the most recent version (Bijou & Dunitz-Johnson, in press), specific examples of these four general conditions are elaborated. Studies representing a wide range of research topics are presented to document how specific events or conditions retard development.

Bijou's functional analysis has major implications for teachers, researchers, and curriculum/technology developers. To the extent that behaviorally oriented approaches to education and development have been diffused within the area of retardation, these implications have been generally accepted. First, a focus on observable interactions shifts attention to the present—not to historical variables, particularly those inferred from test performance or other indirect measures. That is, given a student with retarded behavior, the focus is on accelerating behavior from the first point of contact. The child learns or does not learn based on the effect of intervention. Failure to learn is analyzed in the present, not the past. Constructs articulated in this manner: "Ralph's retarded and does not learn because of early childhood emotional trauma," are thus rejected.

Second, once the conditions that retard development are specified, interventionists may look out for and amelioriate them. The movement to "advantage" culturally disadvantaged children by enriching their early years through parent training, supplementary nutritional and health programs, early structured learning programs, and so on, can be viewed from this perspective. Tawney, Knapp, O'Reilly, and Pratt (1979), for example, in their integrated learning system for severely developmentally retarded students, describe how Bijou's functional analysis provides a structure for developing instructional programs to expand the response repertoire of low functioning students.

In summary, Bijou's functional analysis of retarded development, as it has evolved over a period of nearly 20 years, has as yet had little impact on special educators, although the practices that logically follow from this behavior analysis, i.e., studies in applied behavior analysis, have had widespread impact. This discontinuity may have occurred because intervention studies, designed to modify social and academic behaviors with a broad range of handicapped students, have presented as their rationale basic principles of operant conditioning rather than a fundamental theory of child development or retarded behavior. This discontinuity should disappear as special educators increase their efforts to translate theory into practice, as Snell (1977) and others (Tawney et al., 1979) have done.

Theory into Practice

In 1968 Bijou addressed the Division of School Psychologists at the annual meeting of the American Psychological Association. That address, "What Psychology Has to Offer Education—Now," published later (Bijou, 1970), described the contributions that a small minority of psychologists, the applied behavior analysts, could make to education. That paper, dedicated to Skinner, well represents the translation of an experimental analysis of behavior into applied behavior analysis. Further, it described how teachers could apply behavior principles in their classrooms and how they should prepare themselves to do so.

Referring to behavior analysts, Bijou said:

> We can offer a set of concepts and principles derived exclusively from experimental research; we can offer a methodology for applying these concepts and principles directly to teaching practices; we can offer a research design which deals with changes in the individual child (rather than inferring them from group averages); and we can offer a philosophy of science which insists on observable accounts of the relationships between individual behavior and its determining conditions. (Bijou, 1970, p. 66)

His philosophy of science, of course, is the natural science approach. The concepts and principles are derived from the functional analysis of behavioral and environmental interactions, i.e., the principles of operant and respondent conditioning. The research methodology is the study of the single subject. For our purpose, demonstrating a functional relationship between an intervention and a change in student behavior, empirically verified through the use of the most appropriate design, is the training goal of this text.

Bijou referred to the classroom teacher as the "Lone Arranger" of the contingencies of reinforcement and instructional stimuli. He suggested:

> The teacher arranges the contingencies to develop appropriate study behavior, for example, attending to the materials to be learned, and hopefully she arranges the contingencies so that this behavior becomes part of a child's way of dealing with future study tasks. She also arranges contingencies by scheduling the formal academic subjects (the visible programs), and manners and moral behavior (the invisible programs) in such a way that each child makes progress at approximately his own pace and with minimum frustration or aversive consequences. She finds it necessary, at some times, also to arrange contingencies to reduce or eliminate behaviors that compete with acquiring the desired academic and social behaviors. (Bijou, 1970, p. 68)

He suggested teachers should learn the techniques of behavior analysis "with precision."

> It is therefore essential that the practitioner learn from *first sources:* (1) the nature of the concepts and principles and referential supporting data, (2) the methodology of practical application and the basic literature on the behavioral technology of teaching, (3) the individual research methodology, and (4) the assumptions of behavioral analysis and their implications for educational practices. (Bijou, 1970, p. 69)

Bijou proposed these benefits should accrue to the teacher who employs a behavior-analytic approach: additional satisfaction from documentation of student progress, security in knowing that teaching practices are based on demonstrated principles, a common referent for communication with others regarding students' behaviors, accelerated pupil achievement, and ultimately a better educated community (Bijou, 1966, pp. 70–71).

Bijou's work has had widespread impact in behaviorally oriented special education programs. It illustrates the potential continuities from theory to practice within a data-based, or empirically determined, instructional model. It refers to a body of research that supports the concepts and principles of behavior analysis and to then current studies that demonstrated the utility of the behavior-analytic approach as a solution to specific educational problems, e.g., Thomas, Becker, and Armstrong's (1968) demonstration that disruptive student behaviors could be varied by systematically varying teacher behavior. Finally, his paper set the stage for additional applications and demonstrations, presented throughout this text, to illustrate the utility of single subject research design in educational settings.

Bijou at Washington

The work in experimental and applied behavior analysis at the University of Washington began in the mid fifties. From then until 1965, Bijou's contributions included operant studies with normal and retarded subjects, theory development, and methodology for conducting child behavior studies in experimental and classroom settings. Through research grants and positions in the department of psychology, he supported a significant number of graduate students and new faculty.

In 1965 there was a mass exodus of these faculty from Washington. Many moved to the University of Kansas. According to Kazdin (1978, p. 273), this move established the University of Kansas as the center of applied behavior analysis in the United States.

Contributions from the Washington Research Projects

Bijou's contributions to theory have been described. At Washington, he and Baer formulated a theory of child development (Bijou & Baer, 1961), analyzed the first, or universal stage, in child development (Bijou & Baer, 1965) and began a third volume of readings (Bijou & Baer, 1967). Bijou's extension of theory to retarded development was formulated. (Bijou, 1963, 1966).

Bijou (1955) argued for systematic laboratory study of child behavior. He designed an apparatus to measure a simple fixed operant response. A boxlike apparatus was constructed so that when a child dropped a ball in a hole in the top of the apparatus, the response would be recorded and a trinket reinforcer delivered.

In a subsequent publication, he (Bijou, 1957a) presented data on two experiments. In the first, a group of 18 children was subdivided into two groups, one reinforced on a continuous and the other on an intermittent schedule (FR5). Responses during a brief (3.5 minutes) extinction period were measured. In the second experiment, conditions were identical except that the children received one less reinforcer. In both studies, children reinforced on intermittent schedules made more responses during extinction. Bijou indicated these findings were consistent with infrahuman subjects, that future work might be profitable, and that it might be possible later to generalize from laboratory studies to adult-child interactions.

Bijou (1957b) reported revisions in his laboratory procedures, primarily the design of a simple apparatus to measure free operant responding. The squeeze mechanism from a sponge mop was mounted inside a plywood box. Downward presses activated microswitches controlling recording and reinforcing mechanisms. In a series of experiments, Bijou studied schedule control in normal and developmentally retarded children. Bijou (1958) reported children's resistance to extinction after shaping responses on fixed interval schedules. Four children were reinforced, each on a single schedule (FI60, FI30, FI30, FI20); then responses during extinction were measured. Orlando and Bijou (1960) explored children's responding on four basic (FI, FR, VI, VR) and two multiple schedules (mult VR ext and mult FR ext). Data are presented on selected children from among the 46 who participated. Schedule effects similar to infrahuman species and nonretarded subjects were observed (p. 348). Bijou and Orlando (1961) described a four-phase procedure to establish multiple schedule performance (respond when one discriminative stimulus, e.g., red light, is present, do not respond when another discriminative stimulus, e.g., blue light, is present). In essence, this procedure shaped schedule responding by gradual changes in the procedure (successive approximations in today's terminology). The authors suggested that this method might be more efficient than traditional trial and error methods and, further, that the method might be used to analyze individual differences in children and to facilitate rapid development of a discrimination. This series of studies made these contributions to behavior analysis with handicapped students: (1) procedures modeled after those developed for infrahuman species were shown to be effective with humans; (2) the behavior of normal and retarded children on these demonstrations of schedule control was shown to be similar to laboratory studies with animals; hence the lawful nature of behavior principles was demonstrated; and (3) the laboratory methods, much later, served as a model for classroom instructional procedures.

This program of research and a series of studies reported later on the development of token economies contributed to the research program that Bijou established at the University of Illinois. The translation of these experimental programs into a technology of teaching is described next.

Bijou at Illinois   Bijou established a child behavior laboratory at the University of Illinois where the methodology for applied behavior analysis research was elaborated. His work at Illinois was a continuation of work begun at Washington. Bijou's writing at Illinois covered a wide range of topics: the academic problems of retarded students, clarification of the major attributes of a functional analysis of behavior, and development of a technology of teaching.

Work in behavior modification was being conducted at the University of Illinois when Bijou moved there. Leonard Ullmann had published a book of case studies in behavior modification (Ullman & Krasner, 1965) that was well received in the fields psychology and special education. A behavioral reinterpretation of abnormal behavior (Ullman & Krasner, 1969) soon followed. Desensitization studies were being conducted in clinical psychology. One clinical psychologist, Wesley Becker, impressed by Bijou's work (Kazdin, 1978, p. 271), began a program of research that was to have major impact on emerging special education training programs.

At Illinois, Bijou held an appointment in the Institute for Research on Exceptional Children. This association brought him into contact with graduate students in special education. During Bijou's tenure at Illinois, the Children's Research Center was established on a new campus. Conceived by Samuel Kirk and others as a combined research, training, and service delivery laboratory, a facility comprised of three residential cottages for short-term intervention and research was completed in 1967. Research studies with Down's Syndrome and emotionally disturbed children were initiated. Bijou's influence was extensive as students and staff shifted from one project to another and as behavior principles were employed on these projects.

Contributions at Illinois

Bijou's major contributions at Illinois were elaboration of a research methodology, the development of academic programs for retarded students, and a major influence on students and researchers in special education and psychology. Bijou's contributions, through his influence on others, are described in brief here.

Becker and his students (O'Leary, Madsen, Thomas, Kuypers, and Armstrong) developed token economies and studied the manipulation of teacher and child behavior through behavioral techniques. Becker (1971) wrote *Parents Are Teachers,* a programmed text designed to teach parents behavioral techniques to modify children's problem behavior. He became involved in the DISTAR project and moved to Oregon with Englemann where they carried out research in the national Follow-Through program. Positive reinforcement was incorporated into the DISTAR procedures early on. Becker, Englemann, and Thomas (1971) wrote a series of texts on teaching through a behavioral model.

Tawney (1972) conducted his thesis in Bijou's experimental laboratory. He reported the effects of reinforcing preschool children for correct responses to elements of stimuli considered critical or noncritical to letter discrimination. Series of visual stimuli, which progressed from easy to complex in small steps, were presented in a laboratory setting. Statistical analysis of differences among the two groups who received training and a third control group on pre-post responses on a test of letter discrimination showed that the children reinforced for responding to critical features performed significantly better on the test of letter discrimination. It was suggested that direct training on this component of a reading task (visual discrimination) offered an alternative to then popular visual perceptual training materials, a recommendation consistent with a behavior-analysis approach.

Two papers reflect Bijou's contributions to a methodology for child behavior study. Similar in content, though different in focus, they also represent the transfer of child behavior study from Washington to Illiois. Bijou, Peterson, and Ault (1968) describe how to conduct field studies in applied settings. They argue that a natural science approach provides the basic data that may be used by investigators with different philosophical orientations. Conversely, they argue that data collection systems based on observable and nonobservable (interpreted) events cannot be shared among investigators since encoded nonobservables must either be separated out or reinterpreted. This publication specifies how to define the setting, define stimulus and behavioral events, develop observation recording systems, calculate observer reliability, and collect, analyze, and interpret data. In another paper, Bijou, Peterson, Harris, Allen, and Johnston (1969) describe a methodology for *experimental* studies in applied (natural) settings. They describe the A-B-A-B design and the practical considerations in the conduct of experimental studies.

Bijou's (1972) address at the First Annual Symposium on Behavior Modification at the University of Veracruz in Xalapa, Mexico, is representative of his interest in educational programming. It describes the program at the University of Illinois, demonstrates the translation of behavioral principles to instructional programs for handicapped children, and presents the components of a technology of teaching: program planning and modification, management of reinforcement contingencies, modification of social and academic behavior, monitoring of each child's daily activities, and training of the teacher's assistant (pp. 34–36). These general components have provided a framework for the systematic instructional technologies now widely employed (Snell, 1977) in programs for the handicapped.

The Kansas Group

This section describes the contributions of those students and associates of Bijou who went from Washington to Kansas and stayed there. Also included in this group is Lindsley, who studied and worked with Skinner.

The University of Kansas supports a broad range of research units in psychology and human development. There are university campuses in Lawrence and in Kansas City. The Bureau of Child Research carries out programs at Kansas Neurological Institute in Topeka and at Parsons State Home and Training School in Parsons, Kansas. At various times, outreach projects have been conducted from these sites, thus giving individuals involved and the projects statewide and national visibility. The programs conducted since 1965 with normal and handicapped students have made several contributions to the education of handicapped students:

1. Demonstrations of operant principles applied to the development of positive social and academic behaviors of preschool age children,

2. Application of token economies to a living environment for adjudicated delinquents (Achievement Place),

3. A behavioral preschool (Head Start) and early education (Follow-Through) model, later judged as among the most effective of the Great Society programs,

4. Delineation of the field of applied behavior analysis,

5. Advancement of applied behavior analysis through the sponsorship of the *Journal of Applied Behavior Analysis,*

6. Experimental analysis of language behavior of retarded children,

7. Development of a precision teaching model, and

8. Extension of applied behavior analysis to a wide range of environments, e.g., parks and social problems (antilittering).

Not all these efforts are described here. Neither are the research programs of all the investigators who are or have been at the University since 1965. Instead, attention is focused on those efforts judged to have had the most impact on special education practices.

Donald M. Baer   Donald Baer received his doctorate from the University of Chicago and worked at the University of Washington from 1956 to 1965. His contributions to a theory of child development have been described (Bijou & Baer, 1961, 1965).

At Kansas, he was instrumental in developing the *Journal of Applied Behavior Analysis (JABA)* and served as editor of the fourth volume. Analysis of the journal indexes shows that he has sponsored a wide range of thesis research and has written on theoretical and methodological issues.

Baer, Wolf, and Risley (1968) in the first issue of *JABA* defined the scope and elements of applied behavior analysis. They proposed that the scientific analysis of individual behavior might be applied to socially relevant problem behaviors and, in so doing, assist to achieve a better state of society (p. 91). The focus of inquiry is socially relevant behavior, and empirical verification of procedures is achieved through a methodology appropriate for natural settings. Lacking the precise control of the laboratory, a method for the study of behavior and the interpretation of results is suggested. Thus, the subject of study is behavior important to society and the individual. Consistent with a natural science approach, observable behavior, precisely measured, is the datum of interest. Basic experimental procedures (single subject research design) are employed to demonstrate a functional relationship between an intervention and a change in behavior. Confidence in the effectiveness of the behavior change increases when the effect is repeated, shown to occur reliably, and when procedures are spelled out in explicit detail. Effectiveness of an intervention is judged within the context of the setting and the magnitude of desirable change. Finally, the generality of the behavior change is considered important, i.e., a behavior change is effective if it occurs outside the intervention setting. Baer, Wolf, and Risley (1968) cautioned that generalization does not occur automatically and thus may need to be programmed. The issue of generalization, it should be noted, is of a critical concern in newly developing programs for the severely handicapped. Stokes and Baer (1977) analyzed generalization tactics, identified seven specific strategies to establish generalization, commented on the paucity of data, and suggested that specific programming within the behavior analysis model might contribute to the development of a technology of generalization. These recommendations may be viewed in the context of a persistent concern for a functional, i.e., effective, technology of behavior.

Baer contributed to the development of a program to study language in retarded students. With Guess and Sailor, psychologists now teaching in departments of special education, and others, an experimental analysis was extended to language behavior. This research program was based on Skinner's (1957) theoretical analysis of verbal behavior. The basic goal of this research program was to determine the extent to which specific constructions or response units were manipulatable by operant conditioning. Studies were reported on the content of tantrums during experimental sessions (Sailor, Guess, Rutherford, & Baer, 1968), manipulation of plural morphemes (Guess, Sailor, Rutherford, & Baer, 1968), training receptive (motor) responses to comparative and superlative adjectives (Baer & Guess, 1971), development of syntax (Garcia, Guess, & Byrnes, 1973), training generalization in receptive and productive language models (Guess & Baer, 1973), and training question asking (Twardosz & Baer, 1973). The findings from these studies are the focus of important discussion papers (Guess, Sailor, & Baer, 1974). The research findings and methodology are incorporated in a four-part language training program (Guess, Sailor, & Baer, 1976, 1977, 1978). Other representative contributions include the use of time-out to decelerate specific types of inappropriate mealtime behaviors, e.g., stealing, eating with fingers, or pigging (eating spilled food or eating food directly with mouth) in institutionalized retarded children (Barton, Guess, Garcia, & Baer, 1970).

Montrose Wolf

Montrose Wolf received his master's degree and PhD (1963) at Arizona State University where he worked with Staats to develop a reinforcer system, used in a program to teach reading behavior to nonreading individuals (Staats, Minke, Finley, Wolf, & Brooks, 1964). From 1962 to 1964, he was part of the research team at Washington. He spent a year at the University of Arizona before his move to Kansas in 1965. Bijou credits Wolf with the design of the token economy system in the experimental classroom at the Rainier school (Etzel, LeBlanc, & Baer, 1977, p. 592). At Kansas, Wolf developed Achievement Place, a group living environment for adjudicated delinquents, a model replicated in the West and Southwest with delinquent and retarded populations. Wolf's contributions to handicapped students have been in three areas: (1) development of the token economy at Rainier, (2) application of behavior shaping techniques in an autistic child, and (3) the Achievement Place model.

The study that Wolf, Risley, and Mees (1964) conducted has become classic in the special education literature. The subject, Dicky, age 3½ years when the study began, though normal at birth, developed cataracts at age 9 months. Tantruming and sleep disruption occurred. At age 2, the cataracts were removed, glasses were prescribed but never worn, several diagnoses of his problem behavior were sought—and many were offered by professionals. At age 3, Dicky was admitted to a children's mental hospital. The project began after an opthalmologist indicated the child's vision would be lost unless the glasses were worn and after a variety of unsuccessful attempts were made to shape his self-abusive and generally sparse social and vocal behavior. The authors designed a behavior shaping program and trained ward attendants who then trained the parents to follow programs as the child was gradually returned to the home for longer periods. Tantruming and bedtime problems were extinguished by time-out (placing the child in his room with the door closed until tantrums subsided or until he was in his bed). These behaviors were shaped relatively quickly. Shaping glasses wearing, however, was another matter, and little progress occurred until the authors became directly involved in the project.

One of the principles of operant conditioning is that no new response is created. Instead, an existing response in the subject's repertoire is reinforced and strengthened. Complex motor responses in pigeons, for example, are shaped by specifying a target behavior, observing and specifying a shapable response, reinforcing a naturally occurring response, and shaping the topography of the response by successive approximations. Key pressing, once defined, is shaped by waiting until the pigeon is in proximity to the key and makes a forward head movement toward the key; then reinforcers are dispensed. From such a rudimentary beginning, complex chains of smoothly executed responses are shaped; for example, Skinner once shaped a rat, Pliny the Elder, to lift a marble in its front paws, carry it to and drop it in a tube.

Wolf, Risley, and Mees (1964) attempted a similar procedure. Empty glasses frames were placed around the room, and Dicky was reinforced for picking up, holding, and carrying the frames, and for successive approximations of responses which brought them close to his eyes. Since the glasses were assumed to have acquired aversive properties and since the prescription was powerful, the authors planned to use empty frames first, then frames with plain glass lenses, and finally the regular glasses with prescription lenses. Candy and fruit were used as reinforcers.

Major modifications were required in the original program. The nature of the final program and the reasons for the changes had, and still have, significant instructional value for special educators working with severely disruptive students.

First, major changes did not occur until the investigators became directly involved in the project. Second, because the program was written (defined), it was possible to determine discrepancies between the written and the actual intervention. Third, the power of the reinforcers was weak, and it was necessary to control more of the environment, for example, breakfast was made contingent upon appropriate responding. Fourth, careful observation showed that the physical properties of the frames made it difficult for a close approximation to occur. It was necessary to modify the glasses by creating a caplike frame. Once these "engineering" problems were solved, the behavior was shaped within a 30-minute period. Fifth, once shaped, the behavior was maintained by natural consequences, i.e., positive consequences were terminated if the glasses were removed during meal, play, or other "pleasurable" activities. Sixth, once shaped, another problem occurred: glasses throwing. It too proved amenable to control through operant conditioning. Seventh, data records exist to document the success of the program. Where graphs show loss of behavior control, they also specify the correlated events that occurred with the behavior change, e.g., once home, getting out of bed increased at a time when the child suffered from an intestinal disorder. Anecdotal reports indicated that the child's language increased. Several years later, a follow-up found Dicky living a "normal" life. Critical individuals in his environment were not aware that he had been labeled a problem child or that he had been hospitalized. This study, in summary, demonstrated the application of behavior shaping outside the laboratory with a human subject. It showed that the behavior of a severely disruptive child could be modified by operant conditioning and specified the procedures so that they could be replicated.

Achievement Place Model

Achievement Place, designed by Wolf shortly after his arrival at Kansas, started as a group home for predelinquent youth. The model has been widely replicated with other populations. Four characteristics of the program set it apart from then traditional, and now typical, community home settings. It was (1) based on a behavior deficiency model, rather than a mental illness model (Wolf, Phillips, & Fixen, 1972), (2) based on a token economy, (3) data based, and (4) managed by specially trained houseparents, termed a teaching family. The goal of the program was to return the child to the community with a carefully shaped repertoire of academic and social skills.

Wolf, Phillips, and Fixen (1972) describe the basic structure of an Achievement Place type environment. Children/residents begin to participate in a token economy as soon as they are enrolled in the program. Tokens are earned by demonstrating defined behaviors and may be spent for privileges—backup reinforcers present in the natural environment.

Phillips (1968) and his wife—the first teaching family—reported a series of experiments conducted when the model was first developed. Intervention projects included deceleration of aggressive statements, appropriate bathroom cleaning, shaping punctuality, completing homework, and deceleration of a poor grammatical construction, *ain't*. Positive results were obtained, demonstrated on single subject designs. While these experiments were in progress, students received or lost points for a broad class of behaviors, e.g., earning 500 points for keeping clean and neat, losing 300 for arguing, while working for privileges such as snacks (1000), allowance (1000), and permission to stay up past bedtime (1000).

Bailey, Wolf, and Phillips (1970) instituted a program to shape students' school behavior by dispensing reinforcers at home, based on teachers' evaluation of defined student behaviors (teachers simply marked *yes* or *no*, rather than recording frequency counts.) In one experiment, study behavior decelerated and rule violations accelerated during baseline. In a second phase, students received tokens but not differential reinforcement (teacher always marked *yes* in each behavior category.) Again, study behavior was first emitted at a high rate and rule violation at a low rate. When differential reinforcement was added (one *no* check resulted in loss of privileges at Achievement Place), study behavior accelerated and rule violation decelerated to near zero rates. In a withdrawal phase (100% *yes* marks not required), behavioral control was lost. When differential reinforcement was reinstituted, control was achieved. This study demonstrated a convenient way to maintain school and home control. It required no extensive data collection on the teacher's part—just a check mark on a limited number of categories. This proved to be a useful strategy. In the other experiments in this series, control was demonstrated in a regular class setting. In another, daily records were faded out, and students' behaviors were maintained by twice weekly reports.

Phillips, Phillips, Wolf, and Fixen (1973), in a series of nine experiments, studied various forms of group management of the token economy. The effects of purchased (students bid to become manager) or elected managership were evaluated, as well as the effects of different managerial powers (e.g., give and take away points). The authors suggested some reasons why elected managership was preferred and described ways in which manager-group control and counter-control measures operated in the system. These and other studies conducted at Achievement Place are important because they demonstrate that the behavior of difficult students can be brought under control, that strategies exist for home-school collaboration on shaping or maintaining appropriate behaviors, and that it is possible to carry out systematic research in a natural environment when the interventionist is well trained in the principles of operant conditioning and a research methodology. The teaching family concept, in this respect, is a model for the teacher-researcher.

Ogden Lindsley   Ogden Lindsley studied with Skinner in the early fifties. Their work with adult psychotic patients represented one of the first direct applications of operant conditioning with human subjects in an experimental laboratory setting. In a series of experiments, they studied the free operant behavior of their subjects, often over extended periods of time. Their subjects, situated in a 6' × 6' room, pulled a lever (the Lindsley manipulandum) and received a variety of reinforcers. Responses were recorded electronically and displayed on cumulative records. The general goal of these studies was to determine patterns of responding, i.e., cyclic variation over time. Lindsley and Skinner were interested in the methodology of operant conditioning rather than therapeutic intervention.

Azrin and Lindsley (1956), in an interesting experiment, documented that the cooperative behavior of young children could be shaped by operant conditioning. The study was a direct analog of a pigeon shaping demonstration used by Skinner in his classes at Harvard. Where pigeons pecked keys and subject-pairs were reinforced for pressing the same key in each subject's row of keys, child subject-pairs seated across from each other at a small table were reinforced when each placed a stylus in one of three small holes (response keys) in the table. A cooperative response occurred when the two children placed their styli' in the holes positioned directly opposite each other within .04 second. These responses were reinforced with a flashing light and a single jelly bean. Responses were shaped within 10 minutes in each of 10 teams, extinguished during a no reinforcement period, and reinstated during a second reinforcement period. This study is interesting for these reasons: the pigeon peck, human subject press response analog; the demonstration of operant control with human subjects; and control of a complex (cooperative) behavior. One who can visualize the pigeon and human subject pairs at their task can perhaps "see" the extension of operant principles from infrahuman to human subjects.

Barrett and Lindsley (1962) utilized the operant laboratory to study discrimination and differentiation deficits in institutionalized retarded students chronological age (CA) 7 to 20 years. Subjects were reinforced for responding under one condition (pull left manipulandum when left light is on) and not reinforced for responding under three other conditions (left light, pull right lever; right light, pull left lever; right light, pull right lever). As in Lindsley's studies with adult psychotics, subjects' behaviors were recorded over an extended period of time. Of interest to the experimenters were the patterns of responding that emerged over time. They suggested that the methodology had potential for diagnostic purposes, that the automated environment was sufficiently sensitive to show inter- and intrasubject variability, and that long-term study might reveal the effects on performance of drugs, illness, or other critical events. The study, among the earliest extensions of operant conditioning to children, contributed to the development of methodology (instrumentation and procedures) for laboratory studies of discrimination and other complex processes.

Lindsley's work at Harvard focused on the extension of operant conditioning to human subjects in laboratory settings. He wrote a key article, (Lindsley, 1964) described later, on the utility of prosthetic environments to reduce behavior deficits in retarded individuals—an article which had major impact in special education.

Lindsley at Kansas

At Kansas, Lindsley had a major impact on the program in special education. He served as Educational Coordinator of the Children's Rehabilitation Unit of the University of Kansas Medical Center. There he developed a program of research in the behavioral analysis of looking and listening, utilizing a conjugate programming apparatus. In the conjugate system, subject's responding controls the presentation of a "narrative" stimulus, e.g., a movie or television program. Subject may be required to respond rapidly (press a switch) to keep the sound or visual display at full intensity—or conversely, to refrain from responding. In a representative study, Mira (1968) compared looking and listening among 12 normal and 12 learning disabled students. Subjects viewed a film in a small darkened room. During a three-part procedure, which included a within procedure reversal, subjects worked (pressed) to obtain auditory and visual images, then stopped working to obtain each or worked to obtain sound, and stopped to obtain video, or in the final condition, could work to look and stop to listen and thus demonstrate a modality preference. Descriptive information indicated that consistent listening deficits could be identified through the procedure and that they were present in greater degree among the learning disabled students. Perhaps because of the extensive instrumentation requirements, this assessment technique was little used, yet it demonstrated that laboratory procedures could be applied to the study of functional, academic behavior deficits of students.

Contributions to Behavior Principles and Prosthetic Environments

Major contributions to special education practices have been made by psychologists who had no direct role in training special educators. Here, the nature of these contributions and contributors are described.

Differential Probability of Responding

Different responses are emitted at different rates in the natural environment. Some occur infrequently, or have a *low probability* of occurrence; some occur frequently, or have a *high probability* of occurrence. When low probability behaviors (LPB) are followed by high probability behaviors (HPB), the rate of the LPB can be increased. Differential probability of responding, better known as the Premack principle, and more commonly known as "Grandma's Law," has had a major impact on the development of prosthetic environments, or token economies. The discovery that certain behaviors could positively reinforce other behaviors expanded reinforcer "menus," or choices of preferred events, far beyond consumables and obvious reinforcing events such as playing games or watching television in early studies used.

David Premack (1965), most widely known for his work in teaching language to primates, arranged a series of experiments to test some basic assumptions implicit in learning theory and methodology. He observed that some responses—bar pressing in the rat—were considered reinforceable but not considered as potential reinforcers. For others, e.g., water drinking, the opposite was assumed since in typical rat experiments bar pressing was consequated with the opportunity to drink, and rarely, if ever, was drinking consequated by bar pressing. Premack isolated rats in an experimental space for extended periods to determine their patterns of responding under "natural" conditions, i.e., with food or water always available—not response contingent. He was then able to identify some constants; rats typically lick for water at a rate of about 7 times per second. He also found that certain behaviors have a higher probability of occurrence than others and that LPBs would accelerate when consequated with HPBs. These findings created a new perspective on contingencies of reinforcement. It remained for another psychologist, however, to popularize the Premack principle with human subjects.

Lloyd Homme, in a brief article (Homme, de Baca, Devine, Steinhorst, & Rickert, 1963), described a situation that occurred when a group of psychologists attempted to initiate a program of social control with 3-year-old children. Initially confronted with pandemonium (author's term), the authors gained control of LPB (sitting quietly) by establishing an "if then" rule. "If you sit quietly, then you may run and scream." The authors reported that they were able to shape sitting quietly and attending in a short period.

Homme, Csanyi, Gonzales, and Rechs (1970) developed a formal system of contingency contracting. Through the process of teacher-student contracting, academic and social behaviors are shaped by incremental modifications of the *if* (desired performance) . . ., *then* (preferred consequence) components of the contract. Utilizing the structure of a complete instructional (behavioral) objective (Mager, 1961) the terms of the contract are specified clearly—the behavior to be emitted (e.g., words spelled), the conditions under which the behavior occurs (independently at teacher's request), and the criterion measure that defines task completion (90% correct from a randomly selected list of 10). The process creates dialogue between teacher and student as terms of the contract are negotiated. Students are led to higher performance, and perhaps to increased confidence in their ability, as they work harder and more accurately on defined tasks. Then too, as the contracting process progresses, students gain control of the process, as the teacher assists them to define realistic terms for work performance and as the positive reinforcers are "thinned out" of the *then* half of the contract. The student may begin at a very low level of performance, which is highly reinforced, and may complete the process when he "learns for the sake of learning" or is self-reinforced for completing large amounts of academic work quickly with little error. While the contingency statement is implicit in any token economy, or reinforcer system, the contingency contracting process, as Homme et al. (1969) proposed, might be employed with any or all students in a class, on an individual basis, without the structure of a token economy. Contingency contracting has become part of the methodology of special education as reflected in methods texts by Berdine and Cegelka, 1980; Payne, Polloway, Smith, and Payne, 1981; and others. Thus, while Grandma said, "If you drink your milk, (then) you'll get a cookie," it remained for psychologists, starting in the animal laboratory, to formalize a contracting system that is objective and verifiable in the classroom setting.

Prosthetic Environments

At first glance the term *prosthetic environments* may appear archaic or inappropriately applied to the topic—the development of token economy systems. One typically thinks of a prosthetic *device* such as a crutch, a wheelchair, or a hearing aid. However, the term has special significance in the evolution of behavior principles from the laboratory to the natural environment.

Lindsley (1964) stated, "Children are not retarded. Only their *behavior* in average environments is sometimes retarded. In fact, it is modern science's ability to design suitable environments for these children that is sometimes retarded" (p. 62). Thus begins a paper which was widely referenced in the development of behaviorally oriented special education programs.

Lindsley's thesis was that through the design of prosthetic environments, the behavioral efficiency of individuals manifesting retarded behavior might be maximized. The term *prosthetic,* strictly defined, refers to a device designed to replace a missing limb or organ. Lindsley used the term broadly to refer to anything that might assist a person to achieve normal function in an average environment. For example, he suggested that cosmetics are a class of prosthetic devices. Three types of prosthetics were suggested: devices (wheelchairs, artificial limbs), training (physical rehabilitation, physical therapy), and environments (braille books, wheelchair ramps, modified automobiles for people with physical handicaps). Lindsley proposed that prosthetic environments might be designed for higher order behavioral deficits, e.g., discrimination, differentiation, contingency and reinforcer deficits, and reflex integration. From this perspective, Lindsley described how free operant techniques could be used to shape complex behaviors.

Lindsley introduced the SRKC behavior equation and the concept of a *movement cycle.* The S (stimulus) R (response) K (contingency) C (consequences) paradigm was proposed as a formal equation for identifying the nature of a behavioral deficit. In the same way that an algebra equation can only be solved for one unknown, components of the SRKC equation could be manipulated to determine whether the behavioral deficit was failure to attend to stimuli, to initiate a desired response, or insensitivity to the contingencies or consequences of reinforcement.

The components of the behavioral equation constitute a movement cycle—a defined set of events with a beginning and an end. This concept, in general form, has been translated into systematic instruction procedures based on a *learning trial* model, e.g., The Programmed Environments Curriculum (Tawney, Knapp, O'Reilly, & Pratt, 1979) lesson plans that specify antecedents (teacher's commands and selected instructional materials), behavior (the student's response), a latency period (a defined time limit in which a response must occur or else be scored as a *no* response), and consequents (reinforcement for correct or specific correction procedures for error or *no* responses).

Lindsley's concept of a prosthetic environment was drawn from the laboratory studies of psychotics that he had conducted with Skinner and from other laboratory environments. He offered suggestions for designing prosthetic stimuli, response devices, contingencies, and consequences, i.e., the components of the SRKC paradigm. While his suggestions were unique, and not intended perhaps to survive in toto, the concepts have survived in systematic instruction procedures. His suggestions for prosthetic stimuli focused on modifying the intensity, size, and number of discriminative stimuli. Now, it is common to incorporate stimulus fading, careful arrangement of stimuli from step to step in an instructional procedure, to manipulate the temporal contiguity between demonstrations and response requests in time delay procedures, and so on. He described common devices for response building, or physical response deficits, e.g., arm-operated faucets for the physically handicapped, voice-operated telephones, and specially designed typewriter keyboards. More recently, developmental efforts have produced an array of facilitative devices, e.g., the Kurzweil reading machine—a computerized system that "reads" books to the blind. Visual analysis of print is interpreted by the computer, translated into electronic signals fed through a voice synthesizer, enabling the blind person to hear what is printed on the page. Tawney and his associates once designed a prosthetic environment for low-functioning students. A specially designed response console contained interchangeable panels so that a child with one type of physical motor response deficit might respond by hitting one type of device (a palm press switch), while another, capable of only gross random responses might respond by hitting an extended lever that would record a "hit" from any direction, or still another might be required to make a focused, precise response by pressing a button recessed within a small target area. Lindsley's suggestions for prosthetic contingencies and consequences, drawn from the principles of operant conditioning, are reflected in contemporary use of the principles in behavior management and precise instruction strategies.

In essence, Lindsley proposed that prosthetic environments be designed to maximize the functioning of individuals manifesting retarded behavior. He was careful to distinguish between the acquisition and maintenance of behavior and to suggest that careful, data-based monitoring should be implemented so that prosthetic assistance would be faded out as behavioral sufficiency was demonstrated. He argued that acquisition prosthesis was a more valuable strategy than maintenance prosthesis and encouraged educators to consider that efforts be spent in devising acquisition prostheses for new "patients" rather than maintaining larger numbers on "maintenance prosthesis." Or, perhaps he was suggesting that massive intervention systems should be designed so that when their effectiveness was demonstrated, special education support might be faded out.

Lindsley's work made several contributions to special education:

1. It focused, as did Bijou's work, on retarded *behavior*.

2. It described the the components of direct and precise measurement systems.

3. It set the stage for data-based instruction, i.e., the development of system of precision teaching.

4 It reinforced the idea that, through a behavioral system, it would be possible to precisely analyze the nature of deficits in a movement cycle, or learning trial.

His research set the stage for the work he initiated when he moved to Kansas. Through collaborative efforts, this work was transported to the University of Washington where Haring, White, Lovitt, and their associates have continued to refine precision teaching systems.

Token Economics

The concept of a prosthetic environment was critical in the evolution of operant behavior from the laboratory to the natural environment. The first prosthetic environments in the public schools were token economy systems, based on the laboratory work of Lindsley and Skinner, the prosthetic environments suggested by Lindsley, and the demonstrations reported by Ferster and DeMyer (1962).

Ferster and DeMyer (1962) analyzed the behavior of three hospitalized autistic children in a laboratory setting. The authors considered behavior deficits a prominent feature of autism. Their goals, to establish a durable reinforcer system and to shape complex behavior, were experimental rather than therapeutic. In early sessions, children pressed a bar to receive tokens on intermittent reinforcement schedules. In a later phase, children received tokens for correct matches in a match-to-sample discrimination. The children could use their tokens to obtain a variety of reinforcers available in the experimental room. These included television, pinball, a food and trinket vendor, a phonograph, a color wheel, a picture viewer, an eight-column vending machine loaded with a variety of candies, a telephone set, a pigeon or monkey trained to perform, an electric organ, and an electric train that the children could control. All the devices were automatically programmed, and all responses were automatically recorded. Once adapted to the experimental space, the children worked alone in the room. Thus tantrum behavior was not consequated by adult attention. Schedules were shifted gradually, and other changes were introduced slowly to avoid precipitating tantrum behavior. Sample cumulative records for two children showed consistent responding during the bar press phase and a high rate of correct matches during that phase. The demonstration showed that simple and complex responses could be brought under environmental control. As with other studies conducted during this era, the focus was on demonstrating the lawfulness of behaviors among human subjects who manifested impoverished response repertoires.

At Anna State Hospital

A major demonstration of a token economy was conducted at Anna State Hospital, a facility for the mentally disturbed in southern Illinois. Nathan Azrin, who studied with Skinner at Harvard and collaborated with Lindsley (Azrin & Lindsley, 1956) on early demonstrations of operant behavior with human subjects, moved to Anna State Hospital after completing his doctorate in 1956. There he conducted laboratory studies with infrahuman subjects and individual human patients. In 1961 he was joined by Teodoro Ayllon, who received his doctorate at the University of Houston. He, too, used operant conditioning to modify individual patient's behavior. At Anna State they developed a token economy in one ward that housed chronic mental patients, those most resistant to previous treatments. After four years of experimentation and modification, Ayllon and Azrin (1965) reported six experiments. Later they (Ayllon & Azrin, 1968) published *The Token Economy—A Motivational System for Therapy and Rehabilitation*. This program attracted attention from its inception and, according to Kazdin (1978), exerted immediate influence on other programs (p. 260). The basic goal of this long-term project was to test operant learning theory. Ayllon and Azrin (1968) indicate that a mental hospital is a severe test for any theory. General laws and theories, to be shown to be effective (generalizable), must produce an effect in a wide range of patients who manifest an even greater array of problem behaviors or extreme behavior deficits. For many these behaviors, or deficits, are of long-term duration, have persisted in the face of a variety of therapeutic interventions, and thus are resistant to modification.

The Token Economy describes in detail how the token system was initiated and carried out so that others might apply the process to develop similar systems. A minimal systems principle was applied, i.e., no special criteria were applied to the ward personnel who were employed during the project. Natural rather than contrived reinforcers were used, and a minimal amount of environmental engineering was effected.

The general procedure required that the 46 residents of the ward work at jobs (constructive behaviors) for tokens which could be traded (spent) for a variety of reinforcers. Job descriptions were written for the many functions required within the hospital settings, e.g., dietary assistance, food server, sales clerk, laundry assistant, and so on. Specific behaviors within these and other job functions were selected on the basis of functional relevance: Would they be reinforced outside the ward or outside the hospital? Reinforcers were selected following a "Probability of Behavior Rule: Observe what the individual does when the opportunity exists. Those activities that are very probable at a given time will serve as reinforcers" (Ayllon & Azrin, 1968, p. 60). Following the rule, and testing by observing participation/selection during free and token conditions, it was found that events such as religious service attendance, commissary, music activities, movies, request for specific idiosyncratic items, cigarettes, and the like, served as reinforcers. Multiple reinforcers were available to patients, so that when they satiated on one reinforcer, others were available to maintain behavioral control. When jobs were completed, attendants dispersed tokens.

Ayllon and Azrin (1965) reported selected experiments carried out during the token economy experiment. Generally, they reported units of performance per day for the group, within an A-B-A design where A was the reinforcement and B the nonreinforcement condition. Generally, behavior decelerated to a near zero level when tokens were withdrawn and recovered to the original reinforced level when tokens were reinstituted. (It should be noted that in current terminology this procedure would be labeled a B-A-B design since B is the intervention and A is the withdrawal of intervention). The development of this token economy system was a major step, a landmark, in the transition from laboratory studies of convenient (bar press) responses to functional behaviors of human participants in a natural (for them) environment. Ayllon and Azrin (1968) reported that response priming and environmental arrangements facilitated the transfer of two patients from the hospital to a halfway house. They also reported, interestingly enough, that when the opportunity to receive psychotherapy (to meet with psychiatrists) was arranged as a possible reinforcer, only two patients availed themselves of the opportunity, and then only twice.

The token economy of Ayllon and Azrin (1968) stimulated the application of token systems in a variety of settings. It was, and still is, instructive in these areas: (1) careful planning before implementation, (2) response specification, (3) observation to identify potential reinforcers, (4) use of an array of reinforcing events, (5) individualization of reinforcer menus for each participant, (6) reponse shaping (priming), (7) functional (A-B-A design) tests of the effects of the procedure, and (8) system design allowing continual analysis and revision of the system for individual patients.

At the Rainier School

Birnbrauer, Wolf, Kidder, and Tague (1965) described the token system used at the Rainier School. This project was part of the program of research in operant conditioning initiated by Bijou during his tenure at the University of Washington. The objective of the study was to determine the effect of instituting a token system, removing it for a long period, then reinstituting it (p. 220). Each of the 17 students enrolled in this programmed learning experimental program participated. Of those, 8 had been enrolled and participated in a token system during the previous year. Data were reported on 15 of the 17 students who were in regular attendance and who experienced no change in assignment. These students were mildly and moderately retarded (IQ 50 to 72) and ranged in age from 8 to 14 years.

Students attended this experimental program one to two hours per day for instruction in reading, writing, and arithmetic. They worked independently on experimental materials designed and daily revised by staff to achieve about a 90% correct rate of recording. No more than six students were present at any time, and they were instructed by a teacher and three aides. Students were usually reinforced upon completion of specific assignments. The token system was a folder, containing pages of squares that were marked for work completion. Completed pages, of different values (2¢, 5¢), were traded for backup reinforcers such as trinkets, edibles, gum, and pencils. Students received marks for each correct response, paired with verbal praise. During each phase of the project, students received positive reinforcement for appropriate social behavior. Inappropriate behaviors were ignored; disruptive behaviors were consequated with a time-out procedure.

The experimental design was B-A-B (tokens, no tokens, tokens). Thirteen students received 21 days of no tokens, four received 35. Behavior changes were recorded on percent of errors, number of items completed, and amount of time spent in time-out. Three general responses were described:

> Five subjects showed, for all practical purposes, no adverse effects of NT [no tokens], six Ss increased in percentage of errors in NT, but continued to cooperate and to complete the same or a greater number of items. Four Ss increased in percentage of errors, accomplished less work, and became serious disciplinary problems during NT. After tokens were reinstated, most of the Ss completed progressively more work and stabilized at levels of percentage of errors that were lower than at any previous time. (Birnbrauer et al., 1965, p. 225)

Individual graphs and narrative descriptions graphically illustrated the variable effects on Ss. This study, among the first conducted in a classroom setting, demonstrated the potential of a token reinforcement system.

Becker's Studies

Wesley Becker, a clinical psychologist at Illinois, shifted his interests to applied behavior analysis in the mid sixties. He initiated a series of studies on token economies with his students, among them K. Dan O'Leary, who moved to SUNY–Stony Brook and, with Susan O'Leary and others, continued to apply behavioral principles in classroom settings. Subsequently, Becker worked with Englemann in the development of the direct instruction model for preschool (Head Start) and early elementary school education (Project Follow-Through); both moved to the University of Oregon in the early seventies where work on that training model and instructional materials continues.

The Antecedents of Behaviorism in Special Education

Thus far, the growth of behavior analysis in psychology has been described. Major writings, which have had a significant impact in special education, have been summarized. The careers of psychologists have been traced, and the ways they have impacted on education have been described. Here we trace the careers of special educators, those who recognized the contributions of Skinner and Bijou and incorporated them into their own educational models and research.

Norris G. Haring   Haring received his doctorate from Syracuse University in 1956, where he studied with William Cruickshank. Research at Syracuse at the time focused on the study of learning characteristics of brain-injured children. This program was based on the work of Alfred Strauss—work begun in the 1940s at the Wayne County Training Center.

Haring was Director of Special Education in the Arlington, Virginia, school system for a year and then joined the faculty of the University of Maryland from 1958 to 1960. During this period he collaborated with E. Lakin Phillips on a study of the effects of structured learning on the academic and social behavior of emotionally disturbed students. Haring later moved to the University of Kansas. He encouraged Lindsley to join the faculty there. He moved to the University of Washington in 1965, as Bijou was leaving, to serve as head of the Experimental Education Unit (EEU). The work originating from the EEU has had a major impact in special education—extending a technology of behavior to a wide range of student populations through the development of materials and procedures that comprise elements of systematic instruction.

Haring's career began at the end of the reorganization period in special education. The work he began in the late fifties was published early in the contemporary special education era (Haring & Phillips, 1962) and thus was among the first applications of operant conditioning with handicapped students. It is possible, by describing some of his contributions, to show how an early concern with structured learning environments led to the development of a technology of instruction and behavior management for handicapped students.

Structured Learning

The research program at Syracuse led to the development of an experimental educational program. Cruickshank, Bentzen, Ratzenburg, and Tannhauser (1961) studied the effects of a structured educational program on a group of brain-injured students. That study included some students whose problems were principally emotional in nature. Results suggested that the structured approach might be effective with emotionally disturbed students. Haring and Phillips (1962) compared the effectiveness of this approach to a permissive approach and to the performance of emotionally disturbed students in regular classes.

Cruickshank et al. (1961) hypothesized four critical elements of a structured approach:

1. Reduced environmental stimuli,

2. Reduced space,

3. A structured school program and life plan, and

4. Increased stimulus value of the teaching materials. (p. 14).

The structured approach employed by Haring and Phillips (1962) contained these elements:

1. Assignments were geared to student achievement levels, made brief and clear, then increased in magnitude as students demonstrated an ability to respond.

2. Work booths were constructed to reduce the distracting stimuli in the environment.

3. Specific performance standards, or limits, were set, i.e., students assigned academic work as first priority.

4. Free movement limits were set, i.e., students were allowed free movement in the classroom, within defined parameters.

5. Social-emotional conduct limits were set. Essentially, students were ignored when they behaved inappropriately, given a warning when misbehavior continued, and then placed in time-out (isolated).

6. Parent involvement.

The results of this demonstration project showed superior academic achievement for students in the structured group, as well as social behavior improvement as measured by a behavior rating scale.

The antecedents to a technology of instruction are present in Haring and Phillips's (1962) study, but they must be teased out. Couched in contemporary terms, several elements can be abstracted.

1. Break academic tasks into small steps, based on students' skill levels; then increase task performance as students demonstrate competence.

2. Individualize instruction and allow students free movement (independence) within the classroom.

3. Rearrange or engineer the learning environment.

4. State the limits (rules) in the classroom.

5. Extinguish inappropriate behaviors.

6. Limit (control) verbal directions and demonstrate desired responses when appropriate.

7. Keep performance records and use them for continual program revision.

8. Use consequences to shape behavior.

9. Provide immediate feedback on task performance.

Although the report of this project (Haring & Phillips, 1962) does not reference Skinner's work, Haring (1974) in a brief autobiographical sketch, indicates that "by combining Cruickshank's concept of environmental structure and B. F. Skinner's laboratory work in operant learning, Dr. Phillips and I began to apply behavioral principles to environmental structure" (p. 81).

This project made important contributions to contemporary special education. It was timely; the first P.L. 85-926 doctoral fellows were in the midst of training. *Educating Emotionally Disturbed Children* was then a new model—an important part of the content of instruction for these students. Second, it represented a departure from traditional approaches for "treating emotional illness in children." Other approaches were permissive, nondirective, or psychoanalytic in orientation. "Curing the illness" was their goal. In contrast, Haring and Phillips focused on academic behavior development as a strategy to enable disturbed students to achieve academic success and control of their social behavior. Third, the structure of the model was designed for individualization—one tactic for reducing "distracting environmental stimuli" was to reduce opportunities for group interaction. Environmental engineering and programmed, individualized instruction were precursors to the design of token economies and individual behavior modification strategies.

Precision Teaching

From 1960 to 1965, as director of the Children's Rehabilitation Unit at Kansas, Haring encouraged the development of data-based instruction. Lindsley, as noted, joined the Kansas faculty and brought from Harvard the procedures for an experimental analysis of behavior. These included direct and continuous measurement of behavior. At Kansas, with Haring's encouragement, the cumulative record and the automated cumulative recorder were translated into a paper and pencil system for classroom use—the ubiquitous 6-cycle log paper. During this period the precision teaching model was developed and transported to Washington when Haring assumed the directorship of the EEU.

The Scope of Effort at the Experimental Education Unit

As administrator of the Experimental Education Unit (EEU), Haring encouraged the development of innovative programs for children from birth through adulthood, representing mild to severe handicapping conditions and a wide range of learning problems. Products developed at the EEU include assessment devices, curriculum, and textbooks. Fundamental to all of these efforts is the use of systematic instructional procedures, direct measurement, and applied behavior analysis in the classroom setting. The evaluation of the precision teaching model is reflected in a series of chapters and books. Haring and Lovitt (1967), in a chapter in an early methods text, describe the beginning efforts in applied behavior analysis, including Lindsley's SRKC paradigm. In a related text, edited by Haring and Schiefelbusch (1976),

Haring and Gentry (1976) describe components of direct and individualized instruction, including elements of precision teaching. White and Liberty (1976) describe basic steps in precise educational measurements, and Lovitt (1976) describes a program of research in applied behavior analysis, conducted with learning disabled students on problems of reading, spelling, communication, and pupil management. Kunzelmann (1970), in conjunction with teachers from the EEU developed a programmed text, *Precision Teaching.* Haring, Lovitt, Eaton, and Hansen (1978) present a method for conducting applied behavior analysis in the classroom, based on 10 years of research on reading, writing, arithmetic, and social behavior change carried out at the EEU. White and Haring (1980) present detailed procedures for pupil assessment, instructional planning and implementation, and direct measurement of behavior. These texts, when examined in chronological order, represent increasingly sophisticated strategies for instruction and data-based decision making, utilizing the semilogarithmic (6-cycle log) charting system.

Haring and Hayden (1976) carried out a longitudinal study of Down's syndrome students. Other major efforts include a system of development pinpoints (Cohen & Gross, 1979), the Uniform Performance Assessment System (UPAS) (1981), and a program of research with older, multihandicapped individuals, (Johnson & Mithaug, 1978; Mithaug, 1979a, 1979b, Mithaug & Hagmeier, 1978; Mithaug, Hagmeier, & Haring, 1977). Collectively, these efforts represent the consistent application of behavioral principles across populations for an extended period of time. These efforts stand in contrast to the brief, isolated studies or projects which comprise much of the behavioral work in special education.

Hugh McKenzie   Hugh McKenzie received his doctorate from the University of Arizona in 1966, spent a year at the University of Kansas, and moved to the University of Vermont in 1967. His major efforts there focused on developing and refining *the consulting teacher model.*

Implementation of a Token System

At Kansas, McKenzie, Clark, Wolf, Kothera, and Benson (1968) implemented a token system with learning disabled students. Noting the logistical problems that may occur as teachers attempt to implement systems using chips or other token systems, they analyzed the effect of grades as reinforcers. Ten students participated; data were reported on eight. The study was conducted in a typical self-contained classroom. During the baseline period, typical incentives were available to students: recess, free time, and group lunch contingent upon work completion, special privileges for extra effort, contingent teacher praise for appropriate work behavior, and weekly grade sheets sent home to parents. During the experimental phase, all conditions were identical except that students' allowances were paid contingent upon weekly grade performance. Parents were instructed in the procedure; then they set the amount to be earned for a specific grade and the price of reinforcers children would be allowed to purchase. Since points could be subtracted for incomplete or poor work, students could owe their parents at the end of the week. Children's attending behavior during reading and arithmetic was recorded; the difference in group attending behavior between baseline and intervention was calculated statistically, and significant differences were found. The program was judged effective with seven of eight students, even when some returned to the regular class. McKenzie et al. (1968) suggested that this system benefitted teachers since management was at home under parental control. This study represented one variation on the application of reinforcement procedures within a classroom setting.

The Consulting Teacher Model

McKenzie's consulting teacher model deserves attention since it represents the design of a behavioral intervention system on a statewide basis. The program was initiated in the 1968–1969 school year, as a joint project conducted by the University of Vermont and the Vermont State Deparment of Education. Eight regular elementary teachers in one county completed the first of a two year master's training program. Fifty handicapped learners were served in regular education classes. From this beginning, a statewide service delivery system developed and continues at present.

McKenzie, Egner, Knight, Perelman, Schneider, and Garvin (1970) described the basic components of the consulting teacher program. Critical features are the statewide scope of the project, state department of education and university cooperation, local district-university preplanning to develop the model, local district financing of teachers' salaries while in training and university subsidy of tuition and other support, locally supported release time for teachers to work with other teachers, and provision of consultant services to teachers to help them maintain handicapped students in the regular classroom.

The content of training for consulting teachers included:

1. Principles of behavior modification,

2. Application of these principles to meet the needs of handicapped children in regular classrooms,

3. Precise daily measurements and monitoring of a child's progress to ensure that contingencies, methods, and materials are effective,

4. Procedures for training parents and teachers in the principles and application of behavior modification techniques,

5. Research training to increase skills in devising and evaluating education tactics,

6. Development of supplementary materials suited to the particular needs of handicapped learners, and

7. Methods of advising elementary school teachers in the management and education of handicapped learners.

Those who completed this program were specially certified as consultant teachers, employed by local districts, and awarded an adjunct appointment in special education at the university.

At the local district, the consulting teacher transmits these newly acquired skills to regular education teachers through in-class consultation, workshops, and formal courses (taught by consulting teachers), enabling recipients to receive graduate credit from the university. Teachers who avail themselves of these programs learn principles of behavior analysis, techniques of individualized instruction, content (task) analysis, goal setting for students, on a monthly basis through the school year, skills in developing supplementary instructional packages for students failing to meet timelines (Christie, McKenzie, & Burdett, 1972), and strategies to verify the effect of instruction through multiple baseline research design.

The consulting teacher model has received national attention. Descriptions of the program have appeared in the literature as the model has evolved (Egner & Lates, 1975; Knight, Christie, Egner, Paolucci, & Lates, 1976), and, in general form, applied to the training of teachers of the multihandicapped (Fox, Williams, & Fox, 1977).

A major criterion for consultant teacher trainees and teachers enrolled in courses is documentation of child behavior change. The 1968–1969 Report of the Consulting Teacher Program (Volume 2) contains 50 child behavior change projects conducted by the first year consultant teacher trainees on teachers requesting consultant teacher services. These studies, written in a brief, standard format, generally using a A-B-A-B design demonstrate behavior change on social and academic tasks. External evaluations appear to support the effectiveness of the program. Knight, Meyers, Paolucci-Whitcomb, Hasazi, and Nevin (1981) report a four-year comparison of the academic perform-ance in students enrolled in schools receiving or not receiving consulting teacher services. Statistical analysis of between group raw and percentile scores on reading and math achievement tests showed significant differences in favor of the students enrolled in schools receiving consulting teacher services. Students were those scoring in the lowest 12th percentile on achieve-ment measures. Preintervention test scores (achievement tests administered in the spring of fifth grade) showed no between-group differences, and the authors report no major differences between groups on other population variables. Results showed that, with consulting teacher service beginning in the sixth grade, significant differences emerged at the end of that school year and were maintained after grades seven and eight when only intermittent service was provided.

The consulting teacher program has these unique characteristics: it was begun by a psychologist, on a statewide basis, diffusing applied behavior analysis techniques and demonstrating a functional relationship between intervention and child behavior change. Further, the model focuses on *teachers training teachers* to work with handicapped students who remain in regular class placements.

Richard Whelan   Whelan, a student of Haring's, was a teacher and then an administrator at the famous Menninger Clinic before he entered the doctoral program at the University of Kansas. While a doctoral student he first worked as a classroom teacher of emotionally disturbed students and then received an appointment as an instructor. Later he was appointed Education Director at the Children's Rehabilitation Unit and eventually department chairman. Thus, as student and instructor, he was one of the first special educators trained with a behavioral orientation; and at the same time, he contributed to the training of other special educators.

Whelan's work focused on refining Haring's structured approach and ex-tending the experimental analysis of behavior into the classroom. Although Haring left Kansas in 1965, he and Whelan collaborated on various projects. Haring and Whelan (1966), for example, sponsored a symposium held in 1965 focusing on the learning environment, thus bringing together Lindsley,

Homme, Bijou, and others to explore extensions of the experimental analysis of behavior to the classroom environment. Whelan and Haring (1966) reviewed the small literature in practical applications of operant conditioning in the classroom, presented a general overview of behavioral principles, and described how they were being applied at the Children's Rehabilitation Unit. This brief article describes the state of the art in behavior modification at that time. Whelan and Gallagher (1972), in a chapter representative of Whelan's interests at the time, described the components of a behavioral program for teaching behavior disordered students. They argued for a functional definition of "emotional disturbance" based on the direct observation of behavioral excesses or deficits; they referenced Lindsley's (1966) paper on direct measurement and prosthesis of behavior as a framework for behavior analysis chains (antecedents, behaviors, consequents); they presented basic strategies for accelerating or decelerating behaviors and for recording and displaying the outcomes of intervention—in essence, a short course on behavioral intervention. In 1972, Whelan went to Washington, D.C. where he headed the Division of Personnel Preparation in the Bureau of Education for the Handicapped and where he encouraged development of systems to evaluate the quality of the performance of students enrolled in those funded programs. Subsequently, he returned to Kansas where he has served in administrative roles.

Thomas Lovitt

Thomas Lovitt completed his doctorate at the University of Kansas and moved immediately to the Experimental Education Unit at the University of Washington where he has directed a long-term research program on the application of behavior principles to the academic problems of school-aged (learning disabled) students. At Kansas he worked with Lindsley; his dissertation (Lovitt, 1966) was among those exploring the use of the conjugate reinforcement procedure and the classroom application of behavior principles. Looking at his publications over a period of nearly 20 years, it might be said that his experiences in the doctoral program shaped a high and durable rate of research/writing behavior. Haring and Lovitt (1967) reviewed current work in behavioral principles. Lovitt (1967) introduced the concept of behavioral assessment in the area of learning disabilities. This article was a noteworthy contrast to typical practices then (and now). Lovitt suggested problems with traditional assessment procedures and then developed a four-part procedure which included baseline assessment of behavioral components (following Lindsley's SRKC paradigm), analysis of the goals and abilities of the person referring the child for assistance, and generalization of assessment providing the referring agent with functional information. Lovitt suggested that this procedure would have two major benefits: it circumvents a search for hidden causes and focuses responsibility for remediation on the interventionst. Further, he suggested that the system provided a frame of reference for continuous monitoring of student performance and program revision. These were startling notions in 1967.

Lovitt and Curtiss (1968), in a series of three experiments, studied the effect of self-verbalization of problem solving on an 11-year-old boy's math performance. The boy was required to solve different, increasingly more complex subtraction problems in each experiment; an A-B-A design (no verbalizations, verbalizations, no verbalizations) was used in each experiment.

Rates of correct and incorrect error responses were recorded. Correct responses increased and errors decreased in each of the experiments. In the third phase, no verbalization, correct response rates continued to increase. This early, exploratory study demonstrated that through an experimental analysis it was possible to determine if a commonly used strategy was, in fact, an effective procedure.

Lovitt and Curtiss (1969) compared the effect of teacher and self-imposed contingencies on a 12-year-old student's rate of responding on academic problems. The study was carried out in an experimental class structured on a contingency-managed system. In a series of three experiments, the student received points for units of work completed on regular academic assignments following the regular class schedule. In the first study, the student's response rate was recorded during a baseline period. During the first phase of the intervention, the teacher explained the contingent relationship between performance and points, specified the point values, placed the contingency contracts on the student's desk, and then scored the work and awarded points. In the second phase, the student stated the terms of the contract. In the third phase, teacher-imposed contingencies were reinstated. The second experiment replicated the first. In the third experiment, the teacher imposed contingencies across the three phases; however, the point values available during the first and third phases were those used in the first experiment; during the second phase the teacher imposed values self-selected by the student during the second experiment. Thus, this third experiment attempted to separate the locus of control from the magnitude of reinforcement. The student's increased rate of responding in Phase 2 of Experiments 1 and 2 and decreased rates in Phase 2 of Experiment 3 indicated that self-imposed contingencies accelerated performance, not magnitude of reinforcement. These preliminary studies illustrated that it is possible to empirically test common assumptions, e.g., "solve the problem out loud before you write it," by subjecting them to an experimental analysis and, further, that academic problem behavior could be remedied without reference to hypothetical constructs or process training.

Lovitt's major contributions in special education include the extension of an analysis of behavior to the problems of students labelled learning disabled by others, a behavioral or functional analysis of learning disabilities, management of the longest program of systematic research (systematic replication) of applied behavior analysis of academic problems in a classroom setting, translation of research findings into information useful to classroom teachers (Haring, Lovitt, Eaton, and Hansen, 1978; Lovitt, 1976).

SUMMARY

This chapter traces the evolution of applied behavior analysis from theory to application. Several key events have been described: Skinner's development of a theory of operant conditioning, the emergence of an experimental analysis of behavior, the shift from the experimental laboratory to the natural environment as an "experimental space," the application of experimental procedures to human subjects, and the growth of applied behavior analysis to illustrate these key events. We have referenced critical elements of Skinner's works and described major studies of others. These studies, some of which may seem obscure now, were chosen because at the time they were published they represented a major contribution to theory, methodology, or unique applications to the subject population. These studies also provide a review, of sorts, of behavioral terminology and procedures. We have assumed a fundamental knowledge of operant conditioning. Readers who possess this knowledge should find the content of the chapter provides an S^D for review. Those who find the content foreign should, perhaps, review basic texts in operant procedures.

This chapter describes how contemporary special education acquired its strong behavioral base and technological orientation and identifies the contributions of many who applied these principles to the academic and social behavior problems of handicapped students. We have tried to show how these pioneers influenced the students they trained and how their students then trained others in special education.

3

THE ELUSIVE DATA BASE FOR SPECIAL EDUCATION PRACTICES

Special education is a creature of political invention. The field has survived in spite of itself. It has experienced good times and bad times. It began modestly, grew rapidly, and now faces many challenges. It has survived, for the moment, but not because it has been a demonstrably effective effort. Indeed, though it has endured many cycles of change and transformation, it has yet to enter an era of empiricism. Perhaps, as the field responds to recent criticisms, it will enter that era.

Over the years, special educators have regularly confronted certain fundamental questions.

- What *is* special education?
- What is *special* about special education?
- Do special education programs *make a difference* in the academic achievement of the students enrolled?
- Do special education programs make a *significantly greater difference* in academic performance than an alternative program (or, no program at all)?

Some of these questions are philosophical in nature; others can be answered empirically. The "difference" questions have been asked since programs first were established in the United States. Unfortunately, results of various studies in the past have shown "no significant difference" in favor of special education programs or practices.

Why have special educators endured in the face of these findings? Is there reason to believe that positive effects exist but have not yet been found? Is it possible that researchers have been looking in the wrong place? Or, more to

This chapter was written by **James W. Tawney** and **David L. Gast**.

the point, is it likely that they have utilized a research methodology that does not match the problem at hand? Is there a better way to look at the problem of measuring child behavior change to verify the effects of intervention? Obviously we believe there is a better way. However before we present a case for single subject research methodology we will review efforts to document the effectiveness of special education. After our historical review, we will describe what special education should do and how single subject methodology can contribute to the goal of individualized education.

Our analysis of the history of "no significant differences" in special education practices begins with the analyses of Samuel Kirk, who established the Institute for Research on Exceptional Children (IREC), "the first active research and graduate training department in the country or abroad" (Kirk & Bateman, 1964, Foreword). The IREC was established before the era of contemporary special education. Kirk's analyses of existing research and educational programs set the direction for many early research and curriculum development efforts.

The Efficacy Studies

The story of the effectiveness of special education has been told in research reviews published in the sixties (Guskin & Spicker, 1968; Kirk, 1964; Quay, 1963). Though each is instructive in its own right, Kirk's 1964 review will serve as our focal point. Guskin and Spicker's (1968) review followed Kirk's and analyzed the work of Kirk's associates. Quay's (1963) review is instructive in that it reflects attitudes then prevalent concerning the abilities of lower functioning students. Quay restricted her analysis to educable students because "the retarded at the lower end of the intelligence scale (IQ below 50) have not been demonstrated to be capable of developing academic skills to any appreciable extent" (p. 664). (This attitude on the part of the educational community was partly responsible for the parent activism which resulted in the formation of the National Association for Retarded Children in 1950). Collectively, the three reviews identified the measurement problems encountered in group comparative research.

Looking back, these early studies were concerned with two issues: the effectiveness of special programs for retarded students and the educability of intelligence, i.e., the nature-nurture controversy. We are concerned with the first question.

Kirk's (1948) first analysis was conducted at the request of the editors of the *Psychological Monographs* journal. He analyzed a study by Schmidt (1946) that reported major gains in IQ scores of students in special education classes. He compared the data reported to the data in the school system files and found major discrepancies. This experience occurred before he began his own study of the effects of early intervention, a study he began in 1949 and published in book form in 1958, as *Early Education for the Mentally Retarded.*

Kirk studied the effects of early intervention on retarded children in different living environments. He reported data on statistical comparisons of groups and extensive individual case histories as well. Children in the experimental condition were tested before, during, and after the intervention, and again in follow-up periods of at least one and as many as four years later. Matched contrast subjects were evaluated following the same pattern. Among the many findings, Kirk documented that children receiving the experimental intervention scored significantly higher than the contrast group at the end of the intervention period. While these students maintained their gains on follow-up scores (after first grade), the performance of the contrast group accelerated as a function of preschool intervention. Kirk cautioned that the statistical differences presented a limited perspective on the effects of intervention. He noted that the effect of the intervention was different for subjects with presumed organic (brain) damage than for students who did not appear so impaired. This finding led to the development of another project conducted by Gallagher to determine if tutoring was effective with brain-injured children.

Kirk's study was influential for several reasons. First, the outcomes of the study were presented from two perspectives, case history and statistical data. Second, Kirk was able to make some observations about the nature-nurture controversy, i.e., that both play a part in development. Third, the results were used to generate other intervention and evaluation programs, thus contributing to the advancement of science (or at least educational practice). Fourth, the results, published in 1958, provided direction for early intervention programs that evolved during the 1960s. For example, the Institute supported two programs: (1) Karnes' structured approach to early intervention, work that continues to this day, and (2) the structured approach of Bereiter and Englemann, work that resulted in the Direct Instruction programs in reading, arithmetic, language, and spelling and work that continues at the University of Oregon under the leadership of Engleman, Becker, and Carnine. Finally, this study contributed to the development of another comparison of mentally retarded students in special and regular class placements, the Goldstein, Moss, and Jordan study (1965), in progress when Kirk wrote his 1964 review.

The efficacy question received further attention when federal research funds were made available under P.L. 83-531, enacted in 1954. Research in the area of the handicapped was funded beginning in 1957 (Moss, 1968). Some of these efforts were efficacy studies designed to ask the effectiveness question with improved experimental designs. These studies attempted to control for previously uncontrolled variables. As Kirk (1964) noted in his review, that goal was not achieved. Kirk also reviewed studies of the effects of intervention with trainable retarded students. The outcomes were negative: once again no significant differences were found. Kirk's recommendations, discussed shortly, have been of particular interest during the eighties, as programs for severely retarded children have been evolving.

Explanations for the Lack of Significant Findings

Many explanations have been offered for the lack of strong positive effects in special education programs. Most are summarized in the reviews and critical research articles.

1. Special education was in its infancy. There was no clearly defined intervention program in the early studies.

2. The typical invervention was a watered down approach, i.e., a traditional curriculum was taught at a simpler level and slower pace. Thus it was reasonable to expect an increasingly greater validity problem. The longer students remained in special education, the farther behind they would fall on grade equivalent achievement measures.

3. If a watered down approach was not used, the goals of the program might be described as facilitating social development, a focus that also created a validity problem when evaluating the effects of an intervention.

4. There was a lack of suitable instruments to properly evaluate an intervention.

5. The population was not necessarily part of the normative population of standardized tests, and thus these tests were inappropriate.

6. The reliability and validity of specially constructed tests was suspect.

7. Teachers were improperly trained and thus unable to provide a "special" education.

8. The studies suffered from nonrandom assignments of subjects to treatment conditions. When retarded students who remained in regular grades were compared to those placed in special classes, two different populations were being studied. Though equated on test scores, the functional behaviors of the two groups were very different.

9. Traditional experimental procedures were insufficient to document fully the changes in heterogeneous groups of subjects.

10. Studies were generally short term. Evaluation occurred before there was a chance for the intervention effects to manifest themselves.

Kirk's (1964) summary of evaluations of programs for trainable students reflects the essence of the criticisms:

> In general, the results did not show significant benefits from the special-class programs, which were hurriedly assembled with staff which had had little previous training or experience with this type of child. The instruments of measurement were generally improvised by the investigators. It is the reviewer's opinion that research in this area was initiated without adequate preparation in terms of structure, theory, adequate hypotheses, or adequate measuring instruments. It is possible that intensive case studies, even with a sample of one in some cases, would have served a better purpose at this stage of development than the attempt to use complex statistical procedures on uncontrolled variables. (p. 93)

Guskin and Spicker (1968) expressed their opinion on the subject of educational research with the retarded in a somewhat different view: "It is to be hoped that a review of this field in 1980 would find many investigations which go far beyond the current style of research, which, as yet, has contributed pitifully little that is of value for the educational practitioner" (pp. 272–273).

In summary, when the question of how the programs survived is asked, the answer is clear. There was political impetus to maintain the programs. The findings could be explained away by saying that it was too soon to evaluate, that the studies were methodologically flawed, and that, generally, the investigators went about the task in the wrong way.

Importance of the Early Studies

Theoretically, humans learn from past mistakes. Two factors make it imperative that we pay careful attention to the lessons that may be learned from history. A new field, educating the severely handicapped, has been added to the public education system, and, at the same time, special education has suffered a fall from grace.

Applying Lessons from History to Mandated Programs for the Severely Handicapped

The studies of programs for educable retarded students should have provided direction for the evaluation of programs for the trainable retarded if viable alternatives existed at the time. Apparently, that was not the case.

A search for alternative strategies is critical now as programs for severely handicapped/severely developmentally retarded students, initiated in the 1970s as part of the right to education movement, develop in the 1980s. Because these programs serve students who manifest severely limited repertoires of behavior, the curriculum departs significantly from the traditional definition of "education." Further, their cost is high because they are labor-intensive. These factors make them susceptible to criticism and vulnerable to efforts to remove them from the public school environment. Thus it is reasonable to expect that there will be demands to show that these programs are effective, i.e., that they produce documented performance change.

How can this be accomplished? Tawney and Smith (1981) analyzed a forum of three articles (Burton & Hirshoren, 1979a, 1979b; Sontag, Certo, & Button, 1979) that addressed issues in the education of the severely and profoundly retarded. Tawney and Smith (1981) provided another view of the status of the field in 1980, i.e., whether this new field could provide effective programs:

> In summary, in the context of Kirk's (1964) review of research on programs for trainable retarded students, educational efforts for severely and profoundly retarded individuals seem prepared to provide effective programs. There are clearly identified theoretical approaches, theories which translate into intervention strategies, highly structured intervention programs, representative teacher training programs focusing on specific teacher skill acquisition, and in situ research. There are even measurement strategies which compensate for the lack of "reliable, valid assessment instruments." Collective wisdom and the experience from the efficacy studies should have taught the field to abandon experimental-control comparison studies and to focus on single-subject case report strategies to document skill acquisition. What is needed now is to integrate technologies, to begin to provide birth-onward intervention, and to store longitudinal data in computer systems in order to look at the effect of intervention over extended periods of time. (p. 14)

Special Education's Fall From Grace

Contemporary special education experienced a jarring turnaround in its infancy. As special classes grew in number in the sixties, so did the civil rights movement. As more attention was paid to the education and social condition of the minority groups, it became apparent that, in some areas, minority students were overrepresented in special classes. Thus, it was charged that special education classes had become a form of de facto segregation.

In 1968, Lloyd Dunn, one of the first special educators trained at the University of Illinois, published an article which had major impact on the field. Dunn questioned whether special education class placement was the proper approach.

This expensive proliferation of self contained special schools and classes raises serious educational and civil rights issues which must be squarely faced. It is my thesis that we must stop labeling these deprived children as mentally retarded. Furthermore, we must stop segregating them by placing them into our allegedly special programs.

The purpose of this article is twofold: first, to provide reasons for taking the position that a large proportion of this so called special education in its present form is obsolete and unjustifiable from the point of view of the pupils so placed; and second, to outline a blueprint for changing this major segment of education for exceptional children to make it more acceptable. (p. 6)

Dunn's call for an American Revolution in Special Education led to debate and self-examination within the field. Then, in the 1970s, from outside the field, parents initiated a barrage of civil rights litigation. In the eastern United States parents of severely retarded students filed suit to get their children *into* special education. On the West Coast parents sued to get their children *out of* special education, charging that minority children, many from non-English-speaking homes, were being inappropriately classified as retarded by the use of discriminatory testing practices. Across the country, the suits proliferated. Some, when settled, forced states to modify their educational laws for handicapped students. This momentum, in turn, led to the enactment of P.L. 94-142, The Education for All Handicapped Act of 1975. The many provisions of this law, and the extensive regulations which followed, were designed to remedy specific inappropriate and discriminatory practices. These actions have set a revolution in motion. If the forward movement continues, the effects of this revolution will be felt for many years to come.

The Source of Dissatisfaction

Parents and their advocates, speaking through the courts and Congress, have clearly expressed their dissatisfaction with special educators. In essence they have said:

• You deny our children equal educational opportunity.

• You use tests that discriminate against children from our culture.

• You place our minority and non-English-speaking children in special education and thus perpetuate a unique form of discrimination.

• Your educational programs are inappropriate and do not meet our children's needs.

• You place children in special education when a less drastic alternative might be used.

• You make decisions that affect the lives of our children and you do not tell us.

• You make all the decisions about our children's education, and you do not consult us.

• You do not spend enough money on our children. We demand our fair share—enough to provide an appropriate education.

• You deny our children educational and related services and thus reduce their chances to develop to their maximum.

The force with which parents have spoken through P.L. 94-142 has been reflected in the specificity of their directions to the public schools—and to classroom teachers and others responsible for educational programming. This is not the place for a full discussion of each element of the law and/or the specific sections of the federal regulations. However, within the context of "a fall from grace," it is instructive to note that, as reflected in current regulations, parents acting through the courts, then Congress, then through the federal bureaucracy, have made their presence known in the classroom. They have specified:

1. The conditions under which children must be evaluated,

2. Who shall participate in the development of a child's individual education plan and program,

3. That children's long-term educational goals must be made public,

4. The elements of an individual plan: behavioral objectives, outcome measures, criteria for successful completion of objectives, time estimates for reasonable completion of objectives.

P.L. 94-142 requires parents to sign the individual plans and permits them to revoke the plans at any time by withdrawing their approval.

P.L. 94-142 stops short of being an accountability law—but in a way that is ambiguous. One section of P.L. 94-142 states that it is *not* an accountability law, i.e., a teacher suffers no penalty for failure to complete written objectives within the projected time frame. On the other hand, parents' right to approve their child's individual program and their prerogative to withdraw consent create a powerful accountability system.

Mainstreaming: A Solution, Then Yet Another Problem

The first major effect of P.L. 94-142 was to return mildly handicapped students to the regular classroom—referred to in popular terms as mainstreaming. When the critical mainstreaming studies were reviewed (Semmel, Gottlieb, & Robinson, 1979) the result was "no significant differences":

> There is little evidence that mainstreaming practices result in superior perform- ance among handicapped children. There is an absence of a conclusive body of evidence which confirms that special education services appreciably enhance the academic and/or social accomplishments of handicapped children beyond what can be expected without special education. The lack of empirical evidence for the effect of special education appears to be equally true regardless of whether special services are delivered in mainstreamed or self-contained settings. (p. 267)

Thus, it seems we have more work to do, to document the effectiveness of special education practices.

Lessons from the Past

History tells us that traditional measures have not provided the necessary data to justify the continuation of special education programs. The justifications that sustained special education programs are no longer valid. The political climate that fostered the growth of special programs in the sixties has dis- appeared. The political climate that generated the mainstreaming movement has dissippated, not due to a lack of data, but due to a new view of the federal role in education and a reduction in the flow of federal funds to support these programs. The political activism which created support for P.L. 94-142 also created resistance to its implementation from virtually every segment of the school community, from parents of nonhandicapped students, and from a society that has only grudgingly acknowledged the rights of those who fall outside the white, middle- and upper-class cultures. Future special education will proceed in a very different climate. While special educators may promote the view that services to children are now justified on the basis of a constitutionally interpreted right to a free appropriate education, others may say, in one form or another "OK, but where's your data?"

The remainder of this chapter describes what special education should *do* and how single subject methodology contributes to the goal of individualized education.

Moving Forward

During the seventies, Dunn's call for revolution and other forces created an evolution in the development of products and intervention programs, including tests to identify instructional problems of learning disabled students, the development of process-oriented intervention programs such as the diagnostic-prescriptive teaching model, growth in public school programs for emotionally disturbed (behavior disordered) students, periodic attention to the special problems of gifted students, new (behavioral) approaches applied to the problems of children with communication disorders, advancement in the development of prosthetic devices for physically impaired students, and technology development for sensory impaired children. These developments came about as a result of a movement from general to specific approaches, an increasing emphasis on the behavior of the individual, and the steady growth of a technology of instruction.

Change in Perspective

These developments have been accompanied by a change in perspective. In the sixties, a fundamental question was "What is *special* about special education?" The first edition of Kirk's (1962) introductory text contained a section devoted to that topic (pp. 29–31), later editions do not. An introductory text by Smith and Neisworth (1975) described the factors that led professionals to reevaluate special education priorities and offered this definition, "Special education is that profession concerned with the arrangement of educational variables leading to the prevention, reduction, or elimination of those conditions that produce significant defects in the academic, communicative, locomotor, or adjustive functioning of children." (p. 13)

Educators are now focusing on the environmental *variables* that may effect a change in the functional *behaviors* of exceptional children. Similarly, publishers' catalogs are being filled with texts entitled *Teaching the (categorical label)*. And yet there are other publications that focus on instruction, e.g., White and Haring's (1980) *Exceptional Teaching*, which presents a method for what is commonly called *precision teaching*. This shift in perspective represents a trend to focus on the behavior of the teacher, rather than the deficits of children. This shift is based on the assumption that if teachers *teach* (and utilize the procedures of a sophisticated instructional technology), student behaviors will change in a positive direction. Conversely, when student behavior does not change, attention focuses on faults in the technology or the instructional agent, not on the inferred deficits of the child.

The Status of the Field Today

The field of special education, however defined, currently faces greater challenges than it has at any time in the past. In addition to the change in perspective, there is a growing dissatisfaction with public education and programs for the handicapped are no exception. The altruism which provided past impetus for special programs is gone. Arguments for programs, based on the equal opportunity interpretations of the Constitution, have been overshadowed by the decline of the economy. As a result programs for the handicapped are increasingly being called upon to justify their existence. The accountability provisions of P.L. 94-142 have placed teachers in contact with parents who are making greater demands for documentation that their children are learning at relatively error free rates on increasingly more complex academic tasks.

Even if P.L. 94-142 were to be repealed, current regulations and past events have set the stage for a critical analysis of special education practices. Parents are looking for the data, and programs have been developed to help them. The first author has been directing a national project to train parents to monitor the quality of IEPs and programs and to ask simple, but critical, questions in order to determine whether the elements of the instructional process are in place and whether there is documentation of child performance change.

Components of an Instructional Technology

Instructional technology is sufficiently developed to enable the field to respond positively, to satisfy parents' requests for documentation of child performance change. The elements of an instructional technology have been identified by Tawney and Cartwright (1981):

1. Defining what is taught
   a. Stating the conditions of instruction
   b. Response specification
   c. Stating criterion performance
2. Careful analysis of prerequisite skills
3. Precise behavioral assessment
4. Precise skill or content analysis
5. Fine-grain instructional sequencing—or programming for errorless learning
   a. Specification of teacher statements, cues, and prompts
   b. Specification of correction procedures
   c. Use of reinforcer systems
6. Data-based instruction—immediate decision making based on student's correct and error responses
7. Empirical verification of the effects of an educational intervention
8. Direct and daily measurement of student responses
9. Defined decision rules for program branching or program modification
10. Systematic programming through all phases of learning: acquisition, proficiency, maintenance, and generalization. (p. 6)

These elements are found in varying degrees in the DISTAR materials, in the HI-COMP materials; in the EDMARK reading program prepared to teach a sight word vocabulary to moderately retarded students; and in the Programmed Environments Curriculum, designed for use with severely developmentally retarded students. The tasks or skills needed to implement an instructional technology are widely represented in "methods" texts, e.g., Berdine and Cegelka (1980), Payne, Polloway, Smith, and Payne (1981), Snell (1983), and White and Haring (1980). Although these texts carry recent copyrights, the principles on which they have been structured have been pervasive in the field since Skinner's *Technology of Teaching* was published in 1968.

An example of a lesson, taken from a curriculum representing a highly structured approach and containing all the elements necessary for an instructional technology is shown in Figures 3-1 and 3-2 (pages 60–64).

The examples of curriculum, texts, lessons, and data sheets shown in this section have been included to document the pervasive influence of instructional technology, not to infer that only those who use this approach are in a position to document their teaching effectiveness. However, our bias in favor of technologically oriented approaches is clear. When used as the lesson is taught, a permanent record of response-by-response child performance data is accumulated.

Teacher Competency

We have made no statements about the competence of special education teachers because there have been few serious attempts to define competence and consequently few attempts to measure it. This situation is painfully clear to the first author who once implemented an experimental project to provide special education certification to teachers certified in regular education. It was demonstrated that, with intensive technical assistance, teachers could meet the major evaluation criterion—a random sample of their students' work performance over at least a 30-day period showed 90% of the students were responding at 90% current responding over 90% of the days in the work sample (Tawney, 1980). However, the project, like others in the competency-based education movement of the seventies, did not move beyond the experimental stage. Although this project did not change the world, it offered some lessons. To parents, the question to the teacher is not "Are you competent?" but "Where's the data?" Thus it seems important to help teachers answer the question satisfactorily and then answer the next logical question, "Is there a functional relationship between (your) instruction and child behavior change?"

A Brief Look into the Future

In a very short time, the computer technology will exist to enable every teacher to develop an extensive data base on each student she teaches. It will be possible to enter daily records of students' progress into a computer that will generate a graphic display of performance, in every subject area, for any predetermined number of days, e.g., any n consecutive days, or for any 1–nth set of days. Thus it will be possible to look at students' progress over

Identifying Objects

4/5 Data

Cycle

Skill:

In this program the child learns to recognize the names of objects he uses often in his environment. He learns to select an object from a group through a process which includes introducing then fading auditory and visual cues that enhance the discriminability of the object. The child who learns the skill will follow verbal commands without additional cues.

Entry Behaviors:

1. S uses a variety of common objects with minimal assistance (e.g., self-help skills). If S cannot use objects because of physical limitations, he should be able to indicate in some way that he is aware of the uses of the objects (e.g., opens his mouth when he sees a spoon or cup).

2. S responds to a variety of cued commands for routine tasks (e.g., Following Cued Commands). Although S may or may not be able to comprehend the specific words of a command, he is usually able to perform the desired action by using your model, gestures, or other cues to understand what is expected of him. Typically, S associates a specific word with a specific reinforcing event and anticipates the event whenever that word is spoken (e.g., Responding to Signal Words).

3. S visually discriminates between different objects. Usually S demonstrates this skill by spontaneously using different objects correctly (he shows he can tell a sock from a mitten by attempting to put each one on correctly, without direction). S may also demonstrate visual discrimination by matching objects that are similar in appearance (e.g., Matching-Objects). If S is visually impaired, he should be able to discriminate objects by touch. Adapt the program by having him feel the objects, perform an activity with them if necessary, then select the indicated object.

4. S hears the command, or can lip-read. If S is hearing impaired, you may adapt the program, using signing instead of or in addition to vocal language.

5. S makes some motor response to indicate his choice (points to a specified object, looks at it, picks it up). Select a response appropriate to S's capabilities.

Objective:

When presented with a choice of three objects, S selects the specified object. S must initiate his response within 5 seconds of the command and respond correctly 4 out of 5 trials for each of two different objects that are specified at random.

FIGURE 3-1 Sample lesson from a highly structured curriculum. (From Tawney, J.W., Knapp, D.S., O'Reilly, D.O., and Pratt, S.S. Programmed environments curriculum. Columbus, Ohio: Merrill, 1979, pp. 33–36. Reprinted by permission.)

object = an item that can be easily handled and for which there is a duplicate available. (This program is not appropriate to teach objects that are large or do not have a duplicate that can be used. See Cycle and Follow-Up for suggestions for teaching large objects.)

Cycle:

Record each object S can identify. Each cycle teaches two objects. Repeat as needed to teach other small, easily handled objects. Once S recognizes the names of a variety of familiar objects and can associate those objects with their pictures (e.g., Identifying Simple Pictures), repeat the program to teach large objects (especially those not readily available), using pictures instead of the real objects.

Follow-Up:

Have S respond to a variety of commands that include each new word he learns. Help S generalize these new concepts by teaching him to recognize a variety of objects of the same class (e.g., cup--short red one with a handle; large green cup). Teach S to recognize the pictures of objects he has learned (e.g., Identifying Simple Pictures). Teach S to imitate the names of the objects he has learned (e.g., Shaping Words) and to name the object on his own (e.g., Naming Objects). Have S help with household or school tasks by sorting the objects he has learned (e.g., Sorting). Informally introduce the names of other objects that S sees or uses daily, such as bed, sink, or tree. Encourage S to say the names of these objects.

FIGURE 3-1 (continued)

Program for Receptive Skill 6

Materials:

Select two objects (called targets) to be taught. Obtain a duplicate for each (called samples). In addition, have at least three other objects available to use as distractors.

Chart:

Common Objects Chart, page 457.

GENERAL STRATEGY

Cue:

<u>present sample</u> = select a visual characteristic of the target and its sample (the roundness of a ball, the bristles of a brush). Point out this attribute and describe it ("Look how round the <u>ball</u> is," as you circle the ball with your finger). Then hold up the sample or give it to S, and say its name emphatically... "<u>Ball</u>." If S is vocal, have him try to say the word.

Arrangement:

Display three choices, both targets and one distractor.

Command:

Give an appropriate command for S to indicate one of the targets ("GIVE ME THE <u>CUP</u>" or "POINT TO THE <u>SPOON</u>").

Latency:

S must initiate his response within 5 seconds of the command or delayed cue.

Correction:

Use general correction procedures.

Natural Consequence:

Allow S to interact with the object. Guide S to use the object appropriately (brush his hair with the hairbrush, pretend to drink from the cup).

Other Trials:

Repeat the strategy. Vary trials between the two targets to be identified. Note that S must always meet criterion on both targets. Also, vary the distractor and the arrangement of choices.

Modification:

S has not met step criterion after four errors.

FIGURE 3-1   (continued)

CONDITIONS	BEHAVIOR	CRITERIA
	S selects the specified target...	for each target
PRE Display the choices, and give the command. Present the natural consequence.	unassisted	4 correct out of 5 trials (each target)
S/1 Present the <u>sample</u>. Display the choices, and give the command. Correct if needed. Present the natural consequence.	with sample present	4 correct out of the last 5 trials for each step (each target)
S/2 Present the <u>sample</u>; then <u>remove</u> it. Display the choices, and give the command. Correct if needed. Present the natural consequence.	with sample present, then removed	
S/3 Display the choices, and give the command. If S does not begin to respond correctly, present the <u>sample</u>, and then <u>remove</u> it, repeating the command. Correct if needed. Present the natural consequence.	with delayed sample, which is removed	
S/4 Display the choices, and give the command. Correct if needed. Present the natural consequence.	unassisted	
POST 1 Same as PRE	unassisted	4 correct out of 5 trials for each test (each target)
POST 2 New Command		
POST 3 New Objects (Same type of object, such as a different cup and spoon)		

MODIFICATIONS

When you present the sample, demonstrate the appropriate use of the object at the same time. Allow S to perform the appropriate action with the object. Then give the command. After S's response, present the natural consequence as described.

FIGURE 3-1   (continued)

Data Sheet

4/5 AND RATE DATA PROGRAMS

PROGRAM: _____   STUDENT: _____

REINFORCERS: _____   TEACHER: _____

MATERIALS: _____   SESSION TIME: _____

Date	Min.	Step	Responses* (+, −, θ)	Comments

*SYMBOLS   + = Correct Response
            − = Incorrect Response
         θ = No response
          =   (count as error)

SUMMARY INFORMATION (fill in when applicable):
Total # of Trials: _____

# of Correct: _____

# of Incorrect: _____

% of Correct: _____

Total # of Minutes on Program: _____

FIGURE 3-2. **Data sheet for a highly structured lesson.** (From Tawney, J.W., Knapp, D.S., O'Reilly, D.O., and Pratt, S.S. Programmed environments curriculum. Columbus, Ohio: Merrill, 1979, p. 447. Reprinted by permission.)

extended time periods. Higher functioning students, who are independent learners, will interact directly with the computer to enter this data base. For lower functioning students, whose instruction is guided physically by the teacher, it may be necessary to develop simple, auxiliary keyboards so that teachers can enter data as direct instruction sessions are being conducted.

The storage capabilities of inexpensive and increasingly more sophisticated microcomputers are making it possible for the classroom teacher to conduct a visual analysis of child performance data on a daily basis, at little cost in terms of time per student. The teacher may plot acceleration/deceleration lines and follow a formal decision-making process incorporated into a precision teaching system, or she may simply analyze data for significant deviations from typical performance. This capability permits constant reanalysis and modification of teaching procedures. It also permits teachers to sequence carefully the timing of behavior probes (pretests) and the introduction of new learning activities to show that behavior change occurs as a function of instruction. Teachers will be able to answer both questions: "Where's the data?" and "Are you responsible for the behavior change?" The chapters which follow suggest how research studies can be carried out in the classroom and how daily classroom instruction can be research based.

SUMMARY

Everyone takes data. Food servers do, so do service station attendants. Every clerk in every store takes data. In stores that use sophisticated computer systems, the simple entries of the clerk at the dry goods counter translate into data used for a variety of decisions: inventory management, employee scheduling, quality control, and so on.

It is unfortunate that special education developed without a data collection tradition. The ongoing development of an instructional technology, however, has been making it possible to reverse this earlier tradition. Teachers are gaining access to new instructional management tools: applications of a growing computer technology. And the messages from the public suggest, finally, that these tools be put to good use. Special education practices have been challenged. The forces of change are dictating major changes in the way the field proceeds. The procedures covered in the remainder of this text will enable teachers to move in one direction: to document child performance change as a function of instruction.

4
SCIENTIFIC RESEARCH IN THE CLASSROOM SETTING

- Education is an art.
- Education is a science.
- Education is an art that is being transformed into a science.
- Educational research is psuedoscientific.
- The best technology makes for the best education.
- The growth of technology in education reflects the anti-intellectual attitude that permeates contemporary public education.

Which of these statements you believe depends entirely on where you stand as you look at the problems that confront public education. Or, in other words, your response to these statements is a function of the events that constitute your history. Whatever set of beliefs a student holds, it soon becomes apparent in the early stages of graduate study that educational research is considered to have little impact on educational practice. Generally students who seek links between theory and educational practice will be disappointed. So will those who seek empirical verification of theories translated into educational practice. The intrepid student who approaches a school system with the question "What data influenced the decision to adopt x materials or y methodology?" is likely to be disillusioned by the answers he receives. Thus, a strong case can be made that education, however defined, has benefitted little from the application of *the scientific method* to events which occur in classroom settings. This sad state of affairs is largely responsible for the current disaffection with public education.

In this chapter we intend to state the goals of science and of education. Then we will discuss the integration of science and education and the

This chapter was written by **James W. Tawney** and **David L. Gast**.

pragmatics of classroom-based research as they apply to the use of single subject research designs in educational settings.

The Goal of Science

The *Oxford American Dictionary* (1980) defines *science* as "a branch of knowledge requiring systematic study and method, especially one of those dealing with substances, animal and vegetable life, and natural laws; *natural sciences*, biology, geology, etc.; *physical sciences*, physics, chemistry, etc." *Webster's New Collegiate Dictionary* (1975) defines *science* as "possession of knowledge as distinguished from ignorance or misunderstanding; knowledge attained through study or practice." Simply put, the goal of science, is to advance knowledge. In the popular view, within a discipline the accumulation of knowledge proceeds in a somewhat haphazard fashion. From the efforts of many come the grand discoveries of the few, the findings that move society forward. As the process unfolds, the major body of research yields findings that may go unnoticed for years. Some findings are of immediate interest and generate new research programs that may be abandoned when more fruitful approaches appear on the horizon. Thus, while the individual scientist follows a defined set of procedures applied systematically to an area of inquiry and moves from one logical question to another, science itself advances in a less orderly fashion. Sidman (1960) illustrates the point from the perspective of the scientist:

> It sometimes seems that a brilliantly creative experimenter does not possess the qualities of patience and plodding thoroughness that most of us feel are vital for scientific progress. While it would, of course, be desirable for all investigators to be simultaneously brilliant and plodding, such a combination is, in fact, rare. Most of us are elaborators of other workers' discoveries; a few of us are creators; only a handful are both. We are all necessary, for even the most creative scientist builds upon an established foundation. A scorn for the everyday scientific laborer will blind the student to the immensely valuable and necessary contributions that can come only from hard and often uninspired "pick and shovel" work. On the other hand, if the student is taught, as many are, that pick and shovel labor *is Science*, then he will inevitably fail to appreciate the results of important, but unelaborated, discoveries. (p. 24)

To the student-researcher, his contribution to the advancement of science may seem small. A replication of a published study, the application of a standard procedure in a new environment or with a new population—these efforts may seem minor in the grand scheme of science. Yet they are a very necessary part of the elaboration of a general system of behavior and the growth of applied behavior analysis.

The Goal of Education

The goal of education is to change behavior in a positive direction. One need not be a behaviorist to adopt this definition, although many educators would disagree with the definition, and with that assumption. A brief example will illustrate this point.

Many years ago, when proponents of "behaviorism" and "humanism" were tilting at each other over the "proper approach" to education, the first author was asked to consult with a group of regular and special educators in a small college. The invitation was tendered because of the author's work in the area of "competency based teacher education." The task was to develop a philosophy statement, a set of general goals, and a set of specific competencies to be demonstrated by graduates of this teacher training program. After the amenities, and the coffee, the group set about its first task—developing a philosophy statement. There was little discussion, not uncommon at the beginning stage of a group project. Finally the consultant raised the question, "What is the fundamental goal of education?" Then, to end the silence that followed, he asked, rhetorically, "Isn't the goal of education to change behavior?" No silence this time! A distinguished committee member jumped to his feet, threw down his working materials, shot a withering glance at the consultant, shouted "Oh, my God no! You're one of those behaviorists!" He wheeled and left the room, never to return. At the very least, those actions broke the ice, and the committee proceeded. Being or not being a "behaviorist," of course, had nothing to do with the task at hand—though few, other than the consultant, would have agreed at that point. The lesson to be learned was that long-time educators, however they defined their work, did not define it as changing behavior. However, there is a general social expectation that the educational process will produce a change in children's behavior. Students are expected to "know more" at the end of the school year. Further, teachers are expected to be responsible for that change. The legal contract between a teacher and the employing district is the observable manifestation of a social contract that offers a livelihood in return for the enhancement of the next generation. Whether one chooses to describe the contract in euphemisms or concrete terms, the expectation is the same. For the clasroom teacher the goals of education are clear: to produce a positive change in students' behavior and, at the same time, to establish some personal responsibility for the change.

Integrating Science and Education in the Classroom

Is it possible to incorporate scientific methodology into the daily routine of the classroom environment? It is, but it's not an easy task. We have stated the benefits of this strategy in general terms: to advance science, to document child performance change, and to establish teachers' responsibility for the change. Before moving on to the research task itself, we would like to restate and elaborate on the importance of these goals.

Advancement of Science

Through the work of Skinner and Bijou, we have described a system of behavior analysis. The elements of this system include a philosophy of behavior development, a general theory, a methodology for translating theory into practice, and a specific research methodology.

This system is new in the scope of human evolution and the advancement of science. It will gain acceptance and verification through the successful application of concepts and principles. One general "test" of the system is the demonstration of effectiveness in a variety of settings, in basic and applied applications.

Baer, Wolf, and Risley (1968) have suggested some benefits which may occur from an analysis of individual behavior.

> A society willing to consider a technology of its own behavior apparently is likely to support that application when it deals with socially important behaviors, such as retardation, crime, mental illness, or education. Such applications have appeared in recent years. Their current number and the interest which they create apparently suffice to generate a journal for their display. That display may well lead to the widespread examination of these applications, their refinement, and eventually their replacement by better applications. Better applications, it is hoped, will lead to a better state of society, to whatever extent the behavior of its members can contribute to the goodness of a society. Since the evaluation of what is a "good" society is in itself a behavior of its members, this hope turns on itself in a philosophically interesting manner. However, it is at least a fair presumption that behavioral applications, when effective, can sometimes lead to a social approval and adoption. (p. 91)

Applied behavioral analysis has been adopted and made an integral part of special education. Classroom-based research, derived from a system of behavior analysis and focused as specific problems of learning and reinforcement, has the potential to support the elaboration of a system of behavior analysis. In this way the student-researcher or teacher-researcher may contribute to the advancement of science.

Advancement of Educational Practice

Public education *can* make a difference. The researcher who demonstrates positive changes in children's behavior, in academic performance as well as in social behavior, produces evidence of a benefit of the instructional process. When looking at special education, one does not have to look far to learn that most child-use materials have not been tested thoroughly, that there is a limited data base on instructional procedures, and that much of the existing research was carried out in controlled environments and not in the classroom. Thus, there are many research possibilities in the classroom environment, and any positive outcomes will result in a sorely needed advancement in educational practice.

Empirical Verification of Instructional Behavior

Successful teachers will have to meet new standards in the future. They should expect that increasingly informed parents will ask for data on child performance change, and then will ask for some demonstration that the teachers' efforts were responsible for the change. Computer and instructional technologies have been developed sufficiently to enable an effective teacher to meet these requests for data; although, at the present time, software development and diffusion of these technologies does not put this capability in the hands of all teachers who might want it. However, we are confident that these tools will be commonplace for the next generation of teachers. In the present generation, those teachers who utilize a precise instructional technology, who develop simple data recording systems, and who use the research designs shown in the next section will be able to answer the questions parents ask. The task may require extra effort, but the data should provide sufficient reinforcement to maintain these teaching and research behaviors.

Problems Common to Classroom-based Research

Researchers encounter common problems when seeking data in the classroom environment. In chapter 14 we will describe some of the logistical problems that confront the student researcher, such as getting into the schools with the resources necessary to complete a project. Here, we focus on the day-to-day problems of conducting research in the classroom. Some of these logistical problems translate into design problems, which are discussed in subsequent chapters.

Obtaining Resources for Research

The classroom is, or can be, rich in resources for the teacher-researcher. In the "old days" it was common for a special education teacher to report that he began the school year with students, desks, some chalk, and nothing more. Today that complaint is heard, but infrequently.

The classroom is where the kids are. Instructional materials are the stimuli for experiments. The students emit a wide array of behaviors. Some are of ecological concern, particularly when children emit them with such intensity or frequency that they interfere with personal development and/or the order of the classroom environment. Reinforcement techniques have so long been a part of instructional technology that the materials for reinforcement systems are no longer considered foreign or difficult to obtain. If a student-researcher wished to establish a token economy in a class, philosophical objections might be a more formidable barrier than the task of selecting and acquiring the materials.

Unless a study requires specially constructed equipment, e.g., an electronically controlled match-to-sample apparatus, the resources required for research projects are limited and low cost. Simple forms can be mimeographed in the schools, at little expense to the student and at no expense to the classroom teacher. Digital watches used for time-sampled observations are common and inexpensive. Pocket calculators with elapsed time recording capabilities are relatively inexpensive. Graduate students can serve as volunteer observers for each other. Depending on the school's philosophy and age range of pupils, it should be possible to obtain volunteer student support. In the same way that peers have been used to tutor each other, they can be trained to conduct interobserver reliability checks. If the teacher wishes to verify that an instructional procedure has been followed exactly as written, a principal, supervisor, or parent volunteer can be trained to observe fidelity to the written procedure.

The resources listed above are illustrative, not exhaustive. They are intended to serve as suggestions to generate other likely alternatives. To the student-researcher or classroom teacher who wishes to proceed with a study, but questions whether there are sufficient resources, we say, "Look around you, most of the materials are at hand."

The Pragmatics of Classroom-based Research

Here we consider what happens when "nothing proceeds as planned." Figure 4-1 and the following examples illustrate how reality impinges on the ideal outcome of a study—good, clean data that clearly demonstrate a powerful effect. There are solutions for some of the problems, but in other instances there is no alternative but to start over again. Figure 4-1 represents only two

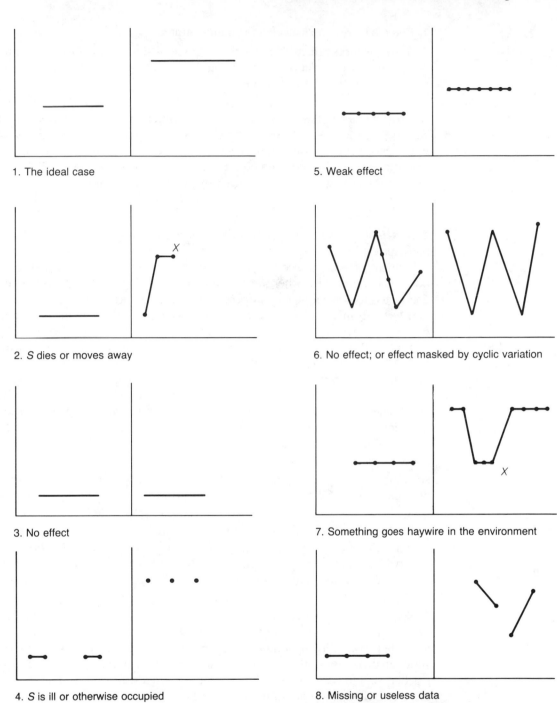

1. The ideal case

2. *S* dies or moves away

3. No effect

4. *S* is ill or otherwise occupied

5. Weak effect

6. No effect; or effect masked by cyclic variation

7. Something goes haywire in the environment

8. Missing or useless data

FIGURE 4-1   Ideal and real classroom-based research problems.

conditions, observation and intervention, which are meant to represent any type of research design. Graph 1 represents the ideal; the subsequent graphs show reality.

1. *The ideal case.* A clear effect is demonstrated.

2. *S dies or moves away.* The ideal, of course, is that once initiated the study is brought to completion. Here, *x* signifies that the study had been interrupted due to the loss of the subject.

3. *No effect.* Graph 3 shows no effect, *S*'s behavior is not brought under control. Whatever has happened, the experimenter (*E*) has started in the wrong place and is very far off base. In some circumstances, a pilot study might have provided direction. When might such a problem occur? Suppose that the intervention represented the academic performance of a child with a moderate learning problem and that *S* had been poorly assessed. An intervention program requiring performance far beyond *S*'s functional skill level might produce such a result.

4. *S is ill or otherwise occupied.* This is a variation on Graph 2. Here *S* participates, but only sporadically. When an intervention is begun to remedy a problem of ecological concern, the strategy may have to be shifted to the home environment (or wherever *S* is when not in school). When the research is conducted to solve a problem of concern to the researcher and it is possible to select *S* from a pool of *S*s, it is important to ask questions about attendance *first*. Sometimes the absences will be due to other factors, e.g., teacher strikes or the weather. The first author once conducted a curriculum field test that spanned a 3-year period. In the first (pilot test) year a threatened strike influenced the start of the project. During the two years of full-scale testing, the country experienced the most severe winters of a century, and in some locales the intervention was interrupted for 30 or more school days. Fortunately, the winter was not severe all across the country, and fewer days were lost at sites outside of New England.

5. *Weak effect.* There appears to be a differential effect, but it is weak. This situation also requires an intensive analysis of procedures to determine possible reasons for *S*'s failure to respond positively to the intervention.

6. *No effect; or effect masked by cyclic variation.* Here it is impossible to tell if there is an effect. There is extreme variability in the observation phase as well as during the intervention. Any effect is masked by failure to extend the observation phase until a pattern is established. The extreme range of responses during the intervention suggests that target behavior is not under conrol.

7. *Something goes haywire in the environment.* Here *x* represents something that happens that is outside of *E*'s control. While *x* may be explained (if it is identified easily), it will require an extension of the study to provide a more substantial demonstration. In the classroom setting, *x* might be a substitute teacher, or the pandemonium of school celebrations, e.g., running sessions close to holidays, visitors in the class, and the like.

8. *Missing or useless data.* Theoretically, in the small-scale projects that are the focus of this text, data should not disappear. The sad fact is that they do. Sometimes *S* eats the data sheets, or they may be lost or misplaced during the course of a busy school day. Sometimes human error in recording renders the data useless. Or, suppose that *E* is following a written procedure and inadvertently makes an error, one that persists until the next periodic observa-

tion by a third party. In this case it is prudent to drop all these days or sessions from the data base. Some of these problems can be alleviated by maintaining strict control of the raw data, for example, securing data sheets on a clipboard hung above the reach of the tallest student. Adherence to procedures can be maintained by practicing until the procedure is automatic and by scheduling more frequent observations. In other words, preplanning can prevent some of these problems. Good research and good teaching both require management skills.

Teaching Behavior and Research Behavior

Similarities

Knowing that teaching and research are considered by many to be antithetical, we would like to draw some parallels between the behaviors we consider to be fundamental to both science and education.

A teacher must:

1. Analyze individual students' performance to identify the instructional level; a form of hypothesis testing.

2. Specify instructional objectives that contain antecedents, behaviors, and defined criterion performance levels.

3. Define instructional procedures, whether they are as general as self-study assignments or as precise as direct instruction procedures based on a learning trial model.

4. Conduct content analysis and task analysis of instructional sequences for individual learners.

5. Implement instruction.

6. Collect data on child performance.

7. Make decisions based on data.

8. Maintain data records.

9. Manage the instructional system.

10. Conduct instruction within professional/ethical guidelines.

A researcher must:

1. Identify a problem.

2. Generate hypotheses in the form: "If I do this, what might happen?"

3. State specific research program objectives.

4. Define the elements of the research procedure: stimuli, apparatus, subjects' response topography, consequent events.

5. Write specific, replicable research procedures.

6. Implement procedures and verify fidelity to procedures, including accurate recording of subjects' responses.

7. Maintain data records.

8. Manage the research program.

9. Analyze and report findings that suggest succeeding steps in the research process.

10. Conduct research in an ethical manner.

The similarities in these sets of behaviors are apparent. They can be synthesized by noting that both the teacher and researcher must (1) be able to identify and analyze problems, (2) generate creative solutions (3) implement an intervention in a systematic manner, (4) document the effect of the intervention, and (5) act on the data.

Some Differences   Though we have proposed that classroom-based research can advance the goals of education and of science, the classroom is obviously not a Skinner box, nor does it approximate a sterile experimental space consisting of a table, a chair for E and S, and a stimulus management device (e.g., a Wisconsin General Test Apparatus). A look at the differences will sensitize the student-researcher to the problems encountered when one attempts to initiate a research project in someone else's classroom. Conversely, the classroom teacher who is about to initiate a research project may be sensitized to the need to create more rigorous conditions for data collection and environmental control.

The Environment

In the research laboratory, the experimenter may work with one subject at a time in a controlled space that contains no distracting stimuli. The classroom, on the other hand, may be rich in stimuli. If a study requires that Ss attend to stimuli and make complex discriminations, some effort must be initiated to create a laboratory-like space within the classroom. Often the use of folding screens or the arrangement of desks and materials in a quiet corner of the room may be necessary to reduce the amount of distracting stimuli present during an experimental session.

The Number of Subjects

There is more than one student/subject in a classroom. The number may preclude meaningful research effort by the classroom teacher; similarly, an excessive number may preclude meaningful instruction. The student-researcher who is concerned with the behavior of 3 of 25 students in a regular third grade must be aware that life proceeds around him.

The Stimuli

In learning studies, the same set of stimuli are presented in a predetermined order to subjects who respond to them until they meet a defined criterion. This is the *trials to criterion* model. Nothing changes except S's performance. In contrast, instructional stimuli should change from day to day as S progresses through sequentially more complex learning activities. When student progress over instructional units is the objective of a research program, the experimenter must be careful to define the unit of instruction and to account for the magnitude of difficulty from one unit to the next.

The Learning Trial Model

In a laboratory experiment using a discrete or fixed trial operant model, (a) stimuli appear, (b) a time interval lapses, and (c) a response does or does not occur. Correct trials are consequated according to a determined rule. Incorrect responses or a failure to respond are consequated according to different rules. We have described a learning trial model for direct instruction, which is based on a laboratory model. The use of this model appears to be on the increase for certain types of students, for example, the moderately or severely handicapped. The model is promoted among advocates for direct or systematic instruction. Yet the model applies to only a portion of the subject population. Older students who manifest only mild forms of learning problems may work "independently," collecting work folders (stimuli) in the morning and returning them, tasks completed, later in the day. Consequation—marks, tokens, or credit transactions—may be counted and recorded after the work is completed, and thus there is no immediate temporal contiguity among antecedents, behavior, and consequent events. Or, students may respond to teacher requests in group settings, where there appears to be no relationship among teacher questions, student responses, and teacher's praise or correcting statements. While this may be yet another fruitful area of inquiry, task analyzing the elements of the process so that they can be accurately measured may be a difficult task.

Defining the Topography of the Response under Study

It is easy to define the motor response required to depress a Plexiglass response panel to activate a microswitch in an electronically controlled discrimination learning apparatus. It is somewhat more difficult to define out-of-seat behavior in a class of active students who make only occasional contact with their physical environment and even less contact with reality (however that is defined).

The Response Unit

A laboratory study may be designed to measure a simple motor response to a standard set of stimuli. Or, an experimenter may wish to describe how S responds, using a simple motor movement, when stimulus control is shifted from a circle to an ellipse. Or, the experimenter may be interested in the effect of contingent electric shock on the frequency of occurrence of self-destructive behaviors such as skin tearing or eyeball gouging.

Classroom instruction is somewhat more complex. When a teacher says, "Ralph has learned what a cup is," learning may be defined as criterion performance, for example, 90% correct responding during these phases: (a) initial acquisition of the response, (b) repeated demonstration with more and more complex exemplars of instances and not-instances of the concept; (c) continued demonstrations over time, with decreasing instances of behavior probes (posttests); and (d) demonstrations over an increasing range of settings and occasions for responding. Research may be conducted across these phases or on any phase.

Measuring Responses

This task may be done automatically in the laboratory. The presence of the experimenter is often not required. These conditions may soon be approximated in the classroom, as students work on academic research problems on microcomputers that automatically record and store data on each subject's performance. In some circumstances, the teacher-researcher will have access to simple response counting devices. Some of these may be wired into microcomputers so that teachers can record responses for students who lack the motor dexterity to self-record or who are emitting responses not easily recorded, for example, discriminably different vocal responses.

Management Responsibilities

Simply put, the student-researcher is responsible for the materials, the logistics of conducting the study, and the behavior of those participating in the experiment. The classroom teacher is responsible for the management of the research he has initiated and for the instructional management of the whole class as well.

SUMMARY

We have defined the goals of science and education and shown how they can be carried out so that both fields are advanced. Possible benefits from extensive programs of classroom-based research have been described. We have listed some common problems and have suggested how some of them might be avoided.

The classroom is a dynamic system. Teachers, students, and a cast of others continuously interact in ever-changing patterns. The task of the researcher—the graduate student or the classroom teacher—is to impose a systematic procedure on some aspect of child-environment interactions and to bring those elements under control. Then it will be possible to state with confidence that the behavior change is a function of carefully planned and sequenced interventions. To the extent that the researcher is able to document that procedures were followed as written, that data were recorded accurately, and that there has been an *effect*, science and education will be advanced.

SECTION TWO

MEASUREMENT ISSUES

5

GENERAL FACTORS IN MEASUREMENT AND EVALUATION

If educators are to effectively design, implement, and evaluate instructional programs, they must measure the effects of their instruction on student behavior. Just as applied research requires the systematic and repeated measurement of behavior (Baer, Wolf, & Risley, 1968), so does effective instruction. The similarities between applied research and data-based instruction are far greater than their dissimilarities. Each of the following characteristics, which distinguish applied research from nonapplied research, also differentiate data-based instruction from non-data-based instruction.

1. The subject or society benefits from the intervention.

2. Intervention focuses on observable events.

3. The effect the intervention has on behavior is "believable."

4. Procedures are described in sufficient detail to permit replication.

5. Terminology used to describe the intervention is conceptually systematic with the literature.

6. The effects of the intervention are large enough to be of practical value to the subject.

7. Behavioral change is maintained over time and generalizes to the natural environment.

This chapter will describe general issues in measurement, with emphasis on (1) direct and systematic measurement of behavior through the use of direct observational recording systems, (2) reliability, and (3) validity.

This chapter was written by **James W. Tawney** and **David L. Gast**.

Characteristics of Measurement and Evaluation

Measurement

In recent years educators have increasingly emphasized the development of systems for monitoring student progress toward instructional objectives. This interest in educational accountability has necessitated that educators become proficient in objectively measuring student behavior.

Measurement may be defined as the systematic and objective quantification of objects, events, or behaviors according to a set of rules. Basic steps or rules to be followed in the measurement process include (1) identifying what is to be measured, (2) defining the behavior or event in observable terms, and (3) selecting an appropriate data-recording system for observing, quantifying, and summarizing behavior.

Identifying What Is to Be Measured

What an applied researcher or teacher measures will depend directly upon the research question or targeted instructional objective. Several sources are available to help the teacher determine what to measure. In addition to using personal observations of student behavior, the teacher can consult with parents, other teachers, support personnel (e.g., occupational therapist, speech pathologist, psychologist), as well as examine previous student assessments. Ideally, a recent individual education plan (IEP) will incorporate the instructional priorities from each of the above sources, facilitating the process.

Defining What Is to Be Measured

In accordance with the behavioral approach to teaching, teachers define target behaviors in observable and measurable terms. Rather than define a student's behavior in such global terms as "disruptive," "bored," or "passive" without further behavioral elaboration, the teacher should describe the behavior(s) which she had observed in specific terms. For example, if a teacher frequently has observed a student leaving her desk without permission, talking with classmates during class presentations, and dropping pencils and books, one would have a much clearer idea as to what the teacher considers disruptive behavior. With this greater behavioral specificity the teacher can more effectively document observations and communicate them to colleagues, the student, and the student's parents. In addition, the focus on observable actions permits others the opportunity to observe the occurrence (or nonoccurrence) of the behavior in question.

Selecting a Data-Recording System

After having identified the behavior to be measured and defining it in observable terms, the teacher must decide upon a method for quantifying the behavior. There are a variety of recording systems available to behavior analysts, each with its own advantages and disadvantages. The teacher must decide what it is about the behavior that deserves attention (i.e., frequency, duration, latency, intensity, magnitude, or accuracy) and then select a recording system that is both practical and reliable. Several direct observational recording systems are available, including event recording, duration recording, interval recording, and time sample recording. Variables that require consideration before selecting a data-recording system include (1) the target behavior identified, (2) the objective of the academic or behavioral intervention program, and (3) the practical constraints of the setting(s) in which the behavior is to be measured. No single recording system is appropriate for all behaviors, all educational objectives, or for use in all settings.

Evaluation

Before discussing the parameters of measurement it is important to make a distinction between measurement and evaluation. *Measurement* was defined in the previous section. *Evaluation* is the analysis or comparison of data, collected during the measurement process, upon which instructional decisions can be based. When the basic rules of measurement have been adhered to and when an accurate analysis of the data has been conducted, program evaluation generates information that facilitates a teacher's understanding of the relationship between student performance and teaching strategy (instructional arrangement, task sequence, pace, materials, instructional method, etc.). Through such understanding, a teacher can better individualize instruction by objectively deciding whether to maintain or modify the teaching strategy.

There are two basic requirements for evaluating the relationship between student performance and the instructional program or intervention strategy. First, accurate, reliable, and frequent measures of student performance are needed. Second, the measurement system must be paired with a rapidly changing single subject research design. This chapter highlights the parameters of measurement, while later chapters detail the various single subject experimental designs appropriate for evaluating behavior. Only when both requirements are met can a functional relationship (i.e., cause-effect relationship) between the independent variables be isolated. Without such pairing, measurement at best yields only correlational information.

Summative Evaluation

A frequently used edcuational evaluation strategy for measuring student performance is the pretest/posttest paradigm. Representative of this evaluation procedure is the annual assessment of student progress toward short-term instructional objectives as specified in the IEP. The literature pertaining to the IEP repeatedly cites the need to objectively evaluate pupil progress toward reaching the goals stated in the IEP "for determining, on at least an annual basis, whether the short term instructional objectives are being achieved" (Section 121a.346, Federal Register, 1977). For many educators, however, the qualifier *at least* has been overlooked and, as a result, evaluations are annual *at best*. Such summative methods for evaluating pupil performance should be viewed only as the peripheral ends of a continuum for monitoring and evaluating individual progress and educational program effectiveness.

The pretest/posttest evaluation paradigm represents what is commonly referred to as a summative evaluation strategy. *Summative evaluation*, a static process, is the documentation of pupil progress by measuring and comparing student performance at two points in time. It evaluates teaching and learning post hoc, i.e. after teaching and learning have occurred. Both the teach-test and test-teach-test paradigms, in which data are *not* collected during the teaching process, are representative of the summative evaluation strategy. Summative information is used by school districts and teachers to provide an appropriate individualized educational program for each special student. Such information is commonly used to determine an appropriate educational placement, develop long-term and short-term educational objectives, and evaluate student performance. The third use, the evaluation of student performance, is the most controversial. As is the case when a child is tested at an educational assessment clinic or in the office of an educational diagnostician or school psychologist, several uncontrolled variables come into play which may adversely affect how a child performs during the test situation. Consider for a moment the following conditions under which educational testing often takes place:

• The child is separated from familiar persons, removed from familiar surroundings, and taken to a strange room.

• Due to crowded conditions in some school buildings (and at some assessment clinics) evaluations are sometimes conducted in noisy hallways, converted broom closets, on gym stages, and at the back of cafeterias.

• "Ideal" testing rooms, equipped with two-way mirrors, microphones, video cameras, barren walls, overhead fluorescent lighting, hard chairs and a table, bring images of police interrogation rooms.

• An evaluator (most likely never seen by the child before) takes the child through a series of activities ranging from requesting responses to questions like "Do bananas fly?" to buttoning, lacing, and zipping the appendages of a polka-dot octopus.

Without belaboring the point, it should be clear that even under the best of conditions (familiar examiner, familiar setting, or after a period of adaptation to a new person and environment) the data gathered from such assessments can only approximate those representing the student's actual capabilities. One cannot ignore the potential adverse influence of these novel variables on student performance. Summative information obtained under these conditions should be approached with caution. An alternative approach for acquiring summative information is to observe and evaluate student performance on functional tasks in the student's natural environment (classroom and/or home) using familiar materials, over an extended period of time (2–4 weeks). This latter evaluation approach is likely to generate information that more accurately reflects a student's educational strengths and weaknesses.

Formative Evaluation
In order to go beyond perfunctory "paper compliance" by conducting annual static assessments of student progress, it is necessary to measure and evaluate the appropriateness of students' programs on a more frequent and regular basis. Formative evaluation is an alternative to, or a strategy to be used in conjunction with, summative evaluation. Formative evaluation, a dynamic or ongoing process, emphasizes the frequent and repeated measurement of student performance on functional and age-appropriate tasks, assessed under natural conditions, over time. Unlike summative data, formative data can be used to guide instruction by providing the teacher with a frequent measure (i.e., gathered at least weekly) of student performance toward a particular objective. Such information allows the teacher to modify the instructional program (e.g., the teaching arrangement, pace, task sequence, materials, reinforcers) in a systematic manner when deterioration of student perform-

ance is first evident. In addition, formative data can confirm student achievement, thereby reassuring the teacher that her instructional programs are appropriate for the student's level of functioning.

Of course many variables must be considered before determining whether student progress is real or contrived. Assuming that the instructional or behavioral objectives are appropriate, appropriate dependent measures have been selected, and the data collected are reliable, frequent and repeated measures of student performance can be both informative and reinforcing to the teacher. However, the simple recording of student performance at frequent and regular intervals does not in itself merit the label of formative evaluation. Only if these data are analyzed and used to determine whether to maintain or modify the teaching process is the evaluation strategy considered formative. For example, consider two special education teachers who have identified the skill of untying shoelaces as an appropriate educational objective for one of their students. Both teachers have consulted available curriculum guides and have identified an appropriate task analysis. Both teachers are collecting trial-by-trial data on their respective students' performance on each step of the task analysis. Teacher 1 regularly summarizes the data after each instructional session by recording the percentage of trials the student performed correctly at each available prompt level and plotting the data on a graph. Then she evaluates the trends in the data and notes how many sessions the student has been on that particular step. Based on this analysis the decision is made to reanalyze the task and build in an additional step. Teacher 2, on the other hand, does not summarize the daily data after each session, nor does she graph or analyze the data for the purpose of guiding the teaching process. Both Teacher 1 and Teacher 2 are engaged in the frequent and regular measurement of student performance toward the objective of untying shoelaces. However, only Teacher 1 is conducting a formative evaluation of student progress, and only Teacher 1 is using the data to determine whether to maintain or modify the instructional program.

Formative Evaluation: Objections and Considerations

The idea of keeping precise and reliable data often is seen as prohibitive by many special and regular educators who are required to assume responsibility for teaching children with a wide range of individual educational differences. The changes demanded of school systems and their teachers via judicial mandates, though not insurmountable, nevertheless are extensive. Teaching behaviors that handicapped individuals need in order to function in less restrictive environments requires methodological and strategical changes from typical modes of instruction used previously in special education and regular classrooms. Although many teachers recognize the need to implement procedures to help them deal effectively with individual differences in their classrooms, concern and confusion about appropriate procedures are rampant.

There is little room left to argue against the premise that each child's educational needs warrant (much less necessitate) "tailor-made" programming. In addition, teachers are required to demonstrate that these programs are beneficial and appropriate for the child; otherwise, alterations must be made.

The success of an exceptional child's instructional program should be evaluated on the basis of the rate at which she moves towards functioning more effectively in more normal environments (Deno & Mirkin, 1977). Child progress cannot be evaluated adequately on the basis of information provided by standardized tests or other summative evaluations administered biannually or annually; rather, it is necessary to gather empirical information on a frequent basis.

One challenging and creative aspect of teaching is identifying instructional programs that match each student's style of learning (instructional arrangement, pace, materials, reinforcers, etc.). Only through frequent, systematic, and reliable program evaluation can teachers determine the efficacy of their instructional decisions. The decision to measure program effectiveness does not require adherence to any particular theoretical orientation. Systematic data collection on student performance represents a teacher's interest in determining the effectiveness of an educational program for appropriate program decision making.

When requested to collect child performance data, a typical teacher response is "I don't have time to collect data; I have to teach." Such an argument reveals a misconception that teaching and data collection are incompatible behaviors. This need not be the case. When appropriate preparations are made, formative evaluation can save teacher and student instructional time by confirming the effectiveness, or signaling the ineffectiveness, of an intervention strategy.

Formative program evaluation has one purpose: to assist the teacher in deciding whether to maintain or modify a program (Bijou, 1977). It serves no purpose to collect data on the effectiveness of a program unless the data are used to help in the decision-making process. In fact, teachers should avoid the "trap of recording any and all behavior, simply for the sake of data collection" (Scott & Goetz, 1980, p. 66). A critical question to ask before collecting performance data is "To what practical end can the data be used?" Practicality is a key factor when deciding what type of data to collect, how frequently the data should be collected, and what method for collecting the data should be used. If the teacher has a thorough understanding of measurement options (dependent measures, recording systems, continuous and intermittent data collection procedures) and knows how to analyze the data, the systematic and frequent measurement of student behavior need not be a time-consuming and aversive process.

Common Objections
Common objections by teachers to the systematic observation and evaluation of student performance have been addressed by Bancroft and Bellamy (1976). They include such statements as:

> Classroom data focuses attention on behaviors which are easy to measure, but ignores important aspects of learning and development.

> Classroom data is not necessary for most teachers because they know where their students are without systematic and formal measurement.

> Direct measurement procedures are too rigid and time consuming and thus detract from teaching itself.

> Since it can be determined easily whether a child has acquired a given skill, daily data collection is not necessary for a teacher to evaluate the effectiveness of the procedures. (Bancroft & Bellamy, 1976, pp. 26–28)

There is, or can be, some truth in each of these objections when a teacher is not well informed about measurement alternatives.

Focus of classroom data collection. It is not uncommon, for example, for teachers to focus their measurement efforts on behaviors (or behavioral objectives) which are "easy" to measure at the expense of measuring "more important" aspects of learning. This objection relates directly to the way in which the teacher defines instructional objectives. Though a great deal of teacher time may be spent measuring a particular student response during an instructional session, this need not be the only condition under which data are collected. This is not to say that collecting data on a student's acquisition of a new behavior under well-defined stimulus conditions is not important; it most certainly is. However, for some students an appropriate instructional objective may be to increase the frequency of a response under novel stimulus conditions (e.g., in different settings, with different teachers, using different materials). In addition to measuring response generalization, a teacher may define an instructional objective to focus attention on the stimulus conditions or prompt levels necessary for a student to learn a particular skill. Cuvo, Leaf, and Borakove (1978), for example, measured the least prompt level necessary for severely handicapped adolescents to successfully perform a series of chained janitorial skills. Similar studies have been conducted in which the focus of the data collection process was not on the topography of the target response but the level of assistance necessary for students to complete the response (e.g., Bellamy, Horner, & Inman, 1979, Horner, 1971; Horner & Keilitz, 1975). The point is that the focus of classroom data collection should be directly related to the instructional objective targeted by the teacher. Some types of data are more easily collected than others. Provided the teacher has a thorough understanding of the systematic observation of behavior, there is no reason that more complex aspects of learning cannot be the focus of educational researchers.

Is systematic measurement necessary? Regarding the objection that teachers know where their students are without systematic and formal measurement, Bancroft and Bellamy (1976) cite studies by Wahler and Leske (1973) and Leslie (1974) which indicate to the contrary. Both studies evaluated the effects of systematic and nonsystematic observation procedures on the accuracy of observers' perceptions of student behavior change. They reported that the results for both studies showed that those observers who used systematic observation procedures noted greater improvement in student behavior than those using nonsystematic observation procedures. Consider for a moment the teacher of 8 severely handicapped students for whom progress is slow and in small steps and the learning disabilities teacher who has 15–20 students in her classroom. What is the probability of their accurately "knowing" where each student is, on each program, without adopting a systematic measurement system? It is extremely unlikely that either teacher could accurately monitor each student's performance and initiate appropriate program modifications at appropriate times by using a nonsystematic observation approach.

Time considerations. The objection that direct measurement procedures are too rigid and time consuming, and thus detract from teaching itself is well known to teacher consultants and teacher trainers. As with the previous objections, there may be some justification for this argument if the data collected are summative and if the data are not used to modify instruction. Summative evaluations tend to be time consuming and rigid and, therefore, it is understandable why some teachers object to collecting such data. In contrast, formative evaluation can assist the teacher during the instructional process. The direct and systematic observation of behavior can facilitate a teacher's: (1) understanding of each student's strengths and weaknesses, (2) general observational skills, (3) awareness of emerging or recurring behaviors, (4) interactions with ancillary personnel (speech therapists, physical therapists, school psychologists) by providing more accurate information, and (5) objective monitoring of program effectiveness, permitting program modification, if necessary, before valuable teacher and student instructional time is wasted (Scott & Goetz, 1980).

The initial implementation of systematic measurement procedures may prove time consuming and cumbersome; however, the benefits derived from the time spent in the initial phases of the data collection process will justify the effort. The amount of time necessary to implement a classroom data collection system will depend directly on a teacher's familiarity with direct measurement procedures and the organization of the classroom. The more familiar the teacher is with direct observational recording methods and the more organized the classroom (e.g., activity schedules, staff responsibilities), the less time it will take and the less cumbersome it will be to implement an effective and efficient data-based classroom.

Scott and Goetz (1980) found there to be some justification to the argument that data collection could interfere with or detract from teaching. In one of the few studies that has evaluated the effects of teachers as data collectors on student behavior and the teaching process, Scott and Goetz's preliminary findings suggested that student-teacher interactions may be affected, but to an "insignificant degree," and certainly not to the extent that the teachers had predicted. Their position is clear; the advantages of data collection to both student and teacher far outweigh the minimal inhibitive effects data collection may have on student-teacher interactions. As teachers become more proficient in their selection and use of observational recording systems, the response cost to teachers will be minimized.

Data collection must be individualized (i.e., the type of data collected and the recording system employed will depend upon the type of information sought). *Parsimony coupled with practicality* should be the rule. Collecting data that will not be used and the use of recording systems which lack simplicity and economy should be avoided. The measurement system should be as simple as possible and still provide the necessary information upon which program decisions can be based. As Bancroft and Bellamy (1976) have pointed out, objections to systematic direct measurement "result from an inability to structure classroom activities for efficient measurement or an unwillingness to use the resulting data to modify a 'tried and true' technique" (p. 28).

Is daily data collection necessary? The fourth common objection to systematic measurement relates to the apparent disinterest of some educators in evaluating the effects of their teaching. The argument that since it can be determined easily whether a child has acquired a given skill, daily data collection is not necessary for a teacher to evaluate the effectiveness of the procedures, illustrates some teachers' disinterest in determining whether their teaching is responsible for behavior change, or whether some extraneous variable or event outside the teaching setting is responsible for the change. This apparent disinterest in evaluating the cause-effect relationship between the intervention strategy and student behavior may not always be the fault of the teacher. Historically, few teacher preparation programs have adequately prepared their graduates to evaluate the effectiveness of their instructional programs.

Many special educators who agree that frequent and systematic observations of student behavior are beneficial to the teaching process still are concerned about whether daily data can be collected in light of the increasing responsibilities being assumed by classroom teachers. It would be naive to presume that all teachers in all classroom settings, regardless of the number of students enrolled or the staffing patterns, should and could collect trial-by-trial data on all programs for all students. This simply is not practical, and as discussed previously, practicality is important to the measurement process. A general rule for determining how frequently a student's performance should be evaluated "frequently, but only after the program has had a fair chance to operate" (Bijou, 1977, p. 11). Although daily measures are considered ideal, they may prove to be impractical because of time constraints. Weekly measures typically are considered the minimum acceptable frequency for evaluating student progress. Failure to evaluate progress weekly increases the risk of continuing an ineffective program which wastes student and teacher time, and which may produce inappropriate interfering student behaviors.

Continuous measurement (i.e., daily, session-by-session or trial-by-trial data) can provide the teacher constant feedback upon which to base program decisions. A number of teaching systems, such as Precision Teaching (White and Haring, 1980), Directive Teaching (Stephens, 1976), Responsive Teaching (Rieth & Hall, 1974), and Data-Based Program Modification (Deno & Mirkin, 1977), include continuous measurement of student progress as an integral part. Although continuous measurement yields a wealth of information upon which teachers can base their program decisions, such rigor may at times prove too cumbersome and too time consuming to be practical.

An alternative to continuous measurement is noncontinuous or intermittent measurement. For example, rather than evaluating a student's performance every instructional session, progress is measured every other session. Although data are not collected daily, they are collected frequently, allowing the teacher to modify the program, if necessary, without wasting instructional time. As with continuous measurement, noncontinuous measurement requires that the data be collected systematically and reliably, using one of the many direct observation recording systems to be discussed. The implementation of a noncontinuous measurement strategy will provide the teacher with information relative to student progress. If data are variable and difficult to analyze, a continuous measurement strategy can be adopted. The particular recording system employed will depend upon the type of information sought and the intensity and precision of the teacher's programming. Weekly measures, using a noncontinuous measurement strategy, will generally suffice to provide the teacher with feedback regarding student progress. However, if the instructional program is part of an applied research project, continuous data are required.

To summarize, teachers have expressed several objections to the systematic and formative evaluation of their instruction. Each of the four arguments presented are in part justified considering: (1) the typical teacher preparation curriculum which has failed to teach teachers how to objectively evaluate their teaching, (2) the increasing demands placed on teachers as a result of recent legislation, and (3) high student-teacher ratios which are being adopted by many state departments of education and local educational agencies. In spite of these constraints, it is incumbent upon special educators to individualize instruction and to document student progress toward instructional objectives.

Guidelines

To accomplish this goal it is necessary that teachers become competent in the selection, implementation, and evaluation of data-recording systems and single subject research designs. By familiarizing oneself with the strengths and weaknesses of each recording system and research design, the teacher is in a better position to select a data collection procedure and design that is efficient, effective, and reliable. General guidelines to follow in the measurement and evaluation of student performance include:

1. Define the target behavior in observable terms.

2. Collect data only to the extent that the data will be used to guide instruction, i.e., avoid the trap of collecting data on all programs and behaviors.

3. Measure that aspect of a student's objective which is of interest, i.e., don't restrict data collection to simple responses and ignore more interesting and important aspects of student behavior.

4. Familiarize yourself thoroughly with data collection and research design alternatives.

5. Select a measurement system which is practical and which can be consistently and reliably used within the constraints of the classroom.

6. Structure the classroom (daily schedule, staffing assignments, etc.) to facilitate data collection as well as teaching.

7. Evaluate data regularly and base instructional decisions to maintain or modify the program on the data.

8. Collect performance data frequently to yield an accurate measure of program effectiveness.

The direct and frequent measurement of behavior, when paired with a single subject research design, can yield information that can facilitate the instructional and learning process. It can assist the teacher in the early identification of learning/behavior problems, provide information on program effectiveness, signal the need for program modification, increase the rate with which a student attains instructional objectives, and facilitate communication with students, parents, administrators, other teachers, and support personnel. Systematic data collection is the "foundation of pragmatic instruction and an antidote to dogmatic and theoretical teaching" (Bancroft & Bellamy, 1976, p. 29).

Reliability and Validity

When student performance is modified through single subject research, two fundamental issues must be confronted: *reliability* and *validity* of measurement. These terms have different meanings in science, evaluation, and general usage. These key terms are considered here. Specific applications are considered throughout the following chapters on measurement and research design.

Reliability

In the vernacular, when you ask "Is she reliable," you mean "Can we count on her?" In the field of test construction and evaluation, "to be reliable" means that a test will yield the same results if administered more than one time. These two referents are reflected in Webster's (1975) definitions: "suitable or fit to be relied on," "giving the same result on successive trials." Within the context of single subject research design, there are two referents for the term *reliability*. The first concerns one's confidence that the outcome of an intervention is "real"; that is, that if the experiment is repeated, the outcome will be the same. Or, if one repeats the same experiment many times, would the outcomes be similar across the series of experiments? To determine if results are reliable, experiments are repeated, or replicated. A full treatment of replication is provided in Chapter 6.

The second referent concerns what one "sees" or records during the course of a study. In a general sense, the question is posed this way: "Are the data accurate?" If the data are products, e.g., the students' answers to worksheet problems, it is important that they are scored accurately. To verify that they are accurate is a simple matter of checking the scores or asking another person to double-check your work. However, many studies are concerned with the observable behavior of children as they interact with the teacher and/or other children in the educational environment. The target behavior occurs in a stream of events which are lost to history, unless they are permanently recorded. Sometimes they are captured on videotape, which can be checked again and again just like an arithmetic worksheet. Many researchers, however, rely on human observers to document that a targeted behavior occurs. Usually, a second observer is employed to determine whether observations are recorded reliably. In this context, the question is "to what extent does the written record correspond with reality (what really happened)?" Sometimes two observers are employed to obtain an estimate of *interobserver reliability*. Then the question is "to what extent did the observers agree that targeted behaviors occurred or did not occur?" These are critical questions because, obviously, if it is not possible to determine the frequency, or duration, of behavior with some degree of precision, then the experimenter will have little basis for claiming that an intervention was successful. Very simple procedures have been developed to calculate reliabilities. However, there is lively debate on which is the *best* method. Many complex solutions have been proposed to yield a better or less biased estimate. Methods for calculating interobserver reliability measures are discussed in the next chapter.

Validity

In the vernacular, you may ask if someone has a *valid* reason for an action. Generally, you mean "Can you justify what you are doing?" Webster offers many definitions, roughly paraphrased, "legal authority to act," "a conclusion reasonably drawn from the evidence," "appropriate to the end in view." The last definition is most closely related to our concern for social or ecological validity of a procedure.

In the field of test construction and evaluation, *validity* is a critical concern. Here, there is one basic question, "Is the test appropriate to use in a given situation?" In the area of achievement testing, the proper variation of the question is "Does the test measure what was taught?" The answer is *judgmental* even though that judgment may be supported by a statistical analysis. With regard to this most basic question, the issue is *content validity*. The judgment can be made only by examining the content of instruction to determine whether there is a match between the content and the items on the test. Poor scores (low student achievement) may occur when a radically new curriculum is introduced but student performance is evaluated on a traditional measure. The same result can occur when a traditional curriculum is significantly altered but the program is evaluated with traditional measures. This content validity problem was discussed in depth in earlier chapters with reference to the efforts to determine the efficacy of special education.

There are variations on this basic validity question: If two similar tests are administered, will students achieve equivalent scores on both tests (*concurrent validity*)? Can a theory be confirmed by the patterns of students' responses to test items (*construct validity*)? From among a set of measures, is it possible to abstract general performance clusters (*factorial validity*)? These are all interesting questions that receive full treatment in texts on test construction and psychological testing. Here our concern is with another form of validity: the social importance of an intervention.

Social Validity

The concern for *social validity* has been paramount since the inception of applied behavior analysis. Baer, Wolf, and Risley (1968) set the stage for this concern when they specified that the domain of applied behavior analysis was "behaviors that are socially important, rather than convenient for study" (p. 92). Wolf (1978) reaffirmed this concern in his essay on the use of subjective measures in applied behavior research. His article, which should be considered fundamental to a clear understanding of the topic, argued that subjective feedback data have a place in applied behavior analysis since they represent "an attempt to assess the dimensions of complex reinforcers in socially acceptable and practical ways" (p. 213). He suggests there are three levels of social validation: goals, procedures, and effects (p. 207). For the classroom-based researcher, these translate into a limited set of questions. Is a desired behavior change important in the social environment? During the sixties, behavior modification programs were instituted in classrooms for preschool- and early school-age disadvantaged students. Some of the targeted behaviors were considered to be prerequisite to success in regular elementary schools, e.g., sitting quietly and paying attention. Winnett and Winkler (1972) challenged those goals, charging that behavior modification was being used to maintain the "law and order" aspect of public education and suggesting that modifying behaviors relevant to the British open education system might be more appropriate. O'Leary (1972), in a companion article, suggested that when the spectrum of behavior modification studies was examined, the targeted behaviors were diverse and that many targets, e.g., increased self-confidence (operationally defined), were important to subjects. Two reviewers commented on these articles, offering clarification on the goals of education. Together they raised important concerns about the application of behavior modification in educational settings. At this level, then, social validation is a *philosophical* issue.

Having decided to apply intervention to an academic or social target, the researcher is confronted with these questions: Is the intervention appropriate? Is it humane? Is it the most efficient and least intrusive method to produce the desired outcome?

Risley (1968) applied contingent shock to suppress the climbing behavior of an autistic child. Although the procedure was effective, and although the side effects were positive rather than negative, the procedure has not been applied in educational settings presumably because there are social sanctions against such controversial procedures. This issue is further elaborated in Chapter 14. At this level, the issue is one of *ethics*.

The third level of social validation is concerned with the magnitude of effect. After an experiment, the basic question is "So what?" Is life appreciably better for the disruptive child and those who care for the child? If a major change occurred, is everyone happy with the change and with the intervention? Suppose that a major project is initiated to shape the "independent living behaviors" of moderately retarded young adults, enabling them to move from their parents' homes to apartments or group homes. Such a transition requires a repertoire of behaviors which may subsumed under the term *independent thinking (behaving)*. The transition from dependence to independence may bring some surprises to parents who have been caring for their children for many years. These surprises may generate side effects, e.g., parents' dissatisfaction with a program that is, by other measures, achieving its goal. One side effect, which the first author once observed in a similar situation, was a concentrated effort to remove the administrator of the program. In a similar vein, Wolf (1978) noted that when consumer satisfaction measures were added to the Achievement Place model, the program was not "summarily 'fired' from the community" (p. 211) when the model was replicated outside of Kansas City. He and his associates had achieved social acceptance, or *practical success*, which is the basic issue at the third level of social validation.

Ecological Validity

Throughout this text, we refer to two types of school targets: academic and social behaviors. With regard to the latter, we have referred to a specific set of disruptive or destructive behaviors as problems of ecological concern. By this we mean those behaviors, e.g., head banging, flesh tearing, which demand immediate attention in a crisis situation. The social validity of these targets is unquestionable, and we might say that they represent yet another type—*ecological validity*. We introduce this term to identify a subset of social behaviors whose severity and intensity represent a clear threat to the individuals who emit them, or to others in the immediate environment. To parallel Wolf's (1978) format, the *goal* of the interventionist is to reduce an immediate threat to the health of the subject and the health or well-being of others immediately affected by the subject's actions. There is likely to be little question about the importance of the problem or the need to modify the behavior. The behavior may require a procedure that is drastic, e.g., the use of contingent shock. The ethical questions which will be raised about this or another procedure will be balanced by the consequence if the behavior is left untreated. Thus, these behaviors will be modified within the framework of the ethical guidelines discussed in Chapter 14. The *effect* of an intervention program will be evaluated on a more direct measure of consumer satisfaction. Parents and interventionists have an objective basis for discussion when graphed data show that a behavior has been reduced to a predetermined and operationally defined criterion level. Scratched or torn flesh which is transformed into a healed surface, or scar tissue, represents another measure. When physical assaults to others are reduced in a school setting, an unobtrusive measure, reduction in the number of formal accident reports filed per week, may provide objective data. Finally, since the procedures used to modify the behavior require parent consent to an intervention plan which must contain fallback contingencies (modify the program after n days if there is no change), there is an internal test for evaluating the magnitude of effect and an ultimate test of satisfaction, defined by parents' right to withdraw consent for the program.

Internal and External Validity

There are two validity issues that are of paramount importance in single subject research: *internal* and *external* validity. The basic questions they ask are stated here. Both terms, in essence, are the focus of the following chapter on direct and systematic replication.

When we ask "Does this study demonstrate *internal* validity?" we are really asking "Is the intervention *and only the intervention* responsible for the change in behavior?" The question is critical because in the universe of events that occur during the course of a study, some are likely to influence the outcome of a study. Controlling for possible sources of confounding from these factors is a major consideration in the selection of a research design.

Two questions are basic to the consideration of *external validity*. The first is specific to the effectiveness of an intervention program: "Given that an intervention produced a dramatic effect with this subject, will it work with other subjects, in other environments, when implemented by other experimenters, and when implemented with minor variations in the basic procedure?" Chapter 6 addresses this question in depth.

The second question strikes at the heart of the field of applied behavior analysis and its single subject methodology. "Is it ever possible to make statements about generality when single subject designs are employed in a study?" Those who ask this question are often proponents of large n contrast group designs who may be disinclined to accept *yes* as an answer.

Threats to Validity

Two concepts are important to an understanding the pragmatics of experimental control. First, it is impossible to control every possible threat to internal validity. Second, a possible threat may not be an actual threat in any situation. Kratochwill (1978) provides a case in point. He presents a table that shows by a + (presence) or − (absence) which of 9 threats may be present in 24 single subject designs. Thus there are 24 × 9 or 216 "cells" in his table. Of those, a + is assigned to 186 columns (pp. 18–19). This news should not be disheartening to the beginning researcher, for, just as there is no free lunch, there is no perfect experiment. Instead, there are carefully designed experiments, which are executed as carefully as they were planned and which provide "adequate and proper data" (Campbell & Stanley, 1966, p.2) for analysis. The researcher's task is to describe what happened during the course of the experiment and to be able to account for planned and un-planned outcomes—those which may have influenced the findings.

History. *History* refers to events that occur during an experiment that may influence the outcome. Suppose that in a traditional experimental-control study, two groups were pretested on achievement in the fall and in the spring to determine which of two instructional programs produced a greater effect. Suppose that a flu epidemic closed down school for one group and those instructional days were reduced. The uneven number of days is a *historical* threat. Similarly, suppose that a single subject study was carried out to determine if a teacher skill (use of soft reprimands) would reduce talk-outs for three disruptive students, using a multiple baseline design, sequenced so that for the first S, observation occurred on days 1–5 and intervention on days 6–30. For the second S, the schedule was observation, 1–10, intervention, 11–30; and for the third S, observation, 1–15, intervention, 16–30. Then suppose that a substitute teacher assumes responsibility for the class for a few days (7–8–9) and that all control is lost in the class. A dramatic change in the behavior of S_1 will not show in the records of S_2 and S_3, who are still in the observation phase. This is a historical threat that can only be accounted for by the researcher's description of the situation. If the same event occurred in the last phase of the project, when all Ss were in an intervention phase, and if each were equally affected, then there will be three demonstrations that document the assertion that this confounding factor was responsible for the changes.

Maturation. *Maturation* refers to changes that occur in subjects during the course of an experiment. While the term *maturation* typically refers to physical growth, it applies equally to becoming fatigued during the course of a session. In a short duration study physical maturation might play little part in the ability of a 10-year-old to compute more correct math responses in 10-minute sessions. Conversely, if one were teaching a slow developing 6-year-old a dressing skill in a study that extended for a long time period, maturation would likely be a major threat.

Testing. *Testing* is a threat in any study that requires the S to respond to the same test repeatedly. In traditional situations the assumption is that test scores will improve with repeated administrations. Kratochwill (1978) cau-tions that reactivity to the intervention should be considered in single subject research. He refers to any major event which might cause Ss to behave differently (p. 14) as a "testing" threat.

Instrumentation. *Instrumentation* threats occur when there is some shift in the measuring devices. Mechanical and human observers each represent a unique set of measurement problems. Cumulative recorders break down at unexpected times. Human observers become fatigued or bored and thus fail to see the same events.

Loss of subjects. Subject attrition creates unique problems in single subject research, where some studies are carried out with one, two, or three Ss for an extended period of time. We discussed this problem in Chapter 4.

Multiple intervention interference. Interference can occur when the same subjects receive multiple interventions or multiple "treatments." The term refers to the interactive effect of one on the other. This threat is reduced by the use of counterbalanced designs, as described in Chapter 12.

Instability. The term *instability* is self-explanatory. It refers to the cyclic variation of a behavior and is discussed further in regard to the decisions that must be made when variation requires extending baselines. It also refers to failure to demonstrate a strong effect; that is, if an intervention produces an immediate and clear effect for a few days, then the behavior returns to its preintervention level, then increases, and so on, it is difficult to conclude that the effect is strong or stable.

Intervening when the behavior is likely to change naturally. Suppose that "something happens," e.g., an aggressive child is introduced into a classroom mid-year and succeeds in upsetting the whole class. An intervention is implemented when students have not yet adapted to their disruptive peer and the class's behavior reduces to its "normal" level. This change may be due either to the intervention or the adaptation process. This source of confounding may not be accounted for by the research design, and there are two possible reasons for the behavior change.

SUMMARY

We have focused on general factors or issues in measurement and evaluation. We have emphasized the distinction between collecting objective information (measurement) and making decisions based on that data (evaluation). We have shown some critical differences between formative or ongoing evaluation and summative (end of intervention) evaluation. Possible benefits of, as well as teachers' objections to, formative evaluation have been identified. Specific guidelines for continuous measurement and evaluation of student performance have been listed.

We have defined the terms *reliability* and *validity*, paralleling the general usage of the terms with their specific use in the context of single subject research design. The terms *social validity* and *ecological validity* were introduced. Common threats to validity were listed.

Our general discussion has presented concepts that are used repeatedly throughout the remainder of the text. The issues we have addressed apply to classroom teaching and to research. They set the stage for the design of research studies and data-based classroom instruction.

6

REPLICATION

Replication means repetition. When the term *replication* is used in the context of a research program, it refers to a series of studies executed to determine if an experimentally produced effect will occur a second, third, or *n*th time. Though replication is a necessary component of the scientific process, the topic has received little attention in applied behavioral texts. Sidman (1960) provided the definitive word on *direct* and *systematic replication*. Hersen and Barlow (1976) relied upon Sidman's definitions in their treatment of the subject, to which they added a third type, *clinical replication*.

Why Replicate?

Replication studies are conducted to answer simple questions. Suppose that an experimenter conducts one study, e.g., using an A-B-A-B design with a single subject and suppose further that the data show a clear effect. The experimenter's reaction will be an enthusiastic and joyful "I did it and it worked!" to which the scientific community will (or should) reply "Yes, but . . . ?" The next question, then, is "If you repeat the experiment, will you get the same effect?" In other words, "Are your results *reliable*?" Suppose that in response the experimenter repeats the experiment with the same subject (direct replication) and obtains the same results. Will these data quiet the scientific community? No. The next questions will be "Will you get the same effect with different subjects?" "Will you get the same effect outside the original experimental environment?" "Will other experimenters obtain the

---

This chapter was written by **James W. Tawney** and **David L. Gast**.

same effect if they follow your procedures, in their environment, with other subjects?" "How broadly will the results *generalize* beyond the original experiment?" If the results of an intervention are spurious and cannot be reproduced reliably, those who attempt to use the procedure will find their efforts wasted. Similarly, an effect that can be produced with a limited range of subjects in a narrowly proscribed experimental space may have little general utility. It is much better to demonstrate an effect across subjects and across species. For example, Terrace (1966) reported results of studies in errorless discrimination, using pigeon subjects responding to narrow wavelengths of color projected onto response keys. His studies provided an interesting alternative view of the problem of stimulus control. But how far might one generalize from pigeons, responding to stimuli purposely matched to the species' unique visual acuity, to other populations, e.g., human students in classroom environments? Fortunately, there is a partial answer, and in this instance it is positive. Sidman and Stoddard (1966) applied Terrace's principle that errors create more errors to research with humans. They developed a laboratory procedure used with young normal children, retarded children, and one 40-year-old institutionalized microcephalic male. Thus, they applied the procedure to a different environment and a different species using a different type of stimulus materials. This was a major step, even for experienced investigators with a long history of laboratory research. Equally bold was their suggestion that it might be fruitful to spend hundreds of hours of development time on teaching programs similar to theirs, but more immediately relevant to everyday living (Sidman & Stoddard, 1966, p. 183). Their work and that of others has been incorporated into instructional procedures designed for error free learning (Tawney, Knapp, O'Reilly, & Pratt, 1979), another large step subsequently justified by data showing mean percent correct responding at greater than 90% with severely developmentally retarded subjects in a variety of educational settings. These three research programs represent application of a principle, rather than replication as it is later defined.

Why replicate? We have provided one answer—to demonstrate the reliability and generality of data. Are there other reasons? Sidman (1960) offers some reasons, succinctly and cogently:

> To the neutral observer it will be obvious that science is far from free of human bias, even in its evaluation of factual evidence. Experimental findings, furthermore, are so fragile when considered within the total matrix of natural phenomena from which they are lifted, and conclusions from such data often so tenuous, that one can only feel surprise at the actual achievements of experimental methodology. What must we work with in any experiment? Uncontrolled, and even unknown, variables; the errors of selective perception arising out of theoretical and observational bias; indirect measurements; the theory involved in the measurement techniques themselves; the assumptions involved in making the leap from data to interpretation. In short, we have a margin of error so great that any true advance might be considered an accident were it not for the fact that too many genuine advances have occurred in too short a time for the hypothesis to be entertained seriously. (p. 70)

Replication, then, reduces the scientist's margin of error and increases confidence that findings that withstand repeated tests are real, not accidental.

Types of Replication

Direct Replication Sidman (1960) defines direct replication as "... the repetition of a given experiment by the same experimenter" (p. /5). In one type, intrasubject replication, everything remains the same—the subject, the stimuli, the consequent events, and the experimental space. In a second type, intersubject replication, everything remains the same except the subject.

Direct replication is conducted only in laboratory studies using infrahuman subjects. For it is only under these conditions that everything remains the same (intrasubject replication). The experimental psychologist, using a rat or pigeon subjects, may repeat an experiment again and again. The data will show whether an original finding is reproducible, and, if so, will indicate that the procedure is sufficiently powerful to bring the behavior under control. Failure to replicate will require careful analysis of the data and perhaps modification of the procedure. Then, when another series of studies demonstrates an effect, the experimenter is confident that, for this subject, the problem of control has been solved. Science has advanced by some small increment (or a large one), and the experimenter will move on to another question, the direction determined by some aspect of this series of experiments. The experimenter will have gained confidence in his findings, but at a price: repeating the same experiment consumes the same amount of resources as moving forward from one interesting question to the next. Further, once a replication series is initiated, the experimenter must confront the question, "How many replications are enough?" The ability to balance costs and determine when to move forward is basic to the repertoire of the good scientist.

Intersubject replication is conducted to insure that the results of an intrasubject series are not unique to a single subject. To the extent that results are reproducible across a number of subjects in the same species, the data permit increased confidence in the intervention.

Systematic Replication Systematic replication is more difficult to define. Sidman's (1960) chapter gives the procedure a name, states how it is different from direct replication, and defines only by example. He notes the fundamental dictum of science is that all subjects be treated alike except for the independent variable. Yet that rule "strangles systematic replication as a primary method for establishing reliability and generality" (Sidman, 1960, p. 111). He states simply, "systematic replication demonstrates that the finding ... can be observed under conditions *different* from those prevailing in the original experiment" (p. 111). He suggests, in essence, that the experimenter's judgment (history) will dictate how far one can move from the original experiment and that systematic replication is a gamble, one which, if successful, "will buy reliability, generality, and additional information" (p. 112). Yet, he cautions:

> The chief commodity of experimental science is data. For the investigator, economy of time, space, and available budget are important determinants of his experimental program. The scientist is faced with the perpetual problem of using his resources for maximum productivity while maintaining the quality of his product. Systematic replication is a time-tested method for increasing both the quantity and the quality of one's work. An original experiment may have been long and arduous.

Direct replication would not only occupy a large segment of the experimenter's time but also tie up costly apparatus that might be used to obtain other important information. (p. 112)

Hersen and Barlow (1976) defined systematic replication "as any attempt to replicate findings from a direct replication series, varying settings, behavior change agents, behavior disorders, or any combination thereof" (p. 339).

This definition presents some problems and requires some additional explanation. First, Hersen and Barlow's context is the clinical laboratory setting, one dealing with mental health clients, hence the phrase "behavior disorders." Second, they earlier included experimentation with *human* subjects in their definition of direct replication; thus they require that systematic replication follow from a direct replication series. This qualification, however, places a severe limitation on the definition, i.e., if systematic observation can *only* follow from a direct replication study, what is the status of studies designed to replicate another researcher's single study—one that has shown interesting and promising results? This restriction notwithstanding, the phrase "any attempt to replicate" is at the same time, perhaps too broad. To illustrate, Hersen and Barlow (1976) presented a table of systematic replication studies in the reinforcement of children's differential attention (pp. 346–349). These 55 studies were conducted by many investigators and were reported from 1959 through 1972. It is doubtful that these studies meet Hersen and Barlow's definition of systematic replication. Whether, collectively, they are systematic replication is a matter of personal opinion.

Jones (1978), in his review of Hersen and Barlow's *Single Case Experimental Designs* (1976), offers a clear analysis of the replication process:

Replication is clearly a canon of applied behavioral science, and is discussed frequently, but executed less frequently. Despite the exemplar series of studies described by Hersen and Barlow as illustrative of replications in applied behavior analysis, this reviewer is concerned that replications may be labelled as such, but in fact not be replications. Absolutely pure replication probably happens seldom, if ever. Pure replication would require a point-by-point duplication of a research design, varying nothing except the time the study was conducted. Such replication is considered trivial by most researchers and probably unpublishable as well. When behavioral interventions lead to large and dramatic effects, and there is no question about the experimental control demonstrated in the study, then such pure replication *is* trivial. But, when researchers change procedures (the inherent flexibility of single-case designs), plan to use the technique with different kinds of subjects in different settings, or anticipate changing any salient aspect of the design, then pure replication, of course, is impossible. Replication then becomes more a matter of repeating the work with systematic modifications. Modified procedures, subject populations, measurement systems, *etc.*, are tested to see if comparable results occur. The value of replication in single-case experimentation occurs when there is a substantial accumulation of parallel or convergent findings from a set of similar, but not identical, procedures, techniques, measurement devices, subject samples, *etc.* In the end, convergence among results from many such replications determines the generality of findings. This is the big goal to be achieved by the field of applied behavior analysis. (p. 313)

In our view, *systematic replication*, as applied to research conducted in educational settings, is an attempt by a researcher to repeat his own procedure, employing variations in the procedure, with the same or different subjects. Or, it is a series of planned experiments, conducted by one researcher that utilizes the same basic procedure, but systematically varies it based on results of the first experiments. Or, it is an attempt by a researcher to reproduce the published findings of others, adhering closely to the original procedure.

We consider ours a functional definition. It reflects the reality that in classroom-based research, very little is the same from day to day, and from study to study. It focuses on the goal of the researcher—to try again a procedure that has been successful (or at least seems promising). Or, viewed from the perspective of the teacher-researcher, "If x intervention has been used with students like mine, will it work for me?"

Clinical Replication

Hersen and Barlow (1976) introduce a third type of replication, which they define "as the administration of a treatment package containing two or distinct treatment procedures by the same investigator or group of investigators ... administered in a specific setting to a series of clients presenting similar combinations of multiple behavioral and emotional problems, which usually cluster together" (p. 336). They refer to this as an advanced process, the end of years of research in "technique building." Again, we note that their context is the clinical laboratory and that their subjects are individuals with many types of "emotional" problems. They consider clinical replication to be a form of direct replication, i.e., the clinical analog of the experimental laboratory procedure. Within this context we can observe their view of the scientific process, as it relates to the field of clinical psychology. It is a three-stage process. First, a researcher working with a series of clients with a similar problem establishes that an intervention produces behavior change. This is direct replication. Next, in clinical replications the researcher (and associates), combining techniques, demonstrate the effectiveness of an intervention package with subjects who demonstrate similar clusters of problem behaviors, e.g., autistic children. The outcome of this long-term process is an empirically verified intervention program (package): a product, in the broad sense, that may be ' 'tested" by others in systematic replications. The outcome of the whole process would be, we infer, a demonstrably effective "psychological" intervention program that "works" with ranges of client populations. This goal is different from replication as Sidman describes it, in regard to the scientific process. It is not so different from the goal of education as we described it in Chapter 4.

Clarifications

In certain types of concept learning, instances of the concept are defined by stating what "it" *is* and what "it" *is not*. Since our definition of systematic replication is relatively open ended, we present here some clarifications and examples.

Direct replication, by definition, is limited to the experimental laboratory. In applied research, in the classroom or similar educational environments, only systematic replication will occur, if replication occurs at all. Systematic replication, defined as planned series of applied behavior studies, is not a common practice, but one that should be encouraged. For example, in our definition we have included the phrase "an attempt ... to reproduce the findings of others." Yet the cumulative index of *JABA*, from its inception through volume 14 shows only three entries (Greenwood, Hops, Walker, Guild, Stokes, Young, Keleman, & Willardson, 1979; Hannah & Risley, 1981; Liberman, Ferris, Salgado, & Salgado, 1975) that are clearly identified as replications.

We have referred to the replication of *experiments* to distinguish the repetition of phases (A-B-A-B) within an experiment from the replication of studies which might incorporate those phases. This may seem a small point, hardly worthy of consideration. However, it seems logical that the beginning student in applied behavior analysis might ask "Isn't A-B-A-B a form of replication?" Yes, but it is not a systematic *replication of experiments.* If a student-researcher conducts one A-B-A-B experiment with a student and then repeats the study with another subject, that is systematic replication.

Does systematic replication, clearly defined as such, appear at all in applied behavioral research? The answer is yes. The place to look for replication, clearly defined, is in journal articles that report more than one experiment. The narrative describing the second study will begin with a statement like "Experiment 2 was conducted to replicate the results of Study 1." Or, "Experiment 2 was conducted to increase the reliability of (confidence in) the findings of Experiment 1." Or, "Experiment 2 was conducted with (another population or another setting) to determine the generality of the original findings." Though we have not conducted an analysis of all such articles, we tend to believe that the majority of these report thesis research.

Beyond these instances, what else constitutes systematic replication? When a researcher carries out a planned series of studies that incorporate systematic changes from one study to the next and identifies them as a replication series, that is clearly systematic replication. If a researcher tries another's procedure and states his intent to replicate, that is another instance.

Suppose that a researcher initiates a study based on current findings in an area, such as time delay, and develops an intervention that contains elements of existing procedures. Is this an instance of systematic replication? It is at this point that the definition of systematic replication is in the mind of the beholder. Suppose the researcher combines elements of three time delay studies as a foundation for an intervention. Then nothing is the same; we have a new experimenter, different subjects, a different environment. We would not consider this an instance of systematic replication. It might be called "doing research in an interesting area," and while there may be a link to the previous research, there is no single common element. The situation is different if (a) the researcher sets out to replicate, (b) states an intent to replicate, (c) contacts the researcher whose work he wishes to replicate in order to verify correspondence with a published procedure, and then (d) carries out the study, (e) reporting results that can be evaluated in relationship to the original work.

This is a more restricted definition than Sidman offers. However, in the experimental laboratory serendipity plays a larger part than it does in the educational environment. For while the scientist approaches a problem with the question "What will happen if . . . ?" the applied researcher, especially in the classroom environment, will approach the problem of behavior change with the question, "How can I make x work" or, as noted, "How can I do y better?" Or, "If x worked for someone else, how can I produce more powerful effect?"

TABLE 6-1   Replication Studies.

Variable	Study		
	1967	1968	1969
Setting	adjustment class	adjustment class	2nd grade class
Subject	17 9-year-olds	6 3rd graders 6 4th graders	7 of 21 students in class
Design	A-B	A-B-A	8-phase study*
Observation System	20 sec observe 10 sec record	20 sec observe 10 sec record	20 sec observe 10 sec record
Independent Variable	(a) average % deviant behavior for group (b) % deviant for individual Ss	(a) average % deviant behavior (b) % deviant for individual Ss	(a) average % deviant behavior for group (b) % disruptive of individual Ss across phases
Intervention	(a) token system; ratings (points) received for rule following, e.g., in seat, face front; points exchanged for small prizes, candy, toys; requirements and costs increased during intervention (b) ignore disruptive students and praise approriate behavior of others	(a) token system; ratings (points) received for rule following, e.g., in seat, face front; points exchanged for small prizes	(a) 8 phases; in token and backup phase, points were exchanged for small prizes
Teacher Training	teacher enrolled in psychology course taught by team member; in-class consultation with experimenter	none	(a) teacher received credits for participation in study (b) teacher required to demonstrate 8 types of behavior to adhere to experimental procedures; teacher received feedback on "adherence to instructions/procedures"
Outcomes	(a) statistically significant results on analysis of variance		(a) statistical differences among conditions (b) mixed effects across the 7 Ss

TABLE 6-1   (continued)

Variable	Study		
	1967	1968	1969
Outcomes *(continued)*	(b) clear evidence of effect observable on group and individual graphs		(c) drop in disruptive behavior of 5 Ss in Token I and equivalent drop in Token II
Other		(a) study terminated at teacher's request; no differential reinforcement by teacher, as in first study. (b) 4 of 6 Ss were in the earlier study.	

*8-phase study: baseline, add classroom rules, add educational structure and maintain rules, add praise and ignore the rules and structure, add tokens to all previous conditions, withdraw tokens and backups, reinstitute tokens and backup, follow-up by withdrawing tokens and backup and leaving all other conditions in effect.

Replication Studies

The Illinois Studies

In the historical development of applied behavioral analysis in special education, we described the work of Becker and his associates at the University of Illinois. The O'Leary and Becker (1967) study, was the *first report* of a token economy system used in a special education classroom setting. O'Leary, Becker, Evans, and Saudargas (1969) reported a *replication* and *systematic analysis*. Kuypers, Becker, and O'Leary (1968) reported a *failure to replicate* a token economy system. These studies were carried out under the same research grant by a core research team in the same school system. Each was an attempt to study the effect of a token economy system on the behavior of selected subjects within a classroom. The variables of interest are shown in Table 6-1.

These studies represent programmatic research. They were planned and are clearly identified as replications. They represent an interesting study in the problems of large-scale research and systematic research/replication in public school settings. The classrooms were special classes for children with adjustment problems in two cases. In each study data were collected on disruptive members of the class. The recording system remained the same across studies, and the dependent variable was the same. There the similarities end. In the first study, O'Leary and Becker (1967) wanted to observe the effect of a token economy in a classroom setting under the direction of the teacher. They noted that previous investigations had used small teacher-pupil ratios, e.g., 4 teachers in a class of 17 students (p. 637). Kuypers, Becker, and O'Leary (1968) attempted a replication without specific teacher training. They sought to approximate the conditions that might exist if a teacher read about token economies and tried to develop one on his own (p. 102). O'Leary, et al. (1969) studied the separate effects of the elements that constituted their total intervention program (p. 3).

The designs increased in sophistication. In the first, a withdrawal and reinstitution (A-B-A-B) was not attempted because the investigators were concerned that a negative reaction would influence their total program. The second study was terminated at teacher request during the withdrawal period. The "praise and ignore" phase of the third study was prematurely terminated because disruptive behaviors during this condition made the situation intolerable (p. 9). Thus the investigators' initial concern was justified.

There are procedural differences among the studies that are not reflected in Table 6-1. The definition of deviant behavior expanded, and specific definitions became more precise. Since teacher judgment determined the points (ratings) students received, there was variability from teacher to teacher. Time of day and scheduling affected the implementation of the point system. In the second study, students were not reinforced for progress toward appropriate behaviors, as they were in the other studies. And, despite extensive preplanning, carefully developed procedures, and intensive training of observers, the second study was terminated because of inappropriate observer behaviors and other administrative failures (p. 108). Finally, the variable *teacher training* was different across the three experiments. None of the studies employed a teacher who was highly trained in behavior modification techniques and had demonstrated skilled execution of the procedures. But the studies were alike on another dimension, which is clear when the studies are read at the same time. They were all maximally intrusive on the classroom environment. There were as many as five observers in the classroom at the same time. While necessary for experimental reasons, they took their toll on teacher participation.

We have described these pioneering studies in order to illustrate clear examples of systematic replication. It should be noted that there was a parallel and interrelated set of studies carried out by the same investigators at approximately the same time. These manipulated specific teacher behaviors to determine their effects on classroom control, e.g., teacher attention and praise (Becker, Madsen, Arnold, & Thomas, 1967); rules, praise, and ignoring (Madsen, Becker, & Thomas, 1968); teacher reprimands (O'Leary, & Becker, 1968); the use of loud and soft reprimands (O'Leary, Kaufman, Kass, & Drabman, 1970). Within this series, the second study is identified as a systematic replication of the first. The fourth study is a further analysis of the procedures used in the third. Collectively, they provided tentative findings that translated into teacher recommendations for applying certain behaviors (skills) to reduce disruptions in the classroom.

Pass

Greenwood et al. (1979) reported a replication of the Program for Academic Survival Skills (PASS), "a standardized intervention package" (p. 25).

PASS is the product of a large-scale, long-term research program conducted at the University of Oregon. In general, the history of PASS can be traced to an early effort (1966–1970), the Engineered Learning Project, to develop a token economy utilizing highly structured academic programs (Walker & Buckley, 1974, p. 5). From that beginning, there emerged working papers, grant reports, journal articles, PASS, the related product Contingencies for Learning Academic and Social Skills (CLASS) (Hops, Fleischman, & Beickel, 1976), and subsequently a text (Walker, 1979). The reference notes and references in the Greenwood et al. (1979) paper illustrate the scope of the research program from which PASS evolved. This study, a group comparison, is of interest not only because it is one of the few clearly defined classroom-based replication studies, but because systematic research, on many dimensions, preceded the study and because the scope of the replication effort was so broad.

PASS may be described, after Hersen and Barlow's (1976) terminology, as a multi-element treatment package, or as a multi-element intervention program. Teacher consultants were trained; then they trained classroom teachers to implement a group contingency management system which, in turn included a timer, data-recording systems, and training manuals. The PASS replication was conducted to answer several questions:

1. Could consultants trained in a 2-day workshop by the authors, using prepared program manuals and materials, select appropriate classrooms and train teachers to successfully implement the PASS program?

2. Could teachers trained in the PASS program by consultants successfully implement PASS in their classrooms during reading and/or mathematics instruction?

3. In contrast to equivalent control subjects in the natural settings and local normative data, would PASS teachers and students significantly improve their performances on measures of observed teacher skill, observed student behavior, teacher ratings of student behavior problems, and academic achievement?

4. Would the PASS group report satisfaction with the program during and following its implementation up to one year later?

5. Would these results be sufficiently powerful to demonstrate replication of effects across two geographically separate school sites in the Western United States? (p. 237)

The study was conducted in two states. A total of 25 consultants and 50 teachers were trained; 1,144 students were enrolled in the classes. Consultants randomly assigned teachers for whom they were responsible to experimental or control (no PASS) conditions. PASS teachers were trained in six 2-hour sessions in which they learned to use a clock light timer to signal student compliance with group contingencies and record intervals of appropriate behavior and then to use group contingency and verbal praise techniques. A statistical technique, analysis of covariance, was used to analyze changes in teacher behavior and child behavior and achievement test scores in reading and math. Student, teacher, and consultant satisfaction with the system was analyzed, and follow-up data were collected to determine the extent to which the system would be used after the experiment was completed. From the many comparisons, some general statements can be made. Overall, PASS produced a positive effect, when compared to the no PASS condition. There were differential effects between sites, with more positive effects in the home state. Specific teacher behaviors, e.g., approval statements, increased, and there were more significant increases in the Oregon sites. There were significant increases in appropriate student behaviors. Observations during and after intervention showed above 80% appropriate group behavior. Overall there were no significant differences in classroom achievement. Finally, questionnaires showed a high degree of satisfaction with the program. The authors cite this study as documentation of the generality of the PASS system.

The magnitude of effort needed to carry out this replication can perhaps be appreciated only by those who have engaged in similar efforts. To conduct this study, the investigators employed coordinators at each site, trained the consultants, developed an observer training program, trained groups of observers, arranged for consultants to train teachers, employed individuals to administer the achievement tests, and supported extensive in-class observations. The logistical barriers to such an effort should not be underestimated.

The investigators might have hoped for equivalent effects in both sites and for documentation of an effect on academic achievement. But a strong case can be made that, given the methodology, any positive effect represents a strong effect. For, in contrast to a small-scale project where, for example, a clear effect is demonstrated across three subjects using a time-lagged multiple baseline design under tightly controlled conditions, these investigators trained a group of consultants in a short time (2-day program). The consultants trained the teachers who then applied group control techniques. The effect was evaluated on several behaviors of a group of students rather than on single subjects. In contrast to other studies which focus on specific academic targets and measure daily percent correct responding on these targets, the investigators relied on pre-post measures on general achievement tests. Thus, they tested for generalized effects once removed from their own direct intervention. The confidence with which they initiated this investigation was based, of course, on the many previous positive results of the small-scale studies that preceded the replication. For example, Greenwood, Hops, Delquadri, and Guild (1974) reported a time-lagged multiple intervention study, applying an early version of PASS in three classrooms (see Figure 6-1). After a baseline period, they introduced these conditions: *rules* (teacher defined rules stated to class during work periods); *rules* and *feedback* (rules stated, student-appropriate behavior recorded, relationship of the clock timer to student behavior identified, percent group-appropriate score graphed and posted); *rules, feedback, group contingencies,* and *individual consequences* (to the previous conditions, teacher added group activities available to class contingent on meeting increasingly rigorous group-appropriate behavior scores; teacher gave individualized praise to on-task students). The last condition represented the total PASS package. Results showed clear increases in group-appropriate behavior as a function of the total package. Data reported on teachers' use of appropriate and inappropriate consequences showed clear increases for each teacher on the use of correct consequences. During baseline, two of three teachers showed relatively high rates of incorrect to correct responses. During intervention, and particularly during the total package condition, rates of incorrect responses reduced to near zero level for all teachers. The authors indicated these results *replicated* earlier experiments in the application of group procedures. Further, in relating their research to earlier studies, they made distinctions among the group procedures in use at the time, thus assisting other researchers to clarify significant procedural variations within that body of research.

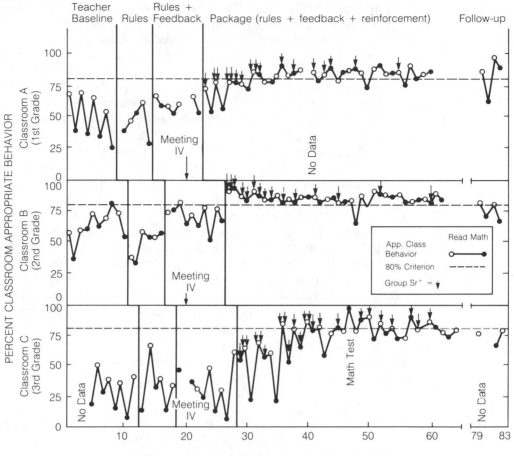

FIGURE 6-1 Precent classroom-appropriate behavior for three classrooms over experimental conditions and stimulus conditions (reading and math).
(Figure 1, p. 420, from: Greenwood, C. R., Hops, H., Delquadri, J., and Guild, T. Group contingencies for group consequences in classroom management: A further analysis. Journal of Applied Behavior Analysis, 1974, 7, 413–425. Copyright by Society for the Experimental Analysis of Behavior, Inc. Reproduced by permission.)

The Good Behavior Game

Barrish, Saunders, and Wolf (1969) developed a simple group behavioral control procedure that has been used often in various forms. This study evolved from two sources. It represented an attempt to develop a reinforcement system that was not artificial, as the authors described the token economies which were then being reported in the literature. At the same time, they noted that the most "natural" reinforcer, teacher attention, might perhaps be insufficient to control students' behavior. Consequently, a team competition "game" was devised and tested.

The study was conducted in a fourth grade class that contained several extremely disruptive students and that represented "a general behavior management problem" (pp. 119–120). Students were divided into two teams. An extensive list of rules (11) was written and made public. Teams received marks when any member was observed to break a rule. The winning team (one receiving fewer marks) received privileges not available to the losing team: wearing victory tags, stars on charts, lining up first for lunch, and 30 minutes of free time at the end of the day (while the losing team continued to work on assignments). If both teams received few marks, both could win. A full week of low marks entitled the groups to an additional 4 minutes of recess for the next week.

The game was in effect first during math instruction and then later during reading. A multiple baseline design was used. During math a baseline period was followed by intervention (the good behavior game). Data (baseline) were recorded in reading during these and subsequent phases. The intervention was withdrawn in math and instituted in reading. After six sessions it was reinstated in math and continued in reading. This represents an A-B-A-B design in math and an A-B design in reading. The simultaneous reversal of conditions in the two study periods, and the resultant behavior change represent an additional demonstration of the effect. Results showed a dramatic reduction in inappropriate behavior during the intervention periods. Percent of intervals in which inappropriate behaviors e.g., talking out, were scored dropped from a median of 96% during baseline to 9% during the intervention periods in math. Interestingly, the authors noted that both teams usually won, i.e., both received less than the daily criterion on 82% of the sessions.

Replications

Medland and Stachnik (1972) replicated the good behavior game *procedure*. This is an important distinction because, within the context of our discussion of what constitutes a replication, only the setting (public school elementary class), statement of rules, and the team competition were the same. The obvious differences were the experimenters, subjects, geographical area, and data recorded. Among the key procedural differences were classroom structure (Ss in each team turned their desks 45° in opposite directions from the front of the room and thus 90° from each other), green and red lights signalled recording procedures, behavior definitions, the experimental design and consequences.

A six-phase design was employed to evaluate the effect of the separate components of the game: baseline$_1$, game$_1$ (all components), baseline$_2$ (return to baseline), rules (only), rules and signal lights (each team's green light signal was replaced by a 30-second red warning signal when a team member emitted an inappropriate behavior), game$_2$ (all components, as in game$_1$). Results showed a dramatic decrease from baseline$_1$ to game$_1$ sessions. Behaviors did not return to their original level after the first intervention, but gradually increased. *Rules* produced a decrease, though behavior was variable during a short phase. Inappropriate behaviors returned to a low rate during *rules and lights,* then decreased further in game$_2$ condition. Perhaps because of the procedural difficulties, the investigators did not offer the study as a clear demonstration of the replicability of the good behavior game. Since the study was short-term (60 days) occurring at the end of the school year, it was not possible to execute other manipulations, e.g., to extend phases to identify cyclic variation or to add phases, e.g., baseline$_3$, game$_3$ or to collect follow-up data.

Harris and Sherman (1973) replicated the Barrish, Saunders, and Wolf (1969) study to determine whether the game would be effective in two classrooms, whether certain components of the game exerted more control than others, and whether the game would have an effect on academic achievement. In the first phase of their study, the basic procedures from the original study were employed. Two behaviors were targeted: defined vocalizations emitted without teacher permission were classified as talking; another set of behaviors was classified as out of seat. The various manipulations can be described, in summary form, in this way: collect baseline data; apply the game to one of the targets but not the other within a class period, e.g., math or English, or apply the game in one class period but not the other; then, withdraw one element of the game from one target, while applying the game in another form to the other target. Data collected were mean daily percent of intervals in which inappropriate behaviors were recorded, represented graphically in histograms, one bar representing each target averaged over the days of the intervention phase. From the many comparisons, several general statements can be made. The game produced dramatic results when applied to a target, in contrast to rate of the nontargeted behavior. For example, in the fifth grade class, talking occurred at nearly 100% during each of two math periods. When the game was applied in the second period but not the first, talking reduced to near 10% and remained at over 90% in the nontargeted period. Overall, the game produced a clear effect. Again in the fifth grade class the game was applied to five subject periods, for 100 school days. Across the 100-day period, talking averaged 8%; out-of-seat behavior averaged 2%. The authors note that over the 133-day period in which the game was in effect in at least one period, both teams "won" the game on 121 days (neither team exceeded the criterion number of marks recorded for inappropriate behaviors in effect for a session).

The manipulations were game, game without consequence (leave school 10 minutes early), manipulate number of marks (8 or 4), game without feedback (marks written or teachers record rather than on blackboard), game without teams (whole class became a team). Generally, a controlling effect was found in all the manipulations except the game without feedback. When the game was played without consequences, disruptive behavior increased, but not to baseline levels. When the criterion was raised from four to eight marks, disruptive behaviors increased. The reduction in disruptive behavior produced no clear effect on academic achievement.

Fishbein and Wasik (1981) adapted the elements of the good behavior game in the library of an elementary school. At the librarian's request, the investigators intervened with one unusually disruptive fourth grade class. After an observation period in the library and the classroom, an A-B-A intervention was introduced. The librarian and students developed a set of rules which they applied to off-task, task-appropriate, and disruptive behaviors. During A conditions (game with reinforcement), the librarian scanned the class periodically and awarded a point if team members were behaving appropriately. If a team scored a point on three of four observations, the reinforcer was delivered—during the last 10 minutes of *class*. The teacher would either read a story or work with students on an art project. In the B condition, the game was played but no reinforcement was delivered. Results showed an increase in appropriate and decrease in inappropriate behavior during the interventions. Some effect was found in the classroom. Since that was where the reinforcer was dispensed, this minor "spillover" effect was not unexpected. When the consequences were removed, the effect was diminished. Though the effect was not strong, overall, in these once-a-week interventions, the authors suggested the technique might be helpful to other librarians who confront the problem of unruly students.

This simple study tests our definition of systematic replication. In our view, it is best described as an application of a general procedure. "Nothing is the same" as the original experiment. The only similarity is that (a) a set of rules were devised, (b) a team competition was initiated, and (c) a consequence was made contingent upon meeting a performance criterion.

What can we say after an analysis of this set of studies employing some version of the good behavior game? The game, applied in the closest approximation to the original, produces dramatic effects across subjects, settings, and different investigators. The game produces the greatest effect when all components are employed; although posting marks on a blackboard probably has little effect if consequences are employed. Not unsurprising, permission to leave school early is a powerful reinforcer; although it may create another set of problems. Two findings are of special interest. When properly structured, both teams can and will win, and the game will produce a strong effect. Further, as Harris and Sherman (1973) demonstrated, the game will produce an effect across the school year. More year-long replications are needed, however, before that claim can be accepted with a high degree of confidence.

Guidelines for Future Replications

The student- or teacher-researcher who wishes to use/replicate the good behavior game should:

1. Read these studies and others that might apply;

2. Develop a chart that identifies the few common elements that apply across the studies;

3. Analyze the specific effects within each study since those have been presented in a general and summary form here;

4. Analyze the authors' suggestions for additional research;

5. Identify the findings that might be most valuable, e.g., Harris and Sherman's findings that "the game" worked across most of the school day and throughout most of the school year.

These five steps apply to any research program, of course, and are discussed in greater detail in Chapter 13. While there are many interesting research topics, some are apparent: Knowing that the game has been used in elementary schools, can equivalent versions be developed in junior and senior high schools? Or, can the game be organized and implemented by the students? Or, will there be differential effects under these conditions: teacher imposed, student designed, or teacher and student mutual selection of rules and reinforcers? Or, how might the basic procedure be modified to produce strong "spillover" effects when the game is applied in only one time period?

Suppose that the student- or teacher-researcher wished to replicate the game. How would we know? Returning to our definition, these conditions would prevail. The title of the report would clearly identify the study as a replication. A reader would be able to identify the commonalities between procedures. The introduction would clearly state that replication was a goal. The discussion section would clearly relate these findings to earlier studies, e.g., "these results confirm the findings of Harris and Sherman (1973) that . . . , but they fail to support the findings of. . . ."

SUMMARY

Replication is a necessary part of the scientific process. Replication establishes the generality of research findings. To the extent that an intervention produces a strong effect across subjects, settings, and experimenters, one has confidence that "x works." Similarly, strong effects obtained many times removed from the original findings increase the external validity of the procedure. In this chapter we have described direct and systematic replication within Sidman's (1960) context—the experimental laboratory. And we have shown how Hersen and Barlow's (1976) concepts of direct, clinical, and systematic replication represent one step away from the experimental laboratory. Our definition of systematic replication has been drawn from the natural environment. We have gone to some lengths to discriminate replication from a general application of a procedure to a problem. The examples of replication studies have been selected to represent different approaches to classroom intervention. Students who read the original studies should be able to develop a clear concept of replication. Further, they may find some avenues for their own research that will, hopefully, advance science and effective educational practice.

SECTION
THREE

RESEARCH
DESIGN

7

DEPENDENT MEASURES AND MEASUREMENT SYSTEMS

Having considered general issues of concern to the teacher-researcher, we now progress to specific steps for measuring students' behavior and conducting applied behavior research. In this chapter we will describe (1) how to select a dependent measure, (2) a systematic recording procedure, (3) design data forms, and (4) systems for insuring reliable measurement. Having acquired this information, teachers and researchers should be ready to conduct single subject research in classroom settings.

Parameters of Measurement

The teacher-researcher must make two decisions before collecting data on student behavior. She must decide (1) what characteristic of a student's behavior should be measured and (2) what method of recording should be used to measure this aspect of behavior.

The first decision relates to the selection of a dependent variable, or dependent measure. White (1971) has defined a *dependent variable* as "a variable which changes as a function of a change in another variable" (p. 186). Dependent variables frequently used by applied researchers and teachers include *number* (e.g., number of words spelled correctly); *frequency* or *rate* (e.g., number of words read correctly per minute); *percent correct* (e.g., percent of addition problems performed correctly per page); *duration* (e.g., number of minutes it takes a student to complete a division problem); and *latency* (e.g., number of seconds it takes a student to return to his desk after instructed to do so by the teacher). Other measures also are available to

---

This chapter was written by **David L. Gast** and **James W. Tawney**.

the classroom teacher but are less frequently reported (e.g., *magnitude, intensity, trials to criterion, errors to criterion*).

The type of dependent measure selected will depend upon the target behavior and the instructional objective. For example, an appropriate objective for a student who reads accurately but slowly would be to increase the number of words accurately read per minute. For another student, who reads at an acceptable rate but who emits a large number of errors, an appropriate objective would be to increase the percentage of words she reads correctly. In selecting a dependent measure it is important to base the decision on the intended purpose of the instructional program (e.g., to increase rate, to increase accuracy, or both).

The "other variable" referred to in White's (1971) definition of the dependent variable is known as the *independent variable*. The independent variable of an experimental investigation or instructional program is a variable that is manipulated or observed by a behavior analyst to determine its effect on the dependent variable. It is equivalent to the intervention, treatment, or experimental conditions under which a behavior is repeatedly measured and evaluated.

Selecting a Dependent Measure

The dependent variable selected will relate directly to the research question and the objective of the intervention. Therefore, it is imperative that the teacher and researcher decide what it is about the behavior under investigation she wishes to change, i.e., frequency, duration, accuracy, latency. The decision as to whether a behavior is occurring at an acceptable or unacceptable level should not be made arbitrarily; it is a decision which should be based on reliable data. Contrary to what some may believe, professional educators and applied researchers do not base their decisions to intervene on subjective evaluations and without conferring with "significant others" (parents, other teachers, ancillary personnel). All decisions, particularly those which focus on decreasing the frequency of a behavior, require an objective (empirical) appraisal of the behavior in addition to parent consultation. To accomplish this the teacher and applied researcher focus their attention on that aspect of the target behavior which is of concern and begin to systematically collect data to verify whether the concern is justified. Only after these initial measures are collected and analyzed is a decision made regarding what course of action to take. This decision is a collective one.

Table 7-1 summarizes the more frequent dependent measures used in classroom research. Each of these measures is defined and exemplified in the remainder of this section.

Number

Number refers to a simple count of the number of times a behavior or event occurs during a constant time period. Number is an appropriate dependent measure only when the observation period during which data are collected is held constant from session to session, or day to day, or when a student has the same number of opportunities to respond on a teacher-paced activity. For example, if each day you read 20 words aloud which students are required to spell correctly within a 10-minute period, the number of words spelled correctly could be used as the dependent variable. In this example both the number of words to be spelled (i.e., opportunities to respond) and the time students have to spell the 20 words are held constant. When number is used to quantify a behavior under free-operant conditions where there is no ceiling or upper limit on the frequency of the behavior, number can be used if the observation period is held constant each day. For example, you could monitor and report the number of talk-outs per day provided the time period

TABLE 7-1   Summary of dependent measures.

Dependent Measure	Definition	Considerations
1. Number	Simple count of the number of times a behavior or event occurs	1.1 Requires constant time across observational periods with free-operant behaviors 1.2 Requires constant number of trials across sessions/days with teacher-paced instruction
2. Percent	Number of occurrences divided by the total number of opportunities for the behavior to occur multiplied by 100.	2.1 Equalizes unequal number of opportunities to respond across sessions/days 2.2 Easily understood 2.3 Frequently used measure for accuracy 2.4 Efficient means for summarizing large numbers of responses 2.5 No reference to the time over which behavior was observed 2.6 Generally, should be used only when there are 20 or more opportunities to respond.
3. Rate	Number of occurrences divided by the number of time units (minutes or hours)	3.1 Converts behavior counts to a constant scale when opportunities to respond or observation time varies across sessions/days 3.2 Reveals response proficiency as well as accuracy 3.3 Reported as responses per minute or responses per hour 3.4 Appropriate for behaviors measured under free-operant conditions 3.5 Cumbersome to use with behaviors measured under teacher-paced conditions
4. Duration (total)	Amount of time behavior occurs during an observation period	4.1 Expressed as the percentage of time engaged in behavior 4.2 Does not yield information about frequency or mean duration per occurrence
5. Duration per Occurrence	Amount of time engaged in each episode of the behavior	5.1 Yields behavior frequency; mean duration per occurrence and total duration information
6. Latency	Elapsed time from the presentation of the S^D and the initiation of the behavior	6.1 Appropriate measure with compliance problem behaviors (long response latency) 6.2 May yield information regarding high error rate when there is a short response latency
7. Magnitude	Response strength or force	7.1 Direct measure requires automated-quantitative instrumentation 7.2 Indirect measure of magnitude possible by measuring effect response has on environment
8. Trials to Criterion	Number of trials counted to reach criterion for each behavior	8.1 Yields information on concept formation (learning-to-learn phenomenon) 8.2 Post hoc summary measure

during which talk-outs are recorded is the same each day. Number has been used most frequently in applied research which has studied free-operant social behaviors, including inappropriate verbal behavior (Luce & Hall, 1981) and aggressive behavior (Bostow & Bailey, 1969; Carr, Newsom, & Binkoff, 1980; Porterfield, Herbert-Jackson, & Risley, 1976). On occasion it has been used with academically related skills, such as the number of assignments completed (e.g., Robinson, Newby, & Ganzell, 1981).

Throughout the applied research literature the term *frequency* has been used interchangeably with *number* to refer to the number of times a target behavior occurs, (e.g., Epstein, Repp, & Cullinan, 1978; Matson & Andrasik, 1982; Strain & Timm, 1974). This substitution in terms is appropriate only when the observation period is constant across days. Generally, when the occurrences of a behavior are tallied it is preferable to use the phrasing "number of occurrences" rather than "frequency of occurrences" to avoid possible confusion with the term *rate*.

Percent

Percent data are perhaps the most frequent dependent measures used by teachers when conducting research. *Percent* refers to the number of times a behavior occurs per total number of opportunities for the behavior to occur, multiplied by 100 (e.g., number "correct" divided by the number of opportunities, multiplied by 100 = percentage of "correct" responses). It is a particularly useful measure when accuracy is of primary concern and when some permanent product is generated, as in the case of many preacademic and academic instructional programs (e.g., percent of addition problems summed correctly on independent worksheets). Percent data also have been used to summarize the number of responses emitted over a series of constant "time-ruled" observation intervals, as when using an interval recording system:

Number of 10-second intervals during which a response occurred.

Total number of observation intervals × 100 = Percentage of intervals the response occurred.

Percent data have several advantages over number and other types of dependent measures (Cooper, 1981; Gentry & Haring, 1976):

1. They convert unequal opportunities to respond across sessions or days to a common scale, thereby "equalizing" the number of opportunities to respond for purposes of data summation and evaluation.

2. They are an efficient means of summarizing large numbers of responses.

3. They are a simple way of summarizing overall performance on a graph or chart.

4. They are more familiar to people than other measures (e.g., rate, latency, magnitude) and therefore facilitate communication of performance.

Percent data, however, do have their disadvantages or limitations:

1. They make no reference to the time over which a behavior was observed, thus limiting what can be said about response proficiency.

2. They place upper and lower limits (i.e., 100% and 0%) on reporting data by not referring to the actual number of responses or opportunities to respond.

3. They can mask trends in the data by not revealing when a response occurs during a particular observation period.

4. They should not be used, generally speaking, when the total number of opportunities to respond is less than 20, in which case one change in the numerator will produce greater than a 50% change.

Rate

Rate has been referred to as the basic datum of science (Skinner, 1966). Synonymous with the term *frequency*, rate refers to the number of times a behavior occurs within an observation period. Unlike number, rate can serve as the dependent measure when a behavior is observed across variable time periods (e.g., Day 1, 10 minutes; Day 2, 7 minutes; Day 3, 12 minutes). The rate of a behavior is calculated by counting the number of times the behavior occurs and dividing the total number of occurrences by the total number of minutes (or hours) during which the behavior was observed.

A distinction has often been made between the terms *rate* and *frequency* based on the manner in which the data are reported. Rate data are commonly reported as the number of responses per minute or hour (Kunzelmann, 1970; White & Haring, 1980) and visually displayed on semilogarithmic graph paper as shown in Figure 7-1.

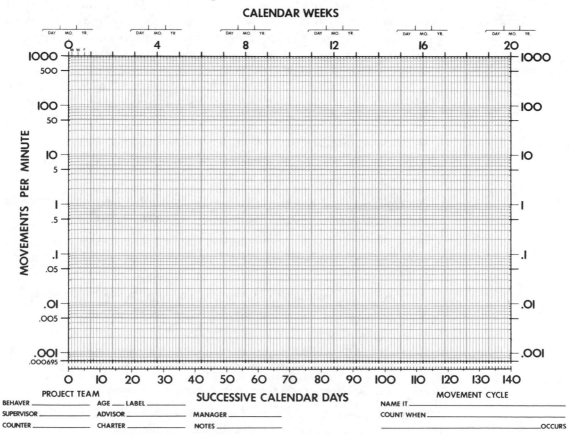

FIGURE 7-1   Semilogarithmic paper.

Although semilogarithmic paper is typically used to display rate data, equal interval graph paper can be used (Hart & Risley, 1968; Repp & Deitz, 1974; Tofte-Tipps, Mendonca, & Peach, 1982). Frequency data are typically reported as the number of responses per total observation period (i.e., data are not converted to responses per minute or hour) and are summarized on the more conventional equal interval graph paper.

Rate is an appropriate dependent measure when it is important to know how often a behavior occurs. It is a particularly useful measure when the intervention focuses on academic and social behaviors under free-operant conditions. Though it may be used during experimenter- or teacher-paced activities, it can become a cumbersome process. If used with teacher-paced instruction (i.e., the teacher controls the presentation of materials, cues, prompts, and consequences), the teacher has to start the stopwatch after the task direction has been presented and stop the stopwatch after the student has responded. By starting and stopping the stopwatch on each trial, an accurate measure of student response frequency can be attained. If this start and stop timing procedure were not employed, the time the teacher took to present task stimuli would be included in the total observation period, thereby affecting the response rate reported and reflecting teacher as well as student proficiency. In such instances the data would reflect changes in either the student's or teacher's rate of responding, or both.

Rate measures have several advantages (Eaton, 1978; Gentry & Haring, 1976; Haring, Liberty, & White, 1980):

1. They are extremely sensitive to behavior changes.

2. They convert behavior counts to a standard or constant scale (e.g., responses per minute), and when plotted on semilogarithmic graphs, they permit behavior comparison across different days and different activities when the amount of time to respond, or the number of opportunities to respond varies.

3. They may be evaluated using "data decision" rules (Eaton, 1978; Haring, Liberty, & White, 1980).

Rate data have two primary drawbacks. First, when the data are displayed visually on semilogarithmic graph paper, many people have difficulty analyzing the data because of their unfamiliarity with standard behavior charts. This disadvantage, however, can be overcome by plotting the rate data on the more conventional and familiar equal interval chart. The second disadvantage of frequency measures relates to their use during teacher-paced instruction. To ensure an accurate measure of student behavior during teacher-controlled instructional activities it is necessary, and often cumbersome, to measure only the actual amount of time the student has to respond. If a second observer is not available to do the timing, you are advised to use percent correct as the dependent measure on teacher-paced activities.

Duration
The choice of duration as a dependent measure is appropriate when you are interested in knowing how long a behavior occurs. There are two types of duration measures: total duration and duration per occurrence. *Total duration,*

which refers to the total amount of time a student is engaged in a behavior during an observation period, may be used to measure such behaviors as the amount of time a student engages in self-stimulatory behavior (e.g., Skiba, Pettigrew, & Alden, 1971) or how long a student is on-task (e.g., Konarski, Johnson, Crowell, & Whitman, 1980). In both cases the data collected are expressed in either the percentage of time or number of minutes engaged in the behavior. In the latter case you would most likely be interested in behavior endurance (i.e., shaping longer and longer periods of on-task behavior). Although appropriate in some instances, total duration typically is paired with some other measure (e.g., number or rate).

Unlike total duration, *duration per occurrence* provides data on both the frequency and the duration of a response. It is the preferred duration measure because it permits one to calculate the frequency of the behavior, the total duration of the behavior, as well as the range, mean, median, and mode duration of the behavior. This combination of frequency and duration measures yields a measure that is sometimes referred to as intensity. Through the use of the duration per occurrence measure both frequency and duration data can be obtained simultaneously. Both measures may prove helpful to a behavior analyst when deciding upon an intervention. For example, if you were concerned about one of your students who "appears" to be engaging in a considerable amount of off-task behavior (e.g., staring at the ceiling) but don't know whether this behavior is characterized by a high frequency and short duration or a low frequency and long duration, by employing a duration per occurrence measure you will be able to identify which of the behavior patterns best characterizes the student's off-task behavior. By having this information available you can then determine whether your intervention should focus on the frequency or duration of the student's off-task behavior. The more information you have on the target behavior, the more likely you are to design and implement an effective intervention package. With this in mind, it is recommended that you record duration per occurrence rather than total duration.

Latency
The latency of a response refers to the amount of time it takes a student to begin a response once the task direction or cue has been presented. Latency is an appropriate dependent measure when a student is slow to initiate a response, as in the case of following teacher directions: "Go to your desk." "Close your book." In addition to signalling a potential compliance problem, a latency measure can provide information regarding a student's understanding of a task's response requirements. A student with a long response latency may require additional instruction or modeling to clarify what response she is to make. In addition to long latencies, you should also be aware of students who have short latencies accompanied by high error rates. You might want to teach a student who manifests this behavior pattern to increase her response latency by requiring that she demonstrate an observing or attending response prior to emitting the terminal task response (e.g., saying the word she is to spell prior to spelling; pointing to the object she is to manually sign prior to signing).

Trials to Criterion

Trials to criterion is a dependent measure that is particularly useful when teaching concepts and operations. It refers to the number of trials (or opportunities to respond) that a student takes to reach a predetermined criterion. Reporting the number of opportunities it takes a student to reach criterion over successive examples of a concept or operation provides the behavior analyst with valuable information regarding the student's forming of a "learning set" (Reese & Lipsitt, 1970). Learning set, sometimes referred to as "learning to learn," is evident when, over successive examples of a concept, fewer trials are required to reach criterion. When a learner responds correctly to a novel example of a concept on the first trial, the learner is said to have learned that concept. Thus, instruction may cease on that concept and begin on another. In the case of motor imitation training, which is intended to teach a child to imitate a teacher's model after the verbal direction "do this," a learning-to-learn phenomenon would be demonstrated if with each new behavior modelled the student requires fewer trials to criterion. When the student can imitate a novel behavior in response to the teacher's model, the student is said to have acquired a generalized motor imitation repertoire. (Figure 8-6 shows how trials to criterion data are frequenty displayed.)

Trials to criterion is an appropriate dependent measure for monitoring student progress through a task analysis sequence (e.g., Feltz, 1980) or when the focus of an investigation is on skill generalization (e.g., Handleman, 1979). One should be aware, however, that trials to criterion measures provide summative, rather than formative evaluation of student progress. For this reason it is advisable that some other dependent measure, such as percent correct, be plotted daily and used to guide instruction.

Magnitude

Magnitude, an infrequently used dependent measure in classroom research, refers to the force or strength of a response. Typically, when magnitude is used as a dependent measure, some automated-quantitative apparatus is required to accurately measure the force of a behavior. Such has been the case in behavior management research designed to reduce classroom noise levels (e.g., Greene, Bailey, & Barber, 1981; Wilson & Hopkins, 1973). In some cases, the magnitude of a response may be determined by evaluating the effect a response has on the environment. For example, muscle strength may be inferred by recording how much weight one can lift, how far one can throw a ball, or how far one can jump. Though an indirect measure of strength, the above measures correlate with more sophisticated automated-quantitative measurement procedures. In addition to these measures of magnitude, the force of a response may be determined as being acceptable or unacceptable according to some criterion included in an operational definition of a behavior. For example, one may define acceptable speech volume on the basis of an observer being able to hear and understand what a student says when positioned no less than 5 feet and no more than 20 feet from the student. As is the case with all dependent measures, the important factor in determining the adequacy of a measure is whether two observers can agree on the occurrence and nonoccurrence of a behavior (i.e., interobserver reliability). For clarity it is best to operationalize a response and state exactly what measure (e.g., distance, weight) is being used to infer response magnitude when a more sophisticated automated-quantitative apparatus is not being used.

Selecting a Measurement Procedure

To this point we have presented a general overview of the basic characteristics and parameters of measurement and evaluation. The remainder of this chapter focuses on the process of systematically recording student behavior. Three basic methods are used to measure and record behavior: (1) automated-quantitative recording, (2) direct measurement of permanent products, and (3) direct observational recording. Emphasis is given to those direct observational recording systems commonly used by teachers and applied researchers that facilitate the reliable measurement of behavior. The present discussion is not intended to be exhaustive. More in-depth discussions on how to measure behavior have been presented elsewhere (Cartwright & Cartwright, 1974; Cooper, 1981; Irwin & Bushnell, 1980).

Automated-Quantitative Recording

Automated-quantitative recording, commonly referred to as automatic recording, is the use of an automatic recording device in which an "organism's response activates an electrical or mechanical apparatus which in turn makes a record, automatically recording each response" (Hall, 1974, p. 1). Though primarily associated with controlled laboratory research, automated-quantitative recording has been used on an experimental basis in home and classroom settings (Tawney, 1977).

Under the sponsorship of a federal contract program, the first author and others designed simple and complex systems to enable students to learn at home and communicate to "learning centers" through electronic transmission systems. Whether simple or complex, it is possible to design communication systems with very basic elements, e.g., press panels or levers that, when pressed, activate microswitches that send signals to an electronic switching apparatus (including microcomputer circuits) that in turn activate response recording devices, reinforcer dispensers, and other devices. As noted later in this chapter, as long as everything works, it is possible to obtain an accurate record of every response of interest to the experimenter.

In spite of its infrequent use in applied research, automated-quantitative recording has the advantage of eliminating the error element associated with human observers. There is, however, no guarantee that these sometimes sophisticated apparatuses will always operate properly. With the recent developments in the microcomputer industry and increasing interest in computer-assisted instruction, it will not be long before classrooms will be equipped with sophisticated automatic recording devices. Already microcomputers are becoming widely available in public school systems, particularly since computer manufacturers offer to give computers to school systems to encourage their use (and of course, to stimulate additional sales).

Students who show mild learning and behavior problems can interact directly with computers as they progress through academic materials. Students with severe physical handicaps can interact directly with computers through specially designed response devices. Aggressive, uncontrollable students can interact with computers through specially built, rugged and simplified response panels, while the computer itself is housed in a protected enclosure. Teachers may use microcomputers to record students' social behaviors by activating simple response counters that are wired into the microcomputer. If trends continue, the potential for computerized data recording and storage should increase dramatically, making it easy for teachers to document what happens in their classrooms.

Direct Measurement of Permanent Products

The direct measurement of permanent products refers to the measurement of some product following a response. It is undoubtedly the most common measurement strategy used by teachers. When teachers grade written assignments (e.g., math worksheets, spelling tests, English themes), evaluate the completion of assembly tasks (e.g., puzzles, bicycle brakes, circuitry boards), or review audio or video recordings of student behavior, they are engaged in the measurement of permanent products. This type of behavior recording is then translated into some numerical term, usually number, frequency, or percent correct.

The direct measurement of permanent products has several advantages for classroom teachers. First, it is practical with a large number of students in the class, a situation in which it is impractical for a teacher to directly observe each student performing each assignment. Second, it is nonintrusive; that is, it does not detract attention from an ongoing lesson. Third, it yields precise records of student behavior which can often be stored for later comparison (e.g., written assignments, audio and video recordings). Fourth, it permits the objective evaluation of interobserver agreement by presenting observers with completed assignments in random order. Fifth, it is conducive to "seat work" and other auto-instructional or independent work assignments.

Generally, the measurement of permanent products is recommended for classroom research that focuses on academic behaviors. In addition, audio and video recordings can prove helpful when conducting research on more basic skills (e.g., oral reading, assembly tasks, self-care skills) and when the focus is on shaping more appropriate social behavior. When a subject's behavior is being recorded continuously through the use of an audio or video recording system (e.g., oral reading of a passage), the dependent measure (e.g., number of mispronounced words) is counted by using one of the direct observational recording systems (e.g., event recording, interval recording).

Direct Observational Recording

Direct observational recording refers to observing and quantifying behavior as it occurs; it is a fundamental component of applied behavior analysis research. There are several types of direct observational recording procedures; the more common ones are summarized in Table 7-2.

Event recording (frequency count). Event recording is the simplest and least time-consuming method for recording the frequency of a behavior. It entails tallying, typically by means of placing a mark on a piece of paper or on a blackboard, every time the target behavior occurs. This results in a count of the number of times the target behavior occurred within the total observation period. Provided one has accurately timed the period of observation, it is possible to calculate and report a subject's rate of responding. For example,

TABLE 7-2   Summary of direct observational recording systems.

Procedure	Operation
Event Recording	Count or tally each time the target behavior occurs within the observation period.
Duration Recording	*a*. Total Duration: Start the stopwatch when behavior begins and stop the stopwatch when behavior ends. Do *not* reset the stopwatch after each occurrence of the behavior. Record the total length of the observation period.
	b. Duration Per Occurrence: Start the stopwatch when the behavior begins and stop the stopwatch when it ends. Record the elapsed time on a data sheet and reset the stopwatch. Repeat the process for the observation period. Record the total length of the observation period.
Latency Recording	Start the stopwatch immediately after the presentation of the S^D (task direction) and stop the stopwatch upon the subject's initiation of the response. Record the elapsed time on a data sheet and reset the stopwatch. Repeat the process for each trial or opportunity to respond.
Interval Recording	Divide the observation period into small equal intervals. Record the occurrence or nonoccurrence of the target behavior *during* each interval.
Time Sample Recording	Divide the observation period into equal or unequal intervals. Record the occurrence or nonoccurrence of the target behavior at the *end* of each interval.
Placheck Recording	Divide the observation into equal or unequal intervals. At the *end* of each interval count the number of subjects engaged in the target behavior (or at each available activity).

when the target behavior is being observed during a free-operant period, the observer need only record the start and stop times of the observational period, subtract the latter from the former, convert the remainder to minutes, and divide the number of behavior counts into the number of minutes in which the subject was observed. This will yield the standard measure of rate (i.e., responses per minute). When the target behavior is being counted during a teacher-paced activity, calculating an accurate rate measure becomes more cumbersome.

Cooper (1981) and Scott and Goetz (1980) have listed several commercially available and teacher-made devices which may facilitate collecting frequency data. These include wrist golf counters, hand tally digital counters, wrist tally boards, masking tape bracelets, beaded tally bracelets, digital counters that attach to pencils, and tally notecards that are taped to students' desks. Figure 7-2 shows a sample data recording form appropriate for collecting frequency data. This data collection form, as well as the above-mentioned frequency count devices, also can be used with audio and video recordings of student behavior when number or rate is the dependent measure.

Duration and latency recording. Duration recording involves collecting data on how long a behavior occurs. As previously discussed, there are two types of duration measures: total duration and duration per occurrence. *Total duration* is recorded by starting a stopwatch when the behavior is initiated

S's Name_____   Date_____

T's Name_____   Behavior_____

Session #_____   Condition_____

Start Time_____ Stop Time_____ = Total Time_____

Directions: Tally number of occurrences

Summary: 1. Total number of occurrences _____

2. Rate (Rs/minute)   _____

3. Reliability percentage   _____%

FIGURE 7-2   Sample event data collection form.

and stopping the stopwatch when the behavior ceases to occur. When the next episode of the behavior is initiated, the observer starts the timing device again *without* resetting the time. At the end of the observation period the observer has data on the total number of minutes (or seconds) the behavior occurred during the observation period. Provided one has an accurate measure of the total observation period, it is possible to summarize the duration data in terms of the percentage of time the subject engaged in the behavior. However, when total duration is the dependent variable, there are no data on the frequency of the behavior. If frequency data are also desired, the observer should use the duration per occurrence recording procedure.

When recording *duration per occurrence,* the observer starts and stops the stopwatch with each occurrence of the behavior. Each time the behavior occurs, the observer records the duration (length of time) of the response. After recording the time on a separate data form, the observer resets the stopwatch and prepares to record the duration of the next behavior occurrence. A primary advantage of the duration per occurrence method is that it yields data on behavior frequency, the duration of the behavior per occurrence, and total duration. Therefore, this procedure provides several alternative methods for summarizing the data: total number of behavior occurences, rate of occurrence, mean duration per occurrence, total duration per observation period, and percentage of time engaged in the behavior per observation period. Duration per occurrence is the preferred duration recording method. Figure 7-3 shows a data recording form appropriate for collecting and summarizing duration per occurrence data.

Duration recording is the appropriate direct observational recording procedure when the target behavior occurs at unacceptable long durations or inappropriate short durations. In both cases the focus of intervention likely would be to positively affect the response duration of the target behavior

```
S's Name_____     Date_____

T's Name_____     Behavior/Task_____

Session #_____     Condition_____

Start Time_____ Stop Time_____ = Total Time_____
```

N	duration/latency per occurrence	N	duration/latency per occurence
1		6	
2		7	
3		8	
4		9	
5		10	

```
Summary:  1. Total number of occurrences        _____

          2. Mean duration/latency per occurrence _____

          3. Range                               _____
```

FIGURE 7-3   Sample latency or duration per occurrence data collection form.

(e.g., decrease the duration of body rocking; increase the duration of working on an assignment unassisted). As a general rule, when one is concerned with how long a student or class engages in a behavior, duration recording should be used (Cooper, 1981).

Latency recording, in contrast to duration recording, focuses on the time elapsed from when a student has an opportunity to respond (e.g., presentation of the task direction "Begin reading aloud") to when the student initiates the response (student reads the first word aloud). This elapsed time, or latency, is recorded by starting the stopwatch immediately after the presentation of the task direction (cue) and stopping the stopwatch when the student initiates the response. The observer then records the elapsed time on a summary data form similar to that presented in Figure 7-3. These data can be used to compute latency per task direction as well as mean response latency. Latency recording is a particularly useful recording procedure when collecting data on students who have a long response latency or students who have a particularly short response latency accompanied by a high error rate. Latency recording may be used with free-operant activities when one is interested in how long it takes a student to respond to another student's presence, as in a free play situation, or how long it takes a student to put in a second puzzle piece after the first puzzle piece is in place. Both latency and duration recording are important direct observational recording systems when response proficiency is of primary concern.

Interval recording. Interval recording is a frequently used data collection procedure in applied research even though it requires the undivided attention of the observer. It has sometimes been referred to as the "workhorse" of applied behavior analysis. Interval recording requires dividing the total

S's Name_____   Date_____

O's Name_____   Behavior_____

Condition_____

Start Time_____ Stop Time_____ = Total Time_____

(Code: √ occurence;   - nonoccurence)

1'				2'				3'				4'				5'			
15"	15"	15"	15"	15"	15"	15"	15"	15"	15"	15"	15"	15"	15"	15"	15"	15"	15"	15"	15"

6'				7'				8'				9'				10'			
15"	15"	15"	15"	15"	15"	15"	15"	15"	15"	15"	15"	15"	15"	15"	15"	15"	15"	15"	15"

Summary: Number of Nonoccurrences_____ Percentage of Nonoccurrences_____%   Number of Occurrences_____ Percentage of Occurrences_____%

FIGURE 7-4   **Sample interval recording data collection form for recording behavior occurrences (√) and nonoccurrences(-) or tallying within intervals.**

observation period into small equal intervals of time and recording the occurrence or nonoccurrence of the target behavior *during* each interval (e.g., Apolito & Sulzer-Azaroff, 1981; Fantuzzo & Clement, 1981; Hauserman, Walen, & Behling, 1973). Figure 7-4 exemplifies a typical interval recording data form.

When using an interval recording system it is important to select an appropriate interval size (e.g., 10 seconds, 15 seconds, 1 minute). The size of the interval during which behavior occurrences will be recorded will determine the maximum behavior frequency which can be reported. For example, the maximum frequency when using a 10-second interval recording system is 6 responses per minute; if a 20-second interval recording system were used, the maximum response frequency would be 3 responses per minute. Therefore, it is important that the interval size chosen approximate the natural frequency and duration of the behavior to be recorded. That is, with high frequency behaviors of short duration, one should use small time intervals (e.g., 10-second intervals (Nordquist & Wahler, 1973); with low frequency behaviors and behaviors with long durations, one should use larger time intervals (e.g., 2-minute intervals) (Hauserman, Walen, & Behling, 1973). It is important to remember that the interval recording system yields only approximations of behavior frequency and duration.

As described thus far, interval recording has been defined as a binary (occurrence-nonoccurrence) recording procedure. There are, however, other ways in which to record behavior using the interval recording system. Two frequently used interval recording procedures are (1) tallying the number of times a behavior occurs during each interval and (2) using an observational code to record the occurrence or nonoccurrence of several target behaviors within an interval.

Tallying has the advantage of yielding a precise measure of response frequency. By using a tally of each behavior occurrence, the observer can determine the appropriateness of the interval size. This is done by noting the number of tallies recorded during each interval and adjusting the interval size accordingly. If, for example, there are several tallies within a large number of single observation intervals, the interval size is too large and should be shortened. The converse is also true; if there are a large number of intervals in which no tallies are recorded, the interval is too short and should be lengthened.

A second, common modification or variation of scoring with the interval recording system is the use of behavioral codes (e.g., Cohen, Polsgrove, Rieth, & Heinen, 1981; Strain & Timm, 1974; VanBiervliet, Spangler, & Marshall, 1981). The use of a behavioral code with the interval recording system entails assigning some code or symbol to each target behavior that is of interest to the observer. If a targeted behavior occurs during the interval, the observer records the appropriate code. As with the binary recording procedure, only one occurrence of each target behavior is recorded in each interval. Figure 7-5 is an example of a behavioral coding data form appropriate for use with an interval recording system. Though potentially cumbersome, behavior coding is particularly useful when collecting data on several behaviors of one subject (e.g., body rocking, finger twirling, head weaving) or when studying the social interactions of several subjects.

A word of caution is appropriate here. When using an interval recording system to monitor several behaviors during the same observation interval, it is advised that a "partial interval" or noncontinous observation control procedure be employed (e.g., Ivancic, Reid, Iwata, Faw, & Page, 1981). Simply described, a noncontinous observation control procedure entails alternating intervals for *observing* response occurrences with intervals for *recording* response occurrences observed in the preceding interval. For example, if a teacher is observing three behaviors using a 10-second interval recording system, the first 10-second interval is used to observe the occurrence of each behavior and the second 10-second interval is used to record which target behaviors occurred during the first 10-second interval. After 10 seconds have elapsed, the observer again observes for another 10-second interval. This alternation of observing and recording periods is used to facilitate accurate recording of behavior since an observer does not record responses during an observation interval. Without such alternation the probability is higher that an observer may not observe the occurrence of a behavior emitted in the first few seconds of each observation interval. This could, of course, adversely effect reliability.

When using an interval recording system, some signalling device is required to mark the beginning and end of an observational interval. Devices used for this purpose have included kitchen timers, audio cassette recorders using tone-cued or "interval-number-cued" audiotapes ("one start-one stop," "two start-two stop," etc.) and "on-off" light-cued devices. It is also possible, and possibly more practical in educational settings, to have a second observer

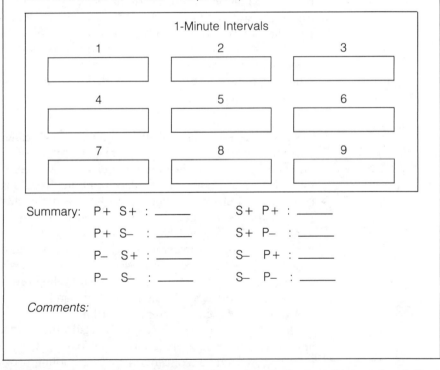

S's Name_____   Date_____

O's Name_____   Behavior(s)_____

Other Students Present   Condition_____

                                 Activity_____

_____ _____
_____ _____
_____ _____

Start Time_____ Stop Time_____ = Total Time_____

Code: + positive   P peer
          − negative   S subject

Directions: For each interaction, record who initiated the interaction (P or S), whether it was appropriate or inappropriate (+ or −), and the response to the initiation (P+ or P−; S+ or S−). (*Note:* Refer to behavioral definitions for + and − responses.)

1-Minute Intervals

1	2	3
4	5	6
7	8	9

Summary: P+ S+ : _____   S+ P+ : _____

           P+ S− : _____   S+ P− : _____

           P− S+ : _____   S− P+ : _____

           P− S− : _____   S− P− : _____

Comments:

FIGURE 7-5   Sample interval recording data collection form using behavioral codes.

with a stopwatch time each observation interval and in some way cue the teacher or primary observer when to move to the next interval. This can be done via manual signs or gestures, or by the second observer using flashcards to signal the start of the next interval. After deciding upon a signalling device, it is important that one practice with it before starting a study and be sensitive to any changes in subject behavior as a function of the device. For example, a tone-cued audio signalling device that can be heard by students could affect their behavior. If one is not sensitive to the potential influence of the signalling device on behavior, one may mistakenly credit the independent variable with affecting change, when in fact the responsible variable may be the students' awareness that their behavior is being observed and recorded. Whenever possible, subjects should be unaware that their behavior is being monitored, except of course when knowledge of being observed is the independent variable. When using tone cues to signal interval changes, one should use an earphone and wear the earphone immediately preceding the study, so that students can adapt to its presence before data collection begins.

As mentioned briefly, the primary disadvantage of interval recording in educational settings is that it requires continuous observer attention during the data collection process. Thus, it is sometimes an impractical procedure because it is cumbersome for teachers to deliver instruction and concurrently record student behavior. It becomes more practical, however, when ancillary teaching personnel are used as observers and when teachers are not required to interact with students during data collection (Cooper, 1981). In spite of this disadvantage, interval recording is a versatile direct observational recording procedure that offers several advantages. First, it provides an estimate of both frequency and duration. Second, it reacts to behaviors of high frequency but with short duration and to behaviors of low frequency but with long durations. Third, interval recording permits more precise statements of interobserver agreement by permitting computation of point-by-point reliability coefficients. When both response frequency and duration are of interest and when a behavior is emitted under free-operant conditions, the interval recording system merits consideration.

Time sample recording. Time sampling, a recording procedure similar to interval recording, provides an estimate of response frequency (and perhaps duration) by periodically sampling behavior. With time sample recording the total observation period is divided into equal (e.g., Fishbein & Wasik, 1981) or variable (Kubany & Sloggett, 1973), time units, at the *end* of which one records the occurrence or nonoccurrence of the target behavior. Unlike interval recording, which requires the observer to continuously monitor behavior during the interval, time sample recording only requires that one look for the occurrence or nonoccurrence of the behavior at the end of each interval. As with interval recording, time sampling requires a signalling device to cue the observer as to when to observe and record the behavior.

A variation of the time sample recording procedure, referred to as *placheck* (Risley, 1971), has been discussed by Hall (1974). *Placheck* is a particularly appropriate recording procedure when one's interest is in recording group behavior. As with the conventional time sampling procedure, the total observation period is divided into equal or variable intervals. At the end of each interval the observer does two things: (1) counts and records the number of subjects engaged in the target behavior (e.g., actively writing on the assignment) and (2) counts and records the number of subjects who should be engaged in the target behavior. By dividing the former by the latter and multiplying the result by 100, one can determine what percentage of subjects in the group was engaged in the behavior at the end of each interval. This information could prove useful to a classroom teacher who is concerned about the on-task behavior of the class as a whole and who wishes to modify the class's on-task behavior.

Placheck has been used in a variety of settings, including day-care centers (Doke & Risley, 1972; LeLaurin & Risley, 1974). In educational settings placheck may be helpful in identifying preferred student activities and toys, i.e., assist in developing reinforcer hierarchies. This could be accomplished by counting the number of students engaged in each available activity (e.g., checkers, computer game, cards, weight lifting, and reading) and dividing the total number of students participating in each activity by the total number of students participating in free time. The result would then be multiplied by 100 and would yield the percentage of students engaged in each activity. This information could assist a teacher to determine the value of each activity prior to establishing a classroom token economy system.

Time sample recording has an important advantage over interval recording relative to collecting data in educational settings. Unlike interval recording, which requires the undivided attention of an observer during the observation period, time sample recording requires that an observer look for an occurrence of the behavior for only a moment at the end of each interval. Because of this procedural difference, time sample recording is a more practical direct observation recording system than is interval recording when a teacher is required to provide instruction and record data concurrently. The data collection formats used with time sample and placheck recording are similar to those used with interval recording (see Figure 7-6).

Designing Data Collection Forms

In Figures 7-2 through 7-6 we have presented several sample data collection forms. You will note that each data sheet presents three types of information: (1) situational, (2) performance, and (3) summary, as recommended by McCormack and Chalmers (1978). Each section or type of information pre-

S's Name_____   Date_____

O's Name_____   Behavior_____

                                   Condition_____

time	occur	nonoccur	time	occur	nonoccur	
1:00			1:30			Summary:
1:05			1:35			Total occurrence _____
1:10			1:40			Percent occurrence _____%
1:15			1:45			Total nonoccurrence _____
1:20			1:50			Percent nonoccurrence _____%
1:25			1:55			

FIGURE 7-6   Sample interval or time sample recording data collection form for recording behavior occurrences (√) and nonoccurrences (-) or tallying within intervals.

sented is important to the data collection and analysis process. Though data sheet formats will vary depending on the type of data collected, the recording system employed, the target behavior and task, the type of observational period (teacher-paced or free-operant), and the intervention strategy, each data form should present at least the information discussed below.

Situational Information

Situational information should reflect the following:

1. Subject's name
2. Date of observation
3. Starting and stopping times of observational period
4. Behavior or task (instructional objective) on which data are collected
5. Experimental condition and phase (Baseline; Training-CRF Schedule; Training-VR3 schedule)
6. Instructor's or data collector's name

Performance Information

The performance information section of a data collection sheet is that portion of the data form where a subject's responses are recorded during the observational period. It is important that this section be as simple as possible, yet provide sufficient information for analyzing a subject's response patterns. Several different performance information sections have been presented in figures 7-2–7-6. Figures 7-7–7-9 present additional performance information section formats commonly used by educators. When recording data during teacher-paced instructional programs, the following information should be provided:

1. Student response code
2. Trial number
3. Discriminative stimulus
4. Stimulus choices
5. Student's response
6. Teacher's consequation of student's response

Summary Information

Summary information should include the following:

1. Total session time
2. Total number of correct and incorrect responses (or total number of occurrences)
3. Percentage of correct responses
4. Reliability coefficient
5. Comments

The importance of the data collection sheet, and an investigator's proficient use of it, cannot be underestimated. It is the vehicle through which a subject's behavior is quantified and analyzed and, therefore, it deserves one's time and careful attention. It is advisable to design data forms so that all reasonable

Trial	S^D		Choices		Student Response	Consequation
1	"spoon"	fork	knife	spoon	+ / −	S^r+
2	___	___	___	___	+ / −	10" TO
3	___	___	___	___	+ / −	
etc.						

FIGURE 7-7   **Sample data sheet performance information section appropriate for match-to-sample or receptive language tasks during teacher-paced instruction.**

Trial	S^D	Student Response	S^r	Consequation Correction	S^r+
1	that	+	√		
2	the	−		√	
3					
etc.					

FIGURE 7-8   **Sample data sheet performance information section appropriate for expressive language tasks during teacher-paced instruction.**

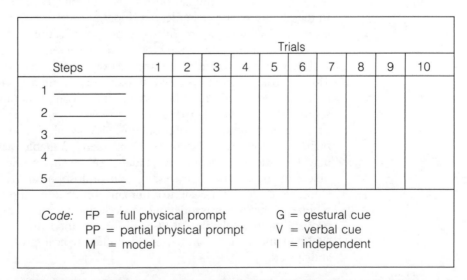

FIGURE 7-9   **Sample data sheet performance information section appropriate for task-analyzed skills during teacher-paced instruction.**

variables that might influence behavior are recorded (e.g., time of day, length of session, consequences delivered, instructor, choice stimuli). Such detail will permit an analysis of errors in the event variable response patterns emerge. If practical constraints require deletion of some information from the data collection form, one should take great care in deciding which information to include and which to exclude. Such caution is warranted because the most obvious data are not necessarily those that provide clues to identifying those variables that influence behavior.

Reliable Measurement

Obtaining reliable measurement is a major task for every researcher. It is a simple matter for the experimental laboratory researcher to describe the physical properties of a Plexiglas press panel and the grams of force required to close a microswitch that is triggered by a peck or paw press. However, that microswitch is attached to complex electronic circuitry and mechanical recording devices, all preprogrammed to self-destruct at different times, each a maximally inopportune time—or so it must seem to the experimenter. Thus, while it is easy to describe behavior in this setting, achieving reliable measurement involves a continual fight against mechanical failure. In the classroom, it may be possible to develop a mechanical recording system for some behaviors, but often it is not practical to do so. Further, there is a wide range of behaviors that cannot be measured by mechanical devices. Consequently, applied behavior research utilizes human observers to record behavioral events.

The use of human observers offers many advantages to the researcher. One observer provides an independent record of data; two or more observers generate additional data. Under certain conditions, it is typical for researchers to report high percentages of agreement between or among observers, and thus increase readers' confidence that the data present a "true picture" of the events that actually occurred. However, using human rather than mechanical recording systems simply trades one set of problems for another. The problems that arise with human observers are easily identified and well reported in the literature. For example, developing observer training programs may be expensive. Observers are intrusive and may require long periods of pre-experiment adaptation in the classroom. Observers' recordings can be biased and may drift (away from a standard) during the course of an experiment. The recording system used will influence an observer's recording; if simple, behavior definitions may be too broad, if complex, (and thus difficult to score) the possibility of error increases. Once recorded, reporting interobserver data presents another set of problems. Simple calculations will present a false picture in some circumstances. Conversely, available statistical procedures may be little understood by student- or teacher-researchers. Others may object to the statistical procedures on philosophical grounds (Baer, 1977). Here, we discuss the design of human observations and behavior recording schemes. Our focus is on how to do it, and further, how to increase the probability that reliable results will be obtained. In essence, we have task analyzed the process and then identified typical problems that might be anticipated.

Selection and Training of Human Observers

Selection of observers is usually done pragmatically, i.e., who's around to do the job? Funded researchers support graduate students who may observe or who may train paid undergraduates. Unfunded graduate students, as we suggest later, may form a pool of peer volunteers, who serve on each other's projects. In the schools, a teacher-researcher might call upon students, parents, or supervisors to conduct reliability checks. Though observer selection is dictated by environmental conditions and though there is no major data base indicating that one group or another represents a better choice of individuals for training, there is sufficient research to identify maximally effective training procedures. The following conditions represent the ideal:

1. Observers should remain naive to the purposes of the experiment.

2. Observers should be trained to a high degree of proficiency *before* the experiment.

3. Observers should be retrained, or "recalibrated," during the course of an experiment, particularly if it extends over a long period of time.

4. Interobserver communication should be constrained, or clearly defined, to limit possible bias or reinterpretation of behavior definitions.

5. The observation training system should be a close approximation of the situation to be observed.

These conditions may be difficult to approximate in ongoing classroom research. Yet, given these standards, the researcher should be able to develop an alternative strategy to compensate for potential weaknesses, e.g., if the purpose of a study must remain hidden, then high school student volunteers would be a better choice than parents, all things considered.

The observer training system should be kept as simple as possible. The researcher should:

1. Develop a training manual, using a minimum number of directions stated in simple sentences.

2. Search relevant studies for commonly used behavior definitions and use, or model from them to avoid ambiguity.

3. Define the rules (etiquette) for observing:
   a. How and when to enter the classroom,
   b. Where to sit,
   c. How to interact or avoid specific topics with school personnel or children,
   d. How to handle problem situations, e.g., ignoring the nontarget *S* who is pulling at your coattail,
   e. what to do with the data, once it has been recorded.

4. Obtain training tapes that are closely related to the setting and circumstances in which the study will be conducted. These tapes might be obtained by:
   a. Contacting other researchers who have conducted similar studies to obtain copies of their tapes.
   b. Seeking out tape libraries in the university or school environment. It is

possible that a university preschool might have a library of tapes of certain types of activities or interactions, and, further, that parental permission has been obtained for professional use of the tapes. Or, the psychology department may have the same type of information. In the schools, the central administration might have copies of "model projects" conducted within the system. Or, individual teachers may have similar records.

c. Obtaining video equipment and develop training tapes on one's own. These may require permissions, as discussed in the chapter on ethical procedures.

5. With the tapes, and the recording system that has been selected, observe tapes with others to develop a scoring chart so that trainees' records can be compared to an accurate, defined standard.

6. Implement the training program.

7. Collect data on observers' trials to criterion since that is a datum little reported in the research.

These basic procedures should result in an observer training program that is clear and simple to learn, the complexity of the recording system notwithstanding. When implemented, the outcome should be a group of observers who can accurately score observations in the presence of a defined standard. Whether these observers will agree when they observe in the classroom is yet another matter. That will depend in large part on the extent to which training conditions match actual conditions and on the nature of the recording system.

Recording System Options

Kelly (1977) analyzed all the articles that appeared in the *Journal of Applied Behavior Analysis,* from its inception through 1975, to identify the type of data-recording systems used in the research reports. As shown in Table 7-3, the majority report observational data. Reliability data were reported in 94%

TABLE 7-3 *JABA* data collection survey.

Information Reported	Percentage of Research Reports	
	293 Published	222 with Observation Data
Observational Data	76%	
Only Mechanically Collected Data	16%	
Only Permanent-Product Data	8%	
Reliability		94%
Reliability on Every Session		9%
Reliability in Each Condition		23%
Event Recording		29%
Trial Scoring		35%
Interval Recording		20%
Time-Sample Recording		21%
Response Duration		9%
Other		6%
Unidentifiable		2%

From: Kelly, M.B. A review of the observational data-collection and reliability procedures reported in the *Journal of Applied Behavior Analysis. Journal of Applied Behavior Analysis,* 1977, *10* (1), 97–101.

of the studies. Since the types of recording systems encompass those in current use, this table serves as the focal point for describing currently used and other recording systems.

The choice of recording system is determined by the topography of the behavior target. Some academic targets, such as correct math problems completed per 10-minute session, can be calculated from permanent products, such as the written responses on the math paper. These are not of concern here since scorers' agreement is straightforward (the answer is correct/incorrect, assuming it is legible). Other academic targets, e.g., correct vocalization of speech sounds, however, will require a different recording system, as social behavior targets. Our focus here is on recording systems that require direct human observation of behavior—not written products.

No recording system will measure everything. Each represents a trade-off; it will "catch" the behavior of interest—most of the time—but will also miss much. The researcher's task is to develop a system that represents the most accurate picture of her target behavior change. To illustrate, the simplest way to record is simply to write down in narrative form everything that occurs. Wright (1967), for example, presents a methodology for analyzing the "behavior stream" of the child in her surroundings. Within the context of the classroom, the observer writes, in simple sentences, what Ralph does all day long (or during math). There are problems with this system. Writing and watching are incompatible behaviors. While the observer is writing, Ralph may be doing something else, and thus the written record is a partial record. Or, Ralph may be emitting a behavior at a high rate, and it is impossible to record each instance. In other words, the flow of the behavior stream is too fast for the observer. Yet another problem is that two observers are unlikely to write equivalent narratives, and thus it may be difficult to obtain an accurate description of the observed behavior. Finally, unless behavior accounts are sparse, "Ralph stood on his head," the observer's judgments may creep into the report. "Under attack, Ralph rapidly ran and hid under the teacher's desk," thus expanding the record to include observations and observer reactions. Bijou, Peterson, and Ault (1968) have commented further on this behavioral recording method, which, with reference to Table 7-3, you will note does not appear in the behavioral literature surveyed by Kelly (1977).

Event Recording

The next most complex system is *event recording*. If a behavior occurs at a low and steady rate it is possible that every event will be recorded; if behavior is emitted at a high rate, e.g., nearly continual fist hits to the forehead, then some instances will be lost. A major problem, described in the next section, is obtaining interobserver reliability. Another problem with this, and all occurrence records, is that an instance of behavior tells nothing about the topography of the response. If a child cries, how long does she cry? Does she wail or just sob quietly? This problem is addressed when the researcher develops the behavior definition, but rarely is it possible to provide an exact and exhaustive record.

Trial Recording

Trial recording provides one way to break the "behavior stream" into quantifiable elements and consequents. A correct response is defined in the behavioral objective. After the S^D (teacher request) the subject (1) responds correctly, (2) makes an error, or (3) does not respond at all; in each case time passes, the trial ends, and the sequence is repeated. This method is useful in certain instructional programs, but much of the instructional universe does not divide itself easily into learning trials. The method typically is not used for social behavior targets.

The recording systems described thus far are continuous systems, that is, observation begins—the subject responds and the events are described or recorded—and then the session ends. They all share two inherent problems. First, the observer must attend throughout the session or risk missing responses. Second, when two observers record simultaneously, it may be difficult to obtain agreement between their records. To compensate for these problems, a number of strategies have been employed to (1) divide the time into smaller units, (2) provide "rest" time for the observer by classifying units as "observe," "record," "rest," etc., (3) allow for more accurate *sampling* across these units.

Interval Recording

Interval recording systems typically divide time into units that are recorded consecutively. *Time* may be continuous, but only the first response that occurs in the interval is recorded. The observer can record that event, then "rest" and record nothing else in the interval. Clearly, this method may provide a distorted picture of reality. If the researcher chooses a long interval, e.g., 1 minute, to record a behavior that occurs at a high rate, e.g., 5 talk-outs a minute, then ⅘ of the data is lost. Or, if the target behavior occurs with extreme cyclic variation, the form of the response curve will be lost. Suppose that the subject's response pattern is typical of that generated by an FI schedule. A recording, derived from an electronically controlled event recorder, would show the typical scallop and then the response bursts at the end of the interval. An interval system as described here will miss (ignore) all the responses in the burst except the first.

Time sampling systems are interval records that contain breaks between observation intervals, e.g., *10* seconds *on* and *5* seconds *off* provides 4 observations per minute, and 20 seconds to rest, reorient, calibrate timers and so on. This is an example of partial interval recording, as defined earlier in this chapter. Behaviors occurring in the *off* periods are lost. If *on* intervals are long, bursts will be lost, just as in interval recording. Conversely, if intervals are short and the break between observation periods is short, the task becomes more difficult, particularly when two observers are attempting to manage a clock or light signal to insure they are recording *on* the same interval. This system is the most complex from a management perspective. The trade-offs are clear. Long observation intervals with reasonable time breaks will make the observer's task easy but will miss a large amount of data. Short intervals with little time between observation intervals will catch most of the data but increase the complexity of the task for the recorder.

Duration Recording

Recording the *duration* of a response is employed when it is important to know how long a behavior occurs. Suppose that a child cries continuously, e.g., the child is put to bed, cries, and maintains her parent's attention, documented by their continual parade in and out of the bedroom to comfort her. Knowing that the behavior lasts for hours, until she falls asleep exhausted, is more critical than the information that she responds one time nightly (frequency). Of course, it is possible to sample across time intervals and find a response occurring 100% of the time. Duration does not provide a measure of the magnitude of the response, a factor which must be accounted for by response (behavior) definition. As noted in Table 7-3, duration is not a frequently used measure.

In summary, there is no best way to develop a recording system. Whatever decision is made, something will be gained and something lost. The student-researcher is advised to read carefully those articles that are closely related to the topic she wishes to study. These will describe the most frequently used systems for that area (target behavior). Narrative accounts in the discussion sections of those articles may tell what the researcher hit or missed and how the recording system may provide an inaccurate view of the effect of an intervention. For example, one of our master's students recently completed a study designed to reduce several behaviors in a day-care program. The recording system, including the behavior definition, was insensitive to the change from wailing to barely audible crying. On that target (crying), there was no documented effect, although there was a change in the topography of the behavior. Finally, the student-researcher should select two or more alternatives, e.g., 10 seconds *on*–5 seconds *off*, 30 seconds on–10 seconds off, and conduct a short pilot test in the environment. These data records and the best advice from the literature will provide a starting point for the development of a maximally representative recording system.

Calculation of Interobserver Reliability

All the efforts described thus far (train observers well; use unambiguous behavior codes; maintain accurate observer recording; develop a recording system that best approximates reality) are intended to produce one outcome. They increase the probability that two observers will observe the same thing and agree on what they saw. For if there is little agreement, then there are two views of reality. The greater the discrepancy between them, the less confidence is permitted the researcher. Without reliability there is no basis for entertaining the validity of an intervention program.

There is extensive literature on the "proper" method for calculating interobserver reliability. It is best described by the title of an article, "Why the 'I've got a better agreement measure' literature continues to grow . . ." (Cone, 1979): a reaction to yet another method for calculating reliability.

The measurement issues can best be viewed within the historical context of the growth of applied behavior analysis. The first token economy studies employed human observers in the classroom setting. The researchers who initiated these programs went to great lengths to establish rigorous control in what was a first venture into the schools for some of them. Observer training was a major part of these research projects, one which consumed time, money, and staff hours to supervise observers. As these studies were implemented, problems arose with human observers. In one instance (Kuypers, Becker, & O'Leary, 1968), a study was terminated partly because of the inappropriate behaviors exhibited by the observers. Due to these problems observer behavior became a subject of research. Then, as observer behavior was manipulated, the correspondence between observer records was closely examined, and, in turn, it became apparent that under some circumstances interobserver reliability measures yielded spurious results. This finding then led to a search for a better reliability measure. This search was stimulated, in part, by a series of articles which appeared in special issues of *JABA* (Vol. 10, No. 1, 1977; Vol. 12, No. 4, 1979).

The problem is that when you ask the question "Did both observers see the same thing (events)?", the answer is not a simple yes or no. Instead, it is "Sometimes they did, and sometimes they didn't." The next question, then, is to what extent did they agree? That answer is influenced by the way the recording system is constructed and how the data from two observer records are compared. Both topics are addressed here.

Event Recording Systems

Event recording, as noted, simply requires that an observer record all the target behaviors that occur during the session, lesson, or specified time period. At the end of the observation, the number of events is tallied. When two observers record during the same period, the agreement between their records is typically obtained by dividing the smaller score by the larger score. This method has frequently been referred to as the *gross method* for calculating reliability. If both record the same number of events, then their agreement is 1.0 or 100%. Any score less than that, multiplied by 100, will yield a percent of agreement. The problem is that this method does not permit the researcher to state that both observers saw the same thing or that the events they agreed on were all the same events. Table 7-4 illustrates the problem. The top row represents the true case. The next row shows that Observer 1 made an *x* for every talk-out she saw (heard). The bottom row contains an *x* for each event Observer 2 recorded. How could this have happened? Suppose that the study was conducted in an old school building in poor repair. Suppose that, just as the teacher announced, "Class, your 30-minute study period will begin now," a large fly slipped through a torn screen and settled on the nose of Observer 1. Preoccupied with the fly, she missed the first five events that were recorded by Observer 2, who recorded all the events until the 16th, when the fly settled on her nose. Given that 20 talk-outs were emitted, what can be said about these records? First, to calculate percent agreements, remember that each observer provides the researcher only with a record of frequencies. Dividing the smaller by the larger, 14 divided by 15 = .93 × 100 = 93% agreement. Not bad—but since we have arranged these records so they can be compared with the true case to show how each observer treated each event, it is clear that the 93% agreement statistic does not tell all there is to know.

Remember that we have created the true case (assume it is a video recording obtained through a permanently installed camera that "caught" all of Grace's talk-outs) for the purpose of illustration. Observer 1 recorded

TABLE 7-4   Grace's talk-outs during 30-minute study periods.

True Case	T	T	T	T	T	T	T	T	T	T	T	T	T	T	T	T	T	T	T	T
Observer 1						x	x	x	x	x	x	x	x	x	x	x	x	x	x	x
Observer 2	x	x	x	x	x	x	x	x	x	x	x	x	x	x	x					

$14/20$ or 70% of the events; Observer 2, $15/20$ or 75%. These percentages are less impressive than the agreement score, but in the typical study these data can never be computed because there is no way to document "the true case." (The situation would be different from that in a clinical psychology laboratory, where the "true case" was first captured on videotape, scored by different observers at some later date).

Now, to look at the record again, to what extent did the observers record the same behavior? Both observers scored 10 of the same events out of 20, or 50%. Much less impressive—but remember that, once again, this statistic cannot be computed since each observer's record is only a series of checks and it is not possible to align them as we have. Because of these limitations, researchers have constructed recording systems that slice time into short intervals and provide some time-sequencing system so that it is possible to document what two observers see or hear "at the same time."

Interval Recording Systems

In an interval recording system, where the first behavior is recorded across continuous time intervals, the data will be influenced by the match between the topography of the behavior and the length of the interval. Long intervals will miss rapidly occurring behaviors. Short intervals will inflate the frequency of long duration behaviors. In the first instance, if Ralph strikes his forehead rapidly, but is measured on 1-minute intervals, only 1 of 50 may be caught. Conversely, if Tyrone is out of seat once and continually across 10 intervals, unless properly defined, his out-of-seat record will be inflated by a factor of 10. In the first case, when two observers are recording, the assumption is that they are both recording the same behavior, but that may not be the case. In the second instance, as is the case with all interval and time sampling procedures, the basic problem is keeping the observers synchronized on the same interval. For if Observer 1 records accurately for each of 50 short intervals, but Observer 2 misses interval 3, and records interval 4 on the line for interval 3 and never corrects the error, then the two observers will be out of sync on 48 out of 50 observations. Thus, interval recording may or may not insure that both observers saw or heard the same event.

When it is important to verify that observers saw *exactly* the same thing, a time sampling procedure identified as momentary time sampling may be used. In contrast to other procedures, this requires that observation points or times be predetermined and that observers score only on these predetermined points in time. Records of these points are compared and calculated in the same ways that interval scores are treated.

One method for calculating interval agreement, commonly referred to as the interval by interval (or point by point) method, is to examine the records of two observers and count 1 for each interval in which there is agreement that a behavior occurred. The sum of this count, divided by the total of agreements plus disagreements multiplied by 100

$$\frac{\text{Agreements}}{\text{Agreements} + \text{Disagreements}} \times 100 = \frac{\text{Percent of}}{\text{Agreement}}$$

yields a percent of agreement measure; one that increases confidence that observers recorded the same behavior at the same time. This estimate may be influenced by the rate of the behavior. Further, the statistic does not account for one part of the data set—agreement that a behavior did not occur. The formula that accounts for that is: $(O + N)/T \times 100 = \%$ score:

1. Count the intervals that show observers agree that a behavior occurred.

2. Count the intervals that show observers agree that a behavior did not occur.

3. Add occurrences (O) and nonoccurrences (N) agreements.

4. Divide the sum of step 3 (O + N) by the total (T).

5. Multiply by 100 to obtain a percent score.

One should calculate two additional reliability coefficients when using either a time sample or interval recording system: (1) occurrence agreement and (2) nonoccurrence agreement. An *occurrence reliability coefficient* (or percentage) should be computed and reported when observers are recording dichotomous events (occurrence/nonoccurrence) and when the target behavior is reported to have occurred in *less than* 75% of the intervals (i.e., low to moderate frequency behaviors). To calculate occurrence agreement use only those intervals in which one or both of the observers record an occurrence. For example, in reference to the data record of two observers presented below, only 4 of the 10 intervals are used to calculate occurrence agreement. The percentage occurrence agreement for these data would be 50%.

Interval	1	2	3	4	5	6	7	8	9	10
Observer 1	+	−	−	+	−	−	−	−	+	−
Observer 2	−	−	−	+	−	+	−	−	+	−

$$\frac{\text{Agreements (2)}}{\text{Agreements (2) + Disagreements (2)}} \times 100 = \frac{2}{4} = 50\% \text{ Occurrence Agreement}$$

Had the point-by-point method been employed, which would use all 10 intervals, interobserver agreement would be reported as 80%, an inflation of the level at which the two observers actually agreed that they saw the behavior occur.

In contrast to occurrence agreement, *nonoccurrence agreement* should be computed when the target behavior is reported to have occurred in *more than* 75% of the intervals (i.e., high frequency behaviors). Calculation of nonoccurrence agreement entails using only those intervals in which one or both observers record a nonoccurrence. For example, the data presented below would yield a nonoccurrence agreement of 33.3%, while the point-by-point method would yield 80% total agreement.

Interval	1	2	3	4	5	6	7	8	9	10
Observer 1	−	+	+	−	+	+	+	+	+	+
Observer 2	+	+	+	−	+	+	+	+	−	+

$$\frac{\text{Agreements (1)}}{\text{Agreements (1) + Disagreements (2)}} \times 100 = \frac{1}{3} = 33.3\% \text{ Nonoccurrence} \\ \text{Agreement}$$

When using an interval or time sample recording system the researcher should calculate two reliability coefficients: (1) total percent agreement, using the point-by-point method, and (2) either occurrence or nonoccurrence agreement, depending on the frequency of the target behavior.

There are objections to these procedures as there are to the others. The major problem is that some agreements are assumed to occur by chance alone. Much of the literature consists of statistical formulas to partial out the effect of chance, e.g., Hartmann (1977). Others have agreed that there is yet no best statistic to estimate chance agreements (Hopkins & Hermann, 1977). Others (Baer, 1977) have suggested that the use of complex statistics is antithetical to the applied behavior analysis tradition. A cursory analysis of the interobserver reliability scores reported in post-1977 issues of *JABA* leaves the impression that the procedures discussed above are predominate in the literature at the present.

SUMMARY

We have focused on two major topics in this chapter. First, we have defined and described dependent measures common to the educational setting. We have described how to select the most appropriate dependent measure and suggested how to design data forms for classroom-based research studies.

In the second section of the chapter we have provided student- and teacher-researchers with a rationale for increasing the reliability of the results obtained in an experiment. We have suggested where to look for behavior definitions appropriate to an area of interest. We have presented strategies for training observers. We have discussed problems in maintaining accurate recording and listed the trade-offs among the various recording systems. We also have presented common formulas for calculating interobserver reliability and referenced other, more complex procedures. We have thus provided the reader with a starting point for developing one part of the procedures for a study. The remainder of this text follows the same format, recommending what to do (sometimes) and how to do it. Across the remaining chapters, the student will find recommendations for selecting appropriate designs, writing procedures, obtaining the resources to carry out studies, and then implementating their research within the framework of ethical procedures.

8

THE VISUAL ANALYSIS OF GRAPHIC DATA

In the preceding chapters we have discussed the parameters of applied research and the importance of the direct, frequent, and reliable measurement of behavior. We have addressed the point that measurement alone does not permit the identification of functional relationships between independent and dependent variables. This is accomplished only when a behavior is measured within the framework of an appropriately chosen single subject research design. Through such pairing it is possible to formatively evaluate a particular intervention's effect on behavior and subsequently use that information to affect positive behavior change with students. In pursuit of this information, applied researchers (1) continuously measure behavior, (2) provide a technological and conceptually systematic description of the conditions under which the behavior is being monitored, (3) evaluate behavior change by employing an appropriate single subject research design, (4) identify those variables which affect the behavior by manipulating only one variable at a time, (5) regularly plot the data on a graph, and (6) conduct a visual analysis of the graphically displayed data, maintaining or modifying the conditions accordingly. Through this sequence of operations applied researchers have been able to isolate variables which influence behavior and, in so doing, further our understanding of human behavior.

In this chapter we discuss the general principles and guidelines adhered to by applied researchers to analyze graphically displayed data. Though there are few hard and fast rules for conducting a visual analysis, there are guidelines which, when followed, increase the probability of an accurate and reliable analysis of data. Specifically, we (1) present a rationale for visual analysis of graphic data, (2) overview general guidelines for graphic representation of data, (3) discuss guidelines for visual analysis of graphic

---

This chapter was written by **David L. Gast** and **James W. Tawney**.

data, (4) outline methods for analyzing behavioral changes within, between, and across conditions, (5) present common data patterns found in single subject investigations, and (6) provide a sample visual analysis of graphic data. This information, in combination with that presented in the preceding chapters, is intended to facilitate both the objective analysis of published single subject research and the design and evaluation of self-initiated research.

Graphic Representation of Data

The Purpose of Graphic Displays

Graphic displays (e.g., line graphs, cumulative graphs, cumulative charts) serve two basic purposes. First, they assist in organizing data during the data collection process, which in turn facilitates formative evaluation. Second, they provide a detailed numerical summary and description of behavior, which in turn allows the reader to analyze the relationship between independent and dependent variables. The underlying purpose or function of the graph is to communicate. For the person collecting the data the graph is a vehicle for efficiently organizing and summarizing a subject's behavior over time. It allows the researcher to analyze, point by point, the effect a particular event has on a subject's behavior. For the behavior analyst "the graph is the primary form of data processing; research decisions, judgments, and conclusions are based almost exclusively on graphed data" (Parsonson & Baer, 1978, pp. 133–134). In addition to the behavior analyst's reliance on graphically displayed data for communication and analysis, teachers and other practitioners will find graphing economical in terms of the time saved by not having to review daily data forms prior to making program decisions and by not maintaining ineffective instructional programs.

The independent analysis of relationships between variables is one of many strengths characteristic of applied behavior analysis and single subject research. By reporting all the data a reader can determine for himself whether a particular intervention has a reliable and "significant" effect on a subject's behavior. The graph, as a compact and detailed data-reporting format, permits independent analysis. Although data could be reported in written narrative day by day or phase by phase, such a format would prove cumbersome. Also, difficulties would arise when attempting to reliably analyze data trends both within and across program conditions. An alternative format for reporting data is the table. Although the table is an efficient format for highlighting and summarizing information, seldom is it used to present point-by-point data; rather, the table is used primarily as a supplemental or secondary data-reporting format. Tables provide an excellent format for summarizing some types of data (e.g., probe trial data, review trial data, direct instructional time information), but they are rarely used as a substitute for graphically displayed data.

Graphic representation of data provides the researcher with an efficient, compact, and detailed summary of subject performance. It communicates to the reader (1) the sequence of experimental conditions, (2) the time spent in each condition, (3) the independent and dependent variables, (4) the experimental design, and (5) the relationship between variables. Therefore, it is not surprising that applied researchers rely heavily on graphs.

Types of Graphic Displays

There are four basic principles which help graphs communicate information to the reader: clarity, simplicity, explicitness, and good design (Parsonson & Baer, 1978). A well-constructed graph will (1) use easily discriminable data points and data paths, (2) clearly separate experimental conditions, (3) avoid clutter by keeping the number of behaviors plotted on one graph to a minimum, (4) provide brief descriptive condition labels and legends, and (5) use appropriate proportions and scales that do not deceive the reader. In addition, it is the responsibility of the researcher to select an appropriate graphic display for presenting the data. The type of display will depend upon the type of data collected and what the researcher wishes to communicate. Generally, behavior analysts present all data (e.g., baseline, intervention, probe, and review data) on one or more types of graphs. By presenting all the data the researcher enables a reader to analyze the data patterns independently.

There are three basic types of graphic displays used by applied researchers: line graphs, bar graphs, and cumulative charts. Although this chapter discusses only the simplest figures within each of the three categories, the reader should be aware that there are numerous variations within each category. Parsonson and Baer (1978) have provided an overview of the various types of line graphs and bar graphs, while Nelson, Gast, and Trout (1979) have discussed the versatility of cumulative charts in educational settings.

Before discussing each type of graph, one should be familiar with the basic components and symbols used in graphic representation. Figure 8-1 presents the major components of a simple line graph, Figure 8-2 presents the basic components of a simple bar graph. As shown, there are several common components across the two types of figures. These include:

• *Abscissa*: horizontal line (X axis) that typically identifies the time variable (e.g., sessions, days, dates)

• *Ordinate*: vertical line (Y axis) that typically identifies the dependent variable (e.g., percentage, frequency, duration)

• *Origin*: common point of intersection of the abscissa and ordinate

• *Tic Marks*: points along both the abscissa and ordinate where values are shown (e.g., 0%, 10%, 20%; Sessions 1, 2, 3)

• *Condition Labels*: one or two descriptive words that identify each experimental condition (e.g., Baseline, Social Reinforcement, Intervention)

• *Condition Change Lines*: solid vertical lines that identify when there has been a change in experimental conditions

• *Key*: one or two words describing each type of data point and path or bar plotted on the graph

• *Figure Number and Legend*: the figure number is used in the narrative to direct the reader's attention to the appropriate graph, and the legend provides a brief and explicit description of the dependent and independent variables

Though not shown in Figures 8-1 and 8-2, most graph paper is printed with a grid. The grid facilitates the accurate plotting of data. When preparing a graph for publication or formal presentation, however, the grid is typically omitted.

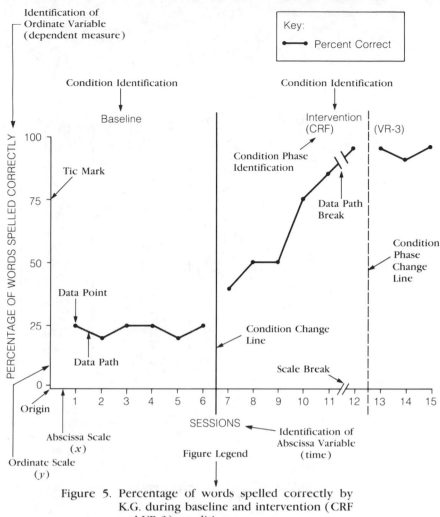

Figure 5. Percentage of words spelled correctly by
K.G. during baseline and intervention (CRF
and VR-3) conditions.

FIGURE 8-1   Basic components of a simple line graph.

Simple Line Graphs

Line graphs represent the most commonly used graphic display for presenting daily data. Figure 8-3 shows two simple line graphs on which three
behaviors (task-relevant, off-task, and disruptive) are concurrently monitored
across two school settings (library and classroom). In the interest of simplicity and clarity, seldom are more than three behaviors plotted on a single
graph.

If additional behaviors are being monitored, as in the case of monitoring the
effect of an intervention on nontargeted behaviors (i.e., response generalization),
additional graphs can be used. Figure 8-4 shows one way to present data on
several nontargeted behaviors that are being monitored concurrently.

   The line graph has several advantages, the most important of which being
that it is familiar to most readers and, thus, is easily read and understood. In
addition, it is easy to construct and permits the researcher or teacher to

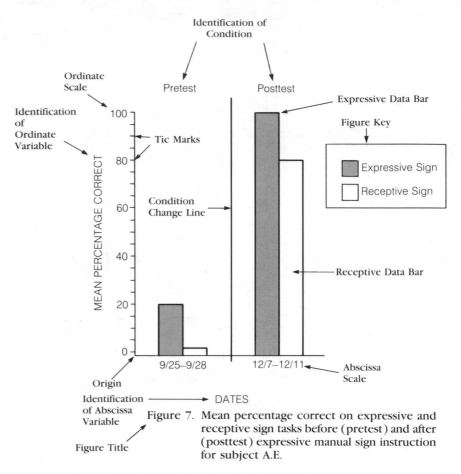

Figure 7. Mean percentage correct on expressive and receptive sign tasks before (pretest) and after (posttest) expressive manual sign instruction for subject A.E.

FIGURE 8-2   Basic components of a simple bar graph.

evaluate continuously the effect an intervention has on the dependent variable(s), thus facilitating formative evaluation and the decision to maintain or modify the intervention.

Simple Bar Graphs

Bar graphs traditionally have been used by applied researchers to display discrete data and comparative information. The great versatility of the bar graph is indicated by its numerous variations. There are two basic types of simple bar graphs: those which present a single bar in an experimental condition and those which present several. As shown in Figure 8-5, the simple single bar graph can be used to summarize a student's performance on a single task which has been presented across several sessions and days. Figure 8-6 shows how the single bar graph can be used to summarize trials-to-criterion data across six behaviors.

Two examples of the simple bar graph in which several bars are plotted for each experimental condition are presented in Figures 8-7 and 8-8. Figure 8-7 presents a simple bar graph which uses two bars to compare pretraining and posttraining conversational ratings of four adolescents.

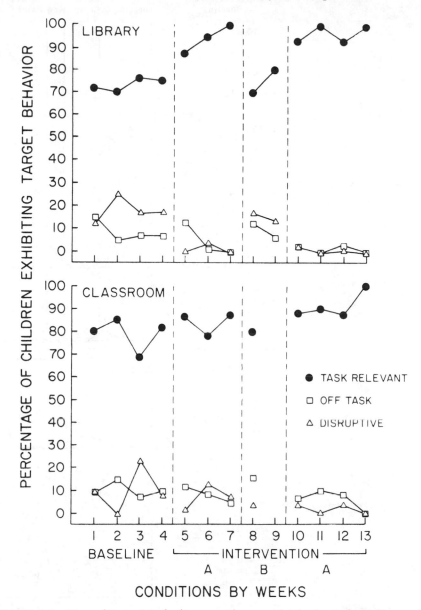

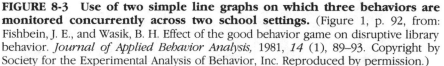

FIGURE 8-3 Use of two simple line graphs on which three behaviors are monitored concurrently across two school settings. (Figure 1, p. 92, from: Fishbein, J. E., and Wasik, B. H. Effect of the good behavior game on disruptive library behavior. *Journal of Applied Behavior Analysis,* 1981, *14* (1), 89–93. Copyright by Society for the Experimental Analysis of Behavior, Inc. Reproduced by permission.)

Figure 8-8 shows how multiple bars can be used to summarize the mean frequency of several behaviors monitored concurrently across conditions. With both types of simple bar graphs the height of the bar indicates the magnitude of the data. When constructing a bar graph it is important to keep the width of each bar identical and thus not perceptually mislead the reader.

A variation of the simple bar graph is the subdivided bar graph. Figure 8-9 shows how the data summarized in Figure 8-7, using two bars, can be plotted

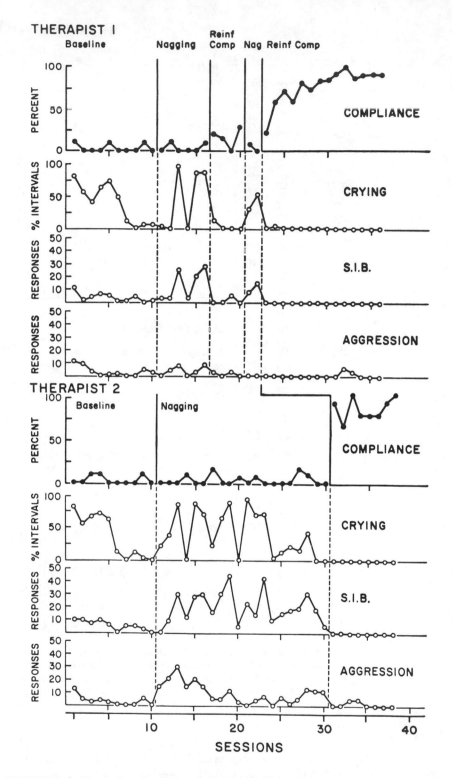

FIGURE 8-4 Use of several simple line graphs to monitor nontargeted but concurrently measured behaviors across two therapists. (Figure 2, p. 216, from: Russo, D.C., Cataldo, M.F., and Cushing, P.J. Compliance training and behavioral covariation in the treatment of multiple behavior problems. *Journal of Applied Behavior Analysis,* 1981, *14* (1), 209–229. Copyright by Society for the Experimental Analysis of Behavior, Inc. Reproduced by permission.)

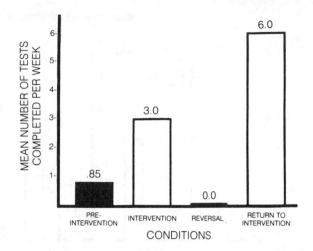

FIGURE 8-5 Use of a simple bar graph to summarize the mean number of reading tests completed per week during each condition. (Figure 3, p. 313, from: Robinson, P. W., Newby, T. J., and Ganzell, S. L. A token system for a class of underachieving hyperactive children. *Journal of Applied Behavior Analysis,* 1981, *14* (3), 307–315. Copyright by Society for the Experimental Analysis of Behavior, Inc. Reproduced by permission.)

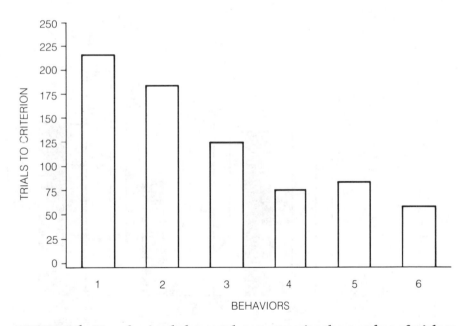

FIGURE 8-6 Use of a simple bar graph to summarize the number of trials to reach criterion across six behaviors.

using the subdivided bar graph format. This method of plotting summarizes the magnitude of the target behavior with a single bar, which permits a quick and easy comparison of the data, in addition to conserving space.

The bar graph provides a simple and straightforward summary of data that is easily understood and analyzed. Though it is not recommended for displaying continuous data, it is an excellent format for displaying and communicat-

MEAN CONVERSATIONAL RATINGS

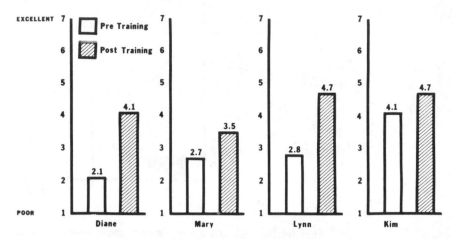
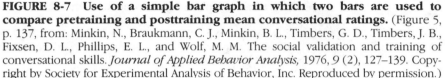

FIGURE 8-7 Use of a simple bar graph in which two bars are used to compare pretraining and posttraining mean conversational ratings. (Figure 5, p. 137, from: Minkin, N., Braukmann, C. J., Minkin, B. L., Timbers, G. D., Timbers, J. B., Fixsen, D. L., Phillips, E. L., and Wolf, M. M. The social validation and training of conversational skills. *Journal of Applied Behavior Analysis,* 1976, *9* (2), 127–139. Copyright by Society for Experimental Analysis of Behavior, Inc. Reproduced by permission.)

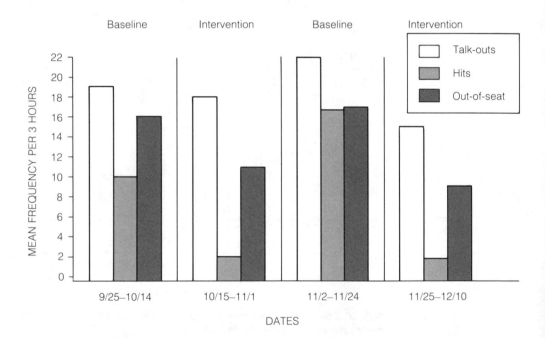
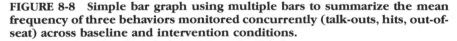

FIGURE 8-8 Simple bar graph using multiple bars to summarize the mean frequency of three behaviors monitored concurrently (talk-outs, hits, out-of-seat) across baseline and intervention conditions.

ing important comparisons in a final research report. In addition to the simplicity and clarity indicative of a well-designed bar graph, it is easy to construct. The bar graph may prove useful to the teacher when communicating a student's progress to his parents.

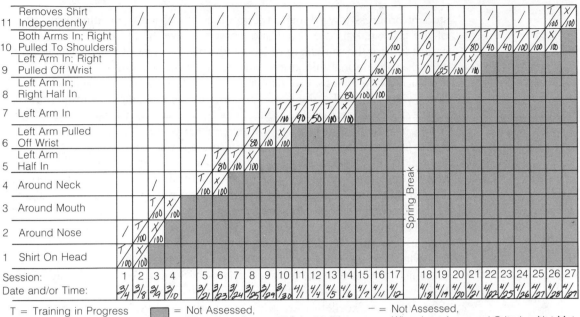

T = Training in Progress   [shaded] = Not Assessed,   − = Not Assessed,
X = Assessed, Criterion Met   When Last Assessed Criterion Met   When Last Assessed Criterion Not Met
/ = Assessed, Criterion Not Met   0–100 = Percentage of Trials Correct on Step

FIGURE 8-9   Data presented in Figure 8-7 replotted using a subdivided bar graph.

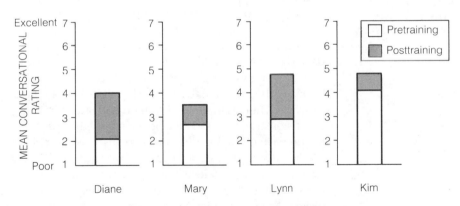

FIGURE 8-10   Use of a cumulative chart to monitor a student's progress in removing a pullover shirt independently.

Cumulative Charts

Cumulative charts have been used less frequently by applied researchers than either line graphs or bar graphs. Few examples are found in the experimental literature. The cumulative chart, however, does provide an excellent visual presentation to summarize child progress toward instructional objectives. Nelson, Gast, and Trout (1979) have discussed how the cumulative chart can be used to monitor and evaluate student progress toward short-term objectives as well as long-term objectives written in a learner's IEP. Figure 8-10 shows how the cumulative chart can be used to monitor and evaluate student progress toward a short-term objective. Along the ordinate the steps of the task analysis are listed and described briefly. Step 1 represents the easiest step for the student, in which the instructor provides the most assistance. As with conventional line graphs, instructional session numbers and/or dates are listed along the abscissa. Rather than plot data points and data paths, as is done with line graphs, the cumulative chart uses a coding system to summarize a student's performance (see "Key"). In addition to using one of the codes, it is helpful to indicate the percentage correct for each session; this assists in the evaluation of student progress on each step of the task analysis. To evaluate the effectiveness of the instructional program (task analysis and procedures), the teacher looks for progress through the task analysis steps in a linear, stepwise progression. When student progress plateaus, this is a signal for the teacher to modify the program.

The cumulative chart has several advantages for the classroom teacher who regularly monitors student performance toward instructional objectives. First, it provides a clear visual picture of student progress by shading in those steps on which the student has reached criterion. Second, it is a versatile visual display which permits the formative evaluation of student performance. Third, it provides an excellent format for monitoring and evaluating student progress through task analysis sequences. And fourth, it facilitates communication between teacher and parents, and among other school personnel.

Guidelines for Selecting and Constructing Graphic Displays

Before analyzing graphically displayed data, it is important that one be able to evaluate the appropriateness of the format used by a researcher to display the data. The primary function of a graph is to communicate without assistance from the accompanying text. This requires that a researcher (1) select the appropriate graphic display (line graph or bar graph) and (2) present the data as clearly, completely, and concisely as possible. How data are presented and how figures are constructed directly influences a reader's ability to evaluate the functional relationship between independent and dependent variables. Though there are few hard and fast rules that govern figure selection, graph construction, and data presentation, there are recommended guidelines for preparing graphic displays (Parsonson & Baer, 1978; *Publication Manual of the American Psychological Association,* 1975; Sanders, 1978). A brief overview of figure selection, graph construction, and data presentation guidelines follows. These guidelines should help you to evaluate graphically displayed data in an objective manner.

Figure Selection

Line graphs are used to present serial data. It is inappropriate to use line graphs to present discrete or nonserial data when the actual data path between two data points is unknown.

Bar graphs are used to present discrete data. For example, when a comparison of pretest and posttest performance is important, a bar graph is often used.

Combination bar and line graphs are sometimes used when baseline (or probe) data are collected over several days (or sessions) on a structured teacher-paced academic task in which there are an unequal number of trials presented each day on each stimulus item, and when continuous data are being collected during the instructional phase of the study. Figure 8-11 shows how Isaac (1979) used a combination bar and line graph to monitor a student's object labeling performance during baseline, probe, and training conditions. Bars were used to summarize the student's performance during baseline and probe test conditions, in which an unequal number of trials were presented on each of the six objects each day (i.e., some objects were presented once and some twice). The height of each bar indicates the mean percentage of correct responses over the "testing" period for each object. The line graph was used to monitor the student's daily performance on the object labeling task being trained using a time delay transfer of stimulus control procedure (Snell & Gast, 1981). The data paths with triangles show the percentage of correct responses emitted by the student before the teacher's prompt (i.e., anticipations). The data paths using circles represent the percentage of correct responses emitted by the student after the teacher's prompt (i.e., waits). When a combination bar and line graph is used, the bar graph is used to present a before and after summary statistic (e.g., mean percent correct for each behavior during the baseline condition) and the line graph is used to present daily training data (e.g., percent correct for each behavior during each session of each instructional condition.)

Graph Construction

The preferred proportion of ordinate (Y axis) to abscissa (X axis) is a ratio of 2:3. The 2:3 ratio is viewed by researchers as limiting the degree of perceptual distortion. If the ordinate scale were longer than this recommended proportion, a steeper slope in the data path would be presented, exaggerating the magnitude of change along the ordinate, while a longer distance between points on the abscissa (in proportion to the ordinate) visually distorts the data by presenting a more shallow data path than if the 2:3 ratio were used.

Separation of experimental conditions is indicated by bold solid vertical lines; a phase change within an experimental condition is frequently separated by a thinner or dashed vertical line. In Figure 8-11 the training condition is divided into two phases: (1) training in isolation and (2) intermixing trained items prior to conducting a probe condition. A dashed line could have been used to separate reinforcement schedule thinning (CRF and VR$_3$) sessions during the intermixed phase of training. All vertical lines used to separate experimental conditions and phases should be drawn between data points.

A scale break is used when the entire ordinate or abscissa scale is not presented. The ordinate scale should show the lower (e.g., 0%) and upper (e.g., 100%) limits of the scale. For example, if the mean percent correct is plotted along the ordinate, both the 0% and 100% levels should be indicated. If the data are consistently below the 50% level, the height of the ordinate may be shortened by placing a scale break above the 50% tic mark, above which the 100% level is marked. Figure 8-12 exemplifies incorrect (a) and correct (b) methods for shortening the height of the ordinate using a simple bar graph.

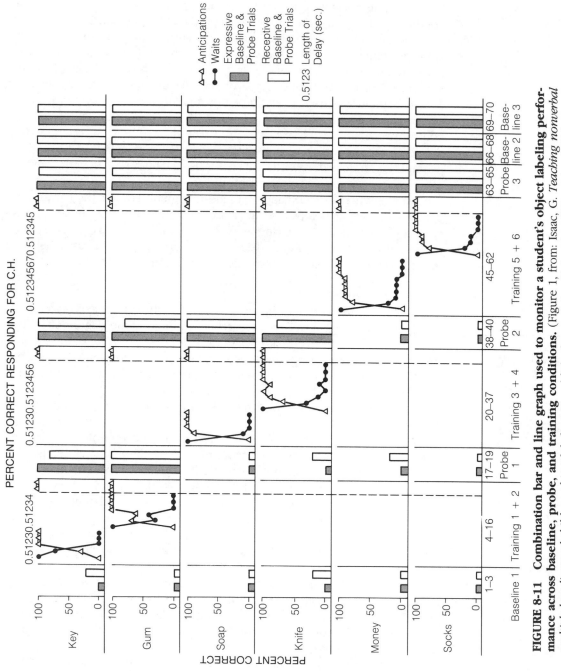

FIGURE 8-11 Combination bar and line graph used to monitor a student's object labeling performance across baseline, probe, and training conditions. (Figure 1, from: Isaac, G. *Teaching nonverbal multiple handicapped children object labeling*. Unpublished manuscript, University of Kentucky, 1979.)

The zero origin tic mark along the ordinate should be placed slightly above the abscissa (see Figures 8-11 and 8-12). When constructing a bar graph, it is particularly important not to mistake a zero level for the absence of plotted data.

The dependent measure should be clearly and concisely labelled along the ordinate. The frequency with which data are collected (i.e., sessions, days, weeks) should be noted along the abscissa.

Figure titles and legends and *experimental condition and condition phase labels* should be concise but explanatory. They should provide sufficient information to allow the reader to identify the dependent and independent variables and the experimental design.

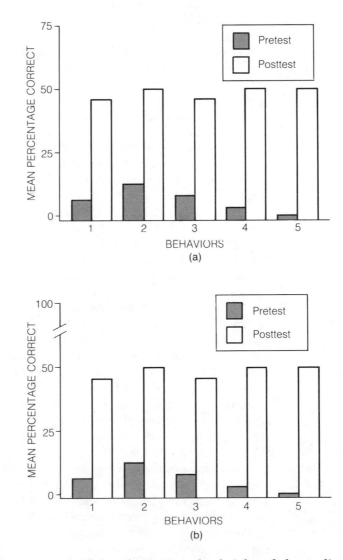

FIGURE 8-12   Method for shortening the height of the ordinate scale.
(a) Incorrect method. (b) Correct method, using a scale break.

Data Presentation

Data points should be marked distinctly using geometric forms (e.g., circles, squares, triangles.) A reader should be able to determine the value of each data point on the ordinate and abscissa scale (e.g., 80% on Day 5).

A *data path* using a solid line to connect two points implies that there is continuity in the data collection process. Dashed or broken data paths are sometimes used to connect discontinuous data. These dashed lines have on occasion been used to connect two points between which no data have been collected (such as connecting data points when the subject has been absent). It is inappropriate to connect data points of two different experimental conditions or condition phases (i.e., data paths should *not* cross experimental condition and phase lines).

When plotting data using a line graph, *no more than three different data paths* should be plotted on the same grid. Additional graphs should be used when more than three data paths are necessary to represent the data.

When logistically feasible, behavioral analysts present *all* data. On occasion, however, when data have been collected over an extended period of time, it may be necessary to condense the data in order to present it on a single grid. A procedure for condensing data, commonly referred to as "blocking," is sometimes used to reduce the number of data points plotted on a graph. This procedure entails calculating the mean performance level of two or more adjacent sessions' data, thereby reducing the length of the abscissa and the number of data points presented on the graph. When blocking has been used, proceed with caution. It is appropriate to block data only if blocking does *not* mask the variability of the data. The procedure is dangerous in that it is possible for a researcher to distort the actual data trends, and therefore it is rarely used. When data points are blocked, the researcher should (1) note that the data have been blocked; (2) specify how many adjacent data points have been blocked within each condition or phase; (3) provide a rationale for blocking, assuring the reader that blocking was not used to mask data variability, but rather to accentuate the data trend and/or reduce the size of the figure due to practical constraints (e.g., not blocking the data would have resulted in an illegible figure when duplicated); (4) present a minimum of three blocked data points for each condition or phase, thereby allowing the reader to evaluate the mean trend within each condition. As a rule blocking is done post hoc; during the course of the research all data are plotted. It is only after the study has been completed, and all data collected, that the researcher can evaluate the appropriateness of the blocking procedure. The general rule regarding blocking is: Don't; if you must, proceed with caution and assure your reader that the blocked data trends parallel and accurately represent unblocked data.

Trend and mean lines may be drawn to supplement the point-by-point data plotted on a line graph; they should not be drawn as an alternative to plotting the actual data points and data paths. Their function is to highlight data trends and averages within and across conditions.

When plotting a statistical average (mean, median, or mode) of a student's (or several students') responses, a researcher generally plots, or specifies in the text, the numerical range of responses. The range of responses for a group of students has sometimes been shown on a figure by drawing a vertical line above and below the plotted data point to the upper and lower levels along the ordinate, thereby showing the two levels between which all students' responses fell. When an individual student's data are averaged within a condition, the range is typically reported in the results section of the research report. The range is an important statistic to a reader when averages are plotted. It permits the reader to evaluate the consistency or stability of an individual's behavior within each condition. When a group average is plotted, the range indicates the degree of variability across students within a condition.

This overview of general guidelines for selecting a graphic display, constructing graphs, and presenting data is by no means comprehensive. Rather, it has highlighted those guidelines that are important to the objective analysis of graphically displayed data. A more comprehensive discussion of guidelines for preparing figures has been presented by Sanders (1978).

Visual Analysis of Graphic Data

Rationale

Educators who are engaged in applied research must be in constant contact with their data if they are to insure that their students are benefitting from involvement in a research project. Provided data are collected continuously on student behavior within the context of an appropriate single subject research design, it is possible for the teacher-researcher to evaluate the effectiveness of a behavior management or instructional program. Formative evaluation of program effectiveness requires a strategy for analyzing data across time and conditions.

The visual analysis of graphic data, in contrast to the statistical analysis of data, represents the most frequently used data analysis strategy employed by applied behavior analysts. The visual analysis strategy has several advantages for special educators and other direct service personnel. First, the visual analysis approach can be used to evaluate the data of individuals or small groups. Second, it is a dynamic process in that the data are collected and analyzed continuously. Third, the visual analysis of graphic data permits a teacher to make data-based decisions throughout a program. Fourth, it focuses on the analysis of individual data patterns, thereby facilitating the individualization of instruction. Fifth, the visual analysis of graphic data permits discovery of interesting findings which may not be directly related to the original research question or program objective. Serendipitous findings (Sidman, 1960; Skinner, 1956) are possible because "primary" data are collected, graphed, and analyzed continuously. Sixth, the graphic presentation of "primary" data permits the independent analysis and interpretation of results, thus permitting others to judge for themselves whether an intervention has merit and whether the findings are reliable and have social validity. Seventh, by graphing and analyzing the data for all students, the effectiveness of an intervention with an individual student is neither overestimated or underestimated. For these reasons the visual analysis of graphic data is the strategy preferred by behavioral researchers working in applied settings. It is an approach which has proven to be both practical and reliable, and therefore it has been adopted by educators and clinicians, as well as researchers, to evaluate data patterns.

Design Notation   Behavior analysts have adopted an "ABC" notation system to assist them in their analysis of single subject research. Through the use of this system they are able to convey information regarding their analyses without having to rely on lengthy narrative descriptions. Though alternative notation systems are used by some researchers (Campbell & Stanley, 1966; Glass, Willson, & Gottman, 1975), the "ABC" notations are used more frequently by applied researchers. Table 8-1 summarizes, and briefly explains, the more common symbols used by behavior analysts in their description of single subject research.

The capital letter A is used to refer to baseline or probe conditions during which the target behavior is repeatedly measured under existing nonexperimental conditions. It is typically the first condition of a single subject experiment. Its primary purpose is to generate data in the absence of intervention, against which data collected in subsequent conditions can be compared. Though the data collected under baseline or A conditions typically represent the natural frequency of the target behavior, as in free-operant research, they need not. The capital letter B is used to refer to the first experimental condition introduced into a data series. Subsequent experimental conditions, which differ procedurally from the first, will be noted with the letters $C, D,$ etc., in the order of their introduction into the study. A single dashed line (-) is used to separate adjacent conditions (e.g., A-B-C-B-C). When two experimental procedures are combined to make a new experimental condition, the letters denoting each of the two procedures are paired without use of the dashed line. For example, if A refers to a baseline condition during which tokens are dispensed noncontingently and B refers to contingent token delivery and C refers to a response cost procedure, then the combination of the contingent token procedure (B) and the response cost procedure (C) would result in the new experimental condition BC. The sequence of conditions in this example might be presented as an A-B-A-BC-A-BC design. Referencing the new condition by using $BC,$ rather than C alone, assists in distinguishing between an experimental condition that introduces a novel

TABLE 8-1   Summary of the "ABC" notation system.

Notation	Explanation
A	Represents a baseline condition in which the independent variable is not present.
B	Represents the first intervention introduced into the data series.
C	Represents the second intervention introduced into the study that is different from the first intervention.
A-B	A dashed line is used to separate adjacent conditions.
BC	Two letters not separated by a dashed line represent the introduction of two interventions in combination.
B'-B''-B'''	Primes are used to show a slight variation from the original procedure.
A_1-B_1-A_2-B_2	A numeral placed at the lower right of a letter notation indicates whether this was the first, second, third, etc., time that this condition was introduced into the data series.

procedure in isolation from an experimental condition that reintroduces a procedure that now is paired with another procedure. This simple differentiation in the labeling of experimental conditions facilitates identification of the relationship between the experimental conditions.

In addition to the above notations, "primes" (e.g., ', '', ''') are added to condition letters (e.g., B, B', B'') to direct attention to slight variations in experimental procedures. For example, an instructional program designed to teach a student a new skill typically begins with the continuous reinforcement (CRF) of each correct response. Upon reaching a predetermined criterion it is desirable to begin thinning the schedule of reinforcement. Reinforcement schedule thinning may entail reinforcing every second correct response (FR-2), followed by reinforcing on the average of every third correct response (VR-3). This process of reinforcement schedule thinning from CRF to FR-2 to VR-3 would be referenced as *B, B',* and *B''*, respectively.

Another helpful notation practice is to number all similar conditions in sequence. For example, when conducting a visual analysis of graphed data presented within the context of an A-B-A-B design, one should number both *A* conditions and both *B* conditions in order (A_1-B_1-A_2-B_2). This assists in differentiating data patterns for similar conditions that were introduced at different points in time over the course of a study.

General Guidelines

This section overviews general guidelines for inspecting and interpreting line-graphed single subject research data. (The guidelines presented should not be viewed as hard and fast rules for interpreting graphic data.) Throughout our discussion we refer to the two basic properties of data that need to be analyzed critically when conducting a visual analysis: level and trend. These terms, and the operations for computing each, are discussed within the context of data plotted on equal interval rather than ratio (logarithmic) graphs. Therefore, our presentation of guidelines for conducting visual analyses is based on absolute rather than relative changes in data patterns. White and Haring (1980), in their discussion of data-based decision rules for teaching, address similar visual analysis procedures but from a Precision Teaching perspective, which advocates the use of ratio charts and thus focuses on relative changes in data patterns. Regardless of which type of graph is used to plot data, equal interval or ratio, adherence to the visual analysis guidelines that follow will result in a reliable evaluation of data.

Though there may be some disagreement among applied behavior analysts regarding what type of graph paper to use, what criterion to use to determine data stability, or when to refer to change in level as abrupt, there is little disagreement regarding what properties of data demand attention. Specifically, behavior analysts attend to (1) the number of data points plotted within a condition, (2) the number of variables changed between adjacent conditions, (3) level stability and changes in level within and between conditions, and (4) trend direction, trend stability, and changes in trend within and between conditions. In the remainder of this chapter we address each of these visual analysis components by defining terminology, describing how to compute each, and pointing out considerations and/or precautions. For the purpose of clarity, visual analysis guidelines are discussed and graphically presented within the context of an A-B design. These same guidelines, however, are used regardless of the conditions being compared (A-B, B-C, B-BC) or the single subject design within which the data were collected.

Condition Length

Condition or *phase length* refers to how long a particular condition is in effect. To determine the length of a condition simply count the number of data points plotted within a condition. A *minimum* of three separate, and preferably consecutive, observation periods are required to determine the level of stability and trend of data. The specific number of observation periods needed will depend on the variability of the data: the more variable the data, the longer the condition should be. Baer, Wolf, and Risley (1968) recommend continuing a condition until "stability is clear." In regard to the length of a baseline condition, however, it is sometimes necessary for applied researchers to take into account both practical and ethical considerations before locking in to the "stability is clear" rule. Some classes of behavior (self-injurious, physically aggressive, and severely disruptive) may require more immediate intervention when the target behavior jeopardizes the health and/or safety of the subject or those who are in close proximity to him. With such behaviors a shorter baseline condition may be justified. When visually analyzing data, or conducting research with these classes of behavior, shorter baseline conditions are understandable and tolerated, though the demonstration of experimental control may be weakened.

Change One Variable at a Time

In order to isolate the influence a particular variable or procedure has on a target behavior, it is necessary to change only one variable when moving from one condition to another. Behavior analysts go to considerable lengths to insure that the independent variable is present in the experimental condition (B) and not present in the adjacent nonexperimental or baseline condition (A). When the only difference between two adjacent conditions is the presence of the independent variable, the researcher can evaluate the influence *that* variable has on the target behavior. To determine how many variables have changed between adjacent conditions, one should read carefully the procedure sections for each condition, noting differences in procedures (e.g., prompting, reinforcement, correction) and conditions (e.g., setting, task format, teachers). Often this information can be obtained from the figure legend and condition labels that accompany the graphs.

Some single subject research focuses on evaluating the effect that a combination of procedures or treatment package has on behavior, rather than the effects of any one procedure. The overcorrection research literature (e.g., Azrin & Wesolowski, 1974; Epstein, Doke, Sajwaj, Sorrell, & Rimmer, 1974; Foxx & Azrin, 1973) exemplifies this line of "treatment package" research. When the purpose of an investigation is to compare the effectiveness of a treatment package against other experimental or nonexperimental procedures, it is important that the only difference between adjacent conditions is the presence of the treatment package. When analyzing data from such research projects, one can only discuss the effect the treatment package as a whole had on the target behavior; one cannot evaluate the relative contribution of any one of its procedures.

As both a designer and reader of experimental research, it is important to attend to this basic rule: *Change only one variable at a time.* If the research is directed at evaluating the effect of an intervention package, rather than a single procedure, still change only one variable when moving from condition to condition. This rule holds true regardless of the condition (Baseline, Intervention 1, Intervention 2, etc.) to which you are moving. Adherence to this principle is fundamental to the identification of cause-effect relationships in single subject research.

Level

The term *level* refers to the magnitude of the data as indicated by the ordinate scale value. When inspecting data, there are two basic aspects of level that are of importance: level stability and level change. *Level stability* refers to the amount of variability, or range in data point values, in a data series. When the range of values is small (low variability), data are said to be stable. Generally, if 80%–90% of the data points of a condition fall within a 15% range of the mean level of all data point values of a condition, applied researchers will consider the data stable. The mean level of a condition is calculated by adding the ordinate values of all data points and dividing the sum by the number of data points. A mean line is then drawn parallel to the abscissa at that value. The specific percentage (5, 10, 12, 15) used to determine level stability varies, depending on such things as the number of opportunities a subject has to respond (as on a teacher-paced task) or the frequency of the target behavior (as with a free-operant behavior). As a general rule, the fewer the number of opportunities a subject has to respond, the larger the percentage used to calculate level stability. If, for example, a student has 20 opportunities to respond during an instructional session, a 10% criterion for calculating stability is not uncommon. If, however, a student has only five opportunities to respond, a stability criterion of 20% would not be unreasonable. When studying a free-operant behavior, the general rule is to use a smaller percentage (10%) to calculate level stability when the data cluster around the uppermost values on the ordinate scale, and use a larger percentage (15%) when the data points fall within the middle or lower range of ordinate values. Thus, before selecting a percentage for calculating level stability, note whether it is a regulated or free-operant behavior and within what range the data fall on the ordinate scale. The question you must ask yourself is whether the data are sufficiently stable to provide a convincing demonstration of experimental control when experimental conditions are changed. The greater the variability in the data series, the greater the risk of not convincing your audience of experimental control.

A second aspect of level of interest to behavior analysts is the amount of change in level within the same condition or phase. The absolute *level change within a condition* is computed by (1) identifying the ordinate values of the first and last data points of a condition, (2) subtracting the smallest from the largest, and (3) noting whether the change in level within the condition is in a therapeutic (improving) or contratherapeutic (decaying) direction, as indicated by the intervention objective. This information is important when determining whether it is appropriate to move to the next planned condition in the design sequence.

The third property of level that receives attention from behavior analysts is the *level change between adjacent conditions.* To compute the absolute change in level between two adjacent conditions: (1) identify the ordinate values of the last data point of the first condition and the first data point value of the second condition; (2) subtract the smallest value from the largest; and (3) note whether the change in level is in an improving or decaying direction. This information will indicate the immediate strength or impact an intervention has on the target behavior. When a large change in level occurs immediately after the introduction of a new condition, the level change is considered abrupt, which is indicative of a "powerful" or effective intervention.

Trend

For the behavior analyst, the trend or slope of a data series is as important as the level of performance. In combination, a careful analysis of level and trend permits a reliable determination of experimental control. *Trend direction* or *slope* refers to the steepness of the data path across time. Typically a trend is referred to as accelerating (increasing in ordinate value over time), decelerating (decreasing in ordinate value over time), or zero celeration (parallel to the abscissa). In addition to referring to the direction of the slope, it is important to note whether the direction of a trend is improving or decaying.

Two methods are commonly used to estimate trend: freehand method and split-middle method. The *freehand method* entails visually inspecting the data of a condition and drawing a straight line that bisects the data points (Parsonson & Baer, 1978). Though this method takes very little time, without considerable practice the reliability of drawing a freehand trend line (sometimes referred to as a line of progress) that accurately depicts the slope of the data series is apt to be low. The *split-middle method,* as described by White & Haring (1980), provides a more reliable estimate of trend and, therefore, is recommended for use with variable data patterns. The split-middle method, which relies on median or middle dates and ordinate values to estimate trend, is outlined in Figure 8-13.
With practice the split-middle method will yield a more accurate and reliable estimate of trend than the freehand method.

Having drawn the line of progress or trend line for the condition one should reinspect the same data to see whether there is more than one *data path within the trend.* Since most conditions of an investigation do not have a sufficient number of data points to calculate a line of progress for each half of a data series, the freehand method is used. If all the data points approximate the direction of the line of progress, one need go no further to analyze the trend within that condition. If, however, two distinct data paths are visible, it is important to identify each (see Figure 8-16, graphs *c* and *d*). The last data path within the trend should guide one's decision to introduce a new condition into a data series (provided there are three to five data points which fall in line). It is important to remember that the trend line itself, as generated by the split-middle method, is an *estimate* of trend and, like the mean line, can divert attention away from the point-by-point data path.

In addition to determining the direction of a trend, it is also important to determine trend stability. Much like evaluating level stability, *trend stability* is evaluated by determining how many of the data points of a condition fall

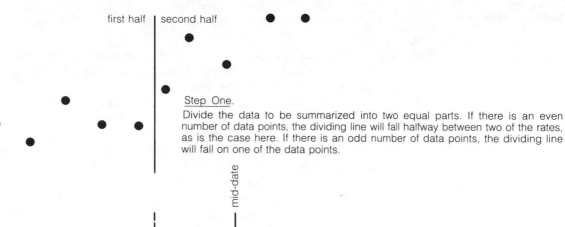

first half | second half

Step One.

Divide the data to be summarized into two equal parts. If there is an even number of data points, the dividing line will fall halfway between two of the rates, as is the case here. If there is an odd number of data points, the dividing line will fall on one of the data points.

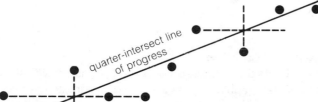

mid-date

mid-rate

mid-date

mid-rate(s)

Step Two.

Find the intersections of the mid-rate and mid-date for each half. In this case, since there are five data points in each half, the mid-rates will be the third data point counting up or down the chart, and the mid-dates will be the third data point counting left or right on the chart. Several data points can all fall on the mid-rate, as illustrated in the first half of this example.

quarter-intersect line of progress

Step Three.

Draw a line through the data which passes through both of the intersections found in step two above. If you stop at this step in the process, you will have found the quarter-intersect line of progress. To find the split-middle line, complete step four below.

split-middle line of progress

Step Four.

Count the number of data points which fall above and below the line drawn in step three above. There should be the same number of data points falling on and above the line as there are falling on and below the line. If not, move the line up or down (keeping it parallel to the original line) until a balance is achieved.

FIGURE 8-13 Split-middle line of progress. (Figure 5-6, p. 118, from: White, O. R. and Haring, N. G. *Exceptional teaching.* Columbus, Ohio: Charles E. Merrill, 1980. Reproduced by permission.)

within a predetermined range along the trend line. Generally, if 80%–90% of the data points fall within 15% (or whatever percentage is used to determine level stability), the trend is considered stable.

After inspecting the data in each condition for trend direction and stability it is necessary to compare conditions, identifying changes in trend and stability brought about by the procedural changes in the investigation. By comparing the differences in slope between lines of progress drawn across two adjacent conditions, it is possible to determine the effect a change in conditions has on the dependent measure. Changes in trend are frequently expressed in terms of "accelerating to decelerating" (see Figure 8-17, graph *f*), "zero celeration to accelerating" (see Figure 8-17, graph *h*), or other similar phrasing. (These and other changes in data patterns are graphically presented and discussed in the next section.) Note whether there was a change, and if there was, whether it was improving or decaying.

Finally, when comparing the data of two adjacent conditions, one should determine the *percentage of overlap* of data point values. Percentage of overlap is calculated by (1) determining the range of data point values of the first condition, (2) counting the number of data points plotted in the second condition, (3) counting the number of data points of the second condition which fall within the range of values of the first condition, and (4) dividing the number of data points which fall within the range of the first condition by the total number of data points of the second condition and multiplying this number by 100. The percentage yielded by this computation reflects the percentage of overlap between the two conditions. Generally, the lower the percentage of overlap, the greater the impact the intervention has on the target behavior.

Common Data Patterns in Single Subject Research

Analysis of Changes within Condition

The visual analysis of data within a condition is concerned primarily with the stability of the data. Figure 8-14, graph *a* depicts a stable data path across five data points. The range of scores is consistently between the 30% and 40% level. With this type of baseline data it would be appropriate to introduce the independent variable in Session 6. Figure 8-14, graph *b*, however, presents variable data. The behavior analyst confronted with these data has two options: (1) to continue measuring student behavior under baseline conditions until the data stabilize or (2) to begin systematically searching for the source(s) responsible for the variability. Figure 8-14, graphs *c* and *d* present data depicting "deteriorating" or decaying trends, i.e., data paths which are in the direction opposite of improvement. These data, despite a consistent change in level across time, are viewed as stable because the data paths are consistently in the direction opposite of improvement. With both types of trends one could implement intervention in Session 6.

Figure 8-15 presents four examples of data paths in which variability is present. Figure 8-15, graph *a* shows an initial period of variability followed by a stabilizing of the data. The initial period of data instability may have resulted from student's not knowing what the task response requirement was or his knowing that he was being observed, which in turn diverted his attention from the task. In other words, the student had not adapted to the new

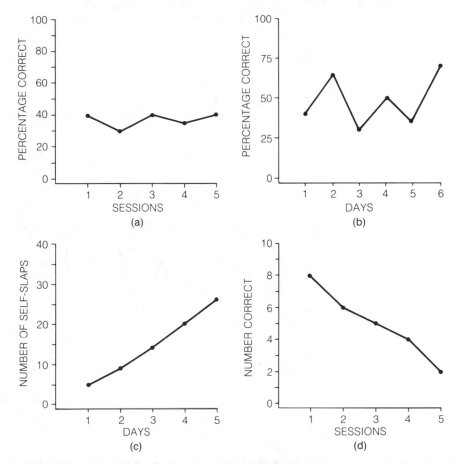

FIGURE 8-14 Common "within condition" data patterns. (a) Stable level and trend (acceptable). (b) Variable level and trend (unacceptable). (c) "Deteriorating" acceleration trend (acceptable). (d) "Deteriorating" deceleration trend (acceptable).

situation and his responding was affected. Once he adapted to the situation his responding stabilized. This type of data path shows that it is sometimes important to continue a condition to give the subject sufficient time to adjust to novel environmental variables. A pattern of this type is acceptable, and it would be appropriate to change conditions in the next session.

Figure 8-15, graph *b* shows a data path that was initially stable but that became variable across time. Such trends pose a difficult problem. Variability may be a function of extraneous events (e.g., problems at home), which may be temporary or permanent, or they may indicate a change in the independent variable (e.g., task analysis step change). Whichever the case, it is recommended that the condition be extended before conducting an experimental analysis.

A data path not uncommon to applied researchers is shown in Figure 8-15, graph *c*. These data show high variability with a gradual trend in the direction of improvement. A change in condition would not provide a convincing demonstration of experimental control even if the data stabilized during the subsequent condition. If for practical or ethical reasons a change in condition

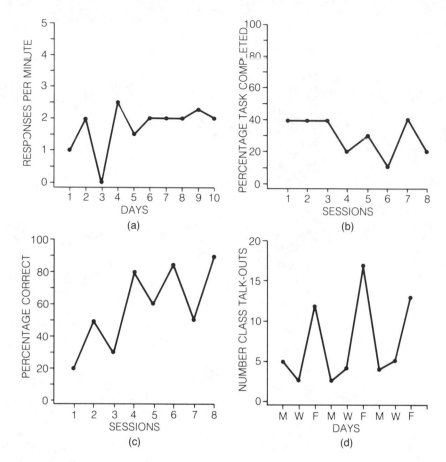

FIGURE 8-15 Common "within condition" data patterns showing variability.
(a) Variable level and trend that stabilizes (acceptable). (b) Stable level and trend that
becomes variable (unacceptable). (c) Variable level and improving trend (unacceptable).
(d) Cyclical variability (unacceptable).

is necessary, drawing a line of progress for each condition will facilitate the
analysis of experimental effect. As a general rule, however, one should
identify and control these sources of variability before one proceeds to the
next condition.

A less common data path confronted by behavior analysts is presented in
Figure 8-15, graph *d*. These hypothetical data, collected on Mondays,
Wednesdays, and Fridays, show an increase in the number of talk-outs on
Fridays. They indicate that there is a regularly recurring event that is responsible for the cyclical variability. When confronted with cyclical variability,
one must identify and control the source before introducing the next scheduled condition.

Figure 8-14, graphs *c* and *d* represent deteriorating trends that are considered acceptable. Figure 8-16, graphs *a* and *b* exemplify unacceptable
"improving" trends in the data. These types of data paths require the researcher to continue the condition until the data stabilize. If the improving
slope is gradual, the behavior analyst may decide to introduce the next

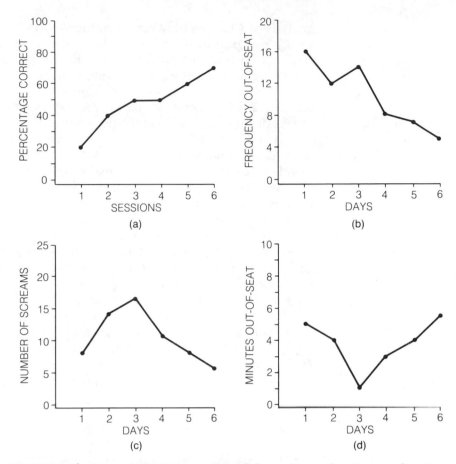

FIGURE 8-16   Common "within condition" data patterns showing accelerating, decelerating, and combination trends. (a) Improving acceleration trend (unacceptable). (b) Improving deceleration trend (unacceptable). (c) Deteriorating-Improving trend (unacceptable). (d) Improving-Deteriorating trend (acceptable).

condition, in which case a line of progress could be drawn to permit a comparison of slopes across adjacent conditions. However, a change in conditions at this time will provide a "less clear" demonstration of experimental control. The preferred tactic is to continue collecting data until the data stabilize.

Figure 8-16, graphs *c* and *d* show a "deteriorating-improving" trend and an "improving-deteriorating" trend, respectively. As noted, whether a trend is acceptable depends upon the target behavior and the intended direction of behavior change. One must look at the dependent measure, listed on the ordinate, to determine whether the trend is acceptable. In figure 8-16, graph *c* the last three data points are in the direction of improvement, and the researcher should withhold treatment until the data stabilize or reverse. Figure 8-16, graph *d* shows that out-of-seat behavior was decreasing (i.e., improving) on the first three days of the condition; however, the trend began to reverse on Day 4 and continued to increase on the following two days; because of this reversal in trend (i.e., the last three days) it would be appropriate to introduce intervention.

Analysis of Changes between Conditions

A stable data path should be present in the condition immediately preceding the condition being analyzed. For example, when baseline data are variable (see Figure 8-17, graph *a*), it is difficult to interpret the experimental effect. The degree of experimental control that can be demonstrated with variable data paths within either condition will depend upon the change in level from one condition to the next and the percentage of overlap in both conditions (Wolery & Harris, 1982). That is, small changes in the dependent variable values during intervention, which follow a variable data path in baseline, provide a weaker demonstration of experimental control than small changes in intervention preceded by a stable baseline data path. Also, the less overlap in the range of the data points of two adjacent conditions, the more convincing the demonstration that the intervention was responsible for the experimental effect. The data patterns presented in Figure 8-17, graphs *a* and *b* depict variable data paths within a condition and data overlap between conditions. Both cases make it difficult for the analyst to make an objective interpretation of the effect of the intervention.

Figure 8-17, graphs *c* and *d* show data patterns frequently encountered by behavior analysts. Figure 8-17, graph *c* represents an increase in level following a stable trend at a lower level in the preceding condition; figure 8-17, graph *d* represents a decrease in level following a stable trend at a higher level in the preceding condition. Figure 8-17, graph *c* presents a data pattern in which there is an immediate and abrupt change in the target behavior

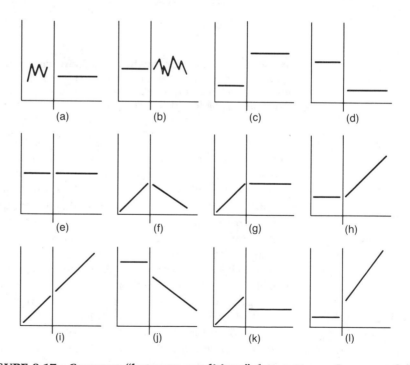

FIGURE 8-17   Common "between conditions" data patterns. Summary of data patterns across two conditions: Graphs (a) and (b), change in variability; Graphs (c) and (d), change in level; Graphs (e) and (i), no change in data; Graphs (f), (g), and (h), change in trend; Graphs (j), (k), and (l), change in level and trend.

upon introduction of the independent variable, a pattern representative of an effective behavior acceleration program. Figure 8-17, graph *d* represents a data pattern of an effective behavior deceleration program. Both patterns are easily interpreted.

Figure 8-17, graph *e* shows no change in the level of the dependent variable across the two adjacent conditions, i.e., the two conditions are functionally equivalent. If these data represent baseline (*A*) and intervention (*B*) conditions, respectively, an applied researcher can treat the two conditions as equivalent and immediately introduce a new intervention (*C* or *BC*). The notation of these two adjacent and functionally equivalent conditions is *A* = *B* rather than *A-B*. When two adjacent conditions are functionally equivalent, it is one of the few times that the researcher is not required to reintroduce *A* before introducing a novel condition.

Generally, readers are more impressed with an intervention that results in a large and abrupt change in response level. Birnbrauer (1981), however, recommends that applied researchers not lose sight of the fact that the level of effect during intervention is directly related to the procedures in effect during a baseline condition. A lengthy baseline, or a baseline condition in which a thin schedule of reinforcement is operating, has a tendency to depress the level of responding. If such baselines are followed by a rich intervention package that includes task novelty, stimulus cues, response prompts, and a dense schedule of reinforcement, there is an increased probability that a large and abrupt change in response level will result. Therefore, when conducting a visual analysis of changes in level, as well as in trend, it is important to pay particular attention to (1) the length of the first condition in the comparison and (2) the procedural differences between the two conditions. When the procedural differences between conditions are small, the change in level need not be large to conclude that the independent variable was effective. When procedural contrast is minimized, it also is easier to isolate the controlling variable.

The remaining graphs in Figure 8-17 (*f, g, h, i, j, k,* and *l*) exemplify the more common changes in trends between adjacent conditions. Graphs *f, g,* and *h* display changes in trend in the second condition (B) that are not accompanied by initial changes in level. Figure 8-17, graph *f* shows that the trend is reversed when intervention is introduced. Figure 8-17, graph *g* shows that the increasing trend levels off. Figure 8-17, graph *h* shows that linear increase occurred when the intervention was introduced. In each example when the intervention was introduced, the data trend was influenced. Whether the change in trend was improving depends upon the objective of the intervention. If the dependent variable in Figure 8-17, graph *h* was the percentage of correct responses in calculating addition problems, these data would represent an improving trend during intervention. If, however, the dependent variable was the number of talk-outs during a 30-minute independent work activity, these data would represent a decaying trend. The acceptability of a trend change cannot be determined without referring to the objective of intervention.

Figure 8-17, graph *i* shows no change in the data trend as a function of the independent variable, i.e., the slope of the data path in intervention is the same as in the baseline condition. These data are interpreted in the same manner as the data presented in Figure 8-17, graph *e*. The independent variable had no effect, and therefore the two conditions are functionally equivalent.

Figure 8-17, graphs *j, k,* and *l* exemplify changes in trend accompanied by changes in level after the introduction of intervention. In all three examples the baseline condition trend is stable; however, the introduction of the independent variable resulted in a decelerating trend in graph *j,* a leveling trend in graph *k,* and an accelerating trend in graph *l.*

The 12 data patterns presented in Figure 8-17 represent the more common patterns encountered by behavior analysts when evaluating single subject research. Figure 8-18 presents three additional patterns, which were discussed by Glass, Willson, and Gottman (1975). These patterns represent: (1) a temporary change in level and trend (Figure 8-18, graph *a*), (2) a delayed change in level and trend (Figure 8-18, graph *b*), and (3) a decaying change in level and trend (Figure 8-18, graph *c*). For each of these three data patterns an example is presented for an acceleration program (graph on left) and a deceleration program (graph on right).

The temporary and decaying change patterns (Figure 8-18, graphs *a* and *c,* respectively) show that the introduction of the independent variable resulted in an abrupt change in level, but over time the data path returned to near baseline levels. Such data patterns may be a function of weak behavior consequences or some extraneous event that coincided with the introduction of the independent variable. When confronted with a temporary or decaying pattern, one should begin an experimental analysis to determine the cause. The delayed change data pattern shown in Figure 8-18, graph *b* could be a function of a weakness in the initial phase of an instructional program or the subject's need for a period of adaptation to discriminate changes among conditions. If the condition lengths were short, it would not be possible to detect such transitory changes. In either case, one must decide whether a more abrupt and rapid change in the subject's behavior is desirable. If it is, a systematic analysis of the initial phase of the instructional program should be conducted.

Analysis of Changes across Similar Conditions

The discussion thus far has focused on the visual analysis of data within conditions and between two adjacent conditions. In order to simplify the presentation of visual analysis guidelines, data were displayed across two conditions (baseline and intervention). As previously mentioned, the A-B design precludes demonstrating a functional relationship between dependent and independent variables. If cause-effect conclusions are to be drawn, the experimental effect must be replicated either through systematic withdrawal and reintroduction of the independent variable (A-B-A-B design) or through systematic introduction of the independent variable across behaviors, subjects, or situations (multiple baseline or multiple probe designs). This replication is necessary to demonstrate a functional relationship between the intervention and behavior change.

The analysis of changes across similar conditions focuses on two questions: (1) Are baseline levels maintained until the independent variable is introduced (multiple baseline or multiple probe design) or retrieved in subsequent baseline conditions (withdrawal or reversal design)? and (2) Do level

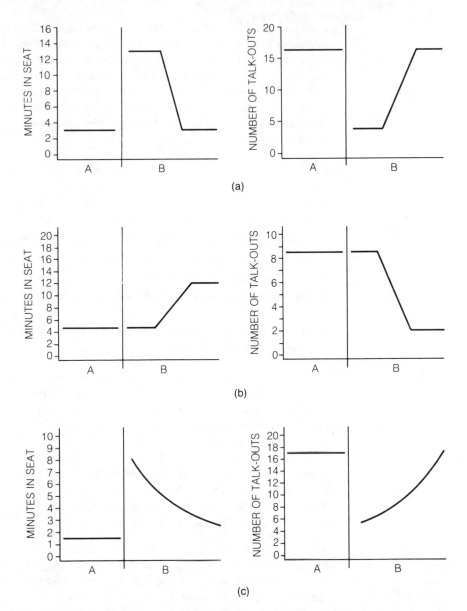

FIGURE 8-18 Temporary, delayed, and decaying data patterns across conditions. (a) Temporary change in level and trend. (b) Delayed change in level and trend. (c) Decaying change in level and trend.

and trend improve after the introduction of the independent variable? If guidelines for analyzing within and between condition data have been followed, and if the answer to these two questions is "yes," then an experimental analysis of the relationship between the target behavior and the intervention has been accomplished.

Due to practical and ethical constraints, however, it is not always possible for an applied researcher to adhere strictly to all recommended guidelines. On these occasions one must decide whether deviations from these guidelines jeopardize the demonstration of experimental control. Some degree of deviation may be acceptable, depending upon the guideline. For example, some degree of data variability may be acceptable; a higher percentage of overlap may be acceptable; and, under some circumstances, shortened condition lengths may be acceptable. Under no circumstances, however, can there be deviations from other recommended guidelines without weakening the demonstration of experimental control. Guidelines that should be adhered to strictly include:

1. The repeated measurement of the dependent variable across time and conditions,

2. The use of a single subject research design which adequately controls for extraneous and potentially confounding variables,

3. The systematic manipulation of only one variable at a time,

4. The maintenance of relatively stable baseline levels until the independent variable has been introduced,

5. The retrieval of baseline levels of responding with reversal and withdrawal designs,

6. The replication of the experimental effect across similar experimental conditions, behaviors, subjects, or situations.

The objective visual analysis of data across similar conditions is extremely important if accurate statements are to be made regarding the internal validity of an experimental effect. By following the previously discussed general guidelines one can determine whether experimental control has been demonstrated. When a visual analysis results in one's questioning a demonstration of experimental control, one must identify why the experimental demonstration was weakened or jeopardized. Through such post hoc analyses behavior analysts can redesign a study, controlling for previously uncontrolled variables. In addition, these analyses provide an excellent source for identifying research questions.

Sample Visual Analysis of Graphic Data

In this section we outline a process for conducting a visual analysis, following the format presented in Table 8-2. Table 8-2 identifies those properties of a data series that we have found helpful when analyzing data within each condition of a study. Table 8-3 lists those between condition comparisons that help to determine the effect of a new experimental condition (or of the withdrawal of an experimental condition) on the target behavior.

To simplify our discussion of the visual analysis process, the hypothetical data presented in Figure 8-19 (page 175) are used. These data represent the number of talk-outs emitted by a student (or classroom of students) collected over two conditions: baseline (A) and intervention (B). For purposes of our example A represents the teacher's verbal reprimand for talk-outs; B represents the teacher's ignoring talk-outs. The objective of our intervention is, of course, to reduce the number of talk-outs emitted by the student. The completed visual analysis of the data graphed in Figure 8-19 is presented in Tables 8-4 and 8-5 (pages 176 and 177). As each component of the visual analysis is discussed we recommend referring to these tables.

TABLE 8-2 Within condition analysis format.

Conditions (In sequence)	1	2	3	4	5	6	7	8
1. Condition Length								
2. Estimate of Trend Direction								
3. Trend Stability								
4. Data Paths within Trend								
5. Level Stability and Range								
6. Level Change								

TABLE 8-3 Between adjacent conditions analysis format.

Condition Comparison	(:)	(:)	(:)	(:)	(:)	(:)	(:)
1. Number of Variables Changed	( ) ( )	( ) ( )	( ) ( )	( ) ( )	( ) ( )	( ) ( )	( ) ( )
2. Change in Trend Direction and Effect	( ) ( )	( ) ( )	( ) ( )	( ) ( )	( ) ( )	( ) ( )	( ) ( )
3. Change in Trend Stability	| to |	| to |	| to |	| to |	| to |	| to |	| to |
4. Change in Level	(–)	(–)	(–)	(–)	(–)	(–)	(–)
5. Percentage of Overlap	___ %	___ %	___ %	___ %	___ %	___ %	___ %

Column heading notes: 2nd condition / 1st condition condition order; for item 2: 1st Trend / 2nd Trend — Effect

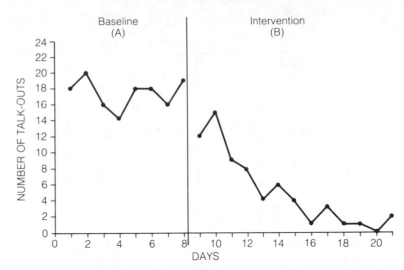

FIGURE 8-19 **Hypothetical data of a behavior management program to decrease the number of talk-outs.**

Component 1: Within Condition Analysis (Table 8-4)

Step 1: Identifying condition sequence. Using the "ABC" letter notation system, assign a letter to each different condition of the study. List these letters, in sequence, across the top row of Table 8-4.

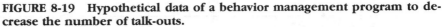

Step 2: Determining condition length. Count the number of data points plotted in condition A and record this number in the A column. Count the number of data points plotted in condition B and record this number in the B column.

Conditions	A_1	B_2
1. Condition Length	8	13

Step 3: Estimating trend direction. Using the split-middle method, estimate the trend for Condition A; for Condition B. (Refer to figure 8-20)

In Row 2 draw an acceleration slope line (Estimate of Trend Direction) for Condition A and a deceleration slope line for Condition B.

Conditions	A_1	B_2
2. Estimate of Trend Direction	╱ ( )	╲ ( )

TABLE 8-4 Summary of visual analysis of hypothetical data plotted in Figure 8-19 (within condition).

Conditions (In sequence)	A / 1	B / 2	3	4	5	6	7	8
1. Condition Length	8	13	—	—	—	—	—	—
2. Estimate of Trend Direction	(−)	(+)	( )	( )	( )	( )	( )( )	
3. Trend Stability	Variable	Stable	—	—	—	—	—	—
4. Data Paths within Trend	(−)	(+) (=)	( )	( )	( )	( )	( )	( )
5. Level Stability and Range	Variable (14–20)	Variable (0–15)	[( )	[( )	[( )	[( )	[( )	[( )
6. Level Change	19–18 (−1)	12–2 (+10)	− ( )	− ( )	− ( )	− ( )	− ( )	− ( )

TABLE 8-5 Summary of visual analysis of hypothetical data plotted in Figure 8-19 (between adjacent conditions).

Condition Comparison	$\dfrac{B_1}{A_1}$ (2:1)	(:)	(:)	(:)	(:)	(:)
						2nd condition / 1st condition / condition order
1. Number of Variables Changed	1					
2. Change in Trend Direction and Effect	(−) (+) positive	( ) ( )	( ) ( )	( ) ( )	( ) ( )	( ) ( ) — 1st trend / 2nd trend / Effect
3. Change in Trend Stability	variable to stable	to	to	to	to	to
4. Change in Level	(18–12) +6	(−)	(−)	(−)	(−)	(−)
5. Percentage of Overlap	7.69 %	___ %	___ %	___ %	___ %	___ %

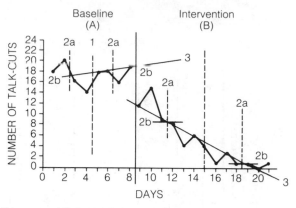

Summary of Split-Middle Method Steps:

Step 1. Divide the data in Condition A in half.

Step 2a. Divide each half in half (mid-date).

Step 2b. Find the middle (median) value (mid-rate) for each
half of the data series (Step 1) and draw a line
parallel to the abscissa that intersects the mid-date
line.

Step 3. Draw a line that passes through the points of intersection found in Step 2b (quarter-intersect line).

Step 4. To find the split-middle line adjust the quarter-
intersect line so that there are an equal number of
data points above and below the line. (In Condition A
no adjustment is necessary.)

Repeat the above steps with the data plotted in Condition B.

FIGURE 8-20   Split-middle method.

Within the parentheses, indicate whether the trend is improving (+) or
decaying (–) in Condition *A*; in Condition *B*. (If the trend line in either
condition was parallel to the abscissa, i.e., zero celeration, you would record
(=).)

Conditions	A_1	B_2
2. Estimate of Trend Direction	/ (–)	\ (+)

Step 4: Determining trend stability. Using a 15% stability criterion, calculate
15% of the highest data point value of Condition *A*.

highest value × stability criterion = acceptable stability range		
20 × .15 = 3.0		

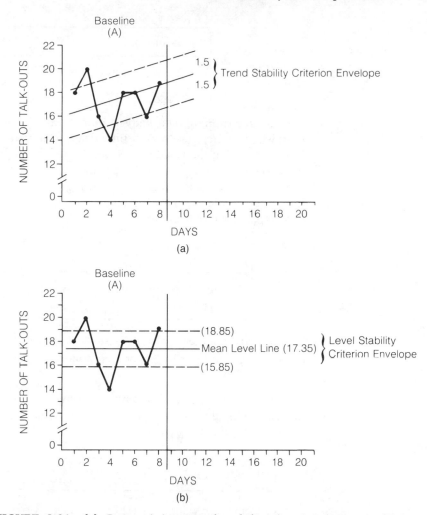

FIGURE 8-21   (a) Determining trend stability for Condition A data presented in Figure 8-19. (b) Determining level stability for Condition A data presented in Figure 8-19.

Draw an envelope around the Condition *A* trend line that represents the acceptable stability criterion. Do the same for Condition *B*. (Figure 8-21, graph *a* exemplifies this operation with Condition *A*.)

Calculate the percentage of data points of Condition *A* that fall within the trend stability range or envelope.

Number of data points within the range	÷	Total number of data points	=	Percent stability
5	÷	8	=	62.5%

If 85%–90% of the data points (e.g., ⅞) fall within the stability criterion range, enter "stable" in Row 3 (Trend Stability); if less than 85%, enter "variable."

Conditions	A⁄1	B⁄2
3. Trend Stability	variable (62.5%)	stable (100%)

Step 5: Determining data paths within trend. Using the freehand method, note whether there are two distinct data paths within the Condition *A* trend line; then within the Condition *B* trend line. If yes, draw lines that represent the two data paths in Row 4 (Data Paths within Trend) and indicate, for each path, whether it is improving (+), decaying (–), or whether it is zero celeration (=). If there is only one data path that approximates the split-middle line, copy the slope line from Row 2.

Conditions	A⁄1	B⁄2
4. Data Paths within Trend	(–)	(+) (=)

(Note: In the intervention condition (*B*), as shown in Figure 8-19, a stable decelerating and improving trend is plotted (Days 9–15) that stabilizes (Days 16–21) near the floor.)

Step 6: Determining level stability and range. Find the mean level of Condition *A* by adding the values of all the data points and dividing the sum by the number of data points.

Condition A	1	2	3	4	5	6	7	8	Total
Data Point Value	18 + 20 + 16 + 14 + 18 + 18 + 16 + 19 =								139

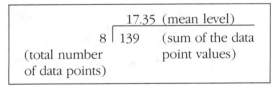

Then, draw a mean line across Condition *A* at the mean level value (17.35). Using the stability criterion (3) for calculating trend stability, draw an envelope around the mean line of Condition *A*. (Figure 8-21, graph *b* shows this operation.) Calculate the percentage of data points that fall within the level stability range.

Number of data points within the range	÷	Total number of data points	=	Percent stability
5	÷	8	=	62.5%

If 85%–90% of the data points (e.g., 7/8) fall on or within the level stability envelope, enter "stable" in Row 5 (Level Stability and Range); if less than 85% enter "variable." To locate the range of values of Condition A identify the data points with the lowest and highest ordinate values. Enter the level range in Row 5 (Level Stability and Range).

Repeat Step 5 with Condition B.

Conditions	A/1	B/2
5. Level Stability and Range	variable 14–20	variable 0–15

Step 7: Determining "absolute" level change. Identify the ordinate values of the first (Day 1) and last (Day 8) data points of Condition A. Subtract the smallest value from the largest and note whether change was in the direction of improvement ($+$), deterioration ($-$), or whether there was no change ($=$).

Largest value – Smallest value = Level				
(Day 8)		(Day 1)		Change
19	–	18	=	1

Enter this information in Row 6 (Level Change). Repeat Step 6 with Condition B.

Conditions	A/1	B/2
6. Level Change	19 – 18 (–1)	12 – 2 (+10)

Table 8-4 summarizes the completed "within condition visual analysis" for the graphic data presented in Figure 8-19.

Component 2: Between Adjacent Conditions Analysis (Table 8-5)

The objective of this component of the visual analysis process is to determine the effect the teacher's ignoring (B) had on the number of student talk-outs. This effect can be identified by comparing the data of Condition B with that of condition A.

Preliminary steps for completing table 8-5.

1. Identify the two conditions to be compared (A and B).

2. Record the second condition in the sequence (B) above the line in the top row labelled "Condition Comparison," and the first condition of the sequence below the line.

Condition Comparison	$^{B_1}/_{A_1}$ (2:1)

(This reads, "comparing the effects of B over A.") Within the parentheses, indicate the order in which the conditions appeared in the sequence of conditions (e.g., B_1 was the second condition in the study; A_1 was the first condition of the study—write 2:1).

3. In most studies we analyze, a particular condition is introduced into a data series more than once (A_1-B_1-A_2-B_2), and frequently a condition will be compared to more than one other condition ($A_{-1}B_1$-BC_1-B_2-A_2-B_3). In such cases, similar condition comparisons ($^{B}/_{A_1}$, $^{B}/_{A_2}$) should be adjacent in the Condition Comparison row. Using the (A_1-B_1-BC_1-B_2-A_2-B_3) condition sequence (or design) as an example, align the condition comparisons according to the following guidelines:

First—Determine which *adjacent* conditions are going to be compared:

$^{B_1}/_{A_1}$, $^{BC_1}/_{B_1}$, $^{B_2}/_{BC_1}$, $^{A_2}/_{B_2}$, $^{B_3}/_{A_2}$

Second—Order the condition comparisons across the top row according to (1) identical condition comparisons ($^{B_1}/_{A_1}$ $^{B_3}/_{A_2}$); (2) similar condition comparisons based on the top condition ($^{B_2}/_{BC_1}$); (3) different condition comparisons ($^{BC_1}/_{B_1}$; $^{A_2}/_{B_2}$).

For the A_1-B_1-BC_1-B_2-A_2-B_3 design, the sequence of condition comparisons would appear as follows:

Condition Comparison	$^{B_1}/_{A_1}$ (2:1)	$^{B_3}/_{A_2}$ (6:5)	$^{B_2}/_{BC_1}$ (4:3)	$^{BC_1}/_{B_1}$ (3:2)	$^{A_2}/_{B_2}$ (5:4)

By ordering condition comparisons in this manner it is possible to identify which conditions were replicated within the same single subject design. This is important when determining the internal validity of the findings and when determining whether correlational or functional conclusions can be drawn.

Step 1: Determining the number of variables changed. To determine the number of variables that change between conditions, carefully read the procedure sections for the two conditions. Attend to both the obvious changes (i.e., introduction or removal of a procedure) as well as the subtle variables that may change (e.g., reinforcement schedule, task format, number of trials per session, teacher proximity to student, time of day, setting). In addition, a descriptive figure legend and descriptive condition labels may prove helpful when identifying changes between conditions. In our example, *A* represents the teacher's attending to each episode of talking-out by his verbal reprimanding of the student, and *B* represents the teacher's systematic ignoring of each talk-out. Assuming all other variables were constant across conditions, enter "1" in Row 1 (Number of Variables Changed).

Condition Comparison	$^{B_1}/_{A_1}$ (2:1)
1. Number of Variables Changed	1

Step 2: Determining the change in trend direction. Copy the information presented in Row 2 of Table 8-4 in Row 2 of Table 8-5 in sequence; i.e., *A* slope followed by *B* slope.

Condition Comparison	$^{B_1}/_{A_1}$ (2:1)	
2. Change in Trend Direction and Effect	(−)	(+)
	Positive	

If two data paths have been identified in the first condition (*A*), enter the slope of the last data path within the condition. This information is obtained from Row 4 of Table 8-4 (Data Paths within Trend).

To determine the effect (positive, negative, or none) of the second condition (*B*) over the first condition (*A*), compare the two slopes for a change in trend direction. In our example, the introduction of *B* resulted in a change in trend from an accelerating-decaying trend in *A*, to a decelerating-improving trend in *B*. Therefore, the introduction of *B* resulted in a positive change in trend direction and "positive" is written in the lower half of Row 2.

Step 3: Determining change in trend stability. In Step 5 of the "within condition analysis" the trend stability of each condition was calculated and noted as being "stable" or "variable." This information was then entered in Table 8-4, Row 3. To identify changes in trend stability between adjacent conditions simply enter the information from Row 3 for the two conditions in Row 3 of Table 8-5.

Condition Comparison	$^{B_1}/_{A_1}$ (2:1)
3. Change in Trend Stability	variable to stable

Step 4: Determining absolute change in level. To determine the change in level from Condition *A* to Condition *B* use the information presented in Row 6 (Level Change) of Table 8-4. In Row 4 (Change in Level) enter the last value recorded under *A* (18) and the first value of *B* (12).

Condition Comparison	B_1/A_1 (2:1)
4. Change in Level	$(18 - 12)$

Then subtract the smallest from the largest value and note whether the change was in the direction of improvement $(+)$ or deterioration $(-)$. If there was no change in level, simply enter 0.

Condition Comparison	B_1/A_1 (2:1)
4. Change in Level	$(18 - 12)$ $+6$

Step 5: Determining the percentage of overlap. To determine the percentage of data point values plotted in A, do the following:

1. Refer to Table 8-4, Row 5 and note the range of values in A (R = 14–20).

2. Refer to Table 8-4, Row 1 and note the number of data points plotted in B (N = 13).

3. Refer to Figure 8-19 and count the number of data points in B that fall within the range of A (N = 1).

4. Divide the number of data points of B that fall within the range of A (1) by the total number of data points in B (13), and multiply by 100.

$$13 \,\overline{\big)\, 1.00} \quad .0769 \times 100 = 7.69\%$$

Enter this percentage in Row 5 of Table 8-5.

Condition Comparison	B_1/A_1 (2:1)
5. Percentage of Overlap	7.69%

Component 3: Guidelines for Writing a Summary of Condition Comparisons

The information presented in Table 8-5 summarizes the major comparisons that should be discussed when evaluating the impact of planned ignoring (B) on the frequency of talk-outs. Having analyzed the graphic data (e.g., Figure 8-19), the next task is to write a clear and concise summary narrative. The following guidelines are presented to assist in this final component of the visual analysis process.

Step 1. Write a brief general statement regarding the impact the second condition of the analysis (*B*) had over the first condition (*A*) relative to the dependent measure (number of talk-outs). Use the descriptive labels of the two conditions rather than the letter notations. Letter notations may be placed in parentheses immediately after the descriptive condition label. (Refer to Table 8-5, Row 2.)

> *Sample:*
> The data presented in Figure 8-19 show a positive change in the number of student talk-outs with the introduction of planned teacher ignoring (*B*).

Step 2. Describe any change in trend direction and stability that occurred when the second condition was introduced. Note whether there were two distinct data paths within either trend. (Refer to Table 8-4, Row 4 and Table 8-5, Rows 2 and 3)

> *Sample:*
> The introduction of planned ignoring resulted in a stable, decelerating-improving trend in the number of talk-outs following a variable, accelerating-decaying trend when the teacher attended to the student's talk-outs.

Step 3. Describe any change in level and indicate whether it was in the direction of the intervention objective. (Refer to Table 8-5, Row 4)

> *Sample:*
> During the first day of intervention (Day 9) 6 fewer talk-outs were observed when compared to the last day of the baseline condition (Day 8).

Step 4. Describe the percentage of overlap between the two conditions. Note whether there was any unusual data point in either condition (high or low value) that may account for a high percentage of overlap. Also, indicate whether the data stabilized at either the ceiling or floor levels. (Refer to Table 8-5, Row 5 and Figure 8-19)

> *Sample:*
> There was a 7.69% overlap in the number of talk-outs between conditions, with the level stabilizing at or below 2 talk-outs per day beginning on Day 18 during intervention.

Step 5. Refer to the graph(s) and tables and write your concerns and recommendations regarding the analysis of these two conditions. This information will be included in the Discussion section of the research report. Focus attention on those things the researcher could have done to strengthen his demonstration of experimental control.

Sample Recommendations:

1. Continue baseline condition for at least two additional days.

2. Replicate the impact of *B* over *A* by expanding the design to an A_1-B_1-A_2-B_2 design. This would strengthen the internal validity of the findings by permitting the researcher to draw functional, rather than correlational, conclusions regarding the influence "planned ignoring" had on the frequency of talk-outs.

3. Replicate the study with other students, other teachers, and in other settings to enhance the external validity of the findings.

Step 6. Steps 1–5 should be followed for each condition comparison listed in Table 8-5.

Step 7. After each individual condition comparison has been written, write one brief paragraph that summarizes all similar conditions. For example, with an A_1-B_1-BC_1-B_2-A_2-B_3 design, write one summary paragraph for each of the following condition comparisons: (1) B to A and B to BC; (2) BC to B and A to B.

SUMMARY

This chapter has overviewed general guidelines for selecting and constructing graphic displays and conducting visual analyses of graphic data. As previously stated, there are few hard and fast rules when it comes to the sequence and format for inspecting data. The three components that have been discussed and the properties of data that we have addressed are familiar to applied behavior analysts. Although the visual analysis sequence and organizational format within each component may vary, the properties of data (level and trend) that require attention do not. In the chapters that follow, detailed visual analyses are presented for each type of single subject research design. As you practice conducting visual analyses on graphic data using the general guidelines outlined in this chapter, you will discover that the process is far less cumbersome than you may now think. Therefore, as you read single subject research investigations and the overviews of studies we present, attempt to complete Tables 8-2 and 8-3—*with practice comes proficiency*.

9

WITHDRAWAL AND REVERSAL DESIGNS

Single subject research methodology is based on what Sidman (1960) and others have referred to as baseline logic. Simply stated, baseline logic refers to the repeated measurement of behavior under at least two experimental conditions: baseline (A) and intervention (B). If there is a measurable change in behavior after the introduction of intervention, when compared with baseline measures, it is probable that the introduction of intervention was responsible for that change (A-B design). To verify this hypothesis the applied researcher can withdraw (or reverse) the condition by returning to the previous baseline condition (A-B-A design). If the student's behavior returns to or approximates the level measured during the initial baseline condition there is a greater likelihood that the intervention was responsible for the behavior change. By reintroducing the intervention condition (A-B-A-B design) a more powerful demonstration of experimental control is possible. The more replications of effect, the greater the probability that the intervention was responsible for the change in the subject's behavior.

The repeated measurement of behavior under baseline and intervention conditions serves as the foundation for all single subject research paradigms. That is, all single subject research designs are mere extensions or elaborations of the basic A-B paradigm. This chapter describes, analyzes, and exemplifies those single subject designs commonly referred to as "reversal" designs. Campbell and Stanley (1966), Glass, Willson, and Gottman (1975), and Birnbrauer, Peterson, and Solnick (1974) have referred to these designs as simple and repeated time series designs. Specifically, discussion focuses on "A", "B", A-B, A-B-A, A-B-A-B, B-A-B, and A-B-C-B designs. Several variations of the A-B-A-B design are presented and discussed.

This chapter was written by **David L. Gast** and **James W. Tawney**.

"A" and "B" Designs

The "A" design and "B" design represent two types of investigations commonly associated with the case-study approach (Kratochwill, 1978). Unlike the traditional case study approach, which relies heavily on descriptive narrative of an investigator's observations (Irwin & Bushnell, 1980), the "A" and "B" designs require that an investigator's observations be summarized and reported in numerical terms. With both designs the investigator pinpoints one or more variables of the behavior or event under investigation and, using some measurement system, quantifies her observations. It is important to note that neither of these paradigms constitutes an experimental design, i.e., an identification of functional relationships between dependent and independent variables is not possible; rather both designs are considered descriptive-observational paradigms.

The "A" design represents a purely descriptive investigation during which an investigator has no plans to intervene or in any way alter the phenomenon under study. Ecological psychologists and sociologists who are often involved in the systematic observation of people in their natural environments, use this approach when mapping behavior patterns relative to ecological variables. Because the investigator does not wish to intrude or intervene during repeated observations of the phenomenon of interest, this descriptive-statistical approach can be viewed as an extended baseline condition; thus the label *"A" design*.

The "A" design has also been used for post hoc analysis of behavior. For example, Weisberg and Waldrop (1972) studied the rate at which Congress passed legislation from 1947 to 1968. Their investigation revealed that "the rate of passage is extremely low three to four months after commencement followed by a positively accelerated growth rate that continues until the time of adjournment" (p. 93). Figure 9-1 presents a cumulative record of the number of bills passed in both sessions of Congress from January 1961 to October 1968. The post hoc analysis of events represents a descriptive-quantitative, rather than an experimental-quantitative, investigation.

The "B" design is a second type of case-study approach. Like the "A" design an investigator who employs the "B" design systematically measures a subject's, or group of subjects', behavior under identified stimulus conditions. Unlike the "A" paradigm, measurement in the "B" paradigm occurs during or soon after an intervention has been introduced—not before. The "B" design does not specify how frequently observations of the target behavior must be made; observations can be made only once, as with a posttest, or as frequently as each day, as with continuous direct observational recording. The more frequent the measurement, the more representative are the data in describing the behavior.

Educators often use the "B" design. For example, a teacher who records weekly spelling test scores after several days of instruction is employing the "B" design. She can determine whether a student has learned the target words, but she cannot verify that her instruction was responsible for the student's achievement. Without preintervention (i.e., baseline) data on the target spelling words, and without adequate measures to control for historical confounding, it is impossible to make an objective empirical evaluation of instructional program effectiveness.

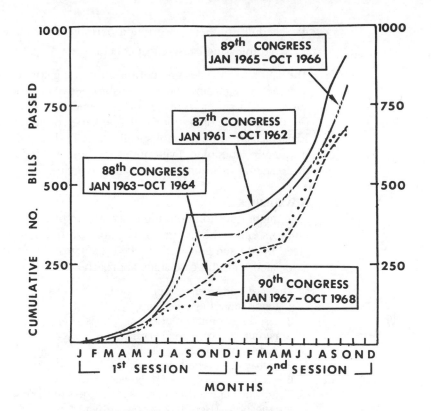

FIGURE 9-1   Cumulative number of bills passed during the legislative sessions of Congress from January 1961 to October 1968. (Figure 2, p. 95, from: Weisburg, P. and Waldrop, P.B. Fixed-interval work habits of Congress. *Journal of Applied Behavior Analysis*, 1972, 5 (1), 93–97. Copyright by Society for the Experimental Analysis of Behavior, Inc. Reproduced by permission.)

Internal and External Validity

At best, the "A" and "B" designs generate descriptive-quantitative information that allows investigators to hypothesize correlational, rather than functional, relationships between a dependent variable and environmental events. Because investigators do not attempt to control for potential confoundings (e.g., history, maturation, testing), the findings cannot be said to be internally or externally valid. Such statements must be derived from an experimental design that replicates a positive effect with the same subject (internal validity) as well as across similar subjects (external validity).

Considerations

Guidelines

An investigator who chooses to study behavior using either the "A" or "B" design should:

1. Behaviorally define the target behavior(s).

2. Select a measurement system that permits an analysis of antecedent and consequent events relative to the target behavior(s).

3. Thoroughly describe the conditions under which the target behavior is measured.

4. Schedule frequent observation periods of the target behavior(s).

5. Avoid inferring cause-effect conclusions.

The "A" and "B" designs permit an investigator to make only correlational statements regarding the relationship between independent and dependent variables. In order to make such statements it is imperative that the dependent variable be operationally defined, the conditions under which the behavior is measured be technologically described, and the observation periods be frequently scheduled. Even under the best of conditions an investigator must avoid stating or implying cause-effect conclusions.

Advantages

One might question both the utility and importance of an investigation which employs either the "A" or "B" design. Lazarus and Davison (1971), as summarized by Hersen and Barlow (1976), suggest the following list of advantages associated with the case-study approach:

> The case study method can be used to:
> 1. foster clinical investigations,
> 2. cast doubt on theoretical assumptions,
> 3. permit study of rare phenomena,
> 4. develop new technical skills,
> 5. buttress theoretical views,
> 6. result in refinement of techniques, and
> 7. provide clinical data to be used as a departure point for subsequent controlled investigations. (Hersen & Barlow, 1976, p. 168)

Both the "A" and "B" designs can be expanded to provide an experimental analysis of the relationship between independent and dependent variables. This can be accomplished by expanding the "B" design to a B-A-B design, provided the dependent and independent variables are operationally defined, the stimulus conditions concisely described, the target behavior repeatedly measured, and the data stable before experimental conditions are changed. Under similar circumstances, with the exception of post hoc studies of events (e.g., Weisberg & Waldrop, 1971), the "A" design may be expanded to an A-B-A or A-B-A-B design. Whether, in fact, these expansions are possible depends upon a number of factors, including practical and/or ethical constraints.

Limitations

The shortcomings of the "A" and "B" designs should be apparent. Neither paradigm permits a functional analysis of behavior. Without measuring a target behavior under both baseline *and* intervention conditions it is impossible to isolate those variables responsible for behavior change. At best, the "A" and "B" designs permit an investigator to report on the level and trend of the data over time and within a broadly defined condition. As a starting point for a more thorough investigation, these "designs" may suffice for the previously discussed advantages.

Concluding Comments

The "A" and "B" designs provide a framework within which a teacher or clinician can objectively measure behavior. Though both are an improvement over the traditional case-study method, neither permits an experimental analysis of behavioral change. There are no occasions in which the "A" or "B" design would be appropriate to evaluate the effectiveness of an instructional program or intervention strategy. The "B" design, however, does permit an objective empirical description of student performance relative to preestablished instructional objective criteria. Determination of whether achievements are due to a teacher's or clinician's intervention strategy requires the use of an experimental design (e.g., A-B-A-B, multiple baseline) that controls for the many potentially confounding variables. There are few occasions when an applied researcher would choose the "A" or "B" design over more rigorous and informative experimental designs.

A-B Design

The A-B design, sometimes referred to as the "simple time series design" (e.g., Birnbrauer, Peterson, & Solnick, 1974), represents the most basic "quasi-experimental" single subject design. This design requires that the dependent variable be measured repeatedly under controlled baseline (A) and intervention (B) conditions. After several observations under baseline conditions, and after the data trend and level have stabilized, the intervention is introduced. During intervention the target behavior continues to be repeatedly measured, noting changes in the dependent variable. Any changes in the target behavior are *presumed* to be a function of the independent variable.

Internal and External Validity

The A-B design is subject to threats to both internal and external validity (Campbell & Stanley, 1966; Glass, Willson, & Gottman, 1975; Kratochwill, 1978). Since the effect is not replicated with the same subject, there is no assurance that the independent variable is responsible for any observed behavioral changes. More specifically, since there is (1) no return to baseline conditions and (2) no concurrent monitoring of similar, yet functionally independent behaviors, the natural course of the target behavior in the absence of the intervention (B) cannot be determined. It may very well be that changes in the dependent variable are occurring naturally or in response to some unidentified and uncontrolled variable (i.e., maturational and historical confounding, respectively). In light of these and other threats to internal validity, the A-B design yields correlational conclusions at best, and then only if abrupt changes in level and trend are observed immediately following the introduction of the independent variable.

Considerations

Guidelines

When using the A-B design, the investigator should:

1. Behaviorally define the target behavior.

2. Collect continuous baseline data (A) over a *minimum* of 3 consecutive days.

3. Introduce the independent variable (B) only after an acceptable stable baseline trend and level have been attained.

4. Continuously collect data on the target behavior during the intervention condition.

5. Avoid inferring cause-effect conclusions.

6. Replicate the experimental effect with similar subjects.

Advantages

The A-B design provides a framework within which behavior can be objectively measured under controlled environmental conditions. It improves upon the "B" design by adding repeated measurement of a targeted behavior under "natural" or baseline conditions prior to the introduction of the independent variable. Though the A-B design does not permit a functional analysis of behavior, it may provide a convincing demonstration that changes in behavior are not a function of the passage of time (i.e., maturation). This may be accomplished when behavioral changes measured in the intervention condition are immediate and abrupt and follow a long and stable baseline data trend. There are circumstances in educational and clinical settings that may preclude the use of more extensive experimental designs that require the repeated withdrawal or reversal of the independent variable. When confronted with such practical and/or ethical constraints the A-B design may be the only evaluation paradigm available to the teacher or clinician for monitoring program effectiveness.

Limitations

Conclusions drawn from studies which employ the A-B design are limited by numerous threats to internal validity (history, maturation, testing, data instability, subject attrition, reactive intervention) and external validity (independent variable description, Hawthorne effect, novelty and disruption effects, experimenter effects, interaction effects of testing, interaction effects of history and intervention, measurement, generality) (Kratochwill, 1978). The most notable limitation of the A-B design is the lack of information on the natural course of the target behavior in the absence of the intervention. Without such information it is impossible to rule out the influence of uncontrolled variables (i.e., historical confoundings) or the passage of time (i.e., maturational confounding) on the dependent measure (Wolf & Risley, 1971).

Let it suffice to say that the A-B design provides weak correlational conclusions; for this reason it has been described as "quasi-experimental." If a full experimental analysis of behavior is desired, it is necessary to extend the design to an A-B-A or A-B-A-B design. Only when the A-B design is expanded in these ways is a functional analysis of behavior possible.

Applied Example: A-B Design

Study I: Severely Handicapped

Azrin, N.H., and Wesolowski, M.D. Theft reversal: An overcorrection procedure for eliminating stealing by retarded persons. *Journal of Applied Behavior Analysis*, 1974, 7 (4), 577–581.

Purpose, subject, and setting. Azrin and Wesolowski (1974) evaluated the effectiveness of an overcorrection procedure, compared to a simple correction procedure, as a deterrent to stealing. The subjects of the investigation were 34 ambulatory and nonverbal severely and profoundly mentally retarded adults (average CA = 41 years; average IQ = 15). The subjects, 16 males and 18 females, were all residents of a state institution. The presenting problem was a high frequency of stealing on the ward, particularly during mealtimes and during commissary periods between meals. The study was conducted in the hospital commissary.

Dependent variable. The dependent variable was the total number of stealing episodes committed by the 34 residents each day. To ensure an accurate detection of each theft the 34 residents were divided into three approximately equal groups; only one group participated in a commissary period at a time. In additon, the two trainers who accompanied the subjects to the commissary independently collected data on the number of stealing episodes during the 30-minute commissary period. These observers were also responsible for consequating any instance of stealing they observed in accordance with the intervention which was in effect at the time. Interobserver agreement on the number of stealing episodes recorded was "almost perfect," with only one disagreement recorded during the course of the study.

Independent variable. The two interventions compared, relative to their impact on the frequency of stealing episodes, were simple correction (A) and overcorrection (B). In the simple correction procedure a staff member required the "thief" to immediately return the stolen food item to the victim. The overcorrection or theft reversal procedure required the offender to return the stolen item to the victim *and* give the victim an additional identical item obtained from the commissary item display area. Both the simple correction and overcorrection procedures included the trainer's (1) verbally reprimanding the thief, (2) verbally instructing her to return or obtain the items, and (3) manually assisting her in doing so if she did not follow the verbal instructions.

Design and condition sequence. A simple A-B time series design was employed to evaluate the effects of the simple correction (A) and overcorrection (B) procedures on the frequency of the residents' stealing. There was no attempt to compare either procedure with a no-intervention condition for ethical reasons. The simple correction condition was in effect for 5 days, followed by 20 days when the overcorrection procedure was administered for each instance of stealing.

Results as reported by authors. Figure 9-2 displays the data on the total number of thefts committed by the 34 residents. During the simple correction condition (A), approximately 20 stealing episodes occurred each day. When the overcorrection procedure (B) was introduced on Day 6, thefts decreased by approximately 50%. By Day 9 (i.e., Day 4 of the overcorrection procedure) no instances of stealing occurred. This trend and level continued over the remaining 16 days of the overcorrection condition. Measures of the amount of time required by staff to complete each correction procedure revealed that the simple correction procedure required an average of 7 seconds (± 2) and the overcorrection procedure 106 seconds (± 17).

Azrin and Wesolowski noted that 27 of the 34 residents committed at least one theft during the course of the study. They also pointed out that 24 of those 27 residents attempted to destroy the item while staff were prompting them to return the item to the victim. They speculated that these offenders intended to "cause distress to the victim, rather than merely possess the item" (p. 579).

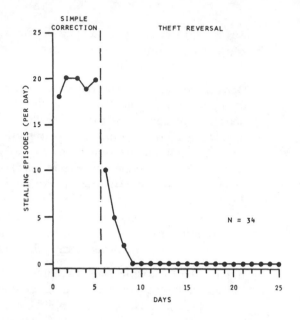

FIGURE 9-2 (Figure 1, p. 579, from: Azrin, N.H., and Wesolowski, M.D. Theft reversal: An overcorrection procedure for eliminating stealing by retarded persons. *Journal of Applied Behavior Analysis*, 1974, 7 (4), 577–581. Copyright by Society for the Experimental Analysis of Behavior, Inc. Reproduced by permission.)

Summary and conclusions. The data presented in Figure 9-2 clearly show a difference in both the level and trend of the number of stealing episodes between the simple correction (A) and overcorrection (B) conditions. The relative effectiveness of the overcorrection procedure compared to the simple correction procedure is, however, at best correlational. Because the effect was not replicated with the same group of residents (i.e., direct intrasubject replication) or with other groups of residents (i.e., direct intersubject replication), the findings have no internal or external validity. This is not to say that the overcorrection procedure was not responsible for decreasing the frequency of thefts; rather there was no experimental demonstration of a cause-effect or functional relationship. If the authors had expanded the A-B design to an A-B-A, and if the frequency of thefts increased during the second baseline or simple correction condition (A_2), then an experimental analysis of the effects of overcorrection on the frequency of stealing would have been possible. The reintroduction of the overcorrection procedure (B_2) would have further strenghthened the internal validity of the findings (i.e., A-B-A-B). An alternative strategy to enhance the believability of the results would have been to replicate the study with additional groups of residents, preferably within the context of a multiple baseline (or multiple probe) design across subjects (see chapters 10 and 11).

Concluding Comments

The A-B design provides a framework for repeated measurement of a targeted behavior during baseline and intervention conditions. Though the design does not permit a functional analysis of behavior, it can be useful to educators and clinicians when practical and ethical constraints preclude the repeated introduction and withdrawal of an intervention. If circumstances permit, and if functional rather than correlational conclusions are desired, an applied researcher should definitely select an expanded version (e.g., A-B-A-B) or variation (e.g., multiple baseline) of the simple A-B design.

A-B-A Design

The A-B-A design represents the simplest single subject research paradigm for demonstrating cause-effect relationships. Like the A-B design, the target behavior is continuously measured under baseline (A_1) and intervention (B) conditions. After the dependent variable has stabilized during intervention, the investigator reintroduces baseline conditions (A_2) to the target behavior. The addition of this second baseline condition enhances the strength of the simple A-B design by allowing functional, rather than correlational, conclusions.

Internal and External Validity

The A-B-A design is preferable to the A-B design, at least from a research standpoint, since it permits an experimental analysis of behavior. Hersen and Barlow (1976) have clearly described how experimental control is demonstrated:

> If after baseline measurement (A) the application of a treatment (B) leads to improvement and conversely results in deterioration after it is withdrawn (A), one can conclude with a high degree of certainty that the treatment variable is the agent responsible for observed changes in the target behavior. Unless the natural history of the behavior under study were to follow identical fluctuations in trends, it is *most improbable* that observed changes are due to any influence (e.g., some correlated or uncontrolled variable) other than the treatment variable that is systematically changed. (Hersen & Barlow, 1976, p. 176)

It is important to note the emphasis on the phrase "most improbable," for though the reintroduction of baseline conditions and the subsequent retrieval or approximation of initial baseline responding levels strengthens the argument that the independent variable was responsible for observed changes in the dependent variable, it does not preclude alternative explanations (e.g., historical confounding). The demonstration of experimental control is strengthened with the A-B-A design, however, when a stable data trend in the intervention condition is followed by an immediate and abrupt change in level and trend in the second baseline condition (A_2). Conclusions can be strengthened further by extending the design to an A-B-A-B design and/or by replicating the experimental effect with other subjects, thereby strenghthening the internal and external validity.

Considerations

Guidelines

When using the A-B-A design the investigator should:

1. Behaviorally define the target behavior.

2. Collect continuous baseline data (A_1) over a minimum of 3 consecutive days.

3. Introduce the intervention (B) only after a stable "contratherapeutic" or zero celeration baseline trend has been established in A_1.

4. Collect continuous data during intervention over a minimum of 3 days.

5. Withdraw (or reverse) the intervention and return to baseline conditions (A_2) only after acceptable stability in level and trend have been established in the intervention condition (B).

6. Replicate the experimental effect with other subjects.

Advantages

The primary advantage of the A-B-A design, when compared with A-B design, is that it allows a functional analysis of behavior. This permits an investigator to conclude with greater certainty that her intervention was responsible for changes in the target behavior. Conclusions can be further substantiated and strengthened when the experimental effect is replicated with similar subjects. Though such replications enhance the external validity of the findings, it is the first change in the dependent variable, when the intervention is introduced for the first time (A_1-B), that is the most generalizable, and hence the most important demonstration of the impact intervention has on the dependent variable (Barlow & Hayes, 1979).

Limitations

Although the A-B-A design permits a functional, rather than correlational, analysis of behavior, it is susceptible to numerous threats to internal and external validity. First, and foremost, is the possibility, however remote, that the introduction and withdrawal of the independent variable coincided with naturally occurring cyclical variations of the target behavior. This threat to internal validity can best be controlled by decreasing or increasing the number of observation periods in the second baseline condition (A_2) and reintroducing the intervention (B_2). This second replication of experimental effect greatly enhances the demonstration of experimental control. Second, there is the likelihood that A_1 dependent variable levels will not be fully retrieved in A_2, though they should be approximated. Such sequential confounding is not uncommon to the A-B-A and A-B-A-B designs. Third, the A-B-A design is not appropriate for evaluating program effectiveness with behaviors which are difficult, if not impossible, to reverse (e.g., academic skills). And fourth, there are practical as well as ethical problems associated with terminating a study in a baseline condition. This criticism is often voiced by teachers and clinicians who are more concerned with improving a student's or client's behavioral repertoire. It is important to remember, however, that there are few occasions when a teacher or applied researcher would select the A-B-A design, a priori, to evaluate the impact of an intervention on a targeted behavior. The A-B-A design appears in the literature primarily due to subject attrition during the course of the investigation; researchers seldom select the A-B-A design at the outset of an investigation.

Applied Example: A-B-A Design

Study I: Mildly Handicapped

Doleys, D.M., Wells, K.C., Hobbs, S.A., Roberts, M.W., and Cartelli, L.M. The effects of social punishment on noncompliance: A comparison with timeout and positive practice. *Journal of Applied Behavior Analysis*, 1976, 9 (4), 471–482.

Purpose, subject, and setting. Doleys et al. (1976) investigated the effects of a social punishment procedure (i.e., a loud verbal reprimand followed by a silent glare) on the noncompliant behavior of four educable mentally handicapped children (CA = 8–10 years). All four children were described by their teachers and parents as being "noncompliant" or "uncooperative." The study was conducted in a room equipped with two tables on which a variety of age-appropriate toys and playthings were placed. These toys and playthings (e.g., coloring books and crayons, plastic cars and trucks, hand puppets) were divided into two groups: Task A toys and Task B toys. All Task A and Task B toys were available each session and assigned to separate tables in the experimental room. Task A toy commands were used to assess response generalization to "familiar" toys, while Task B toys were designated as training toys. In addition to these toys and playthings, a jigsaw puzzle and play telephone were periodically presented during baseline conditions to assess response generalization to "unfamiliar" playthings. Children were seen individually in 30–40 minute sessions by an adult trainer five days per week.

Dependent variables. Data were collected on the subject's "compliance" or "noncompliance" to trainer commands by an independent observer stationed in an adjacent observation room. Noncompliance was defined as a subject's failing to touch the toy specified in the command within 10 seconds. These daily data were converted to a percent of noncompliance for each child. Independent reliability checks were made during 20%–25% of the sessions, depending upon the subject. Interobserver agreement was computed using the scored interval or interval by interval method, yielding a mean percent agreement of 88% to 98%.

Independent variable. During the first session with each child the trainer named and modelled how to play with each toy. In the latter half of the first session and in all subsequent sessions the trainer verbally directed the child to play with one of the Task A or Task B toys every 55 seconds. The mean number of trials presented each session was 24 (range = 18–28). Task A commands (i.e., "familiar" toy probes) were presented in a format similar to "Color in the coloring book with the colors," while Task B commands (i.e., training toys) followed the form "Play with the _____." An equal number of Task A and Task B commands were randomly presented during each session, though only noncompliance to Task B commands was consequated using one of the intervention procedures. The baseline and three intervention conditions were administered as follows:

• *Baseline* (A)—Commands to play with either a Task A or Task B toy were presented every 55 seconds. Periodically subjects were asked to play with one of the two "unfamiliar" probe-toys. There was no consequation for noncompliance, i.e., not touching the appropriate toy within 10 seconds after the command was issued.

• *Social Punishment* (B)—Each noncompliance episode with Task B toys resulted in the trainer (1) firmly grasping the child by the shoulders, (2) verbally reprimanding the child in a "scolding" voice for disobeying, and (3) silently glaring at the child for 40 seconds. Noncompliance to Task A toys was not consequated.

• *Positive Practice* (C)—Each noncompliance response on Task B commands was followed by the trainer manually guiding the child through the commanded task for 40 seconds. If the subject began appropriately play with the toy, manual guidance was removed. Noncompliance to Task A commands was not consequated.

• *Timeout* (D)—Noncompliance to Task B commands resulted in the trainer "calmly" telling the child to sit in the corner of the room for 40 seconds. The trainer led the student to the corner and stood behind her for the duration of the timeout period. Noncompliance to Task A commands was not consequated.

During each session and throughout all conditions the trainer issued commands from one part of the room. He moved around the room if it was necessitated by the experimental condition or to rearrange the toys on the table. The trainer had no other interaction with the subject during sessions except for those required by the interventions.

Design and condition sequence. The order in which conditions were introduced varied across subjects. Keith's noncompliance behavior was evaluated in an A-B-A design, while Paula's noncompliance responses were assessed in an A-C-A-B-A design (see Figure 9-3). Both Ricky and Scott were exposed to all interventions in an A-D-A-C-A-B-A sequence. The A-B-A design used with Keith represents the simplest experimental design. The single subject designs employed with the other three subjects represent two variations of a multitreatment design. (For a detailed discussion of the multitreatment design refer to Chapter *12*). The authors varied the order in which experimental conditions were introduced to subjects to control for historical confounding, i.e., order effect. The decision to introduce an experimental condition (B, C, or D) was based on a preestablished baseline (A) stability criterion of "12% deviation or less in the percent of noncompliance across five sessions" (p. 475).

Results as reported by authors. Figure 9-3 shows the percentage of time Keith and Paula did not follow the trainer's commands across conditions. These data represent the percent of noncompliance with both Task A and Task B toys. These data were combined since noncompliance covaried across tasks. For purposes of our discussion, your attention is directed to Keith's data.

Keith was exposed to two conditions: baseline (A) and social punishment (B). During the first baseline condition (A_1) the mean level of noncompliance over the last five sessions was above 90% Upon introduction of the social punishment condition (B) there was an abrupt positive level change in his percent noncompliance. The two sessions during which the social punishment procedure was in effect yielded a noncompliance level at or below 20%. The reintroduction of baseline conditions (A_2) resulted in a gradual and variable accelerating trend that stabilized at about 80%.

The effect of social punishment on the percent of noncompliance for the other three children was replicated when compared to the preceding adjacent baseline condition (A-B). However, as shown in Figure 9-3, Paula's noncompliance continued to improve during the return to baseline condition. This trend in the final baseline condition that followed the social punishment condition is representative of Scott's data also. For all four subjects the social

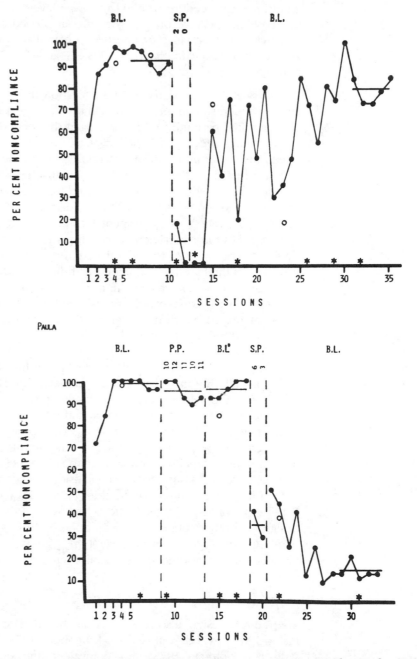

FIGURE 9-3 The percent of noncompliance per session is shown for Keith (upper panel) and Paula (lower panel) across the baseline (B.L.), social punishment (S.P.), and positive practice (P.P.) conditions. The horizontal lines indicate the mean percent noncompliance for the sessions over which they extend; the numbers on the upper portion of each panel represent the number of occasions on which a particular experimental procedure was applied in that session, asterisks mark the sessions when interobserver agreement was obtained, the open circles denote percentage of noncompliance on probe tasks. (Figure 1, p. 476, from: Doley, D.M., Wells, K.C., Hobbs, S.A., Roberts, M.W., and Cartelli, L.M. The effects of social punishment on noncompliance: A comparison with timeout and positive practice. *Journal of Applied Behavior Analysis*, 1976, 9 (4), 471–482. Copyright by Society for the Experimental Analysis of Behavior, Inc. Reproduced by permission.)

punishment procedure resulted in lower levels of noncompliance than did the baseline, positive practice, or timeout procedures. The authors pointed out that noncompliance on the two "unfamiliar" probe-tasks covaried with the levels of noncompliance to Task A and Task B commands across all subjects.

Summary and conclusions. Keith's data show the dramatic positive effect that the social punishment procedure had on his noncompliance. The approximation of initial baseline (A_1) levels during the second baseline condition (A_2) demonstrates the experimental control. i.e., the functional relationship between the social punishment procedure and the percent of noncompliance. The fact that this effect was replicated with three other subjects with more elaborate time series designs adds to the believability that the social punishment procedure was responsible for the decrease in "uncooperative" behavior. The demonstration of experimental control could have been strengthened further if (1) the experimental conditions had been administered for more than two sessions (2) for all subjects the initial baseline levels had been retrieved in the baseline condition that followed social punishment, (3) there had been an abrupt change in level in the first session of the baseline condition that followed social punishment, and (4) the effects of the social punishment procedure had been replicated with each of the four subjects, i.e., direct intrasubject replication.

Concluding Comments

The A-B-A design is more useful than the basic A-B design because it permits an experimental or functional analysis of behavior. However, an applied researcher would seldom select this design at the outset to evaluate intervention effectiveness due to the practical and ethical considerations of ending an investigation in a baseline condition. It would be far more appropriate for an investigator to expand the design to an A-B-A-B, thereby replicating the impact of the independent variable on the target behavior. In order to build a convincing case to support the conclusions generated by an A-B-A design, several intersubject direct replications should be conducted simultaneously. Replication of experimental effects by using either the A-B-A or A-B-A-B design with other subjects has been done by Doleys et al. (1976) and others (e.g., Lutzker, Crozier, & Lutzker, 1981; Van Houten & Lai Fatt, 1981) to increase the believability of intervention effectiveness.

A-B-A-B Design

The A-B-A-B design, also referred to as the "reversal design" (Baer, Wolf, & Risley, 1968), "withdrawal design" (Leitenberg, 1973), "operant design" (Glass, Willson, & Gottman, 1975), and "equivalent time series design" (Campbell & Stanley, 1966; Birnbrauer, Peterson, & Solnick, 1974), is the most frequently used single subject design in behavior modification research (Kratochwill, 1978). Regardless of its label, the A-B-A-B design permits the most powerful demonstration of experimental control because it requires the repeated introduction and withdrawal of an intervention strategy. The most important feature of the A-B-A-B design is that it includes a direct replication of effect, i.e., the last two conditions (A_2-B_2) replicate the first two conditions (A_1-B_1) with the same subject and the same behavior. In spite of the reservations of some educators, therapists, and psychologists, the A-B-A-B design continues to be the simplest and most straightforward evaluation paradigm for showing causality.

Internal and External Validity

The A-B-A-B design demonstrates experimental control when the level and trend of a target behavior improves under intervention conditions (B_1 and B_2) and decays under baseline conditions (A_1 and A_2). With each replication of effect (A-B), the internal validity of the results is strengthened. The internal validity of the independent variable is further strengthened when the magnitude of change in the dependent variable is immediate and abrupt (e.g., correct responding improves from 50% in the last session of A_1 to 90% in the first session of B_1), and when the levels observed in the first baseline condition (A_1) are fully retrived in the second baseline condition (A_2). Though immediate and abrupt changes in both trend and level are desirable, a believable demonstration of casuality is still possible when a gradual reversal in trend is observed and when the first baseline condition level is approached, though not fully recovered. This failure to fully retrieve initial baseline levels within the same number of observation periods of previous conditions is not uncommon to researchers who use the A-B-A-B design. This phenomenon, primarily attributed to historical factors, necessitates changing conditions only after a stable "contratherapeutic" trend has been established. If changes in conditions are based solely on the "equal condition length" guideline, an investigator can seriously jeopardize an otherwise believable demonstration of experimental control.

As with all empirical investigations, the external validity of results is achieved only when cause-effect relationships are replicated with other similar subjects under the same experimental conditions. Consequently many researchers concurrently replicate their investigation from the outset of their study. By so doing they can immediately expand upon the generality of their findings or identify "exceptions to the rule." The importance of this latter point cannot be overstated, for it is through the identification of exceptions that our understanding of human behavior is advanced.

Considerations

Guidelines

When using the A-B-A-B design the researcher should:

1. Behaviorally define the target behavior.

2. Identify, behaviorally define, and concurrently monitor nontargeted behaviors of the same response class.

3. Collect continuous baseline data (A_1) over a minimum of 3 consecutive days.

4. Introduce the intervention strategy (B_1) only after a stable "contratherapeutic" or zero celeration trend has been established in the initial baseline condition (A_1).

5. Collect continuous data during intervention over a minimum of 3 days. (When appropriate, B condition lengths should be the same as A condition lengths.)

6. Withdraw the intervention and return to baseline conditions (A_2) only after

acceptable stability in both trend and level has been established in the first intervention condition (B_1).

7. Reintroduce intervention (B_2) procedures after a stable contratherapeutic or zero celeration trend has been established in the second baseline condition (A_2).

8. Replicate, concurrently if circumstances permit, the experimental effect with similar subjects.

We also recommend that nontargeted behaviors, those behaviors that are functionally or topographically similar to the targeted behavior, be monitored concurrently when using the A-B-A-B design. This strategy may help to identify other changes that occur when the intervention is introduced. Side effects can be either negative (e.g., when head banging, the target behavior, is decreased in frequency, there is a concomitant increase in the frequency of face slapping) or positive (e.g., when sitting at one's desk, the target behavior, is increased in frequency, there is a concomitant increase in the number of assignments completed). Whichever the case, the concurrent monitoring of nontargeted behaviors has practical implications for the educator interested in identifying both appropriate and inappropriate instances of response generalization. Kazdin (1973) has elaborated on the advantages of concurrently monitoring nontargeted behaviors under similar stimulus conditions (i.e., response generalization) and targeted behaviors under different stimulus conditions (i.e., stimulus generalization).

Advantages

The A-B-A-B design provides the most powerful demonstration of casuality available to the applied researcher. It controls for many of the deficiencies associated with the A-B-A design by (1) ending in an intervention condition and (2) providing two occasions during which to replicate the positive effects of intervention (i.e., B_1 to A_1 and B_2 to A_2). By ending in intervention many of the practical and ethical concerns of teachers are dispelled; further, two demonstrations of experimental effect greatly enhance the internal validity of results. As with all single subject designs, the A-B-A-B design can be extended, (e.g., A-B-A-B-C-B-C) thereby permitting the investigator the flexibility of comparing other interventions with the initial intervention. This is a particularly useful option when intervention B results in positive changes in the target behavior which approximate but do not meet the outcome objective. In such cases it would be appropriate for a teacher or researcher to either add to the initial intervention (e.g., A-B-A-B-*BC*-B-BC) or to introduce a totally new intervention (e.g., A-B-A-B-*C*-B-C). These extensions of the A-B-A-B design are discussed and exemplified in Chapter *12* within the discussion of multitreatment designs.

Limitations

The primary limitations of the A-B-A-B design relate to practical and ethical concerns rather than experimental considerations. For many practitioners responsible for programming durable behavior changes (i.e., response maintenance), even a brief withdrawal of an effective intervention strategy may be deemed unethical. This is particularly true when target behaviors are dangerous to the student herself (e.g., eye gouging) or others (e.g., fighting). Such concerns are valid and cannot be discounted. However, one may view condition A_2 (withdrawing the intervention) as a check or "probe." If the target behavior returns to unacceptable levels, that tells the researcher that she will have to plan an additional phase after B_2 is reintroduced. To maintain the response, the researcher may have to thin the reinforcement schedule (e.g., CRF to FR_2 to VR_3) or teach others to carry out the intervention in the natural environment. Rusch & Kazdin (1981) have outlined three startegies (i.e., sequential-withdrawal, partial-withdrawal, and partial-sequential-withdrawal) that may facilitate behavior maintenance if the total withdrawal of the intervention in the second baseline condition (A_2) results in a trend reversal.

Due to ethical concerns, some direct care personnel find it difficult not to apply the intervention during the second baseline condition. If staff and/or parents are not agreeable to withdrawing an effective intervention for even a brief period, the behavior trend probably will not reverse during the second baseline condition, thus jeopardizing a demonstration of experimental control. Therefore, staff and parents should be aware of the purpose of withdrawing the intervention and procedural reliability checks should be conducted during the second baseline condition. Depending upon the availability of staff scheduling of such reliability checks may be impractical.

A third limitation of the A-B-A-B design is that it is not appropriate for evaluating interventions with behaviors that are not likely to be reversed (e.g., writing one's name, completing an assembly task, solving addition problems). The A-B-A-B design can be used in these situations if the reason for failure on such tasks is one of motivation rather than skill acquisition. Otherwise, the multiple baseline or multiple probe design is more appropriate for demonstrating a cause-effect relationship.

Applied Examples: A-B-A-B Design

Study I: Behaviorally Disordered

Luce, S.C., Delquadri, J., and Hall, R.V. Contingent exercise: A mild but powerful procedure for suppressing inappropriate verbal and aggressive behavior. *Journal of Applied Behavior Analysis*, 1980, *13* (4), 583–594. (Experiment 1)

Purpose, subject, and setting. The purpose of the first experiment in this two-experiment investigation was to evaluate the effects of contingent exercise alone on the physically aggressive behavior (i.e., hitting) of a 6-year-old boy who exhibited "autistic behaviors." The study was conducted in a public school classroom in a "regular" neighborhood elementary school. In addition to Ben, the subject for Experiment 1, four to six other students were in attendance. All experimental procedures were administered by the special education teacher and teacher's aide.

In addition to Ben's hitting, he exhibited "high rates of self-stimulatory behaviors, severe tantrums, and abnormal language patterns characterized by repetitive and echolalic responding" (p. 586). During the 2.5 years Ben had participated in the public school program other inappropriate behaviors had been reduced through the use of differential reinforcement of other behaviors (DRO), differential reinforcement of an incompatible behavior (DRI), planned ignoring, restitutional overcorrection with positive practice, and contingent exercise. Although Ben's hitting occurred infrequently at home, his parents requested that his hitting at school be reduced immediately by means of the contingent exercise procedure without a DRO procedure. This request was based on their success with contingent exercise and belief that the DRO procedure was ineffective and time consuming.

Dependent variable. Event recording was used by the teacher or teacher's aide to record the number of times Ben hit throughout the 6-hour school day. A hit was defined as "any hit with an open hand or closed fist" (p. 586). Reliability checks were conducted by a naive adult, stationed outside the classroom, eight times during the course of the experiment across all conditions. The gross method for calculating reliability (smaller number divided by the larger and multiplied by 100) yielded interobserver agreement scores ranging from 87.5% to 100%. The mean reliability score was 97%.

Independent variable. The only experimental procedure in Experiment 1 was contingent exercise. Immediately following each hit the teacher or teacher's aide (1) said, "Ben, no hitting. Stand up and sit down 10 times,"; (2) physically and verbally prompted Ben to stand up and sit on the floor 10 times (physical prompts were used only if Ben did not follow the verbal command); and (3) typically counted aloud or said, "stand up," "sit down," as Ben carried out the exercise routine. If Ben began hitting during contingent exercise the staff began the procedure again.

During baseline conditions no planned procedure was followed after a hitting episode. When fighting that appeared dangerous to the children was observed, staff simply separated the students.

Design and condition sequence. The effectiveness of the contingent exercise procedure (B) was compared to a "no systematic contingencies for aggressive behavior" condition (A) using an A-B-A-B repeated time series design, i.e., withdrawal design. After 17 days of the baseline condition (A_1) the contingent exercise experimental condition (B_1) was implemented for 10 days. A return to baseline condition (A_2) began on Day 28 followed by a reintroduction of the contingent exercise condition on Day 36.

Results as reported by the authors. Figure 9-4 displays the number of hits emitted by Ben across conditions. After a variable baseline data trend, which stabilized at about 30 hits per day over the last 3 days of the condition, the contingent exercise procedure was introduced. Contingent exercise resulted in an abrupt decrease in the number of hitting responses, which maintained at or below 1 hit per day for the last 8 days of the condition. When the baseline condition was reinstated on Day 28, the number of hits remained low for the first 5 days. On Day 33 the frequency of hits began to increase, stabilizing near initial baseline levels. Reinstatement of the contingent exercise condition resulted in an immediate and sustained decrease in the number of hits over the 8 days of the condition. The authors concluded that the contingent exercise procedure was effective in reducing the frequency of Ben's hitting without the use of a DRO procedure. They also pointed out that all staff considered the contingent exercise procedure to be effective.

A detailed analysis of the data. The results of an analysis conducted on the data presented in Figure 9-4 are summarized in Tables 9-1 and 9-2. Table 9-1 shows the results of the "within condition analysis," and Table 9-2 summarizes the "between adjacent conditions analysis."

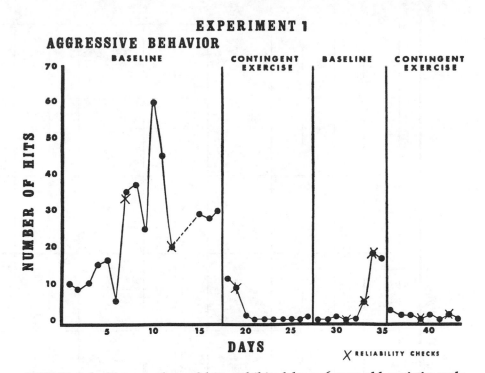

EXPERIMENT 1

FIGURE 9-4   The number of hits exhibited by a 6-year-old autistic male during 6-hour sessions while at school. During *Baseline* the behavior was ignored and no contingencies were provided for aggressive behavior; *Contingent Exercise*, stand up and sit on the floor exercise contingent on hitting. (Figure 1, p. 587, from: Luce, S.C., Delquadri, J., and Hall, R.V. Contingent exercise: A mild but powerful procedure for suppressing inappropriate verbal and aggressive behavior. *Journal of Applied Behavior Analysis*, 1980, *13*(4), 583–594. Copyright by Society for the Experimental Analysis of Behavior, Inc. Reproduced by permission.)

Relative to the first baseline and contingent exercise conditions (A₁-B₁), the introduction of the contingent exercise procedure (B₁) resulted in a positive effect on the number of hitting responses after a variable and accelerating baseline trend (A₁), which stabilized over the last 3 days of the condition (level stability criterion ≤ 10% variability). This positive effect is substantiated by (1) a level change between conditions of +19, (2) a 20% overlap of data points between conditions, which reduced to 0% over the last 8 days of intervention, and (3) a reversal in trend direction immediately upon introduction of the contingent exercise procedure, which stabilized at or near zero.

Relative to the reinstatement of baseline and contingent exercise conditions (A₂-B₂), there was a delayed effect in the reversal of the number of hits upon reintroduction of baseline procedures. During the first 5 days of the second baseline condition (A₂) the frequency of hits paralleled those levels recorded over the last 8 days of the first intervention condition (B₁). This "carryover effect" may have been a function of the subject emitting only 2 hits over the first 5 days of the second baseline condition. Over the last 3 days of this baseline condition, the number of hitting episodes increased, as evidenced by the stable accelerating and contratherapeutic trend over the last 3 days. The

TABLE 9-1   Within condition analysis of a Study I (Luce, Delquadri, & Hall, 1980).

Conditions	$\dfrac{A_1}{1}$	$\dfrac{B_1}{2}$	$\dfrac{A_2}{3}$	$\dfrac{B_2}{4}$	5	6	7	8
1. Condition Length	15^1	10	8	8	—	—	—	—
2. Estimate of Trend Direction	(−)	(+)	(−)	(=)	( )	( )	( )	( )
3. Trend Stability[2]	variable	stable	stable	stable				
4. Data Paths within Trend	(−) (=)	(+) (=)	(=) (−)	(=)	( )	( )	( )	( )
5. Level Stability and Range	variable (5 − 60)	stable (0 − 11)	variable (0 − 19)	stable (0 − 2)	( )	( )	( )	( )
6. Level Change	$\dfrac{10 - 30}{(-20)}$	$\dfrac{11 - 1}{(+10)}$	$\dfrac{0 - 18}{(-18)}$	$\dfrac{2 - 0}{(+2)}$	( )	( )	( )	( )

NOTES: 1. Two absences
2. Ten percent stability criterion equals an acceptable range of 6 hits

TABLE 9-2 Between adjacent conditions analysis of Study I (Luce, Delquadri, & Hall, 1980)

Condition Comparison	$\dfrac{B_1}{A_1}$ (2:1)	$\dfrac{B_2}{A_2}$ (4:3)	(:)	(:)	(:)	(:)	(:)	condition order 1st condition 2nd condition
1. Number of Variables Changed	1	1						
2. Change in Trend Direction and Effect	(=) (+) positive	(−) (=) positive	( ) ( ) ( ) ( )	( ) ( ) ( ) ( )	( ) ( ) ( ) ( )	( ) ( ) ( ) ( )	( ) ( ) ( ) ( )	1st trend 2nd trend effect
3. Change in Trend Stability	variable to stable	stable to stable	__ to __	__ to __	__ to __	__ to __	__ to __	
4. Change in Level	(30 − 11) +19	(18 − 2) +16	(−) |		(−) |		(−) |		(−) |		(−) |		
5. Percentage of Overlap	20 %	100 %	___ %	___ %	___ %	___ %	___ %	

reinstatement of the contingent exercise procedure resulted in an abrupt drop in level ($+16$) and a stable zero celeration trend across the 8 days of the condition. There was 100% overlap in the number of hits between conditions as a result of the low levels recorded during the first 5 days of the preceding baseline condition.

Summary and conclusions. Luce et al. (1980) convincingly demonstrated the effectiveness of contingent exercise alone in reducing the frequency of hits emitted by Ben in his classroom. The direct replication of effect generated with the A-B-A-B withdrawal design provides a believable demonstration of experimental control. This conclusion is based on (1) the abrupt change in level immediately following the introduction of the contingent exercise procedure in both experimental conditions, (2) the maintenance of a low frequency of hitting over the last 8 days of both experimental conditions, and (3) the replication of effect with a second child using a combination withdrawal and multiple baseline design across two behaviors. An even more convincing demonstration of control might have been possible had the authors extended the length of the second baseline condition (A_2), allowing the frequency of hits to more closely approximate original baseline levels or to stabilize for a longer period at the reported levels. For both practical and ethical reasons one can understand why they chose to reinstate the contingent exercise condition when they did. There are those who would question the ethics of returning to baseline procedures having previously reduced the number of hits to zero. One should note that had the second baseline condition not been reinstated, there would have been no data showing the temporary maintenance of effect under baseline or natural environmental conditions. In light of these data an important lesson can be learned, namely, the need to program for maintenance—a lesson which may not have been possible had baseline procedures not been reinstated.

Study II: Mildly Handicapped

Carnine, D.W. Effects of two teacher-presentation rates on off-task behavior, answering correctly, and participation. *Journal of Applied Behavior Analysis*, 1976, *9* (2), 199–206.

Purpose, subject, and setting. The purpose of the Carnine (1976) study was to evaluate the effects of fast and slow presentation rates on the off-task, correct answering, and participation behaviors of two "low achieving" first-grade students. The two subjects who participated in the study (a boy and a girl), along with two other children, comprised the lowest performing first-grade reading group in their school. The children were instructed in reading, using the Level I Distar Program, 30 minutes each day. Instruction took place in a small group in the rear of the classroom while other students worked independently at their seats or received small-group instruction in other areas of the room. Reading instruction was provided by the classroom teacher during the first 33 sessions and by a student-teacher during the last 5 sessions.

Dependent variables. During each instructional session data were collected on each target subject's off-task, correct answering, and participation behaviors by two data collectors. "Off-task" was defined as any occurrence of a subject (1) leaving his or her seat, (2) "blurting out," (3) talking to other children in the group, or (4) ignoring the teacher. Each of these types of off-task behaviors was coded and recorded by the observers. A subject was judged to be participating if he or she responded within 1 second of the teacher's cue. Observers also rated each child's response as correct or incorrect, regardless of his or her participation rating, i.e., a late correct response was scored as answering correctly. Data were collected on one subject at a time. Every 10 trials the observers redirected their attention and collected data on all three dependent measures of the other subject. This alternation of recording between subjects every 10 trials continued until each subject was rated on a total of 30 trials. Different tasks were presented on each trial.

In addition to collecting data on the children's behavior, the observers recorded the task presentation rate. This was done by starting the stopwatches with each new block of 10 trials and momentarily stopping them when children were questioned individually or if there were interruptions. After each block of 10 trials observers recorded the duration of time it took to complete the block of 10 trials and reset the stopwatch. The rate of presentation was calculated by dividing the total instructional time for a session by the number of tasks presented during that session.

Reliability checks were conducted during 87% of the sessions. Interobserver agreement on each of the three dependent measures was calculated using the point-by-point method (i.e., total number of agreements divided by the number of agreements plus disagreements multiplied by 100), which yielded a mean percentage agreement for all measures above 90% (mean range = 90.2%–92.9%). Observer checks on the presentation rates (i.e., procedural reliability checks) revealed a consistent difference across all slow-rate and fast-rate conditions.

Independent variable. The independent variable under investigation was task presentation rate. Two controlled experimental conditions, Slow-Rate Presentation (A) and Fast-Rate Presentation (B), were alternated to assess their effects on the three dependent variables. During the slow-rate presentation condition the teacher silently counted to five after each child's response and then presented the next task. In contrast, during the fast-rate presentation condition the teacher immediately presented the next task after each response. The teacher presented the lesson exactly as it was written in the DISTAR program. The teacher delivered general verbal praise (e.g., "That was really fine") at a constant rate across conditions. This was accomplished by using a preprogrammed tone from an audio cassette recorder, equipped with an earplug, which served as a cue for the teacher to praise. General praise was delivered on a fixed interval 90-second schedule (FI 90 sec.) at the first opportunity after the tone sounded, contingent upon a correct response or attending by both subjects. This constant schedule prevented a confounding of verbal praise and presentation rate.

Design and condition sequence. The effect of slow-rate presentation (A) and fast-rate presentation (B) on both subjects' off-task, correct answering, and participation behaviors was evaluated using an A-B-A-B-A-B design. The certified classroom teacher instructed the reading group during the first 4 phases (A_2-B_1-A_2-B_2), while the student-teacher conducted the group during the last 2

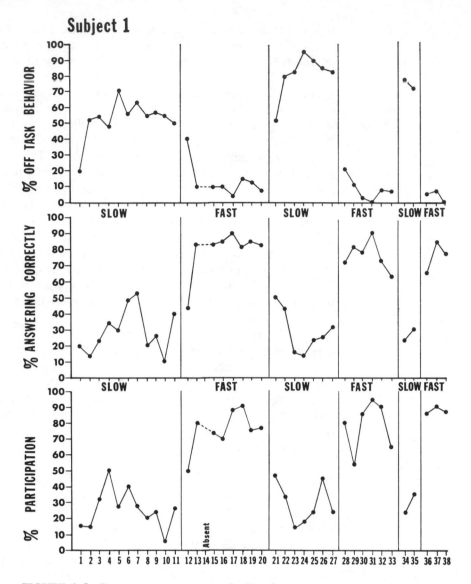

FIGURE 9-5 Percent occurrence of off-task, answering correctly, and participation for Subject 1 during the slow- and fast-rate presentation phases. The dotted lines indicate when Subject 1 was absent. The student teacher taught during the final two phases (Sessions 34 through 38). (Figure 2, p. 204, from: Carnine, D.W. Effects of two teacher-presentation rates on off-task behavior, answering correctly, and participation. *Journal of Applied Behavior Analysis*, 1976, 9 (2), 199–206. Copyright by Society for the Experimental Analysis of Behavior, Inc. Reproduced by permission.)

phases (A_3-B_3) of the investigation. The inclusion of the student-teacher permitted a brief replication across teachers.

Results as reported by the author. Figures 9-5 and 9-6 show the mean percent occurrence of the three dependent measures as recorded by the two data collectors for Subject 1 and Subject 2, respectively. For Subject 1 the means for off-task behavior during slow-rate presentation conditions were: A_1

Subject 2

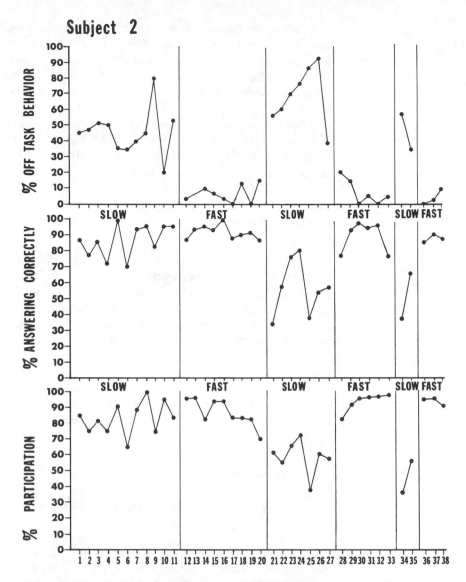

FIGURE 9-6   Percent occurrence of off-task, answering correctly, and participation for Subject 2 during the slow- and fast-rate presentation phases. The dotted lines indicate when Subject 1 was absent. The student-teacher taught during the final phases (Sessions 34 through 38). (Figure 3, p. 205, from: Carnine, D.W. Effects of two teacher-presentation rates on off-task behavior, answering correctly, and participation. *Journal of Applied Behavior Analysis*, 1976, 9 (2), 199–206. Copyright by Society for the Experimental Analysis of Behavior, Inc. Reproduced by permission.)

= 52.6%; A_2 = 81.3%; A_3 = 75.3%. The off-task means during the fast-rate presentation conditions were: B_1 = 13.9%; B_2 = 8.7%; B_3 = 4.5%. The means for correctly answering ranged from 26.6% to 28.0% during the slow-rate conditions and 76.0% and 89.2% during the fast-rate conditions. The slow-rate condition generated a consistently lower mean percentage of participation (A_1 = 25.8%; A_2 = 38.8%; A_3 = 29.1%) when compared to the fast-rate condition (B_1 = 75.4%; B_2 = 76.4%; B_3 = 79.3%).

As shown in Figure 9-6, Subject 2 began the study with a level of off-task behavior comparable to that of Subject 1. On the other two dependent measures, answering correctly and participation, Subject 2 was considerably higher; therefore the introduction of the fast rate condition affected only the off-task behavior. The reinstatement of the slow-rate condition (A_2), however, adversely affected all three dependent measures. The subsequent reinstatement of the fast-rate condition (B_2) resulted in a reversal in trend and level. This pattern of responding on all three dependent measures (A_2-B_2) was replicated with the student-teacher (A_3-B_3). The author concluded "the present study indicated that the faster rate might decrease the occurrence of students' off-task behavior and increase the occurrence of Answering Correctly and Participation. The technique of more rapidly asking questions or giving instruction can be used by teachers in addition to techniques involving contingent consequences" (p. 203).

Summary and conclusions. Carnine (1976) provided an experimental analysis of the importance of task presentation rate on children's off-task, correctly answering, and participation behaviors. The direct intrasubject replication of effect across the two conditions with two different teachers adds to the internal validity of reliability of the findings. The generality of these findings was demonstrated by replicating the different responding patterns with two subjects (i.e., intersubject). Although the generality is somewhat limited due to the similarity of the two children, external validity could have been further enhanced by a systematic replication with different subjects and behaviors. A question in need of investigation is, "What constitutes the optimal presentation rate?" Single subject designs that address comparative questions are discussed in Chapter 12.

Study III: Severely Handicapped

Thompson, G.A., Iwata, B.A., and Poynter, H. Operant control of pathological tongue thrust in spastic cerebral palsy. *Journal of Applied Behavior Analysis*, 1979, *12* (3), 325–333.

Purpose, subject, and setting. This study investigated the effects of an operant approach in the modification of pathological tongue thrust. The subject of the investigation was a 10-year-old, profoundly mentally retarded boy with spastic cerebral palsy, i.e., "moderate spastic and athetoid quadriplegia and general motor dysfunction" (p. 326). Assessments conducted by an occupational therapist indicated he had a "pathological tongue thrust, no effective sucking and no finger feeding or lip closure" (p. 327). Previous attempts to correct his tongue thrust with myofunctional therapy had failed, although on occasion he had been observed to control the behavior. All sessions were conducted during the school lunch period each day.

Dependent variable. Three interdependent child behaviors were measured each session by trained observers: (1) tongue out, (2) food expulsion, and (3) chewing. Each behavior was recorded as occurring or not occurring using a 10-second "partial interval" recording system, i.e., data collectors observed for 7.5 seconds and recorded the observations in the last 2.5 seconds of the interval. After five 10-second intervals observers rested for 10 seconds. In

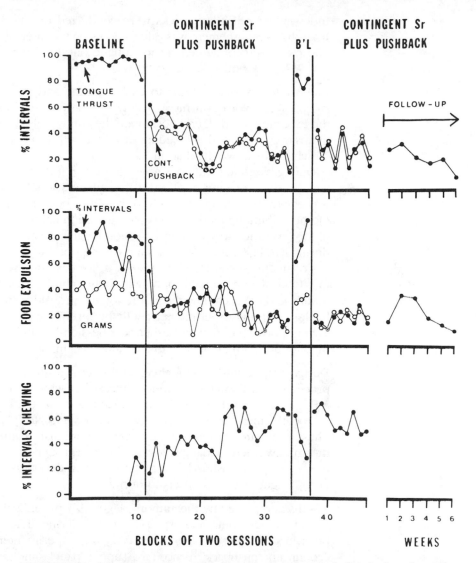

FIGURE 9-7   Percentage intervals of tongue out (target behavior) and contingent pushback (experimenter behavior) across experimental conditions. Also shown are data on food expulsion (both percentage intervals and grams) and chewing (percentage intervals). (Figure 1, p. 330, from: Thompson, G.A., Jr., Iwata, B.A., and Poynter, H. Operant control of pathological tongue thrust in spastic cerebral palsy. *Journal of Applied Behavior Analysis*, 1979, *12* (3), 325–333. Copyright by Society for the Experimental Analysis of Behavior, Inc. Reproduced by permission.)

addition to these child behaviors, observers recorded whether or not the experimenter used the "contingent pushback" procedures. A secondary measure, recorded after each session, was the number of grams of food the child expelled during a meal. This measure was determined by subtracting the presession weight of the catch tray from its post-session weight. All dependent measures, except for the number of grams of food expelled, were reported as the percentage of intervals the behavior occurred (see Figure 9-7).

Independent reliability checks were conducted during 53% of all sessions. Interobserver agreement was calculated using the interval by-interval method. The mean percent agreement for tongue out, food expulsion, and chewing was 93%, 89% and 84%, respectively.

Independent variable. Prior to each baseline and intervention session the subject was involved in myofunctional therapy. After these therapy sessions the experimenter properly positioned the child in his chair and prepared 300 grams of pureed food. All feeding was done with a Teflon-coated spoon while the child's head was held at midline.

During baseline conditions approximately 5 grams of food were presented without regard to the position of the subject's tongue, provided his mouth was empty. The food was removed from the spoon by his upper lip since he did not exhibit lip closure. The feeding session continued until all 300 grams of food were fed to the subject. Session lengths ranged from 9 to 20 minutes during baseline conditions, with a mean session duration of 13 minutes.

Treatment sessions were identical to baseline sessions except that (1) food was presented only when the child's tongue was inside his mouth, and (2) each time the child's tongue protruded beyond the middle of his lower lip the experimenter gently but promptly pushed it back using the Teflon-spoon ("contingent pushback"). Session lengths ranged from 12 to 28 minutes during treatment, with a mean of 17 minutes.

Design and condition sequence. The effects of the "contingent pushback" procedure on the subject's tongue thrust behavior were evaluated using an A-B-A-B withdrawal design. Maintenance was evaluated by collecting data on each of the measures once each week for 6 weeks after the termination of B_2. These follow-up sessions differed from the original treatment sessions in that the child was fed by paraprofessional staff. Throughout the follow-up period the "contingent pushback" or treatment procedure was administered whenever "tongue out" was observed during feeding.

Results as reported by the authors. Figure 9-7 presents data across all conditions for tongue out, food expulsion, and chewing. In addition to these child behaviors, the percentage of intervals the experimenter administered the "contingent pushback" procedure (upper panel) and the amount of food expelled (center panel) are presented. In response to these data the authors concluded: "Present results indicate that the procedures based on operant conditioning principles can effectively control observable components of tongue thrust. Substantial reductions were obtained for tongue out and food expulsion, along with a significant increase in chewing. These gains were maintained by paraprofessional staff during a 2-month follow-up period" (p. 331).

Summary and conclusions. Thompson et al. (1979) successfully reduced the frequency of tongue thrust and food expulsion episodes using an operant treatment package. One cannot conclude, however, that the "contingent pushback" procedure alone was responsible for the decrease in the percentage of intervals during which these behaviors occurred. The authors' description of their treatment condition includes two components not present in the baseline condition: (1) food was presented contingent upon the subject's tongue being inside his mouth and (2) the contingent pushback procedure. Although the authors state that the former procedure was ineffective when used alone, no data are presented to support their claim. Had they implemented the food presentation contingency during baseline and treatment conditions, or excluded this contingency from both conditions, the importance of the "contingent pushback" procedure relative to the contingent food presentation procedure could have been isolated.

This investigation is an important addition to the applied behavior analysis research literature because it shows that behaviors thought by some to be beyond the realm of operant conditioning are in fact amenable to environmental contingencies. Further research with similar behaviors is indeed warranted before conclusive statements can be made regarding the generality of these findings. This investigation is, however, an excellent beginning to what could prove to be an important breakthrough in the treatment of children with general motor dysfunction.

Concluding Comments

The A-B-A-B design represents the clearest and most "powerful" paradigm for demonstrating a functional relationship between independent and dependent variables. It is undoubtedly the most frequently used single subject design in behavior modification research. It improves upon the A-B and A-B-A designs by providing two opportunities to demonstrate casuality with the same subject, thereby strengthening the internal validity of the effectiveness of intervention. When simultaneous studies are conducted using similar subjects, targeting similar behaviors, and employing the same intervention, it is possible to extend the generality or external validity of the independent variable. For this reason it is recommended that, when practical, one should concurrently conduct direct intersubject replications using the A-B-A-B or some other appropriate single subject research design. It is also recommended that nontargeted behaviors be monitored concurrently as a check on response generalization.

Probe measures also can be scheduled in other settings or with other persons to evaluate stimulus generalization. In light of the flexibility of the A-B-A-B design, it deserves serious consideration by teachers, clinicians, and applied researchers engaged in behavior modification research.

Variations of the A-B-A-B Design

All single subject designs, particularly the A-B-A-B design, are extremely versatile paradigms for demonstrating intervention effectiveness. Unlike group research designs, which are static, single subject research designs are dynamic, i.e., rapidly changing. For example, if an investigator designs a study using the A-B-A-B design and discovers that the effect intervention B has on the target behavior is negligible (i.e., A-B), it is not necessary for her to return to baseline conditions (A_2); rather she has the flexibility to introduce a new intervention (C). If intervention C in turn has a measurable positive effect on the target behavior she can proceed by returning to intervention B. In this example the investigator initially chose the A-B-A-B design to evaluate her intervention; however, because intervention B has no effect on the dependent variable, the design was changed to an A-B-C-B design. Because of such flexibility, there are numerous studies in the applied research literature that differ from the basic A-B-A-B design and yet demonstrate experimental control. This section overviews some of the more common variations and extensions of the A-B-A-B design. Specifically, the following designs are described and illustrated: (1) B-A-B; (2) A-B-C-B or A-B-A'-B; and (3) A-B-A-B-C-B. Additional design variations and expansions in which a research question focuses on comparing one intervention with another intervention (e.g., A-B-C-B-C, A-B-BC-B-BC) are discussed more extensively in Chapter 12.

B-A-B Design

The B-A-B design is used frequently by teachers and clinicians with students who exhibit self-injurious or physically aggressive behaviors. To implement this design one must (1) identify a behavior that, if it persists, could result in physical harm to the subject herself or to others with whom she has contact; (2) introduce an intervention immediately upon identification of the behavior without collecting baseline (A_1) data on the natural frequency of the behavior; (3) conduct a "brief" withdrawal of the intervention strategy after the behavior reaches the defined criterion level in the first intervention condition (B_1); and (4) reintroduce the intervention strategy after a brief reversal in trend is observed (B_2). Experimental control is demonstrated when the application of the independent variable results in a decrease in the frequency of the inappropriate and dangerous target behavior (B_1 and B_2) and when an increase in the frequency of the behavior is observed when the intervention is briefly withdrawn (A_2).

When possible it is preferable to collect baseline data, however brief the condition might be, prior to introducing intervention for the first time. Without an initial baseline measure it is impossible to evaluate the effect of the intervention on the natural frequency of the behavior. In contrast to the A-B-A design, however, the B-A-B design has the advantage of ending with intervention and allowing two demonstrations of intervention effectiveness. If practical and ethical considerations permit, a more believable demonstration of casuality is possible with the more complete A-B-A-B design.

Study I: Severely Handicapped

Murphy, R.J., Ruprecht, M.J., Baggio, P., and Nunes, D.L. The use of mild punishment in combination with reinforcement of alternate behaviors to reduce the self-injurious behavior of a profoundly retarded individual. *AAESPH Review*, 1979, *4* (2), 187–195.

Purpose, subject, and setting. The present investigation examined the effects of contingent water squirts and differential reinforcement of other behaviors (DRO) on the self-choking behavior of a 24-year-old profoundly mentally retarded male. The subject had been institutionalized since the age of 8, during which time he exhibited a high rate of self-choking. Immediately prior to the initiation of this study self-chokes averaged 434 responses per school day (range 345 to 458) when a DRO procedure was used by staff. The study was conducted in a variety of settings (classroom, gym, dining room, bathroom, library, school bus) throughout the entire school day. The length of time spent in each setting varied, as did the daily educational activities.

Dependent variable. Different teachers and teacher's aides continuously recorded the number of self-chokes emitted by the subject during school-day activities. The authors defined a self-choke as "any time Peter (the subject) grasped his right shirt collar with his left hand, his left shirt collar with his right hand, and pulled in opposite directions while turning his head from side to side" (p. 190). Data were collected during the entire 6-hour school day, 5 days per week for 12 weeks. Reliability checks were made once every 4 days over the course of the investigation by several independent observers. Interobserver agreement, calculated using the gross method, ranged from 96%–100%, with a mean of 98%.

Independent variable. During intervention sessions self-chokes were consequated by a combination procedure including (1) verbal reprimand ("No choking"), (2) mild punishment (1 cc water squirt of lukewarm tap water from a 1-pint water bottle), and (3) differential reinforcement of an alternative appropriate behavior (DRO—unspecified schedule). Water squirts, which were directed at the area immediately surrounding the subject's mouth, were continued every 2 seconds until self-choking stopped, after which he was told, "That's good," and given a towel to wipe his face. Throughout the day appropriate teacher-cued and -prompted responses were reinforced with social events and edibles.

When the intervention procedures were withdrawn for a brief time (3 sessions), there were no programmed consequences for self-chokes. During this condition the subject was permitted to engage in self-choking and, when he stopped, staff prompted an appropriate response and reinforced its occurrence.

Design and condition sequence. The combined effects of the verbal reprimand, contingent water squirts, and differential reinforcement intervention on self-choking were evaluated within the context of a B-A-B design. The authors omitted the initial baseline condition "because information regarding the preintervention rate of the self-injurious behavior was available from the prior unsuccessful attempt to reduce the behavior using reinforcement of alternate behaviors. To have included initial baseline sessions during this investigation would have wasted resources and would have unnecessarily extended the time that Peter was exposed to nontherapeutic conditions" (p. 191). The initial treatment condition (B_1) was in effect for 24 sessions, followed by a 3-session intervention withdrawal condition (A_1) before reinstatement of treatment procedures (B_2).

Results as reported by the authors. Figure 9-8 displays the number of self-chokes emitted by the subject during each condition of the investigation. The data show that the mean frequency for self-chokes during initial treatment (B_1), withdrawal of treatment (A), and reinstatement of treatment (B_2) conditions was 22, 265, and 24, respectively. The withdrawal of the treatment package resulted in an abrupt and substantial contratherapeutic change in the frequency of self-chokes. This level was reversed immediately upon reintroduction of treatment procedures.

Summary and conclusion. These data show the immediate and dramatic effect of verbal reprimand, contingent water squirts, and reinforcement of alternative appropriate behaviors on the self-injurious behavior of an institutionalized profoundly mentally retarded young adult. Although an initial baseline condition, prior to the introduction of intervention procedures, would have permitted a comparison with the natural frequency of the behav-

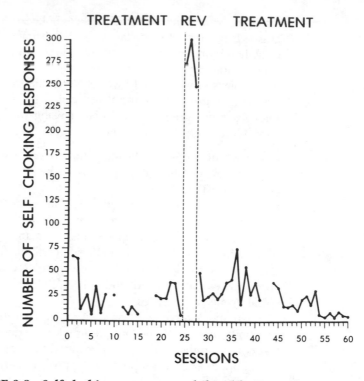

FIGURE 9-8 Self-choking responses exhibited by Peter during each school day across experimental conditions. Missing data points indicate days during which school was not in session. (Figure 1, p. 191, from: Murphey, R.J., Ruprecht, M.J., Baggio, P., and Nunes, D.L. The use of mild punishment in combination with reinforcement of alternate behaviors to reduce the self-injurious behavior of a profoundly retarded individual. *American Association for the Education of the Severely-Profoundly Handicapped Review*, 1979, 4(2), 187–195. Reprinted by permission.)

ior and strengthened the demonstration of experimental control, the abrupt and substantial level changes between conditions give credence to the effectiveness of intervention procedures. The authors' decision to omit an initial baseline condition illustrates the dilemma that sometimes confronts applied researchers who deal with potentially dangerous behaviors in educational and clinical settings.

It is appropriate to point out that within the applied behavior analysis research literature there are studies that report using the B-A-B design with less severe problem behaviors, such as task completion (Robinson, Newby, & Ganzell, 1981; Rowbury, Baer, & Baer, 1976), and on-task behavior (Egel, 1981). Both studies began by introducing an intervention without measuring the target behavior under "preintervention" or baseline conditions. After a positive effect was demonstrated in B_1, both studies reverted to stimulus conditions that approximated those conditions in effect prior to introducing the intervention; thus the "middle" condition was appropriately labeled A. After a stable "contratherapeutic" trend was observed in A, Condition B was reinstated. In both studies the positive effect of intervention on the number of tasks completed was replicated across three similar children, thereby adding to the external validity of their findings. In both studies the designs represent "true" B-A-B designs. However, others have used different labels in comparative designs. Egel (1981) compared the effects of a "constant reinforcer condition" (B) and a "varied reinforcer condition" (C) on the percentage of correct responding and on-task behavior of three "autistic" children. Figure 9-9 shows the design used with each of the three children. For Child 1 the design was reported as a B-C-B; for Child 2 and Child 3 the design was labeled B-C-B-C. The point of contention here is not with the demonstration of experimental control, which there was, but rather with the labeling of the designs. It can only be assumed that the author ascribed to the more conservative defintion of a baseline condition; that being that a baseline condition (A) must represent the "natural frequency" of a target behavior (i.e., responding under "natural" preintervention stimulus conditions). This logic explains why the notation C was assigned to the "varied reinforcer condition" rather than the notation A, but it does not account for the use of the notation B rather than the notation A in the first and third condition of the study. Acceptance of the broader definition of baseline, which views a baseline condition as simply a comparison phase against which subsequent inter-

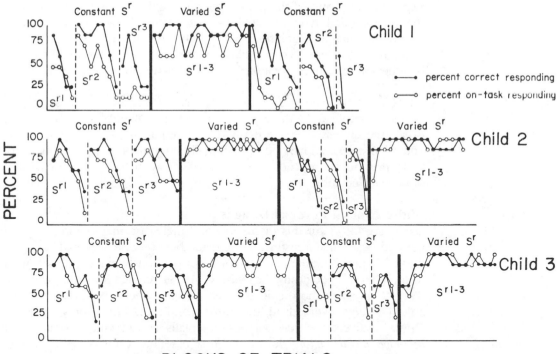

BLOCKS OF TRIALS

FIGURE 9-9 The effects of constant vs. varied reinforcer conditions on correct responding and on-task behavior. The ordinate shows percent correct responding and on-task behavior and the abscissa shows blocks of 8 trials (as the number of trials per condition was not always divisible by 8, the last data point in any given condition reflects 5 to 8 trials). (Figure 1, p. 348, from: Egel, A.L. Reinforcer variation: Implications for motivating developmentally disabled children. *Journal of Applied Behavior Analysis*, 1981, *14*(3), 345–350. Copyright by Society for the Experimental Analysis of Behavior, Inc. Reproduced by permission.)

ventions are evaluated (Birnbrauer, 1981), would have resulted in the design being labeled A-B-A, rather than B-C-B. The A-B-A notation would have been more in keeping with the notation procedures used in other multitreatment comparative investigations.

Clarification

In light of the potential confusion in labeling comparative designs, the following criteria are offered to help clarify when the B-A-B design notation is appropriate. All three criteria should be met.

1. The study must begin and end with the same experimental condition (i.e., identical procedures, location, instructional arrangement, materials, etc.).

2. When compared to the "middle" or A condition, B must have a measurable effect on the target behavior.

3. The A condition must represent the stimulus conditions that were operating prior to introducing the intervention for the first time (i.e., before introducing B_1).

To reiterate, the notation of a design in no way limits a demonstration of experimental control if the person conducting the visual analysis is aware of the number and type of variables that change between conditions. The purpose of directing attention to this rather trivial yet potentially confusing point is to facilitate "conceptually systematic" communication among researchers when using a notation system to describe their experimental design.

A-B-C-B (or A-B-A′-B) Designs

A-B-C-B or A-B-A′-B designs represent a class of single subject designs that are frequently confused with, and subsequently mislabeled, A-B-A-B designs. As previously discussed, the A-B-A-B design requires that A_1 be operationally equivalent to A_2, and B_1 be operationally equivalent to B_2. In other words, there may be no procedural differences between two conditions with the same letter notation.

Withdrawal vs. Reversal Designs

Leitenberg (1973), in his discussion of "single-case methodology," convincingly advocates that a distinction be made between the "reversal" design and the "withdrawal" design, a distinction not previously made by Baer, Wolf, & Risley (1968). Specifically, Leitenberg (1973) restricts the use of the term *reversal design* to those single subject designs where the independent variable is truly reversed in the third condition, not simply withdrawn. Operationalized, the reversal design entails concurrently monitoring two *incompatible behaviors* during the first baseline condition (e.g., hands on desk and hands in lap). After a stable baseline trend is established with both behaviors, the independent variable is applied to one of the behaviors. If the intervention strategy has a positive effect on the target behavior, then it is applied to the concurrently monitored incompatible behavior in the third condition (commonly referred to as A_2). It is at this juncture that the reversal design is distinguished from the withdrawal design. Not only is the intervention withdrawn from the target behavior in the reversal design, but it is applied to an incompatible behavior during the third or "A_2" condition. If there is a decrease in the target behavior and a concomitant increase in the incompatible behavior (or vice versa depending upon the behavioral objective), then a functional relationship between independent and dependent variables is demonstrated. Experimental control is further strengthened by reversing data trends in the fourth (B_2) condition when the independent variable is reintroduced to the target behavior. The key distinction between reversal and withdrawal designs is that the reversal design (1) withdraws or removes the intervention from one behavior and (2) simultaneously applies it to an incompatible behavior. The withdrawal design, on the other hand, simply removes the intervention during the third condition. An easy way to distinguish the two designs is to associate differential reinforcement of an incompatible behavior (i.e., DRI) with the reversal design and extinction with the withdrawal design. Though the reversal design is commonly referred to as a variation of the A-B-A-B design, which it is, it is more appropriate to use the design notation A-B-C-B or A-B-A'-B, rather than the A-B-A-B letter notation, particularly when the first and third conditions are not procedurally identical.

There are few studies in the applied research literatures that have employed a "true" reversal design. The most commonly cited study was conducted by Allen, Hart, Buell, Harris, and Wolf (1964), in which the "isolate" behavior of a nursery school child was modified through the use of contingent adult attention. In the first condition (A_1) baseline data showed that adult attention was being delivered contingent upon the child's isolate behavior. Therefore, intervention (B_1) provided adult attention only when the child was interacting with peers. This redirection of adult attention resulted in a substantial increase in the percentage of peer interactions when compared to baseline data. In the third condition the contingency for receiving adult attention was reversed; that is, isolate behavior resulted in adult attention and peer interaction was placed on extinction—the result, a reversal in the percentage of interactions with peers which approximated levels observed in the first baseline condition. After 5 days in the reversal condition, adult attention was again made contingent upon peer interactions. These data are presented in Figure 9-10.

The distinction between the reversal design (A-B-C-B or A-B-A'-B) and the withdrawal design (A-B-A-B) is small, but nonetheless warranted given the procedural differences relative to the third condition. It is therefore recommended that the A-B-A-B design notation be restricted to those time series designs in which A_2 procedures are identical to A_1 procedures (i.e., withdrawal designs), and that the A-B-A'-B notation be used when the first and third conditions are not operationally equivalent (i.e., reversal designs), though they may be similar.

Multitreatment Designs

Multitreatment designs refer to a class of single subject designs in which two or more planned interventions are compared with one another to determine which has a greater impact on the dependent variable. There are many forms of multitreatment designs, including the comparative designs described in Chapter 12. In many cases the multitreatment design represents an extension of the A-B-A-B design in which an intervention condition C is either added to the design sequence (e.g., A-B-A-B-C-B-C) or combined with condition B (e.g., A-B-A-B-BC-B-BC). In both instances the introduction of C reflects a change in

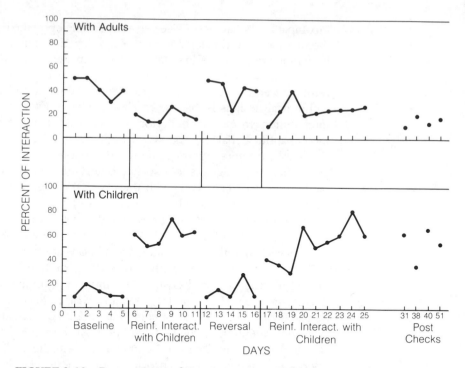

FIGURE 9-10   Percentages of time spent in social interaction during approximately 2 hours of each morning session. (Figure 2, p. 515, from: Allen K.E., Hart, B., Buell, J.S., Harris, F.R., and Wolf, M.M. Effects of social reinforcement on isolate behavior of a nursery school child. *Child Development*, 1964, *35*, 511–518. Copyright by Society for Research in Child Development. Reproduced by permission.)

research interest from comparing condition B to condition A, to comparing condition C to condition B (A-B-A-B-C-B-C) or condition BC to condition B (A-B-A-B-BC-B-BC). The difference between these two comparative designs rests with what an investigator wishes to say relative to intervention B and intervention C. The A-B-A-B-C-B-C design permits an evaluation of B to C and C to B when both are presented in isolation. The A-B-A-B-BC-B-BC design, on the other hand, permits a comparison of B to BC and BC to B. In this latter design no conclusions can be drawn relative to the effectiveness of C to B when presented in isolation. For example, if Condition A represents noncontingent token reinforcement, Condition B contingent token reinforcement, and Condition C response cost, the latter half of the A-B-A-*B-C-B-C* design provides a comparison of contingent token reinforcement (B) with noncontingent reinforcement and response cost (C). The A-B-A-*B-BC-B-BC* design, however, compares the contingent token reinforcement condition (B) with the contingent token reinforcement condition paired with the response cost condition. (BC). The questions are different and thus necessitate different designs.

Abbreviated versions of the multitreatment design can be found throughout the applied research literature (e.g., Foxx & Shapiro, 1978; Van Houten & Nau, 1980). Foxx and Shapiro (1978) compared the effects of "baseline" (A), positive reinforcement (B), and positive reinforcement plus nonexclusionary timeout (BC), on the percentage of time five severely and profoundly retarded children spent engaged in "disruptive classroom behavior" using an

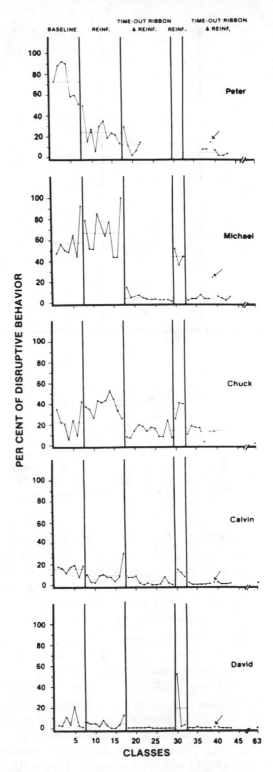

FIGURE 9-11 (Figure 1, p. 130, from: Foxx, R.M., and Shapiro, S.T. The time-out ribbon: A nonexclusionary timeout procedure. *Journal of Applied Behavior Analysis*, 1978, *11*(1), 125–136. Copyright by Society for the Experimental Analysis of Behavior, Inc. Reproduced by permission.)

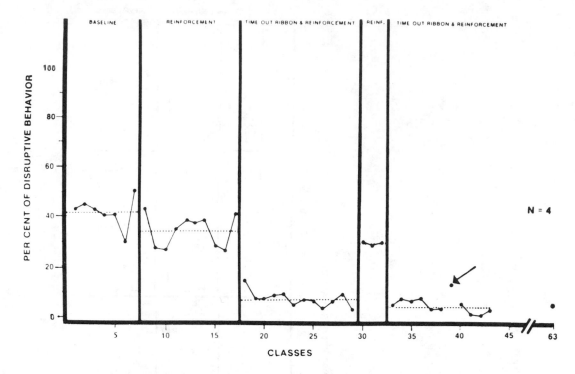

FIGURE 9-12 The mean percent of time spent in disruptive classroom behavior by four of the subjects. (David's data were excluded because of his low base rate of disruptive behavior.) The horizontal broken lines indicate the mean for each condition. The arrow marks a 1-day probe (Day 39) during which the time out contingency was suspended. A follow-up observation of the teacher-conducted program occurred on Day 63. (Figure 2, p. 131, from: Foxx, R.M., and Shapiro, S.T. The timeout ribbon: A nonexclusionary timeout procedure. *Journal of Applied Behavior Analysis*, 1978, *11*(1), 125–136. Copyright by Society for the Experimental Analysis of Behavior, Inc. Reproduced by permission.)

A-B-BC-B-BC design. (The authors, however, refer to the design as an A-B-C-B-C). Figure 9-11 presents the data for each of the five subjects across conditions, while Figure 9-12 summarizes the mean percentage of time four of the five children engaged in disruptive classroom behavior. (Data on the fifth child, David, were omitted due to his low frequency of disruptive behavior during baseline.)

A full discussion of the many variations and extension of the A-B-A-B design is beyond the scope of this chapter. These variations include studies that have compared reinforcement schedules (e.g., Reynolds & Risley, 1968; Van Houten & Nau, 1980) and others that have compared distinctively different interventions (e.g., Cohen, Polsgrove, Rieth, & Heinen, 1981; Favell, McGimsey, & Jones, 1978). Table 12-1 overviews several A-B-A-B design variations that compare two or more different interventions and that are commonly referred to as multitreatment designs. The interested reader is also referred to Cooper (1981) and his discussion of A-B-A-B design variations related to contingent, noncontingent, DRI, and DRO schedules of reinforcement.

SUMMARY

In this chapter we have discussed various designs and presented a list of recommendations for those who are contemplating using one of the designs, namely, "A", "B", A-B, A-B-A, A-B-A-B, B-A-B, and A-B-C-B (or A-B-A'-B). The following basic guidelines are equally important:

1. Introduce a new experimental condition (i.e., baseline or intervention) only after an acceptable data trend has been established in the immediately preceding adjacent condition.

2. Change only one variable at a time when introducing a new experimental condition.

3. Restrict visual analysis to comparing adjacent conditions.

4. Concurrently monitor nontargeted behaviors that may change as a function of applying the intervention to the targeted behavior (i.e., response generalization).

5. Concurrently monitor targeted behaviors under "nontraining" stimulus conditions (i.e., stimulus generalization).

6. Replicate the study with similar subjects to enchance the generality of the findings (i.e., external validity).

The A-B-A-B design, commonly referred to as the "reversal" or "withdrawal" design, represents the most frequently used single subject design in behavior modification research. This chapter has described, exemplified, and visually analyzed the basic A-B-A-B design as well as its more common variations. In spite of some educators' reluctance to employ the A-B-A-B design because of the "brief" withdrawal (or reversal) requirement, it continues to be the most "powerful" and straightforward evaluation paradigm for demonstrating experimental control. Its primary advantage, when compared to abbreviated forms of the design (e.g., A-B, A-B-A, B-A-B), is that it provides two replications of intervention effectiveness with the same subject and the same behavior under similar stimulus conditions. This is also an advantage of the A-B-A-B design when compared to the more popular multiple baseline design.

In the chapters which follow, several alternative experimental designs are discussed. Though each differs from the A-B-A-B design, all represent a rearrangement or elaboration of the more basic A-B design.

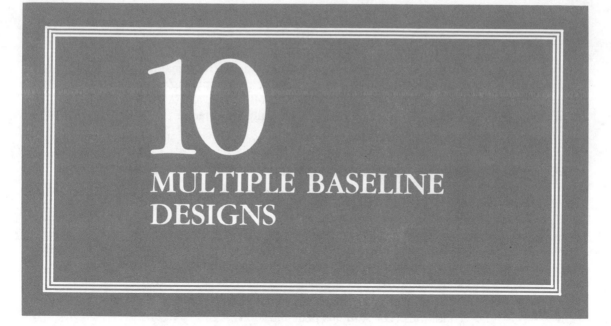

10
MULTIPLE BASELINE DESIGNS

Special educators have been subjected to increasing pressure from consumers, professional organizations, legislatures, and courts to account for their teaching behaviors. They have been asked to provide objective, data-based responses to such social-educational questions as "Are educational objectives appropriate?" "Is each child progressing through the curriculum at an optimum rate?" "When should instructional methods be maintained, modified, or replaced?" "Can a child's progress be attributed to identifiable instructional strategies?" Within the framework of applied behavior analysis, there are a set of single subject research designs appropriate for a demonstration of accountability, namely, the multiple baseline, multiple probe, and changing criterion designs. Each design is flexible (i.e., the learner's behavior controls the pace and choice of programming procedures); is rigorous in its experimental control, allowing for the systematic manipulation of independent variables; and is functional for teachers who want their research efforts to be wholly compatible with their instructional activities. For these reasons, and because the public has mandated individualized education and habilitation plans, the demand for and appreciation of single subject experimental designs will continue to escalate.

This chapter focuses on multiple baseline designs. Rationales for each type of multiple baseline design are presented and implementation procedures described. Education-related studies utilizing these designs are reviewed to illustrate the flexibility of the designs across behaviors, conditions, and individuals representing the wide range of "exceptionality."

This chapter was written by **David L. Gast**, **James R. Skouge**, and **James W. Tawney**

Multiple Baseline Designs

Multiple baseline designs were introduced into the literature of applied behavior analysis by Baer, Wolf, and Risley (1968). Since then the designs have been widely used in educational settings (Gallant, Sargeant, & Van Houten, 1980; Nau & Van Houten, 1981; Schumaker, Hovell, & Sherman, 1977), since they are well suited to the practical requirements of applied research:

1. They lend themselves to program efficacy measures.

2. They have no withdrawal of intervention requirements.

3. They are easy enough to conceptualize and implement to permit teachers and parents to conduct research (Hall, Cristler, Cranston, & Tucker, 1970; Murphey & Bryan, 1980).

There are three principle variations of the multiple baseline design:

1. Across several different behaviors of an individual or group (Kirby, Holborn, & Bushby, 1981; Russo & Koegel, 1977; Savie & Dickey, 1979),

2. Across several different stimulus conditions in which the same behavior of an individual or group is exhibited (Barrish, Saunders, & Wolf, 1969; Chiang, Iwata, & Dorsey, 1979; Lutzker, 1978),

3. Across several individuals or groups displaying the same behavior under the same stimulus conditions (Bornstein & Quevillon, 1976; Gruber, Reeser, & Reid, 1979; Sowers, Rusch, Connis, & Cummings, 1980).

Internal Validity

To demonstrate experimental control with the multiple baseline design, the investigator first collects baseline data simultaneously across three or more data series (i.e., across behaviors, across conditions, or across individuals). When all baseline data series exhibit acceptable stability in level and trend, an intervention is applied to the first baseline series. Logically this intervention should coincide with an abrupt change in the first data series, while the other baselines remain stable. When criterion-level performance is attained in the first data series, the intervention is introduced into the second baseline series. Again the same abrupt behavior change should be demonstrated, while the uninterrupted baseline series remains unchanged. Then the process is repeated in the third, and so on, until the intervention has been applied to each target. To evaluate experimental control remember that "where intervention is applied, change occurs; where it is not, change does not occur" (Horner & Baer, 1978, p. 189). Figure 10-1 provides a graphic prototype of the multiple baseline design where two or more baselines are recorded simultaneously and the intervention is introduced sequentially, one baseline at a time. The multiple baseline design can be conceptualized as a series of simple A-B designs, with the baseline conditions (A) extended for each succeeding behavior until the intervention (B) is finally applied.

Considerations

To demonstrate experimental control, researchers using multiple baseline designs must make two predictions prior to initiating their research: first, that each target behavior (or condition or subject) will be functionally independent, so that the dependent measure will remain stable until the intervention is

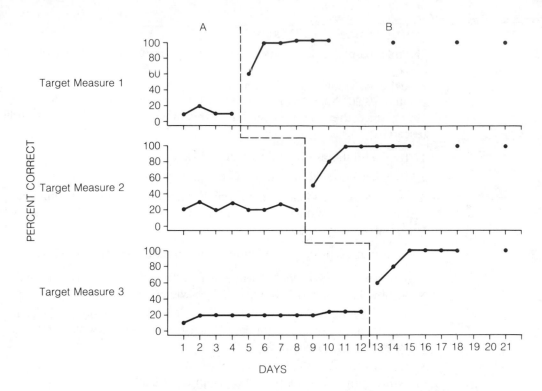

FIGURE 10-1   Hypothetical data using a multiple baseline design.

sequentially applied; and, second, that each behavior (or condition or subject) will be functionally similar and will respond to the same intervention. Should either of these predictions fail, experimental control is lost or, at least, confounded.

In the first case, should behavioral covariation occur within baselines not yet exposed to the intervention, the investigator is left with an ambiguous demonstration of effects, "in which it is evident that change has occurred but not that it was due to the intervention" (Birnbrauer, Peterson, & Solnick, 1974, p. 198). Two questions are left unanswered: (1) Was the intervention effective on the first baseline, with effects generalizing to the unexposed baselines? (2) Was the intervention ineffective, with covarying effects due, instead, to uncontrolled "extra experimental" variables?

In the second case, should one or several of the baselines remain unchanged when the intervention is directly applied, the investigator again is left with an unconvincing demonstration to control, with the intervention appearing to work in one or a few instances, but not in others, i.e., inconsistent intervention effects. Figure 10-2 illustrates both of these threats to experimental control: (a) behavioral covariance across unexposed baselines and (b) inconsistent intervention effects. Strategies to improve predictions and, thus, to minimize these risks are addressed as each multiple baseline design variation is described.

Guidelines

When using the multiple baseline design, the applied researcher should adhere to the following guidelines:

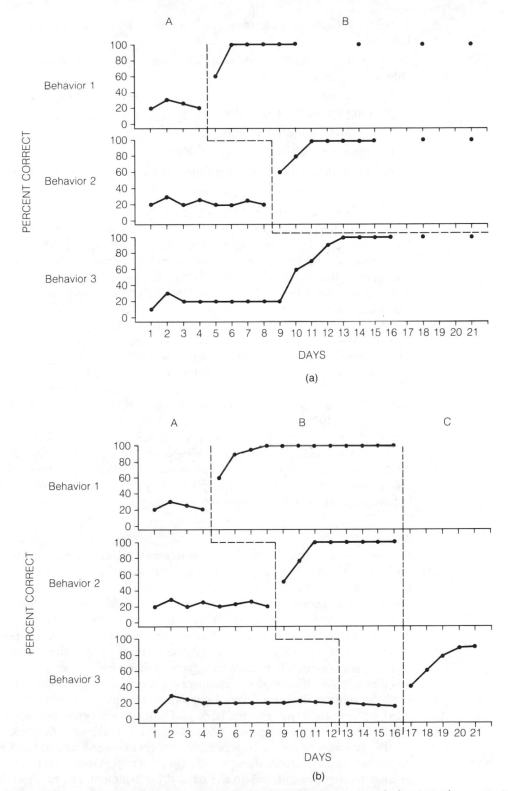

FIGURE 10-2 Hypothetical data for a multiple baseline design across behaviors demonstrating (a) behavioral covariation of Behavior 3, after the intervention is sequentially applied to Behaviors 1 and 2, and (b) a failure of intervention effects for Behavior 3, requiring the addition of a new intervention Condition C for that series.

1. Pinpoint outcome objectives (i.e., criterion levels) before the study is initiated.

2. Apply the intervention only when all baseline data series maintain acceptable stability in level and trend.

3. Apply the intervention to a new baseline series only when criterion-level responding is attained in the already exposed series.

4. Target three or more baselines.

5. Identify functionally independent baselines to avoid "behavioral covariation."

6. Identify functionally similar baselines to avoid "inconsistent intervention effects."

Prior to initiating a study, the investigator should pinpoint outcome objectives (i.e., criterion performance levels) for each targeted baseline series. These preestablished levels serve as standards by which to judge both the magnitude of behavior changes and the pace of application of the intervention. The intervention is introduced only when all baseline series exhibit acceptable stability in level and trend and when criterion-level responding is maintained across all already exposed series.

A believable demonstration of a functional relationship between intervention and behavior change occurs when the effect is replicated across A-B series (Baer, Wolf, & Risley, 1968). Determination of the appropriate number of replications required for believability is complicated by such factors as trend and level stability of the baseline data series and the rate and magnitude of change upon each sequential introduction of the intervention (Kratochwill, 1978). However, provided there are reliable replications of effects, three or four targeted baselines should be satisfactory (Barlow & Hersen, 1973; Kazdin & Kopel, 1975; Wolf & Risley, 1971). A discussion of the guidelines for identifying similar yet functionally independent baselines will follow after each multiple baseline design variation is presented (across behaviors, across conditions, and across subjects).

Advantages

Multiple baseline designs are better suited than A-B-A-B designs to many of the practical demands of applied settings. Perhaps the most significant advantage is that it is not necessary to reverse or withhold a "therapeutic" intervention to demonstrate experimental control (Baer, Wolf, & Risley, 1968; Kazdin & Kopel, 1975; Kratochwill, 1978). This feature can be advantageous: first, because many behaviors are functionally irreversible, including most academic skills (Cuvo, 1979); second, because reversal designs may be ethically inappropriate, especially relative to behaviors that are injurious to the subject or others or to behaviors that demonstrate improvement gains that might not easily be reinstated after a reversal condition (Murphey & Bryan, 1980); and, third, because many parents, teachers, and other practitioners find any reversal requirements objectionable (Cooper, 1981). Additionally, multiple baseline designs require the concurrent measurement of several targeted behaviors, conditions, or individuals, thus providing a closer approximation to the goals of most teacher-practitioners in the natural environment, i.e., to effect multiple and generalized changes in learner responding (Birnbrauer, Peterson, & Solnick, 1974; Hersen & Barlow, 1976; Kratochwill & Levin, 1978).

Limitations

Multiple baseline designs also can be problematic. They require (1) concurrent measurement of several baselines and (2) prolonged baseline conditions. As previously mentioned, multiple baseline designs require the identification and concurrent measurement of several (usually three or four) dependent measures. This requirement can be limiting because it is difficult to identify the requisite number of baseline measures and because the concurrent monitoring of several measures may prove time consuming, expensive, or otherwise impractical (Horner & Baer, 1978; Scott & Goetz, 1980). The extension of baseline measures may result in prolonged, potentially aversive experiences for learners due to boredom, fatigue, competitive responding, and invalidating consequences for the data. Also, the prolonging of baseline measures may be considered ethically questionable when intervention is postponed on behaviors that require immediate attention (e.g., physical aggression directed against self or others) (Kratochwill, 1978; Strain & Shores, 1979; Sulzer-Azaroff & Mayer, 1977).

The Multiple Baseline Design across Behaviors

In the multiple baseline design across behaviors, the investigator identifies a minimum of three similar yet functionally independent behaviors exhibited by one individual, or one group of individuals. Each target behavior is measured concurrently and continuously under the same environmental conditions until a stable baseline trend and level are established. The investigator intervenes on one target while monitoring the other behaviors. When the targeted behavior reaches the criterion level, intervention is introduced on the second target, and then the third. This systematic and sequential application of the independent variable across behaviors continues until all targeted behaviors have been exposed to the same intervention. Targeted behaviors can range from academic behaviors (e.g., number of words read correctly per minute) to social behaviors (e.g., number of object-throwing episodes per 30-minute observation period). The design can effectively evaluate an intervention intended to either accelerate the frequency of an appropriate academic or social behavior or decelerate the frequency of an inappropriate behavior.

Internal Validity   To demonstrate experimental control in a multiple baseline design across behaviors, the investigator must collect acceptable baseline data across each targeted behavior and then apply the intervention to one behavior while maintaining baseline conditions in the others. After criterion-level responding is attained with the first behavior, the intervention is applied to the second. Following replication of criterion attainment with the second behavior, the intervention is applied to the third, and so on. Figure 10-3 presents a graphic prototype of the multiple baseline design across behaviors of an individual or group.

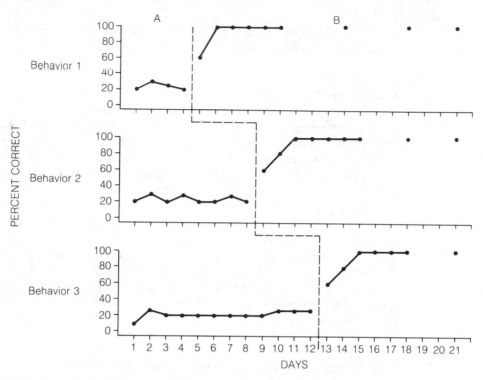

FIGURE 10-3 Hypothetical data using the multiple baseline design across behaviors. Two or more baselines are recorded simultaneously, and the intervention is introduced sequentially, one baseline at a time.

Considerations

Guidelines

When using the multiple baseline design across behaviors, the investigator should:

1. Pinpoint outcome objectives prior to initiating the study.

2. Apply the intervention only when all targeted behaviors exhibit acceptable stability in level and trend.

3. Apply the intervention to a new behavior only after criterion-level responding is demonstrated in the preceding behavior.

4. Target a minimum of three behaviors.

5. Identify behaviors that are functionally independent, yet similar.

The applied researcher who uses the multiple baseline design across behaviors must make two predictions prior to initiating a study: (1) that the targeted behaviors are functionally independent of one another (i.e., behaviors are not members of the same response class), so that baselines will remain stable until the intervention is directly applied, and (2) that the behaviors are sufficiently similar for each to respond, in turn, to the same intervention. There are many academic behaviors that are reasonably certain to be independent of one another, in that they are unlikely to be acquired without direct instruction (e.g., sets of spelling words or sets of arithmetic problems across various math operations). With social behaviors, however, the prediction of independence becomes more problematic. For example, beyond certain thresholds, some behaviors may occasion others (Kazdin & Kopel, 1975), as when a person is taught appropriate grooming skills (e.g., bathing) that, in turn, improve social interactions with peers. This increased frequency of positive interactions increases the probability of the individual learning other appropriate self-care skills, such as oral hygiene and clothing selection, through peer modeling and feedback. In such a case, a multiple baseline design across grooming, oral hygiene, and clothing selection might fail to demonstrate experimental control due to covariation across targeted behaviors. Similarly, the deceleration of some behaviors may result in an acceleration of other inappropriate behaviors if the net result, otherwise, would be a lower overall frequency of reinforcement (Bandura, 1969). For example, a strategy intended to sequentially suppress spitting, hitting, and object throwing might become progressively less effective for each subsequent behavior, unless the intervention provides alternative avenues for the learner to recruit reinforcement (i.e., *differential* reinforcement for appropriate behaviors). Finally, an investigator can provide a more convincing demonstration of experimental control by targeting behaviors that are topographically similar but that are independent of one another. For example, a multiple baseline design across matched phonics skills would be a more convincing demonstration of experimental control than one across three seemingly unrelated behaviors, such as spelling, addition, and out-of-seat.

Advantages

The multiple baseline design across behaviors offers the educational researcher several advantages. First, a return to baseline conditions is not required to demonstrate experimental control. Second, because a reversal condition is not required, the multiple baseline design across behaviors obviates many of the practical and ethical problems associated with reversal designs. Third, it provides a means for evaluating programs designed to teach skills that are irreversible (e.g., spelling, arithmetic, task assembly). Fourth, because most educators are interested in response generalizations and maintenance, the multiple baseline design across behaviors provides a paradigm for continuous monitoring of student progress through these two learning stages.

Limitations

The multiple baseline design across behaviors requires adherence to specific constraints that may present problems for a teacher in some circumstances. First, a minimum of three behaviors must be identified, each independent of one another and yet, each responsive to the same independent variable. Second, the behaviors must be monitored continuously and concurrently, which may prove time-consuming, distracting, cumbersome, or otherwise impractical (Horner & Baer, 1978; Scott & Goetz, 1980). Third, prolonged baseline measures on behaviors not yet receiving instruction may induce extinction effects in the learner(s) (Cuvo, 1979; Horner & Baer, 1978; Murphey & Bryan, 1980) and may raise questions about the ethics of postponing intervention on behaviors that may require more immediate attention (Kratochwill, 1978; Strain & Shores, 1979; Sulzer-Azaroff & Mayer, 1977).

Applied Examples:
Multiple Baseline
Designs across
Behaviors

Study I: Mildly Handicapped

Kirby, K.C., Holborn, S. W., and Bushby, H.T. Word game bingo: A behavioral treatment package for improving textual responding to sight words *Journal of Applied Behavior Analysis*, 1981, *14* (3), 317–326.

Purpose, subject, and setting. Kirby et al. (1981) utilized a multiple baseline design across word groups to assess the efficacy of a word bingo game on the acquisition and retention of oral sight word vocabulary. The students, four girls and two boys, were regular third graders assessed by a resource teacher as especially deficient in sight word pronunciation and overall reading skills. The investigators' intent was to use the bingo game to teach the children four sets of words (labeled set A, B, C, and D), each consisting of 24 sight words randomly selected from a third-grade teacher's manual.

Dependent variables. The dependent measures consisted of the "mean percentage of correct responses" for the group of children on words sets A through D. Each child was assessed individually 3 days per week at the same library location, but at an earlier time (1:00–1:45 P.M.). A child was handed one of the four sets of flashcards (consisting of the 24 sight words in that set) and asked to "flip through" the stack, orally reading one word at a time. Data were collected word by word and scored "correct" if pronounced correctly and "incorrect" if mispronounced or unattempted. While marking the data sheet, the investigator remained silent as the child read, except to say "next word" if the child paused for approximately 3 seconds on any one word. Upon finishing a word set (one trial per word), the child was handed another set and the procedure repeated until all four word sets were assessed. Assessment procedures were somewhat altered, however, during the training of word set C (assessment session 19–24), at which time the investigator began giving word-by-word feedback: words read correctly were consequated with "good" or "right," and errors were corrected immediately by having the child repeat the word correctly while looking at the flashcard. Point-by-point reliability checks were conducted on four occasions with an average interobserver agreement on correct responses of 97.7%

Independent variables. Four separate bingo games (A, B, C, and D) were constructed, one for each word set. The materials for each game consisted of 24 flashcards with one sight word printed on each card, and six bingo cards, each divided into 25 boxes of equal size, with the 24 sight words randomly typed one per box and the center box always marked "free." This provided one card for each child, each card containing the same words but in a different pattern. Before initiating a "round" of the game, the game manager (a teacher's aide) and the children jointly agreed upon a winning bingo combination (e.g., one line in any direction, all outside squares, an   , etc.). The aide then shuffled the flashcards and, drawing from the top of the deck, announced the words at approximately 15-second intervals, until a "bingo" was called. As a word was called, the children were to locate it on their respective cards and to cover it with a chip. The children were encouraged to solicit each other's help in the search process. (Further, when introducing a new word set, the aide both named the word and displayed the flashcard during the 15-second interval; however, by the fourth day of a new game the visual display was faded so that the children were responding only to the oral announcement.) Upon winning a bingo, a child received a star beside his or her name on a publicly displayed poster. Cards were then cleared and a new game begun. During a daily 45-minute session there usually was time for six consecutive games. Further, the same bingo game was played for approximately 12 consecutive school days before the next game was introduced; when a new game was initiated the old games were not played again.

Design and condition sequence. The investigators employed a multiple baseline design across word groups, as illustrated in Figure 10-4. The condition sequence was as follows: set A baseline (A_1) maintained for 4 assessment sessions, followed by set A bingo game (B_1) for 7 assessment sessions; set B baseline (A_2) maintained for 11 sessions, followed by set B bingo (B_2) for 7 sessions; set C baseline (A_3) maintained for 18 sessions, followed by set C bingo (B_3) for 6 sessions; and set D baseline (A_4) maintained throughout the study, 24 sessions.

Results as reported by the authors. As described by the investigators, the group data for word sets A to C demonstrated mean percentages of improvement from A conditions to B conditions of 30.8%, 31.0%, and 32.1% respectively (encompassing a range of 20%–40% for individual children). Furthermore, they suggested that "slight upward drifts" in baselines were not problematic due to (1) abrupt level changes occurring with each new B condition, (2) the absence of overlapping data points across adjacent conditions, and (3) the inconsistent improvement of performance across each B condition until stable 90% or higher correct responding was attained. To further strengthen their case, the authors supplied "representative" individual data for two of the six children to demonstrate that the averaged group data were a fair representation of individual performance.

A detailed analysis of the data. A detailed visual analysis of Figure 10-4 is provided to evaluate the authors' claims, and to supply a model of a strategy that the "research consumer" can use to analyze graphed data. Much of the following discussion is based on information summarized in Tables 10-1 and 10-2, and the reader is encouraged to examine the figure in order to independently assess the tabular data.

Relative to word set A (data series A_1-B_1), the bingo game (B_1) resulted in a positive effect over baseline (A_1), as evidenced by a level change between conditions of +15% correct and by the lack of overlap in scores. A stable, accelerating-improving baseline trend was maintained during intervention until stable, zero-celerating criterion-level responding was attained. *Recommendation:* Ideally, A_1 should have been continued until a clear trend was established showing either a zero-celerating or decelerating slope before introducing B_1. This would have required at least three additional data points. In this case, the investigators introduced the bingo game immediately following a 5% acceleration in performance, as evidenced by comparing the last baseline data point with the preceding one (i.e., an increase from 55% to 60%), providing a less convincing demonstration of the potency of the intervention.

Relative to word set B (data series A_2-B_2), the data provide an excellent replication of effects as indicated by a level change between conditions of

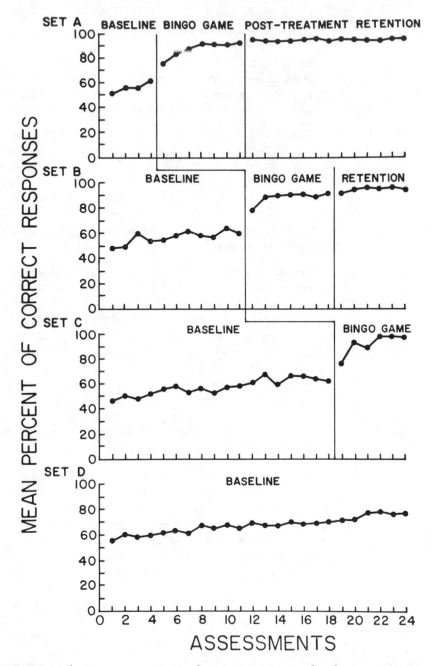

FIGURE 10-4   Mean percentage of correct responses for the group on word sets A through D. (Figure 1, p. 322, from: Kirby, K.C., Holborn, S.W., and Bushby, H.T. Word game bingo: A behavioral treatment package for improving textual responding to sight words. *Journal of Applied Behavior Analysis*, 1981 *14* (3) 317–326. Copyright by Society for the Experimental Analysis of Behavior, Inc. Reproduced by permission.)

TABLE 10-1   Within condition analysis of Study 1 (Kirby, Holburn, & Bushby, 1981).

Conditions	Set A		Set B		Set C		Set D	
	$\frac{A_1}{1}$	$\frac{B_1}{2}$	$\frac{A_2}{3}$	$\frac{B_2}{4}$	$\frac{A_3}{5}$	$\frac{B_3}{6}$	$\frac{A_4}{7}$	$\frac{}{8}$
1. Condition Length	$\underline{4}$	$\underline{7}$	$\underline{11}$	$\underline{7}$	$\underline{18}$	$\underline{6}$	$\underline{24}$	—
2. Estimate of Trend Direction	(+)	(+)	(+)	(+)	(+)	(+)	(+)	( )
3. Trend Stability	stable	stable	stable	stable	stable	stable	stable	
4. Data Paths within Trend	(+)	(+) - (=)	(+) (=)	(+) (=)	(+) (=)	(+) (=)	(+)	( )
5. Level Stability and Range	stable (50–60)	variable (75–90)	stable (50–60)	variable (78–90)	variable (45–65)	variable (75–100)	variable (55–75)	( )
6. Level Change	50–60 (+10)	75–90 (+15)	50–58 (+8)	78–90 (+15)	45–60 (+15)	75–100 (+25)	55–75 (+20)	( )

TABLE 10-2 Between adjacent conditions analysis of Study 1 (Kirby, Holburn, & Bushby, 1981).

Condition Comparison	$\dfrac{B_1}{A_1}$ (2:1)	$\dfrac{B_2}{A_2}$ (2:1)	$\dfrac{B_3}{A_3}$ (2:1)	— (:)	— (:)	— (:)	— (:)	$\dfrac{\text{2nd condition}}{\text{1st condition}}$ condition order
1. Number of Variables Changed	1 game package	1 game package	2 (1 game package plus 1 assessment "feedback" package)					
2. Change in Trend Direction and Effect	(+) (+) no change	(=) (+) positive	(=) (+) positive	( ) ( )	( ) ( )	( ) ( )	( ) ( )	1st trend 2nd trend effect
3. Change in Trend Stability	stable to stable	stable to stable	stable to stable	to	to	to	to	
4. Change in Level	(60–75) +15	(58–78) +20	(60–75) +15	(–)	(–)	(–)	(–)	
5. Percentage of Overlap	0 %	0 %	0 %	___ %	___ %	___ %	___ %	

+20% correct, with no overlap of scores. This data series is more convincing than the preceding A_1-B_1 series because the baseline trend (as evidenced by the last five data points) was zero-celerating prior to introducing intervention. Furthermore, upon intervention, the data showed an accelerating-improving trend that stabilized at the 90% + criterion level.

Relative to word set C (data series A_3-B_3), the data again provide a convincing replication of effects as evidenced by a level change between conditions of +15% correct, no overlap of scores between conditions, and a zero-celerating baseline trend (as defined by the last six data points) followed by an accelerating-improving intervention trend that stabilized at or above the 90% criterion level. The effects of the bingo game were confounded, however, by the "feedback" variable(s) that were simultaneously introduced during the assessment sessions of the B_3 condition. *Recommendation*: No new variables should have been introduced. Assessment procedures, as with the bingo game itself, should have remained consistent throughout all conditions.

Relative to word set D (data series A_4), this uninterrupted baseline data series provided a useful standard by which to demonstrate that the bingo game substantially increased the rate of acquisition above the less than ideal accelerating baseline trends that were evident across all A conditions (including all of the A_1 condition and initial portions of the A_2 and A_3 conditions). *Recommendation*: The bingo game also should have been applied to the word set D series because (1) it would have provided a second replication of effects (given that the A_2-B_2 series were not a "true" replication due to "feedback" variables) and (2) ethically it would seem unfair to the children to subject them to so many assessment sessions (N = 24) without finally delivering instruction.

Summary and conclusions. Allowing for the "feedback" confounding in the A_3-B_3 series (word set 3), it would appear that the investigators' claims were warranted: the bingo game substantially affected the mean percentage of group responding on word sets A, B, and C. The study serves to illustrate, however, that prolonged, continuous baseline assessments may be problematic. The authors rationalized their procedural changes in the third series as the results of (1) the children constantly requesting performance feedback and (2) the fact that several children were perseverating in incorrect answers to one or two of the sight words. Perhaps both of these problems could have been avoided with less frequent testing, an option provided by multiple probe designs. A second purpose of the study was to assess the effects of the bingo game on the students' retention of sight words after intervention. A visual analysis of word sets A and B would indicate criterion-level retention; however, as the authors acknowledged, this high level of responding may have been due to the many practice opportunities associated with frequent assessment. Again, intermittent probe measures, as provided with multiple probe designs, might have permitted a more accurate response to this research question.

In describing the appealing features of the bingo game, the authors noted that it (1) permitted group instruction (2) required little preparation time or expense (3) was manageable by a teacher's aide or an advanced student, (4) encouraged peer modeling and feedback, and (5) was enjoyable for both children and trainer. Given these features and the optimistic indications from the data, it is recommended that the bingo game be systematically replicated both across various mildly handicapped children and other reading and academic skills. Furthermore, the method should be compared with other instructional procedures.

Study II: Severely Handicapped

Savie, P., and Dickie, R.F. Overcorrection of topographically dissimilar autistic behaviors. *Education and Treatment of Children*, 1979, *2* (3), 177–184.

Purpose, subject, and setting. Savie and Dickie (1979) employed a multiple baseline design across four behaviors ("touching face," "touching hair," "taking objects," and "touching others") exhibited by a 12-year-old profoundly retarded "autistic" girl, in order to assess the effectiveness of a briefly applied "overcorrection" procedure to reduce topographically dissimilar behaviors. The child was nonverbal, aggressive toward her classroom peers, self-stimulatory, and self-abusive. For example, she pushed and pulled other children, removed or threw their materials, "mouthed" her fingers after touching her nasal, genital, and anal areas, and pulled and twisted her hair, resulting in bald spots on her scalp. Her measured IQ was 14. The study was conducted in the child's classroom, which included six children, a certified teacher, and a teacher's aide, in a private school for emotionally disturbed children.

Dependent variables. Four dependent variables were targeted: (1) "touching face," defined as mouthing fingers after touching other body areas; (2) "touching hair," defined as pulling, twirling, or flicking her own hair; (3) "taking objects," defined as removing or throwing any materials of her peers; and (4) "touching others," defined as pushing or pulling the other students. Using a continuous frequency count, an independent observer simultaneously recorded the four target behaviors through a one-way mirror, during 1-hour training sessions twice daily for 10 days. Five reliability checks resulted in an average gross interobserver reliability of over 90%.

Independent variable. After five baseline sessions (2½ school days), the classroom teacher intervened on "touching face" by consequating the target behavior with a verbal reprimand and a 3-minute "overcorrection" procedure. Specifically, the teacher responded "No! (specified behavior) is not allowed," and then removed the child to a far corner of the room where she was required to practice "good hands" by sitting at a desk with her hands on the desk top, palms down, with a piece of masking tape loosely affixed across them. This "positive practice" procedure lasted 3 minutes and was applied each time the behavior occurred. In addition, as a continuation of preintervention procedures, the child received intermittent verbal praise for periods of appropriate responding, e.g., "Good girl, Karen! You are a good worker today." After 9 sessions the identical procedures were extended to include "touching hair" and, after 13 sessions, to "taking objects."

Design and condition sequence. The investigators employed a multiple baseline design across behaviors as illustrated in Figure 10-5. The condition sequence was as follows: (1) "touching face"—baseline (A_1), 5 sessions;

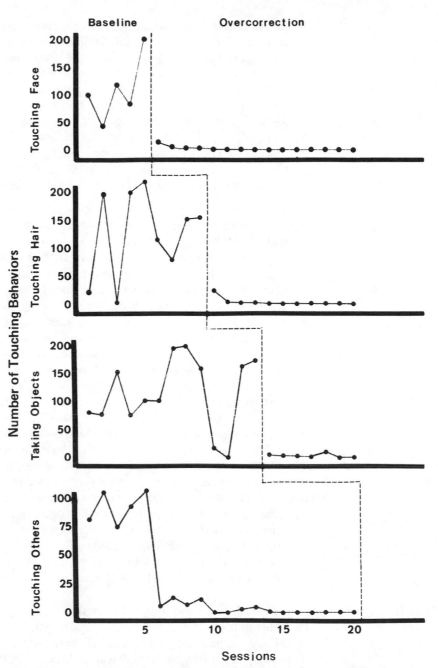

FIGURE 10-5   Inappropriate behaviors during one-hour training sessions.
(Figure 1, p. 181, from: Savie, P., and Dickie, R.F. Overcorrection of topographically dissimilar autistic behaviors. *Education and Treatment of Children*, 1979, *2* (3), 177–184. Reproduced by permission.)

overcorrection (B$_1$), 15 sessions; (2) "touching hair"—baseline (A$_2$), 9 sessions; overcorrection (B$_2$), 11 sessions; (3) "taking objects"—baseline (A$_3$), 13 sessions; overcorrection (B$_3$), 8 sessions; and (4) "touching others"—baseline (A$_4$), 20 sessions.

Results as reported by authors. The investigators reported substantial reductions in the first three behavioral categories upon sequential application of the "overcorrection" procedure and the total suppression of the fourth category without the necessity of direct intervention. Relative to "touching face," the baseline condition (A_1) averaged 102 responses per session compared to a mean of 1.4 during intervention (B_1). Relative to "touching hair," the baseline condition (A_2) averaged 102 responses per session compared to an average 2.9 during intervention (B_2). Relative to "taking objects," a baseline average of 115 per session dropped to 1.7 per session during intervention. And relative to "touching others," an initial level of more than 80 per session was reduced to a zero rate by the termination of the study.

Summary and conclusions. The investigators provide compelling evidence that the "overcorrection" procedure did effectively suppress four topographically different behavioral categories. As with any "package" intervention, however, one is left in doubt as to which package component(s) were critical to success. For example, the observed effects may have resulted from the time-out intervention component, rather than the positive practice supposedly related to the masking tape procedure. Only by changing one variable at a time can such questions be resolved. Additionally, this study would have been strengthened had stimulus, response, and maintenance generalization data been provided: Did the suppressive effects generalize to other natural settings (e.g., lunchroom, playground, bus, home)? Upon decelerating these specific target behaviors, was there a simultaneous acceleration of other equally inappropriate behaviors? Or, on a more optimistic note, were there simultaneous collateral increases in appropriate responding as evidenced, perhaps, by improved peer interactions? Were the behavior changes durable beyond the rather limited 10-day scope of the study? Answers to these types of questions would have provided educators with useful additional information to what, otherwise, appears to be a very potent intervention. Finally, these data illustrate the occurrence of behavioral covariation across unexposed baselines, as evidenced by "transitory" covariation across A_2 and A_3 and complete covariation across A_4, which occurred simultaneously with the introduction of the intervention into the first data series on Session 6. Thus, investigators should target four or more dependent measures in order to insure at least two replications of effects.

Concluding Comments

As discussed, the multiple baseline design across behaviors is applicable to the validation of interventions across many types of learners (spanning the broad range of handicapping conditions), exhibiting a multiplicity of behaviors, in a variety of educational and clinical settings. Table 10-3 summarizes several studies from the applied research literature that employed the multiple baseline design across behaviors.

Gallant, Sargeant, and Van Houten (1980) examined the effects of contingent access to a science activity area on the percent completion and percent accuracy of daily reading and math assignments, for an above-average (IQ = 125), "unmotivated" 11-year-old boy. Using a multiple baseline design across reading and math tasks, the investigators demonstrated that when the contingency was first applied to the reading task, reading accuracy and completion improved immediately, while arithmetic performance remained low. However,

TABLE 10-3 Examples of multiple baseline designs across behaviors.

Reference	Subject(s)	Setting(s)	Dependent Variable(s)	Independent Variable(s)
Gallant, Sargeant, & Van Houten (1980)	a normal functioning, "unmotivated" 6th-grade male (CA = 11; IQ = 125)	regular 6th-grade classroom	"percent completion" and "percent accuracy" across daily reading and math assignments	contingent access to a science activity area
Cooke & Apolloni (1976)	3 males and 1 female labelled "learning disabled" (CA range: 6–9 years)	a "playroom" located adjacent to the subjects' classroom	rate per minute of 4 peer-interactive behaviors: smiling, sharing, positive physical contacting, and verbal complimenting	an instructional package consisting of verbal instructions, modeling, and praise
Clark, Boyd, & Macrae (1975)	4 males and 2 females labelled "delinquent" and "mildly retarded" (CA range: 14–16 years)	a segregated "prevocational" classroom	"percent correct" across 9 job application items (including date, name, address, signature, phone number, birth date, and the name, address, and occupation of a reference)	an instructional package including verbal instructions, modeling, repeated practice, and token reinforcement
Trace, Cuvo, & Criswell (1977)	7 male and 7 female institutional residents, labelled "moderately retarded" (CA range 14–16 years)	a small room in the institution containing 2 chairs and a table	"percent correct" across 6 sets of coin combinations	an instructional package including a graduated hierarchy of prompting and fading
Barton, Guess, Garcia, & Baer (1970)	16 "severely-profoundly" retarded institutionalized males (CA range: 9–23 years)	an institutional dining room	"percent occurrence" of 4 inappropriate mealtime behaviors: "stealing" (removing food from another's tray), eating with fingers, misusing utensils, and "pigging" spilled foods	a time-out contingency, sequentially extended to include each inappropriate behavior

when the contingency was extended to include the math task, there was an immediate replication of effects, leading the applied researchers to suggest that for some children, contingent access to a preferred curricular activity (the Premack principle) may be equally as reinforcing as contingent free time or some other recreational activity, and perhaps more educationally valid. The results would have been more convincing, however, had the investigators provided a second replication of experimental effects (either by adding a third behavior or by implementing a brief reversal in one of the data series) since a multiple baseline design across only two behaviors provides a relatively weak demonstration of control.

Cooke and Apolloni (1976) instructed a group of learning disabled children, three boys, and a girl, ranging in age from 6–9 years, to increase their rates of four prosocial, peer-interactive behaviors: smiling, sharing, positive physical contacting, and verbal complimenting. Utilizing a multiple baseline design across the four behaviors, they sequentially applied an instructional package (consisting of instructions, modeling, and praise) and demonstrated substantial "rate per minute" changes across each behavior when the intervention was applied. Furthermore, the children exhibited generalized prosocial effects when interacting with their untrained peers in the generalization setting.

Clark, Boyd, and Macrae (1975) instructed mildly retarded and "delinquent" youth (four boys and two girls, ranging in age from 14–16 years) to write pieces of biographic information on job application forms including: date, name, address, signature, phone number, birth date, and the name, address, and occupation of a reference. Using a multiple baseline design across the nine responses, the investigators taught the group to produce each item to criterion, using an instructional package that included verbal instructions, modeling, repeated practice, and token reinforcement. The percentage correct for each item substantially improved with training (both on the specifically trained application form and on several untrained "generalization" forms), while the performance level on untrained items consistently remained low. It should be noted, however, that three of the nine baselines exhibited some deterioration, suggesting that prolonged, unreinforced baseline testing may have induced extinction effects.

Trace, Cuvo, and Criswell (1977) designed a program to teach coin equivalencies to moderately retarded institutional residents, seven males and seven females, ranging in age from 14–16 years. Using a graduated hierarchy of prompting and fading, the investigator trained to criterion (as measured by percent correct) six sets of coin combinations (e.g., nickel combinations to 10, 20, 30, ... 50 cents; nickel and dime combinations to 15, 25, 35, ... 50 cents; and nickel, dime, and quarter combinations to 40, 45 and 50 cents). Using a multiple baseline design across the six combination sets, the applied researchers validated their training procedure by documenting replications of effects across each baseline tier.

Barton, Guess, Garcia, and Baer (1970) examined the effect of a time-out procedure on the percent occurrence of four inappropriate mealtime behaviors exhibited by 16 severely-profoundly retarded institutionalized males, ranging in age from 9–23 years. Using a multiple baseline design across "stealing" (removing food from another's tray), eating with fingers, misusing utensils, and "pigging" spilled foods, the time-out contingency first was applied to stealing and then sequentially extended to each succeeding behavior. With each application of the intervention, there was a decrease in appropriate responding and, thus, a convincing demonstration of experimental control.

In conclusion, the multiple baseline design across behaviors is often the design of choice for many applied researchers working in a variety of educational and clinical settings, with a range of academic and social behaviors. It is particularly useful to classroom teachers because it permits continuous monitoring of targeted instructional objectives. Though the design has some limitations (e.g., a prolonged baseline condition for some behaviors), its practical advantages, when compared to the reversal design, have made it a viable and popular evaluation paradigm for those working in special education settings.

The Multiple Baseline Design across Conditions

In the multiple baseline design across conditions, the investigator sequentially applies an intervention across several different stimulus conditions in which the same behavior of an individual or group is exhibited. "Stimulus conditions" can encompass the dimensions of time, instructional arrangement, activity, setting, control agent (i.e., teacher), or composition of peer group. In contrast to the multiple baseline design across behaviors, the multiple baseline design across conditions requires the investigator to target a single behavior and a minimum of three different conditions (e.g., settings) in which the researcher wants the behavior to occur (or not to occur depending upon the objective of the intervention). The target behavior is monitored continuously and concurrently under each of the three conditions until baseline stability is established. The investigator then introduces the independent variable to the target behavior in one condition, while continuing to measure the same behavior in other conditions using baseline procedures. When the behavior stabilizes at or near the criterion level in the first condition, the intervention is then introduced to the same behavior in the second condition. The systematic and sequential introduction of the independent variable across stimulus conditions continues until the criterion level is achieved under all targeted conditions. For example, targeted conditions can range from monitoring the percentage of time on-task across math, spelling, and social studies periods (across activities) to the frequency of "disruptive behaviors" across a classroom, lunchroom, and playground (across settings) to the number of minutes tardy across morning, lunch, and afternoon recesses (across time).

Internal validity   The demonstration of experimental control in the mutliple baseline design across conditions requires the investigator to first collect acceptable baseline data across each stimulus condition and to then apply the intervention in one condition, while maintaining baseline conditions in the others. After criterion-level performance is attained in the first condition, the intervention is applied to the second. Following replication of criterion attainment in the second condition, the intervention is applied to the third, and so on. Figure 10-6 provides a graphic illustration of the multiple baseline design for one behavior of an individual (or group) occurring across different stimulus conditions.

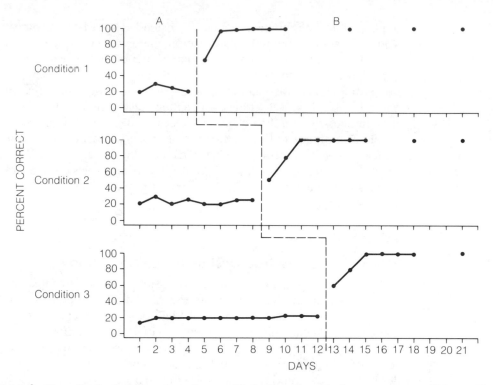

FIGURE 10-6 Hypothetical data using the multiple baseline design across conditions. The same behavior across two or more conditions is recorded simultaneously, and the intervention is introduced sequentially, one baseline at a time.

As with all multiple baseline designs, experimental control is achieved when an acceptable baseline trend is maintained until the intervention is introduced to the target behavior. With the multiple baseline design across conditions there should be no change in the dependent variable until the independent variable is introduced to each stimulus condition.

Considerations

Guidelines

When using the multiple baseline design across conditions, the investigator should:

1. Pinpoint outcome objectives appropriate for each stimulus condition prior to initiating the study.

2. Apply the intervention only when the target behavior is maintained at the acceptable baseline level and trend under all stimulus conditions.

3. Apply the intervention in a new condition only when criterion-level responding is attained in the preceding condition.

4. Target a minimum of three conditions (e.g., settings, teachers, activities).

5. Identify conditions which are functionally independent, yet similar enough to permit the intervention a "fair" chance of working.

When using the multiple baseline design across conditions, the applied researcher must make two predictions (1) that the target behavior will function independently across stimulus conditions, so that baseline data will remain stable and unchanged until the intervention is directly applied, and (2) that the stimulus conditions will be sufficiently similar to permit the replication of effects each time the intervention is applied. There are few guidelines to help researchers predicting that a target behavior will be independent across conditions. Some learners, for example, have reinforcement histories for generalizing across situations, as when a child is reinforced for improved study habits during reading lessons and, in turn, exhibits generalized improvements during spelling and math periods. From a researcher's perspective, however, an optimistic note is that such generalization is often the "exception" rather than "rule." Much behavior is specific to the training situation, unless generalization programming techniques are deliberately applied (Stokes & Baer, 1977).

In regard to the second requirement of identifying similar stimulus conditions, it is important to note that *topographically identical behaviors may be functionally dissimilar* under different stimulus conditions. For example, a child's classroom fighting in the presence of teacher and peers may occur and be maintained by different conditions from fighting at home. Therefore, the probability of demonstrating experimental control may be enhanced by monitoring a behavior across more closely matched stimulus conditions, which share as many setting events as is possible (e.g., across academic periods; across morning, noon, and afternoon recesses; across lunchroom, playground, and halls).

Advantages

The multiple baseline design across conditions is well suited to an important educational consideration: teachers are responsible for the academic and social behavior of children across a broad range of environmental conditions, and it is often necessary to concurrently modify behavioral excesses (or deficits) exhibited in several of those environments. By example, the range of conditions within a classroom includes individual, small group, and large group instructional arrangements across a broad array of curricular domains. Beyond the classroom, educators assume responsibilities for children in buses, lunchrooms, playgrounds, restrooms, hallways, and on field trips. In addition, teachers increasingly are consulting with parents and other care providers to coordinate school-home-community programs. The multiple baseline design across conditions can prove helpful in identifying intervention programs that foster generalized responding across many natural environments (Cuvo, 1979).

Limitations

The multiple baseline design across conditions requires adherence to specific constraints that may be problematic under some circumstances. First, a minimum of three environmental conditions must be identified, each occasioning the same target behavior, yet each independent enough to permit the replication of effects. Second, if the multiple baseline design is across control agents (teacher, teacher associate, and speech pathologist) and/or across settings within a school, individuals responsible for applying the intervention, as well as observers, should be well informed as to the program's purpose and the importance of responding consistently to the behavior. Third, the target behavior must be monitored continuously and concurrently in each condition, a task that may prove time-consuming, distracting, or otherwise burdensome to a teacher (Horner & Baer, 1978; Scott & Goetz, 1980). And fourth, prolonged baseline measures in situations in which the intervention has not yet been introduced may induce extinction effects (Cuvo, 1979; Horner & Baer, 1978; Murphey & Bryan, 1980) and raise questions about the ethics of postponing interventions in environments requiring immediate attention (Kratochwill, 1978; Strain & Shores, 1979; Sulzer-Azaroff & Mayer, 1977).

Applied Examples: Multiple Baseline Design across Conditions

Study I: Moderately Handicapped

Chiang, S.J., Iwata, B.A., and Dorsey, M.F. Elimination of disruptive bus-riding behavior via token reinforcement on a "distance-based" schedule. *Education and Treatment of Children*, 1979, *2* (2), 101–109.

Purpose, subject, and setting. Chiang et al. (1979) employed a multiple baseline design across morning and afternoon bus rides to assess the effects of a driver-implemented token economy on disruptive behaviors exhibited by a 10-year-old retarded boy while riding the bus to school and home. The child (IQ 46) lived with foster parents and attended a public school program for the "severely mentally impaired." He presented a bus-riding history of crying, tantrumming, peer aggression, and self-stimulatory behavior, which often distracted the driver and endangered the safety of the trip. At the time of the study, token management systems were in use both at home and in school, although they had never been extended to include the daily bus commutes. The study was conducted in a standard "Blue Bird" school bus with the driver, an average of 12 other children, and an independent observer in attendance.

Dependent variable. Using a partial interval recording procedure, the independent observer recorded the occurrence or nonoccurrence of "disruptive behavior" within two 10-second intervals per minute for the entire duration of the ride. Data were collected morning and afternoon throughout the study i.e., for 40 school days. "Disruptive behavior" was defined as (1) destruction of property; (2) aggression against others, including slapping, poking, or hitting; (3) self-stimulation, including repetitive hand waving; and (4) inappropriate vocalizations, such as screaming or issuing commands to others. If a disruptive behavior occurred at any time during an interval, the interval was scored "disruptive." The dependent measure, "percent intervals of disruptive behavior," was computed by dividing the number of disruptive intervals in a session by the total number of intervals in the session, and then multiplying by 100. Point-by-point reliability checks were conducted across 12 sessions resulting in a mean agreement of 92%, on both occurrences and nonoccurrences.

Independent variable. The bus driver's route was divided into nine relatively equally spaced intervals, which were identified by landmarks such as stop signs or major intersections. Upon arriving at each new landmark, the driver either (1) praised the child's "good behavior" during the preceding interval and recorded one point on a hand counter mounted on the dashboard of the bus or (2) described to the child the disruptive behavior that occurred during the interval that prevented the awarding of a point. Otherwise, while in-transit the driver ignored disruptive behavior unless it became extreme, in which case she delivered up to two verbal reprimands and then began deducting points from the child's accumulated earnings (response cost). Upon arriving at home or school, the driver issued the child a card identifying the date, time of day (A.M. or P.M.), number of points earned or lost, and anecdotal comments. The child then exchanged the card with parents or teachers for prearranged contingent consequences. Accumulated points were redeemable for small snacks, access to play activities, or privileges such as "running errands" for the teacher. A negative point total, on the other hand, resulted in a brief time-out.

Design and condition sequence. The researchers employed a multiple baseline design across conditions (A.M. and P.M.) as illustrated in Figure 10.7. The condition sequence was: P.M. baseline (A_1) maintained for 17 assessment sessions, followed by token reinforcement (B_1) for 22 sessions; A.M. baseline

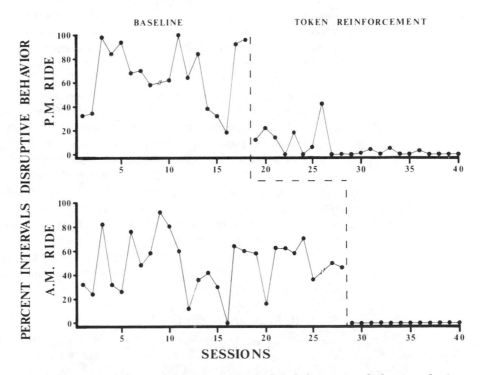

FIGURE 10-7 The percentage of intervals of disruptive behavior during morning and afternoon rides across experimental conditions. (Figure 1, p. 106, from: Chiang, S.J., Iwata, B.A., and Dorsey, M.F. Elimination of disruptive bus-riding behavior via token reinforcement on a "distance-based" schedule. *Education and Treatment of Children*, 1979 *2* (2), 101–109. Reproduced by permission.)

(A_2) maintained for 28 sessions, followed by token reinforcement (B_2) for 12 sessions.

Results as reported by authors. As described by the investigators, substantial reductions in disruptive behavior resulted from each application of the independent variable. For the afternoon data series, the percentage of disruptive behavior during the baseline condition averaged 66% compared to an average 5% during intervention. For the morning series, the baseline condition averaged 48% disruptive behavior compared to 0% disruption during intervention.

Summary and conclusions. It does appear that the investigators' claims were warranted: the token economy substantially reduced disruptive behavior. As with any "package" intervention, however, one is left with doubts as to which specific intervention components were responsible for the observed effects. This becomes especially problematic in a study such as this in which a functional analysis of baseline conditions was never provided. One does not know, for example, what variables may have reinforced or maintained the disruptive behavior prior to intervention. If it was negative attention and reprimands from the bus driver (the rates of which were not provided), perhaps the intervention components of contingent praise and ignoring could have functioned to control the behaviors without including the more "intrusive" token system which, as acknowledged by the authors, should be systematically faded at some point in the program. Answers to such questions can only be provided by changing one variable at a time. Furthermore, the consumers of research are better able to independently assess the appropriateness of an intervention when supplied with functional baseline data. Allowing for these considerations, the fact is that the investigators devised a program that was functional for the bus driver (requiring only 2 hours of training in behavior management and 6 hours of supervised practice on the bus) and that permitted safer transportation for the children. Furthermore, several positive "spin offs" from the intervention were observed informally: (1) the previously disruptive child began interacting more appropriately with his peers, by helping others and conversing with them; (2) the "climate" on the bus became noticeably calmer among all the children; and (3) the driver's interactions with the children became more frequent and positive. Given these features and the optimistic indications from the data, the investigators' suggestions for additional school transportation research are warranted. These include strategies to train bus drivers in behavior management and the use of school-home coordinated group contingencies to manage several or more disruptive children.

Study II: Regular Fourth Grade

Barrish, H.H., Saunders, M., and Wolf, M.M. Good behavior game: Effects of individual contingencies for group consequences on disruptive behavior in classroom. *Journal of Applied Behavior Analysis*, 1969, *2* (2), 119–124.

Purpose, subject, and setting. Barrish et al. (1969) employed a multiple baseline design across academic periods to assess the effectiveness of an interdependent group contingency (the "good behavior game") to manage the behaviors of a disruptive public school fourth-grade class. The group consisted of 24 "normal" children, seven of whom were frequently referred to the principal for leaving their desks without permission, talking out, and otherwise generally distracting the class. In the opinions of both teacher and principal, the overall level of classroom disruption was unacceptable, requiring immediate attention. The "good behavior game" was applied across reading and math periods, each 1 hour long and conducted one after the other every school day morning. Both were very similar in format involving lecture, class discussion, chalkboard work, individual assignments, and quizzes—only the subject content varied.

Dependent variable. Three days a week (Monday, Wednesday, and Friday) one or two observers stationed themselves unobtrusively on one side of the classroom to record the occurrence or nonoccurrence of talking-out and out-of-seat behaviors. Data were collected during half of each academic period (requiring approximately 30 minutes for each) using a 1-minute interval recording system. If at any time during an interval any class member exhibited a target behavior, the interval was scored as an "occurrence" for that particular dependent measure. Thus each interval required two scores, one for talk-outs and one for out-of-seat. *Talking-out* was defined as whispering, speaking, or otherwise vocalizing without teacher permission. *Out-of-seat* was defined as leaving or scooting one's desk without permission. To obtain permission students were required to raise their hands, be recognized by the teacher, and specifically receive her consent. (During seat work, however, students were permitted to leave their desk one at a time either to go to the restroom or to receive assistance at the teacher's desk.) The dependent measures ("percent of intervals scored for behaviors") were computed by dividing the total number of talk-out or out-of-seat occurrences by the total number of session intervals and then multiplying by 100. Point-by-point reliability checks were conducted at least once per condition yielding an average interobserver "occurrence" agreement of 91% for out-of-seat and 86% for talk-outs.

Independent variable. Students were divided by rows into two teams. Each time a student violated one of the talk-out or out-of-seat rules (as defined above), his or her team received a mark on the chalkboard. The object of the game was to accumulate fewer marks than the opposing team and, thus, to win privileges. However, both teams could win if both received fewer than five marks in any one game. Each game lasted for the duration of one class period. Game winners received the following: brightly colored "victory tags" to be worn throughout the school day; a star affixed beside each team member's name on a "winner's chart"; first-in-line privileges for lunch or, if both teams won, early lunch dismissal; and 30 minutes of "special project" time at the end of the school day, with losers remaining at their desks completing additional assignments. As an added incentive, if a team accumulated fewer than 20 marks in one week, the members received a 4-minute early dismissal to a Friday recess.

Design and condition sequence. The researchers employed elements of both A-B-A-B multiple baseline across conditions designs, as illustrated in Figure

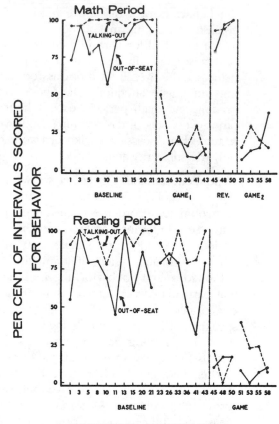

SESSIONS OBSERVED

FIGURE 10-8   Percent of 1-minute intervals scored by an observer as containing talking-out and out-of-seat behaviors occurring in a classroom of 24 fourth-grade school children during math and reading periods. In the baseline conditions the teacher attempted to manage the disruptive classroom behaviors in her usual manner. During the game conditions out-of-seat and talking-out responses by a student resulted in a possible loss of privileges for the student and his team. (Figure 1, p. 122, from: Barrish, H.H., Saunders, M., and Wolf, M.M. Good behavior game: Effects of individual contingencies for group consequences on disruptive behavior in a classroom. *Journal of Applied Behavioral Analysis*, 1969, *2* (2), 119–124. Copyright by Society for the Experimental Analysis of Behavior, Inc. Reprinted by permission.)

10-8. The condition sequence included the following: (1) *math period*—baseline (A$_1$), 21 days; "good behavior game" (B$_1$), 20 days; return to baseline (A$_2$), 6 days; "good behavior game" (B$_2$), 8 days; and (2) *reading period*—baseline (A$_3$) 43 days; "good behavior game" (B$_3$), 14 days.

Results as reported by authors. The authors reported "significant" and "reliable" reductions in both target behaviors when the game was in effect. During math, median baseline intervals for talk-outs and out-of-seat were 96% and 82% respectively, whereas, the rates dropped to 19% and 9% during intervention. During reading, median baseline intervals were 96% and 82% respectively, compared to median intervals of 30% and 10% during intervention.

Summary and conclusions. Group interdependent contingencies can create problems if one or several children misbehave to an extreme and consistently "ruin it" for the group. This was a concern in the present study because of two noncooperative students who occasionally refused to play the game, violated the established rules, and escalated their team scores to the great disappointment of other children. To manage this situation, on six occasions the teacher removed one or both of these children from their respective teams and deducted from the total team score the marks which they had contributed. With this modification a degree of fairness prevailed, and the game was reportedly very successful. It was compatible with naturally occurring classroom activities and goals, relatively easy for the teacher to implement, and well liked by most children (in fact, both teams won 82% of the time). The authors were well advised to suggest future research into the use of games to manage group behavior, including investigations of the relative effectiveness of group contingencies vs. individual contingencies. Finally, this study illustrates two noteworthy components generalizable to other multiple baseline designs: (1) the application of a brief reversal condition to provide an additional replication of effects and (2) the uncluttered visual display of two dependent measures.

Concluding Comments

The multiple baseline design across conditions is applicable to the validation of interventions across many types of learners (spanning the broad range of handicapping conditions), exhibiting a multiplicity of behaviors in a variety of educational and clinical settings. Table 10-4 summarizes several other studies from the applied research literature that have used the multiple baseline design across conditions. Nau and Van Houten (1981) designed a program to reduce the inappropriate classroom behaviors of a group of 31 "noisy" and "disruptive" seventh graders in a junior high school. To evaluate their procedures, the investigators utilized a multiple baseline design across academic periods: math and science. After collecting baseline data (as measured by the "mean percent of disruptive intervals") across both class settings, the investigators intervened in the math class with a "feedback only" condition, in which the teacher publicly recorded the ongoing number of disruptions. Because this intervention produced no noticeable effects ($A_1 = B_1$), it was modified to a "feedback plus detention" condition, in which any student receiving two reprimands would be removed to a detention room for 1–3 days. This added contingency produced a noticeable drop in disruptive behavior during math class. Subsequently, the "feedback plus detention" condition was applied to the science class, upon which an immediate replication of effects occurred. An approximate 30% level change, which occurred across both B conditions, provided a reasonably convincing demonstration of experimental control; however, the study would have been strengthened had the investigators provided a second replication of effects.

Murdock, Garcia, and Hardman (1977) provided articulation training (consisting of oral modeling and descriptive social praise) to remediate several word articulation problems exhibited by an 8-year-old, moderately retarded girl. Four words were targeted for training, and baseline data (as measured by the percentage of correct articulations) were collected across five different environmental settings: the training room, a language development class, a learn-

TABLE 10-4 Examples of multiple baseline designs across conditions.

Reference	Subject(s)	Setting(s)	Dependent Variable(s)	Independent Variable(s)
Nau & Van Houten (1981)	31 "noisy" and disruptive" 7th graders	a junior high school classroom	"mean percent of disruptive intervals" across math and science periods	"feedback plus detention" in which the teacher (a) recorded on the blackboard the ongoing number of disruptions (feedback) and (b) sent to a detention room any student receiving 2 reprimands (detention)
Murdock, Garcia, & Hardman (1977)	2 "moderately retarded" females (8 and 9 years old)	a "training room," language development class, a learning center, a Peabody language group, and the lunchroom of a public elementary school	"percentage of correct articulations" of 4 words targeted across the 5 different school settings	oral modeling and descriptive social praise
Cook, Altman, Shaw, & Blalock (1978)	a 7-year-old, microcephalic, "severely retarded" male	home and special education classroom	"number of daily masturbatory responses during 6 5-minute observation periods"	a squirt of lemon juice into the child's mouth each time behavior occurred

ing center, a Peabody language group, and lunch. As training was conducted in the first setting, "generalization measures" were conducted in the other settings (i.e., baseline conditions were maintained) to determine whether additional training across settings would be required. Of the four targeted words, half required training across three settings, and the other half across two settings, before complete generalization occurred. Thus, the multiple baseline design across conditions functioned both to validate the effectiveness of the intervention strategy and to signal the need for generalization training. Cook, Altman, Shaw, and Blalock (1978) eliminated the public masturbatory behavior of a "severely retarded," microcephalic 7-year-old boy by contingently applying a squirt of lemon juice to the child's mouth each time the behavior occurred. To evaluate the procedure, the investigators employed a multiple baseline design across home and school settings. After collecting baseline data across each setting (as measured by the number of responses during six 5-minute observation periods), the investigators sequentially applied the intervention first at school and then at home. With each application of the intervention, there was a relatively abrupt elimination of the behavior specific to the targeted setting and, thus, experimental control was demonstrated, although a second replication of effects would have been desirable. The choice of the multiple baseline design across conditions was particularly helpful to the mother because the initial intervention at school permitted the clarification of procedures before the parent was required to assume intervention responsibilities at home.

In conclusion, when a teacher or clinician is interested in a student's generalizing a learned skill to different individuals, instructional periods, or places, the multiple baseline design across conditions is appropriate for monitoring student performance and program effectiveness. It has the practical advantage of showing the investigator under what conditions a behavior occurs and does not occur. This information can then be used by the investigator to intervene where appropriate and not to intervene where the target behavior is emitted at an acceptable frequency. However, if stimulus generalization occurs early in a program (i.e., in one of the first three conditions targeted for intervention), an empirical demonstration of program effectiveness is greatly weakened.

The Multiple Baseline Design across Subjects

In the multiple baseline design across subjects or individuals, the investigator sequentially applies an intervention across several individuals who exhibit the same target behavior under similar environmental conditions. In an initial investigation the applied researcher attempts to identify individuals with similar learning histories and who emit the same target behavior at similar frequencies under similar baseline conditions. For example, if a teacher were interested in assessing the effects of token reinforcement on reading rates across individual students, he would initially attempt to identify children of the same chronological age, with similar school backgrounds, and who are currently reading at the same level in the same or a similar classroom. In subsequent investigations, after a series of direct replications, the teacher may choose to evaluate the generality (i.e., external validity) of the intervention by identifying students who vary in one or more ways (e.g., chronological age, skill level) from the students used in the initial study. In these replication efforts, the greater the differences across subjects, the greater the generality of the findings. Initially, however, the prudent researcher evaluates the effect of an intervention on a single target behavior emitted by similar subjects.

The multiple baseline design across subjects differs from both the multiple baseline design across behaviors and across conditions described earlier. In both former paradigms the dependent measure is *intrasubject* (or *intragroup*), in which a single individual (or group) exhibits either several behaviors (multiple baseline across behaviors) or a single behavior across several stimulus conditions (multiple baseline across conditions). In the multiple baseline design across subjects, however, the dependent measure is *intersubject* (or *intergroup*), in which several different individuals (or groups) exhibit the same behavior under the same or similar stimulus conditions.

When employing the multiple baseline design across subjects, the applied researcher identifies a minimum of three subjects who exhibit the same target behavior under similar environmental conditions. Initially the investigator measures the frequency (or duration) of the target behavior emitted by each of the subjects under baseline conditions, until a stable trend and level are established for each. The investigator proceeds by introducing the intervention to the first subject, while continuously monitoring other subjects' responding under baseline conditions. When the target behavior of the first subject attains criterion level, the intervention is introduced to the second subject, while continuing to monitor the target behavior emitted by other subjects under baseline conditions. The systematic and sequential introduction of the independent variable continues until all subjects have been introduced to the same intervention. It is worth noting that typically the investigator continues to monitor each subject until all subjects have reached criterion level. Continuous measurement of postintervention responding serves as a maintenance check and helps the investigator to determine if the experimental effect is durable over time.

Internal Validity

The demonstration of experimental control in the multiple baseline design across subjects requires the investigator to first collect acceptable baseline data across each individual relative to the common target behavior and then to apply the intervention to one individual, while maintaining baseline conditions with the others. After criterion-level performance is attained with the first subject, the intervention is applied to the second. Following the replication of criterion attainment, the intervention is applied to the third, and so on. Figure 10-9 presents a graphic prototype of the multiple baseline design across subjects. Consistent with other multiple baseline designs, experimental control is demonstrated only when there is a positive change in both level and trend after the introduction of the independent variable. Any covariation in behaviors not yet directly exposed to the intervention threatens the demonstration of experimental control.

Considerations

Guidelines

The following guidelines are recommended for those investigators using the multiple baseline design across subjects:

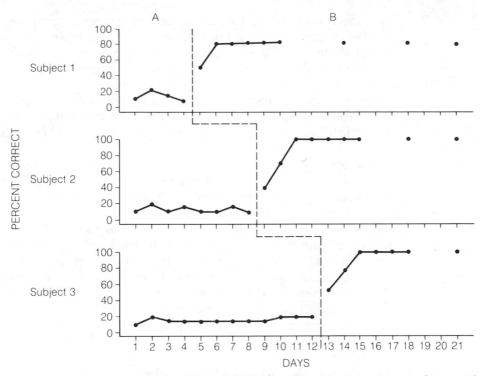

FIGURE 10-9 Hypothetical data using the multiple baseline design across subjects. The same behavior across two or more individuals is recorded simultaneously, and the intervention is introduced sequentially, one baseline at a time.

1. Pinpoint outcome objectives prior to initiating the study.

2. Introduce the intervention only when all subjects exhibit acceptable stability in level and trend under baseline conditions.

3. Apply the intervention to a new subject only when criterion-level responding is demonstrated by the preceding subject.

4. Identfy a minimum of three subjects.

5. Identify functionally independent subjects.

6. Identify similar subjects, i.e., individuals who are similar in chronological age, skill level, and learning history.

The applied researcher using a multiple baseline design across subjects faces two prediction problems: (1) that individuals are functionally independent of one another (relative to the targeted behavior), so that baseline data will remain stable until the intervention is sequentially applied to each, and (2) that subjects are sufficiently similar so that the independent variable will equally affect each person in turn. The selection of the multiple baseline design across subjects is no guarantee against unplanned covariation across baselines. Introducing a behavioral contingency for some individuals may alter the behavior of other individuals in the same situation, through collateral effects of instructions, modeling, and vicarious reinforcement (Bandura, 1969; Kazdin, 1973; Strain, Shores, & Kerr, 1976). One strategy to minimize such effects is to target individuals in similar but separate settings in order to insulate students from the intervention until the designated time (Sulzer-Azaroff & Mayer, 1977). For example, a resource teacher investigating a new instructional tactic in reading might schedule each identified child to receive instruction when the others are occupied elsewhere, or even out of the room. In order to identify an intervention that will equally affect each individual, an investigator should assess carefully the baseline levels of each subject to insure that the intervention objective is appropriate for each subject.

Advantages

The multiple baseline design across subjects is well suited for classroom use for three reasons. First, substantial portions of a school curriculum require different students to master the same skills. Second, students learn at different rates—not everyone is ready to learn the same skill at the same time! Third, teachers are interested in identifying instructional programs and intervention strategies that are effective with several learners. The multiple baseline design across subjects responds to each of these considerations: it targets a common skill across several learners; it staggers instruction to allow for rate differences; and it permits teachers to validate program effectiveness across several of their students, thereby enhancing the generality of the findings (Cuvo, 1979).

Limitations

The multiple baseline design across subjects requires the investigator to adhere to specific constraints that, under some circumstances, may prove problematic. First, a minimum of three similar individuals must be identified, each with similar learning histories and functioning levels as evidenced under similar baseline conditions. Second, the target behavior must be monitored concurrently and continuously across each subject, a task that may prove time-consuming, distracting, or otherwise impractical to the teacher (Horner & Baer, 1978; Scott & Goetz, 1980). Third, prolonged baselines for individuals not yet receiving an intervention may induce extinction effects (Cuvo, 1979; Horner & Baer, 1978; Murphey & Bryan, 1980) and raise questions about the ethics of postponing interventions for individuals ready to learn new skills or otherwise requiring immediate attention (Kratochwill, 1978; Strain & Shores, 1979; Sulzer-Azaroff & Mayer, 1977).

Applied Examples: Multiple Baseline Designs across Subjects

Study I: Moderately Handicapped

Sowers, J.A., Rusch, F.R., Connis, R.T., and Cummings, L.E. Teaching mentally retarded adults to time-manage in a vocational setting. *Journal of Applied Behavior Analysis*, 1980, *13* (1), 119–128.

Purpose, subject, and setting. Sowers et al. (1980) employed a multiple baseline design across individuals to assess the efficacy of an instructional package to teach job-related time management skills to non-time-telling retarded adults. The trainees were three moderately retarded men (IQ range = 43–54) who were being trained in a public cafeteria on a university campus for eventual competitive employment. The study was conducted at each of three work stations in the cafeteria: dishwashing, utility-maintenance, and busing. Each station had its own supervisor and three student trainees. One subject was assigned to each work station for the duration of the study and, thus, the three subjects were unable to observe or communicate with one another during their 6-hour workdays. The investigators' intent was to teach the trainees to use a time card and a standard "sweep-hand" wall clock as prompts for independent activity changes during the work day. Prior to initiating the study none of the trainees could tell time. Each depended, instead, upon the signal of their supervisors.

Dependent variables. Each trainee was assigned four specific daily times for leaving and returning to his work station, including times to (1) go to lunch, (2) return from lunch, (3) go to break, (4) return from break. These time assignments remained constant throughout the study. Four dependent measures were collected daily and computed as the difference between the assigned time and the actual time that the trainee first "attempted" to perform the behavior (i.e., "minutes early and late" to or from lunch and break). "Attempts" were defined either as physical indications of location change, such as leaving the work station in the direction of the break or lunch area, or verbal statements of readiness, e.g., "May I go to lunch now?" For each dependent measure the trainer-observer recorded the exact time that the student first exhibited a behavioral "attempt." From this information he computed the number of minutes early or late (up to a ceiling of 10 minutes) for each time assignment. At least once across all experimental conditions, a second observer independently recorded the time of each behavioral "attempt" (N = 53 reliability checks). Agreements were defined as those occasions when both observers recorded the same time within 60 seconds. The average point-by-point interobserver agreement was 92%; furthermore, they never disagreed by more than 2 minutes.

Independent variables. Students were exposed to four experimental conditions: (1) baseline; (2) pre-instruction, instructional feedback, and time card; (3) instructional feedback and time card; and (4) time card. During the *baseline condition*, at the beginning of each workday the student was verbally informed of his four assigned activity-change times. No other instruction or feedback was provided unless the student was more than 10 minutes discrepant from an assigned time—in which case the trainer delivered neutrally stated feedback, e.g., "It's not lunch (or break) time, go back to work," or "Lunch isn't over yet, take it easy." Beginning with the *second condition*, the student received direct daily instruction in time management. Each morning before going to his work station, he received "pre-instruction" in the use of a time card consisting of pictorial representations of four clock faces, each depicting one of the assigned activity-change times. Each daily session lasted until the student met criterion on two instructional objectives: (1) to correctly identify the time card pictures when randomly named by the trainer (e.g., "Point to the clock face that you use to go to lunch") and (2) to correctly match the time card pictures to a "real" clock hanging on the wall, one with movable hands that were adjusted by the trainer (e.g., "Point to the clock on your card that looks like the 'real' clock"). Following each correct response the student received verbal praise; after each incorrect response the trainer said, "No," and then pointed to the correct choice item. When the daily criterion was reached (eight out of eight consecutive corrects for both objectives), the student was excused to go to his work station. He took his time card with him. Throughout the remainder of the workday, the student

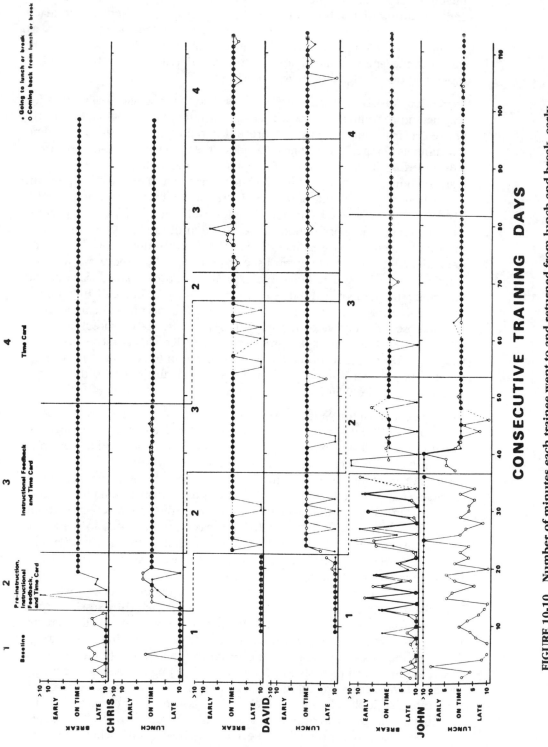

CONSECUTIVE TRAINING DAYS

MINUTES EARLY AND LATE

FIGURE 10-10 Number of minutes each trainee went to and returned from lunch and break, early and late. (Figure 2, p. 125, from: Sowers, J.A., Rusch, F.R., Connis, R.T., & Cummings, L.E. Teaching mentally retarded adults to time-manage in a vocational setting. *Journal of Applied Behavior Analysis*, 1980, *13* (1), 119–128. Copyright by Society for the Experimental Analysis of Behavior, Inc. Reproduced by permission.)

received "instructional feedback," delivered in two forms: praise for correct responding and repeated practice for errors. At each activity location "real" time clocks were visible, and whenever the student attempted an activity change at the exact assigned time, he was praised verbally for his judgment; however, when he responded as little as 1 minute before or more than 10 minutes after the assigned time, he was required to return immediately to his morning "pre-instructional classroom" where he practiced the same pointing and matching tasks until a criterion of four consecutive correct responses for each was attained. Because four activity changes were required each day, a student could and did receive several or more repeated practice sessions per day, especially during the initial days of the condition. The condition was continued until the student responded "on time" to all activities for 3 consecutive work days. The *third condition* was identical to the second, except that the daily "pre-instructional" classes in the morning were deleted. The student went directly to his work station and received performance feedback as required throughout the day. Finally, in the *fourth condition* the feedback procedures were also deleted, so that procedures were identical with the baseline condition, except that the student had continued access to his time card.

Design and condition sequence. The investigators employed a multiple baseline design across individuals. Each individual was exposed to four conditions: baseline condition (A_1); pre-instruction, instructional feedback, and time card (B_1) instructional feedback and time card (B_2); and time card (B_3). The condition sequences for each individual were as follows: *Chris*—A_1 (11 days), B_1 (10 days), B_2 (26 days), B_3 (50 days); *David*—A_1 (14 days), B_1 (14 days), B_2 (28 days), B_1 (5 days), B_2 (21 days), B_3 (17 days); *John*—A_1 (35 days), B_1 (17 days), B_2 (28 days), B_3 (31 days).

Results as reported by authors. During the baseline conditions, Chris and David were consistently late for all activity changes; whereas John exhibited extremely variable behavior, sometimes late and sometimes early, except for consistent attempts to leave early for lunch (averaging 31 minutes before his assigned time). During the first intervention condition (B_1), Chris, and David, and John attained criterion (i.e., 3 consecutive days on time to all activities) after 10, 14, and 17 days, respectively. When pre-instruction was discontinued (B_2), Chris and John continued to be punctual with few exceptions. David, however, began deviating from his assigned break time on the 19th day of the condition. After five violations, pre-instruction (B_1) was reinstated for David. After 5 consecutive days of punctual responding, David was once again exposed to the B_2 condition and henceforth the on-time behavior maintained. Finally, when the trainees were exposed to the time card only condition (B_3); each continued to independently change activities at the assigned times.

Summary and conclusions. Sowers et al. (1980) provide convincing evidence that the independent variable was responsible for each trainee's punctual responding. Behavioral covariation across unexposed baselines was not evident perhaps because modeling opportunities were minimized by (1) assigning different lunch and break times to each trainee and (2) assigning the trainees to different work stations. Strategies such as these are well-advised for users of this design.

This study also illustrates the fact that multiple baseline designs can respond to individual performance variations without necessarily sacrificing experimental control. In this case David began to exhibit a loss of appropriate responding on the 19th day of the B_2 condition, requiring a brief reinstatement of the daily pre-instruction (B_1) condition. This extended intervention sequence apparently met David's needs. It did not threaten the study since experimental control already had been demonstrated by the consistent replication of effects across each A_1-B_1 series.

Study II: Mental Retardation Counselors

Gladstone, B.W. and Spencer, C.J. The effects of modeling on the contingent praise of mental retardation counselors. *Journal of Applied Behavior Analysis*, 1977, *10* (1), 75–84.

Purpose, subject, and setting. Gladstone and Spencer (1977) employed a multiple baseline design across individuals to evaluate the effectiveness of a very simple in-service modeling procedure to increase the delivery rate of response-contingent praise by mental retardation counselors when conducting hygiene training (i.e., toothbrushing and hand-and-face washing) with their severely mentally retarded clients. The counselors, four women and a man, were employees of a large institution for the mentally retarded. They averaged 34 years of age and 10 years on the job. None had received prior formal instruction in behavior modification techniques. Their clients were three boys and one girl, ranging in age from 8 to 15 years, with an average IQ of 37. The children were nonverbal and lacked independent self-help skills. They resided as a family group in an "apartment" that, although located within the institution, was separated physically from the other residences, with the intention of preparing the children for eventual placement in a private, community-based home. Each day, after breakfast and supper, a counselor escorted each child individually into the apartment bathroom for a 5-minute toothbrushing session and a 5-minute hand-and-face washing session. The present study was conducted twice daily during these hygiene sessions.

Dependent variable. For each training program (toothbrushing and hand-and-face washing) two dependent measures were collected: (1) the total number of contingent praise statements delivered by the counselor during the 5-minute sessions and (2) the total number of component responses, as defined by the task analysis, receiving at least one praising statement. Praise statements were defined as verbal responses that included "positive" adverbs or adjectives, e.g., "good," "nice," or "great." Verbal feedback such as "that's it" or "OK" did not satisfy this definition and was not scored as praise. Furthermore, although several praise statements could be scored during any one response component of the task analysis, to be separately tallied a minimum of 2 second's pause between statements was required. Thus, the statement "Good, good, that's great," if delivered without pause, was tallied as a single praise statement. Observer(s) used a recording sheet listing the response components. Each time a praising statement was delivered, its occurrence was tallied next to the appropriate component on the list. Thus data were collected simultaneously for both dependent variables. Interobserver reliability on the "total frequency of praise statements during a session" was computed using the gross method, resulting in percentage agreements of over 90%. Reliability on the "number of components praised during a session" was computed with the point-by-point method, yielding percentage agreements of 89% or greater. Reliability checks were conducted during each condition of the study.

Independent variable. Before the study, the investigators required each counselor to memorize the component sequences of two task analyses, including 10 steps for toothbrushing and 14 steps for hand-and-face washing. Subsequently, during baseline conditions counselors were asked to teach the children the component steps. At this time, no instructions or feedback was provided in regard to training methods; instead, counselors were free to teach as they saw fit. Immediately following each baseline condition, the targeted counselor was exposed to one 5-minute modeling session in toothbrush instruction with one of the children. An investigator, acting as a model, instructed the counselor as follows: "I am going to conduct this toothbrushing session with Robert (for example). Watch me carefully" (p. 78). He then paced the child through the entire response chain, physically or verbally prompting as necessary. During the modeling session no fewer than 14 nor more than 20 response contingent praise statements were delivered, with a minimum of one praise statement modeled for each step of the task analysis. Statements such as "good boy" or "that's right" were spoken with enthusiasm and paired with both a smile and physical contact (such as a pat on the back). Immediately following the single toothbrush-modeling session, the counselor resumed his or her role as trainer by instructing the remaining children in both hygiene tasks—during which, as during the baseline condition, the counselor received no feedback on his or her use of contingent praise or reinforcement. The same modeling procedure was interspersed on three other occasions during each intervention condition—once with each of the remaining children. Thus, each counselor was exposed at some point during intervention to one 5-minute modeling session with each child. All modeling sessions, however, were for the toothbrushing sequence. Hand-and-face washing procedures were never directly modeled by the investigators.

Design and condition sequence. The investigators utilized a multiple baseline design across individual counselors as illustrated in Figure 10-11. The condition sequence was as follows: (1) Counselor 1—baseline (A_1), 4 sessions; modeling (B_1), 11 sessions; follow-up (B_1'), 4 sessions; (2) Counselor 2—baseline (A_2) 8 sessions; modeling (B_2), 6 sessions; (3) Counselor 3—baseline (A_3) 8 sessions; modeling (B_3), 12 sessions; follow-up (B_3') 4 sessions; (4) Counselor 4—baseline (A_4) 16 sessions; modeling (B_4), 10 sessions; follow-up (B_4'), 4 sessions; (5) Counselor 5—baseline (A_5), 36 sessions; modeling (B_5), 12 sessions; follow-up (B_5'), 4 sessions.

Results as reported by authors. Across the five targeted counselors, the investigators reported substantial behavioral changes when the modeling condition was introduced. During baseline conditions the rates of contingent praise during toothbrushing sessions ranged from 1.0 to 3.7 per session, and the number of component reponses praised ranged from 1.0 to 2.5 per session. During the modeling condition, however, the number of praising statements increased to an average of 11.8 per session, and the number of steps praised averaged 5.0 per session. Furthermore, except for Counselor 5,

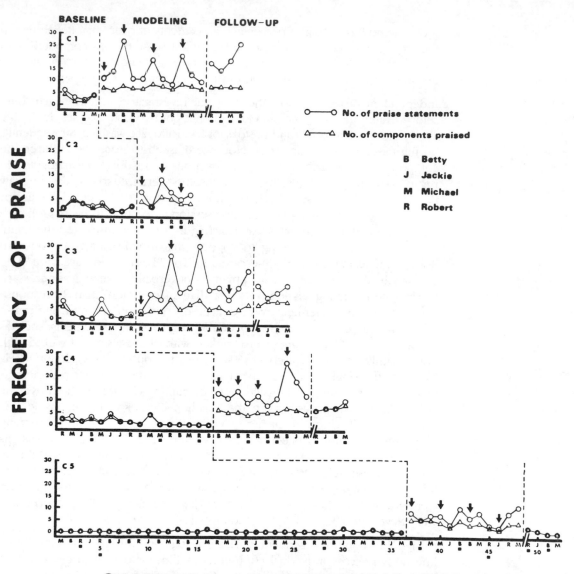

SUCCESSIVE TOOTHBRUSHING SESSIONS

FIGURE 10-11   The number of contingent praise statements and the number of component toothbrushing responses praised by each counselor during baseline, modeling, and follow-up conditions. The letters *B, J, M,* and *R.* located along each abscissa, indicate which child the counselor was training in that session. Squares below the abscissa indicate when reliability checks were made. Arrows identify sessions immediately following modeling sessions. (Figure 1, p. 80, from: Gladstone, B.W. and Spencer, C.J. The effects of modeling on the contingent praise of mental retardation counselors. *Journal of Applied Behavior Analysis,* 1977, *10* (1), 75–84. Copyright by Society for the Experimental Analysis of Behavior, Inc. Reprinted by permission.)

these rate changes were maintained during the follow-up sessions conducted two weeks subsequent to each intervention condition. The data also documented generalized rate gains to the hand-and-face washing sessions (for which no models were provided): the average number of contingent praise statements increased from a baseline rate of 2.0 per session to an intervention rate of 9.0 per session, and the average number of components praised increased from 2.0 to 6.0 per session.

Summary and conclusions. In discussing the external validity of the data, the authors noted several factors that may have influenced the results: first, the model was familiar to and well liked by the counseling staff; second, the targeted responses were simple and conspicuous; third, the counselors had immediate opportunities to practice; and fourth, the continued presence of the observers and the model throughout the study may have functioned to prompt and/or reinforce the targeted behaviors. The authors suggested that "observations of counselor praise when the model was not present would have provided a clearer evaluation of the effects of modeling" (p. 82). Furthermore, although the study attempted to isolate modeling effects from verbal instructions, feedback, and reinforcement, the authors observed that in combination all these components may have resulted in a stronger intervention package. Nonetheless, the study provides a convincing demonstration that professionals can improve their in-servicing credibility by modeling their skills directly with clients.

Concluding Comments

The multiple baseline design across subjects can be used to validate interventions across many types of learners (spanning the broad range of handicapping conditions), exhibiting a multiplicity of behaviors, in a variety of educational and clinical settings. Table 10-5 summarizes several studies from the applied research literature that have used the multiple baseline design across subjects. Schumaker, Hovell, and Sherman (1977) employed a multiple baseline design across three "problem" seventh-grade boys (each exhibiting disruptive in-class behavior, tardiness, occasional truancy, and little or no task completion), in order to assess the effectiveness of contingent home-based praise and privileges for improved school performance (as communicated to the parents by a daily report card from the teacher). Upon application of the school-home program, both the percentage of rules followed and the percentage of class work points earned increased substantially for each child. Additionally, two school guidance counselors systematically replicated the effects across two other students, adding further credibility to the intervention's effectiveness. Horner and Keilitz (1975) designed a program to teach toothbrushing to four mildly and moderately retarded male residents of a state training school, ranging in age from 9–17 years. Using a multiple baseline across subjects, the researchers measured the number of toothbrushing steps completed correctly to demonstrate that a comprehensive task analysis coupled with systematic acquisition-level training (including the presentation and subsequent fading of instructions, models, and physical guidance) could effectively produce criterion-level responding with each individual. Subsequently, the investigators replicated their results with four other similar student-residents. Tucker and Berry (1980) utilized a multiple baseline design across three multihandicapped youth who were severely retarded and sufficiently hearing impaired to require the use of hearing aids (two males and one female, ranging in age from 19–22 years). The purpose of the study was to assess the combined effectiveness of a task analysis and a graduated hierarchy of response prompts to teach students to independently

TABLE 10-5 Examples of multiple baseline designs across subjects.

Reference	Subject(s)	Setting(s)	Dependent Variable(s)	Independent Variable(s)
Schumaker, Hovell, & Sherman (1977)	3 7th-grade males considered to be troublemakers	a public junior high school classroom	"percentage of classroom rules followed" and "percentage of class work points earned"	contingent home-based praise and privileges for improved in-school performance, as communicated by a daily report card
Horner & Keilitz (1975)	4 "mildly" and "moderately" retarded male residents of a state training school (CA range: 9–17 years)	a training room containing 1 sink and a mirror—located within the institution	"the number of toothbrushing steps performed correctly"	a comprehensive task analysis coupled with systematic training, including the presentation and subsequent fading of physical guidance, models, and verbal instructions
Tucker & Berry (1980)	2 males and 1 female, "severely retarded" and hearing impaired (CA range: 19–22 years)	a training room, a classroom, and a residential living unit within a residential institution	"the percent of hearing aid steps performed independently and correctly"	a comprehensive task analysis and a graduated hierarchy of response prompts designed to teach students to independently put on their own hearing aids
Wells, Forehand, Hickey, & Green (1977)	2 fraternal twins variously labelled "severely emotionally disturbed—brain damaged" and "severely mentally retarded—autistic" (CA = 10)	a playroom, located in a segregated school for the "developmentally handicapped"	"percent occurrence of inappropriate direct manipulation, mouthing, hand movements, and other behaviors" (p. 684)	contingent positive-practice overcorrection (a procedure involving manual guidance in appropriate toy use) applied upon the occurrence of any of four inappropriate behaviors

put on their own hearing aids. What is perhaps most noteworthy about the study is that after demonstrating reliable and durable intervention effects within the training setting, the investigators exposed each individual to a generalization probe condition to assess the degree of stimulus generalization to different settings and with new trainers. Two of the three students did not exhibit generalized responding and, therefore, required additional instruction. Wells, Forehand, Hickey, and Green (1977) showed the flexibility of multiple baseline designs by combining the across behaviors design with the across subjects design. In this case, the applied researchers investigated the effects of contingent positive-practice overcorrection (a procedure involving manual guidance in appropriate toy use) on the occurrence of any of four inappropriate behaviors exhibited by two 10-year-old fraternal twins, who were variously labelled "severely emotionally disturbed-brain damaged" and "severely mentally retarded-autistic." Experimental control was demonstrated by the sequential replication of effects across the two children, relative to a reduction in the percent of inappropriate object manipulation (Behavior 1), percent of mouthing (Behavior 2), percent of inappropriate hand movements (Behavior 3), and the percent of "other inappropriate behavior" (Behavior 4). Additionally, the investigators concurrently monitored changes in appropriate toy play throughout the study and demonstrated that for one child a "collateral" generalized effect of the overcorrection was an increase in appropriate play behavior.

In conclusion, when a teacher is interested in modifying the same or similar target behavior emitted by three or more similar students (or groups of students), the multiple baseline design across subjects would be appropriate. It is a design that is well suited for classroom research. In contrast to other multiple baseline designs, the multiple baseline design across subjects addresses the generality of findings by staggering the introduction of an intervention across individuals (i.e., intersubject direct replication) or groups of individuals (i.e., intergroup direct replication). It is a design that can be superimposed over other multiple baseline designs to enhance both the internal and external validity of an intervention, thereby providing a powerful demonstration of experimental control. This pairing of the multiple baseline design across subjects with other multiple baseline designs is particularly advisable when the independence of the behaviors or conditions is in doubt.

SUMMARY

This chapter has overviewed the three types of multiple baseline designs: across behaviors, across conditions, and across subjects. Each multiple baseline design has the distinct advantage of not having to return to baseline conditions to demonstrate experimental control, a characteristic and requirement of the A-B-A-B (reversal and withdrawal) design. To demonstrate experimental control with a multiple baseline design, an investigator systematically introduces the independent variable into each baseline data series (behaviors, conditions, or subjects) in a staggered or time-lagged manner. If, where intervention is introduced, change in the dependent measure occurs and, where it is not, change does not occur, experimental control has been demonstrated.

Multiple baseline designs are well suited to educational and clinical research, particularly when it is not possible or desirable to reverse the effects of an intervention, as with academic and self-injurious behaviors. Though these designs provide an eloquent experimental demonstration of intervention effectiveness, they do not replicate the cause-effect relationship with the same behavior, condition, or subject. Several variations and expansions of the multiple baseline design are discussed in Chapter 11.

11

VARIATIONS OF THE MULTIPLE BASELINE DESIGN: MULTIPLE PROBE AND CHANGING CRITERION DESIGNS

In Chapter 10 we described the multiple baseline design and its three principle variations: multiple baseline designs across behaviors, conditions, and subjects. In this chapter we elaborate on two additional variations of the multiple baseline design: the multiple probe design (Horner & Baer, 1978; Murphey & Bryan, 1980) and the changing criterion design (Hartmann & Hall, 1976). Like the multiple baseline design, multiple probe and changing criterion designs are based on the principle of "time-lagged" control and are particularly appropriate to evaluate the effectiveness of instructional and behavior management programs used in educational settings. In addition, we discuss procedures for resolving some of the more common ambiguities associated with multiple baseline and multiple probe designs.

Multiple Probe Designs

A variation of, and alternative to, the multiple baseline design is the multiple probe design (Cuvo, 1979; Horner & Baer, 1978; Murphey & Bryan, 1980). The multiple probe design is similar to the multiple baseline design in that the independent variable is systematically and sequentially introduced to one behavior (or in one setting or with one subject) at a time. Unlike the multiple baseline design, baseline data are *not* collected on a continuous basis on behaviors that have not yet been introduced to the intervention. Rather, probe trials (i.e., trials that are operationally identical to preintervention baseline trials) are conducted intermittently on behaviors "to be trained." These probe trials, which may be interspersed within instructional sessions

---

This chapter was written by **David L. Gast**, **James R. Skouge**, and **James W. Tawney**.

or across observational periods, provide the applied researcher with data that can be used to evaluate whether a student is improving prior to the introduction of the independent variable. An alternative multiple probe design uses probe sessions rather than single probe trials. With this variation of the multiple probe design baseline, or probe, measures are taken on several behaviors (or in several settings or across several subjects) over the same time period. The intervention is then introduced to the first behavior, provided a stable preintervention level and trend are established. After the first behavior reaches criterion-performance level, one or more probe sessions are again conducted in which all target behaviors are measured. Following this probe condition the independent variable is then introduced to the second behavior. When the second behavior reaches the outcome objective criterion, another probe condition is conducted. This sequence of instructing and probing continues until all behaviors have been introduced to the independent variable. It is important to note that both multiple probe design variations are particularly well suited for a teacher interested in evaluating academic programs, but who is unable to monitor *all* targeted behaviors (or settings or students) on a continuous or daily basis.

Internal Validity   The requirements of demonstrating experimental control with both variations of the multiple probe design are identical to those required with multiple

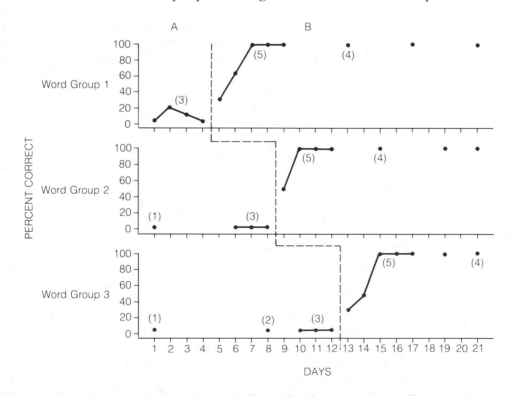

FIGURE 11-1 Hypothetical data using a multiple probe design across spelling word groups: (1) initial probe, (2) probe after criterion, (3) true baseline, (4) review trials, (5) continuous training data. (Figure 4-21, pp. 144–145, from: Cooper, J. O. *Measuring behavior* (2nd ed.). Columbus, Ohio: Charles E. Merrill, 1981.)

baseline designs. That is, if subject responding remains at or near preintervention (baseline) levels across intermittently conducted probe trials and/or probe sessions, and a targeted behavior improves only after the independent variable has been applied, a functional relationship between the independent variable and behavior change has been demonstrated. A note of caution is in order regarding the use of a multiple probe design in which intermittent and interspersed probe trials are conducted. When using intermittent probe trials, rather than a series of consecutive probe sessions, it is important for an investigator to conduct a minimum of three probe trials on each behavior (or with each subject or in each setting) prior to applying the intervention. This represents the absolute minimum number of trials necessary for estimating a data trend, and thus is required for a believable demonstration of experimental control. We recommend going beyond the minimum and suggest that the investigator conduct five or more probes, over a time period. Figure 11-1 provides a graphic illustration of multiple probe design, using intermittent probe sessions, which is in keeping with the recommendations made by Horner and Baer (1978) and Cooper (1981). An alternative multiple probe design, in which a series of consecutive probe sessions is employed rather than intermittent probe trials, is presented in Figure 11-2.

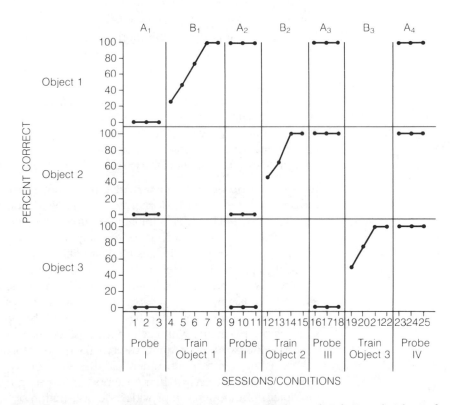

FIGURE 11-2 Hypothetical data using a multiple probe design (with probe conditions) across objects to be signed manually. "A" or probe conditions precede "B" conditions that represent manual sign instruction on each object-sign one at a time in a time-lagged fashion.

Considerations

Guidelines

The guidelines for multiple probe designs are identical to those for multiple baseline designs except for the frequency with which baseline or probe data are collected. That is, the investigator employing a multiple probe design should:

1. Pinpoint outcome objectives prior to initiating the study.

2. Collect probe data across each tier (i.e., behavior, condition, or subject) of the design prior to introduction of the independent variable.

3. Schedule a minimum of three consecutive probe trials and/or probe sessions across 3 consecutive days before introducing the intervention. If interspersed probe trials are used, they should be spaced equally across the time period immediately preceding the introduction of the independent variable.

4. Apply the intervention to a new data series only when all data series show acceptable stability in level and trend.

5. Apply the intervention to a new data series only when criterion-level responding is demonstrated with the preceding data series.

6. Identify a minimum of three behaviors (or conditions or subjects).

7. Identify behaviors (or conditions or subjects) that are similar, yet functionally independent from one another.

8. Collect continuous data on the behavior that is receiving the intervention (i.e., B condition).

Advantages

The multiple probe design offers several practical advantages over the multiple baseline design, while continuing to permit a valid demonstration of experimental control. More specifically, the multiple probe design may prove more appropriate than the multiple baseline design when prolonged baseline measures are either unnecessary, reactive, or impractical.

Intermittent probes are an alternative to "unnecessary" continuous baseline measures (Cooper, 1981; Horner & Baer, 1978; Murphey & Bryan, 1980). To acquire most skills, students initially require systematic direct instruction and reinforcement. Seldom will a student acquire a new skill through repeated practice alone. For example, it is highly unlikely that a student being taught to manually sign the labels for a set of functional, though novel, objects would acquire the targeted manual signs without some level of direct instruction. Similarly, it is improbable that a student who cannot add will be able to multiply or that a student who has not mastered the operation of subtraction will be able to divide. With each of these students a prolonged and continuous baseline would be unnecessary. To quote Horner and Baer (1978), "There is no need to document at the level of well-measured data that behavior does not occur when it cannot" (p. 180). In each of these cases the multiple probe design can provide a demonstration of "baseline stability" and experimental control and thus serve as a practical alternative to the multiple baseline design.

Intermittent probes can avoid inappropriate student behaviors frequently associated with extended baselines. During an extended baseline it is reasonable to expect that students' attention will wander or that students will exhibit inappropriate behaviors when they are repeatedly presented with a task that they cannot solve. Cuvo (1979), in his discussion of the multiple probe technique, states, "Minimal testing is especially reasonable when the baseline level is low or when there is no opportunity for subjects to acquire the target response(s) without direct training" (p. 222), and, "... there is a trade-off between repeatedly administering the dependent measure to establish a stable baseline on one hand and risking impaired performance by subjecting participants to a potentially punishing experience on the other hand" (pp. 222–223). Cuvo suggests that these negative effects can be minimized by administering two probes before introducing the intervention, one preliminary "test" across all behaviors, subjects, or conditions and then one probe test for each subject just before the intervention begins.

Intermittent probes are a practical alternative to continuous baseline measures (Cuvo, 1979; Horner & Baer, 1978; Murphey & Bryan, 1980). Continuous data collection can be a time-consuming endeavor, particularly for a teacher who employs a data-based classroom instructional model and who attempts to collect data on most students and instructional programs. Consequently, any time-efficient evaluation strategy that provides a valid demonstration of instructional effectiveness is valued. The time saved by using intermittent probes rather than continuous baseline measures can be better spent, in most cases, to increase the amount of time a teacher devotes to direct instruction.

Limitations

Just as intermittent and fewer baseline measures can be advantageous, so too can they be disadvantageous. If, for example, there is variability in either level or trend across the probe data series, the prudent researcher must extend her measurement of the dependent variable under baseline conditions. If a researcher does not extend baseline measurement procedures until a stable level and/or trend are established, she risks confounding her results, due to potentially uncontrolled history, maturation, practice, and/or adaptation variables. Second, suppose that after a student has received direct instruction on the first behavior in the multiple probe design tier, practice alone improves her correct responding on other behaviors targeted for training. In such cases intermittent probes may delay, or altogether prohibit, the discovery of response generalization, whereas continuous baseline measures would have alerted the researcher to response covariation from the outset. Thus, the researcher must insure that targeted behaviors, conditions, or subjects are functionally independent and schedule the optimum number of probe trials or sessions before introducing the independent variable.

Applied Examples: Multiple Probe Design

Study I: Multiply Handicapped

Isaac, G.E., and Gast, D.L. *Teaching object naming using a time delay procedure with multiply handicapped students in small group instruction.* Paper presented at the Fifth Annual Conference of the American Association for the Education of the Severely/ Profoundly Handicapped, Baltimore, October, 1978.

Purpose, subject, and setting. Isaac and Gast (1978) employed a multiple probe design across object pairs to assess the efficacy of a *progressive* time delay procedure (Snell & Gast, 1981) for teaching multiply handicapped students to name functional objects. Three students attending a classroom for children labelled "multiply handicapped" received the intervention program. Lisa, a 12-year-old girl, was functionally blind, echolalic, and exhibited stereotypic behaviors, including body rocking, head rolling, and object mouthing. She was functioning at approximately the 30-month level on the LAP-D. Chris, a 14-year-old girl, could verbally imitate but had poor articulation. She too was functioning at about the 30-month level in language on the LAP-D at the onset of the program. She performed numerous self-help skills independently (e.g., toileting, dressing, feeding, washing hands). Dan, a 16-year-old male, had some spontaneous verbalizations ("good boy," "yeah, Dan," "good hands") and could verbally label some objects correctly. He performed at approximately the 24-month level in language on the LAP-D.

Instruction was provided by the classroom teacher in a small group arrangement (i.e., the three students' chairs were arranged in a circle in the corner of the room). Instructional sessions were conducted daily and held to approximately 10 minutes.

Dependent variable. The dependent measure (percent correct) was collected across a series of four measurement conditions: a pretest and three probe conditions. Data were collected separately for each student, and the measure consisted of the percentage of trials on which the student correctly labelled the target object.

The purpose of the program was to teach each student to name six different functional objects. The *pretest* was designed to select six objects for each student that he/she could not verbally label. Before beginning the pretest, each student was first tested on his/her ability to verbally imitate all the object names that would be used in that individual's pretest.

During pretesting, each student was presented with a variety of objects and asked, "What is this?" (Note that in the case of Jean, who was visually impaired, the teacher placed Jean's hand on the object prior to asking "What is this?") Students were allowed 10 seconds to respond on each trial during this condition. The objects were presented one at a time in an intermixed sequence over two sessions on consecutive days. There was a total of 10 trials presented on each object for each student. Only objects that the student could not name (i.e., named at 0 percent correct) were selected as training items (each of the three students had his/her own list of training items).

Probe conditions entailed intermixing all six objects that were targeted for training in the pretest. Each object was presented 10 times during 4 sessions over 2 days, using the same presentation format described for the pretest. To maintain attending during the pretest and probe conditions students were reinforced for "good sitting" or "good looking" with descriptive verbal praise and an edible on the average of every third trial. Reliability checks on student performance were taken at least once during each measurement condition using the point-by-point method, yielding agreement measures ranging from 92% to 100%.

Independent variable. A progressive time delay procedure was used to teach object naming. The teacher presented the object, asked "What is this?", waited the specified delay time, and modeled the correct object name. The delay intervals used were 0", 2", 3", etc. After 10 trials at each delay, the delay time (the time between the teacher asking "What is this?" and her saying the object

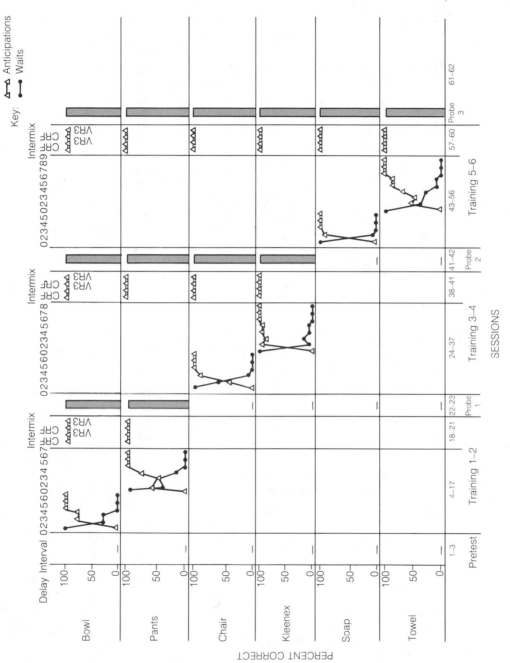

FIGURE 11-3 Percent correct responding on object-naming tasks during probe and progressive time-delay instructional conditions with a visually impaired, severely handicapped student. (From: Isaac, G.E., and Gast, D.L. Teaching object naming using a time delay procedure with multiply handicapped students in small group instruction. Paper presented at the Fifth Annual Conference of the American Association for the Education of the Severely/Profoundly Handicapped, Baltimore, October 1978.)

name) was increased by 1 second for the next block of 10 trials. Training continued until the student could name the object before the teacher's verbal model (a correct anticipation). Both anticipations (correct naming *before* the teacher's model) and waits (correct naming *after* the teacher's model) were immediately followed by teacher praise and an edible reinforcer. However, only correct anticipations were counted toward criterion. Criterion was defined as the student correctly naming an object before the teacher model on 10 of 10 trials over 3 consecutive days. On those occasions when a student responded incorrectly, the teacher simply removed the object, waited 10 seconds, and presented the next trial. For each student, the training objects were paired randomly. After the student was taught to name the first object of his/her pair to criterion, training began on the second object of the pair. After both objects were named at criterion in isolation, they were then intermixed with all previously learned objects (e.g., after training objects 3 and 4 in isolation, they were then intermixed with objects 1 and 2). Students were required to reach criterion (10 consecutive correct anticipations over 2 consecutive days) when reinforced on a CRF schedule and then on a VR-3 schedule before moving to a probe condition. Training sessions were conducted once per day, 5 days per week, and held to approximately 10 minutes. All instruction took place in a small group that included all three students.

Design and condition sequence. The investigators used a multiple probe design across object pairs, as illustrated in Figure 11-3, which presents the session-by session data for Lisa. (The data for the other two students are not presented, though they replicate Lisa's data.) The training sequence for each student was as follows: Pretest–Train Pair 1–Probe 1–Train Pair 2–Probe 2–Train Pair 3–Probe 3.

Results as reported by the authors. All three students learned the name their respective targeted objects only after the instructional procedure was introduced. Only Chris failed to learn one of her initially targeted objects, the "record," due to her inability to verbally imitate the object name. Over a total of 520 training trials, Lisa reached criterion on all six objects trained without an error; over a total of 540 training trials, Chris reached criterion on six of seven targeted objects with only four errors (an accuracy rate of 99.3%); over 390 training trials, Dan reached criterion on all five objects with three errors (an accuracy rate of 99.2%). (Dan was unable to complete training on the final object because he left the school program.)

Summary and conclusions. This study provides a convincing demonstration of experimental effects in that (1) criterion-level responding was attained consistently and promptly after the introduction of the time delay procedure; and (2) prior to the introduction of the time delay procedure, zero percent correct responding was maintained. The choice of a multiple probe design over a multiple baseline design was appropriate for three reasons: first, the six tasks were unlikely to be acquired without direct instruction, thus making unnecessary the daily measurement of unexposed baselines; second, the four interspersed probe conditions required substantially fewer baseline measures, thereby avoiding the potential "reactive" effects of prolonged measures; and third, the design was time efficient because training sessions were not interrupted to measure targets for the unexposed baselines.

Study II: Severely Handicapped

Van Biervliet, A., Spangler, P.F., and Marshall, A.M. An ecobehavioral examination of a simple strategy for increasing mealtime language in residential facilities. *Journal of Applied Behavior Analysis*, 1981, *14* (3), 295–305.

Purpose, subject, and setting. Van Biervliet et al. (1981) employed a multiple probe design across conditions (breakfast, lunch, and dinner mealtimes) to compare the effects of "family style" vs. "institutional style" dining procedures on the rate and quality of mealtime conversation of five mentally retarded residents of a large institution. The residents were moderately and severely retarded men, ranging in age from 16 to 23 years. Each exhibited at least minimal conversational skills, including speech which was clearly understandable to independent listeners. In addition, each displayed appropriate mealtime behaviors relative to utensil use, and neatness. The study was conducted in the institutional dining room during the three standard half-hour mealtimes.

Dependent variable. The principal dependent measure was "average number of verbalizations per minute." To collect these data, two observers sat 5–6 feet behind the dining table and observed each resident, one at a time, for 3-minute intervals—a procedure that was repeated in round-robin fashion throughout the duration of the meal. Each time the observed resident uttered a "comprehensible" verbalization, it was coded within the interval in which it was initiated; thus, each verbalization was recorded only once. Verbalizations were coded as to "type" (i.e., an initiation of conversation or a response to conversation), "content" (i.e., a request for food, a comment about the meal, or miscellaneous conversation), and "direction" (i.e., directed toward staff, observer, or peer). This data collection system permitted the investigators to compute not only the rate of overall verbalizations per minute, but also the specific rates for the three "quality" measures of type, content, and direction. Also, because each resident was observed during separate intervals, the dependent measures could be computed both for the group and for each individual participant. Three reliability checks were conducted within each condition resulting in (1) an average gross interobserver reliability of $\geq$ 90% for the average number of overall verbalizations per minute and (2) an average point-by-point reliability of $\geq$ 85% for the average number of type, content, and direction of verbalizations per minute.

Independent variable. The intervention strategy consisted of a simple manipulation of food serving procedures, i.e., a change from "institutional style" service during baseline to "family style" dining during intervention. During baseline, the institutional style procedures included the following: first, selected residents set the table with silverware, napkins, and glasses; then, the five residents were seated and one at a time (upon hearing his name called) got up to retrieve his preapportioned, food-filled tray; finally, when all had their trays, a prayer was said and eating began. During intervention, the family style procedures presented the following changes: first, in addition to silverware, napkins, and glasses, the tables were set with plates, bowls, cartons of milk and/or juice and food-filled serving platters; after which, the residents were seated, the prayer said, and the food passed around the table, with each resident helping himself to his own chosen portions; finally, when all were served, eating began. Before the family style intervention was initiated the participants were exposed to three 10-minute training sessions during which they practiced requesting food, passing food platters, and thanking the person doing the passing. During the intervention, the investigators provided the participants with feedback on their "food passing" skills; however, no feedback was ever provided on the amount or quality of mealtime conversations. During the baseline and intervention conditions, the residents dined at the same table, consistently ate the same foods, and had available the same half-hour mealtime intervals. Thus, except for the "food

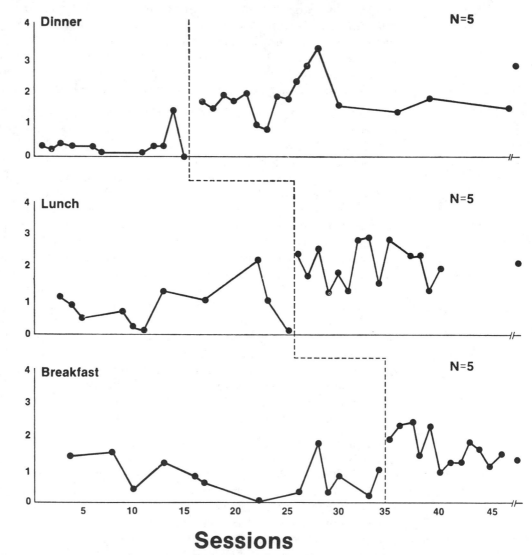

FIGURE 11-4 Average number of verbalizations per minute for all five participants. Frequent gaps between adjacent data points are typical of multiple-probe designs. (Figure 1, p. 300, from: Van Biervliet, A., Spangler, P.F., and Marshall, A.M. An ecobehavioral examination of a simple strategy for increasing mealtime language in residential facilities. *Journal of Applied Behavior Analysis*, 1981, *14* (3), 295–305. Copyright by Society for the Experimental Analysis of Behavior, Inc. Reproduced by permission.)

passing" trainings and feedback, the only significant component of the independent variable was the manner in which food was served.

Results as reported by authors. Van Biervliet, Spangler, and Marshall (1981) reported that "the average number of verbalizations per minute increased during family style meals for all three meals" (p. 299) and "maintained fairly well over an extended period of time" (p. 299). In examining the data for individual residents, the authors found that most of the effects could be explained by increased performances of three residents, whose rates at least doubled during intervention conditions. Regarding the "quality" measures of "direction" and "content," the authors found that (1) increases were peer directed, rather than staff or observer directed and (2) at least four of the

Design and condition sequence. The investigators employed a multiple probe design across conditions (mealtimes) as illustrated in Figure 11-4. The condition sequence was as follows: (1) *"dinner"*: baseline (A_1), 15 sessions; family style intervention (B_1), 12 sessions (plus 5 follow-up probes); (2) *"lunch"*: baseline (A_2), 25 sessions; family style intervention (B_2), 14 sessions (plus 1 follow-up probe); (3) *"breakfast"*: baseline (A_3), 34 sessions; family style intervention (B_3), 12 sessions (plus 1 follow-up probe).

residents exhibited substantial gains in "meal-related conversations" rather than increases in simple "requests for food."

Summary and conclusions. The data (especially in the second and third data series) are variable and thus difficult to interpret. Perhaps a multiple baseline design, requiring more frequent measurement, would have provided a more sensitive representation of the dependent variables than the intermittent baseline probes employed herein. Furthermore, given the relatively small number of targeted residents (N = 5), it would have been helpful to display visually each participant's performance data, as it is difficult to interpret "averaged" data in tabular format. Nonetheless, allowing for these limitations, one is left agreeing with the authors that (1) family style dining service facilitated peer interactions and (2) the procedure is more congruent with the principles of normalization, given that family style service is typical of home settings and affords diners with more control over their own lives. Finally, the procedure was evidently compatible with institutional requirements, as the family style service was subsequently extended to include other unit residents.

Concluding Comments

The multiple probe design is appropriate to validate interventions across many types of learners (spanning the broad range of handicapping conditions), exhibiting a multiplicity of behaviors, in a variety of educational and clinical settings. Table 11-1 summarizes several other studies from the applied research literature that have employed the multiple probe design.

Cronin and Cuvo (1979) illustrated the flexibility of multiple probe designs by combining the multiple probe design across behaviors with the multiple probe design across subjects to teach three sewing skills to "moderately retarded" adolescents. The instructional program consisted of a socially validated task analysis combined with a graduated hierarchy of response prompting and fading procedures. By using a multiple probe design across three behaviors (i.e., the sewing of buttons, hems, and seams), intrasubject experimental control was demonstrated, as measured by replicated increases in the percentage of task steps performed independently across each target behavior.

TABLE 11-1 Examples of multiple probe designs.

Reference	Subject(s)	Setting(s)	Dependent Variable(s)	Independent Variable(s)
Cronin & Cuvo (1979)	"moderately retarded" adolescents, 4 males and 1 female (CA range: 17–20 years)	a public school "TMR" classroom	"the percentage of sewing tasks performed independently" across three behaviors (the sewing of buttons, hems, and seams)	a socially validated task analysis combined with a graduated hierarchy of response prompting and fading procedures
Neaf, Iwata, & Page (1978)	5 "mildly" and "moderately" retarded males (CA range: 18–24 years)	a classroom in the Kalamazoo Valley Multihandicap Center	"the number of task steps performed correctly" relative to locating a bus, signalling it, boarding and riding, and exiting	role playing, manipulating a simulated model, and verbally describing slide sequences
Van den Pol, Iwata, Ivancic, Page, Neef, & Whitley (1981)	3 "mildly" and "moderately" retarded, "multiply handicapped" males (CA range: 17–22 years)	a classroom and actual fast food restaurants	"the percentage of task steps completed correctly" relative to 5 restaurant skills: locating, ordering, paying, eating, and exiting	modeling, role playing, and slide identification
Risley & Cuvo (1980)	2 males and 1 female, "mildly" and "moderately" retarded (CA range: 26–52 years)	an office of a sheltered workshop	"the percentage of task steps completed independently" across 3 emergency phone calls: fire, police, and doctor	a socially validated task analysis combined with a graduated hierarchy of "least prompts," feedback, and social praise
Kleinert & Gast (1982)	a multiply handicapped male—severely hearing impaired, "mild" to "moderate" retardation, and cerebral palsy (CA = 31 years)	a 4m × 4m classroom located in a sheltered workshop	"percent correct" of 6 vocationally relevant manual signs: work station, restroom, break, supervisor, time clock, and supplies	a constant time-delay transfer of stimulus control procedure

Furthermore, by combining this intrasubject demonstration with a multiple probe design across subjects, the effectiveness of the intervention was strengthened as each learner, in turn, demonstrated mastery of the three targeted skills.

Neef, Iwata, and Page (1978) used a multiple probe design across subjects to assess the efficacy of a classroom training procedure to teach independent bus-riding skills to retarded persons. Five mildly and moderately retarded male youth, ranging in age from 18 to 24 years, received sequential instruction across four task-analyzed program components: locating the bus, signalling it, boarding and riding, and exiting. Training procedures consisted of role playing, manipulating a simulated model, and verbally describing slide sequences. Initially, baseline probe measures were taken on the number of task steps performed correctly across the five individuals, and training was then introduced in a time-staggered fashion. The demonstration of experimental control would have been strengthened had the investigators waited until criterion-level responding was attained with one subject before intervening with a new subject. Instead, training was applied to a new student as soon as a positive trend was observed with the preceding student; nevertheless, with each application relatively abrupt positive changes in responding were obtained. Concurrent with the classroom instruction, generalization data were collected relative to student performances on real buses in the natural environment and, as in the classroom, each youth demonstrated criterion-level responding. Furthermore, when compared with an "in vivo" training program (in which similar students were taught the same skills on city buses, rather than in the classroom), the in-classroom procedure proved less time-consuming, less expensive, and equally effective.

In a somewhat similar study, Van den Pol, Iwata, Ivancic, Page, Neef, and Whitley (1981) employed a multiple probe design across subjects to evaluate a classroom-based training procedure to instruct "restaurant skills" to multiply handicapped persons. Three mildly and moderately retarded, multiply handicapped male youth, ranging in age from 17–22 years, received sequential instruction (including modeling, role playing, and slide identification) across five task-analyzed skill components: locating, ordering, paying, eating, and exiting. Baseline and training probes were conducted in a McDonald's restaurant where the percentage of task steps completed correctly was measured. Stable baseline trends were established across each student, prior to initiating intervention; however, as with the Neef, Iwata, and Page (1978) study, the demonstration of experimental control was weakened because training was initiated with subjects prior to attaining criterion-level responding with the preceding subject; nonetheless, relatively abrupt changes to criterion-level responding for each student were obtained. Follow-up data indicated that students generalized skills to a Burger King restaurant, and covert probe measures a year later documented the durability of the behaviors at McDonald's.

Risley and Cuvo (1980) employed a multiple probe design across subjects to evaluate a classroom-based training program to teach mentally retarded individuals to place emergency phone calls to fire stations, police stations, and doctors' offices. Their subjects were mildly and moderately retarded adults, two men and a woman, ranging in age from 26–52. Each person received sequential instruction (using the system of least prompts, feedback, and social praise) across 82 validated task-analyzed steps. Experimental control was demonstrated, as stable baseline trends were established across each student, and relatively abrupt changes to criterion-level responding were replicated across each. However, the study provided only two "baseline" probe sessions for each student, one at the outset of the study and one immediately prior to the application of training. Two or three successive probe sessions (i.e., a "true baseline") immediately prior to training would have provided a stronger demonstration of behavior stability.

Kleinert and Gast (1982) employed a multiple probe design across behaviors to measure the efficacy of a constant time-delay transfer of stimulus control procedure to teach a 31-year-old severely hearing impaired young man (with mild to moderate retardation and cerebral palsy) to produce six vocationally relevant manual signs: work station, restroom, break, supervisor, time clock, and supplies. The manual signs were taught in pairs, using photographs, using the following training sequence: two consecutive "baseline" probe sessions were conducted across each of the six target signs (measuring percent correct); instruction was then sequentially applied to the first two signs, until criterion-level performance was attained for each; consecutive baseline probe sessions were again conducted across the six behaviors; the intervention was then applied to the next sign-pair, followed by a third baseline probe, and so on, until all six manual signs attained criterion. Experimental control was demonstrated by replicating the effects across each sign-pair. Furthermore, the worker learned to produce the signs in near errorless fashion and, after training, was able to label actual people, places, and objects in the work environment and to comprehend the manual signs when others presented them to him.

The multiple probe design is an appropriate alternative to the multiple baseline design when continuous baseline measures are unnecessary or impractical. A common complaint raised by teachers who use the multiple baseline design is that prolonged baseline conditions frequently result in the emergence of inappropriate competing behaviors. In addition, it is not uncommon for teachers to voice concern over extended test conditions that prevent students from receiving feedback on their performance. For the classroom teacher and clinician the multiple probe design may set these concerns to rest. As Cuvo (1979) and others (Cooper, 1981; Horner & Baer, 1978; Murphey & Bryan, 1980) have argued, the multiple probe design offers the applied researcher an efficient way to evaluate the effectiveness of an instructional program while circumventing many of the practical limitations associated with the multiple baseline design.

Resolving "Ambiguities" of Multiple Baseline and Multiple Probe Designs

Internal Validity Issues

An essential requirement for any experiment or investigation is internal validity. As previously discussed, internal validity is attained when a researcher demonstrates that (1) an intervention has an effect on the dependent variable and (2) the effect is replicated within the study. Regardless of the single subject design used to evaluate a functional relationship between independent and dependent variables, a number of threats to internal validity are possible. For the applied researcher who uses either the multiple baseline or multiple probe design the following threats to internal validity must be controlled: history, maturation, testing, instrumentation, data variability, and reactive intervention (Campbell & Stanley, 1968; Glass, Willson, & Gottman, 1975; Kratochwill, 1978). In addition to these potentially confounding variables an investigator must also attend to procedural contrast, i.e., the number and magnitude of differences between the procedures employed in two adjacent conditions (Cuvo, 1979). The literature contains suggestions for controlling threats to internal validity. Here, we describe other strategies to prevent confounding due to history, testing, and procedural contrast.

History

Historical confounding refers to extraneous events (i.e., uncontrolled "extra" experimental variables) that occur concurrently with the introduction of the independent variable and that influence the dependent variable (Kratochwill, 1978). Multiple baseline and multiple probe designs control for historical confounding by demonstrating abrupt changes in the dependent variable across data series over time. However, behavioral covariation (i.e., response generalization) across untreated or baseline data series threatens a demonstration of experimental control. Additionally, two procedural "shortcuts," the use of "delayed" multiple baseline designs (Watson & Workman, 1981) and the early introduction of the independent variable into an untreated data series, potentially threaten and most assuredly weaken a demonstration of experimental control.

Behavioral covariation may be prevented from interfering with a demonstration of experimental control if the researcher: (1) carefully targets behaviors (or conditions or subjects) that are as functionally independent as possible; (2) identifies, a priori, four or more behaviors (or conditions or subjects) rather than the minimum recommendation of three; or (3) combines the multiple baseline (or probe) design across behaviors with the multiple baseline (or probe) design across subjects. Figure 11-5 presents Cronin and Cuvo's (1979) data using the combination design preventative strategy. The graph shows the use of a multiple probe design across three sewing skills (i.e., the sewing of buttons, hems, and seams) that is sequentially replicated across five subjects. Had intrasubject behavioral covariation occurred across the three skills, the demonstration of experimental control would not have been lost due to the consistent replication of effects across subjects.

In the event behavioral covariation emerges during the course of an investigation a "brief" reintroduction of baseline conditions with the last data series introduced to the intervention may salvage a demonstration of experimental control (Kazdin & Kopel, 1975). With this "return to baseline conditions strategy" the investigator closely monitors the effect of the reversal (or withdrawal) on all the data series. If other data series also show a reversal in trend and level, these data provide evidence of a generalized intervention effect. This effect is further verified by the subsequent reapplication of the independent variable and reversal in trend. Figure 11-6 provides a graphic illustration of the use of a reversal condition in the presence of behavioral covariation. Additionally, the reader is referred to Russo and Koegel (1977) for an applied example from the literature.

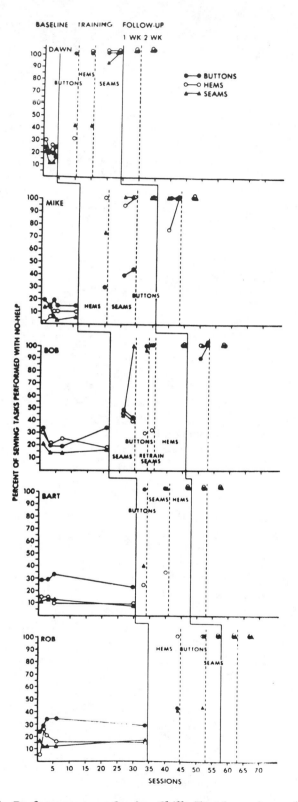

FIGURE 11-5 Performance on Sewing Skills Test in various phases of the experiment for five mentally retarded adolescents. (Figure 1, p. 405, from: Cronin K.A. and Cuvo, A.J. Teaching mending skills to mentally retarded adolescents. *Journal of Applied Behavior Analysis*, 1979, *12* (3), 401–406. Copyright by Society for the Experimental Analysis of Behavior, Inc. Reproduced by permission.)

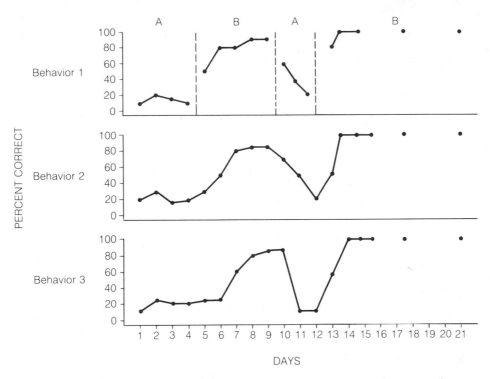

FIGURE 11-6 Hypothetical data illustrating the use of a reversal condition in the presence of behavioral covariation to demonstrate "true" generalized intervention effects.

Though the addition of a reversal (or withdrawal) design to the multiple baseline design may be the only way to salvage experimental control, there are, however, circumstances that may preclude its use. First, the targeted behavior(s) may not respond to a reversal of conditions once they are learned (e.g., academic skills). Second, practical constraints, such as parent and/or staff resistance, may prohibit the reversal (or withdrawal) of an effective intervention. Third, ethical constraints, as with a child who exhibits self-injurious or dangerously aggressive behaviors, may prevent a reintroduction of baseline conditions for even a brief period. The decision to include a "partial reversal" must be determined by weighing the experimental advantages over the practical and ethical disadvantages. This may be one of the *few* occasions where an applied researcher will have to decide between an empirical verification of intervention effectiveness and professional ethics when using the multiple baseline design. It is imperative to consult the student's parents or guardian before one decides to return to baseline.

In an effort to reduce the length of baseline conditions and to increase flexibility to include new behaviors (or conditions or subjects) as they become available, some researchers (e.g., Watson & Workman, 1981) have proposed the use of what they term a *delayed multiple baseline design*. This design obviates the need for concurrent data collection across baseline data series. When using the delayed multiple baseline design, an investigator collects baseline data on the first behavior (or subject or in the first condition) before collecting data on the second behavior, on the second behavior before collecting data on the third behavior, and so on, in a sequential and delayed fashion. Figure 11-7 illustrates the staggered and nonconcurrent measure-

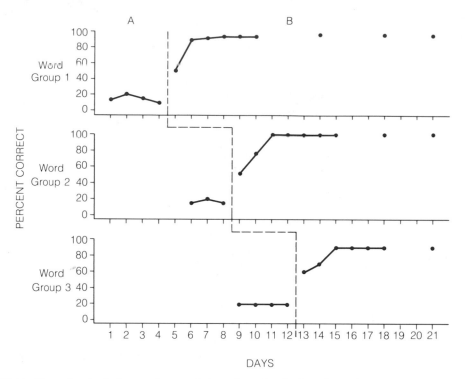

FIGURE 11-7 **Hypothetical data using a *delayed* multiple baseline design across spelling work groups.**

ment of the dependent variable under baseline conditions (A) associated with the delayed multiple baseline design.

Advocates of the delayed multiple baseline design say that it has the advantage that new baselines (e.g., behaviors, conditions, or subjects) can be added as they become available, and thus the risk of prolonged and potentially "reactive" baselines can be avoided. What these advocates have overlooked, however, is the design's failure to meet the basic requirement of demonstrating that the target behaviors are functionally similar yet independent of one another. Without at least an initial concurrent baseline measures across *all* targeted behaviors, in addition to the measures that immediately precede the introduction of the intervention, historical confounding cannot be discounted. In Figure 11-7 for example, it is impossible to estimate the data trend and level for Word Group 2 (over Days 1 through 5) and Word Group 3 (over Days 1 through 8) without the data on each group for the first 3 days of the investigation. It may very well be that the percentage correct was higher for both word groups early in the condition. Although the delayed multiple baseline design may have more flexibility than the traditional multiple baseline and multiple probe designs, it does not, and cannot, provide as convincing a demonstration of experimental control because it fails to concurrently evaluate all targeted behaviors (conditions or subjects) in the initial sessions of the investigation. The visual analysis of such data is limited to a simple A-B design, with all its shortcomings, followed by a series of A-B replications across data series.

Another shortcut, which may have an adverse influence on a visual analysis, is the *early or premature application of the independent variable* into a

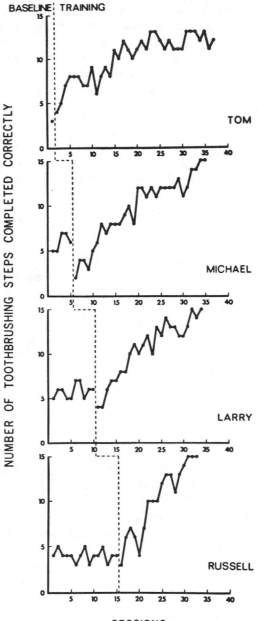

FIGURE 11-8   The number of toothbrushing steps performed correctly by the four subjects in the first group. The broken line through the individual graphs indicates termination of baseline and the beginning of training for each subject. (Figure 1, p. 306, from: Horner R.D. and Keilitz, I. Training mentally retarded adolescents to brush their teeth. *Journal of Applied Behavior Analysis*, 1975, *8* (3), 301–309. Copyright by Society for the Experimental Analysis of Behavior, Inc. Reproduced by permission.)

baseline data series. Several examples of this strategy have been described earlier (Horner & Keilitz, 1975; Neef et al., 1978; Van den Pol et al., 1981). The Horner and Keilitz (1975) data are presented in Figure 11-8. The graph illustrates the early introduction of the independent variable across subjects before criterion-level responding was documented with the preceding subject. Like the delayed multiple baseline design this strategy fails to control for the threat of historical confounding due to an inadequate demonstration of independence across data series. To demonstrate this independence across data series, it is necessary to postpone intervention with new targets until the effect is clearly demonstrated on the existing targets.

Testing and Procedural Contrast

The multiple baseline design is particularly susceptible to confounding of the contrast between baseline testing and intervention procedures. Confounding due to prolonged testing, using untrained items, may generate two distinctly different patterns of responding: (1) it can suppress student responding, resulting in a data path that resembles an extinction curve typical of a nonreinforced baseline; (2) it can enhance student responding, generating a data trend that resembles a learning curve typical of a reinforced baseline. The type of baseline data trend will depend upon such variables as the frequency of observation periods, response requirements (e.g., task difficulty), and the procedures employed in the baseline condition (e.g., reinforcement schedule). In several of the studies discussed previously it was suspected that such "testing and procedural contrasts" accounted for subject behavior patterns (e.g., Clark, Boyd, & Macrae, 1975; Gruber, Reeser, & Reid, 1979; Kirby, Holburn, & Bushby, 1981). These potential side effects have been advanced as rationales for using the multiple probe design rather than the multiple baseline design; however, it is unfair to suggest that multiple baseline designs necessarily evoke reactive responding from learners. As preventive measures, Cuvo (1979) suggested; (1) to minimize the length of baseline sessions by including fewer items and/or fewer trials while still validly sampling learner performance; (2) to maintain as dense a reinforcement schedule during baseline as during intervention by reinforcing appropriate "test-taking behaviors" (e.g., attending to task or by interspersing previously learned "competency items" for which correct responding can be reinforced); and (3) to delete unnecessary components of an intervention package by using, for example, the system of least prompts. By following such guidelines, the risks of confounding due to prolonged baselines are minimized, whether one chooses a multiple baseline or a multiple probe design.

Group Data

Multiple baseline (or probe) designs apply equally well to the behavior of individuals or groups. The treatment of group data, however, can be problematic since variability across individuals may be masked when the group is treated as a single organism by averaging individual data points. To resolve this problem, the researcher may (1) provide and maintain several graphs: one summarizing the average group performance and others documenting the individual performances of group members (an approach used by Kirby et al., 1981); or (2) plot the individual data paths for each participating group member on one graph, as shown in Figure 11-9. These suggestions are most appropriate for smaller groups since too many data paths would be time-consuming to maintain and would clutter a visual display. Further, when the

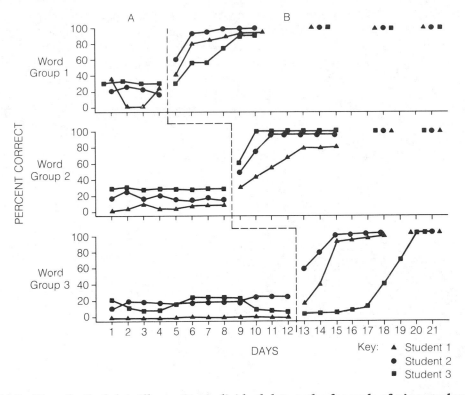

FIGURE 11-9 Hypothetical data illustrating individual data paths for each of nine students (three per baseline). (From Kelly, J.A. The simultaneous replication design. *Journal of Behavior Therapy and Experimental Psychiatry*, 1980, *11*, 203–207.)

behavior of the group is of paramount interest (regardless of individual variability), group data are most appropriate (e.g., Barrish, Saunders, & Wolf, 1969).

External Validity Issues

Applied research, by definition, is concerned with socially important issues (Baer, Wolf, & Risley, 1968; Birnbrauer, Peterson, & Solnick, 1974). The external validity of a study depends both upon the demonstrated practical value of the behavior change for the individual learner (intrasubject generality) and the applicability of findings to different individuals, functioning in different settings, with different change agents (interindividual generality).

Intrasubject Generality

Measures of intrasubject generality include assessment of the durability of behavior change over time (i.e., maintenance), the degree of stimulus generalization (e.g., across settings, teachers, materials, or instructions), and the degree of response generalization across related behaviors. In a recent random survey of empirical studies cited in the applied behavior analysis literature, fewer than 20% of the studies were found to include a systematic series of generalization probes (Kendall, 1981), a fact that is particularly distressing given ample evidence that much behavior is "specific" to the training situation, unless techniques are applied to promote generalization (Stokes & Baer, 1977).

In this and the preceding chapter, we have emphasized that, with multiple baseline (and multiple probe) designs, experimental control may be confounded by premature generalization (covariation) across untreated baselines. This is not to suggest, however, that the designs are confounded by generalized effects across *nontargeted* stimulus conditions or behaviors. Cooke and

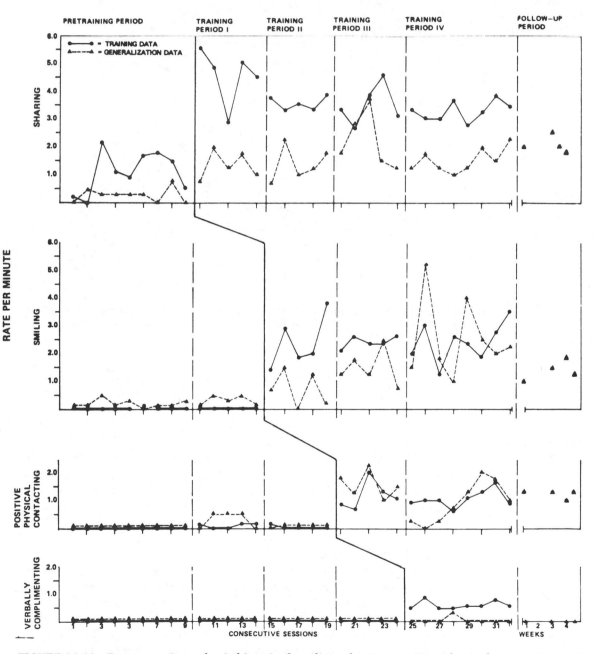

FIGURE 11-10   Rate per minute by Subject 2 of smiling, sharing, positive physical contacting, and verbally complimenting for each training and generalization session. (Figure 2, p. 71, from: Cooke, T.P. and Apolloni, T. Developing positive social-emotional behaviors: A study of training and generalization effects. *Journal of Applied Behavior Analysis*, 1976, *9* (1), 65–78. Copyright by Society for the Experimental Analysis of Behavior, Inc. Reproduced by permission.)

Apolloni (1976) provided an excellent example of concurrent monitoring of stimulus generalization that occurred during the social training of a learning disabled child, as presented in Figure 11-10. The graph shows that as the child improved his social interaction skills in the training session, he concurrently generalized his interaction skills with untrained peers in a "generalization setting."

As an alternative to daily, concurrent monitoring of stimulus generalization, Kendall (1981) recommended adding a series of generalization probes after the experimental effects have been demonstrated in the training setting, as illustrated in Figure 11-11. The graph shows that the intervention was effective. Subsequently, three targeted behaviors were assessed simultaneously across three generalization-probe conditions: G_1, representing a different instructor; G_2, the home instead of school; and G_3, the presence of different peers in the classroom. From these probes, it is evident that complete stimulus generalization occurred for Behavior 1; whereas Behaviors 2 and 3 require further programming across one or more of the test situations. Other studies we have discussed also provide examples of stimulus generalization measures (e.g., Murdock, et al., 1977; Neef et al, 1978; Tucker & Berry, 1980; Van den Pol et al., 1981).

It is equally important for investigators to monitor response generalization since a change in nontargeted behaviors could have implications for instructional programming (Kazdin, 1973; Kratochwill, 1978). For example, using a

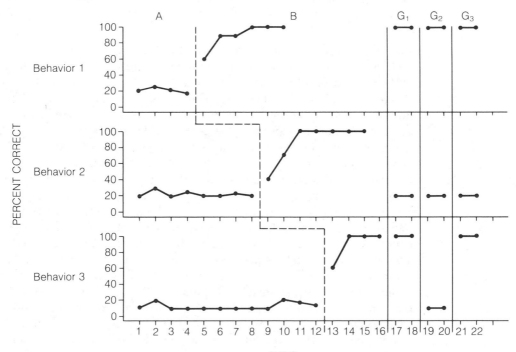

FIGURE 11-11 **Hypothetical data using a multiple baseline design across behaviors, including probes across three generalization conditions (G_1 = different instructor; G_2 = home instead of school; G_3 = different peers).**

multiple probe design across behaviors (e.g., sets of matched spelling words), a teaching strategy may appear to be successful if a child sequentially masters each objective when the independent variable is applied. Suppose, however, that the intervention is so "obtrusive" that it calls attention to the child's errors and invites ridicule. A research design that fails to probe for such nontargeted effects may do a disservice to the child and may misrepresent the external validity of the study. On the other hand, teachers may shortchange themselves by failing to document appropriate generalization as it occurs, a problem that has been noted in studies we described earlier (e.g., Clark et al., 1975; Gladstone & Spencer, 1977; Kleinert & Gast, 1982; Wells et al., 1977).

Perhaps the greatest challenge in conducting generalization probes is to determine which stimulus conditions or responses to monitor. Given the current scarcity of available empirical evidence, an investigator is advised to solicit the opinions of socially relevant judges within the learner's natural environment (including the client herself) and, ultimately, to rely on one's own best professional judgment (Kazdin, 1973; Kendall, 1981; Miller, 1973).

Intersubject Generality

In single subject research, generality is established and limited by the systematic replication of internally valid studies, across individuals, conditions, and behaviors (Birnbrauer, 1981; Birnbrauer et al., 1974; Sidman, 1960). As Birnbrauer (1981) explained:

> Generality is established, or more likely limited, by accumulating studies which are internally valid and by placing the results into a systematic context, i.e., seeking out the principles and parameters that particular procedures appear to be enunciating. (p. 122)

Consistent with this requirement, several of the studies described previously included direct and systematic replications of effects (e.g., Horner & Keilitz, 1975; Schumaker, Hovell, & Sherman, 1977; Tucker & Berry, 1980; Russo & Koegel, 1977). However, there are many occasions when investigators wish to know not only if, and under what conditions, an intervention works, but if one intervention is superior to another. Unlike multitreatment, alternating treatments, and simultaneous treatment designs (to be discussed in Chapter 12), multiple baseline and multiple probe designs do not permit direct comparisons of alternative intervention strategies; however, indirect comparisons are encouraged (Cuvo, 1979). Users of the multiple baseline and multiple probe designs should document the efficacy of their research efforts by including measures of direct instructional time, trials to criterion, monetary expenses, and anecdotal records, so that as studies are replicated using alternative intervention strategies, data accumulate that permit inferences regarding the relative value of instructional options. Two studies described earlier warrant particular mention. Kleinert and Gast (1982) provided "efficiency data," including minimum number of trials to criterion required, number of trials to criterion above minimum, number of errors to criterion, and total training time to criterion. Such data are helpful to investigators wanting to identify both cost effective and time efficient interventions. Neef, Iwata, and Page (1978) provided an excellent example of the use of such efficiency data to argue the superiority of an "in-classroom" public transportation program compared with an "in vivo" program conducted on city buses. The reader is referred to these two studies as models for documenting and reporting secondary measures to help identify effective and efficient intervention strategies.

Changing Criterion Designs

Sidman (1960) described a research design that Hall (1971) named the changing criterion design. This may be appropriate for teachers and other applied researchers who wish to evaluate instructional programs that require gradual, stepwise changes in target behavior performance. Hartman and Hall (1976) describe the changing criterion design as follows:

> The design requires initial baseline observations on a single target behavior. This baseline phase is followed by implementation of a treatment program in each of a series of treatment phases. Each treatment phase is associated with a stepwise change in criterion rate for the target behavior. Thus, each phase of the design provides a baseline for the following phase. When the rate of the target behavior changes with each stepwise change in the criterion, therapeutic change is replicated and experimental control is demonstrated. (p. 527)

Though the changing criterion design has not been widely cited in the applied research literature, Hartman and Hall (1976) have suggested it may be useful to monitor a wide range of programs, e.g., increasing correct math problem completion and decreasing the number of cigarettes smoked per day.

Internal Validity To demonstrate experimental control using the changing criterion design an investigator must show that each time the criterion level is changed (increased or decreased), there is concomitant change in the dependent variable. This change should be immediate and should follow a stable level and trend in the data in the preceding phase. It is imperative to demonstrate stability before changing the criterion level, for each phase serves as a baseline measure for the subsequent phase. A replication of effect (i.e., internal validity) is demonstrated if each stepwise change in criterion level results in a behavior change to the new criterion level. Figure 11—12 illustrates a demonstration of experimental control using the changing criterion design.

Considerations ### Guidelines
Hartman and Hall (1976) have recommended that applied researchers attend to the following design requirements:

1. Introduce the intervention (i.e., the first criterion change) only after the initial baseline data show acceptable stability.

2. Change the criterion level only after stable criterion-level responding has been attained in the preceding phase.

3. Plan, at minimum, four changes in criterion level (i.e., replications).

4. Pinpoint criterion levels, or strategy for determining criterion levels, prior to initiating the study.

5. Vary the magnitude of criterion changes.

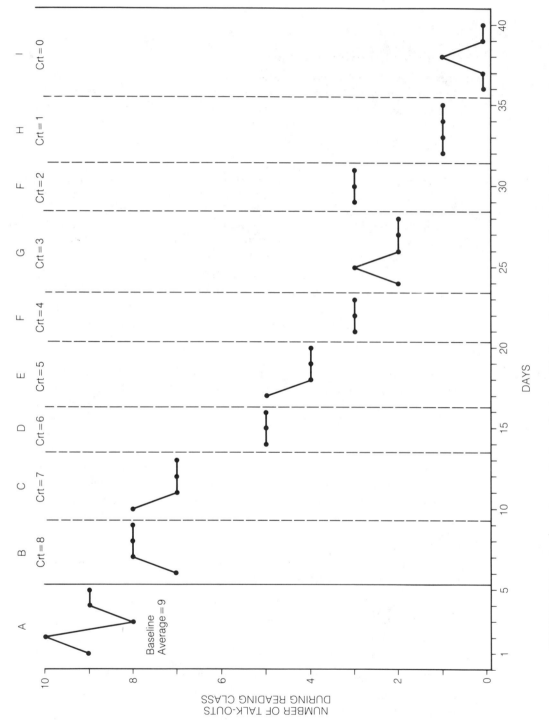

FIGURE 11-12 A changing criterion design with hypothetical data illustrating the number of talk-outs by a "disruptive" fourth grader during baseline (A) and intervention (B), when free time is made contingent upon changing criterion levels of performance.

6. Vary the length of time, across phases, that a subject must maintain responding at a criterion level.

7. Revert to a former criterion level at some point in the stepwise progression.

The strength of the changing criterion design is in its demonstration of a close correspondence between criterion-level change and behavior change. It is possible, however, that the correlation between the two could be explained by naturally occurring, uncontrolled historical, maturational, or measurement factors. These guidelines are intended to dispel such a possibility.

The most essential prequisite to a demonstration of experimental control is the stepwise replication of stable, criterion-level responding (i.e., guidelines 1–3); however, there are additional strategies to increase believability (i.e., guidelines 4–7). To minimize the risks of bias, the investigator optimally should pinpoint criterion levels, or a strategy for determining criterion changes before initiating a study. These predictions are, however, subject to change, depending upon the ongoing variability of the data (e.g., the greater the variability, the larger the required criterion change in order to demonstrate visible differences across phases). As additional assurances of experimental control, the investigator is advised to: vary the length of each phase, vary the magnitude of each criterion change, and revert to a former criterion at some point in the progression to insure that changes in the dependent variable are not naturally occurring. If the data consistently follow each of these criterion demands, there is a higher probability that the intervention is responsible for changes in the target behavior.

Advantages

The changing criterion design is appropriate to evaluate programs designed to shape behaviors that, although in the subject's repertoire, do not occur at an acceptable rate. For the most part the design has been employed to monitor programs in which motivational or compliance problems are responsible for a subject's failure to meet a specified criterion. It can be used to evaluate both acceleration programs (e.g., assignment completion, on-task behavior) and deceleration programs (e.g., talk-outs, out-of-seat, abusive language). Unlike the multiple baseline and multiple probe designs across behaviors, the changing criterion design has the advantage of requiring only one target behavior. In contrast to the A-B-A-B design, no reversal or withdrawal condition is required, though one return to a preceding criterion level is recommended and can strengthen the demonstration of experimental control. Most important, at least from an educator's perspective, the changing criterion design, through its small-step increments in criterion level, permits a student to change her behavior without being "overwhelmed" by an initial, seemingly impossible criterion demand.

Limitations

There are, perhaps, two reasons that the changing criterion design has been little used in the applied research literature: first, it is limited to a relatively small range of target behaviors and instructional procedures and, second, a demonstration of experimental control depends upon the "subjective" prediction of criterion levels, which may or may not conform to the data. The changing criterion design is not an appropriate paradigm to validate "acquisition stage" instructional procedures because any procedural alterations (e.g., stimulus shaping and fading, response prompting and fading, or response chaining) across design phases would alter the intervention and, thus, confound the demonstration of experimental control. Consequently, the design is limited to programs that manipulate consequences for the purpose of increasing or decreasing the frequency of behaviors already established in a subject's repertoire.

A second problem associated with the changing criterion design pertains to the setting and changing criterion levels. Whenever a teacher or researcher is required to specify a criterion level of acceptable performance, there is always some degree of subjectivity or "professional guesswork" involved. The investigator who uses the changing criterion design has the tedious responsibility of making criterion changes that are large enough to be "detectable" though small enough to be "achievable," but not so small that the behavior will far exceed the criterion level. In other words, a demonstration of experimental control depends upon an a priori prediction or strategy for setting a progression of criterion levels, a prediction that may or may not prove appropriate.

Applied Example: Changing Criterion Design	**Study I: Mildly Handicapped** Johnston, R.J., and McLaughlin, T.F. The effects of free time on assignment completion and accuracy in arithmetic: A case study. *Education and Treatment of Children*, 1982 *5* (1), 33–40.

Purpose, subject, and setting. Johnston and McLaughlin (1982) employed a changing criterion design to assess the effect of contingently dispensed free time on improved arithmetic assignment completion. The child, a 7-year-old female enrolled in a regular, self-contained second-grade classroom, presented an average, daily math worksheet completion rate of 35%—a level far below her expected ability, given that she consistently scored above her grade level on achievement tests and, in fact, averaged 100% correct on the daily worksheet problems which she attempted. The present study was conducted during her daily 35-minute arithmetic lesson.

Dependent variables. Daily assignments ranged from 6–43 items, including computational and thought problems. The two dependent variables were: (1) the percentage of problems completed per daily assignment and (2) the percentage correct per assignment. To provide interobserver reliability checks a parent-aide re-graded at least one daily assignment during each phase of the study. For both measures, point-by-point (i.e., problem-by-problem) reliability checks yielded 100% agreement.

Independent variable. During an initial 10-day baseline condition the second-grade teacher (1) presented the child with her daily math assignment, (2) worked one of the problems as a model, and (3) asked the student to complete as many problems as possible within the 35-minute session. At the end of this baseline period, an average daily baseline completion rate was computed that, in this case, was 35%. A changing criterion procedure was then introduced in which the investigators "successively changed the criterion for reinforcement, usually in graduated steps, from baseline level until the desired terminal behavior was achieved" (p. 35). In this study, most of the new criterion levels required a 5% increment in percent completion above the preceding level (i.e., Phase 1 = 35%, Phase 2 = 40%, Phase 3 = 45%, ... Phase 16 = 100%), for 3 consecutive days. Throughout the intervention condition the teacher continued to present the child with the daily assignment and work one example as a model; however, in addition she informed the child of the minimum number of problems that had to be completed (accurately) in order for criterion to be met and reminded her, that upon meeting the criterion, she was eligible to enjoy free time for the remainder of the 35-minute time period. If she did not meet criterion within the allowable 35 minutes, she was required to remain at her desk until criterion was attained.

Design and condition–phase sequence. Johnston and McLaughlin employed a changing criterion design, shown in Figure 11-13, which included a total of 16 criterion changes during the experimental condition. During Sessions 38–40 a brief reversal in criterion level was instituted to strengthen the demonstration of experimental control. The investigation concluded with a three session follow-up baseline condition extended over 25 days, which permitted a pretest-posttest analysis of the data.

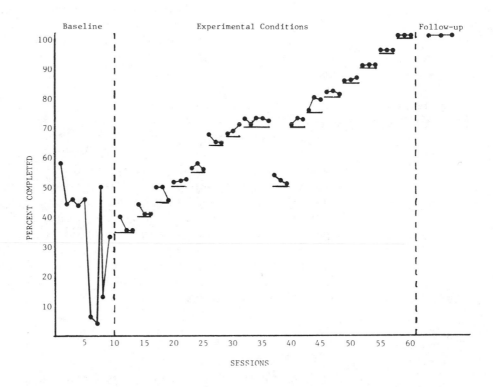

FIGURE 11-13 The percent of problems completed for each assignment during each of the experimental conditions. The solid horizontal lines indicate the reinforcement criterion set for each session. (Figure 1, p. 37, from: Johnston, J.R. and McLaughlin, T.F. The effects of a free time on assignment completion and accuracy in arithmetic: A case study. *Education and Treatment of Children*, 1982, 5 (1), 33–40. Reproduced by permission.)

Results as reported by authors. The authors reported that the student "met or exceeded the criterion each time that it was changed" (p. 36). Whereas her average baseline completion rate was 35%, by the final intervention phase she averaged 100% assignment completion. Furthermore, her accuracy remained stable throughout the study (≥ 95%), even though greater numbers of more difficult problems were being assigned.

Summary and conclusions. Johnston and McLaughlin (1982) provided a simple and convincing strategy to shape a child's rate of task completion, by requiring small increments in performance to insure continued successful responding. Interestingly, after the 60th session the investigator withdrew the free time contingency (i.e., reinstated baseline conditions) and found that 100% task completion and accuracy were maintained when measured by three follow-up probes conducted 5, 15, and 25 days after terminating the experimental condition. This suggests that the use of extrinsic reinforcement can be a temporary procedure useful to initiate new patterns of responding without necessarily "addicting" the student to its continued availability. Furthermore, the authors reported that the free time contingency required very little teacher time or expense. As a final note, one might suspect that the choice of 5% level increments may have been smaller than actually required since the child abruptly reached and often exceeded each new criterion level. Perhaps the outcome objective could have been attained more rapidly had the stepwise requirements been greater. However, this is problematic with all changing criterion designs, i.e., the challenge of identifying criterion levels that will permit the demonstration of experimental control without impeding optimal learning rates.

Concluding Comments

The changing criterion design is one of several experimental paradigms available to educators to evaluate the effectiveness of instructional programs. Though it has not been cited frequently in the applied research literature, it does offer a practical way to monitor student performance when stepwise criterion changes are both desirable and practical. It can be used to monitor programs designed to increase or decrease the rate of a student's responding. The teacher and applied researcher who decide to employ the changing criterion design should follow closely the guidelines previously discussed. One is cautioned to use the changing criterion design only if the target response is in the student's repertoire and the objective of one's intervention is to increase the fluency or rate of responding. Under these conditions the educator and clinician will find the changing criterion design appropriate and useful in evaluating program effectiveness.

SUMMARY

This chapter has described the multiple probe and changing criterion designs. Both designs, which are variations of the multiple baseline design, evaluate the effects of an intervention without having to schedule a reversal or withdrawal condition. In contrast to the A-B-A-B design, the multiple probe design, like the multiple baseline design, requires the concurrent measurement of several target behaviors, conditions, or subjects. Experimental control is demonstrated when there is a change in the data series that has been introduced to the independent variable, with no change in those data series that have not yet been exposed to the independent variable. Multiple probe designs, in contrast to multiple baseline designs, are advantageous when prolonged, continuous baseline measures are unnecessary, impractical, or reactive. Both designs, however, are flexible and pragmatic, as they permit behavior analysts to construct combinations of single subject designs for the purpose of strengthening internal validity (e.g., by reversing or withdrawing the independent variable in the presence of covariation) or external validity (e.g., by combining the across behaviors design with the across subjects design).

The changing criterion design differs from the multiple baseline and multiple probe designs across behaviors in that it requires the identification of only one target behavior. This behavior must be one that is in the subject's repertoire and one that, through the manipulation of consequences, can be modified in a stepwise progression. Experimental control is demonstrated when a change in criterion is followed by a concomitant change in response frequency. The design is limited, however, to a relatively small range of behaviors and instructional procedures.

12

COMPARATIVE INTERVENTION DESIGNS

The preceding chapters contain descriptions of those single subject research designs that have traditionally been used in applied research. Reversal and withdrawal designs provide an excellent demonstration of experimental control by repeatedly showing the impact of an intervention with the same subject and on the same behavior. Multiple baseline and multiple probe designs evaluate the effect of an intervention by staggering its introduction into three or more baseline data series across behaviors, conditions, or subjects. Changing criterion designs permit a researcher to evaluate experimental control by shifting the performance standard or criterion across time in a steplike manner.

Multitreatment, alternating treatments, and simultaneous treament designs comprise another group of single subject designs referred to here as comparative intervention designs. These designs enable the applied researcher to compare the effects of two or more interventions across one or more learners and/or one or more behaviors. The multitreatment design evaluates the effectiveness of two or more interventions introduced singly or in combination with other interventions. The alternating treatments design (ATD) compares the effectiveness of two or more interventions by introducing them over the same time period. The interventions are then counterbalanced across sessions and time of day. The simultaneous treatment design (STD) exposes the learner (or learners) to all interventions at the same time. Counterbalancing across investigators occurs with this design, but all interventions remain available to the learner and he selects the desired one.

This chapter describes comparative intervention designs, specifically the multitreatment, alternating treatments, and simultaneous treatment designs.

This chapter was written by **David L. Gast**, **Carol Chase Thomas**, and **James W. Tawney**.

Internal and external validity, and advantages and disadvantages of each design are considered. Applied examples of studies conducted with a variety of subjects are presented to illustrate the utility of the designs in a variety of educational settings.

The Multitreatment Design

The multitreatment or multiple treatment design is an extension and variation of the reversal and withdrawal (A-B-A-B) design. The multitreatment design is used when an investigator wants to evaluate the effects of two or more interventions upon a behavior. One intervention may be combined with others to determine the effect of a treatment package. These are introduced in a defined sequence and then compared to an adjacent condition. The primary objective is to determine whether any of the interventions are effective, and if so, which is considered the most effective (Birnbrauer, Peterson, & Solnick, 1974). The multitreatment design, then, allows the applied researcher to compare the effectiveness of one intervention over another.

Internal and External Validity

Experimental control in the multitreatment design is demonstrated when the introduction of an intervention is accompanied by a change in the trend and level of the target behavior (Kratochwill, 1978). Internal validity is achieved when the effects of the intervention are replicated with each introduction of the same independent variable. For example, a teacher may wish to evaluate the relative effectiveness of social praise (A), token reinforcement (B), and token reinforcement plus response cost (BC) on a student's rate of work completion. The sequence for introducing these conditions might be: A-B-A-B-BC-B-BC. If token reinforcement (B) results in a reliable positive effect on the student's rate of work completion when compared to social praise, (A), and if token reinforcement plus response cost (BC) consistently increases the rate of work completion over token reinforcement alone (B), internal validity has been achieved. The teacher would conclude that token reinforcement (B) was superior to social praise (A) and token reinforcement plus response cost (BC) was superior to token reinforcement (B) in improving the student's rate of work completion. Note that in this example the A condition refers to an active intervention rather than an observation baseline.

In order for external validity to be demonstrated in a multitreatment design, the effects of the intervention must be replicated in different settings (e.g., classrooms), on different behaviors (e.g., reading rate), and with different subjects (e.g., students with other types of handicapping conditions or in other grades). The replication of the effects of a multitreatment design requires that the investigator provide an accurate and detailed description of the procedures and conditions under which the target behavior was measured (Birnbrauer, et al. 1974; Birnbrauer, 1981).

Considerations

Guidelines
When using the multitreatment design, the investigator should:

1. Identify a target behavior and pinpoint outcome objectives (i.e., criterion levels) prior to beginning the study.

2. Operationally define the procedures that comprise the intervention conditions to be evaluated.

3. Determine the order in which the interventions will be introduced to each subject. Counterbalance the order if the study is being conducted with more than one subject to control for order effects.

4. Collect baseline data (A) for a minimum of three observation periods (days).

5. After stability has been attained in the baseline data, introduce the first intervention (B).

6. Return to the baseline condition (A).

7. Reintroduce the first intervention (B).

8. Introduce the second intervention (C) or intervention package (BC).

9. Introduce succeeding interventions in a systematic fashion keeping in mind that only adjacent conditions can be compared and that each condition must be introduced twice to show a functional relationship.

10. The specific order of conditions will be determined by the conditions one wishes to compare (e.g., A-B-A-C-A-D; A-B-C-B-C-D-C-D). Note that in the first example one can only evaluate the single application of B, C, and D to A.

After an outcome objective for the study has been identified, the applied researcher operationally defines the procedures that comprise the interventions or intervention packages to be evaluated by using the multitreatment design and then determines the order in which the interventions are to be introduced. These decisions may be made on the basis of previous research with different populations. Reviewing the research of others also may provide information about the sequence of interventions or combinations of interventions. In all cases, however, the researcher must remember to change only one variable at a time because changing several variables in one condition precludes the possibility of separating out the effects of a single intervention. For example, in the situation where the investigator wanted to compare the effects of social praise, token reinforcement, and token reinforcement plus response cost on work completion, the investigator introduced only one new intervention in each condition. That is, token reinforcement was introduced singly and then in combination with response cost. If all interventions had been combined and introduced at the same time, it would not have been possible to separate out the effects of response cost from the effects of social praise and token reinforcement.

After the target behavior has been identified and the intervention procedures and sequence determined, the researcher measures the behavior under baseline conditions. Following a stable baseline (A) trend, the first intervention (B) is instituted and is usually followed by a return to the preceding baseline condition (A). After the reintroduction of the baseline condition, the second intervention (C) or package (BC) is introduced. The researcher may then return to baseline (A) or to the first intervention (B). A third intervention (D) may be implemented, followed by a return to baseline conditions (A), to the first intervention (B), or to the second intervention (C). Interventions can also be combined (BC) and compared with baseline

(A) or with an intervention in isolation (B or C or D). The decision to return to A or B or another intervention depends upon the research question. The research question may focus on comparing B to A and C to A, or it may be directed toward comparing C to B, D to B or combinations thereof, such as BC to B. The order in which conditions are introduced depends upon the conditions that the investigator wants to compare. It is important to remember that only adjacent conditions can be compared. Figure 12-1 illustrates the various ways to introduce experimental conditions in a multitreatment design.

Example *a* involves the comparison of three interventions (B, C, D) with baseline (A), Although it appears that D was the most effective in increasing in-seat behavior, the effects may have been due to a sequence effect, i.e., D was more effective because it followed B and C. The interventions can only be compared to the preceding baseline (A) conditions and not to each other because they are not adjacent. Example *b* involves the implementation of three interventions (B, BC, and BCD). The BC and BCD conditions are intervention packages, i.e., combinations of several interventions. The B_1 condition was compared to a baseline condition (A). BC was compared to B (BC_1 to B_1; BC_2 to B_2), and BCD was compared to BC (BCD to BC_2 and BC_3). The intervention package BCD, which was compared to BC_2, can be considered more effective than the BC condition. However, the chance still remains that BCD was effective because it followed B and BC. There is also the possibility that C or D alone would have been effective if implemented separately from B.

Advantages

The major advantage of the multitreatment design is economy of time since a number of interventions can be tested in sequence (Kratochwill, 1978). It also allows comparisons between two different interventions when they are implemented in adjacent conditions.

Limitations

Conclusions drawn from research using a multitreatment design are limited by threats to internal validity and multiple treatment interference. The amount of time required to implement a multitreatment design fosters threats to the internal validity of an investigation because historical and maturational factors may occur during one experimental condition but not another. Multiple treatment interference may result from carryover or sequence effects. If carryover is present, a change observed in the data during the second intervention period may be due to the influence of the first intervention, or it may be due to a combination of the first and second interventions (Kratochwill, 1978). As Birnbrauer, Peterson, and Solnick (1974) cautioned, the sequence of the interventions is important as the effects of earlier interventions may influence the results of those that are implemented later. Furthermore, they stated that the effects of an intervention following a specified baseline or intervention condition can only be compared with that baseline or experimental condition and no other condition. A final limitation of the multitreatment design has to do with interventions which are introduced as part of an intervention package. When two intervention procedures are combined it is not possible to separate out the individual contribution of each procedure.

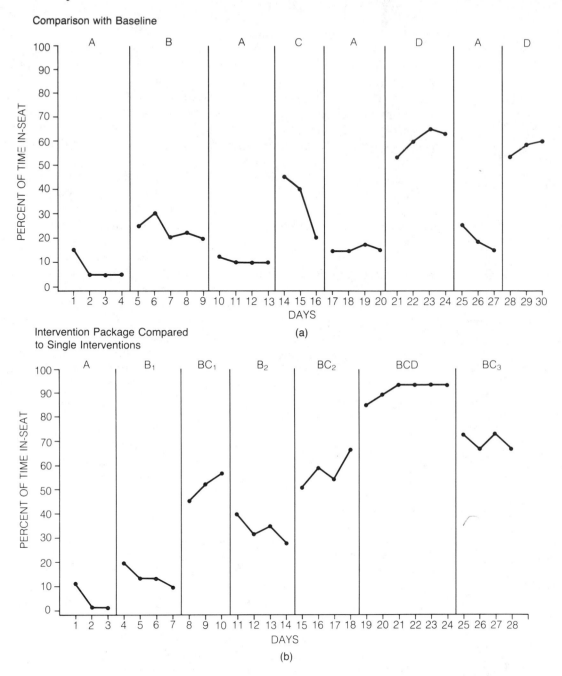

Comparison with Baseline

(a)

Intervention Package Compared
to Single Interventions

(b)

FIGURE 12-1   Illustrations of the multitreatment design.

For example, if social praise paired with free time was effective in increasing
work completion, there is a possibility that social praise or free time would
have been effective if used alone. If these behavior consequences were tested
singly late in the study, the data might lead one to conclude that the intervention of social praise alone (or free time alone) was effective. Once again,
however, the order effect must be considered; social praise alone may have
been effective only because it followed social praise paired with free time or

vice versa. Additional research introducing the interventions in a different order would have to be conducted in such cases.

Applied Examples: Multitreatment Design

Study I

Van Houten, R., Hill, S., & Parsons, M. An analysis of a performance feedback system: The effects of timing and feedback, public posting, and praise upon academic performance and peer interaction. *Journal of Applied Behavior Analysis*, 1975 8 (4) 449–457.

Purpose, subject, and setting. The purpose of this study was to determine the effects of the elements of timing, feedback, public posting of grades, and teacher praise on composition writing. A second purpose was to document performance-related comments by individuals and peers when grades were posted publically by a teacher. The subjects were fourth graders from a low socioeconomic multiracial area of Nova Scotia. The better readers were in Class A (19 students), and the poorer readers were in Class B (20 students).

Dependent variables. The dependent measures were writing rate, on-task behavior, and verbal comments on self-performance or peer performance. Writing rate was determined by counting the number of words written and dividing by the total available writing time. Data on on-task behavior were collected using a time-sampling technique. Each of the five rows in the classroom were sampled for 1 minute. The observer scanned the row from front to back six times per minute, counting the number of children in the row and the number of children on-task in the row. Verbal comments on performance were tallied by an observer who counted audible comments before, during, and after the composition writing period. Reliability checks for all dependent measures were conducted on two randomly sampled days in each experimental phase. The mean agreement on writing rate for Class A was 97%, with a range of 94% to 100%. The mean agreement for Class B was 98%, with a range of 96% to 100%. For on-task behavior the mean reliability for Class A was 98.4%, with a range of 93% to 100%. Mean reliability for Class B was 95.5%, with a range of 93% to 98%. For comments on performance the mean reliability for Class A was 91%, with a range of 83% to 100%. Mean reliability for Class B was 93%, with a range of 79% to 100%.

Independent variables. The independent variables were timing (i.e., announcement of a time limit of 10 or 20 minutes), feedback (i.e., self-counting of number of words written), public posting (i.e., each child's name on a chart indicating the greatest number of words written to date), and praise (i.e., teacher praise for being on-task and for increasing the score on the chart).

Before the experiment began, the teacher for both classes made a list of composition topics that were then randomly ordered and preassigned for each day of the program. Composition writing was conducted 4 days per week. The topic for the day was written on the board and announced by the teacher. The students were instructed to write as much as they could on the topic. The teacher helped the students with spelling of words. Class A was permitted to write for 20 minutes and Class B for 10 minutes. At the end of that time the papers were collected.

Design and condition sequence. The investigators employed a multitreatment design as illustrated in Figure 12-2, examples *a* and *b*. The condition sequence was: baseline (A); timing and feedback 1 (B_1); timing and feedback

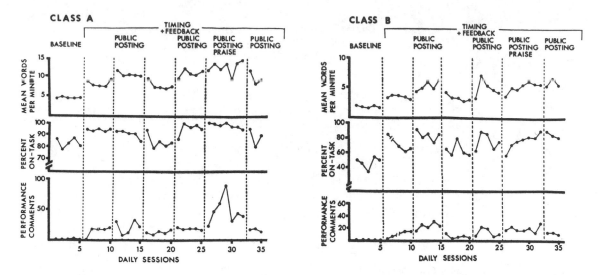

FIGURE 12-2 The mean response rate in words per minute, the mean percentage of intervals on-task, and the number of performance comments in each daily session across all conditions for (a) Class A and (b) Class B. The broken vertical lines represent the introduction of the experimental conditions. The broken data line represents an unrecorded session. (Figure 1, p. 452 and Figure 2, p. 453, from: Van Houten, R., Hill, S., and Parsons, M. An analysis of a performance feedback system: The effects of timing and feedback, public posting, and praise upon academic performance and peer interaction. *Journal of Applied Behavior Analysis*, 1975, *8* (4), 449–457. Copyright by Society for the Experimental Analysis of Behavior, Inc. Reproduced by permission.)

plus public posting 1 (BC$_1$); timing and feedback 2 (B$_2$); timing and feedback plus public posting 2 (BC$_2$); timing and feedback plus public posting plus praise (BCD): and timing and feedback plus public posting 3 (BC$_3$). Condition A was 5 days in length; Condition B$_1$, 5 days; Condition BC$_1$ 5 days; Condition B$_2$, 5 days; Condition BC$_2$, 5 days; Condition BCD, 7 days; and Condition BC$_3$, 3 days.

Results as reported by authors. The authors stated that the timing and feedback condition increased the writing rate of the students to almost double the baseline rates. Introduction of public posting increased the rate even more. The introduction of praise increased the rate for Class A but not for Class B. The increases in writing rate were paralleled by the increases in on-task behavior and number of performance comments. The investigators were uncertain as to why teacher praise was effective with one class but not the other.

A detailed analysis of the data. A visual analysis of the data for the dependent measure of mean words per minute shown in Figure 12-2, example *a*, is provided. The following discussion is based on information summarized in Tables 12-1 and 12-2.

Relative to data series A-B$_1$, timing and feedback (B$_1$) resulted in a positive effect over baseline (A) as indicated by an accelerating-improving trend and a level change of +5 mean words written per minute. Though the data in B$_1$ were variable, there was no overlap in writing rate between conditions.

Relative to data series B-BC, timing and feedback (B) had no effect over timing and feedback plus public posting (BC) (i.e., B$_2$ to BC$_1$). A decelerating-

TABLE 12-1 Within condition analysis of Study I (Van Houten, Hill, and Parsons, 1975).

Conditions	$\dfrac{A_1}{1}$	$\dfrac{B_1}{2}$	$\dfrac{BC_1}{3}$	$\dfrac{B_2}{4}$	$\dfrac{BC_2}{5}$	$\dfrac{BCD}{6}$	$\dfrac{BC_3}{7}$	$\dfrac{}{8}$
1. Condition Length	5	5	5	5	5	7	3	—
2. Estimate of Trend Direction	(=)	(+)	(−)	(−)	(+)	(+)	(−)	( )
3. Trend Stability	stable	variable	stable	stable	variable	variable	variable	
4. Data Paths within Trend	(=)	(−) (+)	(−)	(−) (=)	(+)	(=) (+)	(−)	( )
5. Level Stability and Range	stable (4–5)	variable (7–10)	variable (10–12)	variable (8–10)	variable (10–13)	variable (10–15)	variable (9–13)	( )
6. Level Change	4–4 (0)	9–10 (+1)	12–10 (−2)	10–8 (−2)	10–12 (+2)	12–15 (+3)	13–10 (−3)	( )

TABLE 12-2 Between adjacent conditions analysis of Study I (Van Houten, Hill, and Parsons, 1975).

Condition Comparison	$\frac{B_1}{A}$ (2:1)	$\frac{B_2}{BC_1}$ (4:3)	$\frac{BC_1}{B_1}$ (3:2)	$\frac{BC_2}{B_2}$ (5:4)	$\frac{BC_3}{BCD}$ (7:6)	$\frac{BCD}{BC_2}$ (6:5)	____ / ____ (:)	2nd condition / 1st condition; condition order
1. Number of Variables Changed	1	1	1	1	1	1		
2. Change in Trend Direction and Effect	— (=) / (+) positive	\ (−) \ (−) no change	/ (+) \ (−) negative	\ (−) / (+) positive	/ (+) \ (−) negative	/ (+) / (+) no change	( ) ( )	1st trend, 2nd trend effect
3. Change in Trend Stability	stable to variable	stable to stable	variable to stable	stable to variable	variable to variable	variable to variable	____ to ____	
4. Change in Level	(4–9) +5	(10–10) 0	(10–12) +2	(8–10) +2	(13–10) −3	(12–12) 0	(–) ____	
5. Percentage of Overlap	0 %	20 %	40 %	20 %	33 %	42.8 %	____%	

decaying trend in BC_1 continued across B_2. The data trend across conditions was stable. There was a small change in level between conditions and there was a 20% overlap in values. *Recommendation:* Timing and feedback plus public posting (BC_1) should have been continued until a clear trend had been established either showing a zero celeration or decelerating slope before timing and feedback (B_2) was reintroduced.

Relative to data series BC-B, timing and feedback plus public posting (BC) had a variable and inconclusive effect over timing and feedback (B). Condition BC_1, following B_1, resulted in a change in level of $+2$ with a gradual decelerating and decaying trend across BC_1. There was a 40% overlap in values between the two conditions. Condition BC_2, following B_2, resulted in a level change of $+2$ followed by gradual variable accerating and improving trend across BC_2. There was a 20% overlap in values between BC_2 and B_2. In spite of the consistent change in level across the two (i.e., $+2$), the estimate of trend differed across the comparisons (BC_1 to B_1—decelerating; BC_2 to B_2—accelerating). Therefore, it cannot be concluded that timing and feedback plus public posting (BC) was more effective than timing and feedback (B). *Recommendation:* B_1 should have been continued until the trend stabilized. This would have required at least two additional data points. BC_2 should have been continued until both the level and trend stabilized.

Relative to data series BC-BCD, timing and feedback plus public posting (BC_3) had a negative effect over timing and feedback plus public posting plus praise (BCD) as indicated by a level change of -3 and a variable decelerating data path. There was, however, no clear trend established over the three data points in BC_3. There was a 33.3% overlap in values between BC_3 and BCD. *Recommendation.* BC_3 should have been continued until a stable trend was established.

Relative to data series BCD-BC, the introduction of timing and feedback plus public posting plus praise (BCD) had no effect in changing the level or trend over timing and feedback plus public posting (BC_2). In both conditions a variable accelerating-improving trend was evidenced. There was a 42.8% overlap in values. *Recommendation.* Timing and feedback plus public posting (BC_2) should have been continued until a stable trend was established in the last three data points before introducing timing and feedback plus public posting plus praise (BCD).

Summary and conclusions. Timing and feedback (B) was more effective than the baseline condition (A) in increasing mean words written per minute. In addition, timing and feedback (B) resulted in an increase in percent of time on-task and performance comments. It cannot be determined what effect B had in relation to timing and feedback plus public posting (BC) because of the decelerating trend that continued across the two conditions of BC_1 and B_2. This decelerating trend was also evidenced in the percentage of time students were on-task and by the performance comments. When BC_2 is compared to B_2, the data are variable and decaying for mean words per minute and percent on-task and stable with a minimal decaying effect for performance comments. When timing and feedback plus public posting plus praise (BCD) were introduced, the data were variable but with an improving trend for mean words per minute, stable and decaying for percent of time on-task, and variable and decaying for performance comments. The data should have been allowed to stabilize before the last introduction of timing and feedback plus public posting (BC$_3$). The final condition (BC$_3$) should have been extended until a stable trend was evidenced. When the study was concluded in the BC$_3$ condition, the levels for all three measures were lower than they had been in the BCD condition. The BCD condition should have been introduced again in order to support the authors' statements that timing and feedback plus public posting increased the levels on all measures and that the addition of praise increased the levels even more.

In this study, the authors wanted to determine how each of the intervention packages would affect composition writing and two parallel behaviors. They introduced the packages in a particular sequence and determined that an intervention package comprised of four elements (timing, feedback, public posting, and praise) was the most effective for the students in Class A. However, that combination of interventions was not reintroduced in order to replicate the effects. In addition, it must be remembered that this intervention package was the sixth condition and was instituted 25 days into the study, which raises the possibility that the effects may have been due to sequence and carryover influences. If the authors had wanted to compare the interventions in a shorter amount of time and reduce the possibility of multiple treatment interference, another design (e.g., alternating treatments design) would have been more appropriate.

Concluding Comments

The multitreatment design permits comparisons of the effects of different interventions on specified target behaviors. The design has been used with a number of behaviors, types of learners, and in a variety of educational and clinical settings. Table 12-3 summarizes several studies from the applied research literature that have used a multitreatment design. Cohen, Polsgrove, Rieth, and Heinen (1981) conducted a study similar to the one by Van Houten, Hill, and Parsons (1975) on the effects of self-monitoring, public graphing, and token reinforcement on the acceleration of quiet behavior (one child) and on-task behavior (six children).

Gibson, Lawrence, and Nelson (1976) compared the effectiveness of the three training procedures of (a) modeling, (b) instructions and feedback, and (c) modeling, instructions, and feedback on the verbalization, recreation, and cooperation behaviors of three developmentally disabled adults. Marholin and Steinman (1977) compared the effects of teacher absence and teacher presence under the conditions of unreinforced baseline, reinforcement for being on task, and reinforcement for accuracy and rate on math problem-solving behaviors of fifth- and sixth-grade children with behavior problems. Foxx, Azrin, and their colleagues have used the multitreatment design in a number of studies to compare the effects of overcorrection procedures with other interventions. In an early study, Foxx and Azrin (1973) compared the effects of overcorrection, reinforcement for non-self-stimulatory behavior, physical punishment, a distasteful solution painted on the hand, and "free" reinforcement. The procedures were used with three retarded children and one autistic child who exhibited such self-stimulatory behaviors as object and hand mouthing and hand clapping. The overcorrection procedure was implemented last, raising the possibility that multiple treatment interference (i.e., sequence and carryover effects) may have had an impact on the results.

TABLE 12-3   Examples of multitreatment designs.

Reference	Subject(s)	Dependent Variable(s)	Independent Variable(s)
Cohen, Polsgrove, Rieth, & Heinen (1981)	7 underachieving students enrolled in an after school remedial program	Percent of on-task behavior (6 subjects); percent of quiet behavior (1 subject)	Baseline (A), Self-monitoring (B), Withdrawal (A), Self-monitoring and graphing (BC), Withdrawal (A), Self-monitoring, graphing, and token reinforcement (BCD). A final procedure was used with one student: Self-monitoring, graphing, token reinforcement, and response cost (BCDE)
Foxx & Azrin (1973)	1 autistic, 3 mentally retarded children enrolled in a behavioral day-care program	Number of self-stimulatory behaviors (object mouthing, hand mouthing, head weaving, and hand clapping)	For 1 subject: Free reinforcement (A), Reinforcement for nonmouthing (B), Punishment by a slap (C), Free reinforcement (A), Overcorrection (D). Sequence of conditions counterbalanced across subjects
Marholin & Steinman (1977)	8 5th- and 6th-grade students in a classroom	Percent of on-task behavior and disruptive behaviors; mean number of math problems attempted (rate) and percent correct (accuracy)	Baseline (A), On-task reinforced (B_1), Academic rate and accuracy reinforced (C_1), On-task reinforced (B_2), Academic rate and accuracy reinforced (C_2). In the final 3 sessions of each condition the teacher and aides left the classroom for the last 10 minutes in order to provide a probe measure of stimulus control.
Measel & Alfieri (1976)	2 profoundly mentally retarded adolscents who resided in a state residential institution	Frequency of head slapping and head banging (rate)	Baseline (A), which required verbally instructing subjects in a manipulative task, Reinforcement (B) for attempting the task, and Reinforcement plus overcorrection (BC), which required the same reinforcement procedures and 10 minutes of overcorrection for each episode of self-injurious behavior.
Gibson, Lawrence, & Nelson (1976)	3 developmentally disabled adults in a short-term treatment facility	Number of intervals engaged in appropriate peer interaction	Baseline (A), Instructions and feedback (B), and modeling, instructions, and feedback, (BC). Sequence of treatments counterbalanced across subects

In conclusion, the multitreatment design may have potential for use in applied settings when one wishes to compare several interventions. However, the design is limited by threats to internal validity (e.g., historical and matura-tional factors) and multiple treatment interference (e.g., sequence and carryover effects).

The Alternating Treatment Design

An alternative design for evaluating the effectiveness of several interventions within a single subject (or group of subjects) is the alternating treatments design (ATD). This design avoids many of the interferences and internal validity problems associated with the multitreatment design but still permits comparison of the effectiveness of two or more interventions. The alternating treatments design also has been referred to as a multiple schedule design (Hersen & Barlow, 1976; Leitenberg, 1973), a multielement baseline design (Sidman, 1960; Ulman & Sulzer-Azaroff, 1975), and a simultaneous treatment design (Kazdin & Hartmann, 1978). Barlow and Hayes (1979) have named this paradigm "alternating treatments" and their designation will be used in this chapter.

The basic feature of the alternating treatments design is the fast alternation of two different interventions or treatment conditions with an individual learner or group of learners. The interventions are alternated and counterbal-anced session by session (or within sessions) rather than over time as in a multitreatment design. In contrast to the reversal and multiple baseline designs, both of which require stability in the data before introducing a new condition, a researcher using an alternating treatments design can alternate interventions, regardless of any changes in the target behavior (Barlow & Hayes, 1979; Ulman & Sulzer-Azaroff, 1975).

The important element in the alternating treatments design is stimulus discrimination that permits the subject(s) to identify which intervention is in effect at a certain time. Leitenberg (1973) explained:

> This design is based on discrimination learning principles; that is, if the same behavior is treated differently in the presence of different physical or social stimuli, it will exhibit different characteristics in the presence of these stimuli. (p. 93).

Stimulus discrimination can be facilitated by the use of verbal instructions, color cues, or signs to the learner to indicate which intervention is in effect (e.g., blue coding sheet indicates token economy is in effect; red indicates response cost is in effect).

Internal and External Validity

The data for each intervention in an alternating treatments design are plotted separately to provide a graphic representation of the effects each intervention has on the target behavior. The data are analyzed visually to determine if consistent patterns of responding vary according to the intervention in effect. When the level of responding varies by the alternating conditions, experimen-tal control has been demonstrated (Cooper, 1981; Ulman & Sulzer-Azaroff, 1975). The magnitude of the difference between the experimental conditions can be determined by examining the vertical distance (i.e., ordinate value) between the data paths of the conditions being compared. The greater the vertical distance between condition trend lines, the greater the difference between experimental conditions. If, however, the data paths of the alternating conditions are an overlapping, experimental effect is not evidenced.

Internal validity in the alternating treatments design is demonstrated when one intervention is consistently associated with a different level of responding than other interventions. The internal validity of the alternating treatments design is usually good because the rapid alternation of two interventions controls for the maturational and historical threats that may occur in a multitreatment design. The rapid alternation also reduces sequencing problems because no single intervention is consistently introduced first and maintained for an extended period of time (Barlow & Hayes, 1979; Sulzer-Azaroff & Mayer, 1977).

In order for external validity to be demonstrated in an alternating treatments design, the differential effects of the interventions must be replicated across a different population or group of subjects, across different behaviors, and/or across different conditions (e.g., investigators, settings, instructional arrangements).

Considerations

Guidelines

When using the alternating treatments design, the investigator should:

1. Operationally define all intervention procedures.

2. Determine a schedule for counterbalancing the presentation of the interventions across time (i.e., within sessions, across days).

3. Decide how the intervention procedures will be counterbalanced across teachers, settings, activities, and so on.

4. Collect baseline condition data (A).

5. Introduce the interventions (B and C) in a rapidly alternating fashion in accordance with the counterbalancing schedule. Baseline (A) may be continued for comparison with interventions (B to A and C to A). Continue the alternation of conditions until the experimental effect is demonstrated favoring the effectiveness of one intervention over others.

6. Continue with the most effective intervention (B or C) in the final phase of the study.

After the target behavior has been identified, one should select and operationally define the procedures for each experimental condition to be compared. A schedule for counterbalancing potentially confounding variables (e.g., time, teacher) is determined *a priori*. Baseline condition data are frequently collected before comparing experimental conditions. Following the baseline period (A), two or more interventions (B and C) are administered in an alternating schedule, counterbalanced for such variables as sequence, time of day, and teacher. The interventions are randomly alternated each day within a session, or they are rapidly alternated across days. Each intervention is presented an equal number of times during the experimental or comparison phase of the investigation, in contrast to each intervention being presented alone across a series of experimental phases as in a multitreatment or reversal design. In contrast to a multiple baseline or multiple probe design in which interventions are introduced in a staggered fashion, in an alternating treatments design each intervention is introduced at the same time during the

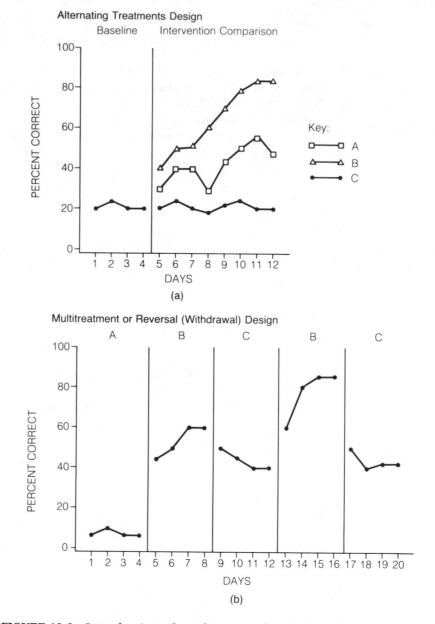

FIGURE 12-3   Introduction of conditions in three types of designs.

same experimental phase of the investigation. Figure 12-3 illustrates the basic differences among an alternating treatments design, a multitreatment or reversal design, and a multiple baseline design in regard to the point at which two interventions (B and C) are introduced. Example *a* illustrates an alternating treatments design which consists of a baseline condition and an intervention comparison phase. The baseline condition (A) was continued throughout the study, which is an optional feature in the alternating treatments design. Conditions B and C were introduced on Day 5 and alternated for the remainder of the study. Example *b* illustrates a multitreatment design which consists of a baseline condition and two comparisons of interventions

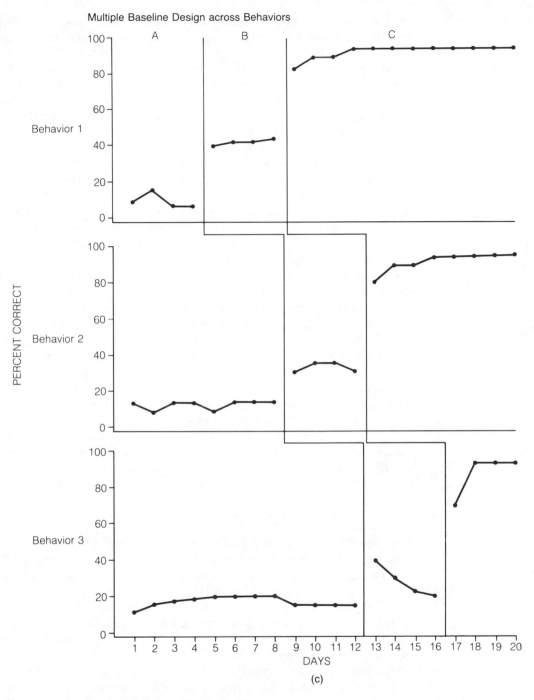

Multiple Baseline Design across Behaviors

(c)

FIGURE 12-3 (continued)

B and C. Condition B was introduced on Day 5 and again on Day 13 in order to provide comparisons with two adjacent C conditions. The multitreatment design requires more time and changing of conditions to permit comparisons than does the alternating treatments design. Example *c* illustrates a multiple baseline design across three behaviors. A baseline condition (A) was used for all three behaviors, and the interventions B and C were introduced after the data had stabilized for the preceding behaviors. The multiple baseline design requires more time and the staggering of implementation of interventions when compared to the alternating treatments design. If a continuous comparison between the baseline condition (A) and the two interventions (B and C) is desired, the investigator may continue to collect baseline condition data for the duration of the study in the alternating treatments design (Barlow & Hayes, 1979; Repp & Lloyd, 1980).

Following the evaluation of the interventions during the comparison phase (i.e., when conditions B and C were in effect), one may choose to continue the study with only the most effective intervention (e.g., B) to determine its effectiveness when presented in isolation. Figure 12-4 illustrates three ways to implement an alternating treatments design. Example *a* illustrates an alternating treatments design which consists of a baseline condition (A), an intervention comparison phase (B and C), and a final phase when the most effective intervention (B) was continued in isolation. The baseline condition (A) was continued through the intervention comparison phase, which is an option with this design. The A, B, C conditions could have been alternated within sessions or within three time periods in a day according to the way the data are graphed for each day. Example *b* illustrates an alternating treatments design which consists of a baseline condition (A), the comparison of two interventions (B and C), and a final phase in which the most effective intervention (B) was continued in isolation. During the intervention comparison phase, the interventions were alternated every other day. Example *c* illustrates an alternating treatments design which consists of a baseline condition (A) and three comparison phases of interventions B and C. In addition, generalization probes were conducted on Day 9 and Day 15. Some researchers have introduced occasional probe conditions (e.g., Barrera, Lobato-Barrera, & Sulzer-Azaroff, 1980), while others have alternated the interventions on a daily basis first and then on other schedules (e.g., Carnine, 1981).

Advantages

The alternating treatments design has several practical advantages when one wants to compare the effectiveness of two or more interventions. First, the alternating treatments design does not require a baseline condition before introducing interventions, although a baseline can be conducted and maintained throughout the study if desired. Second, target behaviors can be treated immediately, instead of waiting for the baseline data to stabilize. Third, behaviors do not need to be reversed in order to demonstrate experimental control, making the alternating treatments design particularly useful when evaluating interventions with nonreversible behaviors. Fourth, the design permits a rapid comparison of several interventions and allows the investigator to conduct a component analysis of a complex procedure (i.e., to separate out the effects of a single component of an intervention package). Fifth, the design minimizes sequencing problems associated with the multitreatment design by rapidly alternating the interventions. And sixth, early termination of a study is less critical with an alternating treatments design than it is with other single subject designs because if differences in intervention effects are going to occur, they typically are evident early in the

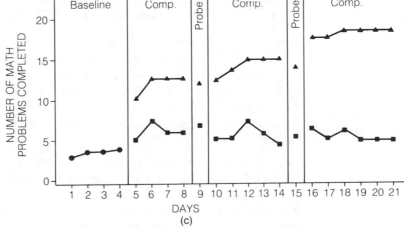

FIGURE 12-4 Three ways of implementing an alternating treatments design.

investigation (Cooper, 1981; Repp & Lloyd, 1980; Sulzer-Azaroff & Mayer, 1977; Ulman & Sulzer-Azaroff, 1975).

Limitations

Although the alternating treatments design is useful when comparing complex interventions, it has some limitations. First, the design requires a high level of consistency across individuals administering the different interventions; therefore, high procedural reliability is of critical importance when evaluating the data. Second, the alternating treatments design is somewhat artificial compared to natural instructional or intervention conditions (Hersen & Barlow, 1976). That is, seldom are two different interventions introduced during the same time period in a rapidly alternating sequence in response to the same behavior in a typical classroom program. Third, depending upon the number of extra-experimental variables that need to be counterbalanced across interventions (e.g., teacher, time of day, sequence for introducing each intervention, instructional locations), controlling for the potential influence of these variables on the target behavior, independent of the interventions, can become cumbersome (Barlow & Hayes, 1979). Fourth, multiple treatment interference (i.e., the influence one intervention has on the apparent effectiveness, or ineffectiveness, of a second intervention) cannot be determined easily (Barlow & Hayes, 1979; Repp & Lloyd, 1980; Ulman & Sulzer-Azaroff, 1975). Fifth, the alternating treatments design may adversely affect the occurrence of behavioral changes if differential intervention effects are not evidenced early in the experimental comparison phase of the study (Kratochwill, 1978). And sixth, the design may not be sensitive to effective though weak interventions when applied over a long period of time. More specifically, an immediate change in the dependent variable, as a function of an intervention, may be masked because the behavior does not maintain across the comparison phase of the study.

Applied Examples: Alternating Treatments Design

Study I: Severely Handicapped

Barrera, R.D., Lobato-Barrera, D., & Sulzer-Azaroff, B. A stimulus treatment comparison of three expressive language training programs with a mute autistic child. *Journal of Autism and Developmental Disorders*, 1980, *10* (1), 21–37.

Purpose, subject, and setting. The purpose of this study was to compare the effectiveness of three language training models. The subject was a 4½-year-old boy diagnosed as autistic and lacking functional expressive language skills. The intervention procedures were implemented in a preschool class for severely handicapped children during the school year. Training was continued at the University of Massachusetts Communication Disorders Clinic during the summer.

Dependent variable. The dependent variable was expressive language (i.e., vocal and gestural responses by the child). Various measures were used to determine which method was most effective in developing expressive language. The authors presented data on the total number of words at critertion, the number of words successfully spoken or signed during daily probe, the percentage of correct responding, and the number of trials to criterion.

Reliability data were collected through analysis of videotape recordings.

The reliability for all three intervention procedures ranged from 85% to 90%, with a combined mean of 87%.

Independent variable. The independent variables were the three language training models of total communication sign training, nonverbal "sign-alone" training, and oral training. Signs were trained using a graduated guidance procedure involving the systematic application and then gradual fading of physical prompts. In the sign-alone training no vocalizations were made by the therapist. During total communication training the therapist orally presented the name of the object and physically guided him to make the signed response. Oral responses were trained using modeling, chaining, and stimulus-fading techniques.

The study was conducted in four phases. Phase I involved adaptation to the treatment environment and the selection of edible reinforcers. Phase II consisted of training on sitting quietly and eye contact. Following these phases, 50 nouns were selected and independently rated by four language specialists on criteria of vocalization and signing difficulty. Thirty nouns were chosen, matched for difficulty, placed into groups of five, and assigned to one of the three training models. In Phase III the child received 20 minutes of training with all three models. The training was continued until the child met a predetermined criterion on all five words within a category. A direct replication of the comparison was conducted on the remaining matched word groups. A criterion verification test was conducted after each comparison to determine that criterion was met on all five words. Phase IV consisted of a period of intensive training using only the procedure that had been the most effective in Phase III. A generalization period following the final phase involved a new therapist, the elimination of training stimuli, and only verbal requests for the child to produce the signs which had been taught using the total communication procedure.

Design and condition sequence. An alternating treatments design was used to compare the effectiveness of the three methods. (The authors used the term *simultaneous treatment* in the title but refer to their design as alternating treatments or multielement in the text of their article.) The order of the presentation of the training procedures was randomized across three time periods each day.

Baseline data are not presented in Figure 12-5; instead the data plotted begin with the alternation of the three treatments on the Group 1 words. Training on Group 1 words lasted for 9 days, followed by a criterion verification check on the 10th day. Training on Group 2 words lasted for 3 days with another criterion verification check on the 14th day. Total communication intensive training involving the introduction of new words and teaching them for 60 minutes each day lasted for a total of 3 days.

Results as reported by the authors. The authors stated that the total communication approach was more effective in developing expressive language skills in the autistic child than either the oral or the sign-alone procedures. The data on all measures demonstrated the superiority of the total communication approach and indicated that the pattern emerged early in the training sequence. The generalization test conducted at the end of training showed that the child responded correctly to all of the words he had been taught with the total communication procedures.

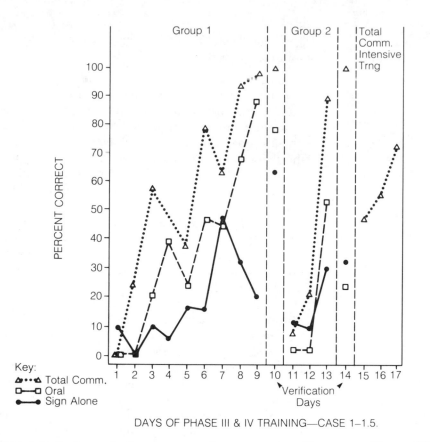

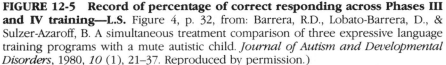

DAYS OF PHASE III & IV TRAINING—CASE 1–1.5.

FIGURE 12-5   Record of percentage of correct responding across Phases III and IV training—L.S. Figure 4, p. 32, from: Barrera, R.D., Lobato-Barrera, D., & Sulzer-Azaroff, B. A simultaneous treatment comparison of three expressive language training programs with a mute autistic child. *Journal of Autism and Developmental Disorders*, 1980, *10* (1), 21–37. Reproduced by permission.)

A detailed analysis of the data. In order to evaluate the authors' statements about their results, a detailed visual analysis of the percentage of correct responding data in Figure 12-5 is presented. The discussion is based on information summarized in Tables 12-4 and 12-5.

Relative to data series A-B, the total communication method (A) was more effective than the sign-alone condition (B) for increasing the percentage of correct responses for both Group 1 (A_1 to B_1) and Group 2 words (A_2 to B_2). Both methods resulted in a variable accelerating-improving trend. The level change (obtained by comparing the final data points in each condition) was a $+8$ for A_1 compared to B_1, and a $+45$ for A_2 compared to B_2. There was a 77% overlap of data points for A_1 to B_1 and a 66% overlap for A_2 to B_2.

Relative to data series A-C, the total communication method (A) was more effective than the oral method (C). The data for Group 1 words using the oral method (C_1) showed a decelerating and decaying trend, while the total communication method (A_1) resulted in a positive effect as demonstrated by an accelerating and improving trend. Both trends were variable. These results

TABLE 12-4 Within condition analysis of Study I (Barrera, Lobato-Barrera, and Sulzer-Azaroff, 1980).

Conditions	Comparison Phase			Replication Phase				
	$\dfrac{A_1}{1}$	$\dfrac{B_1}{2}$	$\dfrac{C_1}{3}$	$\dfrac{A_2}{4}$	$\dfrac{B_2}{5}$	$\dfrac{C_2}{6}$	7	8
1. Condition Length	$\underline{9}$	$\underline{9}$	$\underline{9}$	$\underline{3}$	$\underline{3}$	$\underline{3}$	—	—
2. Estimate of Trend Direction	(+)	(+)	(−)	(+)	(+)	(−)	( )	( )
3. Trend Stability	variable	variable	variable	variable	variable	variable	│	│
4. Data Paths within Trend	(−) (+)	(+)	(=) (−)	(+)	(+)	(−)	( )	( )
5. Level Stability and Range	$\dfrac{\text{variable}}{(\,0\text{–}98\,)}$	$\dfrac{\text{variable}}{(\,0\text{–}90\,)}$	$\dfrac{\text{variable}}{(\,0\text{–}45\,)}$	$\dfrac{\text{variable}}{(\,5\text{–}90\,)}$	$\dfrac{\text{variable}}{(\,0\text{–}55\,)}$	$\dfrac{\text{variable}}{(10\text{–}30)}$	$\dfrac{(\,-\,)}{(\,-\,)}$	$\dfrac{-}{(\,-\,)}$
6. Level Change	$\dfrac{0\text{–}98}{(+98)}$	$\dfrac{0\text{–}90}{(+90)}$	$\dfrac{10\text{–}20}{(+10)}$	$\dfrac{5\text{–}90}{(+85)}$	$\dfrac{0\text{–}55}{(+55)}$	$\dfrac{10\text{–}30}{(+20)}$	$\dfrac{-}{(\,-\,)}$	$\dfrac{-}{(\,-\,)}$

TABLE 12-5   Between adjacent conditions analysis of Study I (Barrera, Lobato-Barrera, and Sulzer-Azaroff, 1980).

Condition Comparison	$\frac{A_1}{B_1}$ (1:2)	$\frac{A_2}{B_2}$ (4:5)	$\frac{A_1}{C_1}$ (1:3)	$\frac{A_2}{C_2}$ (4:6)	$\frac{B_1}{C_1}$ (2:3)	$\frac{B_2}{C_2}$ (5:6)	$\frac{\quad}{\quad}$ (:) 2nd condition / 1st condition condition order
1. Number of Variables Changed	1	1	1	1	1	1	
2. Change in Trend Direction and Effect	(+) (+) no change	(+) (+) no change	(−) (+) positive	(−) (+) positive	(−) (+) positive	(−) (+) positive	( ) ( ) — 1st trend / 2nd trend / effect
3. Change in Trend Stability	variable to variable	variable to variable	variable to variable	variable to variable	variable to variable	variable to variable	___ to ___
4. Change in Level	(98−90) +8	(90−55) +45	(98−20) +78	(90−30) +60	(90−20) +70	(55−30) +25	(−)
5. Percentage of Overlap	77 %	66 %	44 %	33 %	77 %	0 %	___ %

were replicated with Group 2 words (A_2 to C_2). The level change was $+78$ for A_1 compared to C_1, and $+60$ for A_2 compared to C_2. There was a 44% overlap of data points for A_1 to C_1 and a 33% overlap for A_2 to C_2.

Relative to data series B-C, the sign-alone (B) method was more effective than the oral method (C). The data for Group 1 words (C_1) showed a decelerating and decaying trend, while the data for the sign-alone method (B_1) showed a positive effect as demonstrated by an accelerating-improving trend. Both data paths showed variability. These results were replicated with Group 2 words (B_2 to C_2). The level change was a $+70$ for B_1 compared to C_1 and a $+25$ for B_2 compared to C_2. There was a 77% overlap of data points for B_1 to C_1 and no overlap for B_2 to C_2.

Relative to criterion verification checks, the checks supported the effectiveness of the total communication method. The first criterion verification check resulted in 25% more correct responses for words taught by the total communication method compared to those taught by the sign-alone method and 35% more correct responses than were obtained for words taught by the oral method. During the second criterion verification check the percentage correct for words taught using the total communication method was substantially higher than the other two methods. The levels were 65% more correct responses obtained by the total communication method compared to the sign-alone method and 75% more correct responses when compared to the oral method.

Relative to the total communication intensive training data series, this data series shows an accelerating and improving trend with a level change of $+25$ and a range of 45% to 70% correct responses.

Summary and conclusions. The authors' statements about the effectiveness of the total communication method over the sign-alone and oral methods were warranted. The total communication method was consistently more effective on Group 1 words, and the effects were replicated on Group 2 words. Also, scores on criterion verification checks were higher with the total communication method than with either the sign-alone or oral methods. The authors hypothesized that the total communication method may have been more effective than the other two methods because it involved a combination of vocal, visual (gestural), and kinesthetic cues instead of being limited to either vocal or gestural cues alone. The alternating treatments design permitted a quick comparison and replication of the three communication training methods.

Study II: Mildly Handicapped

Ollendick, T.H., Matson, J.L., Esveldt-Dawson, K., and Shapiro, E.S. Increasing spelling achievement: An analysis of treatment procedures utilizing an alternating treatments design. *Journal of Applied Behavior Analysis*, 1980, 13 (4), 645–654.

Purpose, subject, and setting. The purpose of the second study of a two-study investigation was to compare positive practice plus positive reinforcement to more traditional procedures for teaching spelling. The subjects were a girl and a boy hospitalized in a psychiatric facility. The girl (referred to as Child 3) was 13 years old and had been hospitalized due to her aggressive behavior and academic difficulties. The boy (referred to as Child 4) was 12 years old and also had been hospitalized for aggressive behavior. He did not, however, have any significant learning problems. He was included in the study to permit an examination of the generalizability of the intervention procedures to a child who was aggressive but not learning disabled. The procedures were implemented separately for each child by a teacher's aide in a classroom setting.

Dependent variable. The dependent measure was the number of words spelled correctly. The words were taken from the Sivaroti Classroom Reading Inventory, Equivalent Forms A, B, and C. The fourth- and fifth-grade forms were used with the girl and the seventh-grade forms were used with the boy. Eight words were selected from each of three equivalent forms and then were randomly assigned to the three remediation conditions. The accuracy of scoring the daily spelling tests was checked and "near 100% accuracy" was attained. Adherence to the intervention procedures also was checked and revealed that proper procedures were followed in all cases.

Independent variables. During the baseline phase students were instructed to write the spelling words on paper. No feedback on the accuracy of spelling the words was provided. During the positive practice plus positive reinforcement intervention students were required to listen to the word pronounced, pronounce the word correctly, say aloud each letter of the word, and write each misspelled word correctly five times. In addition, the children received a star beside each correctly spelled word and verbal praise from the teacher's aide. During the traditional intervention procedure the teacher's aide placed a check mark beside each misspelled word and wrote out the correct spelling. The child then was told to study the words. For the traditional plus positive reinforcement intervention, the same procedure was followed for the misspelled words, but the aide placed a star beside correctly spelled words and verbally praised spelling accuracy.

Design and condition sequence. An alternating treatments design was used to compare the procedures as illustrated in Figures 12-6 and 12-7. The words from Set A were assigned to the positive practice plus positive reinforcement condition; words from Set B were assigned to the traditional plus positive reinforcement condition; words from Set C were assigned to the traditional-alone condition. During the baseline phase the three sets of words were presented each day in a counterbalanced fashion. Likewise, in the alternating treatments phase the three intervention procedures were administered in counterbalanced order across three time periods. In the final phase, the most effective intervention, positive practice plus positive reinforcement, was used with all three sets of words across all time periods. For Child 3 the baseline phase lasted 5 days, the alternating treatments phase lasted 5 days, and the final phase lasted 6 days. For child 4 the baseline phase lasted 4 days, the alternating treatments phase lasted 5 days, and the final phase lasted 6 days.

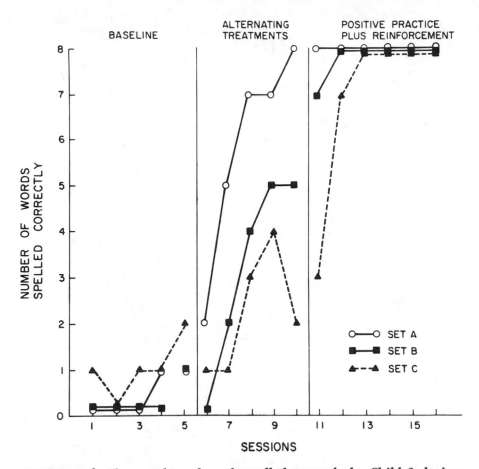

FIGURE 12-6 The number of words spelled correctly by Child 3 during the three experimental phases for the three sets of words. During the alternating treatments phase, words from Set A were assigned to the positive practice plus positive reinforcement condition; words from Set B were assigned to the, traditional plus positive reinforcement condition; and words from Set C were assigned to the traditional alone condition. During the last phase, positive practice plus positive reinforcement was used with all three sets of words. (Figure 3, p. 651, from: Ollendick, T.H., Matson, J.L. Esveldt-Dawson, K., and Shapiro, E.S. Increasing spelling achievement: An analysis of treatment procedures utilizing an alternating treatments design. *Journal of Applied Behavior Analysis*, 1980, *13* (4) 645–654. Copyright by Society for the Experimental Analysis of Behavior, Inc. Reproduced by permission.)

Results as reported by the authors. Positive practice plus positive reinforcement was more effective than the other two interventions during the alternating treatments phase. The traditional plus positive reinforcement condition was more effective than the traditional-alone procedure. When positive practice plus positive reinforcement was implemented in the final phase across all three sets of words and time periods, spelling performance increased and remained at 100% for both children.

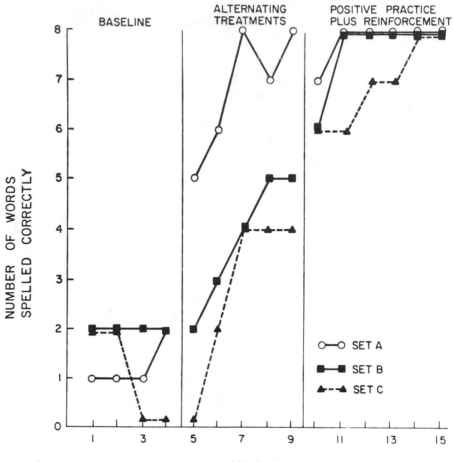

FIGURE 12-7   The number of words spelled correctly by Child 4 during the three experimental phases for the three sets of words. During the alternating treatments phase, words from Set A were assigned to the positive practice plus positive reinforcement condition; words from Set B were assigned to the traditional plus positive reinforcement condition; and words from Set C were assigned to the traditional alone condition. During the lag phase, positive practice plus positive reinforcement was used with all three sets of words. (Figure 4, p. 652, from: Ollendick, T.H., Matson, J.L., Esveldt-Dawson, K., and Shapiro, E.S. Increasing spelling achievement: An analysis of treatment procedures utilizing an alternating treatments design. *Journal of Applied Behavior Analysis*, 1980, 13 (4), 645–654. Copyright by Society for the Experimental Analysis of Behavior, Inc. Reproduced by permission.)

Summary and conclusions. The positive practice plus reinforcement intervention was demonstrated to be the *most* effective of the three procedures. During the alternating treatments phase there was only one overlapping data point for both subjects, thus providing a clear demonstration of experimental effect. The alternating treatments design permitted a rapid determination of which intervention was most effective in increasing the number of words spelled correctly. The most effective intervention was continued in the final phase, bringing mastery levels on all three sets of words to 100% correct.

Concluding Comments

The alternating treatments design permits a comparison of the effects of two or more interventions on a specified target behavior and controls for many of the threats to internal validity that are associated with the multitreatment design (e.g., sequential confounding). As summarized in Table 12-6, the alternating treatments design has been used in a variety of settings and with different population of students. Andersen and Redd (1980) compared the effectiveness of a standard instructional procedure to a generalization training procedure on the percent of appropriate behavior and the percent correct responses for four first graders receiving remedial reading instruction. Carnine (1981) employed an alternating treatments design to evaluate the effects of high and low presentation rates of direct instruction techniques on the academic and on-task behaviors of three preschoolers. Koop, Martin, Yu, and Suthons (1980) compared the effects of minimal social reinforcement and social reinforcement plus edible reinforcement on the number of errors emitted by one moderately retarded and four severely retarded adults in learning an assembly task. Loos, Williams, and Bailey (1977) compared the effects of a helping adult aide, a disciplinary adult aide, a helping fifth-grade aide, and no-aide control on the amount of academic work and the percent of on-task behavior of 54 third graders in two open classrooms. A potential weakness of their study, however, is that their design compared only one type of aide to a no-aide condition rather than alternating the three types of aides with each other and comparing the results. Murphey, Doughty, and Nunes (1979) employed an alternating treatments design to evaluate the effects of response contingent music over a no-music baseline condition on the upright head positioning of six nonambulatory, profoundly retarded, multihandicapped students enrolled in a public school program.

Neef, Iwata, and Page (1980) compared the effects of an interspersed training procedure and a high density reinforcement procedure on the number of spelling words mastered by three mentally retarded students. Redd, Ullmann, Stelle, and Roesch (1979) compared the effects of tutors who provided contingent reinforcement based on school performance and tutors who reinforced noncontingently on the academic performance of four underachieving first graders. Tarpley and Schroeder (1979) compared the effects of differential reinforcement of other behavior (DRO) and differential reinforcement of incompatible behavior (DRI) on the self-injurious behavior of three profoundly retarded institutionalized persons.

In conclusion, the alternating treatments design permits the applied researcher to compare the effects of several interventions in a relatively short period of time. Many of the internal validity problems of history and maturation are avoided because of the rapid alternation of interventions. The sequence effects associated with the multitreatment design are also avoided as a function of interventions being introduced in a counterbalanced order within the same time frame. Carryover effects may be present but can be minimized if stimulus discrimination is achieved. The alternating treatments design is particularly useful when variable baseline data are present and when the target behavior is nonreversible as in the case of academic tasks (Ulman & Sulzer-Azaroff, 1975).

TABLE 12-6   Examples of alternating treatments designs (ATD).

Reference	Subject(s)	Dependent Variable(s)	Independent Variable(s)
Carnine (1981) [multielement research design]	3 normal preschoolers in a preschool classroom	Percentage of correct answers; percent of on-task behavior	Low levels of direct instruction presentation techniques (A) were contrasted with high levels (B). They were alternated daily for the first 10 days and every third day for the next 12 days. B condition was continued for the final two days
Koop, Martin, Yu, & Suthons (1980) [multielement design]	1 moderately retarded, 4 severely retarded adults in an institution	Errors to task criterion in assembly tasks (bicycle brake, fishing reel, Lego building blocks)	Minimal social reinforcement conditions (A) were compared to social plus edible reinforcement conditions (B). Counterbalancing of reinforcement conditions and tasks across clients was used
Loos, Williams, & Bailey (1977) [multielement design]	54 3rd graders in two "open" style classrooms	Academic output (units completed and percentage of on-task behavior)	Three types of aide conditions, helping adult (B), disciplinary adult (C), and helping 5th-grade aide (D), were compared to a standard no aide condition (A). Conditions were randomly sequenced in each class across the 4 language arts periods each week
Murphey, Doughty, & Nunes (1979) [multielement design]	6 nonambulatory, profoundly retarded, multihandicapped students in a public school program	Percent of time the learner's head was in an upright position	A response-contingent reinforcement condition (B) was compared with a baseline condition (A). During condition A no music was available and during condition B music was contingent upon upright head positioning. Conditions were alternated within sessions with the order of presentation counterbalanced across days
Redd, Ullmann, Stelle, & Roesch (1979) [multielement baseline design]	4 underachieving 1st graders receiving tutoring after school	Percent of on-task behavior; number of problems completed	The effects of a tutor who provided material reinforcers after school (B) was compared to a tutor who provided noncontingent reinforcement (A). Sequence of tutors was randomized but each child met with both tutors twice a week
Tarpley & Schroeder (1979) [multiple schedule design]	3 profoundly retarded persons in an institution	Percentage of intervals containing self-injurious behavior	A baseline condition (A) was compared to a differential reinforcement of other behaviors procedure (B)

TABLE 12-6   (continued)

Reference	Subject(s)	Dependent Variable(s)	Independent Variable(s)
			and a differential reinforcement of incompatible behaviors procedure (C). Daily sessions of 36 minutes were used. The DRO (B) and DRI (C) procedures were alternated in the 1st and 3rd positions with baseline (A) in the middle for all sessions.
Anderson & Redd (1980) [multielement design]	4 1st-grade students considered distractible and deficient in reading	Percent of appropriate behavior and percent correct on reading lessons	Standard instruction (A) was compared to generalization training (B) on 2 types of reading tasks. The tasks assigned to the types of instruction were counterbalanced across students. Probes were conducted on both tasks to assess performance levels
Neef, Iwata, & Page (1980) [multielement design]	1 deaf and 2 trainable mentally retarded adults enrolled in an educational program	Cumulative number of spelling words mastered	A high density reinforcement condition (B) was compared to an interspersed training condition (C) following a baseline condition (A). B and C conditions were presented in a randomly alternating order.

The Simultaneous Treatment Design

The alternating treatments design generally encompasses the characteristics of those single subject designs that have been designated in the literature as multiple schedule and multielement designs. Alternating treatments designs also have been referred to (and often confused with) simultaneous treatment designs when, in fact, these two types of designs can be differentiated. Table 12-7 illustrates the similarities and differences between the alternating treatments and simultaneous treatment designs.

The simultaneous treatment design (STD) is sometimes referred to as a concurrent schedule design (e.g., Hersen & Barlow, 1976; Kratochwill, 1978). The design requires the simultaneous or concurrent application of two or more interventions with a single subject (or group of subjects). Like the alternating treatments design, the simultaneous treatment design counterbalances the presentation of interventions. The important distinction between the two designs is the way in which the interventions are presented. In the simultaneous treatment design all interventions are available to the learner at the same time during the experimental or comparison phase, requiring the learner to choose between the interventions. In contrast, the interventions in

TABLE 12-7   Characteristics of alternating treatments and simultaneous treatment designs.

	Alternating Treatments Design	Simultaneous Treatment Design
Other labels used in research	Multiple schedule, multielement baseline simultaneous treatment (the latter is often used erroneously)	Concurrent schedule
Basic feature	Fast alternation of two or more interventions	Simultaneous or concurrent presentation of two or more interventions
Time factor	Interventions can be alternated within sessions, across time of day (morning and afternoon), or across days (Monday/Wednesday and Tuesday/Thursday).	All interventions always available to the subject(s)
Baseline condition	Does not have to be stable before interventions are introduced, baseline can be continued throughout the study if comparisons are desired	Does not have to be stable before interventions are introduced, baseline condition comparison optional
Counterbalancing requirements	Should be counterbalanced across time, teachers, and other variables of interest in a rapidly alternating sequence	Counterbalanced across teachers at designated points so that all personnel administer all interventions to rule out preference for a particular person
Stimulus discrimination	Must be established through the use of verbal instructions, color cues, etc.	Not specifically programmed. Requires subject to discriminate response contingencies.
Experimental control	Demonstrated when patterns of responding vary with the alternating conditions and there is minimal overlap	Demonstrated when patterns of responding vary according to the interventions and there is minimal overlap
Major advantages	Stable baseline not required	Stable baseline not required
	Behaviors do not have to be reversed to demonstrate control	Behaviors do not have to be reversed to demonstrate control
	Several interventions can be compared at the same time	Several interventions can be compared at the same time
	Early termination of a study is less critical	Early termination of a study is less critical

the alternating treatments design are presented in a rapidly alternating counterbalanced sequence. Assume that a teacher is interested in comparing the effectiveness of the contingent delivery of edibles (B) and descriptive verbal praise (C) on the frequency with which an autistic child makes eye contact with an adult in his environment. With the alternating treatments design the delivery of edibles and the delivery of descriptive verbal praise would be rapidly alternated across the comparison phase of the investigation. Each intervention would be paired consistently with a specific stimulus, such as a different colored smock worn by the teacher (e.g., blue smock indicating descriptive verbal praise and a white smock, edible reinforcement). The teacher might choose to conduct two sessions per day, one in the morning and one in the afternoon. On one day edibles would be delivered in the morning and descriptive verbal praise in the afternoon; on the following day descriptive verbal praise would be delivered in the morning and edibles in the afternoon, contingent upon the child's making eye contact with the teacher. If during the course of the study the student's frequency of eye contact with the teacher is consistently higher when one intervention is available (e.g., edible reinforcement), this intervention could then be continued. In contrast, with the simultaneous treatment design the two interventions would be available to the student at all times during the comparison phase of the study. This would require the presence of two adults during each observation, each consistently associated with one of the two interventions. The student would receive either an edible or descriptive verbal praise for eye contact depending upon the teacher he approached. After a consistent pattern of responding was established, the two teachers would switch the consequences they delivered in order to separate the effect of the intervention from the student's preference for a particular teacher. As with the alternating treatments design, the investigator could continue with the intervention that increased the child's eye contact with an adult most effectively.

Internal and External Validity

Experimental control with the simultaneous treatment design is demonstrated in much the same way as with the alternating treatments design. The data for each intervention are plotted separately, and a comparison is made between the individual data paths of each intervention, focusing on differences in level and the percentage of overlap. If one intervention has resulted in consistently higher levels of responding (or lower levels, depending upon the target behavior) and the percentage of overlap in the data for each intervention is minimal, then a reliable experimental effect has been demonstrated. That is, internal validity is achieved when one intervention is consistently associated with higher (or lower) levels of responding over consecutive observation periods. Since all interventions are introduced at the same time, threats to internal validity, such as historical and maturational factors, are equalized for all interventions.

As with all single subject research designs, the external validity of the findings of a simultaneous treatment design is demonstrated when similar results are evidenced with different subjects, on different behaviors, and/or under different stimulus conditions (e.g., settings). As Birnbrauer (1981) has indicated, external validity is not simply an existing element in any type of single subject research; instead, the process of generalization must be pursued actively by researchers interested in determining functional similarities between studies. In all cases, regardless of whether the researcher is using a multitreatment, alternating treatments, or simultaneous treatment design, the baseline conditions, intervention procedures, characteristics of the learners, and a description of the conditions under which the study was conducted should be delineated fully to facilitate replication and, thus, the generality of the findings.

Considerations

Guidelines

When using the simultaneous treatment design one should:

1. Operationally define all intervention procedures.

2. Instruct personnel in the intervention procedures they will be administering.

3. Determine a schedule for counterbalancing all variables which potentially could confound the results.

4. Collect baseline condition data (A).

5. Introduce the interventions (B and C) concurrently, so that all interventions are available to the subject.

6. After a designated length of time, counterbalance the interventions across the personnel, i.e., the person who was administering intervention B now administers C and vice versa.

7. Continue the most effective intervention (B or C) in the final phase of the study.

Once the dependent variable has been identified, interventions to be compared should be defined. Personnel who will be participating in the study should be taught the specific intervention they initially will be administering. After collecting baseline data, introduce two or more interventions (B and C) at the same time and keep them available to the subject for the duration of the experimental comparison phase. The baseline condition may be continued, if desired, to compare baseline performance levels with the levels generated by each intervention. Counterbalancing interventions across personnel, times, and locations should occur at designated points during the investigation to rule out the possibility that any one of these factors is influencing the data during a certain intervention. The subject must be allowed to choose between interventions i.e., make a free-operant response. The intervention period should continue until a consistent pattern emerges. The most effective treatment can then be continued in a final period of the study (Barlow & Hayes, 1979; Browning, 1967). Figure 12-8 illustrates a graphic display of a simultaneous treatment design in which verbal reprimand (A), redirection (B), and DRO (C) are compared. This example illus-

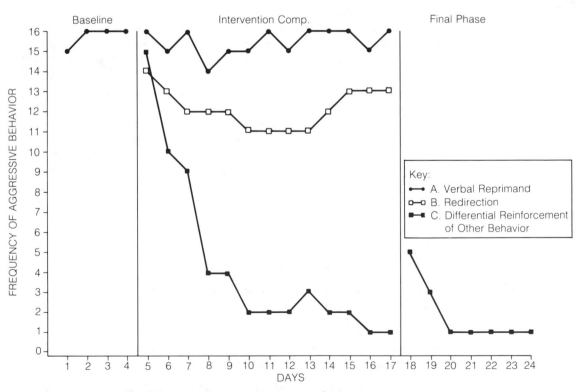

FIGURE 12-8   Example of the simultaneous treatment design.

trates a simultaneous treatment design which consists of a baseline condition (A), an intervention comparison phase (B and C), and a final phase when the most effective intervention (C) was continued in isolation. The data for B and C must appear daily and an equal number of times since they are implemented concurrently and both are always available to the learner. Baseline condition data and total frequency of the behavior could also be plotted through the duration of the study if desired.

Advantages

The primary advantage of the simultaneous treatment design is that it enables a comparison of the effects of different interventions on a target behavior at the same time, thereby controlling for a sequential confounding. In addition, the design is time efficient and does not require a return to baseline conditions or a reversal of behavior (Browning, 1967; Kazdin & Hartmann, 1978).

Limitations

Kratochwill (1978) has discussed several disadvantages associated with the simultaneous treatment or concurrent schedule design. First, the investigator is warned that the design requires extensive planning and monitoring of individuals charged with implementing the interventions. Second, there is the likelihood of confounding in regard to experimenters, time factors, or a combination of the two. Third, there is the possibility that subjects may have difficulty in discriminating which intervention is associated with which investigator when several interventions are available and when investigators switch interventions. A final disadvantage of the simultaneous treatment design is that it may not be logistically feasible to present more than one intervention at a time because of the extra personnel required.

Applied Examples: Simultaneous Treatment Design

Study I: Behavior Disordered

Browning, R.M. A same-subject design for simultaneous comparison of three reinforcement contingencies. *Behavior Research and Therapy*, 1967, *5*, 237–243.

Purpose, subject, and setting. The purpose of this study was to evaluate the effects of three reinforcement contingencies on a child's "grandiose bragging." The subject was a 9-year, 11-month-old male admitted to a residential treatment center with a diagnosis of "psychoneurotic, anxiety reaction." The study was conducted in the treatment center by cottage staff members.

Dependent variable. The dependent variable was the number of grandiose bragging responses by the subject. The bragging behavior consisted of seeking out a staff member and telling a lengthy and untrue story, often related to himself. Staff members periodically checked each other for interobserver agreement but reliability data were not reported.

Independent variable. The independent variables were the reinforcement conditions of positive interest and praise (B), verbal admonishment (C), and purposely ignoring (D). During the positive interest and praise condition the subject was encouraged to tell more about whatever he was bragging about. The verbal admonishment condition consisted of scolding the subject for lying or telling a story that did not make sense. The final condition consisted of ignoring the subject's bragging.

Design and condition sequence. A simultaneous treatment design was used to evaluate the effect each of the three experimental conditions had on the subject's "grandiose bragging." Following a 4-week "uncontrolled" baseline condition, and a 1-week "controlled" baseline condition, during which time staff members ignored each bragging episode while recording its frequency, the simultaneous treatment comparison phase was implemented. The comparison phase continued over a 3-week period. The interventions of positive attention (B), verbal admonishment (C), and purposely ignoring (D) were presented by three groups of staff members, with two staff members assigned to each group. Over the 3-week comparison phase each group of staff members delivered each of the three interventions for 1 week in counterbalanced order. Rotating treatments weekly across staff members controlled for the subject's possible preference for a single staff member. Throughout the simultaneous comparison phase all three consequences for bragging were made available to the subject, though he was exposed to only one of the three treatment conditions depending on which staff member he approached. After 3 weeks of the simultaneous comparison phase, a final experimental phase was implemented during which all staff members responded to bragging occurrences by purposely ignoring (D).

Results as reported by the author. Figure 12-9 shows the weekly mean frequency of the subject's bragging responses throughout the course of the study and for each of the three treatment conditions during the simultaneous comparison phase. Based on these data, Browning concluded that the pur-

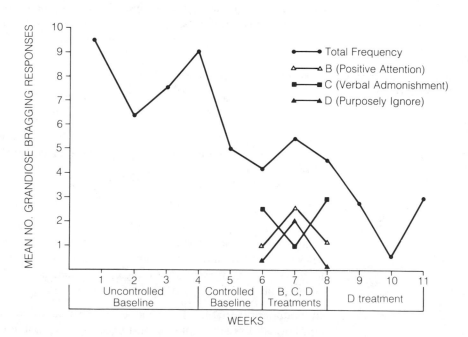

FIGURE 12-9   Total mean frequency of grandiose bragging responses throughout study and for each reinforcement contingency during experimental period. (Figure 3, p. 241, from: Browning, R.M. A same-subject design for simultaneous comparison of three reinforcement contingencies. *Behaviour Research and Therapy*, 1967, *5*, 237–243. Reprinted with permission. Copyright 1967, Pergamon Press, Ltd.)

posely ignoring contingency (D) was more effective than the positive attention (B) and verbal admonishment (C) contingencies in reducing the frequency
of the subject's bragging responses. This finding was statistically significant at
the p = .01 level.

Browning (1967) offered these advantages for the simultaneous treatment
design:

> 1) staff are not required to replicate a baseline period as demanded in the ABAB
> design; 2) several reinforcement contingencies may be compared simultaneously
> by counter-balancing for sequence effects; 3) an appropriate statistical test is
> available for such a same-subject design (Benjamin, 1965); 4) the design satisfies
> the basic requirement of a same-subject study of demonstrating that the behavior
> varies in relation to treatment conditions. (pp. 242–243).

Summary and conclusions. The effectiveness of the purposely ignoring condition over positive attention and verbal admonishment conditions is substantiated by a visual analysis of the blocked data. Except during the second week
of the comparison phase when verbal admonishment resulted in a lower
mean frequency of bragging responses compared to purposely ignoring, the
purposely ignoring contingency was consistently more effective in controlling
the frequency of grandiose bragging.

There are, however, several factors that weaken the experimental findings.
First, the weekly blocking of the data, as presented in Figure 12-9, precludes a
detailed visual analysis of the graphic data. This weakens the study since in
the second week of the comparison fewer responses occurred in the verbal
admonishment condition than in the purposely ignoring condition. This may
have occurred because the subject still approached staff members who had
been associated with another contingency the previous week. Had data been
plotted daily, this hypothesis might have been verified if the two episodes of
bragging to staff assigned to the purposely ignoring condition had been
recorded on the first day of the second week. Second, the overall trend on
the total frequency of bragging episodes was decelerating in a therapeutic
direction over the 11 weeks of the investigation. And third, reliability coefficients were not reported on the subject's bragging responses or on staff
members' adhering to treatment condition contingencies. It should be noted,
however, that the primary contribution of this investigation was not its
experimental findings, but rather its clear description of a new single subject
research design.

The Browning (1967) study remains the only true example of the simultaneous treatment design in the applied rsearch literature (Barlow & Hayes,
1979; Hersen & Barlow, 1976). However, a number of researchers have
conducted studies in which they used a design labelled as simultaneous
treatment. In all cases the procedure involved alternating the presentation of
interventions rather than presenting them concurrently. Therefore, using the
criteria established by Ulman and Sulzer-Azaroff (1975) and Barlow and
Hayes (1979), the designs would be appropriately labelled as alternating
treatments designs rather than simultaneous treatment designs.

A study is presented to describe an alternating intervention that the investigators labelled a simultaneous treatment design. An analysis of this study shows
how the design meets the criteria established for the alternating treatments
design, rather than the simultaneous treatment design.

Study II: Mildly Handicapped

Kazdin, A.E., & Geesey, S.Simultaneous-treatment design comparisons of the effects of earning reinforcers for one's peers versus for oneself. *Behavior Therapy*, 1977, *8*, 682–693.

Purpose, subject, and setting. The purpose of this study was to compare the effects of two different ways of dispensing reinforcers on the attentive behavior of two mentally retarded children. The subjects were male students in a special education classroom. Dick was 9 years old and had a Stanford Binet IQ score of 80. Max was 7 years old and had a Stanford Binet IQ score of 75. The boys were selected because of their inattentive and disruptive behavior during work sessions. The teacher administered the interventions at different times for each subject while they were in the special education classroom.

Dependent variable. The dependent measure was the percent of attentive behavior demonstrated by the subjects. Attentive behavior was equivalent to the child's sitting in his seat and working on his arithmetic or reading workbook assignment. The child had to be attentive for the entire 10 seconds of the observational interval in order for that interval to be counted. Reliability checks were completed on 68.3% of the total observation periods. Interrater reliability ranged from 86.4% to 100% with a median of 92.9%.

Independent variable. During the baseline phase no specific contingencies were used to modify the behavior. During the token reinforcement phase the subject could either earn tokens which could be exchanged for back-up events for himself (self-exchange), or he could earn tokens which could be exchanged for back-up events for himself and the rest of the class (class-exchange). The teacher announced to the class on the first day of the comparative treatments phase that the subject could occasionally earn rewards for the whole group by working hard. For the remainder of the alternating treatments phase the teacher privately told the subject whether he was earning tokens for himself or for the class at the beginning of each observational period. Also during that period a specific card for either self- or class-exchange was marked by the teacher to further signal which contingency was in effect. When the predetermined point value was attained, the subject was allowed to draw a token from a lottery jar to determine the back-up event, and it was administered to the subject or to the entire class depending on which contingency was in effect.

Design and condition sequence. An alternating treatments design was used to compare the effects of the two contingencies, as illustrated in Figure 12-10 (data for Max). The authors referred to the design as a simultaneous treatment design, but, according to the criteria presented in this chapter and by Ulman and Sulzer-Azaroff (1975) and Barlow and Hayes (1979), it meets the requirements of an alternating treatments design. Since the two contingencies were alternated and counterbalanced across time periods rather than presented concurrently, the simultaneous treatment design criteria were not met.

The baseline phase for Max lasted 9 days. The alternating treatments phase, in which the self-exchange and class-exchange token contingencies were counterbalanced across time periods, lasted 8 days. In the final phase, the most effective intervention, class-exchange, was continued for 5 additional days during both time periods.

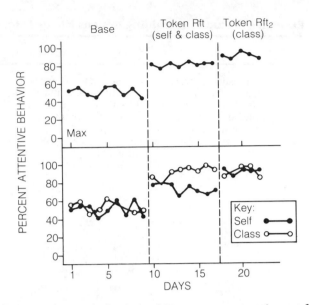

FIGURE 12-10   Attentive behavior of Max across experimental conditions.
Baseline (base)—no experimental intervention. Token reinforcement (token rft)
—implementative of the token program where tokens earned could purchase events
for himself (self) or the entire class (class). Second phase of token reinforcement
(token rft₂)—implementation of the class exchange intervention across both time
periods. The upper panel presents the overall data collapsed across time periods and
interventions; the lower panel presents the data according to the time periods across
which the interventions were balanced, although the interventions were presented
only in the last two phases. (Figure 2, p. 690, from: Kazdin, A.E. and Geesey, S.
Simultaneous-treatment design comparisons of the effects of earning reinforcers for
one's peers versus for oneself. *Behavior Therapy*, 1977, *8*, 682–693. Copyright 1977 by
the Association for Advancement of Behavior Therapy. Reprinted by permission of the
publisher and the author.)

Results as reported by the authors. Kazdin and Geesey (1977) concluded
that the procedure of allowing subjects to exchange tokens for reinforcers for
the entire group was more effective in increasing attentive behavior than
allowing each subject to exchange tokens for activities for himself. The
authors also commented on the utility of the design for comparing interventions in an efficient manner.

Summary and conclusions. The class-exchange contingency was demonstrated
to be the more effective of the two procedures. During the alternating
treatments phase there was only one overlapping data point, strengthening
the demonstration of experimental effect. The alternating treatments design
permitted a rapid demonstration of which contingency was more effective for
increasing the percent of attention behavior. The more effective intervention
was continued in the final phase during both time periods.

**Concluding
Comments**   The simultaneous treatment design permits a comparative analysis of the
effects of several interventions implemented concurrently. As previously
mentioned, the Browning (1967) study is the only true example of the design
in the applied research literature. Several studies that have used designs with
characteristics associated with the alternating treatments design have been

TABLE 12-8   Examples of studies containing designs labelled simultaneous treatment.*

Reference	Subject(s)	Dependent Variable(s)	Independent Variable(s)
Foxx (1977)	1 autistic, 2 severely retarded children enrolled in a day-care intensive learning program	Percentage of trials in which eye contact was made within 5 seconds of a verbal prompt	For 1 learner: Baseline (A) consisting of edibles and praise compared to functional movement training (B). The criterion level for eye contact increased from a glance to 2 seconds; duration of functional movement training was increased from 2 to 5 minutes. Counterbalancing of interventions across therapists was used. Design was combined with a changing criterion design for 2 learners and with a multiple baseline across therapists for 1 learner
Kazdin (1977)	1 educably mentally retarded child in a special education classroom	Percentage of attentive behavior	Experiment 1: Baseline (A), Approval, phase which consisted of reinforcement for 10 seconds of attentive behavior preceded by 20 seconds of inattentive behavior (B) compared to reinforcement for 10 seconds preceded by 20 seconds of attentive behavior (C). C condition was continued in a final phase. Administration of the B and C conditions was counterbalanced across 2 time periods and 2 reinforcing agents
Kazdin & Mascitelli (1980)	2 educably mentally retarded children in a special education classroom	Percentage of attentive behavior	Baseline (A), regular contingency condition (B) in which the child earned tokens for attentive behavior that could be exchanged for back-up reinforcers compared to an earn-off contingency condition (C) in which the child earned tokens exchangeable for reinforcers but also earned himself off the token system for another period. C condition was continued in a final phase. Administration of the B and C conditions was counterbalanced across time periods. Condition in effect at a particular time was announced by the teacher and was indicated by color-coded recording cards

TABLE 12-8   (continued)

Reference	Subject(s)	Dependent Variable(s)	Independent Variable(s)
McCullough, Cornell, McDaniel, & Mueller (1974)	1 1st-grade student in a regular classroom	Percentage of cooperative behavior	Baseline (A), social reinforcement for coopera- tive behavior and ignor- ing uncooperative behavior (B) was compared to social reinforcement for cooperative behavior and time out for uncooperative behavior (C). Condition C was continued in a final phase. Counterbalancing occurred across personnel (teacher and teacher aide) and time (morning and afternoon). The teacher administered B for two days while the aide adminis- tered C. For the next two days they swapped contingencies. The alterna- tion of time periods continued throughout the intervention comparison period.
Brady & Smouse (1978)	1 autistic child receiv- ing services from a state child guidance center	Frequency of correct responses (tapping re- quested object)	Following a baseline condition (A) the three treatment conditions of manual signing (B), vocaliza- tion (C) and total communication (D) were compared. The three treatments were alternated within a single session and counterbalanced across three experimenters. The D condition was continued in the final phase.

*The studies listed in this table meet the criteria presented for alternating treatments designs but were labelled simultaneous treatment by the investigators.

mislabelled simultaneous treatment designs based on others' criteria (Barlow & Hayes, 1979; Ulman & Sulzer-Azaroff, 1975). In these cases, the interventions actually were alternated rather than presented concurrently. Table 12-8 sum- marizes five such studies. Foxx (1977) compared the effectiveness of func- tional movement training (an overcorrection procedure) plus edibles and praise to edibles and praise alone on the development of eye contact in one autistic and two severely retarded children. Kazdin (1977) compared the effects of differential reinforcement on the frequency of inattentiveness and attentiveness that preceded a target response of a mentally retarded child in a special education classroom. Kazdin and Mascitelli (1980) compared a condi- tion permitting the child to exchange tokens for back-up reinforcers to a condition in which the child could earn his way out of the token economy. The percent of attention of two educably mentally retarded children in a special education classroom was compared. McCullough, Cornell, McDaniel, and Mueller (1974) compared the effect of contingent social reinforcement for cooperative behavior and ignoring uncooperative behavior, with social reinforcement for cooperative behavior and time-out for reinforcement for uncooperative behavior with a first grade boy who exhibited disruptive behavior. The results of the McCullough *et al.* (1974) study must be examined carefully since the comparison of the two interventions lasted only 4 days; the most effective intervention, however, was continued in isolation over a third phase of the study, and the results were maintained. Brady and Smouse (1978) compared the effectiveness of total communication, a sign-based approach, and a verbalization procedure on the acquisition of an experimental language by an autistic child. The order of the procedure was alternated within a training session and counterbalanced across three experimenters.

In conclusion, the simultaneous treatment design permits a comparison of the effects of two or more interventions concurrently, Its practical use in applied settings, however, is limited because of the number of individuals needed to implement the interventions and the counterbalancing that must occur in order to separate intervention effects from other variables.

SUMMARY

This chapter has described three types of single subject research designs that enable an applied researcher to compare the effects of several interventions on a targeted behavior. The multitreatment design allows the investigator to examine the effects of interventions that are presented singly or as part of an intervention package; the results, however, may be confounded by sequence and carryover effects. The simultaneous treatment design permits the comparison of several interventions that are implemented concurrently, but it has limited possibilities in applied settings because of the number of personnel required and the degree of counterbalancing that must be accomplished. The alternating treatment design is the most practical of the three comparative intervention designs primarily because it involves the rapid alternation of interventions but avoids many of the problems associated with multiple treatment designs. In addition, it can be employed by one investigator who randomly alternates between interventions and thus it is more practical in terms of personnel time. The alternating treatments design is especially useful in cases where baseline data are variable and where the target behavior cannot or should not be reversed for practical or ethical reasons. For these reasons the alternating treatments design is useful in educational settings when a teacher wants to compare the effects of two or more interventions on academic or social behaviors.

SECTION FOUR

WRITING TASKS AND ETHICAL BEHAVIOR

13
WRITING TASKS FOR
SINGLE SUBJECT
RESEARCH

Earlier chapters have presented a rationale for conducting single subject research in educational settings and described a range of design alternatives. This chapter describes three writing tasks that are a necessary, though perhaps not initially reinforcing, part of the research process: (1) preparing a thesis proposal, (2) writing results for journal publication, and (3) developing proposals for extramural funding. Each product contains the same basic information but is written for a different audience and to accomplish a different objective. Each becomes critically important at different phases in the career of the graduate student who must meet requirements for graduation, who wishes to conduct research in the classroom, and who, after completing advanced degrees finds herself in a position in which publishing and obtaining research funding are major criteria for success. Students who enter short-term programs, e.g., a one-year master's program that requires experimental thesis research, may find that a task that seemed vague and remote when they applied to graduate school becomes real, immediate, and critical as soon as their first term begins. Selecting a topic of interest, preparing a research proposal, and organizing to conduct the research become priority tasks. Students who have lived life fully have undoubtedly encountered one or another of Murphy's laws (nothing proceeds as planned; everything takes twice as long; if anything can go wrong, it will go wrong) and can assume that they apply to the research process. That knowledge may be the impetus to begin the first of these writing tasks early in the program.

The audience for the student research proposal may be the student's advisor, a departmental thesis review committee, and, eventually the institution's human subjects review committee (see Chapter 14). The objectives are to convince the thesis advisor(s) that the idea is sound, that the project has been

This chapter was written by **James W. Tawney** and **David L. Gast**.

thought through fully, i.e., the procedures are sufficiently detailed to convince the advisor(s) that the student knows what she is doing, and that the project is manageable, Then, as described in Chapter 14, the human subjects review committee will want to know that the rights or the subjects have been "assured" and that there is no potential risk.

Writing for journal publication is another matter. The first audience is a review panel, comprised of experts who determine, for the general readership, if a manuscript represents a novel contribution to the field, if the research methodology and procedures are sound, if the results are substantial, whether the results have been interpreted accurately and conservatively, and whether, generally, the information advances science. The second audience, the general readership, is comprised of individuals who have similar interests and who will be evaluating the article, if published, using essentially the same criteria. The difference, in this case, is that the first group determines whether the manuscript is publishable.

Writing for journal publication is a competitive process. Authors compete for space in a journal that has defined parameters, e.g., n pages per issue and n issues per year. As a field grows, e.g., as applied behavior analysis has grown since *JABA* was initiated in 1968, competition increases and predictable outcomes occur, i.e., the number of manuscripts submitted increases, the number of acceptable manuscripts increases, or larger numbers are rejected. If the number increases, but journal size remains the same, a backlog of accepted manuscripts develops and then the journal must either publish special issues to clear the backlog or else the lag between acceptance and publication grows. Then, as specialty areas develop and as publication lags increase, new journals are created. The number of journals listed below documents this phenomenon and, as well, the rapid growth of applied behavior analysis. The student-researcher who hopes to publish should understand the realities of the situation. Generally, this means working closely with the advisor and relying on peer evaluators for technical assistance and feedback.

Behavioral Journals

Journal of Experimental Analysis of Behavior
Behavior Research and Therapy
Journal of Applied Behavior Analysis
Journal of Behavior Therapy and Experimental Psychiatry
Behavior Therapy
Nordisk Tidskrift for Beteendeterapi
Behaviorism
Behavioral Engineering
Behavioral Analysis and Modification
Mexican Journal of Behavior Analysis
Addictive Behaviors
Biofeedback and Self-Regulation
Advances in Behavior Research and Therapy
Behavior Modification
Journal of Organizational Behavioral Management

Journal of Behavioral Medicine
Apprendizaje Y Comportamiento
The Behavior Analyst
Child Behavior Therapy
Behavioral Assessment
Journal of Behavioral Assessment
Les Therapies Comportamentales
Revista Pervana De Analisis De La Conducta
Behavioral Counseling Quarterly
Behavioral Medicine Abstract
Clinical Behavior Therapy Review
Behavioral Research of Severe Developmental Disabilities
Behavioral Psychotherapy
Education and Treatment of Children
Analysis and Intervention in Developmental Disabilities

Applying to federal agencies or private foundations for research funds is an even more competitive process, especially since economic factors have reduced the availability of federal funds. The procedures of the funding agency dictate the audience for whom the proposal is written. Federal agencies solicit proposals annually, or periodically, through an announcement that describes the federal priorities, the nature of research (basic or applied) permitted, and other factors deemed important. When proposals are received at the agency, they may be sent to a group of professionals for review. Those that survive with positive ratings may then be forwarded to another panel of reviewers who rank the proposals according to defined criteria. This information is used by federal project officers when they make their final decision. They follow an internal review procedure, which evaluates decisions at different levels within their administrative unit. The audience, then, is unknown to the person who submits a proposal. It is a review by professional colleagues, though the term is interpreted broadly.

Private foundations employ a variety of strategies, which may range from casual to highly formal. In some cases, a letter outlining a research strategy may be sufficient information for a board composed of the family or business associates of the founders of the organization. In other circumstances, a highly formal process may involve review by a group of the foundation's professional staff, then review by professional consultants, and finally formal review by the foundation's board, which makes decisions based on the professional review. Foundations publish their priorities and often provide examples of the activities they support. Whether one writes to federal or private agencies, it is reasonable to assume that there is intense competition for available funds. In one federal program, once the Research Program of the Bureau of Education for the Handicapped (currently the Research Projects Branch of the Office of Special Education), in a recent annual competition, approximately 300 proposals were submitted. Of those, ten were funded. Because the competition is so intense, grant writers are often supplied with guidelines for preparing proposals. In some cases, the critical elements are transferred into a proposal evaluation sheet, and the components are weighted in order of importance. Although the specific objectives differ from program to program, there are some common questions that guide reviewers' decision making: Does the request fall within the scope of the funding program? Has a critical problem been identified by an exhaustive review of the *pertinent* literature? Does the approach represent a reasonable solution to the problem? Are the procedures written in such detail that reviewers are convinced the investigator knows what she is doing? Will the project generate new and useful information? Is the cost warranted by the proposed benefit? Do the investigator and her sponsoring agency have the resources to carry out the task? If the project delivers what is proposed, will the results be made available to others? These questions are broader in scope than those considered critical to the preparation of thesis proposals and journal articles, reflecting, in part, concern that the funds will produce a payoff; results that have immediate practical application.

In summary, the research process begins when an investigator decides there is something she *wants to know*. To study the problem through systematic research, the investigator must convince others that the need to know can be satisfied without risk or abuse to others and that it is reasonable to spend a certain amount of money to find out. Having answered the question through the proposed research, we assume the investigator is motivated to share the information with others. Having differentiated among the writing tasks needed to be successful in each situation, our attention now turns to developing the written products.

A Caveat

This chapter contains suggestions for writing proposals and manuscripts that may become published articles. That is all they are. They provide guidance through components of the writing task, some of which are well defined by convention or by established guidelines for authors. There is no such thing as a free lunch, and there is no guarantee that following these suggestions will lead to fame, fortune, or a journal publication. At best, we can perhaps increase the likelihood of that event, but that is all.

Prerequisite Behaviors and Tools

The following behaviors, it would seem, should be part of the students' repertoire. They are prerequisites, we believe, to developing proposals and manuscripts. They include the student's ability to:

1. Identify critical research problems from existing literature or from observation of behavioral events.

2. Identify common elements and discontinuities in a body of literature.

3. Follow grammatical rules in ordinary writing.

4. Use standard style manuals, e.g., the *Publication Manual of the American Psychological Association* (1974).

5. Use standard reference tools, including library computer reference systems.

Students who are not confident with their mastery of these skills might:

1. Select a body of research, read recommendations in the discussion sections, and list common recommendations.

2. Analyze a defined set of studies, list agreements/disagreements among findings, list similarities/differences in procedures, identify possible reasons for the findings, and share this analysis with other students or professors for evaluative feedback.

3. Register for a course in technical writing.

4. Acquire a library of style manuals and study them before starting a project.

5. Take advantage of libraries' guided tours and technical assistance services.

Preparing a Thesis Proposal

The following process applies to the development of a basic outline for a master's thesis or doctoral dissertation. While the minimum requirement may be a brief outline of objectives and procedures, and the maximum may be a fully developed study (lacking results and discussion), both have common elements. This section starts with the most basic steps. In essence, these basic steps are expanded or modified, as the thesis proposal develops into a manuscript, or perhaps, forms the nucleus of a proposal for research funding

The frame of reference for this process is a master's level student, with some teaching experience, enrolled in a program designed to teach an advanced set of instructional behaviors. This student, we assume, enters the program with some awareness that during the previous teaching years some things worked and some did not. Or some interventions worked occasionally, but not always. These experiences set the stage for an "attitude of inquiry" or, for verbal statements of this nature: "I would like to know more about _____ teaching procedure." "Under what conditions will _____ correction procedure work?" "Is it possible to conduct an empirical test of the _____ reading program?" Three assumptions are embedded in this context: the student (1) has an experiential repertoire, (2) understands that trying something, even if unsuccessful, represents hypothesis testing in a general sense, and (3) exhibits an active interest in inquiry.

Selecting a Topic   The setting events just described are intended to increase the probability that students recall their teaching experiences and the interesting problems they encountered. Those may serve as the first topics to consider for thesis research. These may focus on a subject population (Down's syndrome infants or third graders), a content area (reading, math, self-help skills), a specific material (teaching DISTAR or EDMARK), or a procedure (time delay, overcorrection, stimulus fading). Each topic will lead the student to a literature filled with research possibilities. Or, perhaps the student has observed that children work inefficiently on certain tasks and has concluded that "there must be a better way" to organize instructional time. Upon reflection, it may be the case that no one knows if and when students work at school. A basic task, and interesting research topic, might be the development and validation of a classroom observation scale. Or, perhaps a student has noticed considerable cyclic variation in the self-stimulatory behavior of an "austistic" child and has wondered if a certain type of intervention, e.g., DRO when the target behavior is at a low rate, might not interrupt the pattern of stereotypy. That might be an excellent and manageable topic or research since (1) there is a body of literature on laboratory studies of autistic children, (2) autism is, at this point in history, puzzling to those who study it, (3) there is disagreement on the issue that autism is a unique syndrome, (4) trying the procedure and finding it effective might make life better for children so labelled, and (5) educational programming (and social programming, for that matter), must honestly be considered in a rudimentary state in the current decade. Thus, this observation suggests a solution to a problem: a solution that is timely, has widespread application if successful, and is humane in that, if successful, it may contribute to enhancing the behavioral repertoires of "autistic" children. These reasons suggest that this is a viable research topic.

It may be that, during the first years of teaching, the graduate student-researcher experienced difficulty using certain instructional materials, questioned their effectiveness, made some general requests for validation or effectiveness data, received none, questioned why they had been purchased, received no satisfactory answer, and then stopped using the materials. This process should not be uncommon since few materials are tested rigorously before they are published. Again, these questions emerge: "Where is the data base on _____ instructional program?" "For whom was the program developed?" "When used as recommended, what results obtained with _____ students?" The first question will be answered as part of the literature search for the study. The data from that search may be compared to the publisher's stated intended audience. A multiple baseline or multiple probe study may be initiated to answer the third question with a small group of students. In some cases, the study may be sufficiently novel to warrant publication. Or, the basic question "Does it work and with whom?" may be a fundable research project.

In other circumstances, the graduate student returns to school to shift interests to another child population or to train for a nonteaching position. Or, the student may enter a graduate program from outside education. In these situations, there is not necessarily a match between past experience and current professional interests. The most efficient way for the student to focus on the research task may be to develop a brief matrix based on a goal statement and specific interests. A simple system is shown in Table 13-1.

In each of these examples, the student should be able to generate behavioral descriptors sufficiently precise to enter computerized resource banks, e.g., the ERIC system. In every case, it should be possible to determine the state of the art in the area of interest in a short period of time. These references will identify critical issues and researchable topics. This process should help students clarify their career goals and focus on a researchable topic.

Once a general topic area is selected, the student must confront certain pragmatic considerations, i.e., such mundane questions as "Is there a target population to work with in the area?" Or, if the focus of interest is improving teacher-child interactions in specific instructional activities, does the equipment exist to videotape interactions for subsequent analysis by independent observers? Or, if one wishes to develop a mini-instructional program on a microcomputer, e.g., using APPLE Pilot (a computer-assisted instruction software author program) and then test it with children, do these resources exist at the university and in the schools to carry out the project?

Having selected those topics that are logistically feasible, the student's next task should be to identify those research topics that are manageable. That decision may best be made in consultation with the thesis advisor. One of the

TABLE 13-1   Over the five years following graduate school, I want to work:

In these Environments	With	Doing
Resource rooms	Moderately retarded adolescents	Prevocational instruction
Regular elementary schools	Regular education teachers	Technical assistance, providing teachers with direct instruction skills
Homes	Parents and their multiply handicapped infants	Parent/infant education
An urban system	Resource teachers	In-class supervision and technical assistance
A private computer firm	Computers	Curriculum development for home-based computer instruction systems

authors (who shall remain anonymous) proposed, as his first doctoral dissertation topic, a study in visual discrimination, using subjects, ages 6, 12, 18, 24, 30, and 36 months, in an appropriate longitudinal design. At the first conference with the thesis advisor, the author was shown, gently, that given the scope of the project, it might take 20 years to answer the question. A less ambitious task, focused on the same basic question, emerged as the final thesis topic.

Students might ask these questions:

• Is a pilot study necessary? (We assume so in most cases.)

• If so, can the pilot and full-scale study be conducted in the —— month time frame of graduate study?

• If subjects will be trained to criterion, does the literature contain data on the typical range of trials found in similar studies with this target population?

• If the study requires in-class independent observers, who will they be, who will pay them, how long will it take to train them to a defined criterion level?

• If the study requires that the investigator-experimenter or teacher use a defined teaching-training procedure, how long does it take to reach criterion?

• If the study utilizes a design that consists of several phases and is replicated (in the broadest sense) across several events (person, places), is there sufficient time to carry out each phase?

• If the study requires subjects with poor attendance (multiply handicapped students with health impairments; delinquent adolescent students who do not attend school regularly or are expelled or incarcerated), is there sufficient time to accommodate repeated absences?

• Are there predictable times or events that will interrupt the study? If so, can they be accommodated? Will teacher strikes close the schools at the beginning of the school year? Will the study be conducted in the winter in an area where schools will be closed for extended periods?

• Does the study contain any elements that represent potential risk? If so, is it likely parents or guardians may withdraw consent, once it is given (see Chapter 14).

• What strategies must be employed to compensate for subject attrition?

• What is the administrative hierarchy in the participating school system? If the study is to be conducted in a large system, will the necessary approvals be processed through the system in time to conduct research?

• If the study requires novel stimuli or instrumentation, who will develop it? If the experimenter must rely on someone else, how will the study be affected if the person fails to deliver on time?

• If the study requires frequent (daily) intervention, at the same time of day, what arrangements must the experimenter make to develop the schedule (register for night classes only during the term)? What accommodations must be made to or with the subjects' school schedule? (It is difficult to schedule intervention daily, five days a week, when the whole class goes swimming on Friday.)

While these questions cut across a variety of logistical problems, confronting them early may help to narrow the focus of the research (able) topic.

Reviewing the Research

This chapter began with the assumption that the student has a basic repertoire of writing and research skills, or will acquire them through extra effort early in the training program. We assume, further, that the student has written a sufficient number of papers, as an undergraduate, so that the review process is not completely foreign. For students who lack information, Borg and Gall (1979) provide a step-by-step process that applies to many areas of educational research. Here the focus is on getting started in the area of applied behavior analysis.

For the thesis proposal, the advisor wants to know whether the student (a) has a fundamental knowledge of key work in the topic area, (b) understands the rationale for the intervention strategy, (c) understands the link between theory and practice, and (d) understands the procedure sufficiently to carry it out accurately in a replication study or to vary it in some way.

In some cases, the student will begin a project, working closely with a faculty member who is conducting research in the topic area. The student's review, then, may begin at a highly focused point and expand from there. The first articles to review may be provided by a faculty member. They may represent her work and others' that is most up-to-date in the field, i.e., the articles may be accepted for publication but not yet published. The review process then begins with the reference lists in these *in press* publications. The titles of articles in the refrence list identify key approaches or procedural variations in the general body of work.

Analyzing these references and their reference lists and repeating the process with other articles may be the fastest method for identifying current, critical research. This strategy will provide the student with a narrowly focused review. Comprehension of the information it contains should be sufficient to answer the questions of concern to the thesis advisor. This is the *starting point* for developing the proposal. The review expands from here, at the same time that other components of the proposal are written.

Not every student will be so fortunate as to start a project at the center of an active research program. Nor will every student have access to faculty who are actively involved in research. Where there are larger numbers of students, there may be little opportunity to develop a working relationship with a faculty member. In these situations, the student must begin the review process in a more traditional manner. The student might do well to start the review process with a rough outline of questions or statements that serve as reference points for the development of the full proposal. Starting with the information obtained from the goal analysis, one alternative is:

I. This is what I want to do (and why)
   A. Work
      1. In the public schools
      2. Teaching third-grade level students who manifest reading problems
      3. Using a novel direct instruction strategy

II. This is what is known about the problem at the present time
   A. Basic instructional approaches are:
      1. Direct instruction
      2. Phonic
      3. Linguistic
      4.

B. Specific training procedures are: (student lists)
1.
2.
3.
4.
C. Critical questions, studied in the area in the last three years are: (student lists)
1.
2.
3.

III. Current research shows
A. These discontinuities in the literature
1. (student lists)
2.
3.
B. Repeated success using these techniques
1. (student lists)
2.
3.
C. Several areas, not yet studied, but recommended by contemporary authors are:
1. (student lists)
2.
3.
D. In summary, the literature suggests: (student writes paragraph summaries of the critical information)
1.
2.
3.

The outcome of this process should be a limited set of topics, or problems, suitable for further study. From these, the student will select a topic of interest and then begin to develop a rationale for that topic.

Justifying the Research Project

Graduate students should include a special section on "justification" in their proposal. It should accomplish these purposes:

1. Demonstrate that the student knows what she is doing,

2. Demonstrate that the project is logically related to an existing body of research, and

3. Demonstrate that the project is a worthwhile endeavor.

The first purpose is the most important at this stage. Master's degree students enter programs without a great deal of contact with faculty, in most cases. They are an unknown quantity, particularly in large programs where the student:faculty ratio is large. Supervising student research, when done properly, requires a large investment of faculty time. The student's first goal, like it or not, is to establish credibility with the faculty who will supervise the project. This goal, while it has little to do with the conceptualization and writing of the research project, has everything to do with getting off to the right start, i.e., establishing the conditions that facilitate rapid development of the project. The second and third goals will be demonstrated by the way the introduction and review of research are written.

Writing the Introduction

At this stage, a brief review of the literature will serve to demonstrate the student has identified a reasonable starting point for a project. The introduction is comprised of three or four parts:

1. A general statement that links the project to the literature

2. A brief review of relevant research

3. A statement that clearly shows what the students wants to *do*

4. A justification section, designed to convince the advisor the student has a grasp of the problem. In some cases, this statement might be included in a separate paper, which accompanies the proposal described at the end of this section.

The Methods Section

The methods section should be as complete as that for a research article, as described in the next section. The basic question for the student-researcher is "*Exactly* what will you *do*?" In some circumstances, the advisor may request the student and a (peer) subject to demonstrate the procedure.

A second question will be "Do you have the resources to carry out the project?"

Expected Outcomes

This should be written in a straightforward manner:

I will use _____ procedure to modify _____ (target behavior). The existing literature suggests the behavior will _____ (accelerate/decelerate). After _____ sessions the procedure will be changed in this way (_____). Then, these possibilities exist (list).

This section should end with a statement that tells how the intervention will permit one to state how an *empirical verification* of the *do* statement (hypothesis) was accomplished.

Other Considerations

The steps described here will generate a working document for the first draft of a thesis proposal. For some students, this will be sufficient to gain approval for the project if, of course, it is well thought out and clearly presented. For other students this will be the starting point. For them the outline of steps for preparation of a manuscript will provide a model for their next revisions. For this reason, that section is most fully developed.

Writing an Overview to Accompany the Thesis Proposal

Students should expect that the thesis advisor's interest in the project will be highly (and positively) correlated with the amount of student effort apparent in the thesis proposal. The student who wanders into the advisor's office with a casual, "Hey, man. I want to study overcorrection," can expect a rather frosty, "Oh, and what *exactly* do you plan to *do*?" The deathly silence that follows such an interchange rarely sets the stage for a positive working relationship. We suggest a better way to start. Prepare a cover letter, a prospectus, designed to establish your credibility as a serious student. Based on your preliminary review efforts, prepare a document that says literally and figuratively "This is what I've done so far (and it represents a major effort)." In this document:

1. Based on your efforts to select and narrow the topics you wish to study,
   a. Describe the general topic area you wish to study;
   b. State why that topic is of interest to you;
   c. State how the project relates to your career goals.

2. State why the topic is important. This statement is part of the justification for the project.

3. List the steps you have already completed to develop the review of research:

   a. List the computer searches you have completed. Include the topic descriptors found, journals searched, and the years searched.

   b. Include a photocopy of the computer search, if it is in a form that can be copied. Or, loan the search document to the professor for a short period.

   c. List the scope of the hand search you have carried out.

   d. Include the research review outline form, filled out legibly, so that the professor can follow your decision-making processes.

4. List the steps you have taken to insure that the child population, the human resources, and other resources are available to document that the project not only is interesting and worthwhile but logistically feasible.

5. List the special skills you have, and that you will acquire, to carry out the study, e.g., if someone must program a microcomputer, can you do it? Or, can you run a portable video system, to collect the video you need for further analysis? (One of the authors once expended a large amount of staff time and funds for ground travel and equipment repair before it was determined that a key project staff person, in fact, did *not* know how to run what was assumed to be a simple system.) Remember, sometimes it's not always possible to go back and tape again or to obtain another group of subjects, if a minor though critical procedural error invalidates the results with the original group of subjects.

Properly developed, this document should convey several messages to the thesis advisor:

• I've found an interesting problem.

• I've found a problem that falls within the domain of applied behavior analysis (as defined by Baer, Wolf, and Risley, 1968).

• I have an active interest in the problem.

• The project clearly relates to my career goals.

• I've invested time and effort to prepare a thesis proposal.

• I've begun to verify the project is feasible.

• I know what I'm doing. (May we proceed?)

If properly developed, the student should be ready to conduct the research project or to develop an extensive proposal, following the model outline.

Preparing a Manuscript for Journal Publication

This section is written from the perspective of preparing a manuscript for publication. The student-researcher has completed a research project, deemed publishable by the faculty advisor. The student will have the primary responsibility for preparing the manuscript, although she will receive technical assistance from the advisor. The first form of assistance may be to provide the student with a set of publication guidelines, such as *JABA* guidelines, illustrated in Figure 13-1.

Further, we assume that, as the student has completed the steps leading to the development of a thesis proposal, she has observed that research articles follow a standard format, with minor variations. First and foremost, the student should have observed that one element is common to most articles. They are *concise*.

Further, we assume the student will start the manuscript preparation task with more information than needed and that the primary task will be to trim this information (e.g., the master's thesis) to fit the journal format. We have chosen not to describe the steps required to develop the thesis document since the requirements vary from university to university.

Finally, we assume that the student's manuscript will be prepared for submission to the journals that publish in the area of behavior analysis, those shown on p. 343. We suggest that students familiarize themselves with a set of journals that publish studies conducted in educational settings. As a final comment, we must acknowledge that there is one tenuous assumption among those described here. Experience has taught us that often, even after students have conducted an extensive review, they have not identified the common elements in a set of research articles. We are led to this conclusion when students request conferences after doing research for a course paper or project. Their initial question is usually stated in this manner, "I've done my research, now how do I write the paper?" Bearing in mind that the directions for the paper were stated in this general form "Follow the *APA Manual,* and *use* a *JABA* article for a prototype," the response to the question is usually, "Did you notice any commonalities in the form of the articles you reviewed?" Students' negative responses are then followed by our request that they go back to the literature for another look. Thus, we suggest that attention to this factor will facilitate students' efforts. In other words, as a student starts her review, she should pay attention to form as well as substance. The following recommendations are designed to facilitate that process.

Introduction   The introduction is composed of three parts:

1. A problem statement,

2. A concise review of key studies, focused on (only) those issues relevant to the study, and

3. A statement of purpose or a hypothesis.

Theoretically, the introduction can be as short as one or two paragraphs. In practice, it may be three.to five paragraphs. An analysis of the first three journals of *JABA* (Volume 14) shows that the introductory paragraphs range in number from 2 to 12. Of the 31 experimental articles, 7 had 3-paragraph

Journal of
APPLIED BEHAVIOR ANALYSIS

GUIDELINES FOR NEW REVIEWERS

The Journal of Applied Behavior Analysis (JABA) publishes reports of experimental research involving applications of the experimental analysis of behavior to problems of social import. Published articles include both within and between subject designs. Occasional discussion articles are also published.

The Tone of the Review

The purpose of the JABA peer review system is to encourage authors to continue their research as well as to select manuscripts for publication. Therefore, it is important that reviewers' comments convey respect for an author's research efforts and include suggestions for improving that research, as well as detailed reasons for suggested revisions or the recommendation that the manuscript be rejected. The tone of a review is as important as the quality of the suggestions given for improving the research. Below are some suggestions of format and wording that may help assure that the tone of a review is not harsh.

The first sentence or paragraph of a review is very important. It should summarize the manuscript and express appreciation for either the research area, the efforts of the author, the difficulties of working in that area, or an aspect of the manuscript that the reviewer liked. In subsequent sentences the recommendations to the Editor (accept with or without revision, reject, etc.) can be conveyed.

Try to minimize use of words that convey a very negative impression, e.g., irrelevant, inadequate, poor, sloppy.

Avoid sarcastic or accusatory comments such as, "Is this finding even worth mentioning?"

Conditionals help soften the tone of a review, e.g., could, would, should, might--in short, words that suggest rather than command.

Below are four examples that contain essentially the same information, but do so in differing tones:

la Most of the introduction is irrelevant to the rest of the manuscript.
lb The introduction could have been more directly related to the aims of the study.

2a It would be impossible for anyone to replicate the procedures.
2b A more adequate description of the procedures would be necessary for replication.

3a The use of the term "co-operative teachers" is very deceiving.
3b A more accurate definition of the term "co-operative teachers" is necessary to avoid confusion.

4a Why didn't you assess the reliability of your measures?
4b It is necessary to report the reliability of your measures in order to allow one to judge the impact of your findings.

Points to Consider

When considering a manuscript and preparing a review you may wish to attend to the following specific points:

Style: The style should correspond to the APA Publication Manual (Second Edition, 1984) and the JABA suggestions for manuscript preparation which appear in the first and third issues of each volume (from Volume 8).

FIGURE 13-1 Publication guidelines. From: *Journal of Applied Behavior Analysis.* Copyright by Society for the Experimental Analysis of Behavior, Inc. Reproduced by permission.)

Abstract: The reader should be able to read the Abstract and then know what the article is about. The Abstract should summarize the purpose of the study, the procedures employed, the results obtained, and the conclusions reached.

Introduction: The introduction should explain the relationship and importance of the study to the field of research, setting the work in the context of the literature from the field of applied behavior analysis and from other research areas.

Procedure: The procedures must be described in sufficient detail to allow the reader with some background in behavioral psychology to replicate the methods.

Measures: Particular attention should be given to the definition of the behavior measured. The definition should be given in terms of observable, physical events. This is not to imply that behavior must be automatically recorded by a transducer, since in many instances human observation is the only way to record a response. In such cases, however, an analysis of reliability of agreement between observers should be included. Furthermore, the description of the observed behavior must allow a reader to record the same behavior reliably. Self-report and questionnaire data may aid in the interpretation of the research and in most instances would be published as supplemental to the behavioral measure(s) rather than as the primary data.

Analysis: The research should include sufficient experimental evidence with appropriate controls to demonstrate that the procedure was directly related to the behavior change reported. Anecdotes or case studies do not meet this requirement. Adequate demonstration will usually involve replication either within or between subjects. It should be recognized, however, that rarely can the demonstration of experimental control be carried out to the level of certainty feasible in the laboratory. Moreover, work in new areas of endeavor will often demonstrate less control than work in established areas. In all cases, social importance and innovation must be weighed against the level of certainty of demonstration reached. Such judgments are often aided by statistical analyses.

Human research involves ethical and legal issues to which reviewers should be alert and which should be fully discussed if relevant.

Results: The presentation of the results should be descriptive and as free of interpretation as possible. Figure captions and labels should be descriptive rather than interpretive. For example, label "voice key operations" as such, rather than as "rate of verbal behavior." Figures should be self-contained with little reliance on the text for their understanding. The reviewer should always check to see that the presentation of results in the text corresponds with the results portrayed in the figures; discrepancies should be brought to the author's attention.

Discussion: The discussion section should integrate and interpret the results and relate them to previous research. The author should be allowed some freedom to develop generalizations, but the reviewer may want to warn the author about statements which might become embarrassing in the future. The conclusions should be based firmly on the results obtained.

OVERALL IMPORTANCE: Will a JABA reader learn something more about the analysis and/or modification of a socially significant behavior from this manuscript?

USE OF UNPUBLISHED MANUSCRIPTS: "An author is protected by common law against unauthorized use of his unpublished work; therefore, an unpublished manuscript is considered a privileged document. Editors and reviewers may not circulate, quote, cite, or refer in writing or orally to an unpublished work, nor may they use any information in the work to advance their own work without the author's consent." (APA Publication Manual, Second Edition, 1974, p. 101)

October 1980

FIGURE 13-1   (continued)

introductions, 8 had 4-paragraph introductions, 6 had 5-paragraph introductions. Clearly, this is not the most extensive part of the writing task. *The challenge is to provide the maximum amount of relevant information in the smallest number of words.* The content of the introduction may be paraphrased by these "topic sentences."

1. The problem is .... (or) The question is....

2. Others have studied these relevant issues. . . .

3. A potential new avenue of research is. . . .

4. Some possible benefits from this new approach are. . . .

5. I propose to. . . . (or) I hypothesize that. . . .

This format is illustrated in Table 13-2 with an article written by Egel, Richman, and Koegel (1981).

Method

The methods section is written in a straightforward manner. The writer's task is to include all the relevant information and exclude all that is not. Unfortunately, the distinction between the two is not always clear. Factors that the authors *consider relevant* are discussed below in the description of the basic elements of the research methodology.

Subjects

Basic information includes:

1. The number of subjects,

2. Subjects' age and sex,

3. General statement of functional level,

4. Specific description of the problem behavior,

5. Physical attributes of the subject that might facilitate or interfere with task performance,

6. Historical events that bear directly on the subjects' current behavioral repertoires,

7. Subject selection criteria, if subjects *are sought* to test an intervention—a situation that is different from applying a potentially helpful intervention to subjects who manifest specific problem behaviors.

Not all of this basic information need be present in every study and, for studies outside the scope of this text, other subject variables may be critical.

The number of subjects, their age, and sex should be included in every study. The description of the functional level of subjects is important to the extent that it influences the outcome of the study. Sidman and Stoddard (1966) reported a series of studies in errorless learning, leading to nearly perfect performance of a 44-year-old lifetime institutionalized subject. His ability to discriminate between circles and ellipses that became "circular" (more round and less oval) was remarkable, given his impoverished history. Equally remarkable was the performance of other young, normal and re-tarded subjects, who made the discrimination when the experimenters could not—unless they measured the stimulus with an ellipsograph.

Reporting intelligence test scores is not likely to be critical to most students of applied behavior analysis (ABA). Academic achievement scores may be important if a study attempts to modify specific academic behaviors, but irrelevant in the description of an intervention designed to modify the disruptive social behavior of third-grade students in regular classes. The selection of terms to describe handicapped students is problematic in this era when issues relating to labelling and classifying have led to the use of

TABLE 13-2   An analysis of the *introduction* to an applied behavioral analysis article.

1. The problem is . . . the question is . . .	As more autistic children are being placed into the "educational mainstream," an important consideration is whether or not the handicapped peers in the classroom can serve as role models for appropriate behavior.
2. Others have studied these relevant issues . . . (or) problems . . .	Extensive work by a number of investigators examining observational learning has demonstrated that peer models for normal children have effected change in a variety of behaviors. These behaviors have included sharing (Elliot & Vasta, 1970; Hartup & Coates, 1967; Igelmo, 1976); sex role behaviors (Kobasigawa, 1968; Miran, 1975); self-reinforcement (Bandura & Kupers, 1964); problem-solving (Clark, 1965; Debus, 1970; Ridberg, Parke, & Hetherington, 1971); and emotional behaviors (Bandura, Grusec, & Menlove, 1967; Bandura & Menlove, 1968).
3. A potential new approach is . . .	The beneficial effects of peer modeling with normal children has invited serious consideration of the possibility that such models might also facilitate learning in handicapped children (Snyder, Apolloni, & Cooke, 1977). Only recently, however, has this concept received any empirical support (Apolloni, Cooke, & Cooke, 1976; Barry & Overman, 1977; Peterson, Peterson, & Scriven, 1977; Rauer, Cooke, & Apolloni, 1978; Talkington, Hall, & Altman, 1973). These studies demonstrated that the responses (e.g., verbal behavior) of retarded children could be brought under the stimulus control of a peer model's behavior.
4. Some possible benefits are . . .	However, there have been some suggestions that normal peer models might be helpful for this population. For example, Coleman and Stedman (1974) described a case history in which a normal peer seemed to serve as a model to modify voice loudness and increase the labeling vocabulary of an autistic child. Other studies, however, have suggested that such positive benefits may not be possible for all autistic children or with all types of models. For example, in a systematic assessment of observational learning with 15 autistic children and adult models, Varni, Lovaas, Koegel, and Everett (1979) found that very low functioning autistic children acquired only a small portion of adult modeled responses. Varni et al. suggested that stimulus overselectivity in lower functioning autistic children may have accounted for those children's failure to learn through observation. They also suggested the possibility that this problem may be less severe for higher level autistic children.
5. I propose (hypothesize) to . . .	In view of the above studies, it seemed plausible that at least some autistic children should be able to benefit from exposure to normal peer models. The present study was therefore designed to test this hypothesis systematically.

Source: Introduction, pp. 3–4, from: Egel, A. L., Richman, G. S., and Koegel, R. L. Normal peer models and autistic children's learning. *Journal of Applied Behavior Analysis,* 1981, 14(1), 3–12. Copyright by Society for the Experimental Analysis of Behavior, Inc. Reproduced by permission.

general terms (learning and behavior disorders) to describe children who manifest very specific problem behaviors. Because of the ambiguities surrounding the use of such terms, the researcher may want to describe students as "those placed in classes for the severely retarded" and "whose repertoire, e.g., language was limited to cries, nonintelligible utterances, and occasional easily discriminable one-word utterances—'Daddy,' 'ball,' 'cup.'" This issue is discussed further in Chapter 14, in the context of communicating clearly with a human subjects review committee.

The description of the problem behavior(s) may be simple or complex. Several behaviors may be described to convey to readers the degree of handicap:

> S was a moderately retarded female, age 15, who demonstrated age appropriate self-help skills, e.g., dressing, grooming, and personal hygiene; who read at the third-grade level; who regularly completed assigned tasks in a job training center but whose social interaction skills were limited and included such work-inappropriate behaviors as swearing, etc.

This description should naturally lead into an intervention to modify those disturbing social behaviors, which would be more specifically defined in the *target behaviors* section of the method.

If the subject manifests physical defects that interfere with task performance, that fact should be included in the description.

Historical factors, relevant to the problem at hand, should be carefully considered. Developing a program to shape the walking behavior of a recently discovered crib-bound 6-year-old requires some description of the environment and the conditions that preceded the study. The repertoire of a feral child, discovered living in inhumane and impoverished conditions, might be very different from that of four profoundly retarded children, enrolled in a day preschool, who were taught to stop crawling and start walking in a program devised by O'Brien, Azrin, and Bugle (1972). On the other hand, certain historical events are generally considered to be irrelevant to a child's current repertoire. Parents' perception of their child's "anxious" behavior during the early childhood years is likely to have little bearing on a reading error modification program.

Students participate in ABA studies for one of two reasons: (1) they manifest problems of ecological concerns (and someone identifies a problem or is sought out to provide assistance), or (2) someone who is seeking to replicate a finding, or try an established technique with a new population, will seek out subjects who manifest certain behavioral characteristics. Those stated criteria are, of course, the focus of the subject description in such studies.

In some studies the subjects and setting are described separately; in others they are combined. Here they have been separated.

Setting

In one or two sentences, describe the critical elements of the environment in which the study was conducted. These include the unique features that might influence the outcome of the study. For example, a university-sponsored preschool, enrolling faculty children in a research-oriented program, may be very different from a preschool enrolling low income children in a storefront school.

It may be appropriate to describe the environment in broad, as well as narrow or specific terms, e.g., a medium sized city in the Midwest; a regular elementary school enrolling special education students in regular classes and special resource rooms; a 1:1 tutorial setting in the corner of the resource room, separated by a movable screen from the other activities taking place during the conduct of the training session. Or, a 6' by 6' tutorial room, devoid of decoration and containing only a small table and two chairs, located in the educational wing of the children's rehabilitation hospital. Or, during math instruction in a third-grade class in an elementary school.

Experimental Procedures

Within the discussion of experimental procedures, these topics are covered: stimulus specification, response specification, consequences of correct and incorrect responses, scripting interactions, and description of the phases of the intervention.

Antecedent stimulus specification. Antecedent stimulus events include unique characteristics of the interventionist, the interventionist's verbal statements, a description of the physical properties of visual stimuli, and the conditions under which these stimuli are presented. The writer should indicate:

1. The interventionist was.... (a trained graduate student, the classroom teacher, a specially trained language therapist)

2. The interventionist said.... ("Give me cookie," "Touch the one that is red," "Do this" as he/she models a response to be imitated)

3. The physical description of the visual stimuli (lessons 1 through 10 of the _____ reading program; worksheets containing 10 math problems requiring the proper use of zero in subtraction; five three-inch-square Polacoated Plexiglas response panels at normal illumination for a standard carousel slide projector)

4. The conditions under which the stimuli were presented (The teacher said, "Look at me," waited for eye contact from S, then said, "Touch the one that is red.") The 3" visual stimuli were ... (back projected onto 4" square response panels which were located on a 24" square interface panel. The top sample panel was located 1" below the top of the interface and 10" from the left and right borders of the interface. The two bottom match response keys were located 1" from the bottom of the interface and thus 12" from the sample key. The left bottom key was located 4" from the left border; the right key 4" from the right border. Thus, the two keys were located 8" from each other.)

When the writer has completed the description of antecedent stimuli, the reviewer/reader should know exactly what the subjects heard and saw before they responded. This component of the procedures can be considered replicable if the reader can:

1. Recreate visual stimuli identical to those described.

2. Identify the same elements, or sections of commercially available instructional materials (units 1–10 of the DISTAR reading program).

3. Say and do what the experimenter said and did in the same sequence.

4. Locate/identify all of the components of an automated instrumentation system and the proper sequence and duration of the stimulus events. From

the examples provided earlier, it would be possible to (a) build a match-to-sample interface using the dimensions listed above, (b) prepare identical slide stimuli using figures included in the text of one's manuscript and the directions for photographing the slides so that, when using a standard carousel projector (as noted) located n inches from the interface, the slides appear as described. Then, the major elements of the electronic circuitry must be listed, e.g., microswitches placed behind response panels, leading to a microprocessor controlling a real time clock which, in turn, controls the stimulus presentation and response intervals and, as well, the sequencing of stimuli, contingent upon correct or error responses.

5. Do *everything* that the experimenter did, that possibly makes a difference in procedures. The experimenter/writer should double-check all the elements of the procedure, e.g., (a) use of neutral vocal tones (no emphasis or inflection) during pretests/posttests, (b) purposeful use of body/facial gestural cues in an educational intervention, (c) saying and signing to hearing impaired or multiply handicapped students.

Response specifications. The procedures may contain a separate section that describes the *target behavior*. This will describe the topography of the response in observable terms. Because students are presumed to be expert in writing descriptions of observable behaviors, we expect that this will be the easiest part of the writing task. The response definition may be as simple as "S will touch the _____ within 5 seconds of the teacher's command." The task becomes more complex when, for example, an observation code must be developed to define a set of social behaviors displayed in varying forms by several target children in a multiple baseline design. In this section, the writer must include the behavior coding system. By the time the experiment is ready for publication, one can assume that the code is clearly written (or the observation reliability data will be nonexistent, and therefore of marginal "publishability").

As a review strategy, the writer should ask these questions to insure that the response definition is complete:

1. Are the conditions under which the behavior occurred described simply? (During math sessions, S's on-task behavior was recorded.)

2. Is the topography of the response clearly defined?
   a. When was the response initiated?
   b. How long did it last?
   c. What terminates the response?
   d. Is the intensity of the response appropriately described? (Did I use a term like *vocalizations,* and find that loud crying decreased to murmured appropriate utterances, yet of the same duration, and thus reflected no change in "minutes of bedtime vocalization per day"?)

3. Was the response defined so that it could be recorded reliably?

Students will note that this list of questions includes some that must be considered before the experiment is initiated. If this list generates some "no" responses, in review, the writer should be prompted to list topics that must be addressed in the discussion section.

Consequent events. It may be helpful to recall that a study may be designed to modify the frequency, intensity, or duration of a *free* operant. A consequent event occurs when the behavior is emitted. That event, or series of consequences, may be described as part of the experimental procedure, part of the experimental design, or in a separate section, e.g., reinforcer systems.

Studies designed to modify academic behaviors are fixed operants or discrete trial responses. In laboratory studies these are most commonly referred to as discrete trials. In educational settings, the procedures may follow a laboratory model, e.g., the *learning trial model* described by Tawney, Knapp, O'Reilly, and Pratt (1979). In these studies, antecedents are presented, a response occurs; or, if no response occurs, a defined time period passes and the trial is terminated. Correct responses are consequated with positive reinforcement. Incorrect or *no* responses are typically followed by correction procedures, extinction, or mild punishers. Each of these events must be described in the manuscript. The writer may describe these series of interactions most clearly by first scripting them and then combining the script into narrative description, as described below.

Scripting the interactions. Scripting is a simple process. It should occur when the study is being designed. It is particularly helpful for communicating with thesis advisors and human subjects review committee members. It requires that the organism-environment interaction be separated into three parts, antecedents (conditions), behavior, and criterion. The sequencing follows an if-then model: "under these conditions, if (*state behavior of S*) occurs, then (*behavior of experimenter*) will occur. Two examples are shown in Tables 3-3 and 3-4.

Describing the experimental procedure. It is an easy step, then, to translate the script into the narrative for the procedures section.

> Instruction took place in a 6′ by 6′ tutorial room located in the children's wing of the rehabilitation hospital. The room contained only a table and two chairs and the instructional materials used during each 15-minute session. The experimenter placed a common spoon and a cup in front of the subject, said, "_____, touch the cup" and waited up to 5 seconds for a response.
>
> A correct response was followed by a sip of juice. The examiner interrupted incorrect motor responses before they were completed, redirected the response to

TABLE 13-3   Free-operant script.

Conditions	Behavior	Consequent Events
During math instruction	Ralph talks out (as defined by observation code: no eye or physical contact, no verbal interaction)	Teacher and class use time-out
	Teacher reinforces an on-task student	
	Every talk-out is consequated as defined here	

TABLE 13-4   Learning trial script (for an academic behavior change program).

Antecedents	Behavior	Consequent Events
Place a common spoon and cup on the table in front of *S*. Say, "_____, touch cup."	*S* completes the motor response within 5 seconds	(a) a sip of juice for every correct response (b) (i) physically interrupt an incorrect motor response and direct *S*'s hand to the correct object; (ii) say, "NO! Touch the *cup*." (c) if no response occurs, wait 5 seconds, rearrange the stimuli, and repeat

the correct object, and said "No! Touch the *cup*." If no response occurred after 5 seconds, the stimuli were repositioned and another trial was initiated. Stimuli were, however, rearranged after every learning trial.

The example builds on information presented in previous sections and adds a critical element, the length of the instructional session. The writer, when starting with the script process, may want to walk through, or talk through, the procedure to insure that the sequence is described fully, e.g., "First I did _____, and *Ss* responded by _____. Then I _____" (and so on through all the steps).

The procedure should include all the relevant information. In review, the writer might ask, "Did I include . . . ?"

1. The length of the session

2. The number of sessions per day

3. The time of sessions

4. The number of trials per session

5. A clear description of the setting

6. A description of all the stimulus events

7. The behavior codes or response definition

8. The consequences for correct, incorrect, or *no* responses

9. The criterion for terminating each phase of the study

10. A description of the reinforcers and the schedule of reinforcement

Observation system response recording and reliability measures. The topic of reliable measurement is covered in Chapter 7. Here the elements of these procedures are listed. The writer should describe:

1. The observers' backgrounds and training,

2. How the observers entered the learning environment and where they were located in proximity to the subjects,

3. The type of observation system used,

4. The specific instruments or strategies used to insure that observers sampled the same intervals,

5. How videotape was used, if it was employed,

6. What was recorded,

7. The method for computing percent of agreements and disagreements,

8. The level of agreement observers reached during their training,

9. The level of agreement obtained during the experiment,

10. The percent of sessions in which interobserver reliability checks were conducted, if two or more observers were not always present.

Not every element will be incorporated in every study. Typically, the information can be presented in one short paragraph.

Describing the phases of the study. An analysis of several applied behavior analysis journals shows that many different strategies are employed to describe the changes across phases of an experiment. Here only the basic elements are considered. Further, this description builds on the previous content of the chapter and thus is limited to the description of phases and phase changes.

A description of the phases of the study should begin with a one-sentence description of the type of experimental design employed. The description of *baseline* should include:

1. The number of days,

2. The reason for lengthening or shortening baseline, if logistical factors require the original plan to be modified,

3. Environmental conditions, if those are important,

4. A general description of subjects' behaviors,

5. The rationale for implementing the next phase,

6. The general sequence for implementing the next phase(s),

7. The conditions in each baseline, if multiple baselines are employed, e.g., A_1 B_1 A_2 B_2 where A_2 represents withdrawal of B and a return to the A_1 conditions,

8. A description of each baseline, if time-lagged interventions are introduced across multiple conditions, e.g., baseline for S, is 5 sessions, S_2 is 10 sessions, S_3 is 15 sessions.

If the elements of the procedure have been clearly written in the separate sections described above, it should only be necessary to describe the differences between phases in a section on experimental design. For example, if social behaviors are consequated with different types of reinforcers across the phases of an experiment, a separate section on *reinforcer options* will describe each option. In the experimental design section, it will be sufficient to name the options as they appear in each phase. These intervention phase descriptions should include:

1. A sequential description of phase changes,

2. A reference to the critical independent variable(s) in or across phases,

3. Critical differences between phases, especially when multiple interventions are manipulated, e.g., A-B-A-B-A-BC-A-BC, and B = tokens, BC = tokens plus praise,

4. Events that determine a phase change,

5. The conditions for generalization or maintenance phases if they are included in the experiment.

Results

The results section should be linked to the graphic representation of data. It should be limited to:

1. A general description of the subjects' behavior(s),

2. Changes in the dependent variable (target behavior across conditions),

3. Descriptions of critical elements of figures and tables,

4. A description of key data points that best represent the magnitude of change within and across conditions,

5. Ranges of performance within conditions,

6. Factors that may influence the results (S_2 is absent from school 5 of 10 days during an intervention phase),

7. Descriptions of S's behavior changes as a function of phase changes.

The results section should be written concisely, devoid of speculation and interpretation. The initial narrative is fairly standard:

• Figure 1 presents. . . .

• During baseline S's behavior was: high–low, variable (erratic-cylic)–stable on the dependent variable (percent correct responding, frequency of talk-outs, etc.).

• Performance was at (define the percent correct responding).
When the intervention was introduced in condition __(B)__,
S^1's behavior: accelerated.
                   decelerated.
                   remained unchanged.

When the intervention was introduced in condition __(C)__,
S^2's behavior: accelerated.
                   decelerated.
                   remained unchanged.

• Across this phase, S's behavior ranged from ____ to ____.

• When conditions were changed, S's behavior changed in this way. . . .

• These unusual events (if any) occurred:. . . .

• These response patterns (if any) occurred:. . . .

From this starting point, the writer will add relevant information that makes this section complete.

Discussion

The discussion section should be developed according to the following rule: *Say no more than the data permit.* The discussion section begins with a brief paragraph summary of the results, i.e. the results show that (this intervention) had (this much) effect on these (describe) subjects.

From this starting point, the discussion focuses on factors relevant to this study. Some, but not all of these, may be helpful to review before the student-writer begins this final task. Bear in mind that the first parts of the manuscript say, in essence, "Here's the problem," "This is how I approached it," "This is what I found." Then, the discussion section says, in essence, "This is what it all means." Within this context, the writer may wish to:

1. Place her findings within the existing body of research, i.e., the findings may be similar to one series of studies, and contradictory to another;

2. Explain the findings with reference to specific procedural similarities and differences in key studies;

3. Describe the unique contribution of this study to the existing literature;

4. Describe the magnitude of effect within and across subjects, conditions, settings, etc.;

5. Identify unanticipated problems which occurred during the course of the study (S^1 died, S^2 moved away);

6. Make public any procedural deviations or errors that occurred;

7. Describe unanticipated effects and any possible reasons for them;

8. Behavioral deviations clearly related to external events (S's performance decelerates when it should accelerate. A figure shows S was out of school, or a naive person, e.g., a classroom aide, interfered with the procedure.);

9. State the questions left unanswered by these research findings;

10. State the implications of the study;

11. List possible next steps in the scientific process;

12. Suggest which next steps are likely to be most important, or most fruitful;

13. Recommend procedural changes in future studies, if these have influenced the results;

14. State the possible benefits others may derive from the results of the study;

15. State the practical applications, or implications, if any, beyond the environment in which the study was conducted;

16. State the cautions that must be taken when interpreting the results of the study;

17. List other possible explanations for the results obtained, if there are areas of ambiguity in the research field;

18. List special abilities/disabilities of the subjects that may have influenced these results, in contrast to other studies conducted in the area of research;

19. List unanticipated negative side effects of the procedure that may caution other researchers to proceed carefully in the area;

20. Describe changes in corollary behaviors that may suggest interesting areas of new research.

When these factors have been reviewed, the student should be able to identify those most relevant, to organize them in logical sequence, and then to write briefly on each topic. The results should be a discussion section that:

1. Relates to issues listed in the introduction,

2. Flows in logical order,

3. Offers a cautious interpretation of the functional relationship between the intervention and behavior change,

4. Discusses interesting findings, and

5. Leads the reader to the next steps in the research process.

The student-researcher, of course, will have received a great deal of feedback on the study, as the thesis proposal was developed, as the study was carried out under supervision, and finally, as the study was defended. These events should assist the student to determine what defines a cautious interpretation and what constitutes a "major" or "dramatic" effect. To the extent that these lessons are learned during graduate training, the student should be prepared to conduct independent research and to seek external funds for research. Before that task is analyzed, however, there are some unfinished elements of manuscript preparation that must be considered.

Petty Details

Four tasks must be completed to prepare a finished manuscript. Some are easier than others; our recommendations are general. The *title*, obviously, should tell what was done, in the least possible number of words. If one applied time-out to the inappropriate eating behavior of retarded subjects in a school cafeteria, the title might be "The Effect of Time-Out on the Eating Behavior of Retarded Students in a Cafeteria Setting."

This brief title tells *what* you did (what procedure you used), to *whom*, and *where*.

We suggest you write the title in two or three different forms, analyze them to insure you have identified the key phrases, then cross out all the words you can without changing the meaning. For example, if you start with "A Study of the Effect of an Extended Time-out Procedure on the Eating, Dish Throwing Behavior ..." you will see that some reduction is possible, e.g., "The Effect of Time-Out on The Eating Behavior. ..."

Writing an *abstract* may be the hardest part of the task; for the whole manuscript must be summarized in the journal's word limit, perhaps 200–250 words. Within this limit, you must state:

1. The general problem area—in one sentence;

2. The procedure used, the type of subjects, the target behavior, and the environment;

3. How behavior change was measured;

4. What you found;

5. The implications, or context, of the research findings.

You will note this brief outline contains 36 words. Students should read the abstracts in the related research areas carefully. They should provide guidelines for expanding their 36-word outline into the required maximum.

Preparing a *reference* list is time-consuming. These suggestions may make this task less aversive:

1. Photocopy the cover page of each article you reference to insure that each reference is accurate.

2. As you develop each section, write a list of references so they can be easily located. If a reference is in a book, code it so it can be located, or make

sure the reference is accurately copied before you return the book to the library.

3. When the manuscript is complete, crosscheck your reference list against it. Have you included references that are not on the list? Have you deleted references from the text, but not from the reference list?

4. Check the reference against the APA style manual. Is every comma, period, and space in place?

5. If you have references that are not represented by example in the APA manual, get expert opinion from someone (your advisor, the graduate school, the secretary to the most prolific researcher in your program).

6. If you have several ambiguous references, treat them consistently, i.e., use the style recommended to you by your expert. Do every one in the same style.

We have saved the easiest step for the last; preparing the *cover page*. It should contain: the title, the author's(s') name(s), and the author's(s') affiliation(s).

It may contain acknowledgments, or they may be prepared on a separate page following the cover page. Author identification *should not* appear on the pages of the manuscript since most journals employ a blind review technique. That is, when reviewed by the editor, the cover page is removed so that reviewers do not know whose work is being evaluated.

Before the manuscript is submitted to any journal, the writer should: (1) review the list of journals presented on p. 000, (2) select those that publish in the area of the study, (3) read the journals' guidelines to authors (including their definition of the types of research they publish), (4) select the *one* journal that most closely matches the topic of the study, (5) prepare the requisite number of copies, (6) add the graphs and figures, and (7) submit to only one journal.

Most journals will accept manuscripts only on the condition that they have not been submitted elsewhere. Essentially, the journal has exclusive rights to the manuscript, once submitted, until the review process is complete. If accepted, the journal may require that it hold copyright rights to the manuscript. If the manuscript is not accepted (heaven forbid), then the author is free to submit it elsewhere.

Writing a Grant Proposal

Writing a grant proposal may appear very far from the daily concerns of the graduate student. However remote it seems at the moment, time passes quickly. Master's degree candidates become doctoral students or move from teaching to administration and find themselves in positions where writing grant applications for special programs is part of the job description. Doctoral students may be required to write proposals for special university funds to support their research or may be encouraged to seek federal support for research. Students who complete their doctorates may find, in their first university position, that many reinforcers are available to faculty who acquire external research funds. Others may find that, whatever position they hold, securing funds from outside sources is necessary for survival. Thus, for many reasons, it seems important to (a) differentiate the focus of grant proposals from thesis research outlines, (b) describe the elements of a funding proposal, and (c) describe the process of grant preparation. This information will provide a basic knowledge repertoire for students, a repertoire that should generalize across a broad range of applications, i.e., funding programs with different priorities and evaluation criteria.

General Considerations

The basic distinctions among thesis proposals, journal manuscripts, and grant proposals are shown in Table 13-5. The general concerns of those who evaluate thesis research and manuscripts have been stated. To review, a thesis committee wants to know if the student has the repertoire to carry out the research. A human subjects review committee wants to insure that the research poses no risk, or carefully controlled risk to the subjects. Journal reviewers must be convinced the research reported in a manuscript is technically accurate, contributes new information, and is reasonably interpreted. Those who evaluate grant proposals have a different set of concerns. A funding agency must be convinced that the research problem is one of *national scope,* that the researcher *can deliver* what she promises, that the potential benefit is *worth the cost* of the project, that the *costs have been reasonably estimated*, and that the *outcomes are potentially the most valuable* of the 30 or 40 proposals that are competing for the same money. If the researcher considers that her proposal is one of 400 that will be evaluated, and that perhaps ten of the 400 will be selected, the grant preparation task comes into clearer focus.

The discussion that follows is based on the assumption that the student has written a thesis proposal, has carried out a research project, and written it in manuscript form. From the student's perspective, the next steps might be to carry out the "recommendations for further research." To do this requires two major tasks: to broaden the scope of the project and to add a management plan (using the term in the broadest sense) that transforms a problem and a set of experimental procedures into a complete grant application. The description here follows the general format required for proposals submitted to the federal agency responsible for programs of research, training, and service for the handicapped.

Elements of a Grant Proposal

Abstract/Overview

This section is an expanded version of the brief abstract required for a journal manuscript. In one or two pages the researcher must:

1. State the problem,

2. Indicate the scope of the problem within the national target population,

3. Describe the status of current knowledge about the problem,

4. Describe the general approach the researcher will take,

5. State the functional utility of the research funding, e.g., how a finding in a discrimination learning study might be applied to the reading problems of school age "learning disabled students,"

6. Emphasize the potential benefits of the study.

TABLE 13-5   Distinctions among critical elements of theses, journal manuscripts, and grant proposals.

Section	Thesis Proposal	Manuscript	Grant Proposal
Introduction			
Problem statement	Find an educationally relevant problem related to student's career interests	Convey the status of research in the topic area	Identify critical problem of national scope
Literature review	Briefly identify a link between the problem and past work	Narrowly focus on accurate interpretations of key problems/issues	Comprehensive analysis of research findings, attempts to solve problems, and/or reasoned analysis of problem
"Do" statements	Describe the contribution you wish to make	State hypothesis or state behaviors to be manipulated across conditions	State hypothesis, describe potential effects of multiple intervention
Project justification	Convince advisor you know what you are doing		Major elaboration of the "critical need" for project funding
Methods	Write as completely as you can; script parts of the intervention	Describe in explicit detail so that readers can replicate the experiment	Describe in explicit detail so that reviewers are clear on the nature of your intervention
Results	What do you expect to find? What range of outcomes is logical?	Complete description of findings	Possible positive outcomes described as "major benefits"
Discussion		Reasonable and conservative interpretations of findings	
Management Plan	General list of resources needed		Comprehensive description of: 1. Major objectives: (a) enabling objectives (b) strategies 2. Timelines 3. Personnel and their qualifications 4. Institutional resources 5. Evaluation plan 6. Budget

Assuming that the reviewers will not always be expert in the area of research, this overview should, in terms familiar to a lay person, identify the problem, the general approach, and the benefits. It should provide the reviewer with an outline of the research plan.

Problem Statement

This section contains four elements:

1. A rationale that presents the problem as one of national scope,
2. An extensive review of research,
3. A rationale for the approach the researcher is proposing, and
4. A summary statement that emphasizes the critical need for the project.

When a reviewer has read this section, she should be led to these conclusions:

1. The researcher has identified a major problem.

2. The magnitude of the problem warrants consideration for federal support.

3. The researcher has, within a few pages, identified the contemporary research on the problem, the known approaches and their relative effectiveness, variations in procedures, etc.

4. The potential benefit warrants spending the money to carry out the research.

Objectives

The proposal should contain a direct statement that tells what the researcher will *do*. In a single subject research study, the objective will follow this general form: to [manipulate (accelerate/decelerate)] the (target behavior) of (subjects) in (setting) by (the intervention strategy).

The proposal should contain an objective for every major, planned activity, e.g., while this chapter was written, the senior author also wrote a *media development* grant proposal that had three objectives: (a) to develop a computer software program, (b) to develop a computer-assisted instruction module, and (c) to produce a 30-minute television program "Johnny's Learning? Show Us Please!" for national public television.

Each objective should be written so that it can be task analyzed and described at two levels—enabling objectives and strategies—and placed in a "workscope," or task table.

Research Method

The research method section is identical in form to the methods section of a thesis proposal, or, except for verb tense, a journal manuscript. It may be included in a separate chapter, or in the operational plan section of a proposal. As noted, students who have progressed this far are assumed to be expert in writing these procedures so that they are accurate, complete, and easy for the reader to follow. This section is different from the operational plan, or "workscope," that is necessary to carry out the logistics of the research program.

Management Plan

The management plan section contains many elements. The grant program announcement may state, in detail, what must be included. Typically, these elements are required:

1. A workscope, or task table,
2. A description of the experience and competencies of the researcher(s),
3. A description of the capabilities of the sponsoring institution,
4. Job descriptions of the individuals employed to carry out the research,
5. An evaluation plan,
6. A budget.

Each is described here.

The workscope. A workscope tells who does what, when, and to what criterion of success. In a sense, it is a collection of behavioral objectives, analyzed, sequenced, and presented in a format that allows reviewers to see the time frame for activities and the criteria for successful completion of tasks.

The workscope may be preceded by a one- or two-page narrative that provides an overview of the general sequence of events.

One common method for presenting the workscope is to prepare a set of tables that contain all of the necessary elements.

Table 13-6 shows an outline for organizing objectives. It shows how an objective (1.0) can be broken into two levels of subtasks: enabling objectives (1.1) and strategies (1.1.1). For each strategy one can specify how every subcomponent will be evaluated and to what criterion.

If the process events (enabling objectives and strategies) are measured by task completion—by a specified date—the workscope may be cumbersome and highly redundant.

The workscope should include the management tasks required by the funding agency. These include submission of periodic reports, interim budget summaries, the final report, and other requirements. Manuscript preparation should be included in the workscope since staff for writing, typing, and submission are part of the costs of the research process.

TABLE 13-6 Model for organizing objectives.

Objective 1.0

Enabling Objective	Strategies	Evaluation Objectives
1.1	1.1.1	1.1.1.1
	1.1.2	1.1.2.1
1.2	1.2.1	1.2.1.1
	1.2.2	1.2.2.1
		1.2.2.2
		1.2.1.3.

When the researcher has analyzed the task and ordered the tasks in workscope format, this preliminary document should be analyzed again, before it is written in final form. The analysis should focus on questions the reviewers are likely to raise:

1. Is every *necessary* activity included?

2. Do the enabling objectives and strategies contain redundant elements that can be deleted?

3. Can the tasks be completed faster?

4. Is sufficient time included to complete certain tasks?

5. If completion of one major objective is contingent upon completion of activities in a parallel strategy, is the timing properly sequenced?

To assist with scheduling, the researcher may wish to employ scheduling aids such as PERT (program evaluation review techniques) and CPM (critical path method). Designed for large, complex projects, these techniques provide a system for estimating completion time for tasks to insure that the total workscope is carried to successful completion. If a beginning researcher, for example, wished to build a new apparatus to carry out a research project, it could be necessary to locate the parts, prepare bid specifications, submit bids through the institution's purchasing department, wait for delivery, assemble the apparatus, test it, and debug it. Then, data collection can begin. Information on strategies to schedule these events, using these techniques, can be found in systems management texts.

When the final management plan is written, the reviewer should have a clear picture of what the researcher plans *to do*. The next questions are "Who will do it?" and "What will it cost?"

Describing institutional resources. The general question "Who will do the work?" represents these specific questions:

1. What will the principal investigator (project director, key researcher) do?

2. Does the principal investigator have the training, experience, and capability to conduct the project?

3. Who else must be employed to conduct the research?

4. What level of training must others have?

5. What is the job description of each funded person?

6. Does the sponsoring agency have the capability to house the research project?

7. What relevant support systems exist within the institution to facilitate the research, e.g., computer systems and access to them?

In order to answer these questions, the researcher should:

1. Prepare a vita, following a standard format, which includes at a minimum (a) degrees and years obtained, (b) relevant positions held, and (c) publications.

2. Prepare a narrative description of relevant research experience, major accomplishments, grants obtained, critical experiences with the target population, and so on. This description should convince the reviewers that

the researcher has the training and competence to bring the project to successful completion.

3. Develop a job description for herself that includes administrative and research responsibilities:
—writing job descriptions for others
—writing position offerings in classified advertising format
—working with the institution's personnel bureau to match the job description to a defined salary level
—recruiting, interviewing, and employing other personnel
—supervising the work of other project staff
—budget planning and management
—preparing bid specifications for equipment, as described earlier
—obtaining written cooperative agreements with participating agencies
—staff training and development
—preparing stimulus materials
—programming computers
—carry out research procedures
—data collection
—data analysis
—preparing research reports (manuscripts)
—preparing project reports required by the funding agency
—maintaining project equipment inventories
—writing staff performance evaluations for the sponsoring institution
—initiating/approving purchase orders for all supplies and materials.

4. Preparing job descriptions for others, following the activity list described in item 3 above.

5. Identify the institutional resources that can be used to conduct the research project. If the researcher is relatively inexperienced, are there others who will provide technical assistance if a problem is encouraged? If computer data analysis is required, does the institution have the systems to do it? If so, is the researcher guaranteed computer time? If time must be paid for, what is the execution time for typical jobs and what does it cost per minute? Does the researcher have most of the "tools" to do the job, and thus show that they need not be purchased? Does the institution have a documented history of successful administration of grants? These are some of the questions that must be addressed.

The evaluation plan. As noted earlier, an evelution plan may be simple or complex. On a small project, completion of the project, written in publishable manuscript form, may be sufficient. On larger projects, extending over several years and closely monitored by the funding agency, timelines for the task completion component for every major activity may be specified. Reviewers may want to know what built-in "signals" there are to warn the funding agency if the project falls seriously behind schedule. If the project requires that products (manuals, computer software, curricula, etc.) be delivered to the sponsoring agency, the evaluation questions will be: Are they delivered as promised? Are they delivered on time?

Budget development. Budget development, at first glance, appears to be a complex task. The researcher, after the first attempt to prepare a budget, may be convinced that it is the most difficult part of the grant writing process. The task does become easier as one identifies the resources that facilitate budget development and as certain standard costs are determined. Eventually, particularly when the research project is small, the process can be viewed as the calculation of a few, easily determined figures. For the beginning researcher, the following recommendations may make the process less difficult. Before any figures are put on paper, the researcher should:

1. Analyze the completed workscope. For each enabling objective and strategy, ask:
   —Who will do it?
   —How long will it take?
   —Does it require materials, equipment, or services?
   —Can the costs be assumed by the institution?
   —What must be charged to the grant?

If the answers are compiled on a preliminary worksheet, the researcher will have a general idea of the items that must be included in the budget.

2. Identify those within the institution who can assist in budget development. In some institutions, an administrator may be charged with the responsibility for assisting to develop budgets. In other places, the researcher is on her own. In that case, the researcher's next step is to seek out experienced colleagues who can provide assistance.

3. Identify the checkpoints in the institution's grant submission. If the proposal must be reviewed at several levels, are there key individuals who will monitor the budget and possibly require budget revisions? If this is the case, do these individuals follow formulas or impose constraints that are written in little known policy manuals? If so, find the constraints ahead of time.

4. Obtain copies of the institution's standard budget preparation worksheets, if these exist.

5. Obtain the formula for calculating the institution's indirect cost rates. These rates represent the service fee, or administrative costs, which the institution charges to sponsor the research.

6. Obtain the institution's purchasing catalogs. These may contain reduced prices for standard items. Further, institutional policy may require that all equipment, office supplies, and other materials be purchased "from"the institution or through its purchasing department.

7. Consult with the resource personnel, if any, to generate these cost estimates.

8. Analyze the funding agency's program announcements or regulations or policy statements. Most have restrictions on "allowable costs," e.g., research programs may not allow capital construction (erecting a building to house the research). Some do not fund equipment purchase, or permit only limited equipment acquisition. Others may require lease, rather than purchase agreements, unless the program is of a long-term duration.

9. Compare the funding agency's and the sponsoring institution's policies and identify possible sources of conflict. At the first author's institution, graduate students receive tuition waivers. On sponsored research, the institution requires that the funding agency pay the tuition, and thus proposals

must contain a line item for graduate student tuition. However, the federal agency that funds research for the handicapped will not pay tuition costs for graduate students. Thus, a "Catch-22" situation exists, and is resolved, term by term, by different policy interpretations within the situation.

Armed with the information obtained through these prerequisite steps, the researcher is prepared to develop a working budget. The first step is to locate the budget sheets that may be part of the funding agency's grant announcement document. The first pleasant surprise is that the budget contains limited set of standard categories. The next sections are organized by standard budget categories. Questions are posed that determine how dollar amounts may be computed. Some questions can perhaps be answered by the funding agency's program officer, although policy guidelines may restrict the information they can provide.

Personnel

The project director's salary. The basic question is "How much time is required to conduct the research *and* administer the project?"

On a small project, the funding agency may recommend a minimum time commitment to insure that sufficient attention is given to the grant. A larger project may require 100% of the project director's time. If the researcher is successful in obtaining several grants that run concurrently, the funding agencies may be diligent in checking to insure that no more than 100% time is committed across all projects.

If the grant program requires cost sharing, is this one expense that the institution will assume, or will the institution require that this expense be budgeted?

Since the salary is projected for the next academic year in a university, or for future budget years in other agencies, is there a maximum amount that the institution will allow as a percent salary increase? If the researcher is due for a promotion and a major salary increase (15%) and institutional guidelines permit only a 5% allowable projection, where will the other 10% come from—if the grant is funded and the potential salary adjustment is received.

Thus, the first budget item contains a known amount and is easy to calculate.

1. Present salary × projected salary increase

2. Estimated next year's salary × percent of time on grant

Professional staff. If the project is of sufficient scope, it may require a doctoral level person in charge of every major research program or professional staff to monitor key workscopes. Generally, these will be funded as full-time positions. As noted, a job description must be developed for each person, in collaboration with the institution's personnel division. Once the basic tasks are described, and the qualifications are specified, a salary range can be determined. Then the researcher may choose to write the position in the budget within that range.

Secretarial/bookkeeping support positions. On a small project, secretarial functions may be limited to typing a few data forms, a manuscript, periodic and final reports. These tasks may be absorbed by the institution's regular secretarial staff. Or, they may be performed by part-time secretarial support, hired on an hourly basis. On larger projects, a full-time secretary may be required.

On small projects, the director, a secretary, and the sponsoring institution's secretaries or administrative aides may collaborate to keep project books. On large projects, a part or full-time bookkeeper may be needed.

For both cases, the salary will be computed on an hourly rate, determined by the institution's salary scale. Once task time estimates are determined, it is simply a matter of computing hours × the hourly rate.

Graduate student support. Assistantships are usually funded on a term basis. There may be a flat payment schedule that applies to all students, or there may be a slight differential for students at different training levels. In either case, these are defined, standardized costs.

Fringe benefits. These are determined by the sponsoring institution. However, they are all paid from project funds. In a university, these may be 25%–30% of faculty positions, which may include social security, state or private retirement funds, medical, dental, vision, and other insurance. For hourly personnel, there may be only a contribution for social security benefits.

Travel expenses. These expenses are subdivided into international, national, and local (intrastate) travel. For the beginning researcher, national and local travel are justifiable expenses. For small projects, one convention presentation may be fundable. Beyond these costs, it may be necessary to budget daily mileage costs from the institution to local school research sites. To compute these costs for national travel, one must determine the cost of a round trip air fare, specify the number of days the trip will take, and calculate the daily *per diem* rate. In some institutions this is a predetermined, fixed cost. In others, it is calculated on the cost of a motel room plus a fixed cost for meals. In any case, the cost of a trip is figured as the cost of transportation plus number of days × a per diem rate. Local travel is computed by multiplying the anticipated number of trips by the round trip distance. For day trips, meals may or may not be a fundable expense.

Supplies and services. Costs may include:

1. Standard office supplies—
   a. typing paper and supplies,
   b. other paper products,
   c. mailing costs.
2. Telephone costs—depending on the scope of the project, telephone costs may be limited to the monthly cost of a single line. Or, if the project must work with agencies located across the country, WATS service may be considered.
3. Special supplies for stimulus materials. These may include:
   a. film and processing for stimuli presented on 35mm slides,
   b. special papers and materials for hand drawn stimulus materials.
4. Graphics—services for designing stimulus materials, brochures that describe the purpose of the project, etc.

5. Minor consumable parts for electronic devices—while major equipment is included in a separate category, minor parts for constructing simple response recording devices, etc., may be included in this section.

Contractual services. This category is used for services provided by contract that are not available through the resources of the institution. These may include leases on office equipment, contracts to build special equipment, and/or consultant fees.

Equipment. This category is appropriate for major equipment purchases. Although there are complex federal regulations which govern the disposition of equipment once a project is completed, in reality the equipment stays with the institution, as long as it is being used for the purpose for which it was obtained. It is, in essence, a gift to the institution. Consequently, agencies may be reluctant to allow costs for equipment. The researcher should, before initiating a request, (1) seek out equipment within the institution, (2) determine the conditions under which existing equipment may be employed, and (3) if the outcome of steps 1 and 2 is negative, proceed with an equipment request.

As noted, if equipment is to be purchased, the researcher will find herself in the midst of a very complex process. The institution may have a standard contract to purchase *one* brand of microcomputers for below the list price. Or, computer purchase may eventually have to be approved by a state agency which monitors the university. In any case, costs and requests are likely to be determined in cooperation with the institution's purchasing department, *and* a strong justification for purchase will need to be written.

Other expenses. This category is used, obviously, for items that do not fit in the others. These may include payments to subject participants, computer time on institutional systems, books and other reference materials, and/or expenses for project advisory committee members.

Total direct costs. The sum of all the budget items listed above is the total direct cost of the project.

Indirect costs. One of the first surprises to confront the beginning researcher is the magnitude of the administrative fee charged by the institution. Universities and private contract corporations usually have a standard fee which has been negotiated with the federal government. The rate may differ, if research is conducted at remote sites. There may be different fees for federal and private funding agencies. Thus, it is not unusual for an institution to add 60% of the total direct costs as *an indirect cost.*

Funding agencies may have limitations on the amount they will allow as an indirect cost rate. If there is a discrepancy, another Catch-22 situation exists.

Total budget. The total budget is the sum of the direct costs and indirect costs.

Completing the Grant Proposal

The process described thus far results in a nearly complete proposal. There are, however, a number of steps that must be carried out before the grant proposal is complete. These vary, of course, among funding agencies. The researcher should:

1. Prepare a cover sheet. Currently federal programs provide a standard form. It requires information that may be difficult to obtain, requiring consultation with others in the institution.

2. Prepare a Table of Contents, following a standard form.

3. Fill out standard forms provided by the funding agency. These may include items related to institutional resources, budget sheets for future award periods, etc.

4. Prepare appendices for:
   a. vitae,
   b. proposed staff positions,
   c. reference materials that do not fit neatly into the body of the grant proposal,
   d. abstracts of related research conducted by the grant initiator,
   e. evaluation instruments,
   f. copies of working agreements with participating agencies,
   g. letters of support from key individuals.

The information included in the appendices should be chosen judiciously. It is easy to expand the proposal by including whatever the researcher deems relevant. In reality, much of this material may go unread.

5. Write a budget justification. This is a narrative description of the need for each category of expenditures. It may be item specific. As noted, some items, e.g., equipment, may require a strong justification. This may be included at the end of the workscope narrative or attached to the line item budget.

6. Arrange for the production of graphs, tables, and charts that are included in the body of the proposal.

7. Compile a reference list

When the draft manuscript is complete, the researcher's next tasks are:

1. Verify the submission deadline for the proposal.

2. Determine the number of copies that must be submitted.

3. Obtain the routing forms that may accompany the proposal as it goes through various levels of institutional review.

4. Arrange the mechanics of production: final typing, reproduction, assembly, and mailing.

5. Insure that the proposal is routed through the institution, and not lying unread on someone's desk.

6. Verify that it is submitted on time.

When these steps are completed, and the proposals have been sent off, the researcher can relax, and prepare for the 6–12 month wait to find out if the proposal is funded.

SUMMARY

This chapter has described three writing tasks in a naturally evolving order in the professional career of a graduate student-researcher. The major differences in the focus of these tasks have been identified. The recommendations have been focused on single subject research projects, although they apply in large part to many other research strategies. The steps in the development of grant proposals have been written so that the information applies across a wide range of funding programs. Thus, while the recommendations are broad in scope and, we believe, specific in detail, they represent only a starting point. The following topics, beyond the scope of this chapter, are ones the enterprising researcher may want to "research."

• What is the shortest possible time a grant proposal can be rushed through institutional review?

• What is the review process within the funding agency?

• What questions are improper and proper to ask program officers within funding agencies?

• Within your institution, who will facilitate your efforts and who will stand in your way when you begin to gather information for a grant proposal?

• What unwritten rules govern the behavior of persons within funding agencies?

• How can you follow shifts in funding priorities within an agency?

This brief list should raise other interesting questions whose answers will enlighten the beginning researcher.

14

ETHICAL PRINCIPLES AND PRACTICES

The student-researcher may be in for a shock upon learning that the research project, independently conceived and carefully designed, must undergo formal scrutiny before it is carried out. Later, in the midst of the institutional review process, it may come as an even greater shock to hear members of a human subjects review team raise serious questions about potential harmful effects as they consider what the student perceives to be a most benign intervention program. Or, review team members may question whether the benefits of the proposed study outweigh the risks, as *they* perceive them. It may seem that some interventions are primarily educational and thus need not be presented for human subjects review. Depending on the interpretation of the university, that may be the case. Yet, any intervention that presumes to alter the social or academic behavior of students, and that presumes to have scientific merit, i.e., to contribute to a knowledge base, raises fundamental ethical and specific procedural questions. Under present federal regulations, sponsoring institutions must "assure" that the rights of the research subjects are protected. These assurances are made only after the proposed study has been brought under public scrutiny through examination by a human subjects review committee.

This chapter presents the ethical issues that must be considered in applied research, describes the steps the student-researcher must go through to obtain institutional approval to conduct thesis research, and, then, describes the guidelines the practicing teacher must follow when utilizing research designs to verify the effectiveness of an intervention.

This chapter was written by **James W. Tawney** and **David L. Gast**.

The Concern for Ethical Behavior

As the 20th century draws to a close, it is apparent that humankind will benefit from, or bear the consequences of (depending on one's point of view), an unprecedented explosion in the growth of science and technology. The advancement of science has made possible the creation of basic forms of artificial life, "test tube babies," *in utero* surgery, and a host of life-sustaining agents. Technology has made possible space exploration and perhaps colonization, increasingly miniaturized and sophisticated computer systems, replacement prostheses for complex organs, and equipment to sustain life under conditions that create new definitions of death. It is also apparent that the moral, philosophical, and ethical issues will be debated, unresolved, long after the practices are firmly in place.

The goal of science is the advancement of knowledge. All forms of scientific inquiry are presumed to be important, whether they seem to offer benefits that are immediate and practical or long range and esoteric. Thus, the scientist pursues knowledge, along whatever path that may take him; at least that is the common view. The physicist or biochemist may work unimpeded and in relative anonymity. Not so the scientist who studies—and attempts to modify—human behavior.

Psychologists and educators engage in their professions within a framework of general standards of conduct. Psychologists have developed ethical principles for conducting research. These serve as a model for social science research and, in large part, address the issues of concern to human subjects review committees. In broadest terms they suggest the researcher acknowledge and evaluate potential risk, conduct research so that risk is minimized, inform human subjects of their rights, and if risk is inevitable, take all steps necessary to reverse the psychological duress imposed. These principles are delineated as follows:

1. In planning a study the investigator has the personal responsibility to make a careful evaluation of its ethical acceptability, taking into account these Principles for research with human beings. To the extent that this appraisal, weighing scientific and humane values, suggests a deviation from any Principle, the investigator incurs an increasingly serious obligation to seek ethical advice and to observe more stringent safeguards to protect the rights of the human research participant.

2. Responsibility for the establishment and maintenance of acceptable ethical practice in research always remains with the individual investigator. The investigator is also responsible for the ethical treatment of research participants by collaborators, assistants, students, and employees, all of whom, however, incur parallel obligations.

3. Ethical practice requires the investigator to inform the participant of all features of the research that reasonably might be expected to influence willingness to participate and to explain all other aspects of the research about which the participant inquires. Failure to make full disclosure gives added emphasis to the investigator's responsibility to protect the welfare and dignity of the research participant.

4. Openness and honesty are essential characteristics of the relationship between investigator and research participant. When the methodological requirements of a study necessitate concealment or deception, the investigator is required to insure the participant's understanding of the reasons for this action and to restore the quality of the relationship with the investigator.

5. Ethical research practice requires the investigator to respect the individual's freedom to decline to participate in research or to discontinue participation at any time. The obligation to protect this freedom requires special vigilance when the investigator is in a position of power over the participant. The decision to limit this freedom increases the investigator's responsibility to protect the participant's dignity and welfare.

6. Ethically acceptable research begins with the establishment of a clear and fair agreement between the investigator and the research participant that clarifies the responsibilities of each. The investigator has the obligation to honor all promises and commitments included in that agreement.

7. The ethical investigator protects participants from physical and mental discomfort, harm, and danger. If the risk of such consequences exists, the investigator is required to inform the participant of that fact, secure consent before proceeding, and take all possible measures to minimize distress. A research procedure may not be used if it is likely to cause serious and lasting harm to participants.

8. After the data are collected, ethical practice requires the investigator to provide the participant with a full clarification of the nature of the study and to remove any misconceptions that may have arisen. Where scientific or humane values justify delaying or withholding information, the investigator acquires a special responsibility to assure that there are no damaging consequences for the participant.

9. Where research procedures may result in undesirable consequences for the participant, the investigator has the responsibility to detect and remove or correct these consequences, including, where relevant, long-term aftereffects.

10. Information obtained about the research participants during the course of an investigation is confidential. When the possibility exists that others may obtain access to such information, ethical research practice requires that this possibility, together with the plans for protecting confidentiality, be explained to the participants as a part of the procedure for obtaining informed consent. (American Psychological Association, *Ethical principles in the conduct of research with human participants*, 1973. Copyright 1973 by the American Psychological Association. Reprinted by permission of the publisher and author.)

These principles were derived after extensive dialogue among groups of psychologists. They are stated in the broadest possible terms since they must apply to basic research in laboratory settings as well as applied research in natural environments. Similarly, they apply to procedures that involve the presentation of noxious or aversive stimuli as well as those that are based on positive consequences. Because they must cover such a broad range of applications, more specific guidance is provided for the individual researcher in a listing of specific problems or issues related to each principle; the implications of possible actions are discussed. In this way, the researcher, hopefully, is guided to make appropriate and ethical decisions. Students should realize that this is a judgmental process and that hard and fast rules do not exist to determine "ethical" research behavior.

Basic Concerns for Applied Research Conducted in Learning Environments

In some instances, research in the classroom, of an educational nature, may be exempted from human subjects review. In other circumstances, all student-researchers may be required to prepare a proposal for institutional review, and the review committee may decide whether the proposal requires full review. Or, independent of university policy, a student's academic advisor may require that educational intervention research be submitted to the review committee as a learning activity for the student. Sensitivity to basic issues related to behavioral interventions may be the critical factor in a decision to request institutional review. These issues are (a) confusion of single subject methodology with "behavior modification" techniques, (b) potential negative effects of a reversal or withdrawal condition, (c) delay of the onset of an intervention in a multiple baseline design.

The growth of applied behavior analyses has not proceeded in the absence of criticism. Criticisms have arisen from (a) basic philosophical issues related to the control of behavior, (b) abuses of behavioral techniques, e.g., the use of token economies with prisoners under conditions that courts have determined to be violations of basic rights, and (c) inappropriate labeling of punitive or coercive techniques as behavior modification. Philosophical issues will continue to be debated, one assumes, as long as behavior modification techniques or behavioral interventions are used. The publicity from documented cases of abuse, primarily with institutionalized retarded populations, has resulted in investigations and prompted the development of guidelines for the use of behaviorally oriented programs. One effort, published by the National Association for Retarded Citizens (May, Risley, Twardosz, Friedman, Bijou & Wexler, 1976), set specific procedures for behavioral interventions. Students should study them before beginning a research project since they provide a perspective on institutional abuse, basic human rights, and constraints on behavioral interventions. These guidelines have prompted further discussion among behaviorists. Sajwaj (1977) described major components of the guidelines and cautioned that they did not, in and of themselves, offer a permanent solution to the problems of abuse. Stolz (1977) argued against the use of specific guidelines, reasoning that a less rigid approach based on an analysis of critical issues might provide more guidance for the researcher. Knowledge of the specific issues and arguments, beyond the scope of this text, are assumed to be prerequisite information for students engaging in behavioral research.

Inappropriate use of the term *behavior modification* has been a persistent problem, one difficult to control and one that may create negative reactions that affect the student-researcher. For example, the first author, many years ago while touring a public school for moderately retarded students, was informed by the principal that the school would make an excellent research and student practicum site because a consultant had trained the teachers in "behavior modification." However, observation revealed that to this group the term was defined by hitting children with hickory sticks. Tactful suggestions that perhaps there had been a misunderstanding were not met with enthusiasm. In this situation, for many parents, perhaps for several years, the term *behavior modification* was synonymous with spanking. The student-researcher who requests to work in such an environment may face intense questioning by review committee members who are parents, too. Making distinctions between what behavior modification is and is not is assumed to be part of the student-researcher's professional repertoire.

There is another distinction that should be acknowledged. As noted, single subject research is generally considered synonymous with behavior modification.

Yet, academic interventions are behavior modification in only the broadest sense of the word. And, while the presumed goal of public education is behavior change in a positive direction, educators typically do not think of themselves as behavior modifiers. Thus, it may be that research projects, representing academic behavior acceleration may be viewed as behavior modification in the most technical sense, when conducted within the structure of a single subject research design. Thus, the student-researcher may be expected to defend an academic intervention program as though it were a high risk behavior change project. A first step, explicit description of the intervention in the human subjects review protocol, should clarify the nature of the target behavior. And that, in turn, is the first step in the process of attaining institutional approval, following the procedure shown in the next section.

Obtaining Institutional Approval to Conduct Student Research

The process outlined here begins after a student has selected a research topic and obtained approval from an academic advisor or thesis research sponsor to proceed with the project. The process of institutional review varies from school to school. Two typical procedures are outlined; one requires researchers to defend a written proposal before a review committee, the other does not. The process starts with a very mundane act: locating the proper forms. The forms will be accompanied, in most cases, by guidelines for preparation of the narrative portion of the protocol. These deserve intensive study by the student. Representative forms from The Pennsylvania State University are shown in Figures 14-1 and 14-2. Also deserving of attention is the submit—revise–resubmit–loop shown in Figures 14-3 and 14-4. Preparation of a clearly written proposal, submitted early, should increase the probability that approval is obtained in sufficient time to conduct the research.

Increasing the Probability of Approval

The best recommendation to increase the probability of approval on the first go-round is to write clearly and succinctly elaborating on those points that are likely to be viewed critically, easily misunderstood, or sensitive. In other words, the skill required to prepare an article for *JABA* will serve to prepare a protocol for human subjects review. The suggestions that follow are elaborations, in part, on the items contained in the guidelines in Figure 14-2.

Special Populations

Students will note that special populations receive specific attention in the checklist portion of the protocol. Since this text was prepared for researchers working with "special students," it is apparent that this is an item of concern for the student-researcher. Currently special students are referred to as "those manifesting learning and behavior of varying degrees of severity." While this terminology is a common referent to special educators and is used in place of specific categorical referents, it is likely to be unfamiliar to review committee members. It will be advisable to follow this general descriptor with a specific referent, e.g., "students traditionally referred to as mentally retarded whose academic performance at age ____ is often that of a first- or second-grade student (in the case of moderately retarded students)." Or, "students who manifest behavior disorders so severe that, without special intervention, they typically disrupt the normal flow of activities in the classroom" or "disrupt or interfere with the learning of their classmates" or "physically assault other students" or "inflict physical injury on themseves or others." Student-researchers are expected to draw on their knowledge of the learning-behavior characteristics of the subjects they wish to work with and to describe the population (a) in general terms, (b) in traditional categorical terms, and (c) with respect to the specific target behaviors that they intend to manipulate.

Guidelines also require a rationale for selecting this special population. An adequate rationale might indicate how or why the target behavior interferes with normal functioning and why the intervention, if successful, will make life better for the subject(s). It might also include a concise reference to an existing literature that verifies that the target behavior is commonly found in the population under study.

Potential Risk

At first glance, it might seem that the issue of potential risk is easily dismissed in a classroom-based academic intervention or in a social behavior change project employing positive consequences. However, risk may be interpreted broadly. Suppose that the researcher engages a student in an intervention during a time when the student would otherwise be receiving academic instruction; then suppose that the intervention does not succeed. The student's behavior is unchanged and he has lost instructional time. If the intervention proceeds for an extended period without positive results, is the researcher responsible for the student's falling behind schedule? Suppose that a traditional and an experimental instructional program are presented alternately to students who perform better under the traditional program. Has the experimental program interfered with more effective instruction and thus disadvantaged the students?

Suppose that the intervention involves physical manipulation of the students, e.g., using physical prompting of motor responses (pointing) with cerebral palsied students. What is the potential risk of physical injury to students who resist or respond defensively? How will the researcher decide if the student/subject is being "harmed" and what alternate plan will be employed to assure that the element of risk is removed?

The authors assume that student-researchers generally will not be permitted to conduct research which involves the presentation of aversive or noxious stimuli and, thus, that is not a topic of concern here. However, suppose that an intervention involves positive consequences for a correct response and a mild reprimand or brief time-out for an incorrect response. What level of risk is present when a mild punishment is used (assuming that it is verified that these stimulus events decelerate the target behavior)?

In response to these issues, the student-researcher might consider that the length of an intervention may constitute only a fraction of a school day and that there may be ways to make up potentially lost instructional time. Further, it is possible to describe how one "feels" physical resistance during prompting,

---

EXPLANATION OF STUDY (INVESTIGATION, EXPERIMENT, PROGRAM)

Ethically and legally consent is not considered to be "informed" unless the investigator discloses all those facts, risks, and discomforts which might be expected to influence an individual's decision to willingly participate as a volunteer in a study.

Inform the human subjects about your study including a "fair" explanation and using language easily understood by lay people. Use whatever space is required to cover the prupose, procedures, etc. You are not limited to one page. The investigator and the subject should sign and date the explanation.

Your consent form may be on one page or on one page and the back of the first page. The length will depend upon the amount of space required for your explanation. and to inform the subjects as outlined in the basic elements of infommed consent (see*).

You should inform the subjects that signed informed consent forms are stored by the Office of the Vice President for Research and Graduate Studies and envelopes with special seals are used for sensitive studies.

Information required in your explanation for informed consent:

* Purpose of Study:
  (In situations where it is not possible to fully disclose the puropse of
  a study, the following statement is optional: "Because the validity of
  the results of the study could be affected if the purpose of the study
  is fully divulged to me prior to my participation, I understand that the
  purpose of the study cannot be explained to me at this time. I understand
  that I will have an opportunity to receive a complete explanation of the
  study's purpose following my participation in the study.")

* Procedures to be Followed:
  (Indicate any which are experimental; inform subjects on data handling
  and procedures used to maintain confidentiality.)

* Discomforts and Risks:

* Alternative Procedures:
  (A disclosure of any appropriate alternative procedures that might be
  advantageous for the subject.)

* Potential Benefits:
  (Of the investigation to the subject or to society. In many investigations
  benefits for the subjects may not exist.)

* Period of Time Required:

_____   _____   _____   _____
Volunteer's Signature   Date   Investigator's Signature   Date

_____   _____
Signature of minor subject's parent or guardian   Date

                    *These items are marked to identify them for
                        investigators as the basic elements of informed consent.

FIGURE 14-1 Human subjects review checklist.

FORM A—Page 2

7. Will any type of electrical equipment be used that will be connected
    to subjects? (If answer is yes, give in the Form D protocol the
    name and qualifications of the individual who will check for
    electrical safety)... NO   YES

8. Will subjects receive any payment for participation (money, course
    credit, etc.)? (If answer is yes, give details in Form D protocol)..... NO   YES

9. Is the project specifically designed to involve subjects who are:
    minors (less than 18 years of age)?.................................... NO   YES
    pregnant women?... NO   YES
    prisoners?.. NO   YES
    mentally retarded?.. NO   YES
    mentally disabled (e.g., brain-damaged, psychiatric patients, etc.)?.... NO   YES
    physically handicapped (e.g., uses wheelchair, walker, etc.)?........... NO   YES
    institutionalized?... NO   YES
    Penn State students?... NO   YES

10. Do procedures include obtaining parental/guardian consent and/or
    institutional authorization for access to subjects if minor, mentally
    retarded/disabled, or institutionalized subjects are involved?.......... NO   YES
                                                                           N.A.

11. Are procedures for maintaining confidentiality of all subjects'
    data fully described?... NO   YES

12. Are procedures for obtaining informed consent fully described?.......... NO   YES

13. Have copies of informed consent documentation been submitted along
    with the protocol (i.e., signature document with explanation of
    study, transmittal letter, debriefing statement, or other)?............. NO   YES

14. Fill in the numer or estimate:
    average amount of time required for subject's participation (in hours).. _____
    if questionnaires are involved, the total number of items............... _____
    number of volunteers (subjects) to be involved in this study............ _____

    The project or activity described in the attached information was planned to adhere
to the University's policies and the institutional assurance with the U.S. Dept. of HEW
regarding the use of human subjects. University review and approval is requested.
Major additions to or changes in procedures involving human subjects that occur after
review of the application will be brought to the attention of the review committee by
the investigator. In addition, the committee will be notified of any unanticipated
events that do or could affect the safety and well being of subjects.

Typed Name   Campus Address   Phone

_____   _____
(Investigator)   (signed)

_____   _____
(Advisor-if applicable)   (signed)

_____   _____
(Dept/Div/Unit Head)   (signed)

FIGURE 14-1   (continued)

PROTECTION OF HUMAN SUBJECTS

FORMAT FOR PROTOCOL (PROCEDURES AND METHODOLOGY)

1. Describe the requirements for a subject population and explain the rationale for using in this population special groups such as prisoners, children, the mentally disabled or groups whose ability to give voluntary consent may be in question.

    What sex? What ages or other characteristics--minors, college students, adults, senior citizens, institutionalized patients: physically or mentally handicapped. Describe any special selection criteria. Describe the mental, medical, and physical status of the subjects and identify any medical, psychiatric, psychological or other treatment they are receiving.

2. Describe and assess any potential risks--physical, psychological, social, legal or other--and assess the likelihood and seriousness of such risks. If methods of research create potential risks, describe other methods, if any, that were considered and why they will not be used.

    Describe your protocol including background, objectives, plans, personnel, materials, equipment, and references. Where and by whom will the experiment be conducted? Identify by name and position all those who will be involved in the experiments, data gathering, or have access to the raw data.

    Where and by whom will questionnaires or instruments be administered? Will there be a follow-up questionnaire or instrument? Identify by name and position all persons administering questionnaires or instruments and those with access to raw data.

    Where and how will raw data be stored? Are the instruments coded? If you have a key for coding, what are the security measures and who has access to the key?

    What will be the disposition of the raw data, instruments, questionnaires, tape recordings, video tapes, photographs and other material which could be identified with individual subjects upon completion of the investigation or study? If your study is collecting sensitive or personal information in which the subjects are not completely anonymous or in which coding is used, tell how long data will be kept and if and when it will be destroyed.

    Be specific about the procedures, methods, experiments, activities, and types of information sought. State frequencies, intensities, durations, types of stimuli or other conditions to be used. Has similar work previously been performed using human subjects? If so, are the procedures generally accepted?

    Can you provide the names of experts in the field with whom the committee members could communicate to discuss potential risks or hazards of your protocol?

3. Describe consent procedures to be followed, including how and where informed consent will be obtained. Attach a copy of the format you intend to use in obtaining informed consent.

    How will subjects be recruited--volunteers from institutional classes, local population, faculty or staff, bulletin board notices, newspaper ads, etc.? Will subjects be paid or receive credit for participation -- how much? Will any motivational devices, coercion, or deception be employed?

    Informed consent must normally be written and contain the basic elements of informed consent including that the subject is free to withdraw his consent and to discontinue participation in the project or activity at any time without prejudice. Informed consent must include a "fair" explanation of the procedures in language easily understood by the subjects. Subjects should be informed of the disposition of identifiable data--instruments, video and tape recordings, photographs, etc.--upon completion of the study.

4. Describe procedures (including confidentiality safeguards) for protecting against or minimizing potential risks and an assessment of their likely effectiveness.

    Provide your guidelines for safeguards used to protect the subject. Detail your criteria for terminating an experiment or for deciding that a subject can no longer participate in an experimental regimen. List the emergency procedures to be employed in case of an accident. Describe how you will maintain confidentiality of information and protect the rights of privacy of your subjects. Provide copies of any questionnaires or instruments to be completed by the subjects. Describe debriefing procedures.

5. Assess the potential benefits to be gained by the individual subject, as well as benefits which may accrue to society, in general, as a result of the planned work.

6. Discuss the risks and benefits of your investigation or activity. If you are submitting a proposal to DHEW, your application may ask you to analyze the risk-benefit ratio. You may provide your answer to DHEW's question for Item 6.

7. Inform the committee of your background and experience which qualifies you to carry out the proposed experiments. Have you previously used this protocol or procedure? How familiar are you with the equipment, devices, or instruments? Biomedical investigations or activities require a faculty member to be responsible for and supervise all investigations. If you are doing behavioral studies or using questionnaires and surveys and are a graduate student, which faculty member is responsible for and is supervising your work? What is the faculty member's experience with the protocol or procedures?

FIGURE 14-2   Directions for completing a human subjects protocol.

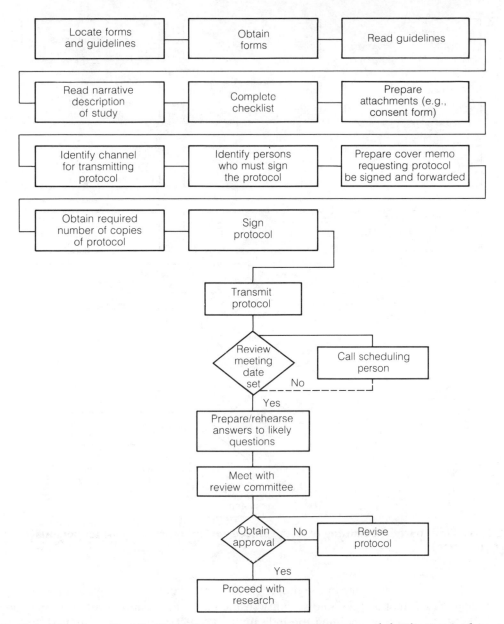

FIGURE 14-3   Flowchart for obtaining human subjects review approval (with personal presentation to committee).

or to list the obvious signs, e.g., emotional responses that signal a researcher that a student is distressed by physical contact. In the case of mild punishers, the researcher might describe the sequence of events, clearly define the punisher, and describe the consequences of *not* employing it. For example, in a small project recently conducted as a course requirement, a professor and a graduate student attempted to shape *drinking from a glass* in a severely developmentally retarded student, one who also manifested physical handicaps. Having observed the child could and sporadically did complete all the

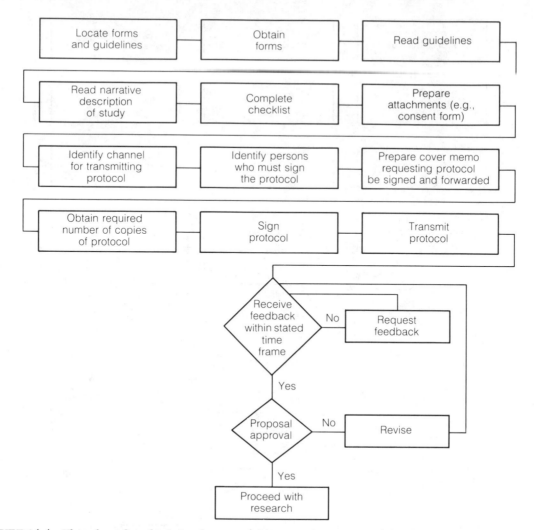

FIGURE 14-4   Flowchart for obtaining human subjects review approval (without personal presentation to committee).

movements in the motor chain, they developed a program to shape a consistent and durable response using physical guidance, time-out (looking away), and withholding the milk until a correct response was emitted. In the midst of the program, the child began to whine, cry, and then tantrum when milk was withheld. At this point, the classroom teacher intervened to terminate the intervention since it was obviously so distressful to the student (in the teacher's opinion). Suppose that this intervention had been a student research project and had been challenged by a human subjects review committee member; the protocol might have been developed in this way:

1. The target is drinking from a glass, without assistance, at every meal.

2. The benefits—the child will acquire a new skill and adults will be freed from the necessity of helping the child with the task.

3. The sequence will be:
   a. Set glass in front of student

   b. Bring student's hand and arm to proper position

   c. Physically prompt drinking by placing hand over the child's and intiating the grasp, lift, tilt, drink motor chain

   d. Gradually withdraw physical assistance (operationally defined)

   e. Praise at each step

   f. When resistance occurs

      i.   remove glass from child's hand,

      ii. turn away for _____ seconds,

      iii. if tantrumming occurs, continue with intervention for _____ sessions or until tantrums are extinguished,

      iv. if the previous steps is unsuccessful after the specified number of sessions, go to plan B (which must be further defined).

This brief outline of a strategy contains two important elements. It acknowledges that an emotional response may occur and sets a limit on the length of time that the behavior will occur before the intervention is modified. This strategy sets the stage for the researcher to account for tantrumming as a typical response in an extinction procedure and then allows for the development of an alternate strategy.

The questions raised here are intended to sensitize the student-researcher to different perspectives on the issue of risk, to raise issues that cannot be answered definitely, and to suggest in one instance a strategy to account for the possibility of duress. Student-researchers may find it helpful to share their protocols with fellow students to identify potential sources of risk and challenge the rationale for engaging in the project.

Defining the Methods and Procedures

The human subjects review protocol requires an abstracted version of the written thesis proposal. While requirements for the scope of the thesis proposal will vary from school to school, from an advisor's verbal approval of a general description of the study to written approval of a fully developed proposal designed for submission for extramural funding, at some point a complete manuscript must be prepared. The authors recommend that the human subjects review prospectus be drawn from a fully developed proposal to insure that the student begin the task of writing early in the research process.

A careful look at Figure 14-2 shows that the human subjects review process focuses on specific elements of the procedures. The protocol requires a complete but abstracted description of the procedures. Then, special attention is directed to two questions, "What will happen to the subjects?" and "What will happen to the data?"

Student-researchers with a background in education or psychology should be skilled in task analysis and should be adept at explicit description of the steps or sequence of events in the research procedure. Students will find it helpful to "walk through" the procedure as they write it and "talk through" the procedures with colleagues. Much of the research conducted utilizing single subject research design will involve discrete trials, making it easy to describe antecedent stimuli, the topography of the subject's response, and the events (correction or reinforcement) which consequate the response. A review committee is less likely to take special interest in antecedent stimuli that are common or easily defined, than in esoteric or potentially noxious stimuli. If academic behavior change projects use common materials, e.g., a well-known basal reading series, it should be sufficient to identify the materials by publisher, content area, and daily "units" of instruction. If academic stimuli are experimental and designed specifically for the study, the researcher might expect to be questioned extensively to determine why they are expected to produce results. If automated equipment is used, the dimensions or parameters of the stimuli should be described, e.g., the subject might discriminate between two tones generated by an audio oscillator preset to a defined frequency and for a constant interval. If visual stimuli are presented and the discriminability of one stimulus is increased by adding, then fading, the intensity of illumination, the degree of illumination, in fading steps, can be described. If a procedure involves a series of statements and actions by the teacher-researcher, these should be written out exactly as they will occur. If the procedure involves physical prompting or guidance, the nature and degree of effort should be described, e.g., "The researcher will say, 'Ralph, touch the ball/block,' and if no spontaneous response occurs, will firmly but gently grasp the student at the wrist and lift the hand/arm so that it drops/rests on the correct object. Physical assistance will be terminated if the student pulls away, cries, or shows other signs of distress." If consequences involve edibles, the review committee is likely to request assurance that the researcher doesn't intend to rot Ralph's teeth. That challenge should be satisfied by describing what is now common practice: observing the child's preferences, consulting with teachers and parents, identifying a menu of nutritional items and sweets (if they are to be used at all), using a schedule of reinforcement, and so on. If noxious stimuli or mild verbal reprimands are part of the procedure, they should be described as completely as possible, e.g, the teacher-researcher will say, "No, pick up the _____," in a firm, neutral voice without facial or other cues indicating displeasure. If an electronically generated stimulus is employed, its physical properties should be described and followed by a statement which provides an easily understood referent, e.g., "after an incorrect response, a buzzer at _____ frequency and amplitude will sound for a half second. This tone sounds much the same as the buzzer on a stove timer or the 'ready' signal on a microwave oven." Thus, there is a common referent, recognizable by most review committee members.

Considerations

The concern for "what happens to the data" is based on three factors: (1) Is the information sensitive? (2) Can the individual subjects be identified? (3) To insure confidentiality, is there a plan to control access to the data and then to destroy it when it is no longer needed?

Most of the data student-researchers collect will not be classified as sensitive information. In the author's view, intelligence test scores constitute the only sensitive data collected on school-age children. Children's records may contain sensitive information on the child and the family, but that data is not collected through single subject research and is unlikely to be of concern to the student-researcher. A case can be made that achievement test scores on individual students are sensitive. The authors would argue against that position. In any case, the student-researcher should expect to yield on that point and treat those scores as the review committee requests. These data are clearly not sensitive:

• Units of academic content, e.g., math problems completed per session;

• Rate of correct verbal responses to teacher's questions;

• Rate or percent correct of motor responses, e.g., point, touch, press responses, to simple or novel visual stimuli, e.g., shape, picture, or letter discrimination;

• Frequency, intensity, or duration of generally acknowledged inappropriate or interfering social behaviors, e.g., hitting, kicking, talking out, self-injurious behavior;

• On-task behavior during study time.

Protecting the anonymity of single subjects is obviously a problem in single subject research—one that is easily solved. The student-researcher should (a) describe how subjects will be coded, e.g., by fictitious initials, (b) verify that the researcher will be the sole holder of the code (or the researcher and academic advisor), and (c) state where the code will be stored (in a locked file in the advisor's office, for example). When a study is prepared for publication, the researcher may use a fictitious name and so label it, fictitious initials, or the real initials of the subject. The location where the study was conducted may be described in ambiguous terms, e.g., a resource room in an elementary school in a medium sized city in the Northeast.

A special problem arises when a study is conducted in a small school or community, when the subject is unique, e.g., the only cerebral palsied child in town, and most of the community is aware of the project. Under these circumstances, the review committee may question the disposition of the final report (master's or doctoral thesis) and the number of individuals who have access to it. Unless the thesis is prepared for publication, few people will actually read it—one or two faculty and a graduate school representative. Review committee members will be well aware of the disposition of the thesis and who will have access to it. If a study is prepared for publication, the committee may question whether anonymity can be sufficiently guaranteed, arguing that any person reading the article would recognize the subject. The journals likely to publish the research are specialized, however, and have a relatively limited circulation. Thus, the probability is low that someone from the local community would have access to the information. Presumably one who did have access would treat the information in a professional manner, but that is outside the scope of concern for the student-researcher.

Confidentiality is an extremely complex issue that arose in universities during the Vietnam era. Students' concerns over government access to their academic records led, eventually, to the enactment of the Privacy of Information Act of 1974. Major components of the confidentiality procedures have been incorporated in P.L. 94-142. Relevant parts of the confidentiality section of the federal regulations (Federal Register, 1977) are shown in Figure 14-5.

The researcher who follows these steps then will have insured confidentiality of the information obtained. At the end of the research project, the student-researcher should have a file of raw data sheets, coded for anonymity, and in a separate place, the key to the code. Whether this information should be destroyed is a matter of judgment. If the study is publishable, good

§ 121a.562   Access rights.

(a) Each participating agency shall permit parents to inspect and review any education records relating to their children which are collected, maintained, or used by the agency under this part. The agency shall comply with a request without unnecessary delay and before any meeting regarding an individualized education program or hearing relating to the identification, evaluation, or placement of the child, and in no case more than 45 days after the request has been made.

(b) The right to inspect and review education records under this section includes:

(1) The right to a response from the participating agency to reasonable requests for explanations and interpretations of the records;

(2) The right to request that the agency provide copies of the records containing the information if failure to provide those copies would effectively prevent the parent from exercising the right to inspect and review the records; and

(3) The right to have a representative of the parent inspect and review the records.

(c) An agency may presume that the parent has authority to inspect and review records relating to his or her child unless the agency has been advised that the parent does not have the authority under applicable State law governing such matters as guardianship, separation, and divorce.

(20 U.S.C. 1412(2)(D); 1417(c).)

§ 121a.563   Record of access.

Each participating agency shall keep a record of parties obtaining access to education records collected, maintained, or used under this part (except access by parents and authorized employees of the participating agency), including the name of the party, the date access was given, and the purpose for which the party is authorized to use the records.

(20 U.S.C. 1412(2)(D); 1417(c).)

§ 121a.564   Records on more than one child.

If any education record includes information on more than one child, the parents of those children shall have the right to inspect and review only the information relating to their child or to be informed of that specific information.

(20 U.S.C. 1412(2)(D); 1417(c).)

§ 121a.565   List of types and locations of information.

Each participating agency shall provide parents on request a list of the types and locations of education records collected, maintained, or used by the agency.

(20 U.S.C. 1412(2)(D); 1417(c).)

§ 121a.566   Fees.

(a) A participating education agency may charge a fee for copies of records which are made for parents under this part if the fee does not effectively prevent the parents from exercising their right to inspect and review those records.

(b) A participating agency may not charge a fee to search for or to retrieve information under this part.

(20 U.S.C. 1412(2)(D); 1417(c).)

§ 121a.567   Amendment of records at parent's request.

(a) A parent who believes that information in education records collected, maintained, or used under this part is inaccurate or misleading or violates the privacy or other rights of the child, may request the participating agency which maintains the information to amend the information.

(b) The agency shall decide whether to amend the information in accordance with the request within a reasonable period of time of receipt of the request.

(c) If the agency decides to refuse to amend the information in accordance with the request it shall inform the parent of the refusal, and advise the parent of the right to a hearing under § 121a.568.

(20 U.S.C. 1412(2)(D); 1417(c).)

§ 121a.568   Opportunity for a hearing.

The agency shall, on request, provide an opportunity for a hearing to challenge information in education records to insure that it is not inaccurate, misleading, or otherwise in violation of the privacy or other rights of the child.

(20 U.S.C. 1412(2)(D); 1417(c).)

§ 121a.569   Result of hearing.

(a) If, as a result of the hearing, the agency decides that the information is inaccurate, misleading or otherwise in violation of the privacy or other rights of the child, it shall amend the information accordingly and so inform the parent in writing.

(b) If, as a result of the hearing, the agency decides that the information is not inaccurate, misleading, or otherwise in violation of the privacy or other rights of the child, it shall inform the parent of the right to place in the records it maintains on the child a statement commenting on the information or setting forth any reasons for disagreeing with the decision of the agency.

(c) Any explanation placed in the records of the child under this section must:

(1) Be maintained by the agency as part of the records of the child as long as the record or contested portion is maintained by the agency; and

(2) If the records of the child or the contested portion is disclosed by the agency to any party, the explanation must also be disclosed to the party.

(20 U.S.C. 1412(2)(D); 1417(c).)

§ 121a.570   Hearing procedures.

A hearing held under § 121a.568 of this subpart must be conducted according to the procedures under § 99.22 of this title.

(20 U.S.C. 1412(2)(D); 1417(c).)

§ 121a.571   Consent.

(a) Parental consent must be obtained before personally identifiable information is:

(1) Disclosed to anyone other than officials of participating agencies collecting or using the information under this part, subject to paragraph (b) of this section; or

(2) Used for any purpose other than meeting a requirement under this part.

(b) An educational agency or institution subject to Part 99 of this title may not release information from education records to participating agencies without parental consent unless authorized to do so under Part 99 of this title.

(c) The State educational agency shall include policies and procedures in its annual program plan which are used in the event that a parent refuses to provide consent under this section.

(20 U.S.C. 1412(2)(D); 1417(c).)

§ 121a.572   Safeguards.

(a) Each participating agency shall protect the confidentiality of personally identifiable information at collection, storage, disclosure, and destruction stages.

(b) One official at each participating agency shall assume responsibility for insuring the confidentiality of any personally identifiable information.

(c) All persons collecting or using personally identifiable information must receive training or instruction regarding the State's policies and procedures under § 121a.129 of Subpart B and Part 99 of this title.

(d) Each participating agency shall maintain, for public inspection, a current listing of the names and positions of those employees within the agency who may have access to personally identifiable information.

(20 U.S.C. 1412(2)(D) : 1417(c).)

§ 121a.573   Destruction of information.

(a) The public agency shall inform parents when personally identifiable information collected, maintained, or used under this part is no longer needed to provide educational services to the child.

(b) The information must be destroyed at the request of the parents. However, a permanent record of a student's name, address, and phone number, his or her grades, attendance record, classes attended, grade level completed, and year completed may be maintained without time limitation.

(20 U.S.C. 1412(2)(D); 1417(c).)

Comment. Under section 121a.573, the personally identifiable information on a handicapped child may be retained permanently unless the parents request that it be destroyed. Destruction of records is the best protection against improper and unauthorized disclosure. However, the records may be needed for other purposes. In informing parents about their rights under this section, the agency should remind them that the records may be needed by the child or the parents for social security benefits or other purposes. If the parents request that the information be destroyed, the agency may retain the information in pargraph (b).

§ 121a.574   Children's rights.

The State educational agency shall include policies and procedures in its annual program plan regarding the extent to which children are afforded rights of privacy similar to those afforded to parents, taking into consideration the age of the child and type or severity of disability.

(20 U.S.C. 1412(2)(D); 1417(c).)

Comment. Note that under the regulations for the Family Educational Rights and Privacy Act (45 CFR 99.4(a)), the rights of parents regarding education records are transferred to the student at age 18.

FIGURE 14-5   Regulations governing confidentiality of information.

scientific practice dictates that the raw data should be kept intact so that other researchers have access to it if they challenge the findings or otherwise wish to examine the data.

Obtaining Informed Consent

Figure 14-6 contains a sample informed consent form, intended as a guide for the student-researcher. The critical elements of informed consent are:

1. Written consent must be obtained from the subject or the subject's parents.

2. The procedure must be described fully.

3. Consent can be revoked at any time, and the subject is free to withdraw from participation.

4. The consent form and the description of the study must be in simple language, clear to uneducated individuals.

In most circumstances, the student-researcher will obtain consent from the child's parents. Students should bear in mind that these parents represent the full range of human variation. The student may be closely questioned by intelligent, informed, and articulate parents who will have many more questions than the human subjects review committee. In many instances, parents will sign a consent form without question because they are willing to participate in any activity that has promise to help their child. In other circumstances, the researcher will confront poorly educated parents of limited ability. In this case, particularly, ethical practice requires that the parents fully understand the intervention.

Parents will be keenly interested in the outcome of the study and, as well, the individuals with whom the results will be shared. Human subjects review requires that that information be provided. In order to conduct a study, at a minimum, the student may be expected to share information with the child's teacher and the principal. Other professionals, e.g., speech and physical therapists, may benefit from knowing the results of the study. The student-researcher should learn what is typical, or expected, in the school system and should be able to list those who will be informed of the outcomes. The student-researcher should decide in advance how detailed an explanation will be given to those who have limited direct involvement with the child. Parents and teachers may request a step-by-step review of the study, focusing on daily sessions where performance was well above or below other data points. Others will be satisfied with a general description of the procedure and the extent to which it was successful. A simple explanation of the sequence of interventions, e.g., three dressing skills taught and empirically verified through a multiple baseline design, focuses on the fact (we will assume) that "no change occurred until intervention was begun. That this occurred three times suggests that the intervention was responsible for the change." This should be easily understood by most people. Finally, parents may wish to know how much information will be shared with others. An explanation should be prepared in advance in the likelihood that the review committee, too, will show a special interest in that information.

Expertise of the Researcher

Human subjects review requests assurance that the researcher knows what he is doing, that he is supervised by knowledgeable faculty, and that the re-

INFORMED CONSENT FORM

The Pennsylvania State University

Title of Investigation:

Investigator(s):   (List Faculty and Graduate Students)   Date:

    This is to certify that I, _____, hereby (give permission to have my child) agree to participate as a volunteer in a scientific investigation (experiment, program, study) as an authorized part of the education and research program of The Pennsylvania State University under the supervision of _____.

    * The investigation and my (child's) part in the investigation have been defined and fully explained to me by _____ and I understand his/her explanation. The procedures of this investigation and their risks and discomforts are described on the back of this form and have been discussed in detail with me.

    * I have been given an opportunity to ask whatever questions I may have had and all such questions and inquiries have been answered to my satisfaction.

    * I understand that I am free to deny any answer to specific items or questions in interviews or questionnaires.

    * I understand that any data or answers to questions will remain confidential with regard to my identity (the child's identity).

    I understand that, in the event of physical injury resulting from this investigation, neither financial compensation nor free medical treatment is provided for such a physical injury and that further information on this policy is available from the Vice President for Research and Graduate Studies, 207 Old Main (865-6331).

    I certify that to the best of my knowledge and belief, I have (the child has) no physical or mental illness or weakness that would increase the risk to me (him/her) of participation in this investigation. (Use this statement if it applies to your investigation.)

    * I FURTHER UNDERSTAND THAT I AM FREE TO WITHDRAW MY CONSENT AND TERMINATE MY (THE CHILD'S) PARTICIPATION AT ANY TIME.

_____ _____   _____
Date   Date of Birth(1)   Subject's Signature

    I hereby consent to the participation of _____, a minor, as a subject in the scientific investigation described.

_____   _____
Date   Signature of minor subject's parent or guardian

    I, the undersigned, have defined and fully explained the investigation to the above subject.

_____   _____
Date   Investigator's Signature

    I was present when the above was explained to the subject in detail and to my best knowledge and belief it was understood.

_____   _____
Date   Witness

(1) Optional for Behavioral and Social Sciences Studies
 * These items are marked to identify them for investigators as the basic elements of informed consent.

FIGURE 14-6   An approved informed consent format.

PROTECTION OF HUMAN SUBJECTS
FORM A—Transmittal to the Vice President for Research and Graduate Studies

                                            Date_____

To: Secretariat, 316 Willard Building

From: Investigator:_____

        Department:_____

Subject (Project Title):_____

_____

Sponsor (Funding Agency):_____

(Please answer all of the following questions; circle the appropriate answer from
among those listed, either No, Yes, or N.A. for not applicable.)

1. This application involves human subjects participating in:
    a. biomedical procedures?... NO   YES
    b. procedures to elicit information (personality tests, question-
        naires, inventories, surveys, observations, etc.)?................... NO   YES
    c. procedures specifically designed to directly modify the knowledge,
        thinking, attitudes, feelings, or other aspects of the behavior
        of subjects?.. NO   YES

2. If biomedical procedures are involved:
    a. are provisions for emergency medical care necessary?
        (If answer is yes, give details in the Form D protocol)............. NO   YES
                                                                                 N.A.
    b. has a qualified M.D. participated in planning the project?
        (If answer is yes, give name in the Form D protocol)............... NO   YES
                                                                                 N.A.
    c. will this study involve drugs or chemical agents (dosages),
        ioning radiation, non-ionizing radiation (microwaves, lasers),
        or high intensity sound?.. NO   YES
                                                                                 N.A.

3. Does this study involve giving false information to subjects?........... NO   YES

4. Are procedures to be used new or innovative (not established and
    accepted)?... NO   YES

5. Will the procedures:
    a. cause any degree of discomfort, harassment, invasion of privacy,
        risk of physical injury, or threat to the dignity of subjects, or
        be otherwise potentially harmful to subjects?...................... NO   YES
    b. if the answer to (a) is yes, have specific provisions been made to
        correct any harmful or adverse conditions that may arise?
        (Give details in the Form D protocol).............................. NO   YES
                                                                                 N.A.

6. Can the potential benefits from the conduct of this study be
    considered to outweigh the risks to subjects?.......................... NO   YES

FIGURE 14-6 (continued)

searcher identify experts outside the university, whom the committee may contact to evaluate the risks of the procedure. Student-researchers who have teaching experience should list and describe the length of the experience and the types of students taught. Generally, the committee may wish to be assured that the researcher has worked with children, has worked in and/or understands the protocol of working in schools, and has pilot tested the procedure. The description of the procedure, included in a previous section, should assure the committee that the antecedent and consequent stimulus events pose no, or limited, risk.

If instrumentation and electronic devices are part of the intervention, the committee may wish to be assured that the researcher is familiar with their operation and thus can verify that they pose no risk to the subjects. If they require no special expertise to operate, that should be noted. If they do, the researcher should explain how that expertise has been acquired. If other personnel are required to operate these devices, their expertise and the nature of their contribution to the project should be clearly stated.

Courteous Research Behavior

Obtaining permission to conduct research by satisfying a human subjects review committee is merely a first step in the process. The student-researcher must follow a specified procedure to obtain permission to enter schools or other learning environments. When the study is in progress, good relations must be maintained with parents and school personnel. After the study is completed, parents, teachers, and other personnel will expect a debriefing. Copies of the final report may be requested by the school or agency as a condition for permission to conduct the research. At every stage, the behavior of the researcher is critical to successful completion of the project. Further, personal interactions between the researcher and others may determine, in large part, whether other researchers are subsequently permitted to work in the system. The authors assume that basic courtesy is a firmly established part of the researcher's repertoire and thus will refrain from sermonizing on how to behave in the schools. Some inherent problems, however, deserve mention.

Following Procedures

Each institution has a set procedure to follow to request permission to work in the schools. In some cases, in a university, a request may be transmitted to a coordinator of field experiences in the College of Education and then transmitted to a specific individual in the schools. In smaller systems, that person may forward the request to the school board for approval; then, if approved, to the principal and classroom teacher. Undoubtedly, the process varies from place to place but in each system there is a clearly defined channel. However, these channels hardly represent reality and therein lies the problem. In an active college of education, which has at least a modicum of rapport with surrounding schools, there are many channels of communication. Many teachers are program graduates, maintain close working relations with former professors, and offer an open invitation to work in their classrooms. On some occasions, teachers will request help directly from the university for problem students who represent eminently researchable challenges. In other situations, when faculty have close working relationships with principals and teachers, it will seem logical to informally discuss a project for teacher/principal reaction which then becomes tacit approval to carry out the research. In other situations, the student-researcher may be encouraged to proceed along formal and informal channels at the same time. Little advice can be offered that applies across settings and situations except that (a) a request to conduct research should be submitted through formal channels as soon as human subjects approval is granted, (b) when invited into the schools informally, specifically ask the person issuing the invitation who should be apprised of the visit, and (c) when discussing a potential study during informal contacts, e.g., when the student-researcher is in the school for other business, stress the fact that the project is only a possibility, describe what stage of development the study has reached, state when it is likely to be formally submitted, and clearly indicate that teacher/principal reaction rather than approval is being sought.

Student-researchers who have taught know full well and thus should be sensitive to the disruption which a research project may cause in the classroom. If the project holds promise of making life more comfortable for the teacher, e.g., an educational intervention provides tutorial instruction for a child and thus frees the teacher for other work, any reasonable disruption is likely to be tolerated. If the benefit is most direct for the researcher and holds only potential benefits for the achievement of science, disruption is less likely to be tolerated. In this circumstance, the researcher should consider how to contribute time or technical assistance to the teacher.

Divulging Information

Divulging information during the study may create a dilemma. Teachers and parents may want to know how things are going. Full, open, and honest disclosure of information is fundamental to ethical practice and the protection of subject's rights. However, specific feedback given frequently may constitute another independent variable in some studies. Suppose that a novel intervention is employed to shape a desired social behavior, that parents request and receive daily progress (Ralph said "please" and "thank you" three more times than yesterday), and that the parents naturally increase the opportunities and reinforcement at home. The change in behavior may occur for two reasons, thus confounding the study. One solution to the problem is to decide ahead of time what type of honest but neutral response will be given ("things seem to be going as expected"). If the project goes badly and parents request that you terminate the project, remember that one element of informed consent is the subject's or parents' right to withdraw participation at any time. Since the response cost of that decision might mean an extra term for the researcher, it is not unreasonable to expect that he will attempt to encourage continued participation. If parents claim an increase in crying or other emotional behaviors at home and attribute that to the intervention, the researcher may have a difficult time convincing them otherwise. If the intervention is being videotaped and it clearly shows that the child smiles often and manifests other signs of pleasure, it is reasonable to show a brief segment of tape and to indicate what percent of the remainder of the tapes show positive interactions. If an independent observer is recording data and can verify that the intervention is positively received, he may be requested to share information with parents. Or, the classroom teacher may be able to see positive change that can be shared. The researcher, in this situation, may walk a fine line between encouragement and coercion and, further, must judge whether sharing information to salvage the project will introduce a potential source of confounding. The situation requires objective analysis and a good sense of ethics.

Researchers should realize that they have an obligation to others who may follow them. One way to meet this obligation and leave the research site on a positive note is to spontaneously provide information about the outcome of the study. Having plotted data daily, complete though rough graphs will be available for discussion as soon as the project is finished. The written narrative from the human subjects review protocol or the written thesis proposal provides a frame of reference to discuss what was done, and the rough graphs provide a referent for the outcome. Immediate feedback to parents and teachers is likely to be highly reinforcing. When the researcher has made commitments to provide written reports, it would seem advisable to provide them before they are due. Hand delivered, with an additional word of thanks for the research opportunity, they should leave a favorable impression and increase the probability that the next researcher will be well received.

Ethical and Legal Considerations for the Classroom Teacher

The ethical considerations described in this first part of this chapter apply, in principle, to the behavior of the classroom teacher who regularly uses single subject research designs to verify the effectiveness of instruction. The procedures and legal requirements, however, are different from those that govern the behavior of the student-researcher.

Data-based Instruction and the Real World

Before considering the teacher's responsibilities in a data-based or research-oriented classrooom, it may be helpful to review typical practice for the classroom teacher.

In regular education, achievement tests may be administered by teachers but are rarely scored by them. Other types of diagnostic information on individual students are collected by psychologists or other professionals. The teacher's responsibility, generally, is to administer unit tests over content, to average grades of the end of the reporting period, to calculate a percent correct statistic, and to assign a letter grade according to the school's standard. In elementary school, teachers are expected to analyze students' error patterns so that they can remedy them. If a child experiences difficulty, the teacher expects concerned parents to request an explanation of the problem and prepares himself to offer specific information. In the advanced grades, the teacher may calculate daily grades and compute an end-of-term grade but does not necessarily expect to offer specific reasons for the low performance of a young adult. In this context, standard achievement test scores are reported annually, and the collective fortunes of the teaching faculty rise and fall in relation to the extent to which students are above or below national norms. A specific group of teachers may be singled out for praise or condemnation if patterns of high or low performance emerge over a period of years. That, however, is as far as teacher accountability for student behavior change extends.

Special education teachers, in the early stages of contemporary special education, did even less data collection than teachers in the regular grades. As noted in Chapter 1, early special education practices slowed down or watered down the regular curricula or changed the focus of instruction to functional or vocationally oriented curricula. Whatever the strategy, the discrepancy from the regular curriculum generally made achievement test scores invalid. As the focus of instruction shifted from academics to social or vocational development, data collection dropped from the repertoire of the special educator. Letter grades were dropped, in favor of general descriptions of performance and certificates of attendance served to indicate the student had regularly progressed through *a* school program. Only recently has data collection been emphasized and primarily for two reasons: (1) the growth of diagnostic-remedial instruction and (2) the growth of applied behavior analysis, or behavior technology, in the classroom setting. A third factor *may* be contributing, but it is too soon to tell. P.L. 94-142 requires teachers of the handicapped to document what they will teach, to what criterion of success, and the extent to which their educational goals are met. While the law stops short of teacher accountability for behavior change on one level, on another teachers must develop educational plans with parents who have the right to request modifications if they are dissatisfied with their child's progress. The administration that passed the law is out of power, and a new administration has yet to signal the extent to which it intends to enforce the law. Rigorous enforcement may bring in-class monitoring by state and federal officials and by parent advocacy groups. Further, certain provisions of the law, those which permit parents to challenge the individual educational plan (IEP) also permit parent school disagreements to proceed to the civil courts, thus placing educational decisions in the hands of the judiciary. The provisions of the law have far-ranging implications for changing teaching practices. In the same way that the student-researcher must make public and justify his research project, the classroom teacher must make public his instructional plans and procedures and must justify them to parents and advocates who may pursue their challenges in the courts. These new demands represent a powerful reason for the classroom teacher to document student progress and, further, to employ single subject research designs to demonstrate that students' behavior changes are a function of a specific intervention. There are other reasons, of course, not the least of which is the personal satisfaction that comes from documenting a functional relationship between teacher effort and child behavior change.

Professional Standards for Classroom Teachers

Teachers are expected to behave in a professional manner, though the dimensions of "professionalism" are nebulous at best. Certain organizations, e.g., the Council for Exceptional Children, have issued professional guidelines from time to time, as shown here:

> Special educators should undertake only those activities which they consider ethical and helpful to exceptional persons. Their employing agencies should support them in due process proceedings when there are potentially serious disagreements about educational programs for exceptional persons. It must be assumed that agencies will not ask their personnel to violate these standards. (1974, p. 62)

Parent groups occasionally publish standards that are, in effect, their expectations. Within the context of civil rights issues, these expectations might better be described as a demand for teachers whose training is equal to that of nonhandicapped students and who are, presumably, equally competent, whatever that may mean.

The National Association for Retarded Citizens first published guidelines for preparing teachers of the mentally retarded in 1963. Recently revised (NARC, 1979) and based, in part, on work in consequence-based teacher certification (certifying teachers only when their students meet defined levels of percent correct responding) (Tawney, 1978), they suggest four areas of expertise:

A competent teacher should:

1. Posess an extensive knowledge of content appropriate to the field of mental retardation (e.g., etiology, history, characteristics, treatments, litigation, etc.);

2. Interact humanely with the retarded learner;

3. Manage the teaching environment so that retarded learners work efficiently; and

4. Produce positive and observable change in retarded learner's performance over time and over increasingly more complex tasks.

These standards suggest that teachers be well prepared, that they create a pleasant learning environment, and that they create learning opportunities that engage children in academic tasks. They go farther than other guidelines by suggesting that teachers produce and document child behavior change. They reflect a growing interest in teacher accountability, an interest that is reflected in the provisions of P.L. 94-142.

Public Law 94-142

P.L. 94-142 was hailed as landmark legislation when it was enacted in 1975. Major efforts were begun on a national basis to implement all the provisions of the law, including a massive infusion of federal funds to state and local education agencies. The law contains these major provisions: (1) that no handicapped child be denied equal educational opportunity, (2) that each handicapped child receive a free, appropriate public education, (3) that handicapped children be educated in the least restrictive educational environment, (4) that an individual educational plan be prepared for each handicapped child, (5) that handicapped children and their parents be provided due process to insure their rights, (6) that parents and children be assured protection during the evaluation process, and that (7) confidentiality of records be assured. The components that bear most directly on teacher behavior are shown here:

121a.346   Content of individualized education program.

The individualized education program for each child must include:
(a) A statement of the child's present levels of educational performance;
(b) A statement of annual goals, including short term instructional objectives;
(c) A statement of the specific special education and related services to be provided to the child, and the extent to which the child will be able to participate in regular educational programs;
(d) The projected dates for initiation of services and the anticipated duration of the services; and

(e) Appropriate objective criteria and evaluation procedures and schedules for determining, on at least an annual basis, whether the short term instructional objectives are being achieved.

121a.349 Individualized education program—accountability.

Each public agency must provide special education and related services to a handicapped child in accordance with an individualized education program. However, Part B of the Act does not require that any agency, teacher, or other person be held accountable if a child does not achieve the growth projected in the annual goals and objectives.

As discussed earlier, these provisions quite specifically describe the legal responsibilities of the classroom teacher.

Ethical Practice   The information in the preceding sections represents general professional expectations for teachers' conduct and performance as well as specific legal responsibilities. It does not, however, relate to the ethics of research in the classroom or consider the teacher's responsibility in conducting empirically verified instruction.

The teacher is likely to use single subject research under two conditions—as part of graduate training or as part of the daily instructional process. In the first instance, the teacher will follow the processes described in the first part of this chapter. In the second instance, the teacher has a somewhat different set of responsibilities.

When single subject research design is used as an integral part of the *instructional* process, the teacher need not seek approval from the school administration. However, since, as this is written, such research represents an innovation, the teacher is well advised to make public the strategies that will be employed. When single subject research design is employed on *social behavior change projects*, and when time-out or other forms of potentially aversive control are employed, ethical considerations for the use of behavior modification must be employed.

The major element of ethical practice that applies to empirically verified instruction is the principle of full and open disclosure of information. Critical elements of P.L. 94-142 require that individual students' programs be planned in conjunction with parents and in collaboration with other specialists and school administrators. The teacher's major tasks are to set up data systems, to explain the logic for the specific research design, and to describe how the design permits certain conclusions. Since these events go beyond typical practice, little disagreement should be encountered; moreover, the additional information obtained should have reinforcing properties.

There are a limited set of special problems that may arise from the use of multiple baseline or multielement designs in instructional programs. If three skills are taught to a severely impaired child, parents may question the need for the extended baselines that precede the second and third interventions and request that instruction begin simultaneously. If the teacher can demonstrate that the child has a full educational program and can provide an estimate of the limited time required to collect baseline, that objection should be removed. If the teacher attempts a new instructional technique in a multiple baseline across three subjects, parents of the second and third students may raise a legitimate concern that their children are being denied an educational opportunity. Again, if the teacher can demonstrate that the children have rigorous programs, that concern should be alleviated. Should the intervention go badly with the first student—so badly that the teacher shifts to another program—the second and third children benefit since they have been spared an ineffective experience. In this situation, the parents of the first child have a legitimate complaint—the student has been subjected to the ineffective program. To counter this objection, the teacher might describe previous research that suggested the program was worth trying and then describe the potential benefit to the students. If there are obvious reasons why the program failed, e.g., the prerequisite behaviors were poorly specified, and if the teacher can describe how the program might be modified (or reintroduced when students have acquired the necessary prerequisites), parental objections should be satisfied. Suppose that there are compelling reasons for restricting an intervention to one setting, e.g., shaping a vocal response using a defined procedure. The teacher might wish to determine if the procedure accelerates the behavior in the instructional setting, record whether generalization occurs spontaneously in other settings, and then systematically introduce the intervention into other settings and document the effect. When written and discussed with parents prior to including it in the IEP, the procedure may seem so simple and attractive that parents decide they should use it at home, too. The counter to this proposition is quite simple, "Let's try it first and see if it works." Since transferring the program to the home is likely to be part of the process, and if that is written into the initial description, the logic of the argument should encourage the parents to delay their assistance until the appropriate stage in the project.

When single subject research is used to verify the effect of a social behavior modification project, particularly when aversives are employed, ethical considerations should be of major concern to the teacher. Since, as discussed earlier, psychologists have chosen not to develop special guidelines for the use of behavior modification, and since there is no special certificate that limits the use of behavior modification to any special professional group, it follows that there are no professional restrictions on the use of behavior modification. Given the legal challenges to behavior modification (Martin, 1975) and the potential for risk to the student, the teacher should initiate such projects only after careful consideration, with caution and with full disclosure of the procedure and with a signed permission from the parent or guardian. These projects should be planned in conjunction with a school psychologist, if that is possible, and to meet the requirements of P.L. 94-142 (based on parental input and parental consent). The major questions that should be confronted are: Is the teacher qualified to develop and implement the project? When is a behavior disruptive or disturbing and to whom? At what point should the use of aversive procedures be considered? What constraints should be written into the behavior change project?

Having stated that there are no professional constraints on teachers' use of behavior modification techniques, why, then, is the issue raised again? The literature on the qualifications of behavior modifiers originates in the field of behavioral psychology and thus does not address the training that classroom teachers should receive before they implement projects in their classrooms. The authors believe that a wide range of expertise exists among special education (and regular) teachers. The proliferation of books on the topic make it possible for one to be self-taught. Because behavioral technology is an integral part of special education, it is reasonable to assume that most teachers-in-training receive some exposure to behavioral principles in general psychology and special methods courses taught by professors who themselves have little direct expertise. In some programs, it is likely that undergraduate and graduate students may progress through basic and advanced courses on behavior modification and through a series of practicum experiences that include training in direct observation, supervised practice in following a written intervention procedure, developing and then implementing—under supervision—single subject behavior change projects using positive consequences, gradually increased responsibility for managing existing token economy systems, and implementing experimental procedures in collaboration with faculty advisors. The authors believe that one's confidence in his ability to implement behavior change projects should be correlated directly with the amount of training and experience received under supervision.

When is a behavior disturbing, and to whom? When a child is tearing his flesh, banging his head, physically assaulting others, or rampaging uncontrolled throughout the school, the decision to intervene is straightforward. When social behaviors are less extreme, the teacher must first analyze the extent to which a behavior is disturbing. Further, one's value systems must be examined. In the late sixties and early seventies, the peak of the compensatory education movement, it was hotly debated whether black preschoolers should be taught "white language" and the social behaviors of the white establishment or should be encouraged to develop skills critical to their culture. At no other time has the culture of the schools been more critically examined. For a time, at least, teachers-in-training were sensitized to their culture and value systems and the subsequent effect those had on their educational decision making. Winett and Winkler (1972), from a slightly different perspective, analyzed selected studies in behavior modification to determine what values were being promoted in the schools, i.e., what social behaviors were being reinforced. They described the model child "as one who stays glued to his seat and desk all day, continually looks at his teacher or his text/workbook, does not talk unless asked by the teacher, hopefully does not laugh or sing (or at the wrong time), and assuredly passes silently in halls" (p. 501).

They concluded that "as currently practiced behavior modification has done very little to change the deplorable state of our schools" (p. 501). O'Leary (1972), in a companion article, suggested that Winett and Winkler had ignored a major portion of the literature and thus developed "a straw man model child" (p. 507). He then described a broader range of behavior change projects and stated the opinion that while certain behaviors, e.g., attending, might be criticized as making children "docile," they had high survival value in the academic environment. This set of articles and accompanying comments by those who evaluated them provide an excellent review of basic issues in the selection of social behavior targets.

At present, determining which social behaviors are disrupting or disturbing is not the sole decision of the special education teacher. As noted, P.L. 94-142 requires parent involvement and collaboration with other professionals. The authors assume that the teacher who intends to initiate a project possesses these prerequisite skills: defining behaviors in observable terms, describing the setting in which the behavior occurs, analyzing behavioral sequences, accurately recording the frequency, duration, magnitude, or intensity of the behavior target. For, when these activities have been completed, the teacher will have a working document (data) from which to develop a rationale for intervention or for deciding that the behavior is disturbing only to him and that, for example, Ralph's talking out on the average of three times a day is hardly intolerable in an otherwise pleasant learning environment.

When should aversive techniques be employed? Only after a series of interventions utilizing positive consequences has been tried, found ineffective, and when data have been collected to verify that this is, in fact, the case.

Model Procedures

What constraints should be written into behavior modification projects? Perhaps the best way to describe these constraints is within the context of the procedures that should be followed to develop social behavior change projects utilizing mildly aversive events. The model procedure that follows is drawn from several sources, primarily the guidelines published by the NARC and from Gast and Nelson's (1977) procedure for using time-out from positive reinforcement. The procedure is written most specifically for the school environment and thus does not contain specific procedures required in institutions for dependent on nonresponsible persons, i.e., the disturbed or retarded. The procedure, readers will note, incorporates the critical elements of P.L. 94-142.

1. Write anecdotal descriptions of potential behavior change targets.

2. Write operational definition of target behavior.

3. Define the context, i.e., write antecedents to and consequents following the behavior.

4. Write/define a procedure for direct observation of the frequency, intensity, duration, or magnitude of the target behavior.

5. Record data for a defined period.

6. Conduct preliminary analysis of data. If data show the problem to be of a lesser magnitude than it appeared or if it is disturbing only to the teacher, STOP.

7. If the problem is severe, in the teacher's judgment, PROCEED.

8. Seek input from parents and others to determine if the problem behavior occurs in other settings and to what extent.

9. Develop a preliminary outline of a plan for modifying the behavior using positive consequences.

10. Obtain parent consent for the plan.

11. Implement the plan.

12. If unsuccessful, terminate the process until a better plan is designed.

13. If unsuccessful, modify the programs using other positive consequences.

14. If unsuccessful, reanalyze the environment and modify the program using positive consequences.

15. Repeat steps 11–14 until all reasonable alternatives, using positive consequences, have been exhausted.

16. Prepare a data summary and graphs to document that positive attempts to modify the behavior have been unsuccessful.

17. Write the steps of the proposed project in brief, outline form.

18. Seek collaboration from specialists if they are available.

19. Consult with parents (assuming there has been constant communication from step 8).

20. Arrange meetings with parents, principal, or other school administrators, and appropriate specialists to verify final form of the intervention.

21. Obtain parents' informed consent (including a provision for withdrawing consent).

22. Verify that the following elements are present in the written plan:
   a) observable description of target behavior
   b) documentation of attempts to change the behavior
   c) explicit description of the aversive stimulus event(s)
   d) the date the intervention will start
   e) the criterion for determining success and thus termination of the project
   f) the maximum length of the project, if it is unsuccessful
   g) dates for review of the project while it is in process by parents and school personnel
   h) a provision for independent observation that the project is being implemented as written
   i) model for graphic display of the data
   j) documentation of related, ongoing activities to expand the child's functional repertoire through positive reinforcement
   k) documentation of relevant research showing that the procedure has been used and is effective.

This is not an inconsequential set of steps. Indeed, there are so many steps preceding the developments of the aversive consequation procedure that the teacher may be inclined to use other, positive strategies to induce behavior change. That possibility weighed heavily in the design of this procedure. Recalling Skinner's interpretation of the essentially punitive climate of the schools, it appears essential that all positive alternatives should be exhausted before others are employed.

Special Problems and Issues

Punishment and Spanking

Teachers with sufficient expertise to confidently undertake the projects described here are fully aware that punishment is an operation defined by its effect on behavior. That distinction is generally unclear to parents and many school personnel. Objections to the use of mild punishers may originate in this confusion. Clarifying the distinction may be a major task for the teacher. The task is made easier by objective definition of the stimulus events to be employed. Parents may find it difficult to accept that spanking is ineffective or may be shown to have positively reinforcing consequences. They may recognize that a firm "no," a mild reprimand, or a water squirt are not highly aversive and may suppress behavior. Defining punishment, describing the physical properties of aversive stimuli in easily understood terms, and showing how the effect of the presentation of these stimuli will be measured may be critical to the distinction between the common and the technical use of the term.

Risk Benefit Factors

To this point, attention has focused on an accurate description of the physical properties of aversives. When developing a rationale for proceeding with a project employing aversives, the teacher will logically describe in an objective manner the effect of the child's actions on himself, other children, or the environment. Again, the limited risk of water squirts to decelerate head banging or eye gouging is apparent. So, too, we presume, are aversives that reduce the number of bruises or bloody noses that classmates suffer or reduce the number of chairs thrown across the room. Other forms of disruption, the number of times a classmate's materials are destroyed and the total amount of time lost (number of students times the number of minutes of studying interrupted by screaming episodes) may require careful description and documentation.

Following Due Process

Due process is a critical factor in P.L. 94-142. The law provides that when parents and the schools disagree, either party may pursue resolution of conflict through a series of hearings which may be appealed to and through the civil courts. Theoretically it is possible for a teacher to insist that a specific intervention be employed, even if the parents object. And, with support from the school adminstration, that course of action might be pursued. In reality, however, the current level of civil rights activism on behalf of the handi-capped makes schools reluctant to pursue such disagreements. Further, expe-rience with the law suggests that mediation and compromise may accomplish more than due process. Thus, while the teacher has the right to exercise his professional judgment, the authors suggest that listening to parents and utilizing their input fully may lead to a more productive outcome.

Time-out

Time out from positive reinforcement has been employed widely in class-room settings and is a controversial procedure. The controversy stems from the frequent misapplication of the procedure and the failure of teachers to obtain parental consent prior to its use. As with any aversive procedure, whether it entails the contingent application of a noxious stimulus or the removal of a reinforcing stimulus, the interventionist must proceed prudently. In the case of time out from positive reinforcement procedures, teachers frequently overlook the need for an identifiable reinforcing event from which the student is contingently removed. Too often a student is removed to a corner of the classroom, a hall, or even a separate room following misbehavior, under the guise of time-out. Such contingent removal qualifies as a time-out strategy only if the activity from which the student is removed is in fact reinforcing. Other misapplications of the time-out procedure have been elaborated by Gast and Nelson (1977), including excessively long time-out periods, failure to use less intrusive time-out procedures (contingent observa-tion and exclusion time-out) before seclusion time-out, use of inappropriate seclusion time-out rooms, and failure to monitor students when in time-out.

To facilitate the effective and ethical use of time out from positive reinforcement procedures Gast and Nelson (1977) have proposed guidelines for the protection of the student, teacher, and agency. To insure that the time out from positive reinforcement procedure is appropriately used and not abused, it is best implemented as a team strategy in which the teacher, the appropriate agency administrators, and the student's parents are active members of the team. Failure to adopt such a strategy could embarass the agency, bring professional censure, or prompt malpractice suits.

SUMMARY

In this chapter we have provided a context for conducting research within a set of ethical principles. We have stated our assumptions about the prerequisite behaviors necessary to conduct academic and social behavior change programs within the framework of single subject research design. Specific procedures have been listed, designed to help the student-researcher obtain approval to conduct research in a manner that protects the rights of his subjects. Brief examples have been provided to show how potential concerns can be explained. Similar information has been provided for the classroom teacher who confronts the same ethical considerations within a different context.

We close by stating again that there are no clear answers to the problems we have raised, and finally, that these guidelines are useful only to those applying mature judgment to the problems they confront.

REFERENCES

Allen, K.E., Hart, B., Buell, J.S., Harris, F.R., & Wolf, M.M. Effects of social reinforcement on isolate behavior of a nursery school child. *Child Development*, 1964, *35,* 511–518.

American Psychological Association. *Ethical principles in the conduct of research with human participants*. Washington, D.C.: Author, 1973.

Andersen, B.L., & Redd, W.H. Programming generalization through stimulus fading with children participating in a remedial reading program. *Education and Treatment of Children*, 1980, *3*(4) 297–314.

Apolito, P.M., & Sulzer-Azaroff, B. Lemon-juice therapy: The control of chronic vomiting in a twelve-year-old profoundly retarded female. *Education and Treatment of Children*, 1981, *4*(4), 339–347.

ARC National Education Committee. *Competency-based teacher education in mental retardation: A model of self-analysis for teacher training programs*. Arlington, Tex. Association for Retarded Citizens, October 1979.

Ayllon, T., & Azrin, N.H. The measurement and reinforcement of behavior of psychotics. *Journal of the Experimental Analysis of Behavior*, 1965, *8,* 357–383.

Ayllon, T., & Azrin, N.H. *The token economy: A motivational system for therapy and rehabilitation*. New York: Appleton-Century-Crofts, 1968.

Azrin, N.H., & Lindsley, O.R. The reinforcement of cooperation between children. *Journal of Abnormal and Social Psychology*, 1956, *52,* 100–102.

Azrin, N.H., & Wesolowski, M.D. Theft reversal: An overcorrection procedure for eliminating stealing by retarded persons. *Journal of Applied Behavior Analysis*, 1974, *7* (4), 577–581.

Baer, D.M. Reviewer's comment: Just because it's reliable doesn't mean that you can use it. *Journal of Applied Behavior Analysis*, 1977, *10*(1), 117–119.

Baer, D.M., & Guess, D. Receptive training of adjectival inflections in mental retardates. *Journal of Applied Behavior Analysis*, 1971, *4*(2), 129–139.

Baer, D.M., Wolf, M.M., & Risley, T.R. Some current dimensions of applied behavior analysis. *Journal of Applied Behavior Analysis*, 1968, *1*(1), 91–97.

Bailey, J., Wolf, M.M., & Phillips, E. Home-based reinforcement and the modification of pre-delinquents' classroom behavior. *Journal of Applied Behavior Analysis*, 1970, *3*(3), 223–233.

Bancroft, J., & Bellamy, G.T. An apology for systematic observation. *Mental Retardation*, 1976, *14* (5), 27–29.

Bandura, A. *Principles of behavior modification*. New York: Holt, Rinehart & Winston, 1969.

Barlow, D.H., & Hayes, S.C. Alternating treatments design: One strategy for comparing the effects of two treatments in a single subject. *Journal of Applied Behavior Analysis*, 1979, *12*(2), 199–210.

Barlow, D.H., & Hersen, M. Single-case experimental designs: Uses in applied clinical research. *Archives of General Psychiatry*, 1973, *29,* 319–325.

Barrera, R.D., Lobato-Barrera, D., & Sulzer-Azaroff, B. A simultaneous treatment comparison of three expressive language training programs with a mute autistic child. *Journal of Autism and Development Disorders*, 1980, *10* (1), 21–37.

Barrett, B.H., & Lindsley, O.R. Deficits in acquisition of operant discrimination and differentiation shown by institutionalized retarded children. *American Journal of Mental Deficiency*, 1962, *67,* 424–436.

Barrish, H.H., Saunders, M., & Wolf, M.M. Good behavior game: Effects of individual contingencies for group consequences on disruptive behavior in a classroom. *Journal of Applied Behavior Analysis*, 1969, *2* (2), 119–124.

Barton, E.S., Guess, D., Garcia, E., & Baer, D.M. Improvement of retardates' mealtime behaviors by timeout procedures using multiple baseline techniques. *Journal of Applied Behavior Analysis.* 1970, *3* (2), 77–84.

Becker, W.C. *Parents are teachers.* Champaign, Ill.: Research Press, 1971.

Becker, W., Englemann, S., & Thomas, D. *Teaching: A course in applied psychology.* Chicago: Science Research Associates, 1971.

Becker, W.C., Madsen, C., Arnold, C., & Thomas, D.R. The contingent use of attention and praise in reducing classroom behavior problems. *Journal of Special Education,* 1967, *1,* 287–307.

Bellamy, G.T., Horner, R., & Inman, D. *Vocational habilitation of severely retarded adults.* Baltimore: University Park Press, 1979.

Berdine, W.H., & Cegelka, P.T. *Teaching the trainable retarded.* Columbus, Ohio: Charles E. Merrill, 1980.

Bijou, S.W. The problem of pseudo feeblemindedness. *Journal of Educational Psychology,* 1939, *30,* 519–526.

Bijou, S.W. The development of conditioning methodology for studying experimental neurosis in the rat. *Journal of Comparative Psychology,* 1942, *44,* 91–106.

Bijou, S.W. The psychometric pattern approach as an aid to clinical analysis—A review. *American Journal of Mental Deficiency,* 1942, *46,* 354–362.

Bijou, S.W. A systematic approach to an experimental analysis of young children. *Child Development,* 1955, *26,* 161–168.

Bijou, S.W. Methodology for an experimental analysis of child behavior. *Psychological Reports,* 1957, *3,* 243–250.

Bijou, S.W. Patterns of reinforcement and resistance to extinction in young children. *Child Development,* 1957, *28,* 47–54.

Bijou, S.W. Operant extinction after fixed-interval schedules with young children. *Journal of the Experimental Analysis of Behavior,* 1958, *1,* 25–29.

Bijou, S.W. Theory and research in mental (developmental) retardation. *Psychological Record,* 1963, *13,* 95–110.

Bijou, S.W. A functional analysis of retarded development. In N.R. Ellis (Ed.), *International review of research in mental retardation* (Vol. 1). New York: Academic Press, 1966.

Bijou, S.W. Studies in the experimental development of left-right concepts in retarded children using fading techniques. In N.R. Ellis (Ed.), *International review of research in mental retardation* (Vol. 3). New York: Academic Press, 1968.

Bijou, S.W. What psychology has to offer education—Now. *Journal of Applied Behavior Analysis,* 1970, *3* (1), 65–71.

Bijou, S.W. The technology of teaching young handicapped children. In S.W. Bijou & E. Ribes-Inēsta (Eds.), *Behavior modification: Issues and extensions.* New York: Academic Press, 1972.

Bijou, S.W. Practical implications of an interactional model of child development. *Exceptional Children,* 1977, *44* (1), 6–14.

Bijou, S.W., & Baer, D.M. *Child development, 2: Universal stage of infancy.* New York: Appleton-Century-Crofts, 1965.

Bijou, S.W., & Baer, D.M. *Child development: Readings in experimental analysis.* New York: Appleton-Century-Crofts, 1967.

Bijou, S.W., & Baer, D.M. *Child development 1: A systematic and empirical theory.* New York: Appleton-Century-Crofts, 1961.

Bijou, S.W., & Dunitz-Johnson, E. *Behavior analysis of retarded development.* Unpublished manuscript. University of Arizona.

Bijou, S.W., & Jastak, J. *Wide Range Achievement Test.* New York: Psychological Corporation, 1941.

Bijou, S.W., & Orlando, R. Rapid development of multiple-schedule performances with retarded children. *Journal of the Experimental Analysis of Behavior,* 1961, *4,* 7–16.

Bijou, S.W., Peterson, R.F., & Ault, M.H. A method to integrate descriptive and experimental field studies at the level of data and empirical concepts. *Journal of Applied Behavior Analysis,* 1968, *1* (2), 175–191.

Bijou, S.W. Peterson, R.F., Harris, F.R., Allen, K.E., & Johnston, M.S. Methodology for experimental studies of young children in natural settings. *Psychological Record,* 1969, *19,* 177–210.

Bijou, S.W., & Ribes-Inēsta, E. (Eds.). *Behavior modification: Issues and extensions.* New York: Academic Press, 1972.

Bijou, S.W., & Werner, H. Vocabulary analysis in mentally deficient children. *American Journal of Mental Deficiency,* 1944, *48,* 364–366.

Bijou, S.W., & Werner, H. Language analysis in brain-injured and non-brain injured mentally deficient children. *The Journal of Genetic Psychology,* 1945, *66,* 239–254.

Birnbrauer, J.S. External validity and experimental investigation of individual behavior. *Analysis and Intervention in Developmental Disabilities,* 1981, *1,* 117–132.

Birnbrauer, J.S., & Lawler, J. Token reinforcement for learning. *Mental Retardation,* 1964, *2,* 275–279.

Birnbrauer, J.S., Peterson, C.R., & Solnick, J.V. Design and interpretation of studies of single subjects. *American Journal of Mental Deficiency,* 1974, *79,* 191–203.

Birnbrauer, J.S., Wolf, M.M. Kidder, J.D., & Tague, C.E. Classroom behavior of retarded pupils with token reinforcement. *Journal of Experimental Child Psychology,* 1965, *2,* 219–235.

Black, M. Some aversive responses to a would-be reinforcer. In H. Wheeler (Ed.), *Beyond the punitive society; operant conditioning: Social and political aspects.* San Francisco: Freeman, 1973.

Borg, W.R., & Gall, M.D. *Educational research: An introduction* (3rd ed.). New York: Longman, 1979.

Bornstein, P.H., & Quevillon, R.P. The effects of a self-instructional package on overactive preschool boys. *Journal of Applied Behavior Analysis,* 1976, *9* (2), 179–188.

Bostow, D.E., & Bailey, J.B. Modification of severe disruptive and aggressive behavior using brief timeout and reinforcement procedures. *Journal of Applied Behavior Analysis,* 1969, *2* (1), 31–37.

Brady, D.O., & Smouse, A.D. A simultaneous comparison of three methods for language training with an autistic child: An experimental single case analysis. *Journal of Autism and Childhood Schizophrenia,* 1978, *8,* 271–279.

Browning, R.M. A same-subject design for simultaneous comparison of three reinforcement contingencies. *Behaviour Research and Therapy,* 1967, *5,* 237–243.

Burton, T.A., & Hirshoren, A. The education of severely and profoundly retarded children: Are we sacrificing the child to the concept? *Exceptional Children,* 1979, *45* (8), 598–602.

Burton, T.A., & Hirshoren, A. Some further thoughts and clarifications on the education of severely and profoundly retarded children. *Exceptional Children,* 1979, *45* (8), 618–625.

Cain, L.F., & Levine, S. Effects of community and institutional school programs on trainable mentally retarded children. CEC Research Monograph B-1, Council for Exceptional Children, 1963.

Campbell, D.T., & Stanley, J.C. *Experimental and quasi-experimental designs for research.* Chicago: Rand McNally, 1966.

Campbell, N.R. Final Report. Committee of the British Association for the Advancement of Science on the Problem of Measurement. London: British Association, 1940.

Carnine, D.W. Effects of two teacher-presentation rates on off-task behavior, answering correctly, and participation. *Journal of Applied Behavior Analysis,* 1976, *9* (2), 199–206.

Carnine, D.W. High and low implementation of direct instruction teaching techniques. *Education and Treatment of Children,* 1981, *4*(1), 43–51.

Carr, E.G., Newsom, C.D., & Binkoff, J.A. Escape as a factor in the aggressive behavior of two retarded children. *Journal of Applied Behavior Analysis,* 1980, *13* (1), 101–117.

Cartwright, C.A., & Cartwright, G.P. *Developing observation skills.* New York: McGraw-Hill, 1974.

Cartwright, G.P., & Cartwright C.A. Gilding the lilly: Comments on the training base model. *Exceptional Children,* 1972, *39* 231–234.

Chiang, S.J., Iwata, B.A., & Dorsey, M.F. Elimination of disruptive bus riding behavior via token reinforcement on a "distance-based" schedule. *Education and Treatment of Children,* 1979, *2* (2), 101–109.

Christie, L.S., McKenzie, H.S., & Burdette, C.S. The consulting teacher approach to special education: Inservice training for special educators. *Focus on Exceptional Children,* 1972, *4,* 1–10.

Clark, H.B., Boyd, S.B., & Macrae, J.W. A classroom program teaching disadvantaged youths to write biographic information. *Journal of Applied Behavior Analysis,* 1975, *8* (1), 67–75.

Cohen, M., & Gross, P. *The developmental resource* (Vols. 1 & 2). New York: Grune and Stratton, 1979.

Cohen, R., Polsgrove, L., Rieth, H., & Heinen, J.R.K. The effects of self-monitoring, public graphing, and token reinforcement on the social behaviors of underachieving children. *Education and Treatment of Children,* 1981, *4* (2), 125–138.

Cone, J.D. Why the "I've got a better agreement measure" literature continues to grow: A commentary on two articles by Birkimer and Brown. *Journal of Applied Behavior Analysis,* 1979, *12,* (), 571.

Cook, J.W., Altman, K., Shaw, J., & Blalock, M. Use of contingent lemon juice to eliminate public masturbation by a severely retarded boy. *Behavior Research and Therapy,* 1978, *16,* 131–134.

Cooke, T.P., & Apolloni, T. Developing positive social-emotional behaviors: A study of training and generalization effects. *Journal of Applied Behavior Analysis,* 1976, *9* (1), 65–78.

Cooper, J.O. *Measuring behavior* (2nd ed.). Columbus, Ohio: Charles E. Merrill, 1981.

The Council for Exceptional Children. *Guidelines for personnel in the education of exceptional children.* Reston, Va.: Author, 1974.

Cronin, K.A., & Cuvo, A.J. Teaching mending skills to mentally retarded adolescents. *Journal of Applied Behavior Analysis,* 1979, *12* (3), 401–406.

Cruickshank, W., Bentzen, F., Ratzenburg, F., & Tannhauser, M. *A teaching method for brain-injured and hyperactive children.* Syracuse, N.Y.: Syracuse University Press, 1961.

Cuvo, A.J. Multiple-baseline design in instructional research: Pitfalls of measurement and procedural advantages. *American Journal of Mental Deficiency,* 1979, *84,* 219–228.

Cuvo, A.J., Leaf, R., & Borakove, L. Teaching janitorial skills to the mentally retarded: Acquisition, generalization and maintenance. *Journal of Applied Behavior Analysis,* 1978, *11* (3), 345–355.

Deno, S., & Mirkin, P. *Data-based program modification: A manual.* Minneapolis, Minn.: University of Minnesota, 1977.

Diana v. *State Board of Education* (C.A. C-70-37 R.F.P.) (N.D. CAL 1970).

Doke, L.A., & Risley, T.R. The organization of day-care environments: Required vs. optional activities. *Journal of Applied Behavior Analysis,* 1972, *5* (), 405–420.

Doley, D.M., Wells, K.C., Hobbs, S.A., Roberts, M.W., & Cartelli, L.M. The effects of social punishment on noncompliance: A comparison with timeout and positive practice. *Journal of Applied Behavior Analysis,* 1976, *9* (4), 471–482.

Dunn, L.M. Special education for the mildly retarded—Is much of it justifiable? *Exceptional Children,* 1968, *35* (1), 5–22.

Eaton, M.D. Data decisions and evaluation. In N.G. Haring, T.C. Lovitt, M.D. Eaton, & C.L. Hansen (Eds.), *The fourth R: Research in the classroom.* Columbus, Ohio: Charles E. Merrill, 1978.

Epstein, L.H., Doke, L.A., Sajwaj, T.E., Sorrell, S., & Rimmer, B. Generality and side effects of overcorrection. *Journal of Applied Behavior Analysis,* 1974, 7 (3), 385–390.

Epstein, M.H., Repp, A.C., & Cullinan, D. Decreasing "obscene" language of behaviorally disordered children through the use of a DRL schedule. *Psychology in the Schools,* 1978, *15* (3), 419–422.

Egel, A.L. Reinforcer variation: Implications for motivating developmentally disabled children. *Journal of Applied Behavior Analysis,* 1981, *14* (3), 345–350.

Egel, A.L., Richman, G.S., & Koegel, R. L. Normal peer models and autistic children's learning. *Journal of Applied Behavior Analysis,* 1981, *14* (1), 3–12.

Egner, A., & Lates, B.J. The Vermont consulting teacher program: Case presentation. In C. Parker (Ed.), *Psychological consultation: Helping teachers meet special needs.* Reston, Va.: Council for Exceptional Children, 1975.

Etzel, B., LeBlanc, J. & Baer, D.M. New developments in behavioral research: Theory, method and application: In Honor of Sidney W. Bijou. Hillsdale, N.Y.: Lawrence Erlbaum Associates, 1977.

Eysenck, H.J. The effects of psychotherapy: An evaluation. *Journal of Consulting Psychology,* 1952, *16,* 319–324.

Fantuzzo, J.W., & Clement, P.W. Generalization of the effects of teacher- and self-administered token reinforcers to nontreated students. *Journal of Applied Behavior Analysis,* 1981, *14* (4), 435–447.

Favell, J.E., McGimsey, J.F., & Jones, M.L. The use of physical restraint in the treatment of self-injury and as positive reinforcement. *Journal of Applied Behavior Analysis,* 1978, *11* (2), 225–241.

Federal Register, 43 (163), Tuesday, August 23, 1977.

Feltz, D.L. Teaching a high-avoidance motor task to a retarded child through participant modeling. *Education and Training of the Mentally Retarded,* 1980, *15* (2), 152–155.

Ferster, C.B., Culbertson, S., & Boren, M.C.P. *Behavior principles* (2nd ed.). Englewood Cliffs, N.Y.: Prentice-Hall, 1975.

Ferster, C.B., & DeMyer, M.K. The development of performances in autistic children in an automatically controlled environment. *Journal of Chronic Diseases,* 1961, *13,* 312–345.

Ferster, C.B., & Skinner, B.F. *Schedules of reinforcement.* New York: Appleton-Century-Crofts, 1957.

Fishbein, J.E., & Wasik, B.H. Effect of the good behavior game on disruptive library behavior. *Journal of Applied Behavior Analysis,* 1981, *14* (1), 89–93.

Fox, W.L., Williams, W.W., & Fox, T.J. *Program planning and development for the multi-handicapped in rural areas; Vermont's service delivery model.* Seventh Annual Invitational Conference: Serving the Severely Handicapped: Are We Meeting P.L. 94-142 Priorities? Minneapolis, Minn.: 1977.

Foxx, R.M. Attention training: The use of overcorrection avoidance to increase the eye contact of autistic and retarded children. *Journal of Applied Behavior Analysis,* 1977, *10* (3), 489–499.

Foxx, R.M., & Azrin, N.H. Elimination of self-stimulatory behavior by overcorrection. *Journal of Applied Behavior Analysis,* 1973, *6* (1), 1–14.

Foxx, R.M., & Shapiro, S.T. The timeout ribbon: A non-exclusionary timeout procedure. *Journal of Applied Behavior Analysis,* 1978, *11* (1), 125–136.

Fredericks, H.D., Baldwin, V.L., & Grove, D.N. *A data based classroom for the moderately and severely handicapped.* Monmouth, Oreg.: Instructional Development Corp., 1977.

Gallant, J., Sargeant, M., & Van Houten, R. Teacher-determined and self-determined access to science activities as a reinforcer for task completion in other curriculum areas. *Education and Treatment of Children,* 1980, *3* (2), 101–111.

Garcia, E., Guess, D., & Byrnes, J. Development of syntax in a retarded girl using procedures of imitation, reinforcement and modelling. *Journal of Applied Behavior Analysis,* 1973, *6* (2), 299–310.

Gast, D.L., & Nelson, C.M. Legal and ethical considerations for the use of timeout in special education settings. *Journal of Special Education,* 1977, *11* (4), 457–467.

Gentry, D., & Haring, N. Essentials of performance measurement. In N.G. Haring & L. Brown (Eds.), *Teaching the severely handicapped* (Vol. 1). New York: Grune and Stratton, 1976.

Gibson, F.W., Lawrence, P.S., & Nelson, R.O. Comparison of three training procedures for teaching social responses to developmentally disabled adults. *American Journal of Mental Deficiency,* 1976, *81,* 379–387.

Gladstone, B.W., & Spencer, C.J. The effects of modelling on the contingent praise of mental retardation counsellors. *Journal of Applied Behavior Analysis,* 1977, *10* (1), 75–84.

Glass, G.V., Willson, V.L., & Gottman, J.M. *Design and analysis of time-series experiments.* Boulder, Colo.: Colorado Associated University Press, 1975.

Goldstein, H., Moss, J.W., & Jordan, L.J. *The efficacy of special class training on the development of mentally retarded children.* (Cooperative Research Project No. 619) Cooperative Research Program of the Office of Education, U.S. Department of Health, Education and Welfare, 1965.

Greene, B.F., Bailey, J.S., & Barber, F. An analysis and reduction of disruptive behavior on school buses. *Journal of Applied Behavior Analysis,* 1981, *14* (2), 177–192.

Greenwood, C., Hops, H., Delquardi, T., & Guild, T. Group contingencies for group consequences in classroom management: A further analysis. *Journal of Applied Behavior Analysis,* 1974, 7 (3), 413–425.

Greenwood, C.R., Hops, H., Delquadri, J., & Walker, H.M. *PASS* (Program for Academic Survival Skills). Manual for teachers, Eugene, Oreg.: Center at Oregon for Research in the Behavioral Education of the Handicapped, University of Oregon, 1974.

Greenwood, C.R., Hops, H., Walker, H.M., Guild, J.J., Stokes, J., Young, K.R., Keleman, K.S., & Willardson, M. Standardized classroom management program: Social validation and replication studies in Utah and Oregon. *Journal of Applied Behavior Analysis,* 1979 *12* (2), 235–253.

Gruber, B., Reeser, R., & Reid, D.H. Providing a less restrictive environment for profoundly retarded persons by teaching independent walking skills. *Journal of Applied Behavior Analysis,* 1979, *12* (2), 285–297.

Guess, D., & Baer, D.M. An analysis of individual differences in generalization between receptive and productive language in retarded children. *Journal of Applied Behavior Analysis,* 1973, *6* (2), 311–329.

Guess, D., Sailor, W., & Baer, D.M. To teach language to retarded children. In R. Schiefelbusch & L. Lloyd (Eds.), *Language perspectives—Acquisition, retardation and intervention.* Baltimore: University Park Press, 1974.

Guess, D., Sailor, W., Rutherford, G., & Baer, D.M. An experimental analysis of linguistic development: The productive use of the plural morpheme. *Journal of Applied Behavior Analysis*, 1968, *1* (4), 297–306.

Guskin, S.L., & Spicker, H.H. Educational research in mental retardation. In N.R. Ellis (Ed.), *International review of research in mental retardation* (Vol. 3). New York: Academic Press, 1968.

Hall, R.V. *Managing behavior: Behavior modification, the measurement of behavior*. Lawrence, Kan.: H & H Enterprises, 1971.

Hall, R.V. *Managing behavior—behavior modification: The measurement of behavior*. Lawrence, Kansas: H & H Enterprises, 1974.

Hall, R.V., Cristler, C., Cranston, S.S., & Tucker, B. Teachers and parents as reasearchers using multiple baselines. *Journal of Applied Behavior Analysis*, 1970, *3* (4), 247–255.

Handleman, J.S. Generalization by autistic-type children of verbal responses across settings. *Journal of Applied Behavior Analysis*, 1979, *12* (2), 273–282.

Hannah, G.T., & Risley, T.R. Experiments in an community mental health center: Increasing client payments for outpatient services. Journal of Applied Behavior Analysis, 1981, *14* (2), 141–157.

Haring, N.G. Early experiences: The evaluation of experimental education. In J. Kauffman & C. Lewis, *Teaching children with behavior disorders: Personal perspectives*. Columbus, Ohio: Charles E. Merrill, 1974.

Haring, N.G., & Gentry, N.D. Direct and individualized instructional procedures. In N.G. Haring & R. Schiefelbusch (Eds.), *Teaching special children*. New York: McGraw-Hill, 1976.

Haring, N.G., Liberty, K., & White, O.R. Rules for data-based strategy decisions in instructional programs: Current research and instructional implications. In W. Sailor, B. Wilcox, & L. Brown (Eds.), *Methods of instruction for severely handicapped students*. Baltimore: Paul H. Brookes Publishers, 1980.

Haring, N.G., & Lovitt, T.C. Operant methodology and educational technology in special education. In N.G. Haring & R. Schiefelbusch (Eds.), *Methods in special education*. New York: McGraw-Hill, 1967.

Haring, N.G., Lovitt, T.C. Eaton, M.D., & Hansen, C.L. *The fourth R: Research in the classroom*. Columbus, Ohio: Charles E. Merrill, 1978.

Haring, N.G., & Phillips, E.L. *Educating emotionally disturbed children*. New York: McGraw-Hill, 1962.

Haring, N.G., & Schiefelbusch, R.L. *Methods in special education*. New York: McGraw-Hill, 1967.

Haring, N.G., & Schiefelbusch, R.L. (Eds.). *Teaching special children*. New York: McGraw-Hill, 1976.

Haring, N.G., & Whelan, R.J. (Eds.). The learning environment: Relationship to behavior modification and implications for special education. *Kansas studies in education*. Lawrence, Kans.: University of Kansas Publications, 1966.

Harris, V.W., & Sherman, J.A. Use and analysis of the "good behavior game" to reduce disruptive classroom behavior. *Journal of Applied Behavior Analysis*, 1973, *6* (3), 405–417.

Hart, B.M., & Risley, T.R. Establishing the use of descriptive adjectives in the spontaneous speech of disadvantaged preschool children. *Journal of Applied Behavior Analysis*, 1968, *1* (2), 109–120.

Hartmann, D.P. Considerations in the choice of interobserver reliability estimates. *Journal of Applied Behavior Analysis*, 1977, *10* (1), 103–116.

Hartmann, D.P., & Hall, R.V. The changing criterion design. *Journal of Applied Behavior Analysis*, 1976, *9* (4), 527–532.

Hauserman, N., Walen, S.R., & Behling, M. Reinforced racial integration in the first grade: A study in generalization. *Journal of Applied Behavior Analysis*, 1973, *6* (2), 193–200.

Hayden, A.H., & Haring, N.G. Programs for Down's Syndrome children at the University of Washington. In T. Tjossem (Ed.), *Intervention strategies for risk infants and young children*. Baltimore: University Park Press, 1976.

Hersen, M., & Barlow, D.H. *Single case experimental designs: Strategies for studying behavior change*. New York: Pergamon Press, 1976.

Homme, L., Csanyi, A., Gonzales, M., & Rechs, T. *How to use contingency contracting in the classroom*. Champaign, Ill.: Research Press, 1970.

Homme, L., deBaca, P., Devine, J., Steinhorst, R., & Rickert, E. Use of the Premack Principle in controlling the behavior of nursery school children. *Journal of the Experimental Analysis of Behavior*, 1963, *6*, 544.

Hopkins, B.L., & Hermann, J.A. Evaluating interobserver reliability of interval data. *Journal of Applied Behavior Analysis*, 1977, *10* (1), 121–126.

Hops, H., Fleischman, D.H., & Beickel, S.L. *CLASS* (Contingencies for Learning Academic and Social Skills). Manual for teachers. Eugene, Oreg.: Center at Oregon for Research in the Behavioral Education of the Handicapped, University of Oregon, 1976.

Horner, R.D. Establishing use of crutches by a mentally retarded spina bifida child. *Journal of Applied Behavior Analysis*, 1971, *4* (3), 301–309.

Horner, R.D., & Baer, D.M. Multiple-probe technique: A variation of the multiple baseline. *Journal of Applied Behavior Analysis*, 1978, *11* (1), 189–196.

Horner, R.D., & Keilitz, I. Training mentally retarded adolescents to brush their teeth. *Journal of Applied Behavior Analysis*, 1975, *8* (3), 301–309.

Howell, K.W., Kaplan, J.S., & O'Connell, C.Y. *Evaluating exceptional children*. Columbus, Ohio: Charles E. Merrill, 1979.

Irwin, D.M., & Bushnell, M. *Observational strategies for child study*. New York: Holt, Rinehart & Winston, 1980.

Isaac, G.E. Teaching non-verbal multiple handicapped children object labeling. Unpublished masters thesis, University of Kentucky, 1979.

Isaac, G.E., & Gast, D.L. Teaching object naming using a time delay procedure with multiply handicapped students in small group instruction. *Fifth Annual Conference of the American Association for the Education of the Severely/Profoundly Handicapped*. Baltimore: October 1978.

Ivancic, M.T., & Reid, D.H., Iwata, B.A., Faw, G.D., & Page, T.J. Evaluating a supervision program for developing and maintaining therapeutic staff-resident interactions during institutional care routines. *Journal of Applied Behavior Analysis*, 1981, *14* (1), 95–107.

Johnson, J., & Mithaug, D. A replication of sheltered workshop entry requirements. *AAESPH Review*, 1978, *3*, 116–123.

Johnston, R.J., & McLaughlin, T.F. The effects of free time on assignment completion and accuracy in arithmetic: A case study. *Education and Treatment of Children*, 1982, *5* (1), 33–40.

Jones, R.R. Invited book review of *Single-case experimental designs: Strategies for studying behavior change* by Michel Hersen and David H. Barlow. *Journal of Applied Behavior Analysis*, 1978, *11* (2), 309–313.

Kantor, J.R. *Interbehavioral psychology*. Bloomington, Ind.: Principia Press, 1958.

Kazdin, A.E. Methodological and assessment considerations in evaluating reinforcement programs in applied settings. *Journal of Applied Behavior Analysis*, 1973, *6* (2), 517–531.

Kazdin, A.E. The influence of behavior preceding a reinforced response on behavior change in the classroom. *Journal of Applied Behavior Analysis*, 1977, *10* (3), 299–310.

Kazdin, A.E. *History of Behavior Modification*. Baltimore: University Park Press, 1978.

Kazdin, A.E. External validity and single-case experimentation: Issues and limitations (a response to J.S. Birnbrauer). *Analysis and Intervention in Developmental Disabilities*, 1981, *1*, 133–143.

Kazdin, A.E., & Geesey, S. Simultaneous-treatment design comparisons of the effects of earning reinforcers for one's peers versus for oneself. *Behavior Therapy*, 1977, *8*, 682–693.

Kazdin, A.E., & Hartmann, D.P. The simultaneous-treatment design. *Behavior Therapy*, 1978, *9*, 812–922.

Kazdin, A.E., & Kopel, S.A. On resolving ambiguities of the multiple-baseline design: Problems and recommendations. *Behavior Therapy*, 1975, *6*, 601–608.

Kazdin, A.E., & Mascitelli, S. The opportunity to earn oneself off a token system as a reinforcer for attentive behavior. *Behavior Therapy*, 1980, *11*, 68–78.

Kelly, M.B. A review of the observational data-collection and reliability procedures reported in the *Journal of Applied Behavior Analysis*. *Journal of Applied Behavior Analysis*, 1977, 10 (1), 97–101.

Kendall, P.C. Assessing generalization and the single-subject strategies. *Behavior Modification*, 1981, *5* (3), 307–319.

Kirby, K.C., Holborn, S.W., & Bushby, H.T. Word game bingo: A behavioral treatment package for improving te: .ual responding to sight words. *Journal of Applied Behavior Analysis*, 1981, *14* (3), 317–326.

Kirk, S.A. *Educating exceptional children*. Boston: Houghton Mifflin, 1962.

Kirk, S.A. Research in education. In H.A. Stevens & R. Heber (Eds.), *Mental retardation: A review of research*. Chicago, Ill.: University of Chicago Press, 1964.

Kirk, S.A. An evaluation of the study by Bernadine G. Schmidt entitled: Changes in personal, social, and intellectual behavior of children originally classified as feebleminded. *Psychological Bulletin*, 1948, *45*, 321–323.

Kirk, S.A., & Bateman, B.D. *Ten years of research at the Institute for Research on Exceptional Children*. Champaign, Ill.: University of Illinois, 1964.

Kleinert, H.L., & Gast, D.L. Teaching a multihandicapped adult manual signs using a constant time delay procedure. *The Journal of the Association for the Severely Handicapped*, 1982, *6* (4), 25–32.

Knight, M., Christie, L. Egner, A., Paolucci, P., & Lates, B. Rate of task completion for evaluating and monitoring a field-based graduate training program. In L. Fraley & E. Vargas (Eds.), *Proceedings of the third national conference on behavior research and technology in higher education*. Atlanta: Georgia State University, 1976.

Knight, M., Meyers, H., Paolucci-Whitcomb, P., Hasazi, S., & Nevin, A. A four year evaluation of consulting teacher service. *Behavior Disorders*, 1981, *6*, 92–100.

Konarski, E.A., Jr., Johnson, M.R., Crowell, C.R., & Whitman, T.L. Response deprivation and reinforcement in applied settings: A preliminary analysis. *Journal of Applied Behavior Analysis*, 1980, *13* (4), 595–609.

Koop, S., Martin, G., Yu, D., & Suthons, E. Comparison of two reinforcement strategies in vocational-skill training of mentally retarded persons. *American Journal of Mental Deficiency*, 1980, *84*, 616–626.

Kratochwill, T.R. Foundations of time-series research. In T.R. Kratochwill (Ed.), *Single subject research: Strategies for evaluating change*. New York: Academic Press, 1978.

Kratochwill, T.R. (Ed.). *Single subject research—Strategies for evaluating change*. New York: Academic Press, 1978.

Kratochwill, T.R., & Levin, J.R. What time-series designs may have to offer educational researchers. *Contemporary Educational Psychology*. 1978, *3*, 273–329.

Kubany, E., & Sloggett, B. Coding procedure for teachers. *Journal of Applied Behavior Analysis*, 1973, *6* (2), 339–344.

Kunzelmann, H. (Ed.). *Precision teaching: An initial training sequence*. Seattle: Special Child Publications, 1970.

Kuypers, D.S., Becker, W.C., & O'Leary, K.D. How to make a token system fail. *Exceptional Children*, 1968, *35* (2), 101–109.

Larry, P. v. Riles, 343 F. Supp 1306 (D.C. Calif, 1972).

Lazarus, A.A., & Davison, G.C. Clinical innovation in research and practice. In A.E. Bergin & S.L. Garfield (Eds.), *Handbook of psychotherapy and behavior change: An empirical analysis*. New York: Wiley, 1971.

Leitenberg, H. The use of single-case methodology in psychotherapy research. *Journal of Abnormal Psychology*, 1973, *82* (1), 87–101.

LeLaurin, K., & Risley, T.R. The organization of day-care environments: "Zone" vs. "man-to-man" staff assignments. *Journal of Applied Behavior Analysis*, 1972, *5* (3), 225–232.

Leslie, D. The effects of systematic observation on the perception of behavior change in children. Unpublished doctoral dissertation, University of Oregon, 1974.

Liberman, R.P., Ferris, C., Salgado, P., & Salgado, J. Replication of the achievement place model in California. *Journal of Applied Behavior Analysis*, 1975, *8* (3), 287–299.

Lilly, S. Special education: A teapot in a tempest. *Exceptional Children*, 1970, *37* (1), 43–49.

Lindsley, O.R. Direct measurement and prosthesis of retarded behavior. *Journal of Education*, 1965, *147*, 62–80.

Lippman, L., & Goldberg, I. *Right to education: Anatomy of the Pennsylvania case and its implications for exceptional children*. New York: Teachers College Press, 1973.

Loos, F.M., Williams, K.P., & Bailey, J.S. A multi-element analysis of the teacher aides in an "open"-style classroom. *Journal of Applied Behavior Analysis*, 1977, *10* (3), 437–448.

Lovitt, T.C. *Narrative rate preferences of normal and retarded males as assessed by conjugate reinforcement*. Unpublished doctoral dissertation, University of Kansas, 1966.

Lovitt, T.C. Assessment of children with learning disabilities. *Exceptional Children*, 1967, *34* (4), 233–239.

Lovitt, T.C. Applied behavior analysis techniques and curriculum research: Implications for instruction. In N. Haring and R. Schiefelbusch (Eds.), *Teaching special children*. New York: McGraw-Hill, 1976.

Lovitt, T.C., & Curtiss, K. Effects of manipulating an antecedent event on mathematics response rate. *Journal of Applied Behavior Analysis*, 1968, *1* (), 329–333.

Lovitt, T.C., & Curtiss, K. Academic response rate as a function of teacher and self-imposed contingencies. *Journal of Applied Behavior Analysis*, 1969, *2* (), 49–53.

Luce, S.C., Delquadri, J., & Hall, R.V. Contingent exercise: A mild but powerful procedure for suppressing inappropriate verbal and aggressive behavior. *Journal of Applied Behavior Analysis*, 1980, *13* (4), 583–594.

Luce, S.C., & Hall, R.V. Contingent exercise: A procedure used with differential reinforcement to reduce bizarre verbal behavior. *Education and Treatment of Children*, 1981, *4* (4), 309–327.

Lutzker, J.R. Reducing self-injurious behavior by facial screening. *American Journal of Mental Deficiency*, 1978, *82*, 510–513.

Lutzker, J.R., Crozier, J.L., & Lutzker, S.Z. The paradoxical effects of "moral" stories on children's behavior. *Education and Treatment of Children*, 1981, *4* (2), 115–124.

MacMillan, D.L., & Morrison, G.M. Evolution of behaviorism from the laboratory to special education settings. In *Advances in special education: Perspectives on Applications* (Vol. 2). Greenwich, Conn.: JAI Press, 1980.

Madsen, C.H., Jr., Becker, W.C., & Thomas, D.R. Rules, praise, and ignoring: Elements of elementary classroom control. *Journal of Applied Behavior Analysis*, 1968, *1* (2), 139–150.

Mager, R.F. *Preparing instructional objectives*. Belmont, Calif.: Fearon, 1961.

Marholin, D. II, & Steinman, W.M. Stimulus control in the classroom as a function of the behavior reinforced. *Journal of Applied Behavior Analysis*, 1977, *10* (3), 465–478.

Martin, R. *Legal challenges to behavior modification*. Champaign, Ill.: Research Press, 1975.

Matson, J.L., & Andrasik, F. Training leisure-time social-interaction skills to mentally retarded adults. *American Journal of Mental Deficiency*, 1982, *86*, 533–542.

May, T., Risley, T.R. Twardosz, S., Friedman, P. Bijou, S.W., & Wexler, D. *Guidelines for the use of behavioral procedures in state programs for retarded persons*. Arlington, Tex.: National Association of Retarded Citizens, 1976.

McCormack, J., & Chalmers, A. *Early cognitive instruction for the moderately and severely handicapped*. Champaign, Ill.: Research Press, 1978.

McCullough, J.P., Cornell, J.E., McDaniel, M.H., & Mueller, R.K. Utilization of the simultaneous treatment design to improve student behavior in a first-grade classroom. *Journal of Consulting and Clinical Psychology*, 1974, *42*, 288–292.

McKenzie, H.S., Clark, M.M., Wolf, M.M., Kothera, R., & Benson, C. Behavior modification of children with learning disabilities using grades as tokens and allowances as back up reinforcers. *Exceptional Children*, 1968, *34* (10), 745–752.

McKenzie, H.S., Egner, A.N., Knight, M.F., Perelman, P.E., Schneider, B.M., & Garvin, J.S. Training consulting teachers to assist elementary teachers in the management and education of handicapped children. *Exceptional Children*, 1970, *37* (2), 137–143.

Measel, C.J., & Alfieri, P.A. Treatment of self-injurious behavior by a combination of reinforcement for incompatible behavior and overcorrection. *American Journal of Mental Deficiency*, 1976, *81*, 147–153.

Medland, M.B., & Stachnik, T.J. Good-behavior game: A replication and systematic analysis. *Journal of Applied Behavior Analysis*, 1972, *5* (1), 45–51.

Miller, L.K. Methodological and assessment considerations in applied settings: Reviewer's comments: *Journal of Applied Behavior Analysis*, 1973, *6* (3), 532–539.

Minkin, N., Braukmann, C.J., Minikin, B.L., Timbers, G.D., Timbers, B., Fixsen, D.L., Phillips, E.L., & Wolf, M.M. The social validation and training of conversational skills. *Journal of Applied Behavior Analysis*, 1976, *9* (2), 127–139.

Mira, M.D. Individual patterns of looking and listening preferences among learning disabled and normal children. *Exceptional Children*, 1968, *34* (9), 649–658.

Mithaug, D.E. A comparison of procedures to increase responding in three severely retarded, noncompliant young adults. *AAESPH Review*, 1979, *4*, 66–80. (a)

Mithaug, D.E. The relationship between programmed instruction and task analysis in the prevocational training of severely and profoundly handicapped persons. *AAESPH Review*, 1979, *4*, 162–178. (b)

Mithaug, D., & Hagmeier, L.D. The development of procedures to assess prevocational competencies of severely handicapped young adults. *AAESPH Review*, 1978, *3*, 94–116.

Mithaug, D. Hagmeier, L.D., & Haring, N.G. The relationship between training activities and job placement in vocational education of the severely and profoundly handicapped. *AAESPH Review*, 1977, *2*, 25–46.

Moss, J.W. Research and demonstration. *Exceptional Children,* 1968, *34* (7), 509–514.

Murdock, J.Y., Garcia, E.E., & Hardman, M.L. Generalizing articulation training with trainable mentally retarded subjects. *Journal of Applied Behavior Analysis,* 1977, *10* (4), 717–733.

Murphey, R.J., & Bryan, A.J. Multiple-baseline and multiple-probe designs: Practical alternatives for special education assessment and evaluation. *The Journal of Special Education,* 1980, *4* (3), 325–335.

Murphey, R. J., Doughty, N., & Nunes, D. Multielement designs: An alternative to reversal and multiple baseline strategies. *Mental Retardation,* 1979, *17*, 23–27.

Murphey, R.J., Ruprecht, M.J., Baggio, P., & Nunes, D.L. The use of mild punishment in combination with reinforcement of alternate behaviors to reduce the self-injurious behavior of a profoundly retarded individual. *AAESPH Review,* 1979, *4*, 187–195.

Nau, P.A., & Van Houten, R. The effects of feedback and a principal-mediated timeout procedure on the disruptive behavior of junior high school students. *Education and Treatment of Children,* 1981, *4* (2), 101–113.

Neef, N.A., Iwata, B.A., & Page, T.J. Public transportation training: In vivo versus classroom instruction. *Journal of Applied Behavior Analysis,* 1978, *11* (3), 331–344.

Neef, N.A., Iwata, B.A., & Page, T.J. The effects of interspersal training versus high-density reinforcement on spelling acquisition and retention. *Journal of Applied Behavior Analysis,* 1980, *13* (1), 153–158.

Nelson, C.M., Gast, D.L., & Trout, D.D. A charting system for monitoring student performance on instructional programs. *Journal of Special Education Technology,* 1979, *3* (1), 43–49.

Nordquist, M., & Wahler, R. Naturalistic treatment of an autistic child. *Journal of Applied Behavior Analysis,* 1973, *6* (1), 79–87.

O'Brien, F., Azrin, N.H., & Bugle, C. Training profoundly retarded children to stop crawling. *Journal of Applied Behavior Analysis,* 1972, *4* (2), 131–137.

O'Leary, K.D., & Becker, W.C. Behavior modification of an adjustment class: A token reinforcement program. *Exceptional Children,* 1967, *33* (9), 637–642.

O'Leary, K.D., & Becker, W.C. The effects of a teacher's reprimands on children's behavior. *Journal of School Psychology,* 1968, *7*, 8–11.

O'Leary, K.D., Becker, W.C., Evans, M.B., & Saudargas, R.A. A token reinforcement program in a public school: A replication and systematic analysis. *Journal of Applied Behavior Analysis,* 1969, *2* (1), 3–13.

O'Leary, K.D., Kaufman, K.F., Kass, R.E., & Drabman, R.S. The effects of loud and soft reprimands on the behavior of disruptive students. *Exceptional Children,* 1970, *37* (2), 145–155.

O'Leary K.K. Behavior modification in the classroom: A rejoinder to Winett and Winkler. *Journal of Applied Behavior Analysis,* 1972, *5* (4), 505–511.

Ollendick, T.H., Matson, J.L., Esveldt-Dawson, K., & Shapiro, E.S. Increasing spelling achievement: An analysis of treatment procedures utilizing an alternating treatments design. *Journal of Applied Behavior Analysis,* 1980, *13* (4), 645–654.

Orlando, R., & Bijou, S.W. Single and multiple schedules of reinforcement in developmentally retarded children. *Journal of the Experimental Analysis of Behavior,* 1960, *3*, 339–348.

Oxford American Dictionary. New York: Oxford University Press, 1980.

Parsonson, B.S., & Baer, D.M. The analysis and presentation of graphic data. In T.R. Kratochwill (Ed.), *Single subject research—Strategies for evaluating change.* New York: Academic Press, 1978.

Payne, J.S., Polloway, E.A., Smith, J.E., Jr., & Payne, R.A. *Strategies for teaching the mentally retarded* (2nd ed.). Columbus, Ohio: Charles E. Merrill, 1981.

Phillips, E.L. Achievement place: Token reinforcement procedures in a home-style rehabilitation setting for "predelinquent" boys. *Journal of Applied Behavior Analysis,* 1968, *1* (3), 213–223.

Phillips, E.L., Phillips, E.A., Wolf, M.M., & Fixsen, D.L. Achievement place: Development of the elected manager system. *Journal of Applied Behavior Analysis,* 1973, *6* (4), 541–561.

Pierce, C., & Risley, T.R. Recreation as a reinforcer: Increasing membership and decreasing disruptions in an urban recreation center. *Journal of Applied Behavior Analysis,* 1974, *7* (3), 403–411.

Porterfield, J.K., Herbert-Jackson, E., & Risley, T.R. Contingent observation: An effective and acceptable procedure for reducing disruptive behavior of young children in a group setting. *Journal of Applied Behavior Analysis,* 1976, *9* (1), 55–64.

Prehm, H.J. Research training and experiences in special education doctoral programs. *Teacher Education and Special Education,* 1980, *3*, 3–9.

Premack, D. Reinforcement theory. In D. Levine (Ed.), *Nebraska symposium on Motivation, 1965.* Lincoln: University of Nebraska Press, 1965.

Publication Manual of the American Psychological Association (2nd ed.). Washington, D.C.: American Psychological Association, 1974.

Quay, L.C. Academic skills. In N. R. Ellis (Ed.), *Handbook of mental deficiency.* New York: McGraw-Hill, 1963.

Redd, W.H., Ullmann, R.K., Stelle, C., & Roesch, P. A classroom incentive program instituted by tutors after school. *Education and Treatment of Children,* 1979, *2* (3), 169–176.

Reese, H.W., & Lipsitt, L.P. *Experimental child psychology.* New York: Academic Press, 1970.

The 1968–1969 Report of the Consulting Teacher Program (Vol. 1). Burlington, Vt.: University of Vermont, 1969.

Repp, A.C., & Deitz, S.M. Reducing aggressive and self-injurious behavior of institutionalized retarded children through reinforcement of other behaviors. *Journal of Applied Behavior Analysis,* 1974, *7* (2), 313–325.

Repp, A.C., & Lloyd, J. Evaluating educational changes with singe-subject designs. In J. Gottlieb (Ed.), *Educating mentally retarded persons in the mainstream.* Baltimore: University Park Press, 1980.

Reynolds, N.J., & Risley, T.R. The role of social and material reinforcers in increasing talking of a disadvantaged preschool child. *Journal of Applied Behavior Analysis,* 1968, *1* (3), 253–262.

Rieth, H., & Hall, R.V. (Eds.). *Responsive teaching model: Readings in applied behavior analysis.* Lawrence, Kans.: H & H Enterprises, 1974.

Risley, T.R. The effects and side effects of punishing the autistic behaviors of a deviant child. *Journal of Applied Behavior Analysis,* 1968, *1* (1), 21–34.

Risley, T.R. Spontaneous language in the preschool environment. In J. Stanley (Ed.), *Research on curriculums for preschools.* Baltimore: John Hopkins, 1971.

Risley, T.R., & Cuvo, A.J. Training mentally retarded adults to make emergency telephone calls. *Behavior Modification,* 1980, *4,* 513–525.

Robinson, H.B., & Robinson, N.M. *The mentally retarded child.* New York: McGraw-Hill, 1965.

Robinson, P.W., Newby, T.J., & Ganzell, S.L. A token system for a class of underachieving hyperactive children. *Journal of Applied Behavior Analysis,* 1981, *14* (3), 307–315.

Rowbury, T.G., Baer, A.M., & Baer, D.M. Interactions between teacher guidance and contingent access to play in developing preacademic skills of deviant preschool children. *Journal of Applied Behavior Analysis,* 1976, *9* (1), 85–104.

Rusch, F.R., & Kazdin, A.E. Toward a methodology of withdrawal designs for the assessment of response maintenance. *Journal of Applied Behavior Analysis,* 1981, *14* (2), 131–140.

Russo, D.C., Cataldo, M.F., & Cushing, P.F. Compliance training and behavioral covariation in the treatment of multiple behavior problems. *Journal of Applied Behavior Analysis,* 1981, *14* (1), 209–229.

Russo, D.C., & Koegel, R.L. A method for integrating an autistic child into a normal public-school classroom. *Journal of Applied Behavior Analysis,* 1977, *10* (4), 579–590.

Sailor, W., Guess, D., Rutherford, G., & Baer, D. M. Control of tantrum behavior by operant techniques during experimental verbal training. *Journal of Applied Behavior Analysis,* 1968, *1* (3), 237–243.

Sanders, R.M. *How to plot data.* Lawrence, Kans.: H & H Enterprises, 1978.

Sajwaj, T. Issues and implications of establishing guidelines for the use of behavioral techniques. *Journal of Applied Behavior Analysis,* 1977, *10* (3), 531–540.

Savie, P., & Dickie, R.F. Overcorrection of topographically dissimilar autistic behaviors. *Education and Treatment of Children,* 1979, *2* (3), 177–184.

Schmidt, B.G. Changes in personal, social, and intellectual behavior of children originally classified as feebleminded. *Psychological Monographs,* 1946, *60,* 1–144.

Schumaker, J.B., Hovell, M.F., & Sherman, J.A. An analysis of daily report cards and parent-managed privileges in the improvement of adolescents' classroom performance. *Journal of Applied Behavior Analysis,* 1977, *10* (3), 449–464.

Scott, L., & Goetz, E. Issues in the collection of in-class data by teachers. *Education and Treatment of Children,* 1980, *3* (1), 65–71.

Semmel, M.I., Gottlieb, J., & Robinson, N.M. Mainstreaming: Perspectives on educating handicapped children in the public school. In D.C. Berlinger (Ed.), *Review of research in education, VI.* American Educational Research Association, 1979.

Sidman, M. *Tactics of scientific research—Evaluating experimental data in psychology.* New York: Basic Books, 1960.

Sidman, M., & Stoddard, L.T. Programming perception and learning for retarded children. In N.R. Ellis (Ed.), *International review of research in mental retardation* (Vol. 2). New York: Academic Press, 1966.

Skiba, E.A., Pettigrew, L.E., & Alden, S.E. A behavioral approach to the control of thumbsucking in the classroom. *Journal of Applied Behavior Analysis,* 1971, *4* (2), 121–125.

Skinner, B.F. The concept of the reflex in the description of behavior. *Journal of General Psychology,* 1931, *5,* 427–458.

Skinner, B.F. Two types of conditioned reflex and a pseudo type. *Journal of General Psychology,* 1935, *12,* 66–77.

Skinner, B.F. Two types of conditioned reflex: A reply to Konorski and Miller. *Journal of General Psychology,* 1937, *16,* 272–279.

Skinner, B.F. *The behavior of organisms: An experimental analysis.* New York: Appleton-Century, 1938.

Skinner, B.F. *Walden two.* New York: Macmillan, 1948.

Skinner, B.F. *Science and human behavior.* New York: Macmillan, 1953.

Skinner, B.F. Some contributions of an experimental analysis of behavior to psychology as a whole. *American Psychologist,* 1953, *8,* 69–78.

Skinner, B.F. *Verbal behavior.* New York: Appleton-Century-Crofts, 1957.

Skinner, B.F. *Cumulative record* (2nd ed.). New York: Appleton-Century-Crofts, 1961.

Skinner, B.F. *The behavior of organisms: An experimental analysis.* New York: Appleton-Century-Crofts. 1966.

Skinner, B.F. *The technology of teaching.* New York: Appleton-Century-Crofts, 1968.

Skinner, B.F. *Beyond freedom and dignity.* New York: Knopf, 1971.

Skinner, B.F. Answers for my critics. In H. Wheeler (Ed.), *Beyond the punitive society; operant conditioning: Social and political aspects.* San Francisco: Freeman, 1973.

Skinner, B.F. *About behaviorism.* New York: Knopf, 1974.

Skinner, B.F. *Particulars of my life.* New York: Knopf, 1976.

Smith, R.M., & Neisworth, J.T. *The exceptional child: A functional approach.* New York: McGraw-Hill, 1975.

Snell, M.E. (Ed.). *Systematic instruction of the moderately and severely handicapped.* Columbus, Ohio: Charles E. Merrill, 1978.

Snell, M.E., & Gast, D.L. Applying time delay procedure to the instruction of the severely handicapped. *The Journal of the Association for the Severely Handicapped,* 1981, *6* (3), 3–14.

Sontag, E., Certo, N., & Button, J.E. On a distinction between the education of the severely and profoundly handicapped and a doctrine of limitations. *Exceptional Children,* 1979, *45* (8), 604–616.

Sowers, J.A., Rusch, F.R., Connis, R.T., & Cummings, L.E. Teaching mentally retarded adults to time-manage in a vocational setting. *Journal of Applied Behavior Analysis,* 1980, *13* (1), 119–128.

Staats, A.W., Minke, K.A., Finley, J.R., Wolf, M.M., & Brooks, L.O. A reinforcer system and experimental procedure for the laboratory study of reading acquisition. *Child Development,* 1964, *35,* 209–231.

Stephens, T.M. *Directive teaching of children with learning and behavioral handicaps.* Columbus, Ohio: Charles E. Merrill, 1976.

Stokes, T., & Baer, D. M. An implicit technology of generalization. *Journal of Applied Behavior Analysis,* 1977, *10* (2), 349–367.

Stolz, S.B. Why no guidelines for behavior modification? *Journal of Applied Behavior Analysis,* 1977, *10* (3), 541–547.

Strain, P.S., & Shores, R.E. Additional comments on multiple-baseline designs in instructional research. *American Journal of Mental Deficiency,* 1979, *84,* 229–234.

Strain, P.S., Shores, R.E., & Kerr, M.M. An experimental analysis of "spillover" effects on the social interaction of behaviorally handicapped preschool children. *Journal of Applied Behavior Analysis,* 1976, *9* (1) 31–40.

Strain, P.S., & Timm, M.A. An experimental analysis of social interaction between a behaviorally disordered preschool child and her classroom peers. *Journal of Applied Behavior Analysis,* 1974, 7 (4), 583–590.

Sulzer,-Azaroff, B., & Mayer, G.R. *Applying behavior analysis procedures with children and youth.* New York: Holt, Rinehart & Winston, 1977.

Tarpley, H.D., & Schroeder, S.R. Comparison of DRO and DRI on rate of suppression of self-injurious behavior. *American Journal of Mental Deficiency,* 1979, *84,* 188–194.

Tawney, J.W. Training letter discrimination in four-year-old children. *Journal of Applied Behavior Analysis,* 1972, *5* (4), 455–465.

Tawney, J.W. Educating severely handicapped children and their parents through telecommunications. In N.G. Haring & L.J. Brown (Eds.), *Teaching the severely handicapped.* New York: Grune and Stratton, 1977.

Tawney, J.W. Explorations in the development of teacher competencies: An outline of procedures. *Teacher Education and Special Education,* 1978, *1,* 66–76.

Tawney, J.W. Explorations in teacher competence: Implementation of a consequence evaluation system. *Teacher Education and Special Education,* 1980, *3,* 3–12.

Tawney, J.W. The future. In P. Cegelka & H. Prehm, *Mental retardation: From categories to people.* Columbus, Ohio: Charles E. Merrill, 1982.

Tawney, J.W., & Cartwright, G.P. Teaching in a technology oriented society. *Teacher Education and Special Education,* 1981, *4,* 3–14.

Tawney, J.W., Knapp, D.S., O'Reilly, C.D., & Pratt, S.S. *Programmed environments curriculum.* Columbus, Ohio: Charles E. Merrill, 1979.

Tawney, J.W., & Smith, J. An analysis of the forum: Issues in education of the severely and profoundly retarded. *Exceptional Children,* 1981, *48* (1), 5–18.

Terrace, H.S. Stimulus control. In W.K. Honig (Ed.), *Operant behavior: Areas of research and application.* New York: Appleton-Century-Crofts, 1966.

Thomas, D., Becker, W., & Armstrong, M. Production and elimination of disruptive classroom behavior by systematically varying teacher's behavior. *Journal of Applied Behavior Analysis,* 1968, *1* (1), 35–45.

Thompson, G.A., Jr., Iwata, B.A., & Poynter, H. Operant control of pathological tongue thrust in spastic cerebral palsy. *Journal of Applied Behavior Analysis,* 1979, *12* (3), 325–333.

Tofte-Tipps, S., Mendonca, P., & Peach, R. Training and generalization of social skills: A study with two developmentally handicapped socially isolated children. *Behavior Modification,* 1982, *6* (1), 45–71.

Trace, M.W., Cuvo, A.J., & Criswell, J.L. Teaching coin equivalence to the mentally retarded. *Journal of Applied Behavior Analysis,* 1977, *10* (1), 85–92.

Tucker, D.J., & Berry, G.W. Teaching severely multihandicapped students to put on their own hearing aids. *Journal of Applied Behavior Analysis,* 1980, *13* (1), 65–75.

Twardosz, S., & Baer, D.M. Training two severely retarded adolescents to ask questions. *Journal of Applied Behavior Analysis,* 1973, *6* (4), 655–661.

Ullmann, L.P., & Krasner, L. (Eds.). *Case studies in behavior modification.* New York: Holt, Reinhart & Winston, 1965.

Ullmann, L.P., & Krasner, L. *A psychological approach to abnormal behavior.* Englewood Cliffs, N.J.: Prentice-Hall, 1969.

Ulman, J.D., & Sulzer-Azaroff, B. Multi-element baseline design in educational research. In E. Ramp & Semb (Eds.), *Behavior analysis: Areas of research and application.* Englewood Cliffs, N.J.: Prentice-Hall, 1975.

Van Biervliet, A., Spangler, P.F., & Marshall, A.M. An ecobehavioral examination of a simple strategy for increasing mealtime language in residential facilities. *Journal of Applied Behavior Analysis,* 1981, *14* (3), 295–305.

Van den Pol, R.A., Iwata, B.A., Ivancic, M.T., Page, T.J., Neef, N.A., & Whitley, F.P. Teaching the handicapped to eat in public places: Acquisition, generalization and maintenance of restaurant skills. *Journal of Applied Behavior Analysis,* 1981, *14* (1), 61–69.

Van Houten, R., Hill, S., & Parsons, M. An analysis of a performance feedback system: The effects of timing and feedback, public posting, and praise upon academic performance and peer interaction. *Journal of Applied Behavior Analysis,* 1975, 8 (4), 449–457.

Van Houten, R., & Lai Fatt, D. The effects of public posting on high school biology test performance. *Education and Treatment of Children,* 1981, *4* (3), 217–226.

Van Houten, R., & Nau, P.A. A comparison of the effects of fixed and variable ratio schedules of reinforcement on the behavior of deaf children. *Journal of Applied Behavior Analysis,* 1980, *13* (1), 13–21.

Wahler, R., & Leske, G. Accurate and inaccurate summary reports: Reinforcement theory interpretation and investigation. *Journal of Nervous and Mental Disease,* 1973, *156,* 386–394.

Walker, H.M. *The acting-out child: Coping with classroom disruption.* Boston: Allyn and Bacon, 1979.

Walker, H.M., & Buckley, N.K. *Token reinforcement techniques.* Eugene, Oreg.: E-B Press, 1974.

Watson, P.J., & Workman, E.A. The non-concurrent multiple baseline across-individuals design: An extension of the traditional multiple baseline design. *Journal of Behavior Therapy and Experimental Psychiatry,* 1981, *12* (3), 257–259.

Webster's New Collegiate Dictionary. Springfield, Mass.: G. & C. Merriam Company, 1975.

Weisberg, P., & Waldrop, P.B. Fixed-interval work habits of congress. *Journal of Applied Behavior Analysis,* 1972, *5* (1), 93–97.

Wells, K.C., Forehand, R., Hickey, K., & Green, K.D. Effects of a procedure derived from the overcorrection principle on manipulated and nonmanipulated behaviors. *Journal of Applied Behavior Analysis,* 1977, *10* (4), 679–687.

Wheeler, H. (Ed.). *Beyond the punitive society; operant conditioning: Social and political aspects.* San Francisco: Freeman, 1973.

Wheeler, H. Introduction: A non-punitive world? In H. Wheeler (Ed.), *Beyond the punitive society; operant conditioning: Social and political aspects.* San Francisco: Freeman, 1973.

Whelan, R., & Gallagher, P. Effective teaching of children with behavior disorders. In N.G. Haring and A. Hayden (Eds.), *The improvement of instruction.* Seattle: Special Child Publications, 1972.

White, O.R. *Glossary of behavioral terminology.* Champaign, Ill.: Research Press, 1971.

White, O.R., & Haring, N.G. *Exceptional teaching* (2nd ed.). Columbus, Ohio: Charles E. Merrill, 1980.

White, O.R., & Liberty, K. Behavioral assessment and precise educational measurement. In N.G. Haring and R. Schiefelbusch (Eds.), *Teaching special children.* New York: McGraw-Hill, 1976.

Wilson, C.W., & Hopkins, B.L. The effects of contingent music on the intensity of noise in junior high home economics classes, *Journal of Applied Behavior Analysis,* 1973, *6* (2), 269–275.

Winett, R.A., & Winkler, R.C. Current behavior modification in the classroom: Be still, be quiet, be docile. *Journal of Applied Behavior Analysis,* 1972, *5* (4), 499–504.

Wolery, M., & Harris, S.R. Interpreting results of single-subject research designs. *Physical Therapy,* 1982, *62* (4), 445–452.

Wolf, M.M. Social validity: The case for subjective measurement or how applied behavior analysis is finding its heart. *Journal of Applied Behavior Analysis,* 1978, *11* (2), 203–214.

Wolf, M.M., Phillips, E.L., & Fixsen, D. The teaching family: A new model for the treatment of deviant child behavior in the community. In S.W. Bijou and E. Ribes-Inēsta (Eds.), *Behavior modification: Issues and extensions.* New York: Academic Press, 1972.

Wolf, M.M., & Risley, T.R. Reinforcement: Applied research. In R. Glaser (Ed.), *The nature of reinforcement.* New York: Academic Press, 1971.

Wolf, M.M., Risley, T.R., & Mees, H., Application of operant conditioning procedures to the behavior problems of an autistic child. *Behavior Research and Therapy,* 1964, *1,* 305–312.

Wright, H.F. *Recording and analyzing child behavior.* New York: Harper and Row, 1967.

Zimmerman, E.H., & Zimmerman, J. The alteration of behavior in a special classroom situation. *Journal of the Experimental Analysis of Behavior,* 1962, *5,* 59–60.

AUTHOR INDEX

SUBJECT INDEX